PREFACE

This is the revised edition of the book on '**Accounting for Management**' or simply called 'Management Accounting'. It is a comprehensive textbook, which provides a good coverage of the fundamentals of Financial Accounting, Cost Accounting and Management Accounting. The discussion on various chapters has been done in a simple and easy to understand manner keeping the students of commerce and non-commerce courses in view. The salient features of this book are: (*i*) a wider coverage of the syllabi of the MBA degree courses of Madras and Anna universities, (*ii*) explanation of various advanced management accounting tools in a very comprehensive manner, and (*iii*) a simple and detailed presentation of the subject matter. A number of problems from past university question papers have been solved. The book will also be useful for the U.G courses of Commerce and MCA degree course. It would be the right book for beginners of accounting.

We, along-with the Publishers, would like to thank Professor CA Geetanjali Pinto, ITM Business School, Navi Mumbai, ITM Group of Institutions, for her valuable feedback on the review of the chapter on *Final Accounts of Companies*.

We hope that the students of MBA and MCA degree courses would derive the maximum benefit out of this book and offer their candid comments. Constructive criticisms and valuable suggestions for the improvement of the book are most welcome.

Dr. N.P. Srinivasan
Dr. M. Sakthivel Murugan

Accounting for Management

(Comprehensive Textbook of Financial, Cost and Management Accounting)

For MBA and MCA Students

Dr. N.P. SRINIVASAN
M.Com., M.Phil., Ph.D.
Retd. Professor & Head
(Presently Visiting Faculty)
Department of Commerce
University of Madras
Chennai, Tamil Nadu

Dr. M. SAKTHIVEL MURUGAN
M.Com., Ph.D.
Reader & Head
Department of Corporate
Secretaryship and Management
D.B. Jain College
Chennai, Tamil Nadu

S. CHAND PUBLISHING

S Chand And Company Limited

(ISO 9001 Certified Company)

S Chand And Company Limited
(ISO 9001 Certified Company)
Head Office: D-92, Sector–2, Noida – 201301, U.P. (India), Ph. 91-120-4682700
Registered Office: A-27, 2nd Floor, Mohan Co-operative Industrial Estate,
New Delhi – 110 044, Phone: 011-49731800
www.**schandpublishing.com**; e-mail: **info@schandpublishing.com**

Marketing Offices:

Chennai	:	Ph: 23632120; chennai@schandpublishing.com
Guwahati	:	Ph: 2738811, 2735640; guwahati@schandpublishing.com
Hyderabad	:	Ph: 40186018; hyderabad@schandpublishing.com
Jalandhar	:	Ph: 4645630; jalandhar@schandpublishing.com
Kolkata	:	Ph: 23357458, 23353914; kolkata@schandpublishing.com
Lucknow	:	Ph: 4003633; lucknow@schandpublishing.com
Mumbai	:	Ph: 25000297; mumbai@schandpublishing.com
Patna	:	Ph: 2260011; patna@schandpublishing.com

First Edition 2004
Subsequent Editions and Reprints 2006, 2007, 2008, 2009, 2010
Revised Edition 2011
Reprints 2018, 2019, 2020, 2022, 2023

Reprint 2024

ISBN: 978-81-219-2344-6 **Product Code:** H8ACM60ACCN10ENZX11R

PRINTED IN INDIA

By Vikas Publishing House Private Limited, Plot 20/4, Site-IV, Industrial Area Sahibabad, Ghaziabad – 201 010 and Published by S Chand And Company Limited, A-27, 2nd Floor, Mohan Co-operative Industrial Estate, New Delhi – 110 044.

ANNA UNIVERSITY
SYLLABUS

1. FINANCIAL ACCOUNTING

1.1. Introduction to Financial, cost and management accounting, generally accepted accounting principles, conventions and concepts. The balance sheet and related concepts, the profit and loss account and related concepts/Introduction to *inflation accounting introduction to human resources accounting*.

1.2. Accounting Mechanics

Basic records, preparation of financial statements, revenue recognition and measurement, matching revenues and expenses, Inventory pricing and valuation. Fixed assets and depreciation accounting, intangible assets.

1.3. Analysis of financial statements

Financial ratio analysis, cash flow and funds flow statement analysis

2. COST ACCOUNTING AND MANAGEMENT ACCOUNTING

2.1. Cost Accounts

Accounting for manufacturing operations, classification of manufacturing costs. Accounting for manufacturing cost.

Cost Accounting Systems : Job order costing, Process costing *Activity Based costing*, Costing and the *value chain*. *Target costing*. Cost-Volume-Profit Analysis, Standard cost system.

2.2. Management Accounting

Relevant cost for decision making, Incremental analysis. Special order decision. Production constraint decisions, Make or buy decisions, sell scrap or rebuild decisions. Joint product decision. *Responsibility accounting and performance evaluation*. Budget : As a planning and control tool.

CONTENTS

1

MANAGEMENT ACCOUNTING – MEANING AND PURPOSE

Learning Objectives

After going through this chapter, you should be able to:

— Explain the meaning and functions of management accounting.

— Discuss the scope, utility, and limitations

— Differentiate management accounting from other accounting systems

— Describe the role and functions of management accountant.

1.1 Concept of Management Accounting

In ordinary language any system of accounting, which assists management in carrying out its functions more efficiently may be termed as management accounting. The Institute of Chartered Accountant of England and Wales has stated that "any form of accounting, which enables a business to be conducted more efficiently can be regarded as Management Accounting." On the same lines, Robert N. Antony has stated, "Management accounting is concerned with accounting information which is useful to management." However, these definitions are very general in nature. Some of the important specific definitions are as follows:

The Institute of Cost and management Accountants, London has defined Management Accounting as the "application of professional knowledge and skill in the preparation of accounting information in such as way as to assist management in the formation of policies and in the planning and control of the operations of the undertakings."

The American Accounting Association has defined as follows: "Management Accounting is the application of appropriate techniques and concepts in processing historical and projected economic data of an entity to assist management in establishing plans for reasonable economic objectives in the making of rational decisions with a view towards these objectives."

In the words of Brown and Howard, management accounting may be defined broadly as that aspect of accounting, which is concerned with the efficient management of a business through the presentation to management of such information as will facilitate efficient and opportune planning and control.

The above definitions clearly indicate that management accounting is concerned with accounting information, which is useful to management. The common thread underlying these definitions is that management accounting is concerned with the efficiency of the various phases of management. However, it should be clearly understood that it does not supplant financial of cost accounting systems; rather it supplements them in order to serve the diverse requirement of modern management.

1.2 Functions of Management Accounting

The basic function of management accounting is to assist the management in performing its functions effectively. The manner in which management accounting satisfies the requirements of the management for arriving at appropriate business decisions may be described as follows:

1. Modification of Data: Accounting data as such are not suitable for managerial decision-making and control purposes. However, they may be used as the basis for making future estimates and projections. In fact management accounting modifies the available accounting data by rearranging the same, by resorting to a process of classification and combination, which enable retention of the similarities of data without eliminating the dissimilarities. For example, the sales figures for different months may be classified to know the total sales made during the period product-wise, salesman-wise, and territory-wise.

2. Analysis and Interpretation of Data: The accounting data is analyzed and interpreted meaningfully for effective planning and decision-making. For this purpose the data is presented in a comparative form. Analytical tools such as Comparative Financial Statements Common-size Statements, Trend percentage, and ratio Analysis are used and likely trends are projected.

3. Facilitating Management Control: Management accounting enables all accounting efforts to be directed towards the attainment of goals efficiently by controlling the operations of the company more effectively. Standards of performance and measure of variation there from are theessential elements of any control system. All these are made possible through standard costing and budgetary control systems, which are an integral part of management accounting.

4. Use of Qualitative Information: Mere financial data and its analysis and interpretation are not sufficient for decision-making purposes. The management may need qualitative information, which cannot be readily converted into monetary terms. Such information may be obtained from statistical compilations, engineering records, case studies minutes of meetings, etc. Management accounting does not restrict itself to financial data alone for helping management; it also uses such (qualitative) information.

5. Satisfaction of Informational Needs of different levels of management: Different levels of management such as top level, middle level, and lower level managements need different types of information. The top management needs concise information covering the entire field of business activities at relatively long intervals. The middle level management requires technical data regularly, and the lower level management is interested in detailed figure relating to the particular sphere of activity at short intervals. Hence, the main function of management accounting is to process accounting and other data in such a way as to satisfied the needs of different levels of management.

1.3 Scope of Management Accounting

The main concern of management accounting is to provide necessary quantitative and qualitative information to the management for planning and control. For this purpose it draws out information from accounting as well as non-accounting sources. Hence, its scope is quite vast and it includes within its fold almost all aspects of business operations. However, the following areas may rightly be pointed out as lying within the scope of management accounting.

- **Financial Accounting:** The major function of management accounting is the rearrangement of modification of data. Financial accounting provides the very basis for such a function. Hence, management accounting cannot obtain full control and coordination of operations without a well-designed financial accounting system.
- **Cost Accounting:** Planning, decision-making and control are the basic managerial functions. The cost accounting system provides necessary tools such as standard costing, budgetary control, inventory control, marginal costing, and differential costing etc., for carrying out such functions efficiently. Hence, cost accounting is considered a necessary adjunct of management accounting.
- **Revaluation Accounting:** Revaluation or replacement value accounting is mainly concerned with ensuring that capital is maintained in real terms and profit is calculated on this basis.
- **Statistical Methods:** Statistical tools such as graph, charts, diagrams and index numbers etc., make the information more impressive and comprehensive. Other tools such as time series, regression analysis, sampling techniques etc., are highly useful for planning and forecasting.
- **Operations Research:** Modern managements are faced with highly complicated business problems in their decision-making processes. O P techniques like linear programming, queuing theory, decision theory, etc., enable management to find scientific solutions for the business problems.
- **Taxation:** This includes computation of income tax as per tax laws and regulations, filing of returns and making tax payments. In recent times, it also includes tax planning.
- **Organization and Methods (O&M):** O&M deal with organizations reducing cost and improving the efficiency of accounting, as also of office systems, procedures, and operations etc.
- **Office Services:** This includes maintenance of proper data processing and other office management services, communication and best use of latest mechanical devices.
- **Law:** Most of the management decisions have to be taken in a legal environment where the requirements of a number of statutory provisions or regulations are to be fulfilled. Some of the Acts, which have their influence on management decisions, are as follows: The Companies Act, MRTP Act, FEMA, SEBI Regulations, etc.
- **Internal Audit:** This includes the development of a suitable system of internal audit for internal control.
- **Internal Reporting:** This includes the preparation of quarterly, half yearly, and other interim reports and income statements, cash flow and funds flow statements, scrap reports, etc.

1.4 Role or Utility of Management Accounting

Management Accounting provides all assistance to the management in all of its functions. By providing the accounting information in the required form and at the required time, it enables management to perform its functions effectively. It makes available the relevant information after modifying the same in suitably for effective planning and decision-making. It helps to replace intuitive decision-making system with scientific decision-making ones. It provides such tools as budgetary control and standard costing, etc. which greatly helps management to exercise its control function effectively. The standard of performance enables management to fix responsibilities and know the weak spots in the enterprise without much difficulty. Coordination among departmental managers is essential to avoid conflicts of interests between them so as to achieve the company's overall objective as planned. Effective coordination could be achieved through departmental budgets and reports, which form an integral part of management accounting.

Organizing is another important function of management. A sound organization entails delegation of authority and fixing of responsibilities without much difficulty. This can be achieved by establishing cost centers, and profit centers. Management accounting assists considerably in establishing such centers, as also in establishing a sound system of internal control and internal audit for these centers.

Communication is yet another function of management, which involves transmission of data, information, results, etc., to both outsiders and insiders. While the decisions of the top management to be communicated to the middle and lower level managements, the results and requirements of the lower level should be reported to the top-level management. Also the results have to be reported to the shareholders, creditors, prospective investors, etc., who wish to know about the company's financial position and progress. Hence, a suitable reporting system is essential for effective communication of relevant facts. Management accounting helps the management in this regard. From these points it is clear that management accounting is useful to management in every field of activity and hence, forms a part of management.

1.5 Enumerate the Limitations of Management Accounting

1. Limitations of Cost and Financial Accounting Systems: Management accounting is mainly concerned with the modification of data and for this purpose; it derives information from financial and cost accounting systems. These accounting systems suffer from certain limitations, as they are prepared on the basis of certain accounting concepts and conventions. Management accounting adopts the information supplied by these systems as such for further processing. Hence, the limitations of these systems may be transmitted to the management accounting system. This may limit its effectiveness and make the information supplied by it a substandard one.

2. Persistence of Intuitive Decision-making: Management accounting assists management in taking decisions scientifically. It includes decision tools such as marginal costing, differential costing, and OR techniques like linear programming, decision theory, etc. It provides all types of information in time. Despite the facilities provided, the management mostly resorts to simple methods of decision-making by intuition or hunch. This makes the management accounting system a waste.

3. Very wide scope: Management requires information from both accounting as well as non-accounting sources, and also quantitative and qualitative information in an endeavour to provide such information management includes many disciplines and deals with a wide range of subject matter. This creates many problems and brings a degree of inexactness and subjectivity in the conclusions obtained through it.

Very Costly: The installation of management accounting system needs a very elaborate organization and numerous rules and regulation. This results in heavy investment, which only big concerns can afford.

5. It invites opposition from within the organization: Management accounting needs a radical change in the accounting organization. It demands rearrangement of personnel and their activities. This is strongly opposed by the people concerned.

6. It is comparatively new discipline and still in the process of development: Hence, it has to face the same impediments, which a new discipline faces – improvement of techniques, fluidity of concepts and sharpening of analytical tools. etc. All this may create doubt about the very usefulness to management accounting.

1.6 Distinctions Between Management Accounting and Financial Accounting

There is close relationship between management accounting and financial accounting. Management accounting draws out a part of the information from the financial accounting and modifies the same for the managerial use. Despite such close relationship between these two, there are certain fundamental differences, which are as follows:

Objective: The main objective of management accounting is to assist management in its task of planning and control. It is so designed as to provide information mainly for internal use by management. Financial accounting is designed to supply information through financial statements to external parties like shareholders, creditors, debenture holders, bank, regulatory bodies, etc. Thus management accounting is primarily an internal reporting system and financial accounting is external reporting system.

Subject matter: Financial accounting deals with the overall performance or position of the business. On the other hand, management accounting deals with the details of the various divisions, departments, products,-types of inventory or other sub-divisions of the enterprise. It s reports are mainly concerned with the profitability or performance of each of the divisions or departments. In short, it provides detailed analytical data for managerial use.

Nature of data used: Financial accounting is concerned with the monetary records of past events, whereas management accounting is concerned with future information. In other words, financial accounting makes use data, which is historical, quantitative, monetary, and objective, while management accounting uses data, which is descriptive, qualitative, statistical, and subjective and relates to the future.

Periodicity of Reporting: The period of reporting is longer in financial accounting when compared to management accounting. Normally financial statements are prepared at the end of the accounting year. But the management requires information at frequent intervals. Hence, greater emphasis is laid in management accounting on furnishing information quickly at short intervals.

Precision: As the information is meant for internal use, there is less emphasis on precision in the case of management accounting. But external parties mean the information provided in financial accounting for use, and therefore, it has to be more precise, as compared to management accounting.

Elements of Compulsion: Financial accounting has more or less become compulsory or statutory for every business. But a business is free to install or not to install a system of management accounting.

Flexibility: The above points of distinctions show that management accounting is highly flexible or less rigid in approach as compared to financial accounting.

1.7 Distinctions Between Management Accounting and Cost Accounting

Cost accounting is not merely a tool for cost ascertainment and cost recording; it is also a good tool for cost control and ascertainment or profitability and for management decision-making. That is why most of the cost accounting concepts are used in management accounting for assisting the management. Although there appeared to be overlapping between cost and management accounting, the following distinctions between the two may be listed:

1. Cost accounting is mostly concerned with cost ascertainment and cost control and employs tools like budgetary control, standard costing and responsibility accounting, etc., for such purposes.

Management accounting is concerned with all such matters in a wider perspective, which would go to assist the management in the formulation of policies, improvement of productivity and profitability and in guiding the management on the point of finance in the day-to-day operations.

2. Cost accounting deals primarily with cost data, while management accounting involves considerations of both cost and revenue. Management accounting is an all-inclusive accounting information system, which covers financial accounting, cost accounting and all aspects of business finance. But it is not a substitute for other accounting functions.

However, one should not be very much concerned with the boundaries of cost and management accounting systems, since both are complementary in nature. Without a well-established cost accounting system, the management accounting system cannot function efficiently. In the absence of cost accounting, details of cost information may not be available easily to the management accountant and his function will lose its significance.

1.8 Role of the Management Accountant

The management accountant plays a vital role in the decision-making process of the organization. He is variously known as Controller of Finance, Financial Controller, Financial Advisor or Chief Accounts Officer, etc. He is responsible for the installation, development and efficient functioning of the management accounting system. He plays an important role in gathering, compiling, reporting and interpreting internal accounting information. He designs the framework of the financial and cost control reports in order to satisfy the information needs of different levels of management. He computes the variances by comparing the actual performance with standards or budget estimates and interprets the results of operations to all levels of management and to the owners of the business.

The management accountant occupies a pivotal position in the organization. He performs staff function and also has line of authority over the accountants and other employees in this office. He educates the executives on the need for controlling information and on the ways of using it. He sifts the relevant information from the irrelevant and reports the same in an intelligible form to the management and sometimes to interested external parties. However, his job is limited to provision of required information in a comprehensive as well as reliable form to the management for decision-making purposes. But the actual decision-making responsibility lies with the management.

1.9 Functions of the Management Accountant

In the USA the management accountant is called Controller or Comptroller. He is considered to be part of the management team since he has the responsibility for collecting vital information, both within and outside the company. He has to design a framework for the management accounting system; therefore he safeguards the accuracy of information and develops devices required for their meaningful organization and interpretation. The functions of the Controller have been laid down by the Controllers' Institute of America. They are typical of the functions of any management accountant by whatever name called. These functions are:

1. To establish, coordinate, and administer as an integral part of management, an adequate plan for the control of operations. Such a plan would provide for profit planning, for capital requirements and financial, sales forecasts, expense budgets and cost standards, together with necessary procedures to effectuate the plan.

2. To compare performance with operating plans and standards and to report the results of operation to all levels of management, and to owners of the business. This function includes the formulation and administration of accounting policy and compilation of statistical records and special reports as required.

3. To consult with all segments of management responsible for policy or action concerning any phase of the operations of the business as it relates to the attainment of objectives, and the effectiveness of policies, organization structures and procedures.

4. To administer tax policies and procedures.

5. To supervise and coordinate preparation of reports to government agencies.

6. To assure fiscal protection for the assets of the business through adequate internal control and proper insurance coverage.

7. To continuously appraise economic and social forces and government influences, and interpret their effect upon business.

It may be noted that these seven functions of a Controller are broad enough to include all phases of policy and organization within the jurisdiction of Controller. This has elevated his position to the top management cadre, to the level of Vice President or Director for Finance.

REVIEW QUESTIONS

1. Explain the concept of management accounting.
2. Describe the functions of management accounting.
3. What is the scope of management accounting?
4. Discuss the utility of management accounting.
5. Enumerate the limitations of management accounting.
6. Distinguish between management accounting and financial accounting.
7. How does management accounting differ from cost accounting?
8. Discuss the role of management accountant.
9. List out the functions of management accountant.

2

FINANCIAL ACCOUNTING – PRINCIPLES

Learning Objectives

After going through this chapter, you should be able to:

— Define the concept of Accounting.
— Describe other aspects of accounting.
— Understand the principles of accounting.
— Describe different systems of book-keeping.
— Know the meaning of some common terms used in accounting.

2.1 Concept of Accounting

Accounting is a means of communicating the results of business operations to various parties interested in or connected with the business viz., the owners, creditors, investors, banks and financial institutions, Government and other agencies. Hence, it is rightly called as the language of business. Accounting is not only associated with business, but also with everybody, who is interested in keeping an account of the monetary transactions. Generally the term 'accounting' refers to financial accounting.

The American Institute of Certified Public Accountants has defined accounting as "the art of recording, classifying and summarizing in a significant manner and in terms of money transactions and events which are, in part at least, of financial character, and interpreting the results thereof". This definition is in keeping with the enlarged scope of accounting.

In the words of Smith and Ashburne, "Accounting is the science of recording and classifying business transactions and events, primarily of a financial character, and the art of making significant summaries, analysis and interpretation of those transactions and events and communicating the results to persons who must make decisions or form judgement. "

Attributes of Accounting

The above definitions bring out the following as the attributes of accounting.

1. Accounting is both an art and science. Analysis interpretations and communication of financial results are the art of accounting requiring special knowledge, experience and judgement. As a science, accounting is governed by certain principles, concepts, conventions and

policies. But it is not an exact science like other physical sciences; rather it is an exacting science.

2. It involves recording, classifying, and summarizing. Recording means systematically writing down in account books the transactions and events reasonably soon after their occurrence. Classifying is the process of grouping of transactions or entries of one nature at one place. This is done by opening accounts in a book called ledger. Summarizing involves the preparation of reports and statements from the classified data [i.e., ledger]. This involves the preparation of final accounts.

3. It records transactions in terms of money. This provides a common measure of recording and increases the understanding of the state of affairs of the business.

4. It records only those transactions and events, which are financial in character. Non-financial events, howsoever important they may be for the business, are not recorded in accounting.

5. It is the art of interpreting the results of operations. It aids to determine the financial position of the enterprise, the progress it has made, and how well it is getting along.

6. It involves communication. The results of analysis and interpretation are communicated to the management and other interested parties.

2.2 Main Objectives of Accounting

From the definitions of accounting, the following may be listed out as the main objectives of accounting:

1. To ascertain the operating results of the enterprise;
2. To reveal the financial position of the business; and
3. To enable control over the operation as well as the resources of the business.

2.3 Functions of Accounting

The following are the major functions of accounting:

(*a*) Keeping systematic records. As a language of business, accounting is to report the results of most business events. Hence, its main function is to keep a systematic record of these events. This function embraces recording transactions in journal and subsidiary books like cashbook, sales book etc., posting them to ledger accounts and ultimately preparing the financial statements [final accounts].

(*b*) Communicating the results. The second main function of accounting is to communicate the financial facts of the enterprise to the various interested parties like owners, investors, creditors, employees, government, and research scholars, etc. The purpose of this function is to enable these parties to have better understanding of the business and take sound and realistic economic decisions.

(*c*) Meeting the legal requirements. Accounting aims at fulfilling the legal requirements, especially of the tax authorities and regulators of the business. It discharges this function in accordance with certain fundamental truths and uniform enforcement of generally accepted accounting principles.

(*d*) Protecting the properties of the business. Accounting helps protecting the property of the business.

(e) Planning and controlling the business activities. Accounting also helps planning future activities of an enterprise and controlling its day-to-day operations. This function is done mainly to promote maximum operational efficiency.

2.4 Various Accounting Systems

Accounting refers to the discipline of recording and classifying the monetary effects of business transactions and events of an enterprise for the purpose of analyzing, and finally reporting the results to variety of interested parties. If the transactions are mostly financial in nature, the accounting system will be termed as financial accounting. On the other hand, if they relate to costing information the system will be known as cost accounting. Financial accounting looks to the interests of external parties who have a financial stake in the concern's affairs - owners, employees, creditors, regulatory authorities, etc. And cost accounting is mainly concerned with the cost information, which is used by the management for cost ascertainment and control purposes. On the other hand, accounting, which is primarily concerned with providing information relating to the conduct of the various aspects of business like cost or profit associated with some portions of business operations, is called as management accounting. However, in the broadest sense, any accounting, which is useful to management, may be termed as management. All financial and cost information generated by accountants is some interest to management. But in practice management accounting differs from other accounting systems in its emphasis upon 'purpose' rather than techniques. Generally accounting refers to the system of financial accounting.

2.5 Users of the Accounting Information

Following are some of the groups of people who would like to make use of the accounting information.

1. Owners. The primary objective of accounting is to provide necessary information to the owners relating to their business. For example, the shareholders of a company are interested in the accounting information with a view to ascertaining the profitability and financial strength of the company.

2. Management. In large business organizations there is a separation of the ownership and management functions. The managements of such concerns are more concerned with the accounting information because of their accountability to the owners for better performance of their concerns.

3. Creditors. Trade creditors, debenture holders, bankers, and other lending institutions are interested in knowing the short-term as well as long-term position of the company. The financial statements provide the required information for ascertaining such position.

4. Regulatory Agencies. Various governments and other agencies use accounting reports not only as a basis for tax assessment but also in evaluating how well various business concerns are operating under regulatory framework.

5. Government. Governments all over the world are using financial statements for compiling statistics concerning business units, which, in turn help in compiling national accounts.

6. Potential Investors. Investors use the information in accounting reports to a greater extent in order to determine the relative merits of various investment opportunities.

7. Employees. Employees are interested in the earnings of the enterprise because their pay hike and payment of bonus depend on the size of profits earned.

8. Researchers. The research scholars in their research in accounting theory as well as business affairs and practices also use accounting data.

In addition, those with indirect concern about business enterprise include financial analysts and advisors, financial press and reporting, trade associations, labour unions, consumers, and public at large. Thus, the list of actual and potential users of accounting information is large.

2.6 What is Meant by the Principles of Accounting?

Accounting is the language of business and information about business is communicated to outsiders through accounting statements. In order to make these statements easily understandable and meaningful, it is necessary that accounting should be based on certain uniform scientifically laid down norms, which are called as accounting principles. The accounting principles are rules of action or a body of doctrine universally adopted while recording the business transactions. Adopting uniform principles in recording the transactions will ensure uniformity, clarity and understanding. If accounting is to serve its purpose more effectively, it should be based on certain uniform and scientifically laid down principles or postulates also termed as accounting standards. The accounting principles can be classified into two categories: (1) Accounting Concepts and (2) Accounting Conventions.

Basic features of accounting principles

The general acceptance of an accounting principle depends on how well it meets the following criteria:

(1) Usefulness or Relevance. A principle is said to be useful if it results in information that is meaningful and useful to its users.

(2) Objectivity. A principle is said to be objective if it results in information, which is not influenced, by the personal bias or judgment of those who furnish it. Objectivity means reliability, trustworthiness and verifiability of accounting system.

(3) Feasibility. A principle is said to be feasible if it can be implemented without undue complexity or cost. Thus, the time, labour and cost of generating accounting data should not exceed its probable use and resulting benefits.

2.7 Accounting Concepts - Meaning and Significance

Accounting concepts are those basic assumptions or conditions upon which the accounting system is based. Some of the important accounting concepts are as follows:

Business Entity Concept: As per this concept, business is treated as a separate entity or unit distinct from that of the proprietor. The significance of this concept is that without such a distinction the affairs of the business will be mixed up with the private affairs of the proprietor and the true picture of the business will not be available. The transactions between the proprietor and the business will be recorded in the business books separately and shown separately under the heading 'capital account'. For example, if when the proprietor invests Rs.50000 in his business, it will be assumed that the owner has given that much money to the business and will be shown as a 'liability' for the business. When he withdraws, say Rs.10000 from the business it will be charged to his capital account and the net amount due to him will be only Rs. 40000.

The concept of separate entity applies to all forms of business organization, viz., a sole trader, a partnership, or a company. The entity concept has three major implications for accounting:

1. All business transactions are recorded from the firm's point of view and not from the point of view of other parties such as owners, managers or customers. For example, when a customer buys goods from the business it is recorded as sales by the firm and not as purchases by the customer.

2. It demarcates clearly the business transactions from the personal transactions of the owner. For example, the household expenses of the owner paid by the business are treated as drawings made by the owner and not treated as business expenses.

Going Concern Concept: As per this concept it is assumed that a business unit has a perpetual succession or continued existence and transactions are recorded from this point of view. Hence, while valuing the business assets, the accountant does not take into account the realizable or market values of the assets. Assets are valued at cost at which they were originally purchased less depreciation till date, which is calculated on the basis of the original cost only.

The concept presumes that the business will continue in operation long enough to charge the cost of fixed assets over their useful life against the business income. It is only on the basis of this concept that a distinction is made between capital expenditure and revenue expenditure. If it is expected that the business will exist only for a limited period, the accounting records will be kept accordingly.

Dual Aspect Concept: Each business transaction has two aspects, i.e., the receiving of a benefit [debit] and giving of a benefit [credit]. For example, if a business purchases furniture, it must have given up cash or have incurred an obligation to pay for it in future. Technically speaking, 'for every debit, there is a credit' this concept is the core of accountancy and upon this the whole superstructure of 'Double entry system of book keeping' has been raised. As each transaction has giving account and receiving account equally, the total assets of a business firm will always be equal to its total equities [i.e., liabilities]. That is

External liabilities + Capital = Total Assets

Total Liabilities = Total Assets

This is called the Accounting or Balance Sheet equation.

Cost Concept: This concept is based on the 'going concern concept'. According to this concept, assets purchased are normally entered in the accounting books at the cost at which they are purchased and this cost is the basis for all subsequent accounting for asset. The market value is immaterial for accounting purpose since the business is not going to be liquidated but is to be continued for a long time to come. This concept also prevents arbitrary values being used for recording purposes, mainly those resulting in the acquisition of assets.

Money Measurement Concept: According to this concept, accounting records only those transactions, which can be expressed in terms of money. Events or transactions, which cannot be expressed in terms of money cannot find place in the books, however important they may be. Qualitative or non-monetary transactions are either omitted or recorded separately. For example a strained relationship between production manager and sales manager, which may affect directly the operating results of the business, does not find place in accounting records.

Realization Concept: According to this concept, the revenue is recognized only when the sale is made. But the sale is a gradual process, which starts with the purchase of raw materials for production and ends with the sale. If no sale is effected, no revenue is recognized.

This is important to stop business firms from inflating their profits. However, there are certain exceptions to this concept like hire purchase sale, or contract etc.

Accrual Concept: This concept is based on the economic premise that all transactions are settled in cash but even if cash settlement has not yet taken place, it is proper to bring the transaction or event concerned into the books. Expenditure incurred during the year but not paid and Income earned but not received is called as accrued items. According to this concept these items will be taken into consideration while arriving at profit or loss. This concept enables to define income and expense.

Matching Concept: The matching concept provides the guidelines as to how the expense be matched with revenues. In other words, costs are reported as expenses in the period in which the associated revenue is reported. Note that costs are matched with revenues, not the other way round. The expense shown in an income statement must refer to the same accounting period, production units, division or department of business unit to which revenue refers.

2.8 Accounting Conventions - Meaning and Significance

Accounting conventions are those customs, usage and traditions that are being followed by the accountants for along time while preparing the accounting statements.

The most important conventions are conservatism, consistency, and material disclosure.

Convention of Conservatism: According to this convention, financial statements are usually drawn up on a conservative basis. While preparing accounts and statements, the accountants are expected not to take into account 'anticipated profits' but to provide for all possible 'anticipated losses.' Window dressing in accounts is not permitted. This practice of accountants acts as a guard against the 'personal judgment' in the preparation of financial statements. It is only on the basis of this convention, the inventory is valued at 'cost or market price whichever is lower'. Similarly provision for bad and doubtful debts is made in the books before ascertaining profits.

Convention of Consistency: According to this convention, accounting practices should remain unchanged for a fairly long time. And they should not be changed unless it becomes absolutely essential to change them. For example, if a particular method of charging depreciation on a particular asset is followed, it should be followed consistently. However, consistency does not prevent the introduction of new improved accounting methods or techniques. If any change is required, such change and its effects should be stated clearly. The aim of this convention is to provide for continuity in accounting practices and methods and enable meaningful comparison of accounting statements over a period or between different firms.

Convention of Material Disclosure: Apart from the legal requirements, good accounting practice demands that all vital information should be disclosed. For example, in addition to asset values, the mode of valuation should also be disclosed. The practice of giving footnotes, references, and parentheses in the statements is in accordance with this convention only. Accountants should report only material information and ignore insignificant details while preparing the accounting statements. If this is not done, the whole accounting process will become highly cumbersome and meaningless. What is material depends upon the circumstances and the discretion of the accountant. Because of this convention only, the cost of asset and its written down value alone shown in the balance sheet. Materiality depends on the amount involved in relation to the asse or to revenues and expenditures or to profit.

2.9 Limitations of Financial Accounting

Financial accounting was able to cope with the needs of business in the initial stages when business was not so complex. But the growth and complexities of modern business have made financial accounting highly inadequate. Most of limitations are mainly due to the cumulative effect of recorded facts, accounting conventions and personal judgments on financial statements. The inadequacies or limitations of financial accounting are as follows:

1. Financial information is incomplete and inexact: The financial statements are essentially interim reports usually prepared for an accounting period. Hence, the financial information as revealed by them is neither complete nor exact. The true financial position or the ultimate gain or loss can be known only when the business is closed down.

2. Qualitative information is ignored: Financial accounting takes into account only the quantitative information, which is expressed in monetary terms. But a number of qualitative factors such as the reputation and image of the management with the public, cordial industrial relations and efficiency of workers, customer satisfaction, competitive strength etc., which cannot be expressed in monetary terms, are not considered by the financial accounting. However, these factors are essential for understanding the real financial condition and the operating efficiency of the business.

3. Financial information is mainly historical in nature: As the financial statements are compiled on the basis of historical costs, they fail to take into account such factors as the decrease in money value, or increase in the price level changes. Since these statements deal with past data, not with the future, they are of little value in decision-making.

4. Financial information is based on accounting concepts and conventions: Accounting concepts and conventions used for the preparation of financial statement make it unrealistic. For example, the value of fixed assets in the balance sheet is shown on the basis of going concern concept. This means that the value put on an asset rarely represents the amount of cash, which would be realized on liquidation. Similarly, the income statement prepared based on the convention of conservatism fails to disclose true income, for it includes probable losses and ignores probable income.

5. Personal judgments influence financial statements: Many items in the financial statements are left to the personal judgment of the accountant. For example, the method of valuation of inventory, the method of depreciation, treatment of deferred revenue expenditure, etc., depend on the personal judgment of the accountant. The true value of such items lies on the soundness of such judgment, which, in turn, depends on the experience, skill, integrity, and competence of the accountant. There is possibility of making improper assumptions either mistakenly or in order to distort the real picture. However such indiscreet personal judgments are controlled to certain extent by the convention of conservatism.

2.10 Different Systems of Accounting for Recording Business Transactions

There are two different system of accounting for recording business transactions. They are cash system of accounting and mercantile system of accounting.

Cash System of Accounting: Under this system, only actual cash received and paid are recorded. No entry is made for a receipt that is merely due; any payment outstanding will be accounted for. Government accounting is based on the cash system only. Professional people like Lawyers, Chartered Accountants, etc., maintain accounts under this system only.

Mercantile System or Accrual System of Accounting: Under this system of accounting, entries are made not only for actual receipt or payment of cash but also for amounts having become due for payment or receipt. In other words, both cash transactions and credit transactions are recorded in the book of accounts. All commercial establishments and even non-trading concerns follow this system only.

Further, accounting records can be prepared under any one of the following systems:

Single-entry system: Under this system only the personal and cash aspects of the transactions are recorded in the books. Normally the impersonal aspects are ignored. It is not based on 'dual aspect concept'. Hence, it is incomplete, inaccurate, and unscientific.

Double-entry system: It is the most common system of bookkeeping whereby the two aspects of every transaction i.e., the receiving aspect [debit] and the giving aspect [credit] are recorded in the books of accounts. It is based on the 'dual aspect concept'. This method of writing every transaction in two different accounts on opposite sides for equal value is known as the double entry system of book keeping. This is the most accurate, complete and scientific system of accounting.

2.11 Advantages and Limitations of Double Entry System

The important advantages of double entry system are as follows:

1. It keeps a complete record of business transactions.
2. It provides complete information concerning the business.
3. It provides a check on the arithmetical accuracy of books of accounts.
4. It discloses the operating results i.e., profit or loss of the business for a given period.
5. It makes possible a meaningful comparison of operating and financial performance over a period of time and enables the businessman to evaluate the progress of his business.
6. It also enables a businessman to plan and control his operations.
7. It reduces the chances of committing fraud.
8. Past details with regard to any account are easily and accurately obtainable in this system.
9. This system is highly flexible and can be adjusted to any specific needs of a business unit.

Limitations of double entry system

Though the system is very methodical, scientific, and accurate, it has a few shortcomings. The biggest limitation is that this method fails to detect errors of the following types:

1. It is not possible to discover a transaction, which is not recorded at all in the books of original entry.
2. If the amount of a transaction is recorded wrongly, there is no way for detecting the error.
3. A compensatory error is also not detected by this system.
4. It involves more clerical labour.

Some Common Terms used in Accountancy

Book keeping: It means recording of business transactions in the books of accounts in accordance with the principles of accounting. In short, it means the recording of of business transactions in a set of account books in a systematic or proper manner.

Objects of Book keeping

(*a*) To know the profit or loss of the business for an accounting year,

(*b*) To know the balances of debtors and creditors of the business,

(*c*) To know the financial position of the business as on the last day of the accounting year,

(*d*) To have information for legal and tax purposes.

Transactions: Transactions are those activities of businessmen, which involve transfer of money or goods or services between two persons or two accounts. These activities may be in the nature of purchase of goods, sale of goods, borrowing from a bank or lending money to some persons, payment or receipt of certain income like dividend or commission etc. They may be in the nature of cash transaction or credit transaction. When cash payment or receipt takes place immediately in a transaction, it is called as cash transaction. When cash is paid or received at a later date, then it will be called as credit transaction. It may be in the nature paper transaction. A paper transaction is a business transaction where there is no payment or receipt of cash either immediately or at a future date. Examples are bad debts written off, loss of goods by fire or theft, depreciation written off, etc.

Entry: An entry is record of a transaction in account books.

Debtor: A person, who received a benefit without giving money or money's worth, is a debtor. Dr. is the abbreviation of debtor.

Creditor: A person, who gives a benefit without receiving money or money's worth, is a creditor. Cr. is the abbreviation of creditor.

Goods: Goods are the articles purchased for the purpose of resale. For example, for a Furniture Mart selling chairs and tables, furniture is considered as goods. Other articles such as computer, a wall clock, or cycle purchased for the office use are not goods, because they are not for sale. They will be called as assets of the business.

Purchases: These are the goods bought for resale to customers.

Purchases Returns: These are the goods returned by the trader to the supplier because of poor quality or defects in the goods supplied. They may also be termed as 'returns outwards' or 'returns to suppliers'.

Sales: These are the goods sold to customers. If it is for cash, it will be termed as cash sales or till takings. If cash for sales is received at a later date, it will be termed as credit sales.

Sales Returns: When the trader receives back goods from the customer for poor quality or defects in the goods sold out, it will be called as 'Sales returns', or 'Returns inwards' or 'Returns from customers'.

2.12 What is an Account?

Account: It is a statement of various dealings that occur between a customer and the firm. It can also be expressed as a clear and concise record of the transactions relating to a person, or a firm, or a property, or a liability, or an income or expenditure. The short abbreviation for account is A/C.

2.13 Classification of Accounts

In order to understand the rules of double entry system, it is essential to know which classes of accounts are affected by a particular transaction. For this purpose, all accounts are broadly classified into two classes: (1) Personal accounts and (2) Impersonal accounts. Impersonal accounts are further subdivided into (*a*) Real account, and (*b*) Nominal account. Thus all the accounts can be classified into 'personal', 'real' and 'nominal' accounts.

Various Types of Accounts

Personal Accounts: These are the accounts relating to persons. A separate account is prepared for each person. Such accounts can take the following forms:

(i) Natural person's accounts, e.g., Krishna's account, Priya's account.

(ii) Artificial person's or body of persons' accounts, e.g., Bank account, any Firm's account, any company's account.

(iii) Representative personal accounts, e.g., Prepaid expenses account, Outstanding wages account.

Real Accounts or Property Accounts: These are accounts relating to a property, an asset, or a possession, e.g., Plant account, Cash Account, Goodwill account, etc. A separate account is prepared for each class of property or asset.

Nominal Accounts: These are the accounts relating to a business expenses or losses and income or gains, e.g., Wages' account, Interest account, Discount received account, Dividends account.

2.14 State the Rules of Double Entry

When closely analyzed, each transaction will reveal two aspects. One aspect will be either 'Receiving Aspect' or 'Incoming Aspect' or 'Expenditure Aspect'. This is termed as 'Debit Aspect'. Another aspect will be 'Giving Aspect' or 'Outgoing Aspect' or 'Income Aspect'. This is termed as 'Credit Aspect'. These two aspects namely 'Debit Aspect' and 'Credit aspect' form the basis of double entry.

The rules of double entry are as follows:

1.	Personal Accounts	-	(a) Debit the Receiver
			(b) Credit the Giver
2.	Real or Property accounts	-	(a) Debit what comes in
			(b) Credit what goes out
3.	Nominal Accounts	-	(a) Debit all expenses and losses
			(b) Credit all incomes and gains

Stages of Double entry system

The following are the three distinct stages of a complete system of double entry:

(*i*) Recording the transactions in the journal.

(*ii*) Classifying the transactions in the journal by posting them to the appropriate ledger accounts and then preparing a trial balance.

(*iii*) Closing the books and preparing the final accounts.

2.15 Distinctions Between Double Entry System and Single Entry System

	Double Entry	Single Entry
1.	The double aspects of a transaction are recorded.	Only one aspect is recorded.
2.	For every debit, there is a credit of equal amount.	There may a debit without a corresponding credit and vice versa.
3.	There are personal accounts, real accounts, and nominal accounts.	There are personal accounts and cash accounts only.
4.	A trial balance can be prepared to test the arithmetical accuracy of accounts.	It cannot be prepared, as the ledger does not contain all accounts.
5.	Trading and Profit and loss account and Balance sheet can be prepared directly.	They cannot be prepared directly.
6.	Actual net profit can be calculated directly.	Approximate net profit can be indirectly calculated.
7.	It involves more clerical labour.	It involves less clerical labour.
8.	It is a perfect scientific system.	It is an imperfect way of bookkeeping.
9.	Tax authorities accept this system.	They do not accept it as such.

Accounting Policies

Accounting policies refer to the particular accounting principles used for the preparation and presentation of financial statements. Different enterprises use different policies. The management of a particular enterprise determines the policy for its enterprise. For example, different accounting policies are adopted in different enterprises for the following items:

(*a*) Valuation of fixed assets and method of depreciation, (*b*) Valuation of inventories, (*c*) Long-term investments, (*d*) Revenue Recognition, (*e*) Retirement benefits, (f) Foreign currency transactions, (*g*) Research and development, (*h*) Deferred Revenue expenditure, (i) Income tax. (*j*) Treatment of contingent liabilities and goodwill.

Accounting Standards

A standard is a particular level of performance, goal or target. It is established by custom, professional or government authorities, common consent, regulatory or legal bodies etc., after extensive observation, testing, research, etc. In accounting, it is the cost yardstick. It is a chosen set of accounting policies about the principles and methods to be adopted.

Essential Features: (*a*) The accounting standards must make the accounting statements more meaningful. (*b*) They should be based on facts or data. (*c*) They must be feasible or achievable.

No accounting standard is universally acceptable. In India, Accounting Standards Board [ASB] is authorized to issue accounting standards. The ASB takes into consideration the international accounting standards for formulating accounting standards. Till date there are 12 accounting standards, which are mandatory. Mandatory means binding on the members of the Institute of Chartered Accountants of India.

2.16 How does accounting differ from bookkeeping?

Bookkeeping refers to the maintaining of the various sets of account books and deals with recording routine and repetitive business transactions in a significant and orderly manner. Assistants usually do it. On the other hand, accounting is more analytical and deals with the designing of accounting system, forecasting, preparation of financial statements and audits, cost analysis, income tax and interpretation of financial statements and reports for decision-making, etc. Senior accountants normally do them. Where bookkeeping ends, accounting starts. Bookkeeping provides necessary data for accounting in the case of big concerns. But in small concerns the same person does both.

REVIEW QUESTIONS

1. Define accounting.
2. What are the attributes of accounting ?
3. State the main objectives of accounting.
4. State the functions of accounting.
5. Explain the various accounting systems.
6. List out the group of people who would like to make use of the accounting information.
7. What do you mean by Principles of Accounting ?
8. State the basic features of accounting principles.
9. Describe the meaning and significance any four accounting concepts.
10. What is the significance of the following accounting concepts:
    (*a*) Going Concern Concept; (*b*) Dual Aspect Concept
    (*c*) Money Measurement Concept
11. What are the various accounting conventions?
12. State the deficiencies of financial accounting.
13. What are the different systems of accounting for recording transactions?
14. What is meant by double entry system of bookkeeping?
15. State the advantages and disadvantages of double entry system.
16. Explain the following terms:
    (*a*) Transaction, (*b*) Account (*c*) Goods (*d*) Bookkeeping
17. How are accounts classified?
18. What are the various types of accounts?
19. State the rules of double entry.
20. Distinguish between double entry and single entry systems.
21. Differentiate bookkeeping from accounting.

3

BOOKS OF ACCOUNTS

Learning Objectives

After completing this chapter, you should be able to:

— Know the various books of accounts used for recording business transactions

— Define journal and describe the procedure for journalizing,

— Pass journal entries.

— Know the meaning of ledger and describe the procedure for ledger posting,

— Do the balancing of ledger accounts,

— State the meaning of trial balance,

— Describe the methods of preparation of trial balance.

Books of accounts mean a set of suitably ruled account books used for recording business transactions. The various books of accounts maintained by a business concern depend upon the method of accounting followed by it. There are two methods, viz., conventional or traditional method and modern or practical method of accounting. The traditional method is suitable for small concerns, which have relatively less volume of transactions. Big concerns, which have a large volume of transactions, find the traditional method inconvenient, and therefore, follow the practical method.

Under the traditional method, a single journal for recording all business transactions and a ledger for maintaining all accounts are kept. But under the modern method, several subsidiary books or special journals are maintained for recording all cash and credit transactions. In addition, one journal proper book is also kept for recording those transactions, which cannot be recorded in the subsidiary books. And a ledger is also maintained for keeping all the accounts of the business. This chapter would discuss the books of journal and ledger and the special journals would be dealt with in the next chapter.

SECTION A: JOURNAL - BOOK OF ORIGINAL OR FIRST ENTRY

3.1 What is a Journal?

A journal may be defined as the book of original or prime entry containing a chronological record of the transactions from which posting is done to the ledger. The transactions are recorded first in the journal in the order in which they occur. The process of recording the transactions in a journal is called as journalizing. The prescribed format of a journal is shown below.

Journal

Date (1)	Particulars (2)	L.F. (3)	Debit (4) Amount	Credit (5) Amount
Year	Name of the A/C to be debited			
Month	Name of the A/C to be credited			
Date	[Narration]			

Explanation

1. **Date:** The date on which the transaction takes place is entered here.

2. **Particulars:** The name of the account to be debited is written in the first line and the abbreviation 'Dr.' is written against it. In the second line, the account to be credited is written preceded by the word 'To'. An explanation of the entry known as 'narration' is also given within bracket explaining briefly about the transaction.

3. **L.F:** stands for Ledger Folio, which means the page number in the ledger in which the entry is posted.

4. **Debit:** In this column the amount to be debited against the 'dr' account is entered.

5. **Credit:** In this column, the amount to be credited against the 'cr' account is entered.

3.2 Describe the Procedure for Journalizing.

From the given business transaction, the receiving aspect and the giving aspect should be identified. Depending upon the nature of account that is affected by the transaction, the rule for journalizing should be selected as follows:

Nature of account	Rule for debiting an account	Rule for crediting an account
Personal Account	Debit the Receiver a/c	Credit the Giver a/c
Real Account	Debit what comes in	Credit what goes out
Nominal Account	Debit all expenses and losses	Credit all incomes and gains

These rules may be used either jointly or separately for journalizing each and every transaction. The examples given below would explain the same.

Transaction 1: 1-1-2002 Vignesh started business with Rs.60,000.

Journal: In this transaction, the receiving aspect is that 'cash' is received by the business, which is distinct from Vignesh's private or personal property and the giving aspect is that Vignesh is the giver. Proprietor's personal account is represented by Capital a/c.

The journal entry in the business books is as follows:

Date	Particulars	L.F.	Debit Rs.	Credit Rs.
1-1-2002	Cash a/c dr.		60,000	
	To Vignesh's Capital a/c			60,000
	[Being capital brought in]			

Debit what comes in, here cash comes in, hence cash a/c is debited. Proprietor is the giver; hence, capital a/c is credited. A short explanation to explain the entry is given within brackets by way of narration. Note that separate rules are used for debiting and crediting the accounts. Real account rule is used for making the debit entry and personal account rule for making credit entry.

Transaction 2

2-1-2002 Furniture was purchased for Rs.20,000.

Journal: In this transaction, furniture is received and cash is paid. The receiving and giving aspects affect the real a/c i.e., furniture and cash, hence, the real account rule i.e., debit what comes in and credit what goes out is to be applied. Furniture comes in and cash goes out. Hence the entry is as follows:

Date	Particulars	L.F.	Debit Rs.	Credit Rs.
2-1-2002	Furniture a/c dr.		20,000	
	To cash a/c			20,000
	[Being furniture purchased for cash]			

Transaction 3

3-1-2002 Bought goods from Raj for Rs.30,000.

In this transaction goods are received and Raj is the giver of goods on credit. Hence, the journal entry is as follows:

Date	Particulars	L.F.	Debit Rs.	Credit Rs.
3-1-2002	Purchases [of goods] a/c dr.		30,000	
	To Raj a/c			30,000
	[Being goods purchased on credit]			

Transaction 4

5-1-2002 sold goods for cash Rs.25,000.

In this transaction, cash comes in and goods go out. Hence, the entry is as follows:

Date	Particulars	L.F.	Debit Rs.	Credit Rs.
5-1-2002	Cash a/c dr.		25,000	
	To Sales a/c			25,000
	[Being cash sales]			

Transaction 5

15-1-2002 paid wages Rs.6,000.

In this transaction, wages being an expense a/c it is debited as per the third rule i.e., debit all expenses and losses and cash is paid for wages, hence it is credited. The journal entry is as follows:

Date	Particulars	L.F.	Debit Rs.	Credit Rs.
15-1-2002	Wages a/c dr.		6,000	

	To Cash a/c [Being wages paid]			6,000

Transaction 6

16-1-2002 Interest received Rs.1,500.

In this transaction, interest being an income, it is credited as per the third rule i.e., credit all incomes and gains. Interest is received in the form of cash; hence it is debited. The journal entry is as follows:

Date	Particulars	L.F.	Debit Rs.	Credit Rs.
16-1-2002	Cash a/c dr. To Interest a/c [Being interest received]		1,500	 1,500

State the accounts involved in the following transactions and which account is to be debited and which account is to be credited.

1. Karthik commenced business with Rs.1,00,000.
2. Purchased furniture for Rs.5,000.
3. Sold goods for cash Rs.5,000
4. Sold goods to Raj for Rs.20,000.
5. Paid salaries Rs.10,000.
6. Purchased goods from Ram for cash Rs.9,000.
7. Commission received Rs.800.
8. Paid outstanding expenses Rs.900.

Answer

Books of Karthik

Sl. No	Accounts involved	Account to be debited	Account to be credited
1.	Cash a/c and Capital a/c	Cash a/c [Real a/c]	Capital a/c [Personal a/c]
2.	Furniture a/c and Cash a/c	Furniture a/c [asset comes in] Real a/c	Cash a/c [asset goes out] Real a/c
3.	Cash a/c and Sales a/c	Cash a/c [Asset comes in] Real a/c	Sales a/c [income] Nominal a/c
4.	Raj a/c and Sales a/c	Raj [receiver] Personal a/c	Sales a/c [Nominal a/c]
5.	Salaries a/c and Cash a/c	Salaries [expense] Nominal a/c	Cash a/c
6.	Purchases a/c and Cash a/c	Purchases a/c [expense] Nominal a/c	Cash a/c
7.	Cash a/c and Commission a/c	Cash a/c [comes in] Real a/c	Commission a/c [income] Nominal a/c

8.	Outstanding expenses a/c and Cash a/c	Outstanding expenses a/c [creditors receive] Personal a/c	Cash a/c [goes out] Real a/c

Illustration 1

Enter the following transactions in the journal of Mr. Ramkumar.

2002 Jan. 1		Rs
1	Started business by investing cash	70,000
2	Purchased land for	20,000
2	Purchased goods for cash	30,000
3	Purchased goods from Ajit on credit	10,000
4	Sold goods for cash	20,000
5	Sold goods to Arun on credit	6,000
6	Paid freight	300
8	Donated to Charities	1,000
11	Paid salaries to Ramesh	1,200
12	Deposited cash into bank	16,000
13	Withdrawn from bank for office use	4,000
14	Withdrawn from bank for private use	6,000
15	Charged Interest on capital	1,000
15	Rent received	2,000
16	Loan from bank	20,000

Solution

Date	Particulars		L.F.	Amount [dr.] Rs.	Amount [cr.] Rs.
2002 Jan. 1	Cash a/c To Capital a/c [Being cash brought in as capital]	dr.		70,000	70,000
2	Land a/c To Cash a/c [Being land bought for cash]	dr.		20,000	20,000
2	Purchases a/c	dr.		30,000	

Date	Particulars		L.F.	Amount [dr.] Rs.	Amount [cr.] Rs.
	To Cash a/c				30,000
	[Being cash purchases]				
3	Purchases a/c	dr.		10,000	
	To Ajit a/c				10,000
	[Being credit purchases]				
4	Cash a/c	dr.		20,000	
	To Sales a/c				20,000
	[Being cash sales]				
5	Arun a/c	dr.		6,000	
	To Sales a/c				6,000
	[Being credit sales]				
6	Freight a/c	dr.		300	
	To cash a/c				300
	[Being freight paid]				
8	Donation a/c	dr.		1,000	
	To Cash a/c				1,000
	[Being donation paid]				
11	Salary a/c	dr.		1,200	
	To Cash a/c				1,200
	[Being salaries paid]				
12	Bank a/c	dr.		16,000	
	To Cash a/c				16,000
	[Being cash deposited into bank]				
13	Cash a/c	dr.		4,000	
	To Bank a/c				4,000
	[Being withdrawal from bank for office use]				
14	Drawings a/c	dr.		6,000	
	To Bank a/c				6,000
	[Being withdrawal from bank for private use]				
15	Interest a/c	dr.		1,000	
	To Capital a/c				1,000
	[Being interest charged on capital]				
15	Cash a/c	dr.		2,000	

Date	Particulars		L.F.	Amount [dr.] Rs.	Amount [cr.] Rs.
	To Rent a/c				2,000
	[Being rent received]				
16	Cash a/c	dr.		20,000	
	To Bank Loan a/c				20,000
	[Being loan taken from bank]				

3.3 What is a Compound Journal Entry?

If two or more transactions of the same nature occur on the same day and either debit account and/or credit account are common in them, then instead of passing a separate entry for each such transaction, one combined entry may be passed. Such type of entry is known as compound journal entry.

For example, if a trader pays postage, stationery, and cartage on the same day, then instead of passing separate entries for each of these three expenses, the following compound entry may be passed:

Postage a/c dr.
Stationery a/c dr.
Cartage a/c dr.
To Cash a/c

3.4 Meaning of Discounts Transactions

Discount is an allowance in the form of reduction in the value of an item. There are two kinds of discounts viz., trade discount and cash discount.

Trade discount is allowed at the time of purchase or sale of goods by one trader to another in order to promote sales. For example, a manufacturer may allow discount on sale of goods to wholesaler or a wholesaler may allow discount to a retailer. It is always allowed as certain percentage on sale price i.e., invoice price. The trade discount is not normally recorded in the books of account. In other words, only the net amount of purchase or sale i.e., invoice price minus trade discount is recorded in the journal.

Example. Mr.X sells goods for Rs. 5000 to Mr.Y at a trade discount of 20%. For recording this transaction the net amount of Rs.4000 [i.e., Rs.5000 – 1000 (20% of 5000)] will be considered by both X and Y.

Entries

			Rs.
Books of Mr.X,			
Mr.Y a/c	dr.	4,000	
To Sales a/c			4,000
[Being goods sold at a discount]			
Books of Mr.Y,			
Purchase a/c	dr.	4,000	
To Mr.X a/c			4,000
[Being goods bought at a discount]			

Cash discount is a discount allowed at the time of making payments or receipts of cash. It is allowed as certain percentage on the amounts due. It is allowed to a debtor by a creditor in order to induce him to pay on time. As the cash discount is calculated on the amounts already recorded in the books, it is shown in the books. Cash discount allowed to a debtor is a loss and it should be debited to discount a/c. Cash discount received from a creditor is a gain and it should be credited to discount a/c.

Example

1. Mr. A owed Rs. 5,000 to the firm. He settled his account in full at a discount of 2%.

The journal entry in firm's books is as follows:

Cash a/c	dr.	Rs.4,900	
Discount allowed a/c	dr.	Rs.100	
To Mr.A a/c			Rs.5,000
[Being A settled his a/c at 2% discount]			

2. Suppose the firm owes Rs.10,000 to Mr.X, who allows a discount of 5% on full settlement of his account.

The journal entry in the firm's books is as follows:

Mr.X a/c	dr.	Rs.10,000	
To Cash a/c			Rs.9,500
To Discount received a/c			Rs.500
[Being X's a/c settled in full at 5% discount]			

Distinctions between Trade discount and Cash discount

	Trade Discount	Cash Discount
1.	It is allowed at the time of making purchases or sales.	It is allowed at the time of making payments or receipts of cash.
2.	It is calculated as certain percentage on the invoice price of goods purchased or sold.	It is calculated as certain percentage on the amounts due to creditors or amounts due from debtors.
3.	It is not shown in the books of accounts. Only the net amount of purchase or sale is recorded in the books.	It is shown in the books: discount allowed as debit entry and discount received as a credit entry.
4.	It is allowed in order to promote more sales or purchases.	It is allowed in order to encourage parties to make payments on time.

Illustration 1

Journalize the following transactions in the books of a trader.

2002 Jan.	1	commenced business with Rs.50,000.
	3	Purchased goods for cash Rs.10,000 at 5% trade discount.
	4	Paid carriage Rs.100
	7	Purchased Machinery for Rs.30,000.
	8	Sold goods to Mani on account for Rs. 15,000.

Solution

Date	Particulars		L.F.	Debit Rs.	Credit Rs.
2002 Jan. 1	Cash a/c	Dr.		50,000	
	To Capital a/c				50,000
	[Being business started with cash]				
3	Purchases a/c	Dr.		9,500	
	To Cash a/c				9,500
	[Being goods bought for cash at 5% trade discount]				
4	Carriage a/c	Dr.		100	
	To Cash a/c				100
	[Being carriage paid]				
7	Machinery a/c	Dr.		30,000	
	To Cash a/c				30,000
	[Being machinery purchased for cash]				
8	Mani's a/c	Dr.		15,000	
	To Sales a/c				15,000
	[Being credit sales]				

Illustration 2

Journalize the following transactions.

Durga of Chennai started business on 1-1-2002 by investing cash of Rs.50,000. She brought goods Rs.20,000 and furniture of Rs.2,500. She borrowed from her friend Priya Rs.25,000 the same day. Her transactions for the month are as follows:

January	1	Purchased goods worth Rs.25,000 less 20% trade discount and 5% cash discount.
	2	Opened a current a/c in State Bank of India with Rs.15,000.
	3	Sold goods worth Rs.15,000 to Vicky and allowed 10% discount.
	4	Received Rs.13,250 from Vicky in full settlement of his account.
	5	Sold goods to Ravi for cash Rs.3,500
	6	Sold goods to Krishna Rs.5,000.
	10	Received Rs.4,925 from Krishna in full settlement.
	15	Paid by cheque: Salaries Rs.2,500 Postage Rs.50 Stationery Rs.175
	16	Repair of furniture Rs.100
	18	Withdraw for personal use Rs.3,500
	20	Goods given in donation Rs.3,500

31 Sold goods to Ram at the invoice price of Rs.10,000 on the terms of trade discount at 20% and cash discount at 10%. He paid half in cash.

Solution

Journal in the Books of Durga

Date	Particulars		L.F.	Dr. Rs.	Cr. Rs.
2002 Jan. 1	Cash a/c	Dr.		50,000	
	Goods [stock] a/c	Dr.		20,000	
	Furniture a/c	Dr.		2,500	
	To Capital a/c				72,500
	[Being cash, goods and furniture brought in to start business]				
1	Cash a/c	Dr.		25,000	
	To Priya's Loan a/c				25,000
	[Being loan taken from Priya]				
1	Purchase a/c	Dr.		20,000	
	To Cash a/c				19,000
	To Discount a/c				1,000
	[Being goods worth Rs.25,000 bought for cash less 20% trade discount and 5% cash discount]				
2	Bank a/c	Dr.		15,000	
	To Cash a/c				15,000
	[Being cash paid into bank]				
3	Vicky a/c	Dr.		13,500	
	To Sales a/c				13,500
	[Being goods worth Rs.15,000 sold at 10% discount]				
4	Cash a/c	Dr.		13,250	
	Discount a/c	Dr.		250	
	To Vicky's a/c				13,500
	[Being cash received less discount]				
5	Cash a/c	Dr.		3,500	
	To Sales a/c				3,500
	[Being cash sales]				
6	Krishna's a/c	Dr.		5,000	
	To Sales a/c				5,000
	[Being credit sales]				
10	Cash a/c	Dr.		4,925	
	Discount a/c	Dr.		75	
	To Krishna's a/c				5,000
	[Being cash received in full settlement]				
15	Salarics a/c	Dr.		2,500	

Date	Particulars		L.F.	Dr. Rs.	Cr. Rs.
	Postage a/c	Dr.		50	
	Stationery a/c	Dr.		175	
	To Bank a/c				2,725
	[Being expenses paid by cheque]				
16	Repairs a/c	Dr.		100	
	To Cash a/c				100
	[Being repairs paid in cash]				
18	Drawings a/c	Dr.		3,500	
	To Cash				3,500
	[Being drawn for personal use]				
20	Donations a/c	Dr.		3,500	
	To Goods [Purchase] a/c				3,500
	[Being donations of goods]				
31	Ram's a/c	Dr.		8,000	
	To Sales a/c				8,000
	[Being goods sold at 20% trade discount]				
31	Cash a/c	Dr.		3,600	
	Discount a/c	Dr.		400	
	To Ram's a/c				4,000
	[Being half amount received at 10% cash discount]				

Illustration 3

An accountant made the following entries in his account books. Are these entries correct? If not, give correct entries.

			Rs.	Rs.
1.	Cash a/c	Dr.	3,500	
	To Raman a/c			3,500
	[Sold goods to Raman for cash]			
2.	Goods a/c	Dr.	6,000	
	To Lakshman a/c			6,000
	[Purchased goods for cash from Lakshman]			
3.	Ravi a/c	Dr.	2,000	
	To Cash a/c			2,000
	[Paid salary to Ravi]			
4.	Purchase a/c	Dr.	1,000	
	To Cash a/c			1,000
	[Furniture purchased for cash]			
5.	Freight a/c	Dr.	350	

	To Cash a/c			350
	[Freight paid on behalf of the purchaser, Raman]			
6.	Charity a/c	Dr.	500	
	To Sales a/c			500
	[Goods given for charity]			
7.	Sathya a/c	Dr.	1,250	
	To Cash a/c			1,250
	[Paid rent to Sathya]			

Solution

All entries are wrong. The correct entries are as follows:

			Rs.	Rs.
1.	Cash a/c	Dr.	3,500	
	To Sales a/c			3,500
	[Being cash sales]			
2.	Purchase a/c	Dr.	6,000	
	To Cash a/c			6,000
	[Being cash purchases]			
3.	Salary a/c	Dr.	2,000	
	To Cash a/c			2,000
	[Being payment of salary]			
4.	Furniture a/c	Dr.	1,000	
	To Cash a/c			1,000
	[Being furniture purchased for cash]			
5.	Raman a/c	Dr.	350	
	To Cash a/c			350
	[Being freight paid on behalf of Raman]			
6.	Charity a/c	Dr.	500	
	To Purchase a/c			500
	[Being goods given in charity]			
7.	Rent a/c	Dr.	1,250	
	To Cash a/c			1,250
	[Being rent paid]			

3.6 What does an Opening Entry Mean?

In a going concern, previous year balances are brought forward at the beginning of new accounting year by means of a composite or compound journal entry. Such an entry is known as opening entry. In journalizing, all the assets accounts are debited and liabilities accounts are credited. The excess of assets over liabilities is credited to Capital account.

Example

Pass the opening entry journal entry and find out the balance in the capital a/c.

The balances as on 31st December 2001 were as follows:

Debit balances: Cash in hand Rs.60,000; Cash at bank Rs.25,000; Stock Rs.90,000; Furniture Rs.35,000; Buildings Rs.1,25,000; Debtors Rs.75,000.

Credit balances: Outstanding rent Rs.2,500; Sundry Creditors Rs.30,000.

Solution

Opening Journal Entry

Date	Particulars		L.F.	Debit Rs.	Credit Rs.
2002 Jan. 1	Cash a/c	Dr.		60,000	
	Bank a/c	Dr.		25,000	
	Stock a/c	Dr.		90,000	
	Furniture a/c	Dr.		35,000	
	Buildings a/c	Dr.		1,25,000	
	Debtors a/c	Dr.		75,000	
	To Outstanding Rent a/c				2,500
	To Sundry Creditors a/c				30,000
	To Capital a/c [balancing figure]				3,77,500
	[Balances brought in from last year]				

REVIEW QUESTIONS

1. Define journal and describe the procedure for journalizing.
2. Illustrate a compound entry.
3. Explain the discount transactions.
4. Distinguish between trade discount and cash discount.
5. Explain the meaning of opening entries giving a few examples.

Review Problems

1. Journalize the following transactions extracted from the books of a bookseller.

May 2002

1	Started business with a capital of Rs.1,50,000.
2	Borrowed from Bank Rs.40,000.
3	Furniture purchased Rs.10,000.
4	Purchased books Rs.50,000 and paper Rs.25,000.
7	Sold books and paper for cash Rs.35,000.

8	Purchased books from Madras Book House for Rs.50,000.
10	Sold books worth Rs.25,000 to Madras University Library.
17	Paid postage Rs.250.
19	Paid Rs.49,500 to Madras Book house in full settlement.
25	Received rent Rs.750 from Rajesh who is using a portion of the shop for his business.
27	Sold books on credit to Prasad Rs.15,000.
30	Paid rent Rs.2 250 and salary Rs.2,500.

2. Pass opening entry and find out the capital from the following balances:

Cash in hand Rs.15,000; Stock Rs.17,500; Debtors - Raj Rs.9,500, and Anu Rs.8,000; Creditors - Geetha Rs.25,000; Prepaid insurance Rs.5,000; Outstanding salaries Rs.6,000.

3. Journalize the following transactions.

2002 Jan.	
1	Rajini started business with a capital of Rs.60,000.
2	He purchased furniture for Rs.8,000.
3	Bought goods on credit from Vicky for Rs.12,000.
12	Sold goods to Umesh for Rs.15,000.
13	Received cash from Umesh Rs.9,000.
14	Purchased goods for cash Rs.12,000.
19	Sold goods for cash Rs.13,000.
20	Purchased stationery for Rs.500.
28	Paid rent Rs.1,200.
31	Paid Vicky Rs.8,000 on account.

4. Give narration for the following entries.

			Rs.	Rs.
(A)	Cash a/c	Dr.	15,000	
	Goods a/c	Dr.	10,000	
	To Capital a/c			25,000
(B)	Luna a/c	Dr.	10,000	
	To Sales a/c			10,000
(C)	Purchase a/c	Dr.	15,000	
	To Subbu a/c			15,000
(D)	Cash a/c	Dr.	9,800	
	Discount a/c	Dr.	200	
	To Luna a/c			10,000
(E)	Subbu a/c	Dr.	15,000	
	To Cash a/c			14,625
	To Discount a/c			375
(F)	Bank a/c	Dr.	4,000	
	Drawings a/c	Dr.	1,000	

	To Cash a/c			5,000
(G)	Charity a/c	Dr.	1,000	
	Drawings a/c	Dr.	2,000	
	To goods a/c			3,000

5. Not all of the following entries are correct. Pass correcting entries wherever necessary.

			Rs.	Rs.
(a)	Purchases a/c	Dr.	4,000	
	To Ajit traders a/c			4,000
	[Being furniture purchased from Ajit traders]			
(b)	Arun a/c	Dr.	1,000	
	To Bank a/c			1,000
	[Being salary paid to Arun by cheque]			
(c)	Sundaram's a/c	Dr.	6,000	
	To Sales a/c			6,000
	[Being goods sold to Sundaram for cash]			
(d)	Ramesh a/c	Dr.	3,000	
	To Furniture a/c			3,000
	[Being old furniture sold to Ramesh on credit]			
(e)	Cash a/c	Dr.	9,000	
	To Sales a/c			9,000
	[Being cash sales for the day]			
(f)	Durga a/c	Dr.	7,500	
	To Purchases a/c			7,500
	[Being goods purchased on credit from Durga]			
(g)	Cash a/c	Dr.	9,800	
	Trade discount a/c	Dr.	200	
	Cash discount a/c	Dr.	100	
	To Sales a/c			10,100
	[Being goods sold for Rs.10,100 and allowed trade discount Rs.200 and cash discount Rs.100]			
(h)	Furniture a/c	Dr.	3,000	
	To Cash a/c			3,000
	[Being furniture purchased for domestic use]			

[**Answer:** Entries (d) and (e) are correct entries. Others are wrong. Correcting entries should be passed.]

6. From the following transactions find out the nature of account and also state which account should be debited and which account should be credited:

(a) Salaries paid; (b) Dividends received; (c) Land purchased for cash; (d) Furniture sold; (e) Outstanding rent; (f) Received cash from Karthik; and (g) Proprietor introduced capital.

SECTION B: LEDGER - BOOK OF FINAL ENTRY

3.7 What is Ledger?

A ledger is a book of main entry and it contains various accounts such as personal accounts, real accounts, and nominal accounts. It is the Principal book of accounts where identical transactions related to specific person or thing are entered. A ledger account is nothing but a summary statement of all transactions relating persons, assets or liabilities, and expenses or incomes, which have taken place during a period of time showing their net effect. Journal records all business transactions separately and as per the order of the date of the transaction. The transaction pertaining to a particular person, asset or expenses are recorded at different places in the journal as they occur on different dates. Hence, journal fails to bring the similar transactions together and it is not useful for any reference. In order to have a consolidated view of the similar transactions, the transactions entered in the journal are transferred to the ledger accounts. The transferring process from journal to ledger is known as posting.

Specimen Ledger Account

Dr. **Name of Account** **Cr.**

Date	Particulars	J.F.	Amount Rs.	Date	Particulars	J.F.	Amount Rs.
Year Month Date	To [Name of credit element]			Year Month Date	By [Name of the debit element]		

This is the standard form of ledger account, which is in "T" form. It is widely used. Each account in the ledger is divided into two equal parts. The left hand side is the debit side [Dr.] and the right hand side is the credit side [Cr.]. Each of the two sides is further divided into four columns for recording the date of the transactions, the name of the account to be debited or credited, folio, and the amount of the transaction. J.F. stands for journal folio i.e., the page number in the journal or subsidiary book from where the posting to the account is made.

Running Balance Form of Ledger Account. This form has six columns, viz., (1) Date; (2) Particulars; (3) J.F.; (4) Dr. Amount [Rs.]; (5) Cr. Amount [Rs.]; and (6) Balance. Commercial banks and some business houses use this type of ledger.

3.8 Advantages of a Ledger

The main advantages of a ledger are:

1. The journal gives information regarding various transactions chronologically. But the ledger gives information regarding all transactions of a particular account in a summary form.

2. In the journal one account is debited and another account is credited at different dates. The final effect of a series of transactions of a certain customer or certain property or

a certain expense is not disclosed by the journal. It is not designed in that way. But the final effect is known at a glance.

3. Similarly the journal could not provide immediately the totality of certain dealings.

3.9 Meaning of a Loose-leaf Ledger

The ledger that is normally used in majority of business concerns is a bound book, so that it can be preserved for a long time. But in bigger concerns bound books may not be used. Appropriately ruled sheets in thick paper are introduced and fixed up with the help of a binder. The sheets can be removed whenever necessary. Therefore, this type of ledger is known as "loose-leaf ledger". There is of course a danger that an unscrupulous employee may remove a sheet. To prevent such removal, this type of ledger is locked and will be with a responsible official.

3.10 How can a ledger be sub-divided?

In small concerns all accounts relating to persons, assets, expenses and income, etc., can be maintained in one ledger and in one Cashbook. In a broad sense, Cashbook is also a part of the ledger. But in bigger concerns, as the accounts are too many, the ledger is further sub-divided. They maintain the following three types of ledgers.

(1) The Creditors Ledger: All accounts of creditors will be found in this ledger. It can also be called as 'Bought Ledger' or 'Supplier's Ledger.' Entries in this ledger are usually made from Purchases daybooks, Purchases Returns book and Cashbook.

(2) The Debtors Ledger: It contains accounts of those customers to whom goods are sold on credit. It is also known as Customers' Ledger or Sales Ledger. Entries in this ledger are usually made from Sales Daybook, Sales Returns book and Cashbook.

(3) General Ledger/Nominal Ledger: It contains all accounts other than debtors and creditors. Accounts of properties, expenses, incomes, capital, drawings, etc., will be found in this ledger. It may also be called as 'Impersonal Ledger'.

Subdivision of Ledger

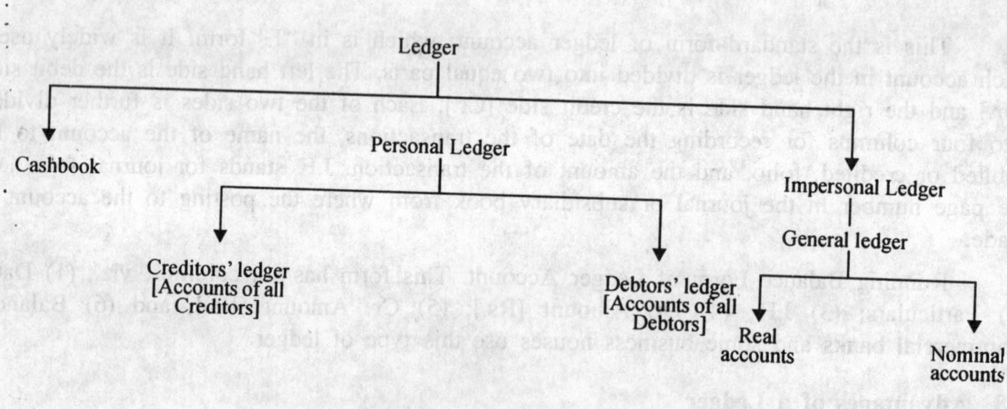

3.11 Procedure for Posting of Journal Entries into Ledger Accounts

Posting means transferring the debits and credits from the journal to ledger accounts. Each amount recorded in the debit column of the journal is posted to the debit side of an account in the ledger. And each amount recorded in the credit column of the journal is posted to the credit side of an account in the ledger.

Separate accounts should be opened in the ledger for posting transactions relating to separate persons, assets, expenses or incomes as shown in the journal.

The concerned account that has been debited in the journal should also be debited in the ledger. While debiting the concerned account, the name of the other account, which has been credited in the journal, is entered in the debit side of this account with a prefix "To".

Similarly, the concerned account that has been credited in the journal should also be credited in the ledger. While crediting the concerned account, the name of the other account that has been debited in the journal, is entered on the credit side of this account with a prefix "By".

The date of the transaction in the date column, the page number of the journal from which the entry is posted in the J.F. column, and the amount of the transaction in the amount columns should be entered in the concerned account.

Finally the concerned account should be balanced in order to find out the net balance in the account.

3.12 What does 'Balancing of an Account' Mean?

The various transactions entered in the journal in the chronological order are posted to the concerned account in the ledger [as explained above]. At the end of a period, say a month, a quarter, or a year, the account will be closed in order to find out the net position shown by it. Totaling the debits and credits of the account separately and finding the difference do this. The difference is entered on the side that is smaller and this difference is the 'closing balance' shown by the account and this will be carried forward to the next period as the 'opening balance' in the account. This process is known as 'balancing the account'. If the debit side total is smaller than the credit side, the difference is entered on the debit side to close the account for the period and the balance is known as the credit balance. If the credit side total is smaller, the difference will be known as the debit balance.

Example 1

On 31st January 2002 Commission paid Rs.5,000.

Journal Entry

31-1-2002	Commission a/c	Dr.	Rs.5,000	
	To Cash a/c			Rs.5,000
	[Being commission paid]			

The concerned accounts to be opened in the ledger are Commission a/c and Cash a/c. In the ledger, the Commission a/c should be debited and the Cash a/c should be credited.

Dr. **Commission a/c** Cr.

Date	Particulars	J.F.	Amount Rs.	Date	Particulars	J.F.	Amount Rs.
2002 Jan. 31	To Cash a/c		5,000	2002 Jan. 31	By balance c/d		5,000

			5,000				5,000
Feb. 1	To balance b/d		5,000				

Dr. **Cash a/c** Cr.

Date	Particulars	J.F.	Amount Rs.	Date	Particulars	J.F.	Amount Rs.
2002 Jan. 31	To balance c/d		5,000	2002 Jan. 31	By Commission a/c		5,000
			5,000				5,000
				Feb. 1	By balance b/d		5,000

Note: C/d is the abbreviation for carried/down. It means that the closing balance in the concerned account is taken [carried] down to the next period as the opening balance.

B/d is the abbreviation for brought/down. It indicates that the closing balance of the previous period has been brought down as the opening balance.

Example 2

On 31-1-2002 Purchased furniture for Rs.5,000 and cash box Rs.3,000 on credit from Exe Ltd.

The concerned accounts are furniture a\c, cash box a/c and Exe ltd. A/c. Furniture a/c and Cash box a/c should be debited and Exe ltd. A/c should be credited.

Dr. **Furniture a/c** Cr.

Date	Particulars	J.F.	Amount Rs.	Date	Particulars	J.F.	Amount Rs.
2002 Jan. 31	To Exe Ltd. A/c		5,000	2002 Jan. 31	By balance c/d		5,000
			5,000				5,000
Feb. 1	To balance c/d	5,000					

Dr. **Cash box a/c** Cr.

Date	Particulars	J.F.	Amount Rs.	Date	Particulars	J.F.	Amount Rs.
2002 Jan. 31	To Exe Ltd. a/c		3,000	2002 Jan. 31	By balance c/d		3,000
			3,000				3,000
Feb. 1	To balance b/d		3,000				

Dr. **Exe a/c** Cr.

Date	Particulars	J.F.	Amount Rs.	Date	Particulars	J.F.	Amount Rs.

2002 Jan. 31	To balance c/d		8,000	2002 Jan. 31	By Furniture a/c		5,000
					By Cash box a/c		3,000
			8,000				8,000
				Feb. 1	By balance b/d		8,000

Illustration 1

Journalize the following transactions, post them in the ledger and balance the accounts as on 31st December 2001.

December	1	Rashmi started business with a capital of Rs.50,000
	2	She purchased furniture for Rs.5,000
	3	Bought goods on credit from Vinod for Rs.8,000
	14	Sold goods to Suresh for Rs.5,000
	15	Received cash from Suresh Rs.3,000
	18	Purchased goods for cash Rs.12,000
	27	Sold goods for cash Rs.8,000
	28	Paid rent Rs.1,200
	31	Paid Vinod Rs.3,000 on account

Solution

Journal of Rashmi

Date	Particulars	J.F.	Dr. [Rs.]	Cr. [Rs]
2001 Dec. 1	Cash a/c Dr. To Rashmi capital a/c [Being capital introduced]		50,000	50,000
2	Furniture a/c Dr. To Cash a/c [Being furniture purchased]		5,000	5,000
3	Purchases a/c Dr. To Vinod a/c [Being credit purchases]		8,000	8,000
14	Suresh a/c Dr. To Sales a/c [Being credit sales]		5,000	5,000
15	Cash a/c Dr. To Suresh a/c [Being cash received]		3,000	3,000
18	Purchases a/c Dr. To Cash a/c [Being cash purchases]		12,000	12,000
27	Cash a/c Dr. To Sales a/c		8,000	8,000

	[Being cash sales]			
28	Rent a/c Dr. To Cash a/c [Being rent paid]		1,200	1,200
31	Vinod a/c Dr. To Cash a/c [Being cash paid]		3,000	3,000

Ledger of Rashmi

Dr. **Cash a/c** Cr.

Date	Particulars	J.F.	Amount Rs.	Date	Particulars	J.F.	Amount Rs.
2001 Dec. 1	To Capital a/c		50,000	2001 Dec. 2	By Furniture a/c		5,000
15	To Suresh a/c		3,000	18	By Purchase a/c		12,000
28	To Sales a/c		8,000	28	By Rent a/c		1,200
				31	By Vinod a/c		3,000
				31	By balance c/d		39,800
			61,000				61,000
1-1-2002	To balance b/d		39,800				

Dr. **Rashmis Capital a/c** Cr.

Date	Particulars	J.F.	Amount Rs.	Date	Particulars	J.F.	Amount Rs.
2001 Dec. 31	To balance c/d		50,000	2001 Dec. 1	By Cash a/c		50,000
			50,000				50,000
				1-1-2002	By balance b/d		50,000

Dr. **Furniture a/c** Cr.

Date	Particulars	J.F.	Amount Rs.	Date	Particulars	J.F.	Amount Rs.
2001 Dec. 2	To Cash a/c		5,000	2001 Dec. 31	By balance c/d		5,000
			5,000				5,000
1-1-2002	To balance b/d		5,000				

Dr **Purchases a/c** Cr.

Date	Particulars	J.F.	Amount Rs.	Date	Particulars	J.F.	Amount Rs.

2001 Dec. 3	To Vinod a/c		8,000	2001 Dec. 31	By balance c/d		20,000
18	To Cash a/c		12,000				
			20,000				20,000
1-1-2002	To balance b/d		20,000				

Dr. **Sales a/c** Cr.

Date	Particulars	J.F.	Amount Rs.	Date	Particulars	J.F.	Amount Rs.
2001 Dec. 31	To balance c/d		13,000	2001 Dec. 14	By Suresh a/c		5,000
				27	By Cash a/c		8,000
			13,000				13,000
				1-1-2002	By balance b/d		13,000

Dr. **Vinod a/c** Cr.

Date	Particulars	J.F.	Amount Rs.	Date	Particulars	J.F.	Amount Rs.
2001 Dec. 31	To Cash a/c		3,000	2001 Dec. 3	By Purchases a/c		8,000
31	To balance c/d		5,000				
			8,000				8,000
				1-1-2002	By balance b/d		5,000

Dr. **Suresh a/c** Cr.

Date	Particulars	J.F.	Amount Rs.	Date	Particulars	J.F.	Amount Rs.
2001 Dec. 14	To Sales a/c		5,000	2001 Dec. 15	By Cash a/c		3,000
				31	By balance c/d		2,000
			5,000				5,000
2002 Jan. 1	To balance		2,000				

Dr. **Rent a/c** Cr.

Date	Particulars	J.F.	Amount Rs.	Date	Particulars	J.F.	Amount Rs.
2001 Dec. 28	To Cash a/c		1,200	2001 Dec. 31	By balance c/d		1,200
			1,200				1,200
1-1-2002	To balance b/d		1,200				

3.13 Meaning of Trial Balance

When the transactions are recorded under *double entry system* there is a credit for every debit. When one account is debited, another account is credited with equal amount. Therefore, it is quite evident that the total of debit balances of the ledger accounts of given transactions will be equal to the total of the credit balances. If a statement is prepared with debit balances in one side/column and credit balances on the other side/column, the totals of the two sides/columns will be equal. Such a statement is called as 'Trial Balance'. Or simply a trial balance may be defined as "a list of balances standing on the ledger accounts and cashbook of a concern".

Features: The following are its main features:

1. It is a tabular statement having separate sides/columns for debit balances and credit balances.

2. Closing balances of the various ledger accounts are brought to this statement.

3. It can be prepared at any date on which accounts are closed and balanced. But it is usually prepared at the end of the accounting year.

4. Trial balance is not an account. It is only a statement.

3.14 Advantages [or Functions] of a Trial balance

The important advantages of a trial balance are:

1. It presents to the businessman a consolidated list of all ledger balances.

2. It is the shortest method of verifying the arithmetical accuracy of entries made in the ledger.

3. If the total of debit side/column is equal to the total of credit side/column, the trial balance is said to agree. Otherwise, it is implied that some errors have been committed in the preparation of accounts.

4. It helps in the preparation of the final accounts i.e., Trading a/c. Profit and loss a/c and Balance Sheet.

3.15 Method of Preparing a Trial Balance

There are two methods of preparing a trial balance. They are: (1) Total Method and (2) Balance Method.

Total Method: In this method, ledger accounts are not balanced. They are totaled. These totals are entered in the debit and credit columns. The grand total of debit column will be equal to the total of the credit column. The format of a Trial balance under this method is as follows:

Trial Balance as on .... [closing date]

Particulars [Name of the Accounts]	L.F	Dr. Total of A/c Amount [Rs.]	Cr. Total of A/c Amount [Rs.]

Balance Method. Under this method, the closing balances of ledger accounts are tabulated in a separate statement. The brought down balances are brought to this statement. All debit balances are shown in the debit column and all credit balances in the credit column. This method is more commonly used one. The format of Trial balance under this method is as follows:

Trial Balance as on .... [closing date]

Particulars [Name of the Accounts]	L.F.	Debit balance Amount [Rs.]	Credit balance Amount [Rs.]

Important Note. All debtors' accounts, Assets or Properties accounts, all expenses or losses accounts will always show debit balances. They will be shown in the debit side/column of the trial balance.

All creditors accounts, Liabilities' accounts, Income or gains accounts will always show credit balances. They will be shown in the credit side/column of the trial balance.

Illustration 2

Prepare a trial balance using the closing balances of ledger accounts prepared for illustration 1.

Solution

The closing balances are as follows: Cash a/c Rs.39,800; Capital a/c Rs.50,000; Furniture a/c Rs.5,000; Purchases a/c Rs.20,000; Sales a/c Rs.13,000; Vinod a/c [cr.] Rs.5,000; Suresh a/c [dr.] Rs.2,000; and Rent Rs.1,200.

Particulars	L.F.	Debit balances Rs.	Credit balances Rs.
Cash a/c		39,800	
Capital a/c			50,000
Furniture a/c		5,000	
Purchases a/c		20,000	
Sales a/c			13,000
Vinod a/c			5,000
Suresh a/c		2,000	
Rent a/c		1,200	
Total		68,000	68,000

Illustration 3

Journalize the following transactions and prepare necessary ledger accounts and verify the arithmetical accuracy of the ledger accounts.

2002		Rs.
January 1	Vicky started business with a capital of	1,00,000
3	Purchased goods from Ajit for cash	30,000
6	Cash sales	2,000
8	Goods sold to Shankar on credit	6,000

10	Purchased goods from Anil on credit	10,000
15	Received from Shankar in full settlement	5,900
20	Paid to Anil	5,000
24	Purchased furniture for office use	4,000
31	Paid shop rent Rs.2,000 and salaries	3,000

Solution

Journal of Vicky

Date	Particulars		L.F.	Amount [Rs.]	Amount [Rs.]
2002 Jan. 1	Cash a/c	Dr.		1,00,000	
	To Capital a/c				1,00,000
	[Being capital introduced]				
3	Purchases a/c	Dr.		30,000	
	To Cash a/c				30,000
	[Being cash purchases]				
6	Cash a/c	Dr.		2,000	
	To Sales a/c				2,000
	[Being cash sales]				
8	Shankar's a/c	Dr.		6,000	
	To Sales a/c				6,000
	[Being credit sales]				
10	Purchases a/c	Dr.		10,000	
	To Anil's a/c				10,000
	[Being credit purchases]				
15	Cash a/c	Dr.		5,900	
	Discount a/c	Dr.		100	
	To Shankar's a/c				6,000
	[Being cash received in full settlement]				
20	Anil's a/c	Dr.		5,000	
	To Cash a/c				5,000
	[Being cash paid]				
24	Furniture a/c	Dr.		4,000	
	To Cash a/c				4,000
	[Being furniture purchased]				
31	Rent a/c	Dr.		2,000	
	Salaries a/c	Dr.		3,000	
	To Cash a/c				5,000
	[Being rent and salaries paid]				

VICKY'S LEDGER

Dr. **Cash a/c** Cr.

Date	Particulars	J.F.	Amount Rs.	Date	Particulars	J.F.	Amount Rs.

2002 Jan. 1	To Capital a/c		1,00,000	2002 Jan. 3	By Purchases a/c		30,000
6	To Sales a/c		2,000	20	By Anil's a/c		5,000
15	To Shankar a/c		5,900	24	By Furniture a/c		4,000
				31	By Rent a/c		2,000
				31	By Salaries a/c		3,000
				31	By Balance c/d		63,900
			1,07,900				1,07,900
1-2-2002	To Balance b/d		63,900				

Dr. **Capital a/c** Cr.

Date	Particulars	J.F.	Amount Rs.	Date	Particulars	J.F.	Amount Rs.
2002 Jan. 31	To Balance c/d		1,00,000	2002 Jan. 1	By Cash a/c		1,00,000
			1,00,000				1,00,000
				1-2-2002	By Balance b/d		1,00,000

Dr. **Purchases a/c** Cr.

Date	Particulars	J.F.	Amount Rs.	Date	Particulars	J.F.	Amount Rs.
2002 Jan. 3	To Cash a/c		30,000	2002 Jan. 31	By Balance c/d		40,000
10	To Anil's a/c		10,000				
			40,000				40,000
1-2-2002	To Balance b/d		40,000				

Dr. **Sales a/c** Cr.

Date	Particulars	J.F.	Amount Rs.	Date	Particulars	J.F.	Amount Rs.
2002 Jan. 31	To Balance c/d		8,000	2002 Jan. 6	By Cash a/c		2,000
				8	By Shankar a/c		6,000
			8,000				8,000
				1-2-2002	By Balance b/d		8,000

Dr. **Shankar's a/c** Cr.

Date	Particulars	J.F.	Amount Rs.	Date	Particulars	J.F.	Amount Rs.
2002 Jan. 8	To Sales a/c		6,000	2002 Jan. 15	By Cash a/c		5,900

				15	By Discount a/c		100
			6,000				6,000

Dr. **Anil's a/c** Cr.

Date	Particulars	J.F.	Amount Rs.	Date	Particulars	J.F.	Amount Rs.
2002 Jan. 20	To Cash a/c		5,000	2002 Jan. 10	By Purchases a/c		10,000
31	To Balance c/d		5,000				
			10,000				10,000
				1-2-2002	By Balance b/d		5,000

Dr. **Discount a/c** Cr.

Date	Particulars	J.F.	Amount Rs.	Date	Particulars	J.F.	Amount Rs.
2002 Jan. 15	To Shankar a/c		100	2002 Jan. 31	By Balance c/d		100
			100				100
1-2-2002	To Balance b/d		100				

Dr. **Furniture a/c** Cr.

Date	Particulars	J.F.	Amount Rs.	Date	Particulars	J.F.	Amount Rs.
2002 Jan. 24	To Cash a/c		4,000	2002 Jan. 31	By Balance c/d		4,000
			4,000				4,000
1-2-2002	To Balance b/d		4,000				

Dr. **Rent a/c** Cr.

Date	Particulars	J.F.	Amount Rs.	Date	Particulars	J.F.	Amount Rs.
2002 Jan. 31	To Cash a/c		2,000	2002 Jan. 31	By Balance c/d		2,000
			2,000				2,000
1-2-2002	To Balance b/d		2,000				

Dr. **Salaries a/c** Cr.

Date	Particulars	J.F.	Amount Rs.	Date	Particulars	J.F.	Amount Rs.

2002 Jan. 31	To Cash a/c		3,000	2002 Jan. 31	By Balance c/d		3,000
			3,000				3,000
1-2-2002	To Balance b/d		3,000				

To verify the arithmetical accuracy of ledger accounts, the trial balance should be prepared.

Trial Balance as on January 31, 2002

Particulars	Debit (Rs.)	Credit (Rs.)
Cash a/c	63,900	
Capital a/c		1,00,000
Furniture a/c	4,000	
Purchases a/c	40,000	
Sales a/c		8,000
Anil's a/c		5,000
Rent a/c	2,000	
Discount a/c	100	
Salaries a/c	3,000	
Total	1,13,000	1,13,000

Illustration 4

Arun commenced business with Rs.30,000 cash and Rs.10,000 furniture. Sales amounted to Rs.1,32,000 including Rs.32,000 cash sales and Rs.20,000 sales were outstanding at the end of the year. Purchases amounted to Rs.70,000 including Rs.16,000 cash purchases and Rs.40,000 has been paid to creditors. Salaries paid amounted to Rs.8,000. Drawings were Rs.12,000. Machinery was purchased for Rs.24,000, out of which Rs.8,000 has been paid. Prepare Trial Balance.

Solution

Trial Balance

Particulars (name of the accounts)	Debit (Rs.)	Credit (Rs.)
Capital		40,000
Furniture	10,000	
Sales		1,32,000
Purchases	70,000	
Debtors	20,000	

Particulars	Debit	Credit
Creditors		14,000
Salaries	8,000	
Drawings	12,000	
Machinery	24,000	
Creditor for Machinery		16,000
Cash	58,000	
Total	2,02,000	2,02,000

Workings

Cash a/c

Receipts	Amount Rs.	Payments	Amount Rs.
To Capital	30,000	By Cash purchases	16,000
To Cash sales	32,000	By Creditors	40,000
To Collections from debtors	80,000	By Salaries	8,000
		By Drawings	12,000
		By Machinery	8,000
		By Balance c/d	58,000
	1,42,000		142,000
To Balance c/d	58,000		

Total value of machinery Rs.24,000 less cash paid Rs.8,000 will be Creditors for machinery i.e., Rs.16,000.

	Total Sales	1,32,000
	Less Cash sales	32,000
	Balance credit sales	1,00,000
Less	Debtors at the end	20,000
	Collections from debtors	80,000

Illustration 5

From the following ledger balances, prepare Trial balance.

Opening Stock Rs.30,000; Purchases Rs.3,00,000; Closing Stock Rs.14,000; Debtors Rs.1,20,000;Cash Rs.3,000; Discount allowed Rs.3,400; Bank Rs.5,600; Creditors Rs.90,000; Sales Rs.4,20,000; Salaries Rs.42,000; Rent Rs.9,000; Postage Rs.4,500; Taxes Rs.1,500; Machinery Rs.1,20,000; Drawings Rs.20,000; Capital Rs.1,52000; Purchase Returns Rs.6,000; Sales Returns Rs.9,000.

Solution

Trial Balance as on ....

Debit balances	Amount Rs.	Credit Balances	Amount Rs.

Opening Stock	30,000	Purchases Returns	6,000
Purchases	3,00,000	Sales	4,20,000
Sales Returns	9,000	Creditors	90,000
Salaries	42,000	Capital	1,52,000
Rent	9,000		
Postage	4,500		
Taxes	1,500		
Debtors	1,20,000		
Discount allowed	3,400		
Drawings	20,000		
Cash	3,000		
Bank	5,600		
Machinery	1,20,000		
Total	6,68,000	Total	6,68,000

Note: Closing Stock is not included in the above trial balance because it is an item of adjustment and its value is ascertained only after closing the ledger accounts.

Illustration 6

The following Trial balance contains certain obvious errors. Point out the errors and prepare a correct Trial balance.

Name of the accounts	Debit (Rs.)	Credit (Rs.)
Purchases	70,000	
Sales		1,00,000
Purchase Returns	4,000	
Sales Returns		8,000
Opening stock	60,000	
Closing stock		56,000
Trade expenses	8,000	
Outstanding expenses	4,000	
Cash in hand	10,000	
Bank overdraft	50,000	
Debtors		56,000
Creditors		12,000
Carriage inwards	4,000	
Carriage outwards		6,000
Discount received	10,000	
Loan from Chaco	30,000	
Capital		1,12,000
Buildings	1,00,000	
Total	3,50,000	3,50,000

Solution

Obvious Errors. The following credit balances have been shown in the debit column: Purchases Returns, Outstanding expenses, Bank overdraft, Discount Received, and Loan from Chaco. These items should be shown in the credit column.

The following debit balances have been shown in the credit column: Sales Returns, Carriage Outwards. They should be shown in the debit column.

Closing Stock, being an adjustment item, should not be shown in the trial balance.

Correct Trial Balance as on ………

Name of the Accounts	Debit (Rs.)	Credit (Rs.)
Purchases	70,000	
Sales		1,00,000
Purchases Returns		4,000
Sales Returns	8,000	
Opening Stock	60,000	
Trade expenses	8,000	
Outstanding expenses		4,000
Cash in hand	10,000	
Bank overdraft		50,000
Debtors	56,000	
Creditors		12,000
Buildings	1,00,000	
Carriage inwards	4,000	
Carriage outwards	6,000	
Discount received		10,000
Loan from Chaco		30,000
Capital		112,000
Total	3,22,000	3,22,000

REVIEW QUESTIONS

1. Explain the meaning of ledger and give a specimen of a ledger account.
2. What are the advantages of a ledger?
3. What is a loose-leaf ledger?
4. State the procedure for posting of entries into ledger accounts.
5. Explain the balancing of a ledger account.
6. Explain the meaning and func· ons of a trial balance.
7. Illustrate the preparation of a trial balance.

REVIEW PROBLEMS

1. Journalize the following transactions and post them to various ledger accounts. Also prepare a Trial Balance as on 31st December 2001.

December 1	Raj started business with a capital of Rs.50,000.
2	He purchased computer for office use for Rs.24,000
3	Bought goods on credit from Vignesh for Rs.18,000.
15	Sold goods to Subbu on credit Rs.15,000.
18	Purchased goods for cash Rs.12,000.
19	Sold goods for cash Rs.9,000.
27	Received cash from Subbu Rs.3,000.
28	Paid rent Rs.1,500.
31	Paid Vignesh Rs.9,000 on account.

2. Mr.Nirmal commenced business on Jan.1, 2002 with Rs.50,000 borrowed from his friend Ramesh. Her transactions for the month of January were as follows:

January 1	Deposited in Bank Rs.20,000.
3	Purchased goods worth Rs.25,000 from Meeran for cash who allowed 20% trade discount and 10% cash discount.
4	Sold goods for cash Rs.20,000.
7	Purchased good from Raju Rs.20,000.
10	Returned goods to Raju worth Rs.2,000.
11	Paid Rs.17 500 to Raju in full settlement.
20	Purchased furniture from Raghav Rs.5,000. He paid freight Rs.200 on our behalf.
21	Paid rent Rs.2,500.
27	Received commission Rs.800.
31	Paid salaries Rs.3,000.

Pass journal entries and post them to various ledger account.

3. From the following information, prepare the Trial balance of Mr.Karthik for the year ended on 31st March, 2002.

Names of Accounts	Rs.	Names of Accounts	Rs.
Capital account	25,000	Sales account	30,900
Furniture & fittings	1,280	Bank [cr.balance]	5,700
Motor Car	12,500	Purchase Returns	250
Buildings	15,000	Commission [Cr.]	750
Debtors	7,600	Sales returns	400
Creditors	5,000	Advertisement	500
Bad debts	250	Interest account [Dr.]	236
Opening Stock	6,920	Cash balance	1,300

Purchases	10,950	Insurance & Tax	2,500
		Salaries	8,164

(Answer: Total of Trial balance Rs.67,600)

4. The following Trial balance has certain errors. Point out the errors and prepare the correct Trial balance.

Particulars	Debit (Rs.)	Credit (Rs.)
Capital account	1,00,000	
Furniture		10,000
Deposit with Bank		75,000
Interest received		10,000
Miscellaneous receipts		7,625
Sundry creditors	12,500	
Sundry debtors	35,000	
Cash in hand		3,375
House rent	2,500	
Office expenses		4,250
Total	1,50,000	1,10,250

(Answer: Total of correct Trial balance Rs.1,30,125)

5. Enter the following transactions in Journal, post them in Ledger and prepare a Trial balance.

2000 June 1	Rajesh commenced business with the following assets: Machinery Rs.1 25,000 Land 45,000 Furniture 32,500, Cash 2,500
2	Sold goods to Anil 20,000
3	Purchased goods from Mouli 32,500
4	Anil paid cash 12 500
7	Damaged goods returned to Mouli 900
10	Paid Mouli on account 14,100
15	Purchased goods from Hariharan 27,000
18	Sold goods to Ravi 37 500
20	Received cash from Ravi 30,000
27	Goods returned by Ravi 2,000
28	Paid Hariharan 18,000
30	Salaries paid 3,750
30	Rent paid 1,250

(Answer: Trial balance total Rs.2,89,900) (M.C.A., Madras University, Nov. 2002)

4

SUBSIDIARY BOOKS

Learning Objectives

After completing this chapter, you should be able to:

— Understand the meaning and advantages of subsidiary books,

— Describe the preparation of various subsidiary books,

— Answer what a journal proper is,

— Know how to reconcile the cashbook and passbook balances,

— Know the meaning and types of accounting errors.

4.1 Basic Accounting Records Maintained by a Business Firm

In small business concerns where the numbers of transactions are few the basic accounting records are mainly the journal book, ledger and a cashbook. One person can maintain all books and record all transactions in these books. However, in big firms having numerous transactions, in addition to these three books separate books are maintained for recording credit purchases, credit sales, bills transactions, etc. They are Purchases Day book, Sales Day book, Returns Inward and Outward books, Bills Receivable and Payable books, and Petty Cash book.

4.2 What does 'Subsidiary Books' Mean?

Subsidiary Books are those books of original entry in which transactions of similar nature are recorded at one place and in chronological order. In a big concern, recording of all transactions in one Journal and posting them into various ledger accounts will be very difficult and involve a lot of clerical work. This is avoided by sub-dividing the journal into various subsidiary journals or books. The subdivision of journal into various subsidiary journals for recording transactions of similar nature are called as 'Subsidiary Books.' The different subsidiary books and their purpose are shown below:

1. Purchases Day Book - for recording credit purchase of goods only. Cash purchase or assets purchased on credit are not entered in this book.

2. Sales Day Book - for recording credit sales of goods only. Assets sold or cash sales are not recorded in this book.

3. Purchases Returns Book - for recording the goods returned to the suppliers when purchased on credit.

4. Sales Returns Books - for recording goods returned by the customers when sold on credit.

5. Bills Receivable Book - for recording the bills received [Bills Receivables] from customers for credit sales.

6. Bills Payables Book - for recording the acceptances [Bills Payables] given to the suppliers for credit purchases.

7. Cash Book – for all receipts and payments of cash.

8. Journal Proper - for recording any transaction which could not be recorded in the above-mentioned subsidiary books. For example, assets purchased or sold on credit and opening entry etc., are entered in this book.

4.3 Advantages of Subsidiary Books

The following are the advantages of Subsidiary books or Special journal:

1. Saving of Clerical Labour: Subsidiary books effect considerable saving of clerical labour in postings and narration. Transactions of any one class such as credit purchases, credit sales, cash transactions etc., are recorded through separate subsidiary journals and there is no need for giving narration. For example, by recording the transactions in the Purchase Day book 50% of the labour in postings is saved. The periodical total of this book is to be debited to the Purchases a/c. Only the personal accounts of the suppliers are to be credited.

2. Division of Clerical Work: As separate journals are used for recording the transactions of each particular type, the division of clerical labour amongst several office clerks becomes possible. This makes speedy record of day-to-day transactions practicable.

3. Minimizes Frauds: These books make possible the introduction of internal check system under which the system of rotation of writing up books can be adopted. This helps minimizing errors and detecting frauds.

4. Facilitates further reference: As transactions of similar nature are grouped together in a separate book, the further reference to any particular item is considerably facilitated.

4.4 Preparation of various Subsidiary Books

Preparation of Purchase Day Book

This book is maintained mainly to record credit purchases of goods. The term 'goods' refers to all such commodities and services in which the firm normally deals. Hence, cash purchase of goods or purchases of assets are not recorded in this book. Entries are made in this book from inward invoices of credit purchases. The ruling of this book is given below:

Date	Particulars [Names of suppliers]	Invoice No.	L.F.	Details Rs.	Amount Rs.

Date column records the date of purchase.

In the particulars column, the name of the supplier of goods is entered and the details of goods purchased are also given in this column.

Invoice number refers to the number of Inward Invoice.

Ledger Folio refers to the page number of the ledger.

In the Details column, the amount of purchase of each type of goods is given.

In the amount column, the total amount for a given transaction is recorded.

The total of this book will give the total credit purchases made during the month.

Postings: Each Supplier's personal account is credited in the ledger with its respective amount with the words "By Purchases a/c." The monthly total of this book is debited to Purchases a/c in the ledger with the words "To Sundries" as per Purchases Book.

Illustration 1

From the following particulars, prepare the Purchase Book of a general merchant:

2001, December 1	Bought from K & Bros., at 10% trade discount
	3 doz pens at Rs.120 per doz.
	20 doz ink bottle at Rs.30 per doz.
7	Purchased for cash 50 reams of ruled paper at Rs.40 per ream from RS Paper House.
11	Purchased from Mani Stores:
	6 doz packets Glucco biscuits at Rs.5 per packet.
	15 doz. Packets salto biscuits at Rs.2.5 per packet.
18	Purchased from Saraswathi Stores:
	6 doz. packets Deluxe erasers at Rs.2.40 per packet.
	20 doz. Penholders at Rs.7.50 per doz.
27	Bought from Deluxe Furniture Mart on credit:
	12 Godrej chairs at Rs.200 per chair

Solution

PURCHASES DAY BOOK

Date	Particulars	Invoice No.	L.F.	Details Rs.	Amount Rs.
2001	K & Bros:				
Dec.1	3 doz. pens @ Rs.120 per doz.			360.00	
	20 doz. Ink bottles @ Rs.30 per doz.			600.00	
				960.00	
	Less trade discount at 10%			96.00	864.00
	Mani Stores:				
11	6 doz. Packets biscuits at Rs.5 per packet			360.00	
	15 doz packets salt biscuits at Rs.2.50 per packet			450.00	810.00
	Saraswathi Stores:,				
18	6 doz. Packets Deluxe erasers at Rs.2.40 per packet			172.80	
	20 doz. Penholders at Rs.7.50 per doz.			150.00	322.80
					1996.80

The transaction on 7th is cash purchases and on 27th is assets purchased. Hence these transactions are not entered in the Purchases Day Book.

Preparation of Sales Day Book

This book is maintained mainly to record credit sales of goods. Hence, the cash sales of goods and assets sold are not entered in this book. Entries in this book are made from the 'outward invoice' of credit sales. The ruling of this book is similar to that of Purchases Book. In the Particulars column of Sales Book, the name of the customer together with details of sales made to him will be entered. The invoice number in this book refers to the number of Outward Invoice sent to the customer. The total of this book will show the total credit sales made during the period.

Postings: Each customer's personal account is debited in the ledger with its respective amount with the words "To Sales a/c". The periodical total of this Book is credited to Sales a/c with the words "By Sundries" as per Sales Book.

Illustration 2

Prepare the Sales Day Book from the following particulars extracted from the books of Meenu Electricals.

2002, January

6 Sold on credit to Malathi:
100 Phillip lamps at Rs.50 per lamp.
200 Mysore lamps at Rs.45 per lamp.
200 Sylvania lamps at Rs.40 per lamp.

10 Sold to Rani for cash:
10 electric iron boxes at Rs.180 per iron box.
5 electric stoves at Rs.156 per stove.

14 Sold to Viji:
6 table lamps at Rs.30 per lamp.
6 Orient fans at Rs.400 per fan.
12 Kaissal [36"] fans At Rs.480 per fan.

18 Sold furniture to Amala on credit Rs.1000.

30 Sold to Janshi Traders
10 Toasters at Rs.90 per toaster.
12 Phillips tube at Rs.50 per tube.
10 Table lamps at Rs.30 per lamp.

Solution

SALES DAY BOOK

Date	Particulars	Invoice No.	L.F.	Details Rs.	Amount Rs.
2002,					
Jan.6	Malathi:,				
	100 Phillip lamps @ Rs.50.00			5000	
	200 Mysore lamps @ Rs.45.00 per lamp			9000	
	200 Sylvania lamps @ Rs.40.00 per lamp			8000	22000
	Viji:,				
14	6 table lamps @ Rs.30			180	
	6 Orient fans @ Rs.400			2400	
	12 Kassels fans @ Rs.480			5760	

				8340	
	Less 5% trade discount			417	7923
	Janshi Traders:,				
30	10 Toasters @ Rs.90			900	
	12 Phillip tubes @ Rs. 50.			600	
	10 Table lamps @ Rs. 30			300	1800
					31723

Preparation of Returns Outward or Purchase Returns Book

This book is maintained to record the returns of goods purchased earlier from the suppliers on credit. When goods are returned, a debit note is made out and sent to the supplier to whom goods are returned. Entries are made in this book from the debit note giving a reference to the number of debit note. The ruling of this book is given below:

Purchase Returns Book

Date	Particulars	Debit Note No.	L.F.	Amount Rs.

Postings: Each supplier's account mentioned in the Purchase Returns Book is debited in the ledger with its respective amount with the words "To Purchase Returns a/c". The periodical total of this book is credited to the Purchase Returns a/c with the words "By Sundries" as per Purchase Returns Book.

Preparation of Returns inward or Sales Returns Book

This book is maintained mainly the returns of goods sold to customers on credit. On receipt of the goods, the firm prepares a 'Credit Note' in the name of the customer and sends its original copy to the customer. Entries are made from Credit Note Book into the Sales Returns Book. The ruling of Sales Returns Book is given below:

Sales Returns Book

Date	Particulars	Credit Note No.	L.F.	Amount Rs.

Posting: Each customer's personal account [as given in the Sales Returns Book] is credited with the amount of goods returned by him with the words "By Sales Returns a/c". The sales returns a/c in the ledger gets the debit with the periodical total of Sales Returns Book with the words "To Sundries" as per Sales returns Book.

Preparation of Bills Receivables Book

This book is maintained to keep a detailed record of all the bills receivable received by the firm. This book provides a medium for posting bills receivable transactions. The ruling of this book is given below:

BILLS RECEIVABLE BOOK

Date when received	Drawer	Acceptor	Where payable	Date of bill	Term	Due date LF	Amount Rs.	Remarks

Postings: The personal account of the person from whom the bill is received , is credited with the amount of that bill and the periodical total of the Bills Receivable Book is debited to Bills Receivable a/c in the ledger.

Preparation of Bills Payable Book

This book is maintained to keep a detailed record of all bills payables accepted by the firm. The ruling of this book is given below:

BILLS PAYABLE BOOK

Date of acceptance	To whom given	Payee	Where payable	Date of bill	Term	Due date	L.F.	Amount Rs.	Remarks

Postings: The personal account of the person whose bill is accepted is debited with the amount of that bill and the periodical total of the Bills Payables Book is credited to Bills Payables a/c in the ledger.

Illustration 3

Enter the following transactions in the proper subsidiary books and post them in the ledger.

2002 January	
1	Bought goods from Bala Rs.15,000.
2	Sold goods to Prem Rs.25,000 and for cash Rs.10,000.
9	Sanjay sold goods to us Rs.10,000 at a trade discount of 10%.
14	Sold goods to Mahesh Rs.12,000.
18	Received goods returned by Prem Rs.500.
20	Returned goods to Sanjay worth Rs.900.
31	Returned goods by Mahesh Rs.1,200.

Solution

Purchases Book

Date	Particulars	L.F.	Inward Invoice No.	Amount Rs.
2002				
January 1	Bala			15,000
9	Sanjay			9,000
				24,000

Sales Book

Date	Particulars	L.F.	Inward Invoice No.	Amount Rs.
2002 January 2 14	Prem Mahesh			25,000 12,000
				37,000

Purchases Returns Book

Date	Particulars	L.F.	Inward Invoice No.	Amount Rs.
2002 January 20	Sanjay			900
				900

Sales Returns Book

Date	Particulars	L.F.	Inward Invoice No.	Amount Rs.
2002, January 18 31	Prem Mahesh			500 1,200
				1,700

Ledger

Bala A/C

Date	Particulars	J.F.	Amount Rs.	Date	Particulars	J.F.	Amount Rs.
				2002 Jan. 1	By Purchases a/c		15,000

Sanjay A/C

Date	Particulars	J.F.	Amount Rs.	Date	Particulars	J.F.	Amount Rs.
2002 Jan. 20	To Purchases Returns a/c		900	2002 Jan. 9	By Purchases		9,000

Prem A/C

Date	Particulars	J.F.	Amount Rs.	Date	Particulars	J.F.	Amount Rs.
2002 Jan. 2	To Sales a/c		25,000	2002 Jan. 18	By Sales Returns a/c		500

Mahesh A/C

Date	Particulars	J.F.	Amount Rs.	Date	Particulars	J.F.	Amount Rs.
2002 Jan. 14	To Sales a/c		12,000	2002 Jan. 31	By Sales Returns a/c		1,200

Purchases A/C

Date	Particulars	J.F.	Amount Rs.	Date	Particulars	J.F.	Amount Rs.
2002 Jan. 31	To Sundries		24,000				

Sales A/C

Date	Particulars	J.F.	Amount Rs.	Date	Particulars	J.F.	Amount Rs.
				2002 Jan. 31	By Sundries		37,000

Purchase Returns A/C

Date	Particulars	J.F.	Amount Rs.	Date	Particulars	J.F.	Amount Rs.
				2002 Jan. 31	By Sundries		900

Sales Returns A/C

Date	Particulars	J.F.	Amount Rs.	Date	Particulars	J.F.	Amount Rs.
2002 Jan. 31	To Sundries		1,700				

Preparation of Cash Book

In most of the business concerns, the number of cash transactions will usually be large. Hence, a separate Cash Book is maintained for recording such transactions. This book keeps a record of transactions of cash receipts and cash payments. Cash Book plays a dual role. It is both a book of original entry as well as a book of final entry [i.e., ledger]. It is a book of original entry because all cash transactions are first of all recorded in the cashbook and then posted to various accounts in the ledger. It also acts as a ledger account since the receipts of cash are entered on the debit side and payments of cash on the credit side. So it is not necessary to have a Cash Account in the ledger.

Types of Cash Book

Cash Book with different rulings is used in different concerns depending upon the nature of the business and the manner in which cash is dealt with. However, the following are the most common forms:

1. Simple Cash Book
2. Two-column Cash Book
3. Three-column Cash Book
4. Petty Cash Book

Simple Cash Book: This is the simplest form of Cash Book and is used in businesses where payments are made and received mostly in cash and where usually no cash discount is received or given. However, if there are any discount or cheque transactions, it is recorded in a separate account in the ledger. The ruling of a Simple Cash Book is like an ordinary cash account.

Cash Book

Date	Particulars	J.F.	Amount	Date	Particulars	J.F.	Amount

Posting: All the items on the debit side of the Cash Book are posted to the credit and those on the credit side are posted to the debit side of the respective ledger accounts affected. The Cash Book is balanced regularly, mostly daily and the balance should be equal to cash in hand. The cashbook will always show debit balance only.

Illustration 4

Enter the following transactions in a Cash Book.

2002			Rs.
March	1	Balance of cash in hand	15,000
	4	Received from Kanna	10,000
	7	Purchased goods for cash	17,000
	11	Cash Sales	18,000
	15	Deposited into Bank	3,000
	18	Bought furniture for cash	4,000
	22	Paid Salaries	1,500
	25	Withdrew from Bank	2,500
	27	Cash Sales	14,000
	30	Paid to Ram	8,000
	31	Rent paid	1,000

Solution

Cash Book

Date	Particulars	LF	Amount	Date	Particulars	LF	Amount
2002 March 1				2002 March 7			
	To balance b/d		15,000		By Purchase a/c		17,000
4	To kanna a/c		10,000	15	By Bank a/c		3,000
11	To Sales a/c		18,000	18	By Furniture a/c		4,000
25	To Bank a/c		2,500	22	By Salaries a/c		1,500
27	To Sales a/c		14,000	30	By Ram a/c		8,000
				31	By Rent a/c		1,000
				31	By balance c/d		25,000
			59,500				59,500
April 1	To balance b/d		25,000				

Two-column Cash Book: This type of cashbook has two columns, viz., cash column and discount column. Usually cash discount is allowed or received when payment is made. So, it is necessary to record this fact at the same place where the cash transaction is recorded. This type is similar to Simple Cash Book, except that one additional column on each side is provided for recording cash discount. As discount is a nominal account, discount allowed being a loss is shown on the debit side and discount received being a gain is shown on the credit side.

Illustration 5

Enter the following transactions in a Double Column Cash Book:

2002, March		Rs.
1	Cash in hand	11,000
5	Received from Krishna	38,000
	Allowed him discount	2,000
7	Bought goods for cash	40,000
9	Cash paid to Yusuf	7,000
	Discount allowed by him	500
12	Goods sold for cash	17,000
14	Withdrawn from Bank	52,000
18	Credit purchases from Mukesh	25,000
22	Paid to Mukesh in full settlement	24,000
25	Received interest on investments	27,000
28	Deposited into Bank	40,000
31	Paid salaries	5,000

Solution

Cash Book

Date	Receipts	LF	Dis. Rs.	Amount Rs.	Date	Payments	LF	Dis. Rs.	Amount Rs.
2002					2002				
Mar 1	To balance b/d			11,000	Mar 7	By Purchase a/c			40,000
5	To Krishna a/c		2000	38,000	9	By Yusuf a/c		500	7,000
12	To Sales a/c			17,000	22	By Mukesh a/c		1000	24,000
14	To Bank a/c			52,000	28	By Bank a/c			40,000
25	To Interest a/c			27,000	31	By Salaries a/c			5,000
					31	By balance c/d			29,000
			2000	145000				1500	145000
Apr 1	To balance b/d			29,000					

Note. Transaction on 18th March is omitted because it is a credit transaction [credit purchases].

Three-Column Cash Book

In modern times, banking habit has become so widespread and is so convenient and safe that a large number of payments of big concerns are made and received through cheques. In such cases, the Cash Book with bank column in addition to the cash and discount columns is found convenient. Such type of cashbook is known as three-column cashbook. In such a Cash Book, cash columns and bank columns represent cash a/c and bank a/c respectively.

Contra Entries. When a transaction affects both the sides of the Cash Book, such a transaction is entered on both the sides and is called as contra entry. For example, when cash is deposited into bank, it is entered in the debit side of the Cash Book by writing "To Cash" and entering the amount in the bank column. The other entry is on the credit side by writing "By Bank" and entering the amount in the Cash column. When the cash is withdrawn from the bank, the reverse entry is made, i.e., by writing "To Bank" in the debit side and entering the amount withdrawn in the cash column and the other entry is on the credit side by writing "By Cash" and entering the amount in the bank column of the Cash Book. Entering the letter "C" in the L.F. column indicates such entries. As the double entry is complete for such transactions in the Cash Book itself, no further posting is required in the ledger.

Rules for recording transactions in the Cash Book

1. All items of cash receipts are entered in the cash column of the receipt side; cash payments in the payment side. Discount allowed on the debit side and discount received on the credit side of the Cash Book [in the discount columns].

2. When cheques are received from customers and deposited immediately they are entered in the bank column of the Cash Book [debit side]. If they are sent to the bank at a later date, it becomes deposit of money into bank and, therefore, a 'contra' entry. It is shown on the bank column on the debit side and cash column on the credit side.

3. If cheques are received by the business and endorsed to creditors, they are taken into cash columns as cash receipt and cash payment.

Illustration 6

Enter the following transactions in a three-column Cash Book and find out the balances as on 16th January, 2002. .

2002 Jan. 1	Cash in hand Rs.3,000; balance at bank Rs.10,000.
3	Sold goods for cash Rs.10,000.
4	Deposited into bank Rs.8,000.
5	Received from Nattu Rs.4 000; And allowed him discount Rs.100.
6	Paid House rent by cheque Rs.1,000
7	Paid to Shyam Rs.5,000; and received discount Rs.50
9	Withdrew from bank for office use Rs.5,000.
10	Received a cheque of Rs.470 from Mohan in full settlement of his account Rs.500.
11	Cash sales deposited into bank Rs.2,500.
12	Cash sales Rs.1,000.
13	Paid Arun by cheque against his claim of Rs.2,000. @ a discount 5 %.
14	Paid traveling expenses Rs.700.
15	Draw a cheque for personal use Rs.1,000.

Solution

Cash Book

[With Cash, Bank, and Discount columns]

Date	Particulars	LF	Dis.	Cash	Bank	Date	Particulars	LF	Dis.	Cash	Bank
2002						2002					
Jan.1	To bal b/d			3000	10000	Jan.4	By Bank	C		8000	
3	To Sales			10000		6	By Rent				1000
4	To Cash	C			8000	7	By Shyam		50	5000	
5	To Nattu		100	4000		9	By Cash	C			5000
9	To Bank	C		5000		13	By Arun		100		1900
10	To Mohan		30		470	14	By T. exps			700	
11	To Sales				2500		By Drawing				1000
12	To Sales			1000		16	By bal. C/d			9300	12070
	Total		130	23000	20970		Total		150	23000	20970
16	To bal b/d			9300	12070						

Illustration 7

Make out a Cash Book with discount, cash and bank columns.

2002 March	
1	Cash in hand Rs.2800; Cash at bank Rs.8100.
3	Received from Jaya Rs.1500 and allowed her discount of Rs.20.
7	Paid into bank Rs.4000.
8	Received for sales cash Rs.100 and cheque Rs.190.
10	Paid Guhan by cheque Rs.570 in full settlement of his account Rs.600.
11	Cash purchases by cheque Rs.700.
15	Drew for office use Rs.350.
17	Advertisement expenses Rs.50.
20	Somu paid direct into our bank account Rs.620.
22	Withdrew cash for personal use Rs.170.

26	Paid rent by cheque Rs.200.
27	Received from Raja a cheque for Rs.490 and allowed him discount Rs.10.
29	Received commission by cheque Rs.220.
30	Cash in excess of Rs.400 was paid into bank.

Solution

Cash Book with Cash, bank, and Discount columns

Date	Particulars	LF	Dis. Rs.	Cash Rs.	Bank Rs.	Date	Particulars	LF	Dis. Rs.	Cash Rs.	Bank Rs.
2002 May						2002, May					
1	To balance B/d			2800	8100	7	By Bank	C		4000	
3	To Jaya		20	1500		10	By Guhan		30		570
7	To Cash	C			4000	11	By Purchase				700
8	To Sales			290		15	By Cash	C			350
15	To Bank	C		350		17	By Advt.				
20	To Somu				620	22	By Drawings			50	
27	To Raja		10	490		26	By Rent			170	200
29	To Commission			220		30	By Cash	C		1030	
30	To Cash	C			1030	31	By Balance b/d			400	11930
	Total		30	5650	13750		Total		30	5650	13750
Jun.1	To Balance c/d			400	11930						

4.5 Preparation of Petty Cash Book

In all businesses, numerous small or petty payments like postage, cartage, printing and stationery, cleaning etc., are made. If all such payments are recorded in the main Cash Book, recording would be cumbersome, and time consuming. Hence, such petty expenses may be recorded in a separate book known as Petty Cash Book. The person maintaining this book is known as petty cashier.

What is Analytical Petty Cash Book?

In large business concerns, the petty cash book is maintained in columnar [or analytical] form, with a separate column for each usual item of expense and a column for total. This type of Petty Cash Book is known as Analytical Petty cash Book. This type enables the businessman to know the information about the amount being spent on each head of petty expense. It also saves time in posting each item of petty payments unnecessarily in the ledger; only totals of various columns are to be posted in the ledger. The ruling of analytical petty cashbook is given below.

Analytical Petty Cash Book

Amount Received Rs.	Date	Particulars	Vou. No.	Total Amount Paid	Post-age	Stationery	Carriage	T.exps.	Sundry Exps
		Total							

What is Imprest System of Petty Cash?

Imprest system of petty cash is a system where the petty cashier is given a lump sum in cash [often called a float] keeping in view the possible needs of the business to meet its petty expenses for a stated period, e.g., a week, or a month. At the end of this period, the petty cashier submits the accounts for the amount spent by him during the period and gets from the main cashier the exact amount of petty cash disbursed, thus bringing his cash balance to the original starting figure. This system is known as *imprest system.*

4.6 Advantages of Imprest System

1. The money in the hands of petty cashier is limited to the imprest amount, thus the risk of misuse of cash or fraud is minimized.

2. While reimbursing the petty cash expenses, the main cashier will necessarily examine the Petty Cash Book to make sure that the amount is correctly arrived at. Discrepancies will be revealed and mistakes soon be rectified.

3. At any time the amount of cash in hand plus expenses not reimbursed must equal the imprest amount, thus facilitating a simple check.

4. The liability of petty cashier in this system can never exceed the imprest amount. As his account is checked weekly or monthly, there is no possibility of his being required to account for transactions that occurred in the distant past.

Illustration 8

Write out an analytical petty cash book from the following:

2002 March 1 Gave an imprest cheque for Rs.100 to the petty cashier. During the month the petty cashier made the following disbursements:

March 7	Bought postage stamps Rs.20.
10	Paid for stationery Rs.6.75.
15	Paid for carriage Rs.7.50.
20	Paid for Taxi hire to sales manager Rs.15.50
22	Sent a telegram to Delhi Rs.5.50
23	Bought ink and paper Rs.7.50.
25	Paid for coolie Rs.20.
27	Tea to traveling agent Rs.3.50.
31	Cash purchases from stationery mart Rs.9.25.

Balance the Petty Cash Book at the end of the month.

Solution

Analytical Petty Cash Book

Amount received Rs.	Date	Particulars	V. No	Total amount paid Rs.	Postage Rs.	Carriage & coolie Rs.	Stationery Rs.	T. Exps Rs.	Sundry expenses Rs.
	2002								
100	March 1	To Bank a/c							
	7	By postage		20.00	20.00				
	10	Stationery		6.75			6.75		
	15	Carriage		7.50		7.50			
	20	Taxi hire		15.50				15.50	
	22	Telegram		5.50	5.50				
	23	Ink &paper		7.50			7.50		
	25	Coolie		20.00		20.00			
	27	Tea exps.		3.50					3.50
	31	Stationery		9.25			9.25		
				95.50	25.50	27.50	23.50	15.50	3.50
4.50	April 1	To balance c/d		4.50					
95.50		To Bank							
100.00									

4.7 What is Journal Proper?

Journal proper [or General Journal] is a simple book of chronological record of business transactions. The use of this book is very much restricted in modern accounting system. Only those transactions, which cannot be conveniently recorded in any of the other books of original entry i.e., subsidiary books or which are not sufficiently numerous to necessitate a special book being devised for them, are recorded in this book. This journal is now used to record the following transactions only.

(a) **Opening Entries.** These entries are needed for opening accounts in the beginning of the financial year. All assets accounts are debited and all liabilities accounts credited and the difference is credited to Capital account.

(b) **Transfer Entries.** These entries are needed to record transfer from one account to another. For example, an asset purchased is wrongly debited to purchases account, then to rectify the mistake the following entry will have to be passed.

Asset a/c To Purchases a/c	Dr.		

(c) **Rectification Entries.** When certain errors are committed in the books. These entries are passed in order to nullify the effect of errors. For example, goods sold for Rs.5000 to Mr. Ram has been entered in the Sales Day Book as Rs.500. This mistake is corrected by passing the following rectifying entry.

Ram a/c To Sales a/c	Dr.	Rs. 4500	Rs. 4500

(d) **Adjustment Entries.** When accounts are closed at the end of a financial year, before preparing final accounts certain adjustments have to be made relating to certain items like depreciation, outstanding expenses, interest on capital, etc. For example, if rent is outstanding for one month say, Rs.500, then the following entry will be passed in order to charge one full year's rent to final accounts.

Rent a/c To Outstanding Rent a/c	Dr.	Rs. 500	Rs. 500

(e) **Closing Entries.** These entries are needed at the end of accounting period to close certain accounts. Transferring their balances to some other accounts does this. For example, transferring its balance to Profit and loss account closes the petty cash account.

(f) **Compound Entries.** Sometimes, compound entries are passed through journal proper to make the record of the transaction more clear. For example, goods sold for cash after allowing trade and cash discounts can be recorded in this journal.

(g) **Casual Entries.** Journal Proper may also used to record such transactions, which do not occur so frequently so that a separate book may not be provided for them. For example, if sales returns are rare, then instead of opening a Sales Returns Book, such rare cases can be recorded in Journal Proper.

Illustration 9

Pass necessary entries in Journal Proper for the following transactions:

1. Opening balances;

Cash a/c Rs. 10,000; Stock a/c Rs. 20,000; Debtors a/c Rs. 80,000; Buildings a/c Rs.160,000; Creditors a/c Rs.10,000; and Bills Payable a/c Rs.40,000.

2. Transfer Rs.2000 from the credit of X a/c to the credit of Y a/c.
3. Rs.400 repairs to furniture debited to Furniture a/c by mistake.
4. Provide 10% depreciation on Buildings.
5. Rent unpaid Rs. 2400.

Solution

JOURNAL PROPER

Date	Particulars		LF	Debit Rs.	Credit Rs.
1	Cash a/c Stock a/c	Dr. Dr		10,000 20,000	

	Debtors a/c Dr		80,000	
	Buildings a/c Dr.		160,000	
	To Creditors a/c			10,000
	To Bills Payable a/c			40,000
	To Capital a/c (bal fig)			220,000
	[Being opening balances]			
2	X a/c Dr.		2,000	
	To Y a/c			2,000
	[Being transfer]			
3	Repairs a/c Dr.		400	
	To Furniture a/c			400
	[Being repairs wrongly debited to Furniture a/c, now rectified],			
4	Depreciation a/c Dr.		16,000	
	To Buildings a/c			16,000
	[Being provision for depreciation]			
5	Rent a/c Dr.		2,400	
	To Outstanding Rent a/c			2,400
	[Being rent unpaid]			

4.8 Bank Pass Book

Passbook or Bank Statement is a copy of the account of the customer as it appears in the bank's books. When a customer deposits money and cheques into his bank account or withdraws money, he records these transactions in the bank column of his cashbook immediately. Correspondingly, the bank records them in the customer's account maintained in its books. Then they are copied in a passbook and given to the customer. With the computerization of banking operations, bank statements (in lieu of passbook) are issued to the customers periodically. Thus passbook is a record of the banking transactions of a customer with a bank. All entries made by a customer in his cashbook (bank column) must be entered by the bank in the passbook. Hence, the balances as per bank column of the cashbook must agree with the balance as per passbook. Of course the balances will be equal and opposite in nature. For example, if the cash book shows a debit balance of Rs.5 000, then the passbook must show a credit balance of Rs.5 000 and vice versa. But in most cases, these two balances may disagree on account of various reasons.

Format of a Bank Passbook or Bank Statement

Name of the bank____________

Address of the bank____________

Account No. ____________

Customer Name:____________

Address of the customer____________

Date	Particulars	Cheque No.	Withdrawals (debits)	Deposits (credits)	Balance	Initials

Causes for Disagreement

The major cause for the disagreement is that certain items have been entered in one book only (i.e., cash book or pass book only). In other words certain debits or credits made in one book (say in cashbook) are omitted to be entered in the other book (say in passbook) and vice versa. Such items may be listed as follows:

1. Cheques sent for collection or deposited into the bank but not yet collected. When a customer deposits cheques into bank, he makes entries (debit bank account) immediately in his cashbook. But the bank will credit the customer account in the passbook only when the cheques are realized. In that case the balances will disagree and cashbook balance will be more than the passbook balance.

2. Cheques issued by the customer but not presented to the bank for payment. When a customer issues cheques to his suppliers/creditors, he will enter the transaction (credit bank account) immediately in his cashbook. But the banker will debit customer account only when the suppliers/creditors present the cheques for payment. Due to this gap, the two balances will disagree and cashbook balance will be more than the passbook balance.

3. Bank charges and interest on overdraft are first debited in the passbook and recorded in the cashbook afterwards. This will cause for the disagreement and cashbook balance will be more than the passbook balance.

4. Interest on bank credit balance and interest on investment, dividends, etc., and bills collected by the bank on behalf of the customer are first credited in the passbook and recorded in the cashbook later on. This makes the two balances to disagree and cashbook balance will be less than the passbook balance.

5. Items like direct payments made by the bank as per standing instructions of the customer and dishonor of a bill discounted with the bank, etc., are first debited in the passbook and recorded in the cashbook later on. This will make the two balances to disagree and cashbook balance will be more than the passbook balance.

6. Commitment of errors such as errors of omission or commission or in casting, carry forward, balancing, etc either in the passbook or cashbook or in both will cause for the disagreement in these two balances.

4.9 Bank Reconciliation Statement

When the customer finds the balances shown by the Cashbook and Bank Passbook different, he will prepare a statement in order to reconcile these two balances. Such a statement is called as Bank Reconciliation Statement. The main purpose of such a statement is to explain the causes of difference between these two balances and find out whether any errors have been committed in the cashbook or passbook and rectify them immediately. This statement is prepared usually at the end of a period on a particular date in order to confirm that the cashbook balance is correct.

Guidelines for preparing the Bank Reconciliation Statement

1. Usually the heading is given as follows:

Bank Reconciliation Statement as on - particular date ----

2. The starting point shall be either 'Balance as shown by the Cashbook' or 'Balance as shown by the Passbook'. The ordinary bank balance in the cashbook is debit balance and in the passbook it is credit balance. On the other hand, the overdraft balance in the cashbook is the credit balance and in the passbook it is the debit balance.

3. The various causes for the disagreement between the two balances should be ascertained by comparing the entries made in theses two books during the concerned period.

4. The effect of the particular cause on the balance shown by the other book should be studied in terms of increase or decrease in the balance.

5. If the result is increase in balance shown by the other book (say, passbook balance), then the amount of such increase should be added to the starting balance (say, cashbook balance). On the other hand, if the result is decrease in passbook balance, then the amount of such decrease should be deducted from the cashbook balance.

Thus by adjusting all 'increase' and 'decrease' items to the starting balance, the balance as shown by the other book will be arrived at. When the balances shown by the cashbook and passbook agree as per Bank Reconciliation Statement, then it will be construed that there are only differences but no errors in the entries made in these two books. These guidelines are explained through the following illustrations.

Illustration 10

From the following particulars, prepare a Bank Reconciliation Statement showing the balance as per Passbook as on 31st March 2002. As on that date the cashbook of Mr.Raman showed a bank balance of Rs.8, 850. On verifying the passbook, the following facts were ascertained:

(a) Cheques deposited into bank before 31st March 2002, but not credited by the bank amounted in all Rs.1850.

(b) Cheques issued but not presented for payment before 31st March 2002 amounted to Rs.2500.

(c) The bank has charged Rs.150 as bank charges and credited Rs.350 as interest.

(d) The bank has given a wrong debit for Rs.450.

(e) A customer has paid directly into bank account a sum of Rs.590 on 30tk March 2002, which has not been into the cashbook.

(f) A cheque for Rs.275 sent for collection and returned unpaid has not been entered in the cashbook.

Solution

Bank Reconciliation Statement of Mr. Raman as on 31st March 2002

		Rs.	Rs.
	Bank Balance as per Cashbook		8,850
Add:	1. Cheques issued but not presented for payment	2,500	
	2. Interest credited in the passbook only	350	
	3. Amount directly paid into bank but not entered in the cashbook	590	3,440
			12,290
Less:	4. Cheques deposited into bank but not credited in the Passbook	1,850	
	5. Bank charges debited in the passbook only	150	
	6. Wrong debit given by the bank	450	

7. Cheques dishonoured entered in the passbook but not in the cashbook	275	2,725
Bank Balance as Passbook		9,565

Explanatory notes: Cause - item no.1 entered in the cashbook only; effect - the bank balance as per cashbook is less. Hence, it is added to cashbook balance to arrive at passbook balance.

Cause - item no.2 entered in the passbook only, effect - passbook balance is more. Hence, it is added to arrive at passbook balance.

Cause - item 3 entered in the passbook only, effect - passbook balance is more. Hence, it is added to arrive at the passbook balance.

Cause - item 4 entered in the cashbook only, effect - cashbook balance is more. Hence, it is deducted from the cashbook balance to arrive at the passbook balance.

Cause - item 5entered in the passbook only, effect - the passbook balance is less. Hence, it is deducted to arrive at the passbook balance.

Cause - item 6 entered in the passbook only, effect - the passbook balance is less. Hence, it is deducted to arrive at the passbook balance.

Cause - item 7 entered in the passbook only, effect - the passbook balance is less. Hence, it is deducted to arrive at the passbook balance.

Except item no.6, which is an error, all other items are causes for the difference, which may occur in the normal course

Illustration 11

Assist Mr. Raja in ascertaining his cashbook balance as on 30th June 2002 for No. I Account from the following information:

(a) His passbook No. I Account showed a balance of Rs.10,500.

(b) Cheques issued on 25th June were for Rs.3,800; out of which Rs.1,200 only had been presented for payment before 30th June.

(c) Rs.6,200 paid into bank on 27th June was wrongly credited to another account.

(d) A bills receivable for Rs.800 was collected by the bank on 28th June, but no corresponding entry was made in the cashbook.

(e) A payment of Rs.500 from another account had been wrongly debited by the bank to this account.

(f) A credit of Rs.400 relating to some other account appeared in the passbook.

(g) The bank has recovered an insurance claim of Rs.2,500 and incurred Rs.150 as charges and commission. The entries for these were made only in the passbook.

(h) The bank has credited interest Rs.400 and debited Rs.90 as bank charges.

Solution

Bank Reconciliation Statement of Account No. I as on 30th June 2002

		Rs.	Rs.
	Bank balance as per Passbook		10,500
Add:	Cash paid in but wrongly credited to another account	6,200	

Wrong debit given to No. I account by the bank	500	
Charges and commission on insurance claim debited In the passbook only	150	
Interest credited in passbook only	400	7,250
		17,750
Less: Cheques issued but not presented for payment (Rs.3,800 - 1,200)	2,600	
B/R collected by the bank not entered in cashbook	800	
Insurance claim credited in passbook only	2,500	
Wrong credit given by the bank to No. I account	400	
Bank charges debited in the passbook only	90	6,390
Bank balance as Cashbook		11,360

Hint: If the effect of causes for difference between cashbook and passbook balance is 'increase' in passbook balance or 'decrease' in cashbook balance, then such items have been added to Passbook balance to arrive at the Cashbook balance.

If the effect of causes for difference between these two balances results in 'decrease' in passbook balance or 'increase' in cash book balance, then such items have been deducted from the Passbook balance to arrive at the Cashbook balance.

Illustration 12

From the following particulars, prepare a Bank Reconciliation Statement of Mr. Shyam as on 31st December 2002:

	Rs.
Overdraft balance as per Cashbook (credit balance on 31st December)	14,380
Interest on overdraft debited in the Passbook only	320
Bank charges debited 'n the Passbook only	140
Cheques drawn but not cashed before 31st December 2002	2,540
Cheques sent for collection but not collected before 31st December 2002	4,420
A B/R discounted with the bank was dishonored on 31st December 2002	1,200

Solution

Bank Reconciliation Statement of Mr. Shyam as on 31st December 2002

	Rs.	Rs.
Overdraft balance as per Cashbook (credit balance)		14,380
Add: Interest on overdraft debited in the Passbook only	320	
Bank charges debited in the Passbook only	140	
Cheques paid into bank but not cleared	4,420	
B/R dishonored debited in the Passbook only	1,200	6,080
		20,460
Less: Cheques issued but not cashed	2,540	2,540
Overdraft balance as per Passbook (debit balance)		17,920

Hints: If the effect of cause for the difference between cashbook and passbook (O/D) balances results in 'decrease' in cashbook balance or 'increase' in passbook balance, then such items have been added to cashbook balance to arrive at passbook balance.

If the effect of cause for the difference between two balances results in 'increase' in cashbook balance or 'decrease' in passbook balance, then such items have been deducted from the cashbook balance to arrive at passbook balance.

Illustration 13

From the following particulars, prepare a Bank Reconciliation Statement and ascertain the balance as per Cashbook as on 31st December 2002:

(a) The bank passbook showed an overdraft balance of Rs. 25,200.

(b) Cheques drawn in December 2002 amounting in all Rs. 25,000, of which Rs. 16,000 worth have been cashed in the same month, a cheque of Rs Rs. 6,000 has been cashed on 4th January 2003, and the rest have not been presented at all.

(c) Out of cheques of Rs. 16,400 deposited on 27th December 2002, Rs. 11,400 worth appear to have been credited in the passbook only on 3rd January 2003.

(d) A cheque of Rs. 1,200 paid into my bank account has been wrongly credited to another account.

(e) Interest on overdraft Rs. 1,200 and Bank charges Rs.150 debited in my passbook on 31st December 2002 have been credited in my cashbook only on 3rd January 2003.

(f) Interest on investments amounting to Rs. 1,500 has been credited in my passbook only.

Solution

Bank Reconciliation Statement as on 31st December 2002

	Rs.	Rs.
Overdraft (debit) balance as per my Passbook		25,200
Add: Cheques issued but not presented for payment before 31st December 2002	9,000	
Interest on investments credited in Passbook only	1,500	10,500
		35,700
Less: Cheques paid into bank but not realized before 31st December 2002	11,400	
Cheques paid into bank wrongly credited to another Account	1,200	
Interest on overdraft debited in Passbook only	1,200	
Bank charges debited in the Passbook only	150	13,950
Overdraft (credit) balance as per my Cashbook		21,750

Hints: If the effect of cause for the difference between two balances results in 'decrease' in passbook balance or 'increase' in cashbook balance, then such items have been added to Passbook (O/D) balance to arrive at the Cashbook balance.

If the effect results in 'increase' in passbook balance or 'decrease' in cashbook balance, then such items have been deducted from the Passbook (O/D) balance to arrive at the Cashbook balance.

4.10 Meaning of Accounting Errors

Accounting errors are the mistakes committed in bookkeeping and accounting. The mistake may be one relating to routine or one relating to principle. They may occur in entering the transactions in the journal or subsidiary books or they may creep at the time of posting into the ledger. Thus, errors may be committed while recording, classifying or summarizing the accounting transactions. The error may be the result of an act of omission or commission.

4.11 Classification of Errors

Depending upon the nature of errors, they may be classified into the following four types: (1) Errors of Omission; (2) Errors of Commission; (3) Errors of Principles; and (4) Compensating Errors.

1. **Errors of Omission:** When a transaction is not recorded by mistake in the books of accounts, it is called an error of omission. The omission may be partial or complete.

Partial Omission may happen in relation to any subsidiary book. Here the transaction is entered in the subsidiary book but not posted to the ledger. For example, goods returned by a customer has been entered in the sales returns book but not posted to the credit of customer's account. Similarly, cash paid to the supplier has been entered in the payment side of the Cash Book but not posted to the debit of supplier's account.

Complete omission can happen when the transaction is completely omitted from the books of accounts. For example, a bookkeeper failed to enter an invoice from the sales daybook.

2. **Error of Commission:** When a transaction is entered in the books of accounts, it might be entered wrongly. It may be entered partially or incorrectly. Such error is called an error of commission. These errors arise often due to the ignorance or negligence or absent-mindedness of the accountant. It may be of different types. Examples of such errors are as follows:

(a) Errors relating to subsidiary books. These are three types:

(i) Entering wrong amount in a subsidiary book, e.g., a purchase of Rs.430 may be entered in the Purchase Day Book as Rs.340 due to wrong transposition of figures.

(ii) Entering the transaction in a wrong subsidiary book, e.g., a purchase transaction may be entered in sales daybook and a sales transaction may be entered in the purchase daybook.

(iii) Wrong casting or carry forward of a subsidiary book. Casting refers to the process of totaling the daybooks periodically. A mistake in relation to totaling is called 'error in casting'. If there is excess totaling, the error is 'over casting' and short totaling is 'unde. casting'. Sometimes, error may be the result of wrong carry forward of the total from one page of the daybook to another, e.g., the total of a page may be Rs.235 and carried forward to the next page as Rs.325.

(b) Errors relating to ledger. These errors may be subdivided broadly into two types. They are: errors of posting and errors in balancing.

Error of posting may be further be subdivided as follows:

(i) Posting wrong amount on the right side of an account. Example. Sale of Rs.560 to Mr.Raja is entered as Rs.650 in the debit side of his account from the Sales Day Book.

(ii) Posting the same amount twice to an account. Example. A cash receipt of Rs.1000 from Mr.Ram is credited twice to his account.

(iii) Posting the correct amount to the wrong side of the right account. Example. A purchase of goods from Mr. Raj for Rs.1000 is debited to his account [instead of crediting].

(iv) Posting wrong amount to the wrong side of right account. Example. A purchase of Rs.1000 from Mr.Sam is debited to his account as Rs.10,000.

(v) Posting the correct amount to the wrong account but on the right side. Example. A sale of goods to S.Anish for Rs.1000 is wrongly debited to G.Anish a/c.

(vi) Posting correct amount to the wrong account and on the wrong side. Example. A sale of Rs.1000 to S.Anish is wrongly credited to G.Anish a/c.

Errors in balancing: Errors may arise in balancing the account resulting in excess or short balance of the account.

3. **Errors of Principle:** These errors occur when entries are made against the principles of accounting. Example. Purchase of computer for office use is wrongly entered in the Purchases Day Book. Capital expenditure should not be treated as revenue expenditure. These errors may be committed (a) due to the inability to make a distinction between revenue and capital items; (b) due to inability to make a difference between business expenses and personal expenses; (c) due to inability to make a difference between productive expenses and non-productive expenses, e.g., wages paid for production may be debited to salaries a/c or salaries paid to office employees may be debited to wages a/c.

4. **Compensating Errors:** These are the errors, which compensate themselves in the net results, i.e., over debit of one account is neutralized by an over credit in some other account to the same extent. Similarly a wrong credit might have been compensated by some wrong debit in some other account. For example, if tax paid Rs.2,500 is debited in Tax a/c as Rs.3,000 and interest received Rs.3,500 is credited in the interest a/c as Rs.4,000, the excess debit of Rs.500 in tax a/c is compensated by an excess credit of Rs.500 in interest a/c. This type of error may be committed in combination of different errors in different accounts. Normally the presence of this type of errors will not be revealed by the trial balance.

4.12 Impact of Errors on Trial Balance

The agreement of the Trail balance is proof as to the arithmetical accuracy of the books of accounts. But it is a final proof of accuracy of books of accounts. it simply assures that for every debit there is a corresponding and equal credit. If trial balance does not agree, it is a clear indication that there are certain errors in the books of accounts. Even if the trial balance agrees, there may be errors in the books of accounts. Hence, the errors may be classified, depending upon the agreement of trial balance, as follows:

(a) Errors that do not affect the agreement of the trial balance.

(b) Errors that affect the agreement of the trial balance.

Errors that are not disclosed by Trial balance or not affect the agreement of the Trial balance are mainly the errors of principle, errors of complete omission, errors of commission and compensation errors. Certain errors like entering a transaction in two subsidiary books or writing a wrong amount in a subsidiary book or mis-posting to the wrong account but correct side, etc. locating such errors are quite difficult and such errors can always be rectified by means of journal entries.

Errors that are disclosed by trial balance or affect the agreement of the Trial balance are mainly the errors of wrong or omission of posting, wrong totaling of subsidiary books, wrong carry-forward and wrong balancing of ledger accounts, etc. Wrong posting may be in the forms of posting a wrong amount to a ledger account or posting to the wrong side of an account or double posting. As these errors affect mostly only one side of ledger accounts, they will be revealed by the trial balance through disagreement of debit and credit totals.

4.13 Procedure for Rectifying Accounting Errors

Broadly speaking, there are two methods of rectification of errors. They are as follows:

1. **Striking of the wrong entry.** Under this method wrong entry is erased or struck out as and when it occurs or noticed. But this method is not advisable because it helps perpetration of fraud. It is also objectionable because it affects the legal value of books of accounts and makes them appear clumsy. Besides, it is complicated because often correction of one mistake will necessitate erasion in different sets of books. Hence, this method is not adopted.

2. **Making appropriate entries to correct the errors.** This method is applicable to Errors of Omission, Commission, or Principle. If the error is of full omission, then the full-omitted entry is passed. If it is of partial omission, the entry left out is made. If the error is one of commission, rectifications are made either by additional entry or by opposite entry taking into account the nature of the error. This method is scientific and hence preferred one.

Procedure for Rectification. The following three steps may usually be adopted while attempting to rectify an error.

(a) Ascertain what has actually been done, i.e., what the error is.

(b) Make sure what should be done, i.e., the correct record.

(c) Decide what correct entry is to be made and pass, rectification.

Certain errors affect only one side of an account. These one-sided errors do not require journal entries for rectification. In the case of such errors, an entry should be made on the debit side of an account to increase the debit value or reduce the credit value of that account. Or an entry should be made on the credit side of an account in order to increase the credit value or reduce the debit value of that account.

There are errors that affect both the accounts found in a transaction. These two-sided errors can be rectified by appropriate journal entries designed either to record an omission or to rectify an error of commission or principle.

Rectification of One-sided errors

Errors in totaling of subsidiary books: This type of errors will affect their respective ledger accounts. Hence, they should be rectified accordingly.

Example 1.

(a) Purchase book has been over cast by Rs.600 [for the month of January.]

(b) Sales book has been under cast by Rs.300.

(c) Purchase Returns Book has been over cast by Rs.150.

(d) Sales Returns Book has been under cast by Rs.60.

Rectification

(a) Over casting of Purchase Book will result in excess debit of purchases a/c, hence, it should be credited with Rs.600.

(b) Under casting of Sales Book will result in under crediting of sales a/c, hence the sales a/c should be credited with Rs.300.

(c) Over casting of Purchases Returns Book will result in over crediting of Purchases Returns a/c, hence the purchases returns a/c should be debited with Rs.150.

(d) Under casting of Sales Returns Book will result in under debiting of sales returns a/c, hence it should be debited with Rs.60.

Errors of Carry forward: This type of error is committed by taking a wrong figure from one page to another page.

Example 2.

(a) A total of Rs.596 in the purchases book has been carried forward as Rs.695.

(b) The total of sales book Rs.484 on page 20 was carried forward to page 21 as Rs.448.

(c) Purchase returns book was carried forward as Rs.1220 instead of Rs.1120.

(d) Sales Returns Book was carried forward as Rs.678 instead of Rs.768.

Rectification

(a) The effect of this error is that purchase a/c will be debited more by Rs.99 (695 – 596). Hence purchase a/c should be credited with Rs.99.

(b) The effect of this error is that the sales a/c will be credited less by Rs.36 (484 – 448). Hence the sales a/c should be credited with Rs.36.

(c) The effect of this error is that the purchases returns a/c will be credited more by Rs.100 (1220 –1120). Hence the purchases returns a/c should be debited with Rs.100.

(d) The effect of this error is that the sales returns a/c will be debited less by Rs.90 (768 – 678). Hence the sales returns a/c should be debited with Rs.90.

Errors of Posting: These errors, known as errors of commission, may occur as

(a) Failure to post to the personal account in the ledger

(b) Posting wrong amount on the correct side of the ledger

(c) Posting the correct amount on the wrong side of the ledger

(d) Posting a wrong amount on the wrong side of the ledger

Example 3

(a) Purchases from Anish for Rs.2000 have not been posted to his personal a/c.

(b) Sales to Priya for Rs.3600 have been posted to her account as Rs.6300.

(c) Purchases from Durga for Rs.1500 have been posted to the debit of her a/c.

(d) Sales to Meena for Rs.4200 have been posted to her credit as Rs.2400.

Rectification

(a) Anish a/c should be credited with Rs.2000.

(b) Priya's a/c should be credited with Rs.2700.

(c) Durga's a/c should be credited with double the amount i.e., Rs.3000.

(d) Meena's a/c should be debited with Rs.6600 (i.e., Rs.4200 + 2400).

Rectification of Errors that affect two or more accounts

Example 4

	Error	Rectification	Rs.	Rs.
(a)	Error of Principle: Purchase of Furniture for Rs.5000 has passed through Purchases Day Book.	Furniture a/c Dr. To Purchases a/c	5000	5000
(b)	Error of complete Omission: A credit purchase of Rs.20,000 from Vicky was omitted from the books.	Purchases a/c Dr. To Vicky/s a/c	20,000	20,000
(c)	Wrong amount recorded in the subsidiary book: A credit purchase of Rs.20,000 from Vignesh was recorded in the Purchase Daybook as Rs.2000.	Purchases a/c Dr. To Vignesh a/c	18,000	18,000
	A credit purchase of Rs.20,000 from Vignesh was entered in the purchases book as Rs.2,00,000.	Vignesh a/c Dr. To Purchases a/c	1,80,000	1,80,000
(d)	Wrong Posting: Goods returned by Rani & Co Rs.2000 was posted to Vani & co a/c.	Vani & co a/c Dr. To Rani & co a/c	2,000	2,000
	Rent paid Rs.4,500 for proprietor's house was debited to Rent a/c.	Drawings a/c Dr. To Rent a/c	4,500	4,500
(e)	Recording in a wrong subsidiary book: A credit purchase of goods for Rs.20,000 from Ramu & Co. was passed through the Sales Day Book.	Sales a/c Dr. Purchase a/c Dr. To Ramu & Co a/c	20,000 20,000	40,000

4.15 What does Suspense Account mean?

Errors that affect one account will affect the agreement of the Trail balance. If the errors cannot be located immediately and rectified, then the difference in trial balance is kept in a separate account called 'suspense account'. Suspense account is a temporary and imaginary account, which is closed later when the errors are located. The artificial tallying of the trial balance by the introduction of suspense account enables the Final Accounts to be prepared even before the location of errors. If the suspense account shows debit balance, it is shown in the asset side of the balance sheet. If it shows credit balance, it is shown in the liability side. On locating the errors in the beginning or in the course of next year, rectifying entries would be passed and when all the errors have been completely rectified the suspense Account will show no balance. In the case of one-sided errors, if they are to be rectified through journal entries, the suspense account can be used for the required debit or credit depending upon the nature of error. For example, the purchase book is under cast by Rs.500. In this case the purchase a/c is to be debited with Rs.500. But to rectify through a journal it needs a credit entry; for which the suspense a/c may be used as the credit a/c. the entry would be as follows:

	Dr.	Cr.
Purchase a/c Dr.	Rs.500	
To Suspense a/c		Rs. 500
[Being under casting of Purchase Book rectified by crediting suspense a/c]		

Mostly arithmetical errors are rectified through suspense a/c. For other errors suspense a/c will not be involved. Moreover, if the errors are located after the preparation of the Suspense Account, all those errors can be rectified only by means of suitable journal entries.

Illustration 14

A bookkeeper having failed to tally the Trial balance on 31st May 2002 opened a Suspense a/c and transferred the difference of Rs.1709 to the credit of Suspense a/c. the following errors were later discovered. Give journal entries and show the Suspense a/c:

(i) Sales book was under cast by Rs.2000.

(ii) Purchase of machinery for Rs.3000 was passed through the purchases book.

(iii) Goods sold to Vijaya for Rs.45 was posted to her account as Rs.54.

(iv) Purchase returns book was over cast by Rs.200.

(v) The total of sales book was carried forward from page 5 to 6 as Rs.1222 instead of Rs.1122.

Solution

Rectification Entries

			Rs.	Rs.
(i)	Suspense a/c	Dr.	2000	
	To Sales a/c			2000
	(Being under casting of sales rectified)			
(ii)	Machinery a/c	Dr.	3000	
	To Purchases a/c			3000
	[Wrong debit to purchases rectified]			
(iii)	Suspense a/c	Dr.	9	
	To Vijaya a/c			9
	(Excess debit to Vijaya a/c rectified)			
(iv)	Purchase Returns a/c	Dr.	200	
	To Suspense a/c			200
	(Over casting of Purchase Returns Book rectified)			
(v)	Sales a/c	Dr.	100	
	To Suspense a/c			100
	(Excess carry forward of the total of sales book rectified)			

Suspense a/c

2002		Rs.	2002		Rs.
May 31	To Sales a/c	2000	May 31	By Difference in Books	1709
	To Vijaya a/c	9		By Purchase Returns a/c	200
				By Sales a/c	100
		2009			2009

Illustration 15

The following errors were discovered in the books of Ghosh on 31st July, 2002.

(a) Rectify the errors without opening suspense a/c.

(b) Given that the difference in Trial balance Rs.2610 was debited to Suspense a/c; give journal entries with Suspense a/c.

(c) Show the Suspense a/c.

(i) The total of purchase book for December had been under cast by Rs.1000.

(ii) Rs.760 paid for repairing machinery had been debited to Machinery a/c.

(iii) Cash Rs.390 received from Geetha, though entered in the cashbook had not been posted to Geetha's a/c.

(iv) The sales book has been over cast by Rs.500.

(v) A sale of Rs.4000 to Ram has been passed through the purchase book.

(vi) Goods returned by Mani Rs.750 have been entered in the returns outwards book. However, the Mani's account is correctly posted.

Solution

Rectification without Suspense account

(i) Purchase a/c should be debited with Rs.1000.

(ii) Repairs a/c Dr. Rs.760

To Machinery a/c Rs.760

[Wrong debit to machinery a/c rectified.]

(iii) Geetha's a/c should be credited with Rs.390.

(iv) Sales a/c should be debited with Rs.500.

(v) Ram's a/c Dr. Rs.8000

To Sales a/c Rs.4000

To Purchase a/c Rs.4000

[Entry to rectify a sales transaction wrongly entered in Purchase book.]

(vi) Returns Outward a/c should be debited with Rs.750.

Returns Inwards a/c should be debited with Rs.750.

[Wrong credit given to returns outwards a/c rectified]

Rectification with Suspense account

			Rs.	Rs.
(i)	Purchases a/c	Dr.	1000	
	To Suspense a/c			1000
	(Under casting of purchase book rectified)			
(ii)	Repairs a/c	Dr.	760	
	To Machinery a/c			Rs.760
(iii)	Suspense a/c	Dr.	390	
	To Geetha's a/c			390
	(Partial omission to personal account rectified)			
(iv)	Sales a/c	Dr.	500	
	To Suspense a/c			500
	(Over casting of sales book rectified)			
(v)	Ram's a/c	Dr.	8000	
	To Sales a/c			4000
	To Purchases a/c			4000

	(Wrong entry in Purchases Book rectified)			
(vi)	Returns Outwards a/c	Dr.	750	
	Returns Inward a/c	Dr.	750	
	To Suspense a/c			1500
	(Wrong entry in Returns Outwards Book rectified)			

Suspense A/c

Dr.	Rs.		Cr Rs.
To Difference in Books	2610	By Purchases a/c	1000
To Geetha's a/c	390	By Sales a/c	500
		By Returns Outwards a/c	750
		By Returns Inwards a/c	750
	3000		3000

Illustration 16

Rectify the following errors.

(a) Bills received from Raman for Rs.500 passed through Bills Payables Book.

(b) An item of Rs.150 relating to Prepaid Insurance was not brought forward from last year.

(c) Rs.400 paid to Mehta against our acceptance was debited to Mehta's a/c.

(d) Rs.150 relating to purchase of stationery has been wrongly to the personal account of the owner.

(e) The total of the Discount column on the debit side of the cashbook has been cast short by R.30.

Solution

			Rs.	Rs.
(a)	Bills Receivable a/c	Dr.	300	
	Bills Payable a/c	Dr.	300	
	To Raman a/c			600
	(Being wrong entry in Bills Payable Book rectified)			
(b)	Prepaid Insurance a/c	Dr.	150	
	To Suspense a/c			150
	(Being prepaid insurance brought forward from last year)			
(c)	Bills Payable a/c	Dr.	400	
	To Mehta's a/c			400
	(Being wrong debit to Mehta rectified)			
(d)	Stationery a/c	Dr.	150	
	To Drawings a/c			150
	(Being wrong debit to personal a/c rectified)			
(e)	Discount allowed a/c	Dr.	30	
	To Suspense a/c.			30
	(Being under casting of debit column of discount rectified)			

REVIEW QUESTIONS

1. What are subsidiary books? What are its advantages?
2. Describe the preparation of Purchase Day Book.
3. How is Sales Book prepared?
4. Give the specimen of Returns Inward and Outward Books.
5. Describe the various types of Cash Book.
6. Describe the preparation of Three-Column Cash Book.
7. State the meaning and advantages of Imprest System of Petty Cash.
8. Mention a few transactions that are entered in Journal Proper.
9. Describe the various types of errors giving suitable examples.
10. Explain the impact of accounting errors on Trial balance.
11. Illustrate the rectification of one-sided errors.
12. Illustrate the rectification of errors that affect more than one account.
13. What is Suspense Account?

REVIEW PROBLEMS

14. Enter the following transactions in the proper subsidiary books and post them in the ledger.

2002 May 1	Bought goods from Ramesh Rs.35,000.
3	Sold goods to Raja Rs.25,000 and for cash Rs.10,000.
8	Purchased goods from Sanjay Rs.20,000 at a trade discount of 5%.
12	Received goods returned by Raja Rs.600.
15	Sold goods to Mathesh Rs.24,000.
19	Returned goods to Sanjay worth Rs.800.
30	Purchased office furniture from Exe & Co for Rs.4000 on credit.
31	Returned goods by Mathesh Rs.1000.

[Refer illustration 3]

15. Enter the following transactions in a Cash Book with cash and discount columns.

2002 March 1	Opening cash balance Rs.5000.
3	Received from Sam Rs.600 and allowed him a discount of Rs.15.
4	Bought goods for cash Rs.1800.
8	Paid Guhan Rs.200 and was allowed a discount of Rs.20.
10	Purchased office furniture for Rs.250
12	Cash sales Rs.1300.
16	Bought stationery Rs.40.
18	Raj settled his account for Rs.535 by paying Rs.500.
22	Paid rent Rs.175.
25	Received from Rakesh Rs.400 and allowed him a discount of Rs.10.
28	Paid Gopi Rs.700 in full settlement of his account for Rs.717.
31	Paid salaries and wages Rs.120.

[**Answer**: Closing cash balance Rs.4515. Discount [Dr.] Rs.60 & [Cr.] Rs.37]

16. Enter the following transactions in a Three-column Cash Book.

2002 April 1	Commenced business with Rs.10,000; paid into bank Rs.8000.

2	Bought office furniture by cheque Rs.3000.
6	Cash sales Rs.1000.
9	Paid Arun Rs.600 and was allowed a discount of Rs.60.
13	Rajesh paid by cheque Rs.690 in full settlement of his account Rs.700; the cheque was deposited into bank.
17	Withdrew from bank for office use Rs.1000.
25	Cash sales received by cheque Rs.1200.
30	Drew for personal use cash Rs.100; salaries paid Rs.500.

[**Answer:** Closing balances –Cash Rs.4000; Bank Rs.4690. Discount [dr.] Rs.10 & [cr.] Rs.60]

17. A petty cashbook is kept on imprest system, the amount of imprest being Rs.100 and has six analytical columns for postage, stationery, traveling expenses, repairs, office expenses and ledger accounts. Enter the following transactions:

September 1	Opening petty cash balance Rs.19.44
1	Received the cash to make up the imprest
7	Purchased stamps Rs.9.50
8	Paid railway fare Rs.14.50.
	Paid bus fare Rs.2.10
12	Paid to Somu Rs.35.00
18	Paid for cleaning toilets Rs.6.00
20	Paid rickshaw charges Rs.6.50
26	Paid for repairs to type writer Rs.4.00
	Paid for stationery Rs.3.50
30	Paid office expenses Rs.8.00

[**Answer:** Closing cash balance Rs.10.90]

18. An Accountant while balancing his books found that there was a difference [excess credit] of Rs.860 in the trial balance. The difference was placed in the suspense account and the books were closed. The following errors were disclosed afterwards:

(a) Rs.3000 sales proceeds of old machinery have been posted to sales a/c.

(b) Rs.600 the price of goods purchased from Ratan, had been shown on the credit side of his account as Rs.60.

(c) Rs.50 discount received from Ram, had been shown in his account, but not posted to discount account.

(d) A sum of Rs.500 owed to Krish had not been included in the list of creditors.

(e) Account of Reka had been debited with Rs.100 on account of goods returned by her.

Give journal entries to correct these errors and prepare the suspense account.

5

PREPARATION OF FINAL ACCOUNTS

Learning Objective

After going through this chapter, you should be able to

— State the meaning of final accounts.

— Describe the Income Statement and Balance Sheet.

— Classify the various assets and liabilities

— Differentiate balance sheet from trial balance

— Make adjustments to the final accounts

— Work out problems in final accounts

5.1 Meaning of 'Final Accounts'

Final Accounts refers to the final statements of accounts prepared in order to ascertain and report the results of the financial activities of a business. Having prepared the Trial balance, which establishes the accuracy of books of accounts, the next step is to ascertain the operating results and financial position of the business. For this purpose, the final accounts are prepared, which include mainly the Trading and Profit and loss account, also called as Income Statement and Balance sheet. The preparation of trading account reveals the gross profit earned or gross loss incurred, the profit and loss account reveals the net profit or loss earned and that of the balance sheet would reveal the financial position of the business. Many parties such as the owners, creditors, investors, employees, and regulatory authorities, etc are interested in the financial information provided by the final accounts.

5.2 Class of Concerns from Accounting Point of View

Broadly the concerns may be classified into business concerns and non-business concerns. Business concerns mainly function with the profit motive and the non-business concerns, though they make some profits while doing their activities, do not have profit making as their main motive. Hence, these concerns may also be classified as profit making concerns and non-profit making concerns.

Business concerns may further be classified as trading concerns, manufacturing concerns, and service organizations. Trading concerns do mainly trading business, i.e., buying and selling of goods. Example: wholesale and retail organizations, super markets, mega stores etc. Manufacturing concerns mainly engage in manufacturing activities. They buy raw materials, convert them into finished products and then sell them to customers directly or indirectly. Example: Industrial concerns manufacturing various products. Service organizations mainly provide services to the customers. They do not normally engage in any of the trading or manufacturing activities. Examples: banking companies, Insurance companies, etc. These concerns may further be classified, depending their size and area of operation, as small, medium, and large-scale organization. Depending upon the forms of organizations, they may be classified as sole trading concerns, partnership organizations, company type and co-operative organizations.

Whatever may be the type, all concerns maintain books of accounts adopting double entry system of book keeping. All of them prepare final accounts at the end of the accounting or financial year in order to find out the results of their operating performance and financial position. However, depending upon the nature of business, the items of income and expenditure will vary and also the scope of final accounts will vary. For example, a trading concern will prepare trading and profit and loss account to find out the profit or loss earned during the accounting year. A manufacturing concern will prepare a manufacturing account in order to find the cost of production and then trading and profit and loss account to ascertain the gross profit and net profit. A service organization, say a banking company, will prepare only the profit and loss account to find out the net profit. A non-profit making institution will prepare an Income and Expenditure Account in the place of Profit and Loss account. However, in all cases the income statement would be followed by a Balance Sheet. But the composition of assets and liabilities will vary from business to business. Further there are no statutory forms for final accounts in the case of sole trading and partnership organizations. But there are statutory forms in the case of company type of organizations.

5.3 What is Trading Account?

An income statement of a trading concern has two parts, viz., Trading Account and Profit and loss Account. Trading accounting is an account prepared to ascertain the trading results of a business i.e., the gross profit earned or gross loss incurred from buying and selling of goods during a particular period. The excess of net sales [total sales less returns] over cost of goods sold is termed as gross profit. Adding together the opening stock, purchases and direct expenses on purchase of goods or manufacturing the goods less closing stock computes the cost of goods sold. When the cost of goods sold is more than the net sales, the difference is termed as gross loss. The gross profit or loss is transferred to Profit and Loss Account. The specimen of a Trading account is given below:

Trading Account for the year ended 31st December 2002

Dr. Cr.

Particulars	Amount	Particulars	Amount
To Opening Stock		By Sales xxxxx	
To Purchases xxxxx		Less Returns xxx	
Less returns xxx		By Closing Stock	
To Direct Expenses			
To Gross Profit transferred to P & L A/c			

Explanation of the debit side items of the Trading A/c

Opening Stock: This is the stock of goods in hand at the beginning of the accounting period. Generally this item will appear in the Trail balance. Sometimes it may consist of stock of raw materials, work in process, and finished goods.

Purchases: This item includes total purchases less trade discount and returns. Goods taken out by the proprietor for personal use are also deducted from purchases and debited to drawings account. Purchase of assets is not included in this item.

Direct Expenses: All expenses incurred in connection with purchases and making them ready for sale are termed as direct expenses. A few items of direct expenses are: Carriage inwards, Import duties, customs duties, wages, Power charges, Manufacturing expenses, Consumable stores and royalties, etc.

Explanation of credit side items of Trading A/c

Sales: This item includes the total sales less returns. Items of assets sold are not included in sales.

Closing Stock: It is the amount of goods, which remain unsold at the end of the accounting period. Generally it is shown outside the trial balance. This item is entered in two places in final accounts, i.e., credit side of trading account and asset side of the balance sheet.

5.4 Give the Closing Entries for Trading Account

Closing entries are the journal entries necessary to close the various ledger accounts by transferring them to final accounts. Transferring them to the trading a/c closes the balances in the opening and closing stocks, purchases and sales and direct expenses. The following closing entries are passed for the same:

For transfer of Opening stock, net purchases, and direct expenses to Trading A/c

Trading a/c Dr.
  To Opening Stock a/c
  To Purchases a/c
  To Direct Expenses a/c

For transfer of net sales and closing stock to Trading a/c

Sales a/c Dr.
Closing Stock a/c Dr.
  To Trading a/c

For transfer of gross profit

Trading a/c Dr.
  To Profit and loss a/c

OR

For transfer of gross loss,

Profit and loss a/c Dr.
  To Trading a/c

Example 1

From the following ledger balances taken out at the close of a trading year ended 31st December 2001, prepare trading account and pass necessary closing entries.

	Rs.		Rs.
Opening Stock	16000	Carriage Inwards	2400
Purchases	40000	Wages	6600
Sales	160000	Freight and Dock charges	4800
Returns Inwards	3000	Stock on 31 12-2001	14000
Returns Outwards	800	Salaries	30000

Solution

Trading Account for the year ended 31st December 2001

		Rs.			Rs.
To Opening Stock		16000	By Sales	160000	
To Purchases	40000		Less Returns	3000	157000
Less Returns	800	39200	By Closing Stock		14000
To Carriage Inwards		2400			
To Wages		6600			
To Freight & dock charges		4800			
To Gross Profit to P & L a/c		102000			
		171000			171000

Note: Salaries, being an Office expense, is not included in the Trading a/c.

Closing Entries

For transfer of debit side items to trading a/c

		Rs.	Rs.
Trading a/c	Dr.	69000	
To Opening Stock			16000
To Purchases			39200
To Carriage Inwards			2400
To Wages			6600
To Freight & dock charges			4800

For transfer of credit side items to trading a/c

Sales a/c	Dr.	Rs. 157000	
Closing Stock a/c	Dr.	14000	
To Trading a/c			Rs.171000

For transfer of gross profit to Profit and loss a/c

Trading a/c	Dr.	Rs. 102000	
To Profit & Loss a/c			Rs. 102000

5.5 What is Profit and Loss Account?

Profit and loss a/c is an account, which is prepared to calculate the final profit or loss of the business. All operating expenses and other non-operàting income and expenditures and losses are charged to P&L a/c to find out the net profit. Operating expenses such as office and administration expenses, selling and distribution expenses and financial charges are indirect in nature and incurred to carry on business profitably. Non-operating income such as dividends received; interest received etc., and non-operating expenses and losses such as donations paid, fire losses etc., are also charged to P&L a/c in order to arrive at the final net profit or loss earned by the business. This account is a nominal account and its balance - net profit or loss is transferred to Capital account. The specimen P&L a/c is given below:

Profit and Loss Account for the year ended 31st December 2002

Particulars	Amount Rs.	Particulars	Amount Rs.
To Gross Loss [transferred from Trading a/c] To Salaries To Rent To Commission To Advertisement To Discount allowed To Interest paid To Postage To Printing and stationery To Depreciation To Net Profit transferred to Capital a/c		By Gross Profit [transferred from Trading a/c] By Dividend received By Interest received By Discounts received By Commission earned By Net Loss transferred to Capital a/c	

Explanation of debit side items of P&L a/c

Office and Administration Expenses: Salaries paid to office staff. Godown and warehouse staff, office rent, municipal rates and taxes, other office expenses like postage, stationary etc.

Selling and Distribution Expenses: Salesmen's salaries, selling commission, advertisement, carriage outwards, bad debts, discount allowed, etc.

Financial Charges: Interest on loans, overdrafts and bills overdue etc.

Depreciation and other non-operating expenses, and abnormal losses.

Explanation of credit side items of P&L a/c

Non-operating income: Interest on Investments, Rent received, discounts received, commission earned and other abnormal gains. In short, except sales income all other items of income are credited to P&L a/c.

Items not to be shown in P&L a/c

Domestic and household expenses: All personal expenses of the proprietor are treated as drawings and not shown in P&L a/c. Income tax and life insurance premium paid are the personal expenses of the proprietor and added to drawings.

Closing Entries

(a) For transfer of various items of expenses to P&L a/c

Profit and Loss a/c Dr.

To Various Expenses a/c

(b) For transfer of various items of income and gains to P&L a/c

Various income and Gains a/c Dr.

To Profit and Loss a/c

(c) To transfer Net Profit

Profit and Loss a/c Dr.

To Capital a/c

To transfer Net Loss

Capital a/c Dr.

To Profit and Loss a/c

Example 2

From the following balances taken out at the close of a year ended 31st December 2002, prepare a Profit and Loss Account.

	Amount [Rs.]		Amount [Rs.]
Gross Profit	102000	Discount [dr.]	1000
Carriage outwards	5000	Apprentice Premium [cr.]	3000
Salaries	11000	Printing and Stationery	500
Rent	2200	Rates and taxes	700
Insurance Premium	1800	Traveling expenses	400
Bad debts	4200	Depreciation	12000
Sundry Trade Expenses	600	Repairs and maintenance	5600

Solution

Profit and Loss Account for the year ended 31st December 2002

Particulars	Amount [Rs]	Particulars	Amount [Rs]
To Carriage outwards	5000	By Gross Profit b/d	102000
To Salaries	11000	By Apprentice Premium	3 000
To Rent	2200		
To Insurance Premium	1800		
To Bad debts	4200		
To Sundry Trade Expenses	600		
To Discount	1000		
To Printing and Stationery	500		
To Traveling expenses	400		
To Rates and taxes	700		
To Depreciation	12000		
To Repairs and maintenance	5600		
To Net Profit transferred	60000		
To Capital a/c	105000		105000

5.6 What is Manufacturing Account?

Industrial concerns, in order to find out the cost of production, prepare a separate account called *manufacturing account.* This account includes all expenses relating to manufacturing operations such as raw materials consumed, semi-manufactured goods, productive wages, power and other manufacturing expenses. The cost of goods produced is transferred to trading a/c. Trading a/c deals with the sale of goods and debited with the cost of production instead of purchase of goods as in the case of trading concerns. Some concerns combine trading a/c with manufacturing a/c and calculate the Gross Profit or Gross Loss of the manufacturing operations. The specimen form of manufacturing account is given below:

Manufacturing Account for the year ended 31st December 2002

Particulars	Amount [Rs.]	Particulars	Amount [Rs.]
To Opening Stock: Raw materials Goods in process To Purchase of materials To Manufacturing wages To All Factory expenses To Repairs to Plant & Factory Buildings To Depreciation of Plant & Factory Buildings		By Closing Stock Raw Materials Goods in process, By Cost of Production transferred to Trading a/c [Balancing Figure]	

5.7 Distinguish between Manufacturing Account and Trading Account

	Manufacturing Account	Trading Account
1.	It is prepared by manufacturing concerns only.	It is prepared by trading concerns
2.	The purpose of preparing this account is to find out cost of production.	The purpose of preparing this account is to find out trading results - gross profit or loss.
3.	It is debited with raw materials consumed, productive wages, all factory expenses, and other manufacturing expenses.	It is debited with purchase of finished goods, carriage inwards and other trading expenses.
4.	The cost of production is transferred to Trading a/c in order to find out the manufacturing profit or gross profit or loss.	The gross profit or loss is transferred to P&L a/c in order to find out the net profit or loss of the business.

Example 3

From the following balances extracted from the books of Arun for the year ended 31st December 2002, prepare Manufacturing Account.

Particulars	Rs.	Particulars	Rs
Opening Stock:			
Raw materials	20000	Gas and Water	6000
Semi-finished goods	10000	Return of materials	2600
Finished goods	52000	Coal and fuel	6600
Purchases:		Factory power	25000
		Fire insurance	2600
Raw materials	160000	Sales returns	24000

Finished goods	34000	Depreciation on factory buildings	2400
Carriage inwards:			
Raw materials	6000	Closing Stock:	
Finished goods	700	Raw materials	16000
Manufacturing		Semi-finished	26000
wages	20000	Goods	
Factory rent	14000	Finished goods	44000
Salary of Supervisor	7200	Sales	440000

Solution

Manufacturing Account for the year ended 31st December 2002

Particulars	Amount (Rs.)		Particulars		Amount (Rs.)
To Opening Stock:			By Closing Stock		
Raw materials	20000		Raw materials	16000	
Semi-finished goods	10000	30000	Semi-finished		
To Purchase of			Goods	26000	42000
Raw materials	160000		By Cost of		
Less Returns	2600	157400	Production, transferred to Trading a/c		
To Carriage inwards		6000			235200
To Manufacturing wages		20000			
To Factory expenses:,					
Salary of supervisor	7200				
Factory Rent	14000				
Gas and water	6000				
Coal and fuel	6600				
Factory power	25000				
Fire insurance	2600				
Depreciation	2400	63800			
		277200			277200

Note: Items relating to finished goods i.e., sales, sales returns, opening stock and closing stock are not entered in the Manufacturing a/c since they are items to be entered in the Trading a/c.

Example 4

From the following figures relating to the year 2002, prepare Manufacturing a/c, Trading a/c, and Profit and Loss a/c.

Particulars	Amount (Rs.)	Particulars	Amount (Rs.)
Stock on 1.1.2002:		Depreciation: Machinery	50000
Finished goods	66000	Office Equipment	16200
Raw materials	32000	Sundry Expenses: Factory	10600
Work in progress	22000	Office	35600
Purchase of materials	301800	Sales	720000
Carriage on Purchases	8200	Stock on 31-12-2002:,	
Wages	130000	Finished goods	55000
Factory Salaries	52000	Raw materials	36000
Office Salaries	36000	Work in progress	18600

Repairs: Machinery	16600	
Office Equipment	3400	

Solution

Manufacturing Account for the year ended 31st December 2002

Particulars		Amount (Rs.)	Particulars	Amount (Rs.)
To Opening Work in progress		22000		
To Materials consumed:			By Cost of Production transferred to Trading a/c	568000
Opening Stock	32000			
Add: Purchases	301800			
	333800			
Less: Closing Stock	36600	297200		
To Carriage on Purchases		8200		
To Wages		130000		
To Factory Expenses:				
Salaries	52000			
Machinery repairs	16600			
Depreciation of Machinery	50000			
Sundry expenses	10600	129200		
		586600		
Less Closing Work in progress		18600		
		568000		568000

Trading Account for the year ended 31st December 2002

Particulars	Amount (Rs.)	Particulars	Amount (Rs.)
To Opening Stock of Finished Goods	66000	By Sales	720000
To Cost of Production transferred from Manufacturing a/c,	568000	By Closing Stock in finished goods	55000
To Gross Profit transferred to Profit and Loss a/c	141000		
	775000		775000

Profit and Loss Account for the year ended 31st December 2002

Particulars	Amount (Rs.)	Particulars	Amount (Rs.)
To Office salaries	36000	By Gross Profit transferred from Trading a/c	141000
To Repairs of Equipment	3400		
To Depreciation of Equipment	16200		
To Sundry office expenses	35600		
To Net Profit transferred to Capital a/c	49800		
	141000		141000

5.8 What is Balance Sheet?

A balance sheet [B/S] may be defined as "a statement drawn upon a given date, generally at the end of each accounting year, to measure the exact financial position of a business, setting forth the various assets and liabilities of the concern at this date." From this definition it may be understood that the B/S is a statement of assets and liabilities as on a particular date. Its assets on a given date and its liabilities indicate the financial position of a concern on that date. Excess of assets over liabilities represents the capital and is indicative of the financial soundness of a company. A B/S is also described as a 'statement showing the sources and application of capital.' It is a statement and not an account. It is prepared from real and personal accounts.

On the left hand side of the B/S, the liabilities and capital are shown. On the right hand side, all the assets are shown. Therefore, the two sides of the balance sheet must always be equal. Otherwise, there is an error somewhere in the books of accounts. A properly drawn up balance sheet gives information relating to (a) the nature and value of asset; (b) the nature and extent of liabilities; (c) whether the firm is solvent; and (d) whether the firm is over trading. In short, it explains the financial condition of the concern.

5.9 Describe the nature of a Balance Sheet and give the specimen format of a B/S.

(a) The B/S is prepared as on a particular date. The information furnished by the B/S is true only on that date and not before or later. The capital position of a concern keeps on changing from time to time. Hence, it is never prepared to cover a period.

(b) A B/S is not an account. It is a statement showing the assets, liabilities and capital of a particular concern.

(c) A B/S is intended to reveal the financial position of a concern. It shows the nature and value of assets, the nature and value of liabilities and the amount of capital.

A specimen format of a Balance Sheet is given below:

Balance Sheet of (firm's name) as on (closing date)

Liabilities	Amount	Assets	Amount
Current Liabilities:		**Current Assets:**	
Bills Payables		Cash in hand	
Sundry Creditors		Cash at bank	
Bank Overdraft		Sundry debtors	
Outstanding Expenses		Bills Receivables	
Income received in advance		Prepaid Expenses	
Long-term Liabilities:		Accrued Income	
Mortgage Loans		Closing Stock	
Debentures		**Investments:**	
Owner's Equity:		Government Securities	
Reserves and Surplus		Other investments	
Capital		**Fixed Assets:**	
Add Net Profit		Furniture	
Interest on Capital		Plant and Machinery	
Less Drawings		Land and Buildings	
Income tax		Patents	
		Goodwill	

		Miscellaneous expenses	

Note for any contingent liability, if any.

Form of Balance Sheet

There is no prescribed form of B/S for a sole trader and partnership concern. However, the assets and liabilities may be shown either in the liquidity order or permanency order. Under liquidity order, the assets, which can be converted into cash, are shown first and those, which cannot be converted into cash come next and so on. Similarly, those liabilities, which are to be paid immediately, are shown first and others payable later come next and so on. Under permanency order the arrangement of assets and liabilities will be reversed. Assets, which are used permanently in the business, are shown first and the most liquid asset is shown at the bottom. The arrangement of assets and liabilities in any one of these methods is called as "marshalling of the Balance Sheet". In the case of joint stock companies the B/S is prepared as per the prescribed form given in the Companies Act.

5.10 How can Assets be Classified?

Assets represent every thing, which a business owns and has money value. In other words assets represent the possession and properties of the business. They are valuable resources owned by a business entity that benefit future period. Land and buildings, plant and machinery, stock, cash, debtors, etc., are some examples of assets. Depending upon the nature of assets they are classified as follows:

Fixed Assets: Assets, which are acquired and held permanently and are used for the purpose of earning profits are called fixed assets. Land and buildings, plant and machinery and furniture, etc., are some examples of these assets.

Current Assets: Those assets such as cash, debtors, stock, etc., that can be converted into cash, or consumed in production of goods and services are called current assets. They are normally owned by a business not more than one accounting year. As their values are constantly floating from one form to another [for example cash into stock, stock into debtors and so on], they are also called as floating assets

Liquid Assets: Those assets, which are in the form of cash or readily converted into cash are liquid assets. Examples are cash, bank, bills receivables, marketable securities, etc.

Tangible Assets: These are definite assets that can be seen, touched and have volume such as cash, stock, machinery, etc. On the other hand, intangible assets cannot be seen and touched or felt, e.g., goodwill, copyrights, etc.

Fictitious Assets: These assets have no real value and are losses not written off, e.g., P&L a/c debit balance, Preliminary expenses, Discount on issue of securities, etc.

Wasting Assets: Those assets such as mines, quarries, etc., that become exhausted or reduce in value by their working are called wasting assets.

Contingent Assets: Contingent asset is an asset the existence, value and ownership of which is dependent on the occurrence or non-occurrence of a specified act or an uncertain future event. Suppose a firm has filed a suit for some specified property now in possession of someone else. If the suit is decided in firm's favour, the firm will get the property. At the moment, the specified property is a contingent asset. Contingent liability in respect of a contract for capital expenditure already entered into will give rise to an asset on payment, at present; it is only a contingent asset. Similar would be the position of a patent applied for arising of a firm's on research effort.

5.11 How can Liabilities be classified?

All claims that the business owes are liabilities. They include the credit balances of personal and real accounts together with the proprietor's capital. A liability is a claim by an outsider on the assets of the business and an amount that a business is legally bound to pay. Liabilities may be classified into four categories.

Fixed Liabilities: Those liabilities that are payable only on the termination of the business are called fixed liabilities. It mainly includes the proprietor's equity such as paid up capital, reserves and surplus.

Long-term Liabilities: Those liabilities, which are payable over a long period of time, say five to ten years, are called as long-term liabilities. Debentures, Mortgage loans, Term loans, etc., are a few examples of long-term liabilities.

Current Liabilities: Those liabilities that are payable out of current assets within the next accounting period usually a year or already due are called current liabilities. Sundry creditors, bills payables, short-term bank overdraft and outstanding expenses, etc., are some examples of such liabilities.

Contingent Liabilities: A contingent liability is one, which is not an actual liability but will become an actual one on the occurrence of some future uncertain event. It has two characteristics: (a) uncertainty as to whether the amount will be payable or not, and (b) uncertainty about the amount involved. Some examples are law suits against the company for environment pollution, patent infringement, trademark violation, etc., arrears of fixed cumulative dividend, uncalled liability on partly paid up shares, and bills of exchange, guarantees given against particular firm person.

5.12 Distinguish between a Trial Balance and Balance Sheet

	Trial Balance	Balance Sheet
1.	It is a list of balances of all ledger accounts; no account with a balance can be left out.	It is a statement of assets and liabilities; only personal and real accounts appear here.
2.	Its object is to check the arithmetical accuracy of the ledger balances.	Its object is to reveal at a glance the financial position of the business concerns.
3.	It includes the opening stock.	It includes the closing stock.
4.	It is prepared whenever desired or at the end of every month or quarterly, half yearly, or annually.	It is usually prepared at the end of a trading period or accounting year.
5.	It does not give information about the net profit or net loss.	It gives information about the profits and the capital balance includes the profit.
6.	It is not absolutely necessary to prepare the trial balance. It can be dispensed with.	Preparation of balance sheet is absolutely necessary to complete the accounting process.

7.	It is generally prepared without giving effect to any adjustment.	It cannot be prepared without making adjustmetns for outstanding and prepayments.
8.	It contains the headings 'debit' and 'credit'.	It contains the headings 'liabilities' and assets'.

Example 5

From the following particulars, prepare a Balance Sheet as on 31st December, 2002

Particulars	Rs.	Particulars	Rs.
Capital	100000	Loan to Sumathi	10000
Business Premises	110000	Investments	6000
Furniture & Fixtures	5000	Cash in Hand	400
Bills Receivable	7000	Cash at Bank	7000
Bills Payable	5000	Proprietor's withdrawals	6000
Sundry Debtors	40000	Net profit	77800
Sundry Creditors	31600	Closing Stock	14000
Packing Machinery	9000		

Solution

Balance Sheet as on 31st December, 2002

Liabilities		Rs.	Assets	Rs.
Sundry Creditors		31600	Cash in Hand	400
Bills Payable		5000	Cash at Bank	7000
Capital	100000		Investments	6000
Add Net Profit	77800		Sundry Debtors	40000
			Bills Receivable	7000
	177800		Closing Stock	14000
Less Drawings	6000	171800	Loan to Sumathi	10000
			Packing Machinery	9000
			Furniture & Fixtures	5000
			Business Premises	110000
		208400		208400

Example 6

The following balances are extracted from the books of M/s Durga & Co. on 31st December, 2002. You are required to prepare the Trading and Profit and Loss Account and a Balance Sheet as on that date:

Particulars	Rs.	Particulars	Rs.
Stock on Jan. 1	1000	Discounts (Cr.)	400
B/R	4500	Returns outwards	500

Purchases	39000	Trade Expenses	200
Wages	2800	Office Fixtures	1000
Insurance	1100	Cash in hand	500
Sundary Debtors	30000	Cash at Bank	4750
Carriage Inward	800	Rent & Taxes	1100
Commission (Dr.)	800	Carriage outward	1450
Interst on Capital	700	Sales	50000
Stationery	450	Bills Payable	3000
Returns Inwards	1300	Creditors	19650
		Capital	17900

The Closing Stock was valued at Rs. 25,000.

Solution

Trading & Profit & Loss a/c of M/s. Durga & Co. for the year ended 31st December, 2002

Dr

Particulars		Rs.	Particulars		Rs.
To Opening Stock		1000	By Sales	50000	
To Purchase	39000		Less Returns Inwards	1300	
Less Returns outwards	500				48700
		38500	By Closing Stock		25000
To Wages		2800			
To Carriage Inward		800			
To Gross Profit c/d		30600			
		73700			73700
To Insurance		1100	By Gross Profit b/d.		30600
To Commission		800	By Discounts		400
To Interst on Capital		700			
To Sationery		450	Cr		
To Trade Expenses		200			
To Rent and Taxes		1100			
To Carriage outward		1450			
To Net Profit transferred to capital a/c		25200			
		31000			31000

Balance Sheet of M/s. Durga & Co. as on December 31, 2002

Liabilities	Amount Rs.	Assets	Amount Rs.
Creditors	19650	Cash in Hand	500

Bills payable		3000	Cash at Bank	4750
Capital	17900		Bill Receivable	4500
Add. Net Profit	25200		Stock	25000
		43100	Sundry Debtors	30000
			Office Fixtures	1000
		65750		65750

5.13 Adjustments

The object of preparing the Final Accounts is to find out the true profit or loss for the year under consideration. This requires that all items, which are relevant for the current year, be brought into account. For example, in the case of expenses, all expenses incurred for the current year, whether paid or unpaid must be debited to the P&L a/c. The unpaid amount of a particular expense has to be brought into account. This is known as adjustment. The following are the common adjustments:

Closing Stock. As the value of closing inventories is ascertained at the end of the accounting year, it appears as an adjustment. It should be credited to Trading a/c and shown in the asset side of the B/S. The adjusting entry is:

Closing Stock a/c Dr.

To Trading a/c

Trading Account

			Rs.
		By Sales By Closing Stock	

Balance Sheet

Liabilities	Rs.	Assets	Rs.
		Closing Stock	

Outstanding Expenses: These are the expenses incurred within the accounting year but the payment has not been made. Outstanding or unpaid expenses should be added to the concerned expenses a/c in P&L a/c and will be shown as a current liability in the B/S. For example, the Rent for the month of December 2002 Rs.1,000 remain unpaid. The calendar year is the accounting year.

Adjusting Entry:

Rent account Dr. Rs.1000

To Outstanding Rent a/c Rs.1,000

Profit and Loss Account

			Rs.	
To Rent Account	[11 months rent]	11,000		
Add: Outstanding	[December]	1,000	12,000	

Balance Sheet as on 31st December 2002

Liabilities	Rs.	Assets	
Outstanding Expenses: Rent	1,000		

Prepaid Expenses: These are the expenses, which have been paid, but part of the amount paid extends to the next year. It is also called as 'Un-expired expenses'. Advance amount paid should be deducted from the concerned expenses and be shown as a Current Asset in the B/S. For example, the insurance premium of Rs.2,400 a year was paid on 1st July 2002. The calendar year is the accounting year.

Since one year's premium has been paid on 1st July, the premium for 6 months, i.e., half the amount relates to the current year and the other half relates to the next year. Hence, Rs.1,200 must be treated as prepaid and deducted from the premium paid and be shown as an asset in the B/S.

Adjusting Entry

Prepaid Insurance a/c Dr. Rs.1,200

To Insurance Premium a/c Rs.1,200

Profit and Loss Account

	Rs.	Rs.	
To Insurance Premium a/c	2,400		
Less: Prepaid insurance	1,200	1,200	

Balance Sheet

Liabilities	Rs.	Assets	Rs.
		Prepaid Insurance	1,200

Accrued Income: It is the income that has already been earned [i.e., the service has already been rendered] but the money has not been received. For example, Interest on investments accrued Rs.1,200. The interest for the current year is due at the close of the year. The amount may be actually received in the next year. At present it represents an income, which has become receivable or accrued. Hence it is credited to P&L a/c and being accounts receivable, shown as an asset in the B/S.

Adjusting Entry

Accrued Interest a/c Dr. Rs.1,200

To Interest a/c Rs.1,200

Profit and Loss Account

	By Interest on investments	......	
	Add: Interest accrued	1,200	

Balance Sheet

Liabilities	Rs.	Assets	Rs.
		Interest accrued	1,200

Incomes received in Advance: These are incomes received during the current year, but part of the amount received relates to the next year. Such amount must be deducted from the total amount received in P&L a/c and shown on the liabilities side of the B/S as it represents an amount, which the business is obliged to return. For example, a business concern has received apprentice premium for three years amounting to Rs.6,000. In this amount Rs.2,000 i.e., 1/3 of Rs.6,000 is for current year and should be credited to P&L a/c as income. And the balance Rs.4,000 represents a liability as the business is obliged to return.

Adjusting Entry

Apprentice Premium a/c Dr. Rs.4000

To Apprentice Premium received in advance Rs.4000

Profit and Loss Account

		Rs.	Rs.
	By Apprentice Premium	6,000	
	Less: Received in advance	4,000	2,000

Balance Sheet

Liabilities	Rs.	Assets	Rs.
Apprentice Premium received in advance	4,000		

Depreciation on Assets: Depreciation means diminution or fall in value of an asset due to its constant use. It may also arise on account of wear and tear, lapse of time and obsolescence. It is a loss to the business. It is usually calculated at a certain percentage on the value of asset and the amount so obtained is first shown on the debit side of the P&L a/c and then deducted from the original value of asset in the B/S. For Example, a business has furniture of the value of Rs.50,000. at the end of the year it is depreciated at 5%.

Adjusting Entry

Depreciation a/c Dr. Rs.2,500

To Furniture a/c Rs.2,500

[5% on Rs.50,000 = 2,500]

Profit and Loss Account

	Rs.	
To Depreciation a/c		
Furniture	2,500	

Balance Sheet

Liabilities	Rs.	Assets		Rs.
		Furniture	50,000	
		Less: Depreciation	2,500	47,500

Bad Debts: Debts represent money due from debtors [i.e., uncollected portion of credit sales]. When debts become irrecoverable, it becomes bad debts and is treated as a loss. The amount of bad debts is debited to P&L a/c and is deducted from Sundry Debtors in the B/S. For example, the ledger balance in respect of sundry debtors of a trader shows Rs.20,000 and of this Rs.1,000 is estimated to be irrecoverable.

Adjusting Entry

Bad Debts a/c	Dr.	Rs.1,000	
To Sundry Debtors a/c			Rs.1,000

Provision for Bad and Doubtful Debts: Every business has a lot of dealings by way of credit transactions. This gives rise to a sizable amount of book debts or debtors. But it is seldom that 100 percent of these debts will be recovered. Hence, it becomes necessary to bring down the debtors balance to it true position. The usual practice is to calculate such doubtful debts at a certain percentage, based on past experience on debtors. It is called as Provision or Reserve for Doubtful Debts. However, the provision for bad and doubtful debts is calculated on good debts i.e., after deducting bad debts not adjusted earlier.

Example: The sundry debtors of a trader at the close of the year stood at Rs.21,000. It is estimated that Rs.1,000 is written off as bad debts and 5% provision is created for doubtful debts.

Adjusting Entries

Bad Debts a/c	Dr.	Rs.1,000	
To Sundry Debtors a/c			Rs.1,000
Profit and Loss a/c	Dr.	Rs.2,000	
To Bad Debts a/c			Rs.1,000
To Provision for Doubtful Debts			1,000

Profit and Loss Account

	Rs.		
To Bad Debts	1,000		
To Reserve for Doubtful Debts	1,000		

If there is an old provision for doubtful debts, it should be adjusted [deducted] against the new provision.

Balance Sheet

Liabilities	Rs.	Assets		Rs.
		Sundry Debtors	21,000	
		Less: Bad Debts	1,000	
			20,000	
		Less: Provision for Doubtful Debts	1,000	19,000

Provision for Discount on Debtors: Cash discounts are allowed to debtors in order to encourage them to make prompt payments. After providing for bad and doubtful debts, the balance of debtors represents debts due from sound parties. They may try to pay their dues on time and avail themselves of the cash discounts permissible. Hence, this discount should be anticipated and provided for. It is, therefore, the usual practice in business is to provide for discount on debtors at certain percentage on good debts.

Example. Suppose a trader has sundry debtors amounting to Rs.20,000 and he estimates that after a provision of 5% for doubtful debts, a provision for discounts at 2% is desirable. Then, on the sound debts, i.e., Rs.19,000 a provision of 2% is made as Reserve for Discount on Debtors.

Adjusting Entry

Profit and Loss a/c	Dr. Rs.380	
To Reserve for Discount on Debtors a/c		Rs.380

Profit and Loss Account

	Rs.	
To Bad Debts		
To Reserve for Doubtful Debts	1,000	
To Reserve for Discount on Debtors	380	

Balance Sheet

Liabilities	Rs.	Assets		Rs.
		Sundry Debtors	20,000	
		Less: Provision for Doubtful Debts	1,000	
			19,000	
		Less: Provision for Discounts on Debtors	380	18.620

Provision for Discount on Creditors: Creditors represent the amount owed by the business to suppliers of goods on credit. Sound business concerns make it a practice to settle accounts with creditors in time to earn goodwill of the creditors and also the discount allowed by them. In that case the liability in respect of sundry creditors can be reduced to the extent of discounts anticipated. Based on the past practice, a certain percentage on creditors balance is calculated as Provision for discounts and deducted from the creditors balance in the B/S and the same amount is credited as gain in the P&L a/c.

Example. A trader had sundry creditors at Rs.10,000 on 31st December 2002. It is desired to make a provision of 3% on this amount for discounts.

Adjusting Entry

Reserve for Discounts on Creditors a/c	Dr. Rs.300	
To Profit and Loss a/c		Rs.300

Profit and Loss Account

	Rs.		Rs.
		By Reserve for Discount on Creditors	300

Balance Sheet

Liabilities	Rs.			
Sundry Creditors	10,000			
Less: Reserve for Discounts	300	9,700		

Interest on Capital: Often, interest at a normal rate is allowed on the capital of the proprietor employed in the business. This is necessary in order to assess the efficiency of the business. Otherwise the profits would include the interest and appear at a higher rate. The interest so charged is a loss to the business and gain to the proprietor. So it is debited to the Profit and Loss a/c and added to the capital in the Balance Sheet.

Adjusting Entries

Interest on Capital a/c Dr.
 To Capital a/c

Profit and Loss a/c Dr.
 To Interest on Capital a/c

Interest on Drawings: Drawings are money withdrawn by the proprietor from his capital. Just as the business allows interest on capital, it charges interest on drawings. It is a gain to the business and a loss to the proprietor. So, it is credited to the Profit and Loss a/c and deducted from the capital in the Balance Sheet.

Profit and Loss Account

	Rs.		Rs.
To Interest on Capital		By Interest on Drawings	

Balance Sheet

Liabilities	Rs.		
Capital Add: Interest on Capital Less: Drawings Interest on Drawings			

Guidelines for the Preparation of Final Accounts

When a trial balance and adjustments are given for the preparation of Final Accounts, the following points should be kept in mind:

1. Trial balance items should be entered into Final Accounts in only one place. Debit balances should be debited to Trading a/c or Profit and Loss a/c or Balance Sheet asset side. For example, Wages given in trial balance should be debited to Trading a/c and Salaries to Profit and Loss a/c and Furniture in the asset side of the Balance Sheet.

Similarly credit balances should be credited to Trading a/c or Profit and Loss a/c or shown in the Liability side of the Balance sheet. Examples: Sales given in the trial balance should be credited to Trading a/c; Interest received to Profit and Loss a/c and Capital a/c shown in the liability side of the Balance sheet.

2. Adjustment items should be entered in two places in the Final Accounts in order to complete the double entry principle. They are entered into books of accounts for the first time.

3. Guidelines for making adjustments in the Final Accounts.

Adjustment	Profit and Loss a/c	Balance Sheet
Outstanding Expenses [Current Liability]	Add to the concerned item of expense in debit side	Show all Outstanding Expenses in the Liability side.
Prepaid or Unexpired expenses [Current Asset]	Deduct from the concerned item of expense in the debit side.	Show all prepaid expenses in the Asset side.
Accrued or Outstanding income [Current Asset]	Add to the concerned item of income in the credit side.	Show the accrued income in the Asset side.
Income received in advance [Current Liability]	Deduct from the concerned item of income in the credit side.	Show the income received in advance in the liability side.
Closing Stock [Current Asset]	Credit Trading a/c with the value of closing stock.	Show the closing stock in the Asset side.
Stock destroyed by fire [Abnormal loss]	Credit Trading a/c with full value of stock destroyed. Debit P&L a/c with the actual loss [total stock destroyed less insurance claim]	Add the claim received in cash with Cash a/c OR show the Insurance Company a/c in the Asset side.
Depreciation [Operating loss]	Debit with the amount of depreciation of individual asset.	Deduct the amount of depreciation from the concerned item of asset Or add the amount with the Depreciation Reserve in the liability side.
Bad Debts [Operating loss]	Debit the amount of bad debts.	Deduct the amount of bad debts from Sundry Debtors.
Provision for Bad and Doubtful Debts [Reserve]	Debit the provision	Deduct the amount from Debtors.
Discount allowed and Provision for Discounts	Debit both the items.	Deduct from Debtors discounts allowed first and then deduct the provision.
Discounts received and Provision for Discounts received.	Credit both the items.	Deduct from Creditors discounts received first and then deduct provision.
Interest on Capital	Debit the amount of interest on capital.	Add the interest to the Capital a/c.
Interest on Drawings	Credit the amount of interest on drawings.	Deduct the interest from Capital a/c.

Illustration 1

From the following trial balance of EverGreen and Company, prepare trading and profit and loss account and balance sheet.

Trial Balance as on 31st December 1995

Particulars	Debit [Rs.]	Credit [Rs.]
Cash in hand	2400	
Purchases	240000	
Stock on 1st January 1995	70000	
Debtors	100000	
Plant and Machinery	120000	
Furniture	30000	
Bills Receivable	40000	
Rent and Taxes	20000	
Wages	32000	
Salaries	37600	
Capital		200000
Bills Payable		44000
Creditors		48000
Sales		400000
	692000	692000

Additional Information

(a) Closing Inventory as on 31st December 1995 Rs.50,000.

(b) Outstanding wages Rs.5,000.

(c) Depreciation on Plant and Machinery at 10 percent and Furniture at 5 percent.

[M.C.A., November,1998, Madras University, Old Regulations]

Solution

BOOKS OF EVERGREEN AND COMPANY

Trading Account for the year ended 31st December 1995

Particulars		Rs.	Particulars	Rs.
To Opening Stock		70000	By Sales	400000
To Purchases		240000	By Closing Stock	50000
To Wages	32000			
Add Outstanding	5000	37000		
To Gross Profit c/d		103000		
		450000		450000

Profit and Loss account for the year ended 31st December 1995

Particulars	Rs.	Particulars	Rs.
To Salaries	37,600	By Gross Profit b/d	1,03,000
To Rent and Taxes	20,000		
To Depreciation:			
Plant &Machinery	12,000		
Furniture	1,500		
To Net Profit carried to Capital a/c,	31,900		
	1,03,000		1,03,000

Balance Sheet as on 31st December 1995

Liabilities		Rs.	Assets		Rs.
Creditors		48,000	Cash in hand		2,400
Bills Payable		44,000	Debvtors		1,00,000
Outstanding Wages		5,000	Bills Receivable		40,000
Capital	2,00,000		Stock		50,000
Add Net Profit	31,900	2,31,900	Furniture	30,000	
			Less Depreciation	1,500	28,500
			Plant & Machinery	1,20,000	
			Less Depreciation	12,000	1,08,000
		3,28,900			3,28,900

Illustration 2

The following is the trial balance of Raja Jewelers as on 31st December 1995.

Debit balances	Rs.	Credit balances	Rs.
Opening Inventory	72,000	Capital	5,00,000
Purchases	2,25,000	Sales	3,50,000
Furniture	15,000	Purchase Returns	1,800
Motor Car	30,000	Ram	32,000
Buildings	4,25,800	Shyam	24,000
Sanjay	12,000	Commission	7,500
Kishore	20,000		
Raghav	18,000		
Advertisement	22,000		
Repairs and maintenance	13,000		
General expenses	16,000		
Insurance	7,000		
Cash in hand	3,500		
Cash at bank	6,000		
Salaries	30,000		
	9,15,300		9,15,300

You are required to draft Profit and Loss account and Balance Sheet as on 31st December 1995 after taking into account the following adjustments:

(a) Closing Inventory as at 31.12.1995 Rs.80,000.

(b) Interest on Capital at 6 percent.

(c) Prepaid advertisement Rs.2,000.

(d) Goods used for domestic purpose Rs.1,800.

(e) Outstanding Salaries Rs.3,000.

(f) Depreciation on buildings at 5%, on furniture at 5%, and motorcar at 10%.

[M.C.A., November 1998, Madras University]

BOOKS OF RAJAN JEWELERS

Trading and Profit and Loss Account for the year ended 31.12.1995

Particulars		Rs.	Particulars	Rs.
To Opening Inventory		72,000	By Sales	3,50,000
To Purchases	2,25,000		By Closing Inventory	80,000
Less Returns	1,800			
	2,23,200			
Less Drawings	1,800	2,21,400		
To Gross Profit c/d		1,36,600		
		4,30,000		4,30,000
To Salaries	30,000		By Gross Profit b/d	1,36,600
Add Outstanding	3,000	33,000	By Commission	7,500
To Advertisement	22,000			
Less Prepard	2,000	20,000		
To Reparis and maintenance		13,000		
To General Expenses		16,000		
To Insurance		7,000		
To Depreciation:				
Furniture		750		
Motor Car		3,000		
Building		21,290		
To Interest on Capital		30,000		
To Net profit to Capital a/c		60		
		1,44,100		1,44,100

Balance Sheet as on 31.12.1995

Liabilities		Rs.	Assets		Rs.
Capital	5,00,000		Building	4,25,800	
Add Interest on capital	30,000		Less Depreciation	21,290	4,04,510
Net Profit	60		Furniture	15,000	
	5,30,060		Less Depreciation	750	14,250
Less Drawings	1,800	5,28,260	Motor Car	30,000	
Sundry Creditors:			Less Depreciation	3,000	27,000
Ram	32,000		Closing Inventory		80,000
Shyam	24,000	56,000	Sundry Debtors:		
Outstanding Salaries		3,000	Sanjay	12,000	
			Kishore	20,000	
			Raghav	18,000	50,000
			Prepaid Advertisement		2,000
			Cash at bank		6,000
			Cash in hand		3,500
		5,87,260			5,87,260

Note: Goods used for domestic purpose should be treated as drawings.

Illustration 3

The following is the trial balance of Kamal Enterprises for the year ended 31st December 1996. you are required to prepare a Profit and Loss a/c and Balance Sheet after taking into account the adjustments given below.

Debit balances	Rs.	Credit balances	Rs.
Cash in hand	500	Sales	1,50,300
Cash at bank	1,200	Purchase returns	5,000
Office furniture	6,000	Accounts Payable	12,000
Accounts Receivables	15,000	Bills Payable	8,000
Commission	1,200	Discount received	1,000
Bills Receivables	3,500	Dividend received	2,000
Power and fuel	6,000	Rent receive	3,500
Plant and Machinery	24,000	Capital	27,000
Office expenses	2,000		
Carriage inwards	1,200		
Carriage outwards	3,500		
Rent, rates, and taxes	1,700		
Leasehold Premises	25,000		
Wages	30,000		
Salaries	7,000		
Opening Inventory	12,000		
Sales Returns	2,000		
Purchases	60,000		
Drawings	7,000		
	2,08,800		2,08,800

Adjustments:

1. Closing Inventory as on 31.12.1996 Rs.18,000
2. Depreciate Plant and Machinery at 10%.
3. Salaries outstanding Rs.1,000; Power and fuel outstanding, Rs.2,000.
4. Rs.5,000 was spent on erection of plant and machinery, but wrongly included under wages.
5. Provide for bad and doubtful debts for Rs.1,500.
6. Discount earned but not received Rs.100.
7. Commission due but not recorded Rs.200.
8. Rent received includes Rs.500 received in advance.

[M.C.A., May 1998, Madras University]

Solution

BOOKS OF KAMAL ENTERPRISES

Trading and Profit and Loss account for the year ended 31-12-1996

Particulars		Rs.	Particulars		Rs.
To Opening Inventory		12,000	By Sales	1,50,300	
To Purchases	60,000		Less Returns	2,000	1,48,300
Less Returns	5,000	55,000	By Closing Inventory		18,000
To Carriage inwards		1,200			

To Wages	30,000				
Less Erection charges	5,000	25,000			
To Power and fuel	6,000				
Add Outstanding	2,000	8,000			
To Gross Profit c/d		65,100			
		1,66,300			1,66,300
To Salaries	7,000		By Gross Profit b/d		65,100
Add Outstanding	1,000	8,000	By Discounts received	1,000	
To Commission	1,200		Add Outstanding	100	1100
Add Outstanding	200	1,400	By Dividends received		2,000
To Office expenses		2,000	By Rent received	3,500	
To Carriage outwards		3,500	Less Received in advance	500	3,000
To Rent, rates and taxes		1,700			
To Depreciation on Plant		2,900			
To Provision for bad debts		1,500			
To Net Profit transferred to Capital Account		50,200			
		71,200			71,200

Balance Sheet as on 31.12.1996

Liabilities		Rs.	Assets		Rs.
Accounts Payable		12,000	Cash in hand		500
Bills Payable		8,000	Cash at bank		1,200
Outstanding expenses:			Accounts Receivables 15,000		
Salaries	1,000		Less Provision for bad debts	1,500	13,500
Power and fuel	2,000				
Commission	200	3,200	Bills Receivables		3,500
Rent received in advance		500	Closing Inventory		18,000
			Discounts earned but due		100
Capital	27,000		Furniture		6,000
Add Net Profit	50,200		Plant and Machinery		
	77,200		Add Erection charges	24,000	
				5,000	
Less Drawings	7,000	70,200		29,000	
			Less Depreciation	2,900	26,100
			Leasehold Premises		25,000
		93,900			93,900

Illustration 4

From the following particulars taken from the books of Nirmal Traders, prepare Trading and Profit and Loss account for the year ended 31st December 2000 and the Balance Sheet as on that date.

Ledger balances	Rs.	Ledger balances	Rs.
Land and buildings	94,000	Plant	70,000
Cash	4,600	Patents	24,000
Debtors	7,600	Funiture	9,400
Sales	1,89,000	Travelling expenses	17,000
Bills Receivable	2,400	Salesmen's commission	2,600
Purchases	33,600	Carriage inwards	800
Wages	47,800	Packing	1,200
Creditors	10,400	Advertising	3,600
Salaries	33,000	Bank balance	1,200
Sales returns	800	Loans	84,800
Loss by fire	1,000	Trucks	37,000
Discounts received	400	Capital	1,30,000
Opening stock	13,000		

Provide for 15% depreciation on Plant. Write off Patents by a third. An amount of Rs.1,700 was due to workers. An overpayment of Rs.400 made to the salesman towards commission. The Insurance Company agreed to meet the losses by fire in totally. Closing stock was valued at Rs.7,400.

Solution

Trading Account for the year ended 31st December 2000

Particulars		Rs.	Particulars		Rs.
To Opening stock		13,000	By Sales	1,89,000	
To Purchases		33,600	Less Returns	800	1,88,200
To Wages	47,800		By Closing stock		7,400
Add Outstanding	1.700	49,500			
To Carriage inwards		800			
To Gross Profit c/d		98,700			
		1,95,600			1,95,600

Profit and Loss Account for the year ended 31st December 2000

Particulars		Rs.	Particulars	Rs.
To Salaries		33,000	By Gross Profit b/d	98,700
To Traveling expenses		17,000	By Discounts received	400
To Salesman's commission	2,600			
Less Prepaid	400	2,200		
To Packing		1200		
To Advertising		3,600		
To Depreciation:				
Plant	10,500			
Patents written off	8,000	18,500		
To Loss by Fire	1,000			
Less Insurance company	1,000	Nil		
To Net Profit to Capital a/c		23,600		
		99,100		99,100

Balance Sheet as on 31st December 2000

Liabilities		Rs.	Assets		Rs.
Creditors		10,400	Cash		4,600
Loans		84,800	Bank		11,200
Outstanding wages		1,700	Bills Receivable		2,400
Capital	1,30,000		Debtors		7,600
Add Net Profit	23,600	1,53,600	Insurance company [loss by fire]		1,000
			Prepaid Commission		400
			Closing stock		7,400
			Patents	24,000	
			Less 1/3 written off	8,000	16,000
			Trucks		37,000
			Furniture		9,400
			Plant	70,000	
			Less Depreciation at 15%	10,500	59,500
			Land and Building		94,000
		2,50,500			2,50,500

Illustration 5

From the following prepare Trading a/c, P&L a/c and Balance Sheet as on 31st December 2000:

Particulars	Debit Balances Rs.	Credit Balances Rs.
Opening stock	10,000	
Cash and Bank	4,000	25,000
Purchases and Sales	70,000	90,000
Returns	3,000	4,000
Debtors and Creditors	30,000	21,000
Buildings	30,000	
Capital		30,000
Furniture and Fittings	7,000	
Bad debts reserve		2,000
Petty cash	200	
Carriage inwards	800	
Salaries	11,000	
Interest charged by Bank	500	
Sundry trade expenses	6,000	
Insurance premium paid for the year up to 30.6.2001	1,000	
Telephone charges	500	
Commission		2,000

Additional Information

(a) Closing stock Rs.15,000.

(b) Buildings and Furniture and Fittings are to be depreciated by 10% and 20% respectively.

(c) Bad debts Rs.1,000 are to be written off and a reserve of 5% is to be kept on remaining debtors.

(d) Commission received in advance Rs.1,000.

[M.C.A., May 2002, Madras University.]

Solution

Trading Account for the year ended 31st December 2000

Particulars		Rs.	Particulars		Rs.
To Opening stock		10,000	By Sales	90,000	
To Purchases	70,000		Less Returns	3,000	87,000
Less Returns	4,000	66,000	By Closing stock		15,000
To Carriage inwards		800			
To Gross Profit c/d		25,200			
		1,02,000			1,02,000

Profit and Loss Account for the year ended 31 st December 2000

Particulars		Rs.	Particulars		Rs.
To Salaries		11,000	By Gross Profit b/d		25,200
To Petty cash expenses		200	By Commission	2,000	
To Interest on Overdraft		500	Less Received in advance	1,000	1,000
To Insurance Premium	1000				
Less Prepaid					
	500	500			
To Telephonic changes		500			
To Sundary Trade expanses		6,000			
To Bad debts	1,000				
Add New Bad debts reserve	1,450				
	2,450				
Less Old Reserve	2,000	450			
To Depreciation: Furniture		1,400			
Buildings		3,000			
To Net Profit to Capital a/c		2,650			
		26,200			26,200

Balance Sheet as on 31st December 2000

Liabilities		Rs.	Assets		Rs.
Creditors		21,000	Cash		4,000
Bank Overdraft		25,000	Debtors	30,000	
Commission received in advance		1,000	Less Bad debts	1,000	
Capital	30,000			29,000	
Add Net Profit	2,650	32,650	Less New Bad debts reserve		
				1,450	27,550
			Closing Stock		15,000
			Prepaid Insurance		500
			Furniture&Fittings	7,000	
			Less Depreciation @ 20%	1,400	5,600

		Buildings	30,000	
		Less Depreciation	3,000	27,000
	79,650			79,650

Illustration 6

From the following trial balance extracted from the books Mr. Ramesh prepare his Trading and Profit and Loss Account and Balance Sheet as on 30th June 1999:

Debit balances	Rs.	Debit balances	Rs.
Cash in hand	540	Cash at oank	2,630
Purchases	40,675	Returns inwards	680
Wages	10,480	Fuel	4,730
Carriage inwards	2,040	Carriage outwards	3,200
Stock [1st July 1998]	5,760	Building	40,000
Machinery	20,000	**Credit Balances:**	**1,76,580**
Goodwill	7,500	Sales	98,780
Salaries	15,000	Returns outwards	500
Insurance	3,600	Capital	71,000
Sundry Debtors	14,500	Sundry Creditors	6,300
Drawings	5,245		
			1,76,580

Take into account the following adjustments:

(a) Depreciate Building at 10% and Machinery at 20%,

(b) Salaries outstanding Rs,2,000.

(c) Create a Reserve for bad and doubtful debts at 5% on sundry debtors.

(d) Closing stock was valued at Rs.6,800. (e) Insurance prepaid Rs.200.

[M.C.A., November 2001, Madras University]

Solution

BOOKS OF RAMESH

Trading Account for the year ended 30th June 1999

Particulars		Rs.	Particulars		Rs.
To Opening stock		5,760	By Sales	98,780	
To Purchases	40,675		Less Retuns inwards	680	98,100
Less Returns outwards	500	40,175	By Cloasing stock		6,800
To Carriage inwards		2,040			
To Wages		10,480			
To Fuel		4,730			
To Gross Profit to P&L a/c		41,715			
		1,04,900			1,04,900

Profit and Loss Account for the year ended 30th June 1999

Particulars		Rs.	Particulars	Rs.
To Salaries	15,000		By Gross Profit b/d	41,715
Add Outstanding	2,000	17,000		
To Insurance	3,600			
Less Prepaid	200	3,400		
To Carriage outwards		3,200		
To Reserve for bad debts		725		
To Depreciation: Building		4,000		
Machinery		4,000		
To Net Profit to Capital a/c		9,390		
		41,715		41,715

Balance Sheet as on 30th June 1999

Liabilities		Rs.	Assets		Rs.
Sundry Creditors		6,300	Cash in hand		540
Salaries outstanding		2,000	Cash at bank		2,630
Capital	71,000		Sundry debtors	14,500	
Add Net Profit	9,390		Less Resserve for bad debts	725	13,775
	80,390		Closing Stock		6,800
Less Drawings	5,245	75,145	Prepaid Insurance		200
			Machinery	20,000	
			Less Depreciation	4,000	16,000
			Building	40,000	
			Less Depreciation	4,000	36,000
			Goodwill		7,500
		83,445			83,445

Illustration 7

Mr. Maharaja gives you the following figures from his books as on 31st December 2002:

Particulars	Rs.	Particulars	Rs.
Capital	50,000	Purchases	48,000
Sundry Creditors	10,000	Discounts received	400
Bills Payable	1,000	Buildings	10,000
General Reserve	5,450	Plant and Machinery	15,000
Provision for bad debts	1,000	Book Debts	16,400
Sales	75,000	Bank balance [dr.]	3,400
Discounts allowed	750	Investments [4%]	10,000

Stock [1st January 2002]	15,000	Bills Receivable	2,500
Audit Fees	2,000	Wages and Salaries	13,000
Office expenses	2,000	Reparis and Renewals	1,800
Furniture	2,500	Interest paid	700
		Bad Debts recovered	200

The value of stock on hand on 31st December 2002 was Rs.18,000; there was a fire, which destroyed goods worth Rs.3,500. The insurers admitted a claim for Rs.2,500. This amount had not been received and no entries have been passed yet. Buildings are to be depreciated at 2 % p.a. and Plant and Machinery at 10% p.a. Rs.2,000 is to be transferred to General Reserve out of profits, if any. Interest on Investments is due for 12 months. The manager is entitled to a commission of 10% of net profits after charging his commission. Prepare the Trading Account, Profit and Loss Account, and Balance Sheet.

Solution

BOOKS OF MR. MAHARAJA

Trading Account for the year ended 31st December 2002

Particulars	Rs.	Particulars	Rs.
To Opening stock	15,000	By Sales	75,000
To Purchases	48,000	By Closing stock	18,000
To Gross Profit c/d	33,500	By stock destroyed by fire	3,500
	96,500		96,500

Profit and Loss Account for the year ended 31st December 2002

Particulars	Rs.	Particulars	Rs.
To Wages and Salaries	13,000	By Gross Profit b/d	33,500
To Office Expenses	2,000	By Bad debts recovered	200
To Audit Fees	2,000	By Interest on Investment due	400
To Repairs and Renewals	1,800	By Discounts received	400
To Interest paid	700		
To Discounts allowed	750		
To Depreciation: Machinery	1,500		
Building	200		
To Loss by Fire	1000		
To Manager's Commission	1,050		
To Net Profit to Capital a/c	10,500		
	34,500		34,500

Balance Sheet as on 31st December 2002

Liabilities		Rs.	Assets		Rs.
Capita'	50,000		Buildings	10,000	
Add Net Profit 10,500			Less Depreciation	200	9,800

Less to Reserve 2,000	8,500	58,500	Plant and Machinery	15,000	
General Reserve	5450		Less Depreciation	1,500	13,500
Add Transfer from Profits		7,450	Furniture		2,500
	2,000		Bills Receivable		2,500
Sundry Creditors		10,000	Stock		18,000
Bills Payables		1,000	Debtors	16,400	
Manager's Commission		1,050	Less Provision for bad debts	1,000	15,400
			Interest on Investments due		400
			Insurance Company		2,500
			Investments [4%]		10,000
			Bank		3,400
		78,000			78,000

Calculation of Commission: Net Profit before charging commission is Rs.11,550.

If Net Profit after charging commission is Rs.100,

The commission would be Rs.10 at 10%.

Net Profit before charging commission would be Rs.110. [100 + 10 = 110]

Actual net profit is Rs.11,550, hence the commission is 11,550 × 10/110 = Rs.1,050.

Loss by fire: Stock destroyed by fire	=	Rs.3,500
Less Insurance claim admitted	=	2,500
Loss by fire	=	1,000

Illustration 8

From the particulars extracted from the books of Gaiter Traders, prepare final accounts for the year ended 31st March 2002:

Particulars	Rs.	Particulars	Rs.
Capital	2,00,000	Land	54,000
Cash at bank	8,000	Sales	5,00,000
Cash in hand	2,000	Carriage inwards	3,200
Buildings	1,20,000	Gas	8,800
Wages	60,000	Sundry creditors	48,800
Salaries	40,000	Sundry debtors	60,000
Rent and rates	7,200	Purchase Returns	8,000
Printing and stationery	4,800	Sales Returns	6,000
Stock on 1.4.2001	32,000	Bills Receivable	16,000
Purchases	2,80,000	Discounts received	1,600
Insurance	3,200	Discounts allowed	2,000
Machinery	48,000	Furniture	12,000
Drawings	24,000	Travelling expenses	7,200
		Loans	40,000

Provide the following

(a) Prepaid insurance Rs.800. (b) Depreciation: (i) Machinery at10% and (ii) Furniture at 5%.

(c) Interest on capital at 3%. (d) Outstanding wages Rs.3,200; outstanding salaries Rs.2,400. (e) Write off bad debts Rs.4,000 and create a Reserve for bad debts at 5% on debtors.

Also create Reserve for discounts on debtors and creditors at 1%. [f] Value of closing stock Rs.40,000.

Solution

BOOKS OF GAITER TRADERS

Trading Account for the year ended 31st March 2002

Particulars		Rs.	Particulars		Rs.
To Opening stock		32,000	By Sales	5,00,000	
To Purchases	2,80,000		Less Returns	6,000	4,94,000
Less Returns	8,000	2,72,000	By Closing stock		40,000
To Wages	60,000				
Add Outstanding	3,200	63,200			
To Carriage inwards		3,200			
To Gas		8,800			
To Gross Profit c/d		1,54,800			
		5,34,000			5,34,000

Profit and Loss Account for the year ended 31st March 2002

Particulars		Rs.	Particulars	Rs.
To Salaries	40,000		By Cross Profit b/d	1,54,800
Add Outstanding	2,400	42,400	By Discounts received	1,600
To Rent and rates		7,200	By Reserve for discounts on creditors	488
To Printing and stationery		4,800		
To Insurance	3,200			
Less Prepaid	800	2,400		
To Discounts allowed		2,000		
To Reserve for discounts on debtors		532		
To Traveling expenses		7,200		
To Depreciation: Machinery		4,800		
Furniture		600		
To Bad debts		4,000		
To Reserve for bad debts		2,800		
To Interest on capital		6,000		
To Net Profit to Capital a/c		72,156		
		1,56,888		1,56,888

Balance Sheet as on 31st March 2002

Liabilities		Rs.	Assets		Rs.
Sundry Creditors	48,800		Cash in hand		2,000
Less Reserve for discounts	488	48312	Cash at bank		8,000
Loans		40,000	Bills Receivable		16,000
Outstanding Expenses:			Sundry debtors	60,000	
Wages		3,200	Less Bad debts	4,000	
Salaries		2,400		56,000	

Capital	2,00,000		Less Reserve for bad debts		
				2,800	
Add Interest on capital	6,000			53,200	
Net Profit	72,156		Less Reserve for discounts		
				532	52,668
	2,78,156		Prepaid Insurance		800
Less Drawings	24,000	2,54,156	Stock		40,000
			Furniture	12,000	
			Less depreciation	600	11,400
			Machinery	48,000	
			Less Depreciation	4,800	43,200
			Building		1,20,000
			Land		54,000
		3,48,068			3,48,068

Illustration 9

The trial balance of Mr.Mani as on 31st December 1994 was as follows:

Ledger balances	Debit [Rs.]	Credit [Rs.]
Purchases	1,62,505	
Sales		2,52,400
Reserve for doubtful debts		5,200
Sundry debtors	50,200	
Sundry creditors		30,526
Bills Payable		3,950
Opening stock	26,725	
Wages	23,137	
Salaries	5,575	
Furniture	7,250	
Postage	4,226	
Power and fuel	1,350	
Trade expenses	5,831	
Bad debts	525	
Loan to Ram at 10% on 1-9-1994	3,000	
Cash at bank	10,000	
Outstanding wages		2,000
Trade expenses accrued but not paid		700
Drawings	4,452	
Capital		10,000
	3,04,776	3,04,776

Adjustments:

(a) Write off depreciation at 10% on Furniture.

(b) Stock on 31st December 1994 Rs.12,550.

(c) Goods of the value of Rs.1,500 were destroyed by fire and the insurance company admitted the claim for Rs.1,000.

(d) Sundry debtors include an item of Rs.500 due from a customer who has become insolvent.

(e) Reserve for bad debts is to be maintained at 5% on debtors.

Prepare Trading and Profit and Loss account and a Balance Sheet as on 31st December 1994. *[B.Sc., March 1996, Madras University]*

Solution

BOOKS OF MR. MANI

Trading Account for the year ended 31st December 1994

Particulars	Rs.	Particulars	Rs.
To Opening stock	26,725	By Sales	2,52,400
To Purchases	1,62,505	By Closing stock	12,550
To Wages	23,137	By Stock destroyed by fire	1,500
To Power and fuel	1,350		
To Gross Profit c/d	52,733		
	2,66,450		2,66,450

Profit and Loss account for the year ended 31st December 1994

Particulars	Rs.	Particulars			Rs.
To Salaries	5,575	By Gross Profit b/d			52,733
To Postage	4,226	By Interest on Loan due [for 4 months]			100
To Trade expenses	5,831	By Old Reserve for bad debts		5,200	
To Depreciation on Furniture	725	Less: Bad debts - old	525		
To Loss by fire [Rs.1,500 - 1,000]	500	- New	500		
To Net Profit to Capital a/c	37,666	New Reserve	2,485	3,510	1,690
	54,523				54,523

Balance Sheet as on 31st December 1994

Liabilities		Rs.	Assets		Rs.
Sundry Creditors		30,526	Cash at bank		10,000
Bills Payable		3,950	Debtors	50,200	
Outstanding Wages		2,000	Less Bad debts	500	
Trade expenses due		700		49,700	
Capital	10,000		New Reserve	2,485	47,215
Add Net Profit	37,666		Stock		12,550
	47,666		Loan to Ram		3,000
Less Drawings	4,452	43,214	Interest on loan due		100
			Insurance company [claim]		1,000
			Furniture	7,250	
			Less Depreciation	725	6,525
		80,390			80,390

REVIEW QUESTIONS

1. What does 'Final Accounts' mean?
2. Explain the various types of concerns from accosting point of view.
3. Explain the following: Trading Account, Profit and Loss Account and Manufacturing Account.
4. Distinguish between Manufacturing Account and Trading Account.
5. Give a specimen format of a balance sheet.

6. How can assets be classified?
7. How can liabilities be classified?
8. Distinguish between a balance sheet and trial balance.
9. Explain the following terms (a) Contingent liability (b) Tangible assets (c) Accrued income (d) Current liabilities.

REVIEW PROBLEMS

1. From the following data, prepare Trading Account of a trader for the year ending 31st March 2002:

	Rs.
Stock on 1.4.2001	24,000
Purchases	6,08,000
Sales	9,50,000
Purchase Returns	8,000
Sales Returns	10,000
Direct Expenses incurred during the year:	
Freight	10,000
Carriage	2,000
Import duty	8,000
Clearing Charges	12,000
Cost of goods distributed as free samples	5,000
Goods taken for personal use	2,000
Stock destroyed by fire during the year	13,000

The cost of unsold stock on 31st March 2002 was Rs.1,20,000, but its market value was Rs.1,50,000.

[**Answer:** Gross Profit Rs.2,08,000]

Hints: Free samples distributed should be deducted from Purchases and shown as selling expense in P&L a/c;

Goods taken for personal use should be deducted from purchases and deducted as drawings from capital; stock destroyed by fire should be credited to trading a/c and actual loss to P&L a/c and insurance claim received in B/S.

2. Prepare Manufacturing and Trading Accounts for the year ending 31st December 2002 from the following information extracted from the books of a manufacturing concern.

	Opening Stock [Rs.]	Closing Stock [Rs.]
Raw materials	1,20,000	80,000
Work in progress	24,000	16,000
Finished goods	86,400	64,000

	Rs.
Materials purchased	4,00,000
Wages	2,50,000
Stores consumed	30,000
Indirect wages	72,000
Factory Rent	24,000
Depreciation on Plant and Machinery	40,000
Sales	11,20,000

Purchase of finished goods 10,000

[**Answer:** Cost of goods manufactured Rs.8,64,000; Gross Profit Rs.2,23,600]

3. From the following particulars, prepare Trading and Profit and Loss Accounts for the year ended 31st December 2002:

Particulars	Rs.	Particulars	Rs.
Stock (on 1.1.2002)	4,00,000	Salaries	60,000
Purchases	5,10,000	Rent, rates and taxes	24,000
Wages	2,00,000	Depreciation	6,040
Carriage	10,000	Repairs	12,000
Purchase Returns	26,500	Discounts allowed	25,010
Export Duty	18,000	Bad debts	18,000
Sales	11,50,000	Advertisement	5,000
Coal & Coke	50,000	Gas and water	3,000
Sales Returns	20,000	Factory lighting	5,000
Printing and stationery	4,500	General expanses	800

Value of closing stock on 31st December 2002 was Rs.6, 00,000.

[**Answers:** Gross Profit Rs.5, 78,500; Net Profit Rs.3,97,950]

4. The following were the balances taken out from the books of Mr. N.Narayanan as on 31st March 2002:

Particulars	Rs.	Particulars	Rs.
Taxes and insurance	2,240	Purchases'	1,26,440
Plant and machinery	50,000	Stock [1-4-2001]	50,000
Creditors	15,840	Narayanan's loan	20,000
Wages	13,560	Motor lorry	6,500
Bad debts	784	Carriage on Purchases	4,600
Land and buildings	27,680	Capital a/c	1,58,800
General charges	2,000	Repairs and replacements	2,400
Salaries	5,726	Drawings	12,600
Advertisement	7,600	Allowance from creditors	4,800
Debtors	16,000	Stock of coal	4,000
Rent received	1,146	Coal consumed	13,436
Sales	1,50,000	Cash at bank	4,000
Cash in hand	1,020		

The value of stock on 31st March 2002 was Rs.60, 000. Prepare Trading and Profit and Loss Account for the year ended 31st March 2002 and a Balance Sheet as on that date.

5. From the following particulars prepare final accounts of Mr.John for the year ended 31st March 2002.

Debit balances	Rs.	Credit balances	Rs.
Cash in hand	1,200	Capital	1,00,000
Purchases	1,20,000	Bills Payable	22,000
Stock (1.4.2001)	35,000	Creditors	24,000
Debtors	50,000	Sales	2,00,200
Plant and Machinery	60,000	Reserve for Bad debts	1,000
Furniture	15,000		
Bills Receivable	20,000		
Rent and Rates	10,000		

Wages	16,000		
Salaries	20,000		
	3,47,200		3,47,200

Additional Particulars: (a) Closing Stock Rs.40,000; (b) Outstanding rent Rs.2,000 and outstanding salaries Rs.4,000; (c) Provide depreciation on Plant and Machinery at 5% and on furniture at 10%.; and (d) Increase Reserve for Bad debts on Debtors to 2.5 percent.

[**Answers:** Gross Profit Rs.66,200; Net Profit Rs.25,450; Balance Sheet Total Rs.1,80,450]

6. From the following trial balance of Mr. Mahesh, prepare Trading and Profit and Loss Account for the year ended 30th June 2,002 and Balance Sheet as on that date.

Particulars	Rs.	Rs.
Capital		60,000
Sundry expenses	5,400	
Manufacturing expenses	1,500	
Reserve for bad debts		1,000
Productive wages	21,500	
Office Rent	2,000	
Plant and Machinery	28,000	
Furniture and Fittings	10,000	
Insurance	1,200	
Bills Receivables/ Payables	3,300	4,200
Factory Rent	4,000	
Salaries	16,000	
Carriages in	1,500	
Carriages out	1,700	
Cash in hand	4,700	
Sundry Debtors/ Creditors	23,500	14,300
Purchases / Sales	68,000	1,40,500
Opening Stock	20,500	
Drawings	7,200	

Take into account the following adjustments:

(a) Closing stock amounted to Rs.27, 000.

(b) Write off Rs.500 as bad debts and maintain the reserve for bad debts at Rs.1, 150.

(c) Unexpired insurance amounted to Rs.300.

(d) Sales include Rs.500 worth of goods taken out by the proprietor for personal use.

(e) Depreciate Machinery by 10% and Furniture at 5%.

[**Answers:** Gross Profit Rs.26,200; Net Loss Rs.3,750; Balance Sheet total Rs.67,550.]

[Hints: for adjustment (d): deduct goods used for personal use from sales as well as purchases in trading account]

7. From the following particulars, prepare Final Accounts for the year ended 31st March 2002:

Particulars	Debit [Rs.]	Credit [Rs.]
Drawings	10,000	
Stock on 1.4.2001	46,000	
Purchases and Returns	1,50,250	600
Cash in hand	3,400	
Cash at bank	22,660	
Freehold Premises	38,600	
Trade expenses	840	
Printing and Advertising	1,640	
Professional charges	280	
Commission		3,300
Investments as on 1.4.2001 @10%	4,000	
Interest on Deposits		200
Debtors and Creditors	36,000	29,000
Wages	25,000	
Salaries	14,000	
Capital		1,14,000
Income tax	1,600	
Discounts	6,300	4,600
Sales Returns and Sales	500	2,08,950
Bills Receivable/ Bills Payable	3,200	10,000
Office Furniture	3,050	
Rent, rates and insurance	4,000	
Bad debts provision		670
	3,71,320	3,71,320

Adjustments: (a) Provide for wages Rs.5,000.

(b) Write off 5% depreciation on Freehold Premises and 10% on Furniture.

(c) Insurance paid in advance Rs.200.

(d) Stock on 31.3.2002 is Rs.52,000.

(e) Charge interest on capital at 5% and on drawings Rs.300.

(f) Further bad debts are Rs.1,000.

(g) Provide for bad and doubtful debts at 5% on debtors.

(h) Make provision for discount on debtors and reserve for discount on creditors at 2%.

[**Answer:** Gross Profit Rs.34,800; Net Profit Rs.6,440; Balance Sheet Total Rs.1,57,600]

8. From the following Trial Balance as on 30th June 2002, prepare Final Accounts for the year ending on 30th June 2002:

Particulars	Debit [Rs.]	Credit [Rs.]
Capital		60,000
Opening stock	20,500	
Purchases	68,000	
Drawings	7,200	
Carriages inwards	1,500	

Sales		1,40,500
Book Debts	23,500	
Trade Creditors		14,300
Cash in hand	500	
Cash at bank	2,200	
Carriages out	1,700	
Salaries	16,000	
Factory Rent	4,000	
Bills Receivable	5,300	
Bills Payable		4,200
Insurance	1,200	
Furniture	10,000	
Machinery	28,000	
Office Rent	2,000	
Manufacturing wages	21,500	
Reserve for bad debts		1,000
Factory expenses	1,500	
General expenses	5,400	
	2,20,000	2,20,000

Adjustments to be considered:

(a) Stock on 1.7.2001 amounted to Rs.27,000.

(b) Write off Rs.500 as bad debts and maintain the provision for bad debts at 5% on Debtors.

(c) Insurance paid in advance Rs.300.

(d) Depreciate Machinery by 5% and by Furniture by 10%.

(e) On 15th June 2002 a fire broke out and destroyed stock of the value of Rs.10,000. The insurance company admitted the claim for Rs.6, 000 only and paid the amount 16th July 2002.

[**Answer:** Gross Profit Rs.60, 500; Net Profit Rs.27,450; Balance Sheet Total Rs.98,750]

9. From the following, prepare the Trading and Profit and Loss account for the year ended 31st December 2002 and the Balance Sheet as on that date:

Debit balances	Rs.	Credit balances	Rs.
Drawings	2,000	Capital	1,76,000
Plant and Machinery	1,00,000	Sales	4,68,000
Furniture and fixtures	12,000	Returns outwards	4,000
Loose tools	20,000	Discounts	6,000
Goodwill	10,000	Creditors	24,000
Stock 1.1.2002	20,000	Reserve for Bad debts	2,000
Purchases	2,12,000	Raja's Loan a/c	20,000
Returns inwards	8,000		
Wages	1,00,000		
Carriage inwards	12,000		
Salaries	41,600		
General expenses and Insurance	72,000		

Rent and Taxes	14,400		
Postage and telegrams	4,000		
Packing [distribution]	8,000		
Sundry debtors	48,000		
Nalini's a/c	2000		
Cash at bank	14,000		
	7,00,000		7,00,000

Adjustments

(a) Stock on 31.12.2002 was valued at Rs.30,800.

(b) Depreciate plant and machinery at 5% and furniture and fixtures at 6%. Loose tools are revalued at Rs.16,000.

(c) Proprietor drew Rs.800 per month, which he charged to salaries account.

(d) Remuneration of Rs.2,000 paid to Nalini, a temporary employee, stands debited to her personal account and the same is to be corrected.

(e) Reserve for bad debts is to be maintained at 5% on debtors. Maintain reserve for discounts on Creditors at 2%.

(f) Unpaid insurance is Rs.400.

[**Answer:** Gross Profit Rs.1,50,800; Net Profit Rs.14,360; Balance Sheet Total Rs.2,22,680.]

Hints: For adjustment (c) treat the amount $12 \times 800 = 9600$ as drawings; deduct from salaries and from capital a/c. For adjustment (d) add the amount i.e., Rs.2000 to salaries a/c and deduct from Nalini's a/c. Nalini's a/c will appear as zero in B/S.

10. The following Trail Balance was extracted from the books of M/s Aurofoods and Co. as on 31st March 1999.

Debit Balance	Rs.	Credit Balance	Rs.
Plant and Machinery	20,000	Capital account	80,000
Mfg. wages	34,500	Sundary Creditors	44,560
Salaries	15,850	Bank loan	15,000
Furniture	10,000	Purchase Returns	1,740
Freight on purchases	1,860	Sales	2,50,850
Buildings	24,000	Reserve of bad debts	2,000
Mfg. Expenses	9,500		
Insurance and Tax	4,250		
Goodwill	25,000		
General Expenses	8,200		
Factory Fuel and Power	1,280		
Sundry debtors	78,200		
Factory lighting	950		
Opening stock	34,200		
Motor car	12,000		
Purchases	1,02,000		
Sales return	3,100		
Bad debts	1,400		

Interest and bank charges	400		
Cash at Bank	4,200		
Cash in hand	1,120		

Prepare Trading and Profit and Loss Account as well as Balance sheet for the year ending March 31, 1999 taking into consideration the follwing information.

(a) Closing Stock Rs. 30,500

(b) Depreciate; Plant and Machinery-10%; Furniture-5%; Motor car - Rs. 1,000

(c) Bring provision for Bad debts to 5% on debtors.

(d) A commission of 1% on gross profit is to be provided for works manager.

(e) A commission of 2% on net profits (after charging the work's manager's commission) is to be credited to the General Manager.

[**Answer:** Gross Profit Rs. 95,700; Net Profit Rs. 58,072; Balance Sheet Total Rs. 1,99,750; Diff in TB Rs. 2,140; M's commission Rs. 1161]

[MBA Nov. 2000, Madras University]

6

DEPRECIATION AND RESERVES

Learning Objectives

After going through this Chapter, you should be able to

— Understand the meaning and objectives of depreciation,

— Explain various methods of depreciation,

— Work out problems in depreciation accounting,

— Distinguish between Provisions and Reserves.

6.1 Concept of Fixed Assets

Business concerns invest their capital mainly in fixed assets and current assets. Fixed assets refer to the various tangible and intangible assets and other facilities used in the business for producing and selling the goods or rendering the services to the customers. Current assets are maintained in the business in order to operate the fixed assets and carry on the business activities. It is also called as working capital. Fixed assets are of two types: (1) Tangible Fixed assets, and (2) Intangible Fixed Assets. Tangible fixed assets include such physical assets as land and buildings, plant and machinery, furniture and fittings, vehicles, etc. Intangible fixed assets include such invisible assets as patents, goodwill, copy rights, leaseholds, trade marks, etc. Fixed assets form and provide such facilities required for manufacturing and selling goods and services to the customers and generate revenues to the business. In this process, they depreciate over a period of time and the resulting loss in their values should be recovered from the revenues generated by such assets. Hence, depreciation is treated as necessary business expenditure. This chapter discusses the different aspects of depreciation.

6.2 Meaning of Depreciation

In common usage the term 'depreciation' refers to a decline in the value of any kind of property. But in Accounting its use is restricted to the expiration of the cost of tangible fixed assets. Except land, all other physical assets have a limited period of useful life. They are used to generate income over its economic life. Hence, their cost should be properly allocated as expense to the accounting periods in which these assets are used. The accounting process for this gradual conversion of the cost of fixed assets into expense is called as 'depreciation'. Depreciation is defined as "a permanent, continuing and gradual shrinkage in the book value of a fixed asset due to use, wear and tear, obsolescence or efflux ion of time."

The Accounting Standard No.6 of the Institute of Chartered Accountants of India (I.C.A.I) defines depreciation as a measure of wearing out, consumption, or other loss of value of a depreciable asset arising from use, efflux ion of time, or obsolescence through technology and market changes. Depreciation is allocated so as to charge a fair proportion of the depreciable amount in each accounting period during the expected useful life of the asset.

6.3 Characteristics of Depreciation

(a) Depreciation refers to fall or shrinkage rather than an increase in the value of an asset.

(b) It refers to a fall in book value of the asset. This value may or may not be equal to the market value or the cost price of the asset.

(c) The fall in book value is a slow and gradual process rather than a sudden event. It is always continuing and a permanent shrinkage.

(d) Depreciation is restricted to the fall in the value of fixed assets. Once a fixed asset is put to use, depreciation begins to occur and it stays there forever.

6.4 Objectives or Need for Providing Depreciation

(a) To ascertain true profits: Depreciation is a charge for capital assets used in earning profits and therefore, it should be viewed as a business expenditure. Unless proper charge for this expense is made in accounts, the correct profit cannot be ascertained.

(b) To show the assets at their proper values: Depreciation must be accounted for in order to show the assets at their proper values and thereby present a true and fair view of the financial position of the business. Unless depreciation is provided, the value of the assets will be overstated in the Balance Sheet and it will not reflect the true and fair view of the business.

(c) To create funds for replacement of assets: Depreciation is a non-cash expenditure. Hence, the amount of depreciation charged to Profit and Loss account remains in the business and the amount thus accumulated during the working life of the asset provides funds for its replacement at the end of the working life of the asset.

(d) To keep the capital in tact: If depreciation is not charged, the amount of profit will be inflated. If such profits are distributed among the owners, then it will amount to the distribution of fixed capital from the business. In the long run it will affect the financial health of the business.

(e) Statutory Need: Provision of depreciation is a statutory need: Section 205 of the Indian companies Act has made compulsory for a joint stock company to provide for depreciation before distributing the profits as dividends.

6.5 Depreciation, Depletion and Amortization Distinguished

The term 'depreciation' is restricted to represent the fall in the book value of the tangible and physical assets, such as land, buildings, plant furniture, etc.

The term 'depletion' is applied to refer to the physical exhaustion of natural resources such as coalmines, ore deposits, oil wells, etc.

The term 'amortization' is used to refer to the write off of long-term investments or intangible assets such as leaseholds, copy rights, patents, goodwill, trade marks, etc.

6.6 Causes of Depreciation

(1) Physical Deterioration: Depreciation is caused mainly from wear and tear when the asset is in use and from erosion, rust, rot and decay when it is exposed to wind, rain, sun and other elements of nature.

(2) Economic Factors: These arise due to obsolescence and inadequacy. Obsolescence means the process of becoming obsolete and out of date. New model and new technology may make the asset obsolete even though it is in good physical condition. Inadequacy refers to the stoppage of asset's usage because of growth and changes in the size of the firm.

(3) Time Factors: Some assets lose their value simply with the passage of time. Intangible fixed assets such as lease, patents, copyrights, etc., lose their working capacity over a period of time, if such assets are not used at all.

(4) Depletion: Some assets like coal mines, ore and oil deposits lose their utility and value due to extraction of deposits from them. The charge of depletion is made on the basis of consumption of the concerned asset.

6.7 Computation of Depreciation

The computation of depreciation charge involves the following factors:

(a) Depreciation Base: Depreciation base refers to the cost to be recovered over a period of time of use. Higher the depreciation base, higher will be the depreciation charge. It depends up on the cost of asset, salvage value and removal cost. In short, it is as follows:

Depreciation base

= Cost of Asset – Salvage value + Removal cost

The cost of asset includes the purchase price plus installation charges.

(b) Useful or Economic life: Estimation of economic life of a fixed asset is a very difficult task. The amount of depreciation depends mainly on the useful working life of the asset. Higher the useful life, lower will be the amount of depreciation charge. Both obsolescence and physical endurance must be considered in estimating the useful life. For accounting purpose, the useful life of an asset is based up on its expected use and replacement policy of the management.

(c) The Depreciation method: The method of depreciation is a very important factor in the allocation of net cost of an asset to each of the accounting periods in which the asset is used. There are a number of methods, which may be used in calculating the periodic depreciation charges. Different methods may give significantly different values. Hence, the method selected in any specific instance should be logical and based on a careful evaluation of the peculiarities of the individual concern.

6.8 Methods of Depreciation

The following are the methods of providing depreciation:

(a) Fixed Installment or Straight line Method

(b) Diminishing Balance or Written down Value Method

(c) Sums of the Digits Method

(d) Annuity Method

(e) Depreciation Fund or Sinking Fund Method

(f) Insurance Policy method

(g) Revaluation Method

(h) Activity Method: (i) Production Unit method, (ii) Machine hour rate method, (iii) Service unit (Hours) method (iv) Depletion method

(i) Repairs and Renewals method

Straight line Method: Under this method, an equal portion (amount) of the cost of the asset is allocated as depreciation to each accounting year over a period of its effective life. This is done so as to reduce the value of the asset equal to zero or its salvage or scrap value. It is based on the assumption that depreciation is a function of time rather than of use and the service potential of the asset is assumed to decline by an equal amount each year. The annual depreciation charge will be computed as under:

Annual Depreciation charge

$$= \frac{\text{Cost of asset} + \text{Erection Charges} - \text{Scrap value} + \text{Removal cost}}{\text{Estimated useful life of the asset}}$$

Example:

A machine is purchased for Rs.50,000 and Rs.1,000 is incurred as erection charges. The machine has 4 years of useful life with a salvage value of Rs.5,000. The removal cost may amount to Rs.1,000. Compute the annual depreciation charge.

Solution

Annual Depreciation charge

$$= \frac{\text{Rs.}50{,}000 + 1{,}000 - 5{,}000 + 1{,}000}{4} = \text{Rs.}11{,}750$$

Rs.11,750 (fixed amount) will be charged as depreciation every year for four years.

Calculation of Rate of Depreciation: The depreciation rate is one, which will charge the entire depreciable cost over the estimated life of the asset. The rate of depreciation can be calculated as follows:

Rate of depreciation

$$= \frac{(\text{Cost} - \text{Salvage} + \text{Erection cum Removal Costs}) \times 100}{\text{Estimated life} \times \text{Cost}}$$

Or Rate of Depreciation

$$= \frac{\text{Annual Depreciation Charge}}{\text{Cost of asset}} \times 100$$

Rate of Depreciation

$$= \frac{(\text{Rs.}50{,}000 - 5{,}000 + 1{,}000 + 1{,}000) \times 100}{50{,}000 \times 4} = 23.50\%$$

$$\text{Or Rate of Depreciation} = \frac{\text{Rs.}11{,}750 \times 100}{\text{Rs.}50{,}000} = 23.5\%$$

Merits

1. It is very simple to operate and easy to understand.

2. Sine the same amount is charged as depreciation every year, it does not take into account the seasonal fluctuations of the use of asset.

3. The asset account can be reduced to zero or its scrap value at the end of the estimated life of the asset, if so desired.

Demerits

1. The depreciation charge and maintenance expenses will be less in the beginning and more towards the end. But the depreciation charged will remain constant every year. Hence this method fails to even out the charges as per actual loss.

2. As the method is based on time factor and ignores the actual usage of the asset, it is illogical. It is not necessary that an asset is put to use equally over its life time. Many factors may necessitate the uneven usage of the asset over the year. In such case, this method proves unsuitable.

3. This method does not take into account the interest on capital invested in the asset.

4. This method creates complications in respect of additions to assets with different life spans requiring separate calculations.

5. It ignores time value of money (discount factor). Hence the reported income may not be true.

Suitability

This method is suitable under the following cases:

(a) When the usage of the asset is uniform from year to year,

(b) When the asset is relatively of small value,

(c) Possibility of obsolescence is very low, and

(d) No large scale repairs and renewals are required during its life time. This method is generally applied for writing down assets like furniture, patents and short leases.

Accounting Treatment

Depreciation can be treated in accounts in two ways:

(a) Charging depreciation to Asset Account – Under this system the amount of depreciation is deducted (credited) from the value of asset account and charged (debited) to Profit and Loss account. The asset account appears in the Balance Sheet at its reduced value (i.e., cost less depreciation up to date). The following accounting entries are passed:

(i) When depreciation is provided, the entry is

Depreciation A/c Dr.
To Asset A/c

(ii) When depreciation account is closed, the entry is

Profit and loss A/c Dr.
To Depreciation A/c

(b) Creating Provision for Depreciation – Under this system, the amount of depreciation is credited to Provision for Depreciation account or Accumulated Depreciation account. The following entries are passed:

(i) When depreciation is provided, the entry is

Depreciation A/c Dr.

To Provision for
Depreciation A/c

(ii) When depreciation account is closed the entry is

Profit and loss A/c Dr.
To Depreciation A/c

Instead of the above two entries, one combined entry may be passed as follows:

Profit and loss A/c Dr.
To Provision for
Depreciation A/c

The Provision for Depreciation account may be shown either on the Liability side of the Balance Sheet or as a deduction from the value of the concerned asset on the asset side.

Illustration 1

On 1st January 1994 a firm purchased machinery worth Rs.50,000. On 1st July 1996, it bought additional machinery worth Rs.10,000 and spends Rs.1,000 on its erection. The accounts are closed each year on 31st December. Assuming the annual depreciation is charged at 10% per annum on original cost, show necessary accounts for five years, when

(a) Asset Account is maintained at written down value, and

(b) Asset account is maintained at cost.

Solution

(a) When Asset Account is maintained at written down value:

Machinery Account

Date	Particulars	Amount Rs.	Date	Particulars	Amount Rs.
1994 January 1	To Bank	50,000	1994 Dec. 31	By Depreciation	5,000
				By Balance c/d	45,000
		50,000			50,000
1995 January 1	To Balance b/d	45,000	1995 Dec.31	By Depreciation	5,000
				By Balance c/d	40,000
		45,000			45,000
1996 January 1	To Balance b/d	40,000	1996 Dec. 31	By Depreciation	5,550
July 1	To Bank	11,000		By Balance c/d	45,450
		51,000			51,000
1997 January 1	To Balance b/d	45,450	1997 Dec. 31	By Depreciation	6,100
				By Balance b/d	39,350
		45,450			45,450
1998 Jan. 1	To Balance b/d	39,350	1998 Dec. 31	By Depreciation	6,100
				By Balance c/d	33,250

		39,350			39,350
1999 January 1	To Balance b/d	33,250			

Depreciation Account

Date	Particulars	Amount Rs.	Date	Particulars	Amount Rs.
31 Dec.94	To Machinery A/c	5,000	31 Dec.94	By P & L A/c	5,000
31 Dec.95	To Machinery A/c	5,000	31 Dec.95	By P & L A/c	5,000
31 Dec.96	To Machinery A/c	5,550	31 Dec.96	By P & L A/c	5,550
31 Dec.97	To Machinery A/c	6,100	31 Dec.97	By P & L A/c	6,100
31 Dec.98	To Machinery A/c	6,100	31 Dec.98	By P & L A/c	6,100

(b) When Asset Account is maintained at cost, a separate Provision for Depreciation account should be maintained.

Machinery Account

Date	Particulars	Amount Rs.	Date	Particulars	Amount Rs.
1 Jan. 94	To Bank	50,000	31 Dec.94	By Balance C/d	50,000
1 Jan. 95	To Balance B/d	50,000	31 Dec.95	By Balance C/d	50,000
1 Jan. 96	To Balance B/d	50,000	31 Dec.96	By Balance C/d	61,000
1 July 96	To Bank	11,000			
		61,000			61,000
1 Jan. 97	To Balance B/d	61,000	31 Dec.97	By Balance C/d	61,000
1 Jan. 98	To Balance B/d	61,000	31 Dec.98	By Balance C/d	61,000
1 Jan. 99	To Balance B/d	61,000			

Depreciation Account

Date	Particulars	Amount Rs.	Date	Particulars	Amount Rs.
31 Dec.94	To Provision for Dep. A/c	5,000	31 Dec.94	By P & L A/c	5,000
31 Dec.95	To Provision for Dep. A/c	5,000	31 Dec.95	By P & L A/c	5,000
31 Dec.96	To Provision for Dep. A/c	5,550	31 Dec.96	By P & L A /c	5,550
31 Dec.97	To Provision for Dep. A/c	6,100	31 Dec.97	By P & L A/c	6,100
31 Dec.98	To Provision for Dep. A/c	6,100	31 Dec.98	By P & L A/c	6,100

Provision for Depreciation Account

Date	Particulars	Amount Rs.	Date	Particulars	Amount Rs.
31 Dec.94	To Balance C/d	5,000	31 Dec.94	By Depreciation	5,000
31 Dec.95			1 Jan.95	By Balance B/d	5,000
	To Balance C/d	10,000		By Depreciation	5,000
		10,000			10,000
31 Dec.96	To Balance C/d	15,550	1 Jan.96	By Balance B/d	10,000
			31 Dec.96	By Depreciation	5,550
		15,550			15,550
31 Dec.97	To Balance C/d	21,650	1 Jan.97	By Balance B/d	15,550
			31 Dec.97	By Depreciation	6,100
		21,650			21,650
31 Dec.98	To Balance C/d	27,750	1 Jan.98	By Balance B/d	21,650
			31 Dec.98	By Depreciation	6,100
		27,750			27,750
			1 Jan. 99	By Balance B/d	27,750

Disposal of asset

When a fixed asset is sold during the accounting period, first the amount of depreciation should be calculated for the period of use (i.e., from the previous date of year ending up to the date of sale). The book value as on the date of sale should be calculated by deducting the amount of depreciation for the period. The difference between the sale price and the book value of the asset will be profit or loss on sale. If the sale price is more than the book value, the difference is profit and the book value minus sale price will be loss. The profit or loss should be credited or debited to P & L a/c. Amount received should be debited to Cash or Bank a/c and the concerned asset sold should be credited. The following entry is passed:

Bank a/c	Dr.	– amount received
Depreciation a/c	Dr.	– depreciation for the period of use
P & L a/c	Dr.	– loss on sale
To Asset a/c	– book value of the asset	

When there is profit on sale, it should be credited to P & L a/c in the above entry. If the asset a/c is maintained at original cost and a separate Provision for Depreciation a/c is maintained, the depreciation on the asset sold for the period of use should be credited to Provision a/c and then the provision for depreciation on asset sold shall be transferred to the concerned asset a/c and thereby the asset a/c is closed. The following entries are passed:

Depreciation a/c	Dr.	– for the period of use
To Provision for Depreciation		
Bank a/c	Dr.	– amount received
Provision for dep. a/c	Dr.	– total depreciation on asset sold
To Asset a/c		– original cost of asset sold
To P & L a/c		– profit on sale of asset

Illustration 2

On 1st January 1998 JB Ltd., purchased five machines for Rs.20,000 each. Depreciation is charged at the rate of 10% per annum on cost. The accounting year ends on 31st December each year. On 31st March 1999 one machine was sold for Rs.16,000 and on 30th September 2000 another machine was sold for Rs.15,000. A new machine was purchased on 30th June 2001 for Rs.24,000. Prepare Machinery Account and Provision for Depreciation account for four years.

Solution

Machinery Account

Date	Particulars	Amount Rs.	Date	Particulars	Amount Rs.
1-1-99	To Bank a/c	1,00,000	31-12-99	By Balance C/d	1,00,000

		1,00,000			1,00,000
1-1-99	To Balance B/d	1,00,000	31-3-99	By Bank a/c	16,000
				By Prov. For Dep. A/c	2,500
				By P & L a/c	1,500
			31-12-99	By Balance C/d	80,000
		1,00,000			1,00,000
1-1-99	To Balance B/d	80,000	30-9-00	By Bank a/c	15,000
30-9-99	To P & L a/c	500		By Prov. for Dep. A/c	5,500
			30-12-00	By Balance C/d	60,000
		80,500			80,500
1-1-01	To Balance B/d	60,000	31-12-01	By Balance C/d	84,000
30-6-01	To Bank a/c	24,000			
		84,000			84,000

Provision for Depreciation Account

Date	Particulars	Amount Rs.	Date	Particulars	Amount Rs.
31-12-98	To Balance C/d	10,000	31-12-98	By Depreciation	10,000
		10,000			10,000
31-3-99	To Machinery a/c	2,500	1-1-99	By Balance B/d	10,000
31-12-99	To Balance C/d	16,000	31-3-99	By Depreciation (on 20,000 for 3 months)	500
			31-12-99	By Depreciation (on 80000 for one year)	8,000
		18,500			18,500
30-9-00	To Machinery a/c	5,500	1-1-00	By Balance B/d	16,000
31-12-00	To Balance C/d	18,000	30-9-00	By Depreciation (on 20,000 for 9 months)	1,500
			31-12-00	By Depreciation (on 60000 for one year)	6,000
		23,500			23,500

31-12-01	To Balance C/d	25,200	1-1-01	By Balance B/d	18,000
			31-12-01	By Depreciation (on 60000 for one year)	6,000
				By Depreciation (on 24000 for 6 months)	1,200
		25,200			25,200

Written Down Value (WDV) Method

It is also known as Reducing Balance or Reducing Installment Method or Diminishing Balance Method. Under this method, the depreciation is calculated at a certain fixed percentage each year on the decreasing book value commonly known as WDV of the asset (book value less depreciation). The use of book value (the balance brought forward from the previous year) and fixed rate of depreciation result in decreasing depreciation charges over the life span of the asset.

While applying the depreciation rate both salvage or scrap value and removal cost are ignored. It is not possible to reduce the book value to zero; but it can be reduced close to its salvage value at the end of its useful ~~life.~~ The rate of depreciation may be determined using the following formula:

$$\text{Depreciation Rate} = 100\left(1 - \sqrt[n]{\frac{S}{C}}\right)$$ where n = number of years

S = Salvage value

C = Cost of asset

For example, if a plant costs Rs. 8,000 with an estimated salvage value of Rs.1,000 at the end of third year of its useful life, the rate of depreciation will be calculated thus:

$$\text{Rate of Depreciation} = 100\left(1 - \sqrt[3]{\frac{1000}{8000}}\right)$$

$$= 50\%$$

Merits

The following are the advantages of this method:

(a) As this method equalizes the total charges of using the asset (i.e., the amount of depreciation plus repair charges) from year to year, it is considered more equitable than straight-line method. This is because depreciation charges decline each year whereas repair charges increase year by year.

(b) It matches the service of the asset with the depreciation charge. When asset is more efficient in the initial years, higher depreciation is charged compared to later years. It is true about fixed assets such as motor vehicles.

(c) It recognizes the risk of obsolescence by charging the major part of depreciation in the early years of the life of the asset.

(d) It results in a better cash flow through tax deferral as under this method, the net income to be taxed is lower in the initial years and higher in subsequent years.

(e) As and when additions are made to the asset, fresh calculations of depreciation are not necessary.

(f) Income-tax authorities recognize this method.

Demerits

The main drawbacks of this method are as follows:

(a) In subsequent years the original cost of the asset is completely lost sight of.

(b) The asset can never be reduced to zero.

(c) This method does not take into consideration the interest on capital invested in the asset.

(d) This method requires elaborate book-keeping. The determination of correct rate of depreciation is a complex task.

Suitability

This method is most suitable to those assets that have more efficiency in the beginning and late on decreases year after year. This method is usually adopted for plant and machinery, fixtures and fittings, motor vehicles, etc.

Accounting Treatment and other problems will be similar to those discussed earlier in the case of Straight-line method. Only the amount of depreciation will be calculated differently.

Illustration 3

On 1-1-99, A ltd., purchased machinery for Rs.1,20,000 and on 30th June 2000, it acquired additional machinery at a cost of Rs.20,000. On 31st March 2001, one of the original machines, which had cost Rs.5,000 was found obsolete and sold as scrap for Rs.500. It was replaced on that date by a new machine costing Rs.8,000. Depreciation is provided at the rate of 15% per annum on the written down value. Show the ledger accounts for the first three years:

(a) When depreciation is written off in the asset account; and

(b) When depreciation is accumulated in a separate account.

Solution

Machinery Account

Date	Particulars	Amount Rs.	Date	Particulars	Amount Rs.
1-1-99	To Bank a/c	1,20,000	31-12-99	By Depreciation a/c	18,000
				By Balance C/d	1,02,000
		1,20,000			1,20,000
1-1-00	To Balance B/d	1,02,000	31-12-00	By Depreciation a/c	16,800
30-6-00	To Bank a/c	20,000		By Balance C/d	1,05,200
		1,22,000			1,22,000
1-1-01	To Balance B/d	1,05,200	31-3-01	By Bank	500
31-3-01	To Bank a/c	8,000		By Depreciation a/c	135

				By P&L a/c	2,977
			31-12-01	By Depreciation a/c (15,238 + 900)	16,138
			31-12-01	By Balance C/d	93,450
		1,13,200			1,13,200
1-1-02	To Balance B/d	93,450			

Depreciation account

Date	Particulars	Amount Rs.	Date	Particulars	Amount Rs.
31-12-99	To Machinery a/c	18,000	31-12-99	By P&L a/c	18,000
		18,000			18,000
31-12-00	To Machinery a/c	16,800	31-12-00	By P&L a/c	16,800
		16,800			16,800
31-3-01	To Machinery a/c	135	31-12-01	By P&L a/c	16,273
31-12-01	To Machinery a/c	16,138			
		16,273			16,273

(b) When depreciation is accumulated in a separate account:

Machinery Account

Date	Particulars	Amount Rs.	Date	Particulars	Amount Rs.
1-1-99	To Bank a/c	1,20,000	31-12-99	By Balance C/d	1,20,000
		1,20,000			1,20,000
1-1-00	To Balance B/d	1,20,000	31-12-00	By Balance C/d	1,40,000
30-6-00	To Bank a/c	20,000			
		1,40,000			1,40,000
1-1-01	To Balance B/d	1,40,000	31-3-01	By Bank	500
31-3-01	To Bank a/c	8,000		By Prov. For dep. A/c	1,523
				By P & L a/c	2,977
			31-12-01	By Balance C/d	1,43,000
		1,48,000			1,48,000

Provision for Depreciation Account

Machinery Account

Date	Particulars	Amount Rs.	Date	Particulars	Amount Rs.
31-12-99	To Balance C/d	18,000	31-12-99	By Depreciation a/c	18,000
		18,000			18,000
31-12-00	To Balance C/d	34,800	1-1-00	By Balance B/d	18,000
			31-12-00	By Depreciation a/c	16,800
		34,800			34,800
31-12-01	To Machinery a/c	1,523	1-1-01	By Balance B/d	34,800
31-12-01	To Balance C/d	49,550	31-3-01	By Depreciation a/c	135
			31-12-01	By Depreciation a/c	16,138
		51,073			51,073

Depreciation Account

Date	Particulars	Amount Rs.	Date	Particulars	Amount Rs.
31-12-99	To Prov. For Dep. A/c	18,000	31-12-99	By P & L a/c	18,000
		18,000			18,000
31-12-00	To Prov. For Dep. A/c	16,800	31-12-00	By P & L a/c	16,800
		16,800			16,800
31-3-01	To Prov. For Dep. A/c	135			
31-12-01	To Prov. For Dep. A/c	16,138	31-12-01	By P & L a/c	16,273
		16,273			16,273

Workings:

	Rs.
Original cost of asset sold as on 1-1-99	5,000
Less: Depreciation @ 15% for 1999 on 5,000	750
Balance as on 1-1-2000	4,250

Less: Depreciation @ 15% for 2000 on 4,250	638
Balance as on 1-1-2001	3,612
Less: Depreciation @ 15% for 3 months	135
(on 3,612)	3,477
Less: Sold as Scrap	500
Loss transferred to P&L a/c	2,977

Asset Disposal Account

When a part of the asset is disposed off, it is better to open an Asset Disposal Account. In that case, if the asset account is maintained at Written down value, the book value of the discarded portion of the asset should be debited to Asset Disposal account and credited to concerned Asset Account. But if the asset account is maintained at original cost, the following two entries will be passed:

(1) Asset Disposal a/c To Asset a/c	Dr.	with the original cost of discarded portion of the asset
(2) Provision for Depreciation a/c To Asset Disposal a/c	Dr.	with the depreciation provision applicable to the discarded portion of the asset

Whether the Asset Account is maintained at written down value or at original cost, the amount realized from the sale of discarded portion of the asset should be credited to Asset disposal Account and then the balance of this account, being profit or loss on this transaction, is transferred to P & L a/c. If however, some portion of the discarded asset could not be sold up to the close of the accounting year, then the estimated realizable value of such unsold asset should be carried down as balance in the Disposal Account.

Illustration 4

The cost of Machinery in use with a firm on 1-1-2000 was Rs.50,000 against which the depreciation provision stood at Rs.19,190 on that date; the firm provided depreciation at 10% per annum on straight line method. The firm started its business on 1-1-1996. On 30-9-2000 two machines costing Rs.3,000 and Rs.2,400 respectively, both purchased on 1-7-1997 had to be discarded because of damage and had to be replaced by new machines costing Rs.4,000 and Rs.3,000 respectively. One of the discarded machines is sold for Rs.1,600; against the other it was expected that Rs.600 would be realized. Show the Machinery Account, Provision for Depreciation Account and Machinery Disposal Account for the year 2000.

Solution

Machinery Account

Date	Particulars	Amount Rs.	Date	Particulars	Amount Rs.
1-1-00	To Balance B/d	50,000	30-9-00	By Machine Disposal a/c	5,400
30-9-00	To Bank a/c	7,000	31-12-00	By Balance C/d	51,600

		57,000			57,000
1-1-01	To Balance B/d	51,600			

Provision for Depreciation Account

Date	Particulars	Amount Rs.	Date	Particulars	Amount Rs.
30-9-00	To Machine Disposal a/c	1,350	1-1-00	By Balance B/d	19,190
31-12-00	To Balance C/d	22,475	31-12-00	By Depreciation a/c (On machinery in use)	4,635
		23,825			23,825
			1-1-01	By Balance B/d	22,475

Machinery Disposal Account

Date	Particulars	Amount Rs.	Date	Particulars	Amount Rs.
30-9-00	To Machinery a/c	5,400	30-9-00	By Prov. For Dep. A/c	1,350
				By Depreciation a/c (On two machines for 9 months)	405
				By Bank a/c	1,600
				By P & L a/c	1,445
			31-12-00	(Balancing figure) By Balance C/d	600
		5,400			5,400
1-1-01	To Balance B/d	600			

Working Notes:

1. Depreciation provided on two discarded machines (Rs.3 000 + 2 400)

For 1997 (for 6 months)	Rs. 270
For 1998	540

For 1999	540	
Total depreciation till 1-1-2000	1350	
Depreciation for 9 months to 30-9-2000	405	

2. Depreciation on Machinery in use:

Cost of Machinery on 1-1-2000	Rs.50,000
Less: Cost of discarded machines	5,400
	44,600
Depreciation for one year on Rs.44,600	4,460
Depreciation for 3 months on Rs.7,000	175
Total depreciation on machinery in use	4,635

Change of Method: Consistency principle of accountancy requires that the accounting policies practiced should be same for all years and there should be no change from one to another. Hence, the same method is adopted throughout the period. But sometimes change of depreciation method becomes inevitable. Such a change may be introduced from the year of change or with retrospective effect. In the former case, one has to find out the changed depreciation base at the beginning of the year and then depreciation for the year is calculated by the changed method on this changed base. But in the later case, wherein change is to be effected with some back date, the value of asset is calculated by the new method on the date of change. It will become the basis of computation of depreciation for periods after the date of change. Further more, in order to adjust depreciation for past periods due to change of method, depreciation should be calculated for the past period of asset by using both the existing method and changed method and the difference is adjusted in the current year's asset account by giving debit or credit to profit and loss account.

Illustration 5

On 1st January 2001, ABC ltd. had Rs.97,200 to the debit of Machinery Account. It depreciated its machinery on diminishing balance method at 10% per annum. During the year 2001, part of the machinery purchased on 1st January 1999 for Rs.8,000 was sold for Rs.4,500 on 1st July 2001, and new machinery at a cost of Rs.15,000 was purchased and installed on the same date incurring Rs.800 as installation charges.

The company wanted to change its method of depreciation from diminishing balance method to straight-line method with effect from 1st January 1999, and adjusts the difference before 31st December 2001. The rate of depreciation remains the same as before. Show the Machinery Account and ascertain the amount chargeable to Profit and Loss Account as depreciation or obsolescence loss in the year 2001.

Solution

Machinery Account

Date	Particulars	Amount Rs.	Date	Particulars	Amount Rs.
2001 January 1	To Balance B/d	97,200	2001 July 1	By Bank (Sale)	4,500
July 1	To Bank (Purchase)	15,800		By Depreciation a/c (On machine sold)	324
				By P&L a/c (loss)	1,656
			Dec. 31	By Depreciation a/c (Depreciation for the year)	11,990
				By P&L a/c (Additional depreciation due to change in method)	1,120
				By Balance C/d	93,410
		1,13,000			1,13,000

Working Notes:

1. Calculation of Loss on Sale of Machinery:

	Rs.
Cost on 1st January 1999	8,000
Less Depreciation for 1999	800
WDV on 1st January 2000	7,200
Less Depreciation for 2000	720
WDV on 1st January 2001	6,480
Less Depreciation for 6 months	324
Book Value on 1st July 2001	6,156
Less Amount realized from sale	4,500
Loss on Sale	1,656

2. Calculation of Depreciation for the current year:

	Rs.
Original Cost of Machinery on 1-1-1999 Rs.97,200 × 100/90 × 100/90 =	1,20,000
Original Cost of Machinery on 1st January 1999 in use Rs. 1,20,000 − 8,000 (sold)	1,12,000
Depreciation on Machinery in use at 10%	11,200
Depreciation on Machinery purchased for 6 months on Rs.15,800	790
Depreciation for the year 2001	11,990

3. Calculation of additional depreciation due to Change of Method:

	Rs.
Depreciation for 1999 and 2000 according to Straight-line method at 10% on Rs.1,12,000	22,400
Depreciation for 1999 and 2000 as per diminishing balance Method at 10%:	

For 1999 on 1,12,000 = 11,200	
For 2000 on 1,00,800 = 10,080	21,280
Additional depreciation charged to P & L a/c	1,120

Sum of the Year's Digits Method

Similar to Diminishing Balance Method, Sum of the Digits Method is also a device for obtaining decreasing depreciation charge. This method uses a constant depreciation base like Straight-line Method. But it applies a constantly reducing rate to the base, which results in decreasing depreciation charge year-by-year. The rate of depreciation in the method is a fraction having the sum of the digits representing the useful life of the asset as its denominator and the individual year digits in descending order each year as its numerator. For example, for an asset having 4 years of useful life, the denominator would be the sum of the digits from 1 to 4 i.e., 1 + 2 + 3 + 4 = 10 and the numerator would be 4 for the first year, 3 for the second year, 2 for the third year and 1 for the fourth year. The merits and demerits of this method are more or less same as the diminishing balance method. However, the computation is a little bit complicated under this method.

Illustration 6

A ltd. purchased a plant on 1-1-2000 for Rs.1,80,000. The useful life was estimated at 10 years, with a salvage value of Rs.15,000. no removable costs are anticipated.

(a) Compute the depreciation charge for each of the years 2000, 2001, and 2002 using (i) Straight-line method and (ii) Sum of the years digits method.

(b) Assuming that the income of A ltd. is taxed at a rate of 50%, how much tax savings will be provided by the use of Sum of the Years' digits method rather than the straight-line method in each of the years 2000, 2001, and 2002.

Solution

Sum of the years' digits for 10 years $= (N \times N + 1)/2$, When $N = 10$, Sum $= (10 + 10 + 1)/2 = 55$

(a) Calculation of Depreciation charge

Year	Depreciation Base (Cost − Salvage)	Straight line	Method	Sum of the	Digits method
	Rs.	Rate	Dep. Charge	Rate	Dep. Charge
2000	1,65,000	1/10 or 10%	16,500	10/55	30,000
2001	1,65,000	1/10 or 10%	16,500	9/55	27,000
2002	1,65,000	1/10 or 10%	16,500	8/55	24,000

(b) Calculation of Tax Savings under the Sum of the Digits Method

Year	Depreciation	Charge under	Difference	Tax Savings
	Straight-line Method (Rs.)	Sum of the Digits Method (Rs.)	Rs.	At 50% Rs.

2000	16,500	30,000	13,500	6,750
2001	16,500	27,000	10,500	5,250
2002	16,500	24,000	7,500	3,750

Annuity Method

Normally various methods of depreciation do not take into account the interest lost on capital invested in the asset. The Annuity Method removes this deficiency. Under this method, the amount spent on the purchase of an asset is considered as an investment, which is assumed to earn interest at certain rate. The interest at this fixed rate on the opening balance of asset is debited to asset account each year and then the cost of asset together with interest thereon is written off equally over the life of the asset. The amount of annual depreciation charge under this method can be ascertained from the Annuity Table. This table indicates the amount of depreciation to be written off every year on an asset valued at Re.1 over a period at certain interest rate. An extract of an Annuity Table is given below:

Periodic payment required to amortize Re.1 and interest

Years	3%	4%	5%	6%
1	1.030000	1.040000	1.050000	1.060000
2	0.522611	0.530196	0.537805	0.545437
3	0.353530	0.360349	0.367209	0.374110
4	0.269027	0.275490	0.282012	0.288591
5	0.218355	0.224627	0.230975	0.237396
6	0.184598	0.190762	0.197017	0.203363
7	0.160506	0.166610	0.172820	0.179135
8	0.142456	0.148528	0.154722	0.161036
9	0.128434	0.134493	0.140690	0.147022
10	0.117231	0.123291	0.129505	0.135868
11	0.108077	0.114140	0.120389	0.126793
12	0.100462	0.106552	0.112825	0.119277
13	0.094030	0.100144	0.106456	0.112960
14	0.088526	0.094669	0.101024	0.107585
15	0.083767	0.089941	0.096342	0.102963

Merits and Demerits: This method treats the purchase of an asset as an investment and charges interest on the same. Hence, it is considered a scientific one. However, it has many limitations. Firstly, this method is a complicated one, as it requires a lot of calculations. In case of additions and extensions the calculations are to be revised each time thus complicating its application and operation. Secondly, the amount of depreciation charged is more since it includes interest cost also. The amount remains constant though the interest charges decreases year after year.

Suitability: This method can be used advantageously for long leases involving considerable capital outlay. It is also suitable for assets requiring frequent additions and replacements.

Accounting Entries

1. When an asset is acquired:
   Asset Account Dr.
   To Bank Account
2. When interest is charged to asset:
   Asset Account Dr.
   To Interest account
3. When depreciation is provided:
   Depreciation Account Dr.
   To Asset Account

Interest account can either be transferred to P & L Account or be deducted from depreciation in the P&L Account.

Illustration 7

A firm purchases a 5-year lease for Rs.30,000. It decided to write off depreciation on the annuity method, presuming the rate of interest to be 5% per annum. If annuity of Re.1 for 5 years at 5% is 0.230975, show the Lease Account for full period.

Solution

The amount of depreciation to be charged every year

$$= 0.230975 \times 30000 = \text{Rs.}6{,}929.25$$

Lease Account

Date	Particulars	Amount Rs.	Date	Particulars	Amount Rs.
1st year	To Bank	30,000.00	1st year	By Depreciation	6,929.25
	To Interest	1,500.00		By Balance C/d	24,570.75
		31,500.00			31,500.00
2nd year	To Balance B/d	24,570.75	2nd year	By Depreciation	6,929.25
	To Interest	1,228.54		By Balance C/d	18,870.04
		25,799.29			25,799.29
3rd year	To Balance B/d	18,870.04	3rd year	By Depreciation	6,929.25
	To Interest	943.50		By Balance C/d	12,884.29
		19,813.54			19,813.54
4th year	To Balance B/d	12,884.29	4th year	By Depreciation	6,929.25

	To Interest	644.21		By Balance C/d	6,599.25
		13,528.50			13,528.50
5th year	To Balance B/d	6,599.25	5th year	By Depreciation	6,929.25
	To Interest	330.00			
		6,929.25			6,929.25

Depreciation Fund Method or Sinking Fund Method

The salient feature of this method is that it provides funds for replacement of the asset. It is suitable for plant and machinery and many other wasting assets, which require replacement. It is designed in such a way that, apart from providing depreciation on the asset, it provides the required funds for the replacement of the asset when the asset is to be replaced by new asset. Under this method, one Depreciation Fund Account is opened and the amount of depreciation is credited to that account. The asset account year after year stands at original cost. At the end of the year, the amount of depreciation is debited and Depreciation Fund Account is credited and the corresponding amount is invested outside in some readily realizable securities in order to provide funds for replacement. Interest received on investments is also invested likewise. The amount that is annually set aside as depreciation is such that this with compound interest will be a sum equal to the cost of asset less residual value, if any. This amount is determined with the help of Sinking Fund Table. The extract of which is given below.

Periodic deposit, which will amount to Re.1 =

Sinking Fund Table

Period	3%	4%	5%	6%
1	1.000000	1.000000	1.000000	1.000000
2	0.492611	0.490196	0.487805	0.485437
3	0.323530	0.320349	0.317209	0.314110
4	0.239027	0.235490	0.232012	0.228591
5	0.188355	0.184627	0.180975	0.177396
6	0.154598	0.150762	0.147017	0.143363
7	0.130506	0.126610	0.122820	0.119135
8	0.112456	0.108528	0.104722	0.101036
9	0.098434	0.094493	0.090690	0.087022
10	0.087231	0.083291	0.079505	0.075868
11	0.078077	0.074149	0.070389	0.066793
12	0.070462	0.066552	0.062825	0.059277
13	0.064030	0.060144	0.056456	0.052960
14	0.058526	0.054669	0.051024	0.047585
15	0.053767	0.049941	0.046342	0.042963

Accounting Entries

First Year

1. For purchase of asset at the time of purchase

Asset A/c	Dr.
To Bank A/c	

2. For providing depreciation at the end of the year

Depreciation Account	Dr.
To Depreciation Fund A/c	

3. For investing the amount of depreciation at the end of the year or beginning of next year

Depreciation Fund Investment A/c	Dr.
To Bank A/c	

4. For transferring depreciation to P & L A/c at the end of the year

P & L A/c	Dr.
To Depreciation A/c	

Second and Subsequent Years

1. For receiving interest on investments at the end of the year

Bank A/c	Dr.
To Interest on Investment A/c	

2. For transferring interest to Fund account

Interest on Investment A/c	Dr.
To Depreciation Fund A/c	

Note: The above two entries may be combined as follows

Bank A/c	Dr.
To Depreciation Fund A/c	

3. For providing the annual installment of depreciation

Depreciation A/c	Dr.
To Depreciation fund A/c	

4. For investing the amount of depreciation and interest received

Depreciation Fund Investments A/c	Dr.
To Bank A/c	

5. For transferring depreciation to P&L Account

P & L A/c	Dr.
To Depreciation A/c	

In the Last Year

These entries will be repeated for the subsequent years. In the last year, the interest on investments received and annual depreciation will be transferred to depreciation fund Account as usual. But the amount is not invested because the investments will be sold at the end of the year and used for the replacement of the old asset. Hence, in the last year entries nos. (1),

(2), and (3) will be repeated but entry no. (4) will not be passed. Thereafter, the following additional entries are passed:

1. For sale of investments

    Bank A/c ... Dr.

    To Depreciation Fund Investment A/c

2. For transfer of profit or loss on sale of investments

    In case of profit

    Depreciation Fund Investment A/c ... Dr.

    To Depreciation Fund A/c

    In case of loss, reverse entry will be passed.

3. For sale of discarded asset

    Bank A/c ... Dr.

    To Old Asset A/c

4. For transferring Depreciation Fund Account to Old Asset Account

    Depreciation Fund A/c ... Dr.

    To Old Asset A/c

5. For transferring the balance of Old Asset Account to P & L Account

    Profit and Loss A/c ... Dr.

    To Old Asset A/c

    Or

    Old Asset A/c ... Dr.

    To Profit and Loss a/c

6. For purchase of New Asset

    New Asset A/c ... Dr.

    To Bank A/c

Illustration 8

A company purchased a lease for four years on 1-1-1997 for Rs.2,01,500. it is decided to provide for the replacement of the lease at the end of four years by setting up a Depreciation Fund. It is expected that investments will fetch interest at 4%. Sinking Fund tables show that to provide the requisite sum at 4% at the end of four years, an investment of Rs.47,450.02 is required. Investments are made to the nearest rupee. On 31-12-2000, the investments are sold for Rs.1,48,500. On 1-10-2001, the same lease is renewed for a further period of four years by payment of Rs.2,20,000.

Show the journal entries and give necessary ledger accounts to record the above.

Solution

Journal Entries

Date	Particulars		Amount Rs.	Amount Rs.
1-1-1997	Lease Account	Dr.	2,01,500	
	To Bank account			2,01,500
	(Being purchase of lease)			
31-12-1997	Depreciation Account	Dr.	47,450.02	
	To Depreciation Fund account			47,450.02
	(Being the annual depreciation charge)			
	Depreciation Fund Investment Account	Dr.	47,450.00	
	To Bank Account			47,450.00
	(Being investment made from depreciation Fund)			
	Profit and Loss Account	Dr.	47,450.02	
	To Depreciation Account			47.450.02
	(Being depreciation charged to P & L A/c)			
31-12-1998	Bank Account	Dr.	1,890.80	
	To Depreciation Fund Account			1,890.80
	(Being interest on investment received credited to Depreciation Fund a/c)			
	Depreciation Account	Dr.	47,450.02	
	To Depreciation Fund Account			47,450.02
	(Being the annual depreciation charge)			
	Depreciation Fund Investment Account	Dr.	49,350.00	
	To Bank Account			49,350.00
	(Being investment made from Dep. Fund)			
	Profit and Loss Account	Dr.	47,450.02	
	To Depreciation Account			47,450.02
	(Being depreciation transferred to P & L A/c)			
31-12-1999	Bank Account	Dr.	3,870.20	
	To Depreciation Fund Account			3,870.20
	(Being Interest received credited to DF A/c)			
	Depreciation Account	Dr.	47,450.02	
	To Depreciation Fund Account			47,450.02
	(Being the annual depreciation charge)			

Date	Particulars		Amount Rs.	Amount Rs.
	Depreciation Fund Investment Account	Dr.	51,320.00	
	To Bank Account			51,320.00
	(Being Investments made from Fund)			
	Profit and Loss Account	Dr.	47,450.02	
	To Depreciation Account			47,450.02
	(Being depreciation charged to P & L A/c)			
31-12-2000	Bank Account	Dr.	5,920.48	
	To Depreciation Fund Account			5,920.48
	(Being interest received credited to Fund)			
	Depreciation Account	Dr.	47,450.02	
	To Depreciation Fund Account			47,450.02
	(Being the annual depreciation charge)			
	Bank Account	Dr.	1,48,500.00	
	To Depreciation Fund Investments A/c			1,48,500.00
	(Being investments realized)			
	Depreciation Fund Investments Account	Dr.	380.00	
	To Depreciation Fund Account			380.00
	(Being profit on sale transferred)			
	Depreciation Fund Account	Dr.	2,01,870.56	
	To Lease Account			2,01,870.56
	(Being balance in Fund A/c transferred)			
	Lease Account	Dr.	370.56	
	To Profit and Loss Account			370.56
	(Being the balance in Lease A/c transferred)			
1-1-2001	New Lease Account	Dr.	2,20,000.00	
	To Bank Account			2,20,000.00
	(Being the purchase of New Lease)			

Ledger Accounts

Lease Account

Date	Particulars	Amount Rs.	Date	Particulars	Amount Rs.
1-1-97	To Bank	2,01,500	31-12-97	By Balance C/d	2,01,500

1-1-98	To Balance B/d	2,01,500	31-12-98	By Balance C/d	2,01,500
1-1-99	To Balance B/d	2,01,500	31-12-99	By Balance C/d	2,01,500
1-1-00	To Balance B/d	2,01,500	31-12-00	By Depreciation Fund A/c	2,01,870.56
31-12-00	To P & L A/c	370.56			
		2,01,870.56			2,01,870.56

Depreciation Fund Account

Date	Particulars	Amount Rs.	Date	Particulars	Amount Rs.
31-12-97	To Balance C/d	47,450.02	31-12-97	By Depreciation A/c	47,450.02
		47,450.02			47,450.02
31-12-98	To Balance C/d	96,790.84	1-1-98	By Balance B/d	47,450.02
			31-12-98	By Bank (Interest)	1,890.80
				By Depreciation A/c	47,450.02
		96,790.84			96,790.84
31-12-99	To Balance C/d	1,48,120.06	1-1-99	By Balance B/d	96,790.84
			31-12-99	By Bank (Interest)	3,870.20
				By Depreciation	47,450.02
		1,48,120.06			148,120.06
31-12-00	To Lease Account	2,01,870.56	1-1-00	By Balance B/d	1,48120.06
			31-12-00	By Bank (Interest)	5,920.48
				By Depreciation	47,450.02
				By D.F Investment A/c (Profit)	380.00
		2,01,870.56			2,01,870.56

Depreciation Fund Investments Account

Date	Particulars	Amount Rs.	Date	Particulars	Amount Rs.
31-12-97	To Bank	47,450	31-12-97	By Balance C/d	47,450
		47,450			47,450
1-1-98	To Balance B/d	47,450	31-12-98	By Balance C/d	96,800
31-12-98	To Bank	49,350			
		96,800			96,800
1-1-99	To Balance B/d	96,800	31-12-99	By Balance C/d	1,48,120
31-12-99	To Bank	51,320			
		1,48,120			1,48,120
1-1-00	To Balance B/d	1,48,120	31-12-00	By Bank	1,48,500
31-12-00	To D.Fund Account	380			
		1,48,500			1,48,500

Depreciation Account

Date	Particulars	Amount Rs.	Date	Particulars	Amount Rs.
31-12-97	To D. Fund A/c	47,450.02	31-12-97	By P&L A/c	47,450.02
31-12-98	To D. Fund A/c	47,450.02	31-12-98	By P&L A/c	47,450.02
31-12-99	To D. Fund A/c	47,450.02	31-12-99	By P&L A/c	47,450.02
31-12-00	To D. Fund A/c	47,450.02	31-12-00	By P&L A/c	47,450.02

New Lease account

Date	Particulars	Amount Rs.	Date	Particulars	Amount Rs.
1-1-01	To Bank A/c	2,20,000			

Illustration 9

In the books of Lakshmi Mills Ltd. the Machinery account stood at Rs.25,00,000. Depreciation Fund amounted to Rs.20,00,000, which was represented by outside investments. The investments are sold for Rs.20,30,000. The machinery is to be replaced by a new machine at a cost of Rs.32,00,000 to be purchased from Tools India Ltd. A part of the old machine was given to Tools India Ltd. for Rs.1,80,000 and the balance was sold for Rs.80,000. The net amount due to Tools India Ltd. was paid by cheque.

Write up necessary accounts in the books of Lakshmi Mills Ltd.

Solution

Machinery Account

Particulars	Amount (Rs.)	Particulars	Amount (Rs.)
To Balance B/d	25,00,000	By Machine Disposal A/c	25,00,000
To Tools India Ltd.	32,00,000		

Depreciation Fund Account

Particulars	Amount Rs.	Particulars	Amount Rs.
To Machine Disposal A/c	20,30,000	By Balance B/d	20,00,000
		By D.F Investments A/c	30,000
	20,30,000		20,30,000

Depreciation Fund Investments Account

Particulars	Amount Rs.	Particulars	Amount Rs.
To Balance B/d	20,00,000	By Bank A/c	20,30,000
To Depreciation Fund A/c	30,000		
	20,30,000		20,30,000

Machine Disposal account

Particulars	Amount Rs.	Particulars	Amount Rs.
To Machinery a/c	25,00,000	By Dep. Fund A/c	20,30,000
		By Tools India Ltd. (exchange)	1,80,000
		By Bank A/c	80,000
		By P & L A/c	2,10,000
	25,00,000		25,00,000

Tools India Ltd. Account

Particulars	Amount Rs.	Particulars	Amount Rs.
To Machine Disposal A/c	1,80,000	By Machinery A/c	32,00,000
To Bank A/c	30,20,000		
	32,00,000		32,00,000

Insurance Policy Method

This method is similar to Depreciation Fund Method. Under this method an Insurance policy is taken from an insurance company. The policy is taken for such a period that it matures when the asset is to be replaced. The procedure is same as the Depreciation Fund Method except that the amount of investment will be in the form premium paid on the insurance policy. The premium is paid at the beginning of each year and debited to Depreciation Fund Policy Account. The annual depreciation will be equal to the amount of annual premium and is debited to Profit and Loss Account and credited to Depreciation Fund Account at the end of the accounting year. Generally interest is not recorded yearly in this method. When the policy matures, the agreed sum is received from the Insurance Company and is used to purchase the new asset. The balance in the Depreciation Fund Policy Account is transferred to Depreciation Fund Account and thereafter; transfer to Old Asset Account closes the balance of Fund Account. Balance of Old Asset account is written off to Profit and Loss Account.

Merits: This method has all the advantages of Depreciation Fund Method. In addition, it has the advantage of protecting the firm against loss on realization of investment. Besides, there is no botheration of selecting proper securities for investment and of realizing and reinvesting the interest on investments.

Accounting Entries

The following two entries in the first and subsequent years:

1. For payment of premium at the beginning of the year
   Depreciation fund Policy Account Dr.
   To Bank Account
2. For providing depreciation at the end of the year
   Profit and Loss Account Dr.
   To Depreciation Fund Account

In the last year in addition to the above two entries, the following entries:

3. For receiving the amount on maturity of Policy:
   Bank Account Dr.
   To Depreciation Fund Policy A/c
4. For transferring profit on policy to Fund Account
   Depreciation Fund Policy Account Dr.
   To Depreciation Fund account
5. For closing down the Depreciation Fund Account:
   Depreciation Fund Account Dr.
   To Old Asset account
6. For realizing the salvage value of Old Asset:
   Bank Account Dr.

To Old Asset Account

7. For transferring the balance of Old Asset Account (in case of loss):
   Profit and Loss Account Dr.
   To Old Asset Account
   In case of profit on sale, reverse entry will be passed.
8. For purchase of new asset:
   New Asset Account Dr.
   To Bank Account

Interest

Profit in the policy account refers to total interest on premium paid. Since interest is earned on premium at the end of each year the policy account on maturity shows accumulated interest as profit. If the interest is considered at the end of each year, the following entry is passed:

Depreciation Fund Policy Account Dr.

To Depreciation Fund Account

(Being interest credited to fund account)

Illustration 10

A company purchased a lease for three years for Rs.1,20,000 on 1st January 1998 and decided to provide for its replacement by means of an insurance policy for Rs.1,20,000. The annual premium is Rs.38,000. On 1st January 2001, the lease is renewed for a further period of three years for Rs.1,20,000. Journalize the above transactions.

Solution

Date	Particulars		Rs.	Rs.
1-1-1998	Lease Account	Dr.	1,20,000	
	To Bank Account			1,20,000
	(Being purchase of Lease)			
	Depreciation Fund Policy Account	Dr.	38,000	
	To Bank account			38,000
	(Being the annual premium paid)			
31-12-1998	Profit and Loss Account	Dr.	38,000	
	To Depreciation Fund Account			38,000
	(Being annual depreciation charge)			
1-1-1999	Depreciation Fund Policy Account	Dr.	38,000	
	To Bank Account			38,000
	(Being annual premium paid)			
31-12-1999	Profit and Loss Account	Dr.	38,000	
	To Depreciation Fund Account			38,000
1-1-2000	Depreciation Fund Policy Account	Dr.	38,000	
	To Bank Account			38,000

	(Being annual premium paid)		
31-12-2000	Profit and Loss Account Dr.	38,000	
	To Depreciation Fund Account		38,000
	(Being annual depreciation charge)		
	Bank Account Dr.	1,20,000	
	To Depreciation Fund Policy A/c		1,20,000
	(Being policy money realized on maturity)		
	Depreciation Fund Policy Account Dr.	6,000	
	To Depreciation Fund Account		6,000
	(Being profit transferred to fund)		
	Depreciation Fund Account Dr.	1,20,000	
	To Old Lease Account		1,20,000
	(Being closure of Fund Account)		
1-1-2001	New Lease Account Dr.	1,20,000	
	To Bank Account		1,20,000
	(Being new lease detained)		

Illustration 11

A & Co. purchased a machine for Rs.5,000, which is expected to last for three years only. They are informed that its scrap value will be Rs.625. They decide to purchase an endowment policy for three years for a sum of Rs.4,375. the annual premium is Rs.1,375 and the rate of interest works out at 3% compound interest. The scrap of machine actually realized for Rs.550. Show the Depreciation Fund account, Depreciation Policy account and Machine Account for all three years. Calculations may be made nearest to rupee only.

Solution

Depreciation Fund Account

Year	Particulars	Amount Rs.	Year	Particulars	Amount Rs.
I (end)	To Balance C/d	1,415	I (end)	By P & L A/c	1,375
				By Dep. Policy A/c (Interest)	40
		1,415			1,415
II (end)	To Balance C/d	2,875	II (Start)	By Balance B/d	1,415
			II (end)	By P & L A/c	1,375
				By Dep. Policy A/c (Interest)	85
		2,875			2,875
III (end)	To Machine A/c	4,375	III (Start)	By Balance B/d	2,875
			III (end)	By P & L A/c	1,375

				By Dep. Policy A/c (Interest)	125
		4,375			4,375

Depreciation Fund Policy Account

Year	Particulars	Amount Rs.	Year	Particulars	Amount Rs.
I (Start)	To Bank Account	1,375	I (End)	By Balance C/d	1,415
I (End)	To Depreciation Fund A/c	40			
		1,415			1,415
II (Start)	To Balance B/d	1,415	II End)	By Balance C/d	2,875
II (End)	To Bank account	1,375			
	To Dep. Fund A/c (Interest)	85			
		2,875			2,875
III (Start)	To Balance B/d	2,875	III (End)	By Bank account	4,375
III (End)	To Bank account	1,375			
	To Dep. Fund A/c (Interest)	125			
		4,375			4,375

Machine Account

Year	Particulars	Amount Rs.	Year	Particulars	Amount Rs.
I (Start)	To Bank account	5,000	I (End)	By Balance C/d	5,000
II (Start)	To Balance B/d	5,000	II (End)	By Balance C/d	5,000
III (Start)	To Balance B/d	5,000	III (End)	By Dep. Fund A/c	4,375
				By Bank account (Sale of scrap)	550
				By P & L A/c (Loss on sale)	75
		5,000			5,000

Activity Method

Under this method the usage of asset is gıven more importance than the passage or efflux ion of time. The depreciable cost of the asset is spread over in various accounting periods in accordance with the extent of use or activity of the asset. If an asset is not used in any one year, then no depreciation will be charged for that year assuming that there is no decline in its service life. This method is suitable in case the use of asset vary from period to period. The activity may take place in different forms and accordingly the methods may be called in different names as follows: (a) Production Unit Method, (b) Machine Hour Method, (c) Service Unit (hours) Method, and (d) Depletion Method.

Production Unit Method: This method is adopted when the economic life of the asset is fixed in terms of units of production. Under this method the depreciation rate is determined by dividing the net cost of the asset by the estimated number of units that are likely to be produced during its useful economic life. The annual depreciation charge is calculated by applying this rate to the number of units produced during an accounting period.

Depreciation Rate per unit

$$= \frac{\text{Cost–Salvage Value}}{\text{Total units produced during the asset's lifetime}}$$

Depreciation for the year

= Number of units produced during the year

× Depreciation Rate per unit

Machine Hour Method: This method is useful when the life of machine is fixed in terms of hours. Hourly rate is determined by dividing the total cost of the machine by total number of hours to be used in its lifetime. The annual depreciation charge is calculated by applying this rate to the number of hours used in an accounting period.

Machine Hour Rate

$$= \frac{\text{Cost–Salvage Value}}{\text{Total estimated machine hours in Machine's lifetime}}$$

Depreciation for the year = Number of Hours used in the year

× Machine Hour Rate

Illustration 12

A Ltd. purchased a machine at a cost of Rs.99,600. It was expected to last for 6 years with a scrap value of Rs.3,000. Find out the depreciation for each of the six years under (a) Production Units Method and (b) Machine Hour Rate Method.

Total estimated life in units of production is 77,280 units and total estimated life in machine hours is 19,320 hours.

Additional data are:

Year:	1	2	3	4	5	6	Total
Units produced:	11,600	13,000	12,400	12,000	13,640	14,640	77,280
Working hours:	2,900	3,250	3,100	3,000	3,410	3,660	19,320

Solution

(a) Production method:

Depreciation Rate per unit

$$= \frac{\text{Cost–Salvage value}}{\text{Estimated life in units}} = \frac{99{,}600 - 3{,}000}{77{,}280} = \text{Rs.}1.25$$

Computation of Annual Depreciation

Year (1)	Units produced (2)	Rate per unit Rs. (3)	Annual Depreciation Rs. (Col 2 × Col 3)
1	11,600	1.25	14,500
2	13,000	1.25	16,250
3	12,400	1.25	15,500
4	12,000	1.25	15,000
5	13,640	1.25	17,050

(b) Machine Hours or Working Hours Method:

Depreciation Rate per hour

$$= \frac{\text{Cost–Scrap Value}}{\text{Estimated life in hours}} = \frac{99{,}600 - 3{,}000}{19320} = \text{Rs.}5.00$$

Computation Annual Depreciation

Year (1)	Working Hours (2)	Rate per Hour Rs. (3)	Depreciation Rs. (2) × (3)
1	2,900	5.00	14,500
2	3,250	5.00	16,250
3	3,100	5.00	15,550
4	3,000	5.00	15,000
5	3,410	5.00	17,050

(c) Service Unit (Hours) Method:

This method is mostly useful for depreciating Transport vehicles. It takes into consideration the 'running time' of the asset for calculating the depreciation. Under this method the depreciation is calculated by dividing the net total cost of the asset by its estimated service life. For example, in the case of car the service life is the effective running mileage or in the case of Aircraft it is the effective flying hours. Then this depreciation is calculated by applying the depreciation rate to the mileage covered or number of hours operated during the accounting period.

For example, the cost of a car is Rs.1,50,000 and its estimated life is 50,000 running hours. The car runs for 1,200 miles in the first year. Compute depreciation for the first year.

Solution

Depreciation Rate per mile

$$= \frac{\text{Total Cost–Scrap Value}}{\text{Estimated life in running miles}} = \frac{1,50,000}{50,000} = \text{Rs.3.00 per mile}$$

Depreciation for the first year

= 1,200 mile × Rs.3.00 per mile = Rs.3,600

(d) Depletion Method

This method is used for allocating the cost of natural resources e.g., mines, quarries, oil and gas deposits, etc. The life of the asset is estimated by geographical survey methods in terms of total units of resource deposits. The depletion (exhaustion) rate per unit is computed by diving the net total cost of natural resource by the estimated available number of units. Then the depreciation for a year is calculated by applying the depletion rate per unit to the total quantity extracted during that year.

Illustration 13

The MM Ltd. leased a manganese ore mine on 30th June 1998 for a sum of Rs. 5,00,000. it is estimated that the total quantity of ore in the mine is 50 000 tons of which 80% may be raised. The annual output is as follows:

Year:	1998	1999	2000
Output (Tons)	2,500	10,000	8,000

Using the depletion method of depreciation, show the Mine Account for the above three years.

Solution

Depreciation Charge per ton

= Total cost/Effective production

= 5,00,000/80% of 50,000 = Rs.12.50 per ton

Mine Account

Year	Particulars	Amount Rs.	Year	Particulars	Amount Rs.
30-6-98	To Bank	5,00,000	31-12-98	By Depreciation (2,500 × 12.5)	31,250
				By Balance C/d	4,68,750
		5,00,000			5,00,000
1-1-89	To Balance B/d	4,68,750	31-12-99	By Depreciation (10,000 × 12.50)	1,25,000

				By Balance C/d	3,43,750
		4,68,750			4,68,750
1-1-00	To Balance B/d	3,43,750	31-12-00	By Depreciation (8,000 × 12.50)	1,00,000
				By Balance C/d	2,43,750
		3,43,750			3,43,750
1-1-01	To Balance B/d	2,43,750			

Revaluation Method

This method is used to depreciate small and diverse items of asset such as bottles, corks, packages, patterns, moulds, trademarks, loose tools, livestock, and etc. under this method, the asset in question is submitted to experts for valuation at the end of every year and the fall in value of the asset is treated as depreciation. This is debited to Profit and Loss account and credited to Asset account. However, if there is an appreciation in value of the asset, it should either be ignored or credited to a Reserve Account. Purchase of asset during the year is recorded in a normal manner.

Example

On 1-1-2001, A Ltd. had a stock of bottles valued at Rs.5,000. On 1st July 2001, the company purchased additional bottles for Rs.3,000. On 31st December 2001 the entire stock of bottles was revalued at Rs.6,500. Show the bottles account for the year 2001.

Solution

Bottles Account

Year	Particulars	Amount Rs.	Year	Particulars	Amount Rs.
1-1-01	To Balance B/d	5,000	31-12-01	By Depreciation (8000 – 6500)	1,500
1-7-01	To Bank A/c	3,000		By Balance C/d	6,500
		8,000			8,000
1-1-02	To Balance B/d	6,500			

Repairs and Renewal Method

Under this method the total repairs and renewal costs are estimated for the whole life of the asset and added to its capital cost (less scrap value) to get an aggregate figure. This figure is then divided by its estimated life, the resultant is the amount that has to be charged to Profit and Loss account each year in respect of repairs, renewals and depreciation. The corresponding credit is given to Provision for Depreciation and Repairs Account. Each year actual amount of repairs and renewals are debited to this Provision Account and not to Profit and Loss Account. The balance of Provision Account shows the net amount set aside for depreciation and by the time the asset becomes useless, the balance should be equal to the difference of its cost and scrap value. At the end of the working life of the asset, transfer to Asset account closes the provision account. If the estimation of total repairs and renewals goes wrong and asset account shows any balance, then it will be transferred to Profit and Loss Account.

Illustration 14

On 1st January 1997, Vignesh Ltd. purchased a machine for Rs.50,000, which was expected to last for 4 years; its salvage value was estimated at Rs.7,500. The repairs and maintenance charges were estimated to be Rs.17,500 during the lifetime of the asset. Actual expenses for repairs and maintenance during 1997, 1998, 1999 and 2000 had been Rs.1,000, Rs.4,000, Rs.5,500, and Rs.6,500 respectively. At the end of fourth year, the machine is sold at Rs.7,500. Prepare necessary accounts using an equitable method of charging depreciation and maintenance expenses.

Solution

Provision for Depreciation and Repairs Account

Date	Particulars	Amount Rs.	Date	Particulars	Amount Rs.
31-12-97	To Repairs & Maintenance A/c	1,000	31-12-97	By P&L A/c	15,000
	To Balance C/d	14,000			
		15,000			15,000
31-12-98	To Repairs & Maintenance A/c	4,000	1-1-98	By Balance B/d	14,000
	To Balance C/d	25,000	31-12-98	By P & L A/c	15,000
		29,000			29,000
31-12-99	To Repairs & Maintenance A/c	5,500	1-1-99	By Balance B/d	25,000
	To Balance C/d	34,500	31-12-99	By P&L A/c	15,000
		40,000			40,000
31-12-00	To Repairs & Maintenance A/c	6,500	1-1-00	By Balance B/d	34,500
	To Balance C/d	43,000	31-12-00	By P&L A/c	15,000
		49,500			49,500

Machine Account

Date	Particulars	Amount Rs.	Date	Particulars	Amount Rs.
1-1-97	To Bank A/c	50,000	31-12-97	By Balance C/d	50,000

1-1-98	To Balance B/d	50,000	31-12-98	By Balance C/d	50,000
1-1-99	To Balance B/d	50,000	31-12-99	By Balance C/d	50,000
1-1-00	To Balance B/d	50,000	31-12-00	By Bank A/c	7,500
31-12-00	To P & L A/c	500	31-12-00	By Provision for Dep.& repairs A/c	43,000
		50,500			50,500

Working Note:

	Rs.
Cost of the Machine	50,000
Less: Scrap value	7,500
	42,500
Add: Estimated Repairs & Maintenance Expenses	17,500
Composite Cost	60,000

Annual cost of depreciation and repairs

$$= \frac{60,000}{4} = \text{Rs.}15,000$$

Provision and Reserve

Accounting convention of Conservatism requires every business to provide for risk and uncertainties. Hence, it is necessary for every business to make provisions and reserves. Though the terms Provision and Reserve are used interchangeably, they have different connotations and purposes.

Provision: Provision is normally a charge against protits. Its purpose is mainly to meet some unknown loss or to provide for some accrued expenses. For example, the provision for bad debts, provision for discounts and provision for contingencies, etc. are created mainly to meet some future losses. In the case of outstanding liability when the exact amount involved is not known then a provision is created for such items like provision for taxation and provision for repairs, etc. A provision is created even if the business incurs a loss.

Reserve: Reserve is an appropriation of profit. It may be created for general or special purpose. It is also created for the purpose of meeting some future losses or some future liability. For example a company may create reserve to redeem a future liability say, debentures, called Denture Redemption Fund. Funds appropriated for redemption purpose may be invested in some outside securities, say, Government securities, which may be called Redemption Reserve Fund Investments. Generally creation of reserves strengthens the financial position of business.

Reserves can be broadly classified into Capital Reserve and Revenue Reserve. Capital Reserve is created out of capital profits such as share premium, profits prior to incorporation, and profits on reissue of forfeited shares, etc. Capital reserve is not ordinarily available for distribution as dividends. Revenue Reserve is created out of revenue profits, such as Reserve fund, Dividend Equalization Reserve, Profit and loss account balance, and Investment Fluctuation Fund, etc. Any reserve, which is generally available for dividends, may be called as revenue reserve.

Distinctions between Provision and Reserve

	Provision		Reserve
1.	Provision is a charge against profits.	1.	Reserve is an appropriation of profits.
2.	It is created to meet some unknown loss or some known expenditure.	2.	It may be created for any general or specific purpose.
3.	It is provided to meet some legal or necessary requirements.	3.	It is created to meet some known liability or strengthen the financial position of the business.
4.	The proprietor has no claim on provision as it is for a specific loss or expenditure.	4.	The proprietor has claim on reserve as it is created out of distributable profits.
5.	Provision may be shown on the liability side or as a deduction from the concerned asset in the asset side.	5.	Reserve is always shown on the liability side under 'Reserves and Surplus'.

Illustration 15

A firm writes of 95% of the cost of machinery acquired over a period of 10 years by straight-line method, leaving 5% as estimated scrap value. Full depreciation is written off even if the machinery is in use only for a part of a year. On 31st December 2001 the original cost of the machinery in use was as follows:

Purchased in 1991 or earlier	Rs.1,20,000
Purchased in 1993	40,000
Purchased in 1997	30,000

On 30th June 2002 a machine, which had cost Rs.10,000 in 1990 was disposed off for Rs.900 and on 30th November 2002; a machine acquired in 1997 at a cost of Rs.15,000 was sold for Rs.5,000. On the same date new machinery was acquired for Rs.45,000.

Prepare the Machinery Account for 2002, the accounts being closed on 31st December each year.

Solution

Machinery Account

Date	Particulars	Amount Rs.	Date	Particulars	Amount Rs.
1st Jan. 2002	To Balance B/d		June 30 2002	By Bank A/c (sold)	900
	Of 1991 6,000		Nov. 30	By Bank A/c (sold)	5,000
	Of 1993 5,800		Nov. 30	By Depreciation (sold)	1,425
	Of 1997 15,750	27,550	Nov. 30	By P & L A/c (loss)	1,450
30th June	To P & L A/c	400	Dec. 31	By Depreciation	9,500
30th Nov.	To Bank A/c	45,000	Dec. 31	By Balance C/d	54,675
		72,950			72,950

1st Jan. 2003	To Balance B/d	54,675			

Working Notes:

Opening balance of Machinery:

Balance of machinery purchased in 1991 (10 years over)

=5% of 1,20,000 = Rs.6,000

Balance of machinery purchased in 1993 (9 years over)

= 2,000 + 1/10 of 38,000 = 5,800

Balance of machinery purchased in 1997 (5 years over)

= 750 + 15,000 = 15,750

Depreciation for 2002

Purchased in 1993 = 95% of 40,000 × 1/10 = 3,800

Purchased in 1997 = 95% of 15,000 × 1/10 = 1,425

Purchased in 2002 = 95% of 45,000 × 1/10 = 4,275

Total = 9,500

Loss on sale of machine: Cost = 15,000

Less Depreciation 95% of Rs.15,000 × 5/10 = 7,125

Book Value = 7,875

Less Depreciation for 2002 (full) = 1,425

Book Value as on 30th November 2002 = 6,450

Less Sold for = 5,000

Loss on sale = 1,450

Illustration 16

On 1.1.2000 the cost of the machinery in use with a firm was Rs.5,00,000 against which the depreciation provision stood at Rs.1,91,900 on that date; the firm provided depreciation at 10% per annum on straight line method. The firm started its business on 1.1.1996. On 30.9.2000, two machines costing Rs.30,000 and Rs.24,000 respectively, both purchased on 1.7.1997 were discarded because of damage and replaced by two new machines costing Rs.40,000 and Rs.30,000 respectively. One of the discarded machines was sold for Rs.16,000; against the other it was expected that Rs.6,000 would be realized.

Show the Machinery Account, Provision for Depreciation account and Machinery Disposal account.

Solution

Machinery Account

Date	Particulars	Amount Rs.	Date	Particulars	Amount Rs.
1-1-00	To Balance B/d	5,00,000	30-9-00	By Machinery Disposal A/c	54,000

30-9-00	To Bank A/c	70,000	31-12-00	By Balance C/d	5,16,000
		5,70,000			5,70,000
1-1-01	To Balance B/d	5,16,000			

Provision for Depreciation Account

Date	Particulars	Amount Rs.	Date	Particulars	Amount Rs.
2000 Sept.30	To Machinery Disposal A/c	13,500	2000 Jan.1	By Balance B/d	1,91,900
Dec.31	To Balance C/d	2,24,750	Dec.31	By Depreciation A/c (On machinery in use)	46,350
		2,38,250			2,38,250
			2001 Jan.1	By Balance B/d	2,24,750

Machinery Disposal Account

Date	Particulars	Amount Rs.	Date	Particulars	Amount Rs.
2000 Sept.30	To Machinery A/c	54,000	2000 Sept.30	By Provision for Depreciation A/c	13,500
				By Depreciation A/c (on 2 machines for 9 months)	4,050
				By Bank A/c	16,000
				By P & L A/c (Balancing figure)	14,450
			Dec.31	By Balance C/d	6,000
		54,000			54,000
2001 Jan.1	To Balance B/d	6,000			

Working Notes:

1. Depreciation provided on two discarded machines:

	Rs.
For 1997 (for six months)	2,700
For 1998	5,400
For 1999	5,400

	Total Depreciation till 1st Jan. 2000	13,500
	Depreciation for 9 months to Sept. 2000	4,050
2.	Depreciation on machinery in use:	
	Cost of Machinery on 1-1-2000	5,00,000
	Less: Cost of discarded machines	54,000
	Cost of Machinery in use	4,46,000
	Depreciation on Rs.4,46,000 for one year	44,600
	Depreciation for 3 months on Rs.70,000	1,750
	Total Depreciation	46,350

Illustration 17

On 1-1-1996 Machinery was purchased for Rs.80,000. On 1-7-1997 additions were made to the amount of Rs.40,000. On 31-3-1998 machinery purchased on 1-1- 1997 costing Rs.12,000 was sold for Rs.11,000 and on 30-6-1998 machinery purchased on 1-1-1996 costing Rs.32,000 was sold for Rs.26,700. On 1-10-1998 additions were made to the amount of Rs.20,000. Depreciation was provided at 10% p.a. on diminishing balance method. Show the Machinery Account for three years 1996 to 1998 (year ended on December 31). (ICWA Inter)

Solution

Machinery Account

Date	Particulars	Amount Rs.	Date	Particulars	Amount Rs.
1-1-96	To Bank A/c	80,000	31-12-96	By Depreciation	8,000
				By Balance C/d	72,000
		80,000			80,000
1-1-97	To Balance B/d	72,000	31-12-97	By Depreciation	11,200
1-1-97	To Bank A/c	40,000	31-12-97	By Balance C/d	1,00,800
		1,12,000			1,12,000
1-1-98	To Balance B/d	1,00,800	31-3-98	By Depreciation	270
	To P & L A/c (Profit transferred)	470		By Bank A/c	11,000
	To P & L A/c (Profit transferred)	2,076	30-6-98	By Depreciation	1,296
1-10-98	To Bank A/c	20,000		By Bank A/c	26,700
			31-12-98	By Depreciation	6,908
				By Balance C/d	77,172

		1,23,346			1,23,346
1-1-99	To Balance B/d	77,172			

Working Notes:

		Rs.
1.	Machinery purchased on 1-1-1997	12,000
	Less: Depreciation for 1997 @10%	1,200
	Balance as on 1-1-98	10,800
	Depreciation for 3 months in 1998	270
	Book Value as on 31-3-98	10,530
	Profit (Balancing figure)	470
	Sold for	11,000
2.	Cost of the Machinery on 1-1-1996	32,000
	Less: Depreciation for 1996	3,200
	Balance on 1-1-1997	28,800
	Less: Depreciation for 1997	2,880
	Balance on 1-1-1998	25,920
	Less: Depreciation for 6 months in 98	1,296
	Book Value on 30-6-98	24,624
	Profit (balancing figure)	2,076
	Sold for	26,700
3.	Depreciation for the remaining machines:	
	Book value of machines on 1-1-98	1,00,800
	Book value of machines on 1-1-98 sold in 1998	36,720
		64,080
	Depreciation for 1998 on 64,080 @10%	6,408
	Depreciation for new machine for 3 months on Rs.20,000	500
	Total	6,908

Illustration 18

A lease is purchased on 1-1-1997 for 5 years at a cost of Rs.50 000. It is proposed to depreciate the lease by annuity method charging 5% interest. Show the Lease Account for 5 years.

Solution

A reference to the Annuity Table shows that to depreciate Re.i by annuity method over 5 years charging interest at 5%, one must write off a sum of Re.0.230975. To write off Rs.50,000, a sum of Rs.11,548.75 (0.230975 × 50,000) should be written off every year.

Lease Account

Date	Particulars	Amount Rs.	Date	Particulars	Amount Rs.
1-1-97	To Bank A/c	50,000.00	31-12-97	By Depreciation	11,548.75
31-12-97	To Interest (5% Rs.50,000)	2,500.00		By Balance C/d	40,951.25
		52,500.00			52,500.00
1-1-98	To Balance B/d	40,951.25	31-12-98	By Depreciation	11,548.75
31-12-98	To Interest (5% on 40,951.25)	2,047.56		By Balance C/d	31,450.06
		42,998.81			42,998.81
1-1-99	To Balance B/d	31,450.06	31-12-99	By Depreciation	11,458.75
31-12-99	To Interest (5% on 31,450.06)	1,572.50		By Balance C/d	21,473.81
		33,022.56			33,026.56
1-1-00	To Balance B/d	21,473.81	31-12-00	By Depreciation	11,548.75
31-12-00	To Interest (5% on 21,473.81)	1,073.69		By Balance C/d	10,998.75
		22,547.50			22,547.50
1-1-01	To Balance B/d	10,998.75	31-12-01	By Depreciation	11,548.75
31-12-01	To Interest (5% on 10,998.75)	550.00			
		11,548.75			11,548.75

Note: At the end of each year, the depreciation will be debited to P & L Account and interest will be credited to P & L Account.

Illustration 19

A collieries ltd. acquired a lease of a mine for 20 years on 1st January 1995 on a lump sum payment of Rs.5 lakhs. It was estimated that the coal deposit of the mine was 20 lakhs tons, 75% of which would be raised within the time period. The company decided to write off the lease account under straight-line method of depreciation. The lease account was shown accordingly for the first five years. On 31st October 2000, the Board of Directors decided to depreciate the lease on depletion method with retrospective effect from 1st January 1995. The annual raisings were:

Year:	1995	1996	1997	1998	1999	2000
No. of Tons:	20,000	30,000	1,00,000	2,00,000	2,00,000	2,00,000

You are required to show the Lease Account from January 1, 1995 to December 31, 2000 showing your calculations clearly.

Solution

Lease Account

Date	Particulars	Amount Rs.	Date	Particulars	Amount Rs.
1-1-95	To Bank A/c	5,00,000	31-12-95	By Depreciation	25,000
				By Balance C/d	4,75,000
		5,00,000			5,00,000
1-1-96	To Balance B/d	4,75,000	31-12-96	By Depreciation	25,000
				By Balance C/d	4,50,000
		4,75,000			4,75,000
1-1-97	To Balance B/d	4,50,000	31-12-97	By Depreciation	25,000
				By Balance C/d	4,25,000
		4,50,000			4,50,000
1-1-98	To Balance B/d	4,25,000	31-12-98	By Depreciation	25,000
				By Balance C/d	4,00,000
		4,25,000			4,25,000
1-1-99	To Balance B/d	4,00,000	31-12-99	By Depreciation	25,000
				By Balance C/d	3,75,000
		4,00,000			4,00,000
1-1-00	To Balance B/d	3,75,000	31-12-00	By P&L A/c (Addl. Depreciation)	58,333
				By Depreciation	66,667
				By Balance C/d	2,50,000
		3,75,000			3,75,000
1-1-01	To Balance B/d	2,50,000			

Working notes:

1. Calculation of Additional Depreciation:

Depreciation Charge on Depletion Method $= 5{,}00{,}000/(20{,}00{,}000 \times 75\%) =$ Re.0.33 per ton. Production for the years 1995 to 1999 = 5,50,000 tons

Depreciation for these years $= 5{,}50{,}000 \times 0.33 =$ Rs.1,83,333

Depreciation as per Straight-line method = 1,25,000

Additional depreciation due to change 58,333

2. Depreciation for 2000 $= 2{,}00{,}000 \times 0.33 =$ 66,667

Additional depreciation due to change in method is to be charged to P & L A/c in the year 2000.

REVIEW QUESTIONS

1. Explain the concept of Depreciation.
2. Discuss the causes of depreciation.
3. What is the need for depreciation?
4. Discuss the factors that are considered for calculating depreciation.
5. State clearly the various methods of depreciation.
6. Discuss in detail the Straight-line method of depreciation.
7. Explain the terms 'Provision' and 'Reserve'.
8. Distinguish between Provision and Reserve.
9. Distinguish between Annuity Method and Sinking Fund Method.
10. Write short notes on:
    (a) Diminishing Balance Method, (b) Repairs and Renewals Method, (c) Depletion Method, and (d) Revaluation Method.

REVIEW PROBLEMS

11. A ltd. purchased a machine on 1st January 1996 for Rs.60,000. On 1st July 1996 the company purchased another machine for Rs.50,000. On 1st July 1997, the company sold the machine purchased on 1st January 1996 for Rs.40,000. It was decided that the machines were depreciated at 10% p.a. on Diminishing Balance Method. Assuming the accounts are closed on 31st December every year, show the Machine Account for the years 1996 and 1997.

    (**Answer:** Balance on 31-12-97 Rs.42,750;
    Loss on sale of machine Rs.11,300;
    Depreciation on machine sold for 6 months Rs.2,700;
    Depreciation for the remaining machine Rs.4,750)

12. Machinery Account in the books of a concern was shown as follows:

Balance as at 1st January 1987	Rs.7,450
Purchase of machinery on 1st July 1987	2,200
Sale of machinery on 1st October 1987	1,000

The original cost of the machinery sold was Rs.3,000 on 1st July 1984. Machinery is being depreciated at 10% p.a. on diminishing balance of the asset. Show the Machinery Account in the books of the concern for the year 1987. The books are closed on 31st December each year.

(B.Com., M.K.U., April 1988)

(**Answer:** Balance on 31-12-1987 Rs.6,718;
Loss on sale Rs.1,135)

13. On 1st January 1993, A Ltd. purchased 6 machines for Rs.15,000 each. The company closes books on 31st December each year. Depreciation at the rate of 10% on initial cost has been charged to Profit and Loss Account and credited to a separate Depreciation Provision Account. On 1st January 1994 one machine was sold for Rs.12,500 and on 1st January 1995 a second machine was sold for Rs.12,500. An improved model, which cost Rs.28,000, was purchased on 1st July 1994. The same rate of depreciation was applied for the new machine as well. You are required to show: (a) Machinery Account; (b) Machinery Disposal Account; and (c) Depreciation Provision Account.

(**Answer:** Balance on 31-12-1995 Machinery Account Rs.88,000; Depreciation Provision Account Rs.22,200;
1-1-1994 loss on sale of machine Rs.1,000; and
on 1-1-1995 profit on sale of machine Rs.500)

14. A company purchased a lease for three years for Rs.30,000 on 1st January 1990 and decided to provide for its replacement by means of an insurance policy for Rs.30,000. The annual premium was Rs.9,500. On 1st January 1993 the lease is renewed for a further period of 3 years for Rs.30,000. Show the necessary ledger accounts.

(Madras University, B.Com., Adapted)

(**Answer:** Profit on realization of Policy Rs.1,500)

15. A concern maintains Sinking Fund for replacement of Machine. The balances in the relevant accounts as on 1-1-1994 are:

Sinking Fund	Rs.80,000
5% Sinking Fund Investments	80,000
(Nominal Value Rs.1,00,000)	
Machine Cost	1,00,000

Annual contribution to Sinking Fund is Rs.15,000. The investments are sold on 1-1-1995 and a new machine is purchased for Rs.1,20,000. Show necessary ledger accounts in the books of the concern.

(**Answer:** Loss on sale of Investments-Rs.10,000;
Balance in old machine to be transferred Rs.5,000)

16. Deluxe Cinema Ltd. acquired a lease of a cinema theatre for 5 years by paying Rs.4,00,000. Depreciation is to be charged by Annuity Method, interest being 5%. If annuity of Re.1 for 5 years at 5% is 0.230975, show the Lease Account for the full period making your calculations to the nearest rupee.

17. A company, whose accounting year is the calendar year, purchased on 1st April 1997 machinery costing Rs.30,000. It further purchased machinery on 1st October 1997 costing Rs.20,000 and on 1st July 1998 costing Rs.10,000. On 1st January 1999, one-third of the machinery, which was installed on 1st April 1997, became obsolete and was sold for

Rs.3,000.

Show how the Machinery Account would appear in the books of the company. The depreciation is to be charged at 10% p.a. on written down value method. (C.A. Inter, Adapted)

(**Answer:** Machinery Account balance-Rs.39,330)

18. On 1-1-1990 a second-hand machine was purchased for Rs.4,00,000; overhauling and installation expenses for the machine amounted to Rs.1,00,000. Another machine was purchased for Rs.2,00,000 on 1-7-1990. On 1-7-1992 the machine installed on 1-1-1990 was sold for Rs.2,50,000. Dismantling charges for the machine sold on 1-7-1992 were Rs.10,000. On the same date another machine was purchased for Rs.8,00,000 and was commissioned on 30-9-1992. The company had adopted calendar year as its financial year. Under the existing practice, the company provides depreciation at 10% p.a. on original cost. In 1993 it has been decided that depreciation will be charged on diminishing balance at 15% p.a. The change is not to be made with retrospective effect. Show Machinery Account for 1990 to 1994. Also show Machine disposal account. (ICWA. Inter adapted)

(**Answer:** Balance in Machinery A/c on 31-12-1994 Rs.6,71,925; Loss on sale of asset in 1992 Rs.1,35,000)

19. A firm purchased machinery on 1st July 2000 for Rs.45,000 and incurred Rs.5,000 as erection charges. The firm closes books on 31st December each year. Assuming that depreciation is written off at the rate of 10% p.a., show the Machinery Account up to 31st December 2002, under (a) Straight-line method and (b) Written down value method.

(**Answer:** Balance on Machinery A/c (a) Rs.37,500, (b) Rs.38,475)

20. A firm desires to debit its Profit and Loss Account with a uniform figure every year in respect of repairs and renewals. It expects that considering the life of the asset in question, Rs.9,000 will be the average amount to be spent every year. Actual repairs are Rs.900 in the first year, Rs.2,100 in the second year and Rs.3,300 in the third year. Show the necessary Ledger Account.

(**Answer:** Provision for Repairs and Renewals Account-Balance 3rd year end Rs.20,700.)

21. The Indian Minerals Ltd. leased on 30-6-1993 an ore mine for a sum of Rs.5,00,000. It is estimated that the total quantity of ore in the mine is 1,00,000 tons. The annual output is as follows:

Year:	1993	1994	1995	1996
Tons:	5,000	20,000	16,000	21,000

Using the Depletion Method of depreciation, show the Mine Account for the above four years.

(**Answer:** Balance in Mine A/c-Rs.1,90,000)

22. The cost of the Machinery in use with B & Co. on 1-1-2002 was Rs.60,000 against which the depreciation provision stood at Rs.20,000 on that date. The firm provided depreciation at 10% on diminishing value. On 1-7-2002, a machine costing Rs.8,000 purchased on 1-1-2000 was sold for Rs.6,000 and on the same date another machine was purchased for Rs.10,000.

Show the following accounts in the books of B & Co. for the year 2002:

(a) Machinery Account

(b) Provision for Depreciation Account

(c) Machinery Disposal Account

(**Answer:** Balances as on 31-12-2002 (a) Rs.62,000;
(b) Rs.22,332; (c) Loss Rs.156)

Illustration 23

A company purchased four years' lease on 1-1-1997 for Rs.2,01,500. It is decided to provide for replacement of the lease at the end four years by setting up a Depreciation Fund. It is expected that investments will fetch interest at 4%. Sinking Fund tables show that to provide the requisite sum at 4% at the end of four years, an investment of Rs.45,450.02 is required. Investments are made to the nearest rupee.

On 31st December 2000, the investments are sold for Rs.1,48,500. on 1st January 2001, the same lease is renewed for a further period of four years by payment of Rs.2,20,000.

Show journal entries and give the necessary ledger accounts to record the above.

(**Answer:** Refer Illustration 8)

7

FINANCIAL STATEMENTS ANALYSIS

Learning Objectives

After going through this chapter, you should be able to

— Explain the meaning, objectives, and nature of financial statements,

— Know the users of financial statements,

— Discuss the importance and limitations of financial statements,

— Describe different types of financial analysis,

— Understand the preparation of Comparative financial statements, Common-size statements, and Trend percentages.

7.1 Meaning of Financial Statements

Financial statements generally refer to four basic statements-the Income Statements (i.e., Trading and P & L a/c], thė Balance Sheet, the Statement of Retained Earnings and the Sources and Uses of Funds Statements. The Financial Statements, taken together, give the accounting picture of the firm's operations and financial position. The package of Financial Statements include such schedules as those relating to fixed assets, long term investments long term debts, Accrued liabilities, Cost of goods manufactured, Selling expenses and Administrative and General expenses. These schedules mainly supplement the information contained in the Financial Statements and are considered essential for the purpose of analysis. In addition, explanatory footnotes are also given as an integral part of Financial Statements when the information given in the financial statements and schedules are inadequate. For example, explanatory notes regarding methods of inventory valuation and of depreciation, description of Contingent liabilities etc., are given as footnotes.

7.2 Objectives of Financial Statements

Different types of people need varied information and fortunately such information may be classified as relating to profitability, liquidity, and solvency. The main objective of financial statements is to satisfy the needs of such people. The Accounting Principles Board of America states the objectives as follows:

(1) To provide reliable financial information about economic resources and obligations of a business and other needed information about changes in such resources and obligations

(2) To provide reliable information about changes in net resources [resources minus obligations] arising out of business activities and financial information that assists in estimating the earning potentials of business.

(3) To disclose, to the extent possible, other information related to the financial statements that is relevant to the needs of the users of these statements

7.3 Describe the Nature of Financial Statements

According to the American Institute of certified Public Accountants: "Financial statement reflect a combination of recorded facts accounting convention, and personal judgement, and the judgement and conventions applied affect them materially." This statement makes clear that the accounting information as depicted by the financial statements are influenced by three factors viz., recorded facts, accounting conventions, and personal judgement

Recorded Facts: This refers to the data recorded in the account books is not usually depicted in the financial statements even if it consists of highly material facts. For example, the cost of fixed assets on the date of their acquisition is shown rather than their market or replacement price, for such price is not recorded in the account book.

Accounting Conventions: Accounting conventions are certain fundamental accounting principles and include those custom and traditions, which guide the accountants while preparing the financial statements. For example, the convention of conservatism makes the accountant feel the need for making a provision for expected loss, but at the same time, to ignore the expected profits.

7.4 Who are the Users of Financial Statements?

Different classes of people are interested in the financial statements analysis with a view to assessing the economic and financial position of any business or industry in terms of profitability, liquidity or solvency.

Such persons and bodies include:

1. Shareholders: Divorce between ownership and management and broad-based ownership of capital due to dispersal of share holdings have made shareholders take more interest in the financial statements with a view to ascertaining the profitability and financial strength of the company.

2. Debenture holders: The debenture holders are interested in the short-term as well as the long-term solvency position of the company. They have to get their interest payments periodically and at the end the return of the principal amount

3. Creditors: Potential suppliers of goods and materials and others doing business with the company are interested in the liquidity position of the company.

4. Financial Institutions and Commercial Banks: These financial institutions are interested in the solvency - short-term as well as long-term - and profitability position of the company.

5. Prospective Investors are interested in the future prospects and financial strength of the company.

6. Employees and Trade Unions are interested in the profitability position of the company.

7. Important Customers who want to make long-standing contract with the company are interested in its financial strength.

8. Tax Authorities are interested in the profits earned by the company.

9. Government Departments dealing with the industry in which the company is engaged are interested in the financial information relating to the company.

10. Economists and Investments Analysts are interested in the financial and other information of the company.

11. Members of Parliament - the Public Accounts Committee and Estimates Committee - are interested in the financial information of the government companies

12. SEBI and Stock Exchanges are interested in the prospects and performance of listed companies with a view to protecting the interests of investors.

13. Managers are interested in knowing through the financial statements the present position and future prospects of the company. This is mainly to review the company's progress and position and take decisions for the future.

7.5 Essential features of Financial Statements

1. The Financial Statements should be relevant for the purpose for which they are prepared. Unnecessary and confusing disclosures should be avoided and all those that are relevant and material should be reported to the public.

2. They should convey full and accurate information about the performance, position, progress and prospects of an enterprise. It is also important that those who prepare and present the financial statements should not allow their personal prejudices to distort the facts.

3. They should be easily comparable with previous statements or with those of similar concerns or industry. Comparability increases the utility of financial statements.

4. They should be prepared in a classified form so that a better and meaningful analysis could be made.

5. The financial statements should be prepared and presented at the right time. Undue delay in their preparation would reduce the significance and utility of these statements.

6. The financial statements must have general acceptability and understanding. This can be achieved only by applying certain "generally accepted accounting principles" in their preparation.

7. The financial statements should not be affected by inconsistencies arising out of personal judgement and procedural choices exercised by the accountant.

8. Financial Statements should comply with the legal requirements if any, as regards form, contents, and disclosures and methods. In India, companies are required to present their financial statements according to the Companies Act, 1956.

7.6 Importance of Financial Statements

The importance of financial statements lies in their utility to satisfy the varied interest of different categories of parties such as management, creditors, public, etc.

1. Importance to Management: Increase in size and complexities of factors affecting the business operations necessitate a scientific and analytical approach in the management of modern business enterprises. The management team requires up to date, accurate and systematic financial information for the purposes. Financial statements help the management to understand the position, progress and prospects of business vis-a-vis the industry. By providing the management with the causes of business results, they enable them to formulate appropriate policies and courses of action for the future. The management communicates only through these financial statements, their performance to various parties and justify their activities and thereby their existence. A comparative analysis of financial statements reveals the trend in the progress and position of enterprise and enables the management to make suitable changes in the policies to avert unfavourable situations.

2. Importance to the Shareholders: Management is separated from ownership in the case of companies. Shareholders cannot, directly, take part in the day-to-day activities of business. However, the results of these activities should be reported to shareholders at the annual general body meeting in the form of financial statements. These statements enable the shareholders to know about the efficiency and effectiveness of the management and also the earning capacity and financial strength of the company. By analyzing the financial statements, the prospective shareholders could ascertain the profit earning capacity, present position and future prospects of the company and decide about making their investments in this company. Published financial statements are the main source of information for the prospective investors.

3. Importance to Lenders/Creditors: The financial statements serve as a useful guide for the present and future suppliers and probable lenders of a company. It is through a critical examination of the financial statements that these groups can come to know about the liquidity, profitability and long-term solvency position of a company. This would help them to decide about their future course of action.

4. Importance to Labour: Workers are entitled to bonus depending upon the size of profit as disclosed by audited profit and loss account. Thus, P & L a/c becomes greatly important to the workers. In wages negotiations also, the size of profits and profitability achieved are greatly relevant.

5. Importance to the Public: Business is a social entity. Various groups of society, though directly not connected with business, are interested in knowing the position, progress and prospects of a business enterprise. They are financial analysts. lawyers, trade associations, trade unions, financial press, research scholars and teachers, etc. It is only through these published financial statements these people can analyze, judge and comment upon business enterprise.

6. Importance to National economy: The rise and growth of corporate sector, to a great extent, influence the economic progress of a country. Unscrupulous and fraudulent corporate managements shatter the confidence of the general public in joint stock companies, which is essential for economic progress and retard the economic growth of the country. Financial Statements come to the rescue of general public by providing information by which they can examine and assess the real worth of the company and avoid being cheated by unscrupulous persons. The law endeavours to raise the level of business morality by compelling the companies to prepare financial statements in a clear and systematic form and disclose material information. This has increased the confidence of the public in companies. Financial statements are also essential for the various regulatory bodies such as tax authorities, Registrar of companies, etc. They can judge whether the regulations are being strictly followed and also whether the regulations are producing the desired effect or not, by evaluating the financial statements.

7.7 Limitations of Financial Statements

Most of the limitations are mainly due to the cumulative effect of recorded facts, accounting conventions and personal judgement on financial statements. Unless they are prepared specially they fail to reflect the current economic picture of business. As such, financial statements have a number of limitations. The important limitations are as follows:

1. **Information is incomplete and inexact.** The financial statements are interim reports usually prepared for an accounting period. Hence, the financial information as revealed by them is neither complete nor exact. The true financial position or ultimate gain or loss, can be known only when the business is closed down.

2. **Qualitative information is ignored.** Financial statements depict only those items of quantitative information that are expressed in monetary terms. But, a number of qualitative factors, such as the reputation and prestige of the management with the public, cordial industrial relations and efficiency of workers, customer satisfaction, competitive strength, etc., which cannot be expressed in monetary terms , are not depicted by the financial statements. However, these factors are essential for understanding the real financial condition and the operating results of the business.

3. **Financial statements mainly show historical information.** As the financial statements are compiled on the basis of historical costs, they fail to take into account such factors as the decrease in money value or increase in the price level changes. Since these statements deal with past data only, they are of little value in decision-making.

4. **Financial statements are based on accounting concepts and conventions.** Accounting concepts and conventions used the preparation of financial statements make them unrealistic. For example the income statement prepared on the basis of the convention of conservatism fails to disclose the true income, for it includes probable losses and ignores probable income. Similarly the value of fixed asset is shown in the balance sheet on the 'going concern concept'. This means that the value of the asset rarely represents the amount of cash, which would be realized on liquidation.

5. **Personal judgement influence financial statements.** Many items in the financial statements are left to the personal judgment of the accountant. For example, the method of inventory valuation, the method of depreciation the treatment of deferred revenue expenditure, etc., depend on the personal judgment of the accountant. If it goes wrong, the real picture may be distorted. However, such indiscreet personal judgement are controlled to a certain extent by the convention of conservatism.

7.8 Explain the Method of Presentation of Financial Statements

Presentation of financial statements should be more meaningful as well as purposeful. The language used and presentation should be simple and easy to understand even by ordinary people. In case of sole proprietary and partnership concerns, there are no prescribed forms. The conventional method of presentation is 'T' or account form or horizontal form. In the case of companies, the Companies Act 1956 has given prescribed forms for the Profit and Loss Account and Balance Sheet in Part I Schedule VI in horizontal forms only. But in recent times they are presented in vertical form i.e., in a single column form. The vertical form enables one to grasp the essential message very quickly. The modern practice is to draw up financial statements in vertical summary form and to give details as required by law in separate schedules. Each schedule is being distinctly numbered giving reference to the schedule in the main financial statements. The Government, by a special notification, has permitted companies to prepare the Balance Sheet either in horizontal form or vertical form. The vertical form of Balance Sheet as per the notification is given below.

Schedule VI - Part I B
Name of the Company ... ...
Balance Sheet as at..

	Schedule No.	Figures as at the end Of current year	Figures as at the end of previous year
I. Sources of Funds			
1. Shareholders' Funds			
[a] Capital			
[b] Reserves & Surplus			
2. Loan Funds			
[a] Secured Loans			
[b] Unsecured Loans			
Total			
II. Application of Funds			
1. Fixed Assets			
[a] Gross Block			
[b] Less: Depreciation			
[c] Net Block			
[d] Capital work in Progress			
2. Investments			
3. Current Assets and Loans and advances			
[a] Inventories			
[b] Sundry Debtors			
[c] Cash and Bank balances			
[d] Other Current assets			
[e] Loans and advances			
Less: Current Liabilities			
[a] Current liabilities			
[b] Provisions			
Net Current Assets			
[f] [a] Miscellaneous expenditure to the extent not written off			
[b] Profit and Loss A/c			
Total			

Notes:

1. Details under each of the above items shall be given in separate schedules. The schedule shall incorporate all the information given under Part I A of Schedule VI read with notes containing general instructions for preparation of Balance Sheet.

2. The Schedules referred to above, accounting policies and explanatory notes that may be attached shall form an integral part of the balance sheet.

3. The figures in the balance sheet may be rounded to the nearest "000" or "00" as may be convenient or may be expressed in terms of decimals of thousands.

4. A footnote to the balance sheet may be added to show separately contingent liabilities.

Part II of Schedule VI states the particulars and information to be given in the Profit and Loss account.

The horizontal form of Balance Sheet as required by Part I of Schedule VI to the Companies Act is given below in an abridged form.

Figures for the previous year	Liabilities	Figures for the current year	Figures for the previous year	Assets	Figures for the current year
	Share Capital			Fixed Assets	
	Authorized			Goodwill	
	Issued			Land and Buildings	
	Subscribed			Plant and machinery	
	Less calls unpaid			Furniture	
	Reserves and surplus			Vehicles, etc.	
	Capital Reserve			**Investments**	
	General Reserve			Government Bonds	
	Other Reserves			Shares, Debentures	
	P&L App. A/c			Immovable Properties	
	Secured Loans			**Current Assets**	
	Debentures			**Loans and Advances**	
	Loans from Banks			Current Assets	
	Other loans			Interest Accrued	
	Unsecured Loans			Stocks	
	Fixed Deposits			Debtors	
	Current Liabilities and Provisions			Cash & Bank balances Loans and Advances:	
	Current liabilities:			Advances	
	Sundry Creditors			Bills Receivable	
	Bills Payable			Advance payments	
	Outstanding expenses			**Miscellaneous**	
	Provisions:			**Expanses**	
				Preliminary expenses	

Income Statement

The format of the Income Statement or Profit and Loss Account is same as that of sole proprietary or partnership concerns and usually prepared in "T" shape. However, in the case of Companies the Manufacturing, Trading and Profit and Loss Account is prepared in horizontal form except with three modifications.

(a) The heading given is only "Profit and Loss Account" in the place of Manufacturing, Trading and Profit and Loss account.

(b) The Net Profit is shown after making provision for taxation in the Profit and Loss account and taken to Profit and Loss appropriation Account.

(c) Figures relating to previous period are also given.

Profit and Loss Appropriation Account

The companies prepare a separate P&L Appropriation A/c in order to explain how the profits earned during the period has been distributed. This statement is also called as the Statement of Retained Earnings. The format is as follows:

Profit and Loss Appropriation Account for the year ending.

Particulars	Amount	Particulars	Amount
To Transfer to Reserve Fund To Sinking Fund		By Balance b/d [balance of profit from last year]	
To Proposed dividends: Preference shares Equity shares		By Net Profit [transferred from current year's P& L A/c]	
To Blance c/d			

7.9 What does 'Analysis and Interpretation of Financial Statements Mean'?

Analysis and Interpretation of financial statements refers to the process of determining the significant operating and financial characteristics from the accounting data with a view to getting an insight into the activities of an enterprise. Myers defines "Financial Statement analysis is largely a study of relationship among the various financial factors in a business as disclosed by a single set of statements, and a study of the trend of these factors as shown in a series of statements". By establishing a strategic relationship between the items of a balance sheet and income statement and other operative data, the financial analysis [as it is simply called] explains the meaning and significance of such items.

The terms *'analysis'* and *'interpretation'* are complimentary to each other, though sometimes they are used distinctively. While *analysis* is used to mean the simplification of data by methodical classification of data given in the financial statements, the term *interpretation* means explaining the meaning and significance of the data so simplified. However, analysis is useless without interpretation, and interpretation becomes difficult without analysis. Hence, as the objective of analysis is to study the relationship among the various items of financial statements by interpretation, many to cover both analysis and interpretation together use it

7.10 Main Objective of Financial Analysis

Different parties are interested in the financial statements for different purposes and look at them from different angles. For example, the debenture-holders analyze the statements in order to ascertain the ability of companies to make regular periodical interest payments and final payment of principal amount on maturity. The prospective shareholders would like to know whether the business is profitable and is progressing on sound lines. Above all, the management is interested in the operational efficiency as well as the financial position of the business. Hence, the main objective of financial analysis is to make a detailed study about the cause and effect of the profitability and financial condition of the firm.

7.11 Different types of Financial Analysis

Financial analysis may be classified into different categories depending upon (i) the materials used, and (ii) the method of operation followed in the analysis. Based on the material used or people interested in the analysis, it may be classified as External vs. Internal Analysis.

External Analysis: People outside the firm do external analysis. In the matter of financial statement analysis, investors, credit agencies, government agencies, shareholders, etc., are outsiders/external parties to the firm. An external analyst usually has only the published information to rely upon. His position has been improved in recent times due to increased governmental regulations requiring business concerns to provide detailed information to the public through audited accounts.

Internal Analysis: Analysis for management purposes is the internal type of analysis. It is done by the Company's finance and accounting departments and is more detailed than external analysis. Executives and employees of the organization also conduct it. Officers appointed by the governmental or court agencies under regulatory and other jurisdictional powers vested in them over the business also conduct the analysis.

Based on the methods of analysis, it may be classified as horizontal vs. vertical analysis.

Horizontal Analysis: It refers to the comparison of the trend of each item in the financial statement over a period of years, or that of companies. The figures for this type of analysis are presented horizontally over a number of columns. Such a column represents a year or a company. This type of analysis is also called as Dynamic Analysis as it is based on data from year to year, rather than on data of any one year.

Vertical Analysis: It is also called as Static Analysis. In vertical analysis the figures relating to a financial statement are presented vertically, i.e., a figure from a year's statement is compared with a base selected from the same statement. This type of analysis is mainly used to study through ratios the quantitative relationship of various items in the financial statement on a particular data, or for one accounting period. It is useful to understand the performance of several companies in the same group, or many divisions or departments in the same company. However this type of analysis is not very conducive to a proper analysis of a company's financial position, for it depends on the data for one time period. In order to make it more effective, it could be conducted both vertically as well as horizontally.

7.12 Major Tools of Financial Analysis

Various tools or techniques are used in the financial analysis. The main objective of any analytical method is simplification and presentation of data in a more comprehensive manner. However, no one type of analysis is sufficient to support overall findings, or to serve all types of users. The most important tools of financial analysis are as follows:

(a) Comparative Financial Statements,

(b) Common Size Statements,

(c) Trend Ratios or percentages,

(d) Ratio Analysis,

(e) Funds Flow Analysis,

(f) Cash Flow Analysis.

7.13 Preparation of Comparative Financial Statements

Comparative Financial Statements refer to the statements of financial position of a business, which are prepared in such a way as to provide a time perspective to the various elements embodied in the financial statements. These statements include two types of analytical statements. They are Comparative Balance Sheets and Comparative Income Statement. In these statements figures are placed side by side for two or more periods in order to facilitate comparison. They also facilitate comparison among two or more firms that belong to the same industry. Comparison may be regarding to profitability and financial soundness.

Preparation of Comparative Financial Statements

Comparative statements mainly show the following information for analytical purposes.

(a) Actual data in absolute money values, as given in the financial statements for the periods under consideration.

(b) Increases or decreases in various items in money values, and

(c) Increases or decreases in various items in terms of percentages

The following examples would illustrate the method of preparation of a Comparative Balance Sheet and a Comparative Income Statement with imaginary figures.

Comparative Balance Sheet
[as on 30th June 2001 and 2002]

[in lakhs of rupees]

Assets	30-6-2001 Rs.	30-6-2002 Rs.	Amount of increase or decrease in 2002 Rs.	Percentage of increase or decrease in 2002 %
Fixed Assets:				
Premises [less dep.]	600	570	– 30	– 5.00
Plant & machinery [less dep.]	400	500	100	25.00
Furniture [less dep.]	100	85	– 15	– 15.00
Total Fixed Assets	1,100	1,155	55	5.00
Investments	200	150	50	– 25.00
Current Assets:				
Stock	300	300	–	–
Debtors	200	150	– 50	– 25.00
Cash & Bank	70	78	8	11.43
Total Current Assets	570	528	– 42	– 7.40
Total Assets	1,870	1,833	– 37	– 2.00
Liabilities	**30-6-2001 Rs.**	**30-6-2002 Rs.**	**Amount of increase or decrease in 2002 Rs.**	**Percentage of increase or decrease in 2002 %**
Capital:				
8% Preference Capital	200	300	+ 100	+ 50.00
Equity Capital	500	500	–	–

Reserves & Surplus	200	250	+ 50	+ 25.00
Total Proprietors' Funds	900	1,050	+ 150	+ 16.67
Secured Loans:				
10% Debentures	350	200	− 150	− 43.00
Current Liabilities:				
Sundry creditors	300	350	+ 50	+ 16.67
Bills payable	200	175	− 25	− 12.50
Taxes payable	120	58	− 62	− 50.00
Total Current liabilities	620	583	− 37	− 5.97
Total Liabilities	970	783	− 187	− 19.28
Total Capital & Liabilities	1,870	1,833	− 37	− 2.00

Tentative conclusions

Total fixed assets have been added during the year 2002 by Rs.55 lakhs [i.e., about 5%] compared to 2001, for which long-term investments worth Rs.50 lakhs have been realized. The level of current assets worth Rs.42 lakhs has been reduced. Despite the increase in fixed assets, the total assets have been decreased by Rs.37 lakhs. It implies that the addition to fixed assets has been partly financed by the sale or reduction of other assets. Increase in fixed assets and decrease in current assets reflect a poor financial policy. The relationship between the total current assets and total current liabilities is not satisfactory.

Increase in the preference share capital of Rs.100 lakhs might have been due to the fresh issue of shares for the redemption of debentures. Also, the increase in reserves may represent the redemption of debentures out of profits.

Comparative Income Statement

Similar to the Comparative Balance Sheet, the Comparative Income Statement contains the same columns and supplies the same type of information. It is illustrated below.

The Comparative Income Statement explains the relationship between sales and cost of goods sold and its effect on gross profit. Increase in selling expenses and office and administration expenses relating to the increase in sale should not be proportional. This will indicate clearly the efficiency of operations by showing changes in absolute figures and also in terms of percentage of the operating profits from one period to another. The Companies Act of India insists that companies should give figures for different items for the previous year together with the current year's figures in the Profit and Loss account and Balance Sheet.

Comparative Profit and Loss Statement
[for the year ended 30th June 2001 and 2002]

[Rs. In lakhs]

Particulars	2001	2002	Amount of increase or decrease in 2002	Percentage of increase or decrease in 2002
	Rs.	Rs.	Rs.	%
Net Sales	600	800	+ 200	+ 33.33
Cost of goods sold	400	500	+ 100	+ 25.00

Gross Profit	200	300	+ 100	+ 50.00
Operating expenses:				
Office expenses	20	20	–	–
Selling expenses	20	30	+ 10	+ 50.00
Total operating expenses	40	50	+ 10	+ 25.00
Operating Profit	160	250	+ 90	+ 56.25

Inferences: while net sales have increased by 33.33%, the cost of goods sold has increased by 25%. The percentage of profits has increased by 50%. The increase in total operating expenses is 25% only, which has increased the net operating profits by 56.25%. The overall performance in 2002 is satisfactory compared to 2001.

The main limitation of Comparative Financial Statements is that they fail to show the changes that have taken place from year to year in relation to total assets, total liabilities and capital or total net sales. Common-size Analysis eliminates this limitation.

7.14 Preparation Common-size Statements

Common-size Financial Statements are those statements in which items reported in the financial statements are converted into percentages taking some common base. In the Common-size Income Statement, the net sales are assumed to be 100% and other items are expressed as a percentage of sales. Similarly in the Common-size Balance Sheet the total assets or total liabilities are assumed to be 100% and other items of assets and liabilities are expressed as a percentage of this total [i.e., 100%]. Common- size statements are also called as "Component Statements" or "100 per cent Statement" because each statement is reduced to the total of 100 and each individual item is expressed as a percentage of this total.

Example

The preparation of Common-size statement is illustrated below based on the imaginary figures used in the examples of Comparative Financial Statements.

Common-size Balance Sheet
[as on June 2001 and 2002]

Rs. In Lakhs

Assets	2001 Amount Rs.	Percentage 100%	2002 Amount Rs.	Percentage 100%
Fixed Assets:				
Premises less depreciation	600	32.09	570	31.09
Plant machinery less depreciation	400	21.39	500	27.27
Furniture less depreciation	100	5.35	85	4.64
Total Fixed Assets [A]	1,100	58.82	1,155	63.00
Investments [B]	200	10.70	150	8.19
Current Assets:				
Stock	300	16.05	300	16.37
Debtors	200	10.70	150	8.18
Bank	50	2.61	60	3.27
Cash	20	1.06	18	0.99
Total Current assets [C]	570	30.48	528	28.81

Total Assets [A + B + C]	1,870	100.00	1,833	100.00
Liabilities	2001 Amount Rs in lakhs.	Percentage 100	2002 Amount Rs. In lakhs	Percentage 100
Capital:				
8% Preference capital	200	10.70	300	16.37
Equity capital	500	26.74	500	27.27
Reserves	200	10.69	250	13.64
Proprietors' funds [1]	900	48.13	1,050	57.28
Secured Loans: [2]	350	18.71	200	10.91
10% Debentures				
Current Liabilities:				
Sundry creditors	300	16.05	350	9.09
Bills payable	200	10.70	175	9.55
Taxes payable	120	6.41	58	3.17
Total Current Liabilities [3]	620	33.16	583	31.81
Total liabilities [2 + 3]	970	51.87	783	42.72
Total Capital and liabilities [1 + 2 + 3]	1,870	100.00	1,833	100.00

Interpretation. The percentage of fixed assets to total assets increased from 58.83% in 2001 to 63% in 2002. At the same time the percentage of current assets decreased from 30.47% to 28.31%. This indicates a poor current assets management policy. The value of investments has also decreased from 10.70% to 8.19%, which may be in order to finance the increase in fixed assets. The preference share capital has increased from10.70% to 16.37% and reserves from 10.69% to 13.64%. but at the same time, the long-term as well as the current liabilities to total liabilities has come down from 51.87% to 42.72%. Compared to total current liabilities the total current assets are inadequate. Hence, the working capital position is not satisfactory. In general the financial policy of the concern is highly unsatisfactory.

Common-size Income Statement
[for the years ended 30th June 2001 and 2002]

Particulars	2001 Amount Rs. In lakhs	Percentage 100	2002 Amount Rs. In lakhs	Percentage 100
Net Sales	600	100.00	800	100.00
Cost of Goods sold	400	66.67	500	62.50
Gross Profit	200	33.33	300	37.50
Operating Expenses:	20	3.33	20	2.50
Office expenses	20	3.33	20	2.50
Selling expenses	20	3.33	30	3.75
Total operating expenses	40	6.66	50	6.25
Operating profit	160	26.67	250	31.25

Interpretation: The gross profit percentage has increased from 33.33 to 37.50. This increase is more than proportionate compared to sales. This is because the increase in cost of goods sold is less than proportional. Similarly the net profit percentage has also increased from 26.67 to 31.25. In general, the overall operating efficiency of the business is highly satisfactory.

7.15 What are Trend Percentages or Ratios?

Trend Analysis refers to the comparison of past data over a period of time with that of a base year. Under this method, percentage relationship that each statement item bears to the same item in the base year is calculated. Any year i.e., the earliest year involved in comparison, or the latest year, or any intervening year, may be taken as the base year. As the purpose of this analysis is to highlight some important changes, the trend percentages are calculated only for some important items that can be connected with each other. The concerned item in the base year is taken to be equal to as 100 and then based on this, trend percentages for the corresponding items in other years are calculated. This method is a horizontal type of analysis of financial statements. The trend percentages are shown in comparative financial statements.

Trend analysis is a useful tool for the management since it reduces large amount of absolute data into a simple and easily readable form. By looking at the trend in a particular ratio one can see whether the ratio is increasing or decreasing or remaining constant. From this a problem is unearthed and good management is observed.

Precautions to be taken

1. The base year selected should be normal and be truly representative of all years involved in the analysis.

2. The financial statements used for the analysis must have been prepared applying consistent accounting principles and practices.

3. The figures of the various accounting statements considered for the analysis should be adjusted for any price level changes, as compared to base year, before computing trend percentages.

4. Trend percentages should be studied along with the absolute figures on which they are based. This will enable us to know whether the change is significant or not. For example, one item may increase from Rs.100 to Rs.200 [i.e., 100% increase] and the other item may change from Rs.10,000 to Rs.14,000 [i.e., 40% increase]. Of these two, the change in the first item is not significant compared to the second item.

The trend ratios for the assets of a balance sheet are illustrated below with imaginary figures:

Comparative Balance sheet as on June 30, 1999 - 2002

Assets	June 30 [Rs. In lakhs]				Trend Percentages Base year 1999			
	1999	2000	2001	2002	1999	2000	2001	2002
Fixed Assets:								
Land	80	100	110	120	100	125.00	137.50	150.00
Plant	160	200	240	240	100	125.00	150.00	150.00
Furniture	20	25	25	25	100	125.00	125.00	125.00
Total Fixed Assets	260	325	375	385	100	125.00	144.20	148.10
Current Assts:								

Cash	20	25	20	30	100	125.00	100.00	150.00
Debtors	40	50	60	80	100	125.00	150..00	200.00
Stock	60	80	70	100	100	133.33	119.67	166.67
Total Current Assets	120	155	150	210	100	129.17	125.00	177.70

Note: A separate column for the base year [1999] need not be provided in the comparative balance sheet.

Interpretation

From the above statement it is clear that both the fixed assets and current assets have registered an increasing trend. This is an indication of the company's growth over the period. Similar to this analysis, trend percentages can be computed for the important items of the liabilities side of the balance sheet and of the Income Statement.

Illustration 1

The comparative balance sheets of ABC Ltd., are given below:
Balance Sheets as on 31st December 2001 and 2002

[Rs. In 000's]

Liabilities	2001 Rs.	2002 Rs.	Assets	2001 Rs.	2002 Rs.
Equity Share Capital	800	1,200	Current Assets:		
Capital Reserve	120	220	Cash	236	20
General Reserve	444	418	Debtors	418	380
Sinking Fund	80	100	Stock	320	260
6% Debentures	400	650	Others	64	26
Current Liabilities:			Investments	540	340
Sundry Creditors	510	234	Fixed Assets:		
Others	14	20	Furniture less depn.	18	36
			Buildings less depn.	620	1,572
			Land	40	60
			Other Assets	112	148
	2,368	2,842		2,368	2,842

Comment upon the significant changes that have taken place during the year 2002.

Solution

Comparative Balance Sheets of ABC Ltd., as on 31st December 2001 and 2002

Particulars	2001 Rs. In Lkahs	2002 Rs. In lakhs	Increase or Decrease Rs. In lakhs	Percentage Increase or Decrease %
Current Assets:				
Cash	236	20	– 216	– 92

Debtors	418	380	– 38	– 9
Stock	320	260	– 60	– 19
Others	64	26	– 38	– 60
Total Current Assets	1,038	686	– 352	– 34
Investments	540	340	– 200	– 37
Fixed Assets:				
Furniture	18	36	+ 18	+ 100
Buildings	620	1,572	+ 952	+ 154
Land	40	60	+ 20	+ 50
Total	678	1,668	+ 990	+ 146
Other Assets	112	148	+ 36	+ 32
Total Assets	2,368	2,842	+ 474	+ 20
Liabilities & Capital				
Current Liabilities:				
Sundry Creditors	510	234	– 276	– 54
Others	14	20	+ 6	+ 43
Total Current liabilities	524	254	– 270	– 52
6 % Debentures	400	650	+ 250	+ 63
Total liabilities	924	904	– 20	– 2
Equity Capital	800	1,200	+ 400	+ 50
Reserves & Surplus:				
Capital Reserves	120	220	+ 100	+ 83
General Reserves	444	418	– 26	– 6
Sinking Fund	80	100	+ 20	+ 25
Total Surplus	644	738	+ 94	+ 15
Total Capital	1,444	1,938	+ 494	+ 34
Total Liabilities & Capital	2,368	2,842	+ 474	+ 20

Comments: Individual as well as total current assets have decreased in 2002 when compared to 2001. The total current assets have decreased by 34%. Investments have also decreased by 37%. Amounts realized from the assets have been mainly used to repay current liabilities [decrease by 52%] and the balance used for the purchase of fixed assets. Fixed assets, particularly buildings have increased significantly by 146% and other assets by 32%. It is heartering to note that these assets have been funded through the issue of debentures by 63% and equity and surplus by 65%. Generally, there is an overall increase in total assets in 2002 over 2001 only by 20%.

Illustration 2

From the following Income Statements of ABC Ltd., prepare a Comparative Income Statement.

Income Statements for the year ending 31st December 2001 and 2002

Particulars		2001 Rs. In Lakhs.		2002 Rs. In Lakhs
Net Sales		6,850		7,210
Less Cost of goods sold		4,190		4,630
Gross Profit		2,660		2,580
Operating Expenses:				
Office expenses	940		910	
Selling Expenses	470		460	
		1,410		1,370
Operating Profit		1,250		1,210
Add: Other Income - dividend		220		250
Less: Other Deductions:		1,470		1,460
Interest paid		220		220
Net Profit before tax		1,250		1,240
Less Income Tax		620		620
Net Profit after tax		630		620

Solution

ABC Ltd.,
Comparative Income Statement
for the years ended 31st December 2001 and 2002

Particulars	2001 Rs. In Lakhs	2002 Rs. In lakhs	Increase or Decrease Amount	Increase or Decrease percentage
Net Sales	6,850	7,210	+ 360	+ 5.30
Less: Cost of goods sold	4,190	4,630	+ 440	+ 10.50
Gross Profit	2,660	2,580	– 80	– 3.00
Operating Expenses:				
Office expenses	940	910	– 30	– 3.20
Selling expenses	470	460	– 10	– 2.10
Total operating expenses	1,410	1,370	– 40	– 2.83
Operating Profit	1,250	1,210	– 40	– 3.20
Add: other Income - dividend	220	250	+ 30	+ 13.64
Less: other deductions:	1,470	1,460	– 10	– 0.70
Interest paid	220	220	Nil	Nil
Net Profit before Tax	1,250	1,240	– 10	– 0.80
Less Income Tax	620	620	Nil	Nil
Net Profit after Tax	630	620	– 10	– 1.60

Illustration 3

Convert the following Income Statement into Common Size Statement and interpret the changes in 2002 in the light of conditions in 2001.

Income Statement

Particulars	2001 Rs.	2002 Rs.
Gross Sales	30,600	36,720
Less: Returns	600	700
Net Sales	30,000	36,020
Less Cost of goods sold	18,200	20,250
Gross Profit	11,800	15,770
Less: Operating expenses		
Administrative expenses	3,000	3,400
Selling expenses	6,000	6,600
Total expenses	9,000	10,000
Operating Profit	2,800	5,770
Add Non-operating Income	300	400
Total Income	3,100	6,170
Less: Non-operating expenses	400	600
Net Profit	2,700	5,500

Solution

Common-Size Income Statement

Particulars	2001		2002	
	Amount [Rs.]	Per cent	Amount [Rs.]	Per cent
Gross Sales	30,600	102.0	36,720	101.9
Less: Returns	600	2.0	700	1.9
Net Sales	30,000	100.0	36,020	100.0
Less: Cost of goods sold	18,200	60.7	20,250	56.2
Gross Profit	11,800	39.3	15,770	43.8
Less: Operating expenses				
Administrative expenses	3,000	10.0	3,400	9.4
Selling expenses	6,000	20.0	6,600	18.3
Total expenses	9,000	30.0	10,000	27.7
Net Operating income	2,800	9.3	5,770	16.1
Add Non-operating income	300	1.0	400	1.1
Total Income	3,100	10.3	6,170	17.2
Less Non-operating expenses	400	1.3	600	1.7
Net Profit	2,700	9.0	5,570	15.5

The analysis of the above income statement enables to draw the following conclusions:

(a) During the year 2002 the cost of goods sold has declined by 4.5% i.e., from 60.7% to 56.2%. This decline may be due to the decrease in cost of raw materials. Owing to this decline, the gross profit ratio has increased from 39.3% to 43.8%.

(b) The operating expenses have declined by 2.3%, which indicates high operating efficiency and economy in expenditure; both administrative and selling expenses have declined less than proportionately despite the increase in these items in absolute amounts.

(c) The combined effect of decrease in cost of goods sold and operating expenses has caused for an increase in net operating income by 6.8% i.e., from 9.3% in 2001 to 16.1% in 2002.

(d) The increase in non-operating income is a welcome feature while the corresponding increase in non-operating expenses proportionately is not desirable.

As final conclusion, it may be said that the company has been operating more efficiently in 2002 as compared to 2001.

Illustration 4

From the following information, interpret the results of operations of a manufacturing concern using trend ratios.

Income Statement for the years ended 1999 to 2002

Amount [Rupees in Lakhs.]

Particulars	1999	2000	2001	2002
Net Sales	100.00	95.00	120.00	130.00
Less: Cost of goods sold	60.00	58.90	69.60	72.80
Gross Profit	40.00	36.10	50.40	57.20
Less Operating expenses	10.00	9.70	11.00	12.00
Net Operating Profit	30.00	26.40	39.4	45.20

Solution

Trend Ratios [1999 = 100]

Particulars	1999	2000	2001	2002
Net Sales	100	95	120	130
Cost of goods sold	100	98	116	121
Gross Profit	100	90	126	143
Operating expenses	100	97	110	120
Net Operating Profit	100	88	131	151

Conclusions:

From the above statement, it is seen that the sales, cost of goods sold and operating expenses have declined in 2000 when compared to base year 1999. But one important point that the decline in sales is comparatively less than the cost and operating expenses. On the other hand, the sales, cost and operating expenses have all increased in 2001 and 2002 as compared to1999. But the increase in cost and operating expenses is lesser than the increase in sales. As a conclusion we may infer from these trend ratios that a larger portion of cost of goods and operating expenses is fixed and they are not affected by change in sales volume. Because of this, we find that the net operating profit is more in 2001 and 2002 as compared to 1999.

Illustration 5

Develop proforma income statement for the months of April, May and June for a company from the following particulars.

(a) Sales are projected at Rs. 4,50,000, Rs. 4,80,000 and Rs. 5,00,000 for April, May and June respectively.

(b) Cost of goods sold is Rs. 1,00,000 plus 30% of selling price per month.

(c) Rent is Rs. 15,000 per month. Administration expenses for April are expected to be Rs. 1,20,000 but expected to rise 1% per month over the previous month's expenses.

(e) The company has Rs. 6,00,000 of 8% loan, interest payable monthly.

(f) Corporate tax rate is 50%.

Solution

Proforma Income Statement for the Months of

For the months of	April Rs.	May Rs.	June Rs.
Projected Sales	4,50,000	4,80,000	5,000
Less:Cost of goods sold	2,35,000	2,44,000	2,50,000
Gross Profit	2,15,000	2,36,000	2,50,000
Less: Operating expenses: Rent	15,000	15,000	15,000
Administration expenses	1,20,000	1,21,200	1,22,412
Selling expenses	13,500	14,400	15,000
	1,48,500	1,50,600	1,52,412
Operating Profit	66,500	4,000	4,000
Less: Financial expenses: Interest on Loan	4,000	4,000	4,000
Net Profit	62,500	81,400	93,588
Less: Income Tax @ 50%	31,250	40,700	46,794
Profit after Tax	31,250	40,700	46,794

REVIEW QUESTIONS

1. Explain the meaning and nature of Financial Statements.
2. What are the objectives of Financial Statements?
3. Explain the essential attributes of Financial Statements.
4. Discuss the importance of Financial Statements.
5. Who are the users of Financial Statements?
6. State the limitations of Financial Statements.
7. Explain the meaning, objectives and importance of analysis and interpretation of financial statements.
8. Explain the various ways of presentation of financial statements.
9. Describe briefly the major tools used in the financial statement analysis.
10. What are Comparative Financial Statements? How are they prepared?
11. What are common-sized Balance Sheet and Income Statement?
12. What are Trend Ratios? How are they computed?
13. State the different types of financial analysis.

REVIEW PROBLEMS

14. The comparative balance sheet for Enpees Ltd., as on 31st December 2001 and 2002 are given below:

Rs. In thousands.

Assets	2001 Rs.	2002 Rs.
Fixed Assets	2,600	3,100
Less: Depreciation Reserve	800	1,100
Net Fixed Assets	1,800	2,000
Current Assets:		
Stock in trade	1,200	1,600
Debtors	200	800
Cash	300	100
Total Current assets	1,700	2,500
Total Assets	3,500	4,500
Liabilities:		
Equity Share Capital	1,000	1,000
Reserves	800	1,200
6% Debentures	200	200
Current Liabilities:		
Sundry Creditors	400	500
Bills Payables	900	1,300
Bank Overdraft	200	300
Total Current Liabilities	1,500	2,100
Total Liabilities	3,500	4,500

Comment upon the significant changes that have taken place during the year 2002.

[Refer illustration 1]

15. From the following information prepare a Common-Size Income Statement and make brief comments:

Income Statements for the years ended 30th June

Particulars	2000 Rs.	2001 Rs	2002 Rs
Net Sales	6,20,000	4,40,000	2,80,000
Cost of goods sold	4,30,000	3,02,000	2,04,000
Gross Profit	1,90,000	1,38,000	76,000
Operating Expenses	1,26,000	69,000	44,000
Net Operating profit	64,000	69,000	32,000
Interest Expenses	6,000	3,500	2,500
Profit before tax	58,000	65,500	29,500
Provision for taxes	25,000	35,000	14,000
Profit after tax	33,000	30,500	15,500

[Refer illustration 3]

16. From the following balance sheets of Shree ltd., compute the trend percentages and make brief comments.

[Rupees in thousands]

Liabilities	2000	2001	2002	Assets	2000	2001	2002
Share Capital	25	20	25	Fixed Assets	20	15	16
Retained Earnings	5	3	2	[less depreciation]			
Accounts Payable	8	9	7	Investments	4	2	4
Accrued Expenses	3	2	1	Stock	5	3	4
Taxes Payable	3	2	3	Debtors	12	13	11
				Cash	3	3	3
	44	36	38		44	36	38

[Refer Illustration]

8

RATIO ANALYSIS

Learning Objectives

After going through this chapter, you should be able to

— Explain the concept of Ratio analysis and its uses and limitations,

— Understand different types of ratios,

— Describe the computation of different ratios and their significance,

— Compute ratios from financial statements and derive financial statement information from ratios.

8.1. Meaning of Ratio Analysis

The term 'ratio' simply means one number expressed in terms of another. It describes in mathematical terms the quantitative relationship that exists between two numbers. The term 'accounting ratio', J.Batty points out, is used to describe significant relationships between figures shown on a Balance Sheet, in a Profit and Loss Account, in a Budgetary Control System or in any other part of the accounting organization. Ratio Analysis, simply defined, refers to the analysis and interpretation of financial statements through ratios. Nowadays it is used by all business and industrial concerns in their financial analysis. Ratios are considered to be the best guides for the efficient execution of basic managerial functions like planning, forecasting and control, etc.

8.2. Nature of Ratio Analysis

Ratios are designed to show how one number is related to another. It is worked out by dividing one number by another. Ratios are customarily presented either in the form of a coefficient or a percentage or as a proportion. For example, the current assets and current liabilities of a business on a particular date are Rs.2 lakhs and Rs.1 lakh respectively. The resulting ratio of Current Assets and Current Liabilities could be expressed as 2 (i.e., 2,00,000/1,00,000) or as 200 per cent. Alternatively in the form of a proportion the same ratio may be expressed as 2:1, i.e., the current assets are two times the current liabilities.

Ratios are invaluable aids to management and others who are interested in the analysis and interpretation of financial statements. Absolute figures may be misleading unless compared, one with another. Ratios provide the means of showing the relationship that exists between figures. Though there is no special magic in ratio analysis, many prefer to base conclusions on ratios as they find them highly useful for making judgments more easily. However, the numerical relationships of the kind expressed by ratio analysis are not an end in themselves but are a means for understanding the financial position of a business. Generally, simple ratios or ratios compiled from a single year's financial statements of a business concern may not serve the real purpose. Hence, ratios are to be worked out from the financial statements of a number of years.

Ratios, by themselves, are meaningless. They derive their status partly from the ingenuity and experience of the analyst who uses the available data in a systematic manner. Besides, in order to reach valid conclusions, ratios have to be compared with some standards that are established with a view to represent the financial position of the business under review. However, it should be borne in mind that after computing the ratios one cannot categorically say whether a particular ratio is good or bad as the conclusions may vary from business to business. A single ideal ratio cannot be applied for all types of business. Speedy compiling of ratios and their presentation in the appropriate manner is essential. A complete record of ratios employed is advisable; and explanation of each, and actual ratios year by year should be included. This record may be treated as a part of an Account Manual or a special Ratio Register may be maintained.

8.3. How can Ratios be interpreted?

Generally four different approaches are available for interpreting ratios. They are as follows:

(a) Interpretation of individual ratio: An individual ratio, by itself, may have significance of its own. For example, a persistent fall in the net profit to sales ratio may indicate inefficiency or waste in the organization. Normally they are to be studied with reference to some standards. However, these standards are mostly approximations, the conclusions derived from deviations of actual ratios from them may be misleading. Hence, this approach is to be combined with others.

(b) Interpretation by referring to a group of ratios: Sometimes, when studied individually, it may be difficult to comprehend the significance of certain ratios fully. In such cases, the analysis could be made more meaningful by computing some of the additional related ratios. A change in one ratio may have significance only when viewed in relation to other ratios. For example, the significance of the Profit Ratio could be made clear by calculating other ratios like return on capital employed, interest coverage ratio, etc.

(c) Interpretation of ratios by trend: Under this method an individual ratio or a group of related ratios are computed and compared over time. The significant trends - increasing, decreasing or constant -are considered for reaching conclusions. Sometimes the average of the ratios calculated for a number of years are used for carrying out the analysis.

(d) Interpretation by inter-firm comparisons: In this approach, the ratios of one firm are compared with the ratios of other firms in the same industry. Such inter-firm comparisons may be significant as some of the other firms considered for comparison may be experiencing the same or similar financial problems. Generally, selected significant ratios are calculated and published by trade associations or credit rating or financial institutions in the form of tables. Individual firms for carrying out the analysis may use such tables.

A full-fledged investigation of the financial and economic position of any business, however, needs the application of all the four approaches. This is essential for generating useful information that will make clear the intrinsic meaning of any ratio.

8.4. Uses or advantages of Ratio Analysis

1. Simplification of mass of accounting data: Ratios enable the mass of accounting data to be summarized and simplified. Besides, they provide the means of showing the interrelationship that exist between various segments of business, as revealed through accounting statements, and thereby prevent any distortions that may result from the study of absolute figures.

2. An invaluable aid to management: Ratio analysis helps management in the discharge of its basic functions such as planning, forecasting, control, etc. The trend ratios may be useful for predicting likely events in the future. The plans made can be 'signposted' by accounting ratios and thereby become an integral part of the standard costing and budgetary control systems.

3. Facilitates better coordination and control: Ideal ratios can be established and the relationship between primary ratios may be used to establish the desirable coordination. Ratios may also be used for control of performance as well as control of costs. They are an effective means of communication and play a vital role in informing the position of and progress made by the business concern to the owners or other parties.

4. A tool to assess important characteristics of business: Ratio analysis is an effective instrument to assess important characteristics of business like liquidity, solvency, profitability, etc. A study on these aspects may enable to draw conclusions relating to the financial requirements and capabilities of business concerns.

5. An effective tool of analysis for intra-firm and inter-firm comparisons: Ratio may also be used as measures of efficiency. It is the main tool of analysis for intra-firm and inter-firm comparisons. By comparing the ratios of different firms one may identify the factors associated with successful and unsuccessful firms or strong and weak firms or overvalued and undervalued firms.

8.5. Limitations of Ratio analysis

1. Limitations of Financial Statements: Ratios are mainly calculated from the information recorded in the financial statements. As financial statements suffer from a number of limitations, such limitations may affect the quality of ratio analysis. For example, the financial statements do not reveal non-financial changes though important for the business. Hence, the ratio analysis may fail to serve its purpose fully.

2. No fixed standards: Ratios gain significance only when they are compared with other ratios or standards. But it is very difficult to lay down fixed standard for ideal ratios. Also ratios share with statistical concepts all the limitations of the latter.

3. Qualitative factors are ignored: Ratios are tools of quantitative analysis only and normal qualitative factors that may generally influence conclusions derived are ignored while computing ratios. For example, a high current ratio may not necessarily mean sound liquid position when current assets include a large inventory consisting of mostly obsolete items. Hence, it is very difficult to generalize whether a particular ratio is 'good' or 'bad'.

4. Lack of standard formulae: There are no standard formulae for working out ratios and it makes comparison very difficult. They are worked out on the basis of different items in different industries. In addition, the number of ratios is so large that the task of selecting appropriate ratios for different units becomes very difficult. Ratios also fail to indicate clearly the point where the error lies.

5. it is no substitute for personal judgment: Ratio analysis is only a beginning and gives just a fraction of information needed for decision-making. It is just an aid and cannot replace thinking and personal judgment employed in the decision-making process.

6. Problems of Price level changes: Ratios fail to reflect the price level changes as they are based on historical data. Hence, they may give misleading results when inflationary conditions are ignored. Comparison of two firms set up in different years through ratio analysis may not be meaningful, since the values of assets and liabilities of the two companies may not be comparable.

7. Ratios alone are not adequate: Ratios computed from historical data are used for predicting and projecting the likely events in the future. Such ratios may provide only a glimpse of a firm's past performance, but the forecast for the future may not be correct since several other factors like management policies, economic and market conditions, etc., may induce future operations.

It may be concluded that ratio analysis, if not done properly or done mechanically, would be both misleading and dangerous. It is an aid to management to take correct decisions, but as a mechanical substitute for personal judgment and thinking, it would be worse than useless.

8.6 Various methods of classification of ratios

Ratios may be classified in a number of ways to suit any particular purpose. Different kinds of ratios are selected for different types of situation. Mostly, the purposes for which the ratios are used and the kind of data available determine the nature of analysis. In general, the following bases of classification are in vogue.

(a) Classification according to accounting statements: This classification is based on the nature of accounting statement on which the items used for compiling ratios appear. Accordingly, the different subdivisions are:

(i) Balance Sheet Ratios: These ratios are also called as financial ratios. The components or items for computation of these ratios are drawn from the Balance Sheet. Examples: Current Ratio (items used for computation are current assets and current liabilities), Debt-Equity Ratio (items are long-term debts and shareholders' funds).

(ii) Profit and Loss Account Ratios: These ratios are also called as operating ratios. The items used for the calculation of these ratios are usually taken out from the income statement i.e., Trading and Profit and Loss Account. Examples are Gross Profit ratio, Net Profit Ratio, Operating Ratio, etc.

(iii) Inter-statement Ratios or Combined Ratios: The information required for the computation of these ratios is normally drawn from both Balance Sheet and Trading and Profit and Loss Account. Examples are Debtors Turnover Ratio, (i.e., a debtor is balance sheet item and credit sales is trading account item). Stock Turnover Ratio, (stock is balance sheet item and cost of sales is trading account item.

(b) Classification according to time: This classification is based on the point of time in relation to which ratios are compiled. Accordingly, they may be classified as follows:

(i) Structural Ratios: The data used for the computation of these ratios normally relate to the same point of time, e.g., ratios of a particular month, quarter or year. In this sense, the balance sheet ratios, and the income statement ratios of a particular year may be termed as structural ratios.

(ii) Trend Ratios: These ratios are computed between items over a period of time and used for the analysis. For example, current ratios for a period of 10 years may be calculated and the trend (long-term changes) observed from these ratios may be used for the analysis.

(c) Classification according to importance: Some ratios when related to the main objective of the business for the purpose of analysis may be more important than others. The British

Institute of Management has recommended this basis of classification for inter-firm comparisons, and the Institute has suggested the following types:

(i) Primary Ratios: The prime motive of any business undertaking is profit and therefore, ratios like Profit to Sales, Return on Capital employed may be termed as primary ratios for such undertaking.

(ii) Secondary Ratios: These ratios are mainly used to explain the primary ratios. They are also known as subsidiary or supporting ratios. Taking the ratio of Return on Capital employed as the primary ratio, the following ratios may be grouped as secondary ratios: (a) Profit and earning ratios; (b) Cost or Expense ratios; (c) Capital and related ratios; and Turnover Ratios.

(d) Classification according to function or tests satisfied: Robert N. Antony suggested that ratios may be grouped on the basis of certain tests, which satisfy the needs of the parties having financial interest in the business concern. These tests are: (i) Test of Liquidity (ii) Test of Profitability and (iii) Market tests

(e) Classification according to nature: Under this classification, ratios are grouped as follows:

(i) Liquidity Ratios: These ratios are used to measure the ability of the firm to meet its maturing obligations or current liabilities. Examples: Current Ratio, Acid Test Ratio.

(ii) Leverage Ratios: These ratios help to measure the financial contribution of the owners compared to that of creditors, as also the risk of debt financing. They are also known as Capital Structure Ratios. Example: Debt to Equity ratio, Fixed Assets to Net Worth, Interest Coverage Ratio.

(iii) Turnover or Activity Ratios: These ratios enable measurement of the effectiveness of the usage of resources at the command of the concern. Examples: Fixed Assets Turnover Ratio, Stock Turnover Ratio. These ratios would also indicate the profitability position of the business.

(iv) Profitability Ratios: These ratios are intended to measure the end result of business operations. Examples: Gross Profit Ratio, Return on Capital employed, and Operating Ratio.

From the above discussion, it may be observed that one basis of classification blends into another. Whatever classification is followed, the ratios should be computed carefully and presented to the management and other interested parties at regular intervals.

ANALYSIS OF LIQUIDITY OR LIQUIDITY RATIOS

8.7. Significance of liquidity ratios or analysis of liquidity

Liquidity ratios play a key role in assessing the short-term financial position of a business. Commercial banks and other short-term creditors are generally interested in such an analysis. However, managements can employ these ratios to ascertain how efficiently they utilize the working capital in the business. Shareholders and debenture holders and other long-term creditors can use these ratios to assess the prospects of dividend and interest payments. This type of ratios normally indicates the ability of the business to meet the maturing or current debts, the efficiency of the management in utilizing the working capital, and the progress attained in the current financial position.

8.8. Describe the principal Liquidity Ratios.

Current Ratio - Meaning

Current Ratio may be defined as the ratio of current assets to current liabilities. It is also known as Working Capital Ratio or 2:1 Ratio. It shows the relationship between the total current assets and total current liabilities, expressed as formula given below:

$$\text{Current Ratio} = \frac{\text{Current Assets}}{\text{Current Liabilities}}$$

Components: Current assets mean cash or those assets convertible or expected to be converted into cash within the accounting year, and current liabilities are those liabilities to be paid within the same time. Current assets normally include the following items: Cash in hand and at bank, Marketable Securities or readily realizable investments, Bills Receivable, Book Debts (excluding bad debts and provision), Inventories and Prepaid Expenses. Current Liabilities include items such as Outstanding or Accrued Expenses, Sundry Creditors, Bills Payable, Bank Overdraft, Provision for Taxation, etc.

General Guidelines: All current assets and current liabilities should be properly valued. Therefore all reserves and provisions created should be deducted from such current assets. Book debts outstanding for more than 6 months and loose tools should be excluded. Investments, which are easily marketable and are meant to be sold for cash should be treated as current assets. Even long-term liabilities, if they are repayable within the accounting year, should be treated as current liability. Bank overdraft, unless specifically stated as a permanent arrangement, should be treated as a current liability. As regards bills receivable, all bills (whether discounted or not) should be treated as current asset and at the same time, discounted bills receivable should be treated as current liability.

Example 1

From the following compute the Current Ratio.

Excerpt from a Balance sheet

	Rs.			Rs.
Sundry Creditors	15,000	Cash		10,000
Outstanding Expenses	2,000	Short-term Investments		20,000
Bills Payable	8,000	Bills Receivable		6,000
Income tax Payable	15,000	Book debts	42,500	
Bank overdraft	35,000	Less Reserve	2,500	40,000
		Inventories		44,000
		Prepaid expenses		5,000
		Loose Tools		5,000
Total	75,000	Total		1,30,000

Total current assets Rs.1,25,000 (loose tools should be excluded). Total current liabilities Rs.75, 000.

$$\text{Current Ratio} = \frac{1,25,000}{75,000} = 1.67 \text{ or } 5:3$$

Interpretation: From the above ratio, it is clear that for every rupee worth of current liabilities, there are current assets worth Rs.1.67. In other words, it connotes that the firm can meet all it s current obligations even by just realizing 60% of its current assets. Though 2: 1 is often referred to as a banker's rule of thumb standard of liquidity for a business, it is suggested that an ideal current ratio could be between 1.5: 1 to 2: 1.

Significance of Current Ratio: Current ratio is an index of the firm's financial stability, i.e., an index of technical solvency and an index of the strength of working capital, which means excess of current assets over current liabilities. The logic behind the current ratio is that cash need not be immediately available to meet all current liabilities on a particular date but there should be good prospects for an adequate inflow of cash indicated by the amounts of individual components of current assets. It is closely connected with the concept of working capital. A high current ratio is an assurance that a firm will have adequate funds to pay current liabilities and other current payments.

However, the main limitation of current ratio is that it fails to indicate the liquidity of individual components of current assets. For example, a high current ratio due to large inventories may not be regarded as an index of liquidity as one that is due to huge cash and bank balances. Even if the ratio is favorable, the firm may be in financial trouble because of more stock and work in progress, which are not easily convertible into cash and therefore, may have less cash to pay off current liabilities. Hence, it is suggested that the current ratio should not be used as the sole index of short-term solvency.

Liquid Ratio - Meaning

Liquid Ratio may be defined as the ratio of liquid assets to liquid liabilities or current liabilities. It is concerned with the relationship between liquid assets and liquid or current liabilities. The other terms used for liquid ratio are 'Quick ratio' and 'Acid Test Ratio'. For the purpose of computation, the current assets and current liabilities could be classified as follows:

Current Assets: (a) Liquid Assets, and (b) Deferred Assets.

Current Liabilities: (a) Liquid Liabilities, and (b) Deferred Liabilities.

Establishing a simple rule that all assets and liabilities are liquid if they are expected to be realized or paid within a month could make this classification, otherwise they belong to 'deferred' category. However, the criterion for such classification depends upon the purpose for which the liquid ratio is used.

Components: Liquid assets normally include cash, bank, sundry debtors, bills receivable, and short-term investments or marketable securities. In other words, they are current assets minus inventories and prepaid expenses. In the same manner, liquid liabilities are current liabilities minus bank overdraft and income received in advance. The formula is as follows:

$$\text{Liquid Ratio} = \frac{\text{Liquid Assets}}{\text{Liquid Liabilities}} \text{ or } \frac{\text{Liquid Assets}}{\text{Current Liabilities}}$$

Some authorities recommend that liquid ratio may be computed comparing current liabilities with liquid assets.

General Guidelines: All guidelines that are applicable to the computation of current ratio are equally applicable to the computation of liquid ratio. That is, current assets and current liabilities should be properly valued and the nature of assets should be kept in view.

Example 2

From the figures given in Example 1, the liquid ratio may be calculated as follows:

Liquid assets = Current assets minus inventory and prepaid expenses.

= Rs.1,25,000 minus (Rs.44,000 + Rs.5,000) = Rs.76,000

Liquid liabilities = Current liabilities minus Bank overdraft

= Rs.75,000 minus Rs.35,000 = Rs.40,000

$$\text{Liquid Ratio} = \frac{\text{Rs.76,000}}{\text{Rs.40,000}} = 1.9 \text{ or } 1.9:1$$

Interpretation: The ratio indicates that by realizing the debtors, short-term investments and bills receivables at their face values along with cash and bank balances, the firm could pay off all liquid liabilities. In other words, the firm could meet its liquid liabilities without resorting to the sale of inventories. Comparing with the standard ratio of 1:1 for liquid ratio, the actual ratio i.e., 1.9:1 is exceptionally good. However, maintaining very high ratio continuously may also indicate too much of idle cash resources.

Significance of Liquid Ratio: Liquid Ratio is a more rigorous test of liquidity than current ratio. A comparison of current ratio with liquid ratio would indicate the degree of inventory held up. A high liquid ratio compared to current ratio may indicate under-stocking while a low liquid ratio may indicate over-stocking. When used in conjunction with current ratio, the liquid ratio gives a better picture of the firm's capacity to meet its short-term obligations out of short-term assets. However, it is difficult to establish a standard without further investigation. A reasonable standard for the liquid ratio may vary from season to season and also from business to business.

For example, a manufacturing company may have a weak liquid ratio in time of prosperity, for increased activity may result in huge stocks and holding of less cash. Hence, it should be remembered while arriving at conclusions that though technically inventories are not immediately available to meet current liabilities, to some extent, they do generate cash during normal course of business. Inventories are converted into cash, debtors, and bills receivable when they are sold in the ordinary course of business. Though this ratio is an improvement over current ratio, the interpretation of this ratio also suffers from the same limitations of current ratio.

Absolute Liquidity Ratio

Absolute liquidity is represented by cash and near cash items. Hence, in the computation of this ratio, only absolute liquid assets are compared with liquid liabilities. These assets normally include cash, bank, and marketable securities. It is to be observed that receivables are excluded from the list of liquid assets.

Formula

$$\text{Absolute Liquidity Ratio} = \frac{\text{Cash + Bank + Marketable Securities}}{\text{Liquid Liabilities}}$$

This ratio gains significance only when it is used in conjunction with the first two ratios. A standard of 0.5: 1 is considered an acceptable norm for this ratio. In other words, this ratio indicates that 50 paise worth of absolute liquid assets are sufficient to meet one rupee worth of liquid liabilities. However, this ratio is not in much use.

The Current Ratio, Liquid Ratio and Absolute Liquidity Ratio generally indicate the adequacy of current assets for meeting current liabilities. This is one dimension of liquidity analysis. The other dimension of liquidity is the determination of the rate at which various short-term assets are converted into cash. Important ratios under the secondary category are as follows:

Debtors Turnover Ratio

Debtors or Receivables normally include both sundry debtors and bills receivable (B/R) and represent uncollected portion of credit sales. Turnover, here, refers to credit sales. Receivables constitute an important component of current assets and therefore the quality of receivables determines the liquidity of a firm to a greater extent. This ratio can be calculated in two ways as follows:

(a) $\text{Debtors Turn over Ratio} = \dfrac{\text{Net Credit Sales}}{\text{Average Debtors + Average B/R}}$

(b) $\text{Average Debt Collection Period} = \dfrac{\text{Months or Days in a year}}{\text{Debtors Turnover Ratio}}$

Alternatively it can be calculated as follows:

$$\text{Average Collection Period} = \frac{\text{Average Debtors + B/R}}{\text{Total Net Credit Sales}} \times \text{Months or Days in a year}$$

OR

$$\text{Average Collection Period} = \frac{\text{Average Debtors + B/R}}{\text{Monthly or Daily Sales}}$$

$$\text{Where monthly or daily sales} = \frac{\text{Total Net Credit Sales}}{\text{12 or No of days}}$$

Components: Book debts and B/R, which arise out of credit sales, should be considered. Adding opening and closing balances of Book Debts and B/R and then dividing the result by two can arrive at average amount. It should be noted that provision for bad and doubtful debts should not be deducted since it may give the impression that some amount of receivable has been collected. When credit sales figure is not given the total sales may be considered for computation. The Receivables Turnover Ratio, when calculated in terms of days or months, is known as Average Collection Period or Debts Collection Period.

Example 3

From the following details compute Debtors Turnover Ratio and Average Collection Period:

	Rs.
Sundry Debtors as on 1-1-2002	30,000
Sundry Debtors as on 31-12-2002	45,000
Bills Receivable as on 1-1-2002	10,000
Bills Receivable as on 31-12-2002	15,000
Total Sales for the year	3,50,000
Cash Sales for the year	50,000
Provision for doubtful debts as on 31-12-2002	2,000

Solution

Average debtors = Rs.30,000 + 45,000/2 = Rs.37,500

Average B/R = Rs.10,000 + 15,000/2 = Rs.12,500

Average Accounts Receivables Rs.50,000

$$\text{Debtors Turnover} = \frac{\text{Net Credit Sales (Total sales} - \text{Cash sales)}}{\text{Average Accounts Receivables}}$$

$$= \frac{\text{Rs.}3,00,000}{\text{Rs.}50,000} = 6 \text{ times}$$

$$\text{Average Collection Period} = \frac{\text{Average Debtors + Bills Receivables}}{\text{Net Credit Sales}} \times 360$$

$$= \frac{50,000}{3,00,000} \times 360 = 60 \text{ days}$$

(It may be assumed for the number of days in a year as 360 or 365)

In fact these two ratios are inter-related. Debtors Turnover Ratio could be obtained by dividing the number of days in a year by the average collection period (i.e., 360 days/60 days = 6). It may be noted that provision for doubtful debts has not been considered for computation.

Significance: Average collection period indicates the quality of debtors by measuring the rapidity or slowness in the collection process. A shorter collection period implies prompt payment by debtors, while longer period implies a too liberal and inefficient credit collection performance. In order to measure the efficiency of the credit collection department this should be compared with the average of the industry. It should be neither too liberal nor too restrictive. When a liberal credit policy may result in more bad debts and over-investment in receivables, a restrictive policy may result in lower sales and resultant lower profits. It is very difficult to establish a standard collection period since it depends on a number of factors such as the seasonal character of the business, nature of industry, credit policy of the firm, etc. However, it is a good supplementary check to be used for judging the adequacy of current ratio.

Creditors Turnover Ratio

This ratio is similar to Receivables Turnover Ratio. It compares the Accounts Payable with the total credit purchases. It signifies the credit period enjoyed by the firm in paying creditors. Accounts Payable include both sundry creditors and bills payable (B/P). It is calculated as follows:

$$\text{Creditors Turnover Ratio} = \frac{\text{Net Credit Purchases}}{\text{Average Creditors + B/P}}$$

$$\text{Average Payments Period} = \frac{\text{Average Creditors + Average B/P}}{\text{Monthly or Daily Purchases}}$$

$$\text{Where Monthly or Daily Purchases} = \frac{\text{Total Credit Purchases}}{12 \text{ months or } 360/365 \text{ days}}$$

Alternatively

$$\text{Average Payment Period} = \frac{\text{Months or Days in a year}}{\text{Creditors Turnover Ratio}}$$

Example 4

From the following particulars, compute the Creditors Turnover Ratio:

Total Purchases during the year 2002	Rs. 3,00,000
Total cash purchases during the year	60,000
Creditors on 1.1.2002	40,000
Creditors on 31.12.2002	60,000
Bills Payable on 1.1.2002	7,500
Bills Payable on 31.12.2002	12,500

Solution

Total Credit Purchases = Rs.3,00,000 – 60,000 = Rs.2,40,000

Average creditors = Rs.40,000 + 60,000/2 = Rs.50,000

Average B/P = Rs.7,500 + 12,500/2 = Rs.10,000

$$\text{Creditors Turnover Ratio} = \frac{\text{Rs.}2,40,000}{\text{Rs.}60,000} = 4 \text{ times}$$

$$\text{Average Payment Period} = \frac{\text{Rs.}60,000}{\text{Rs.}20,000} = 3 \text{ months}$$

$$\text{When average credit purchases} = \frac{\text{Rs.}2,40,000}{12} = \text{Rs.}20,000$$

Significance: A high creditors turnover ratio signifies that the creditors are being paid promptly thus boosting up the credit worthiness of the firm. A very low ratio may signify that the firm is not taking full advantage of credit facilities allowed by the creditors.

Inventory Turnover Ratio - Meaning

Inventory Turnover Ratio is a ratio that establishes the relationship between Cost of Sales and Average Inventory. It is also known as Stock Turnover Ratio. This ratio indicates whether the investment in inventory is within proper limit or not. Besides being an index of liquidity of a firm showing the rate at which inventories are converted into sales and then into cash, this ratio helps the finance manager to evaluate the inventory policy.

Components: Average inventory and Cost of goods sold are the constituents of the ratio. When monthly inventory figures are available, the average inventory is calculated by taking the inventory level at the opening date plus inventory levels at the end of each month, adding them up and then dividing by thirteen. If the monthly figures are not available, then adding could derive the average inventory stock levels at the opening and closing dates and dividing by two. As regards sales, the ratio is best expressed when the average inventory is compared with the cost of goods sold. However, when cost of goods is not known, the ratio of net sales (sales less returns) to average inventory may be used as substitute. Some firms, like departmental stores, which value inventories at selling price under retail method, may compute this ratio comparing net sales to average inventory at selling prices.

Formulae: Stock Turnover Ratio can be calculated by employing any one of the following formulae:

(a) $\dfrac{\text{Cost of goods sold}}{\text{Average inventory at cost}}$

(b) $\frac{\text{Net Sales}}{\text{Average inventory at cost}}$

(c) $\frac{\text{Net Sales}}{\text{Average inventory at selling price}}$

(d) $\frac{\text{Number of sold}}{\text{Average number of units in stock}}$

To be more realistic the ratio should be calculated using the same units as numerator and denominator. Accordingly, the first (both in terms of cost) and third (both at selling price) formulae may be considered more logical. However, the second one may be used where the cost of goods is not known. The fourth formula is useful mainly to eliminate the effect of changing prices.

When the inventory consists of more kinds of items such as raw materials, work in process and finished goods, it is useful to break up the inventory turnover ratio into its main constituent parts to bring out the efficiency or inefficiency at various points. In such cases, the inventory turnover ratio and its constituent parts may be calculated as follows:

$$\text{Inventory Turnover Ratio (Main Ratio)} = \frac{\text{Cost of good sold during the year}}{\text{Average inventory at cost}}$$

Note: Average inventory is calculated by taking the stock levels of finished goods, raw materials, and work in process at the opening and closing dates.

$$\text{Raw Materials Turnover Ratio} = \frac{\text{Materials consumed}}{\text{Average Stock of raw materials}}$$

$$\text{Work – in Process Ratio} = \frac{\text{Cost of completed work}}{\text{Average Work in process}}$$

$$\text{Finished Goods Turnover Ratio} = \frac{\text{Cost of goods sold}}{\text{Average stock of finished goods}}$$

Example 5

From the following particulars calculate Stock Turnover Ratio:

Opening stock of finished goods	Rs. 40,000
Purchases	Rs. 1,20,000
Carriage on purchases	10,000
Sales	2,00,000
Closing sock of finished goods	30,000

Solution

$$\text{Stock Turnover Ratio} = \frac{\text{Cost of Sales}}{\text{Average Stock}}$$

Average Stock = (Opening stock + Closing Stock)/2

= (Rs.40,000 + Rs.30,000)/2 = Rs.35,000

Cost of Sales = Opening Stock + Purchases + Carriage− Closing Stock

= Rs.40,000 + 1,20,000 + 10,000 − 30,000 = Rs.1,40,000

$$\text{Stock Turnover Ratio} = \frac{\text{Rs.1,40,000}}{35{,}000} = 4.00 \text{ times}$$

Significance: Inventory Turnover Ratio is an effective tool to measure the liquidity of inventory and thereby to avoid any danger of overstocking as a prelude to the efficient utilization of a firm's resources. While a high Inventory Turnover Ratio indicates brisk sales, a low turnover ratio may reflect dull business, over -investment in inventory, accumulation of huge stocks, etc. However, it should be remembered that these ratios, standing by themselves, mean absolutely nothing. Hence, for a meaningful analysis, they should be compared with similar ratios in the previous period, or with the ratio of other similar firms. It is very difficult to establish standards for this ratio because it will differ from industry to industry. It is also an index of profitability, where a high ratio signifies more profit; a low ratio signifies low profit. Sometimes a high inventory turnover ratio may not be accompanied by relatively high profits or profits may be sacrificed to push up sales volume by reducing selling price. Similarly a high turnover ratio may be due to under-investment in inventories.

Precautions: The interpretation of inventory turnover ratio should always be done keeping in view the complex circumstances, which have a bearing upon the formulation of inventory policies. When ratios fall out of standards, the reasons for such results should be ascertained, and then conclusions can be arrived at. The following factors may be given due consideration while using the inventory turnover ratio:

Price trends: Increasing or decreasing prices will have their influence on inventories.

Volume of business: An increasing trend in the volume of business may necessitate large inventories, and vice versa.

Supply Conditions: Scarcity conditions may compel firms to pile up stocks for future requirements.

Seasonal conditions: The amount of inventory may differ between seasons. Hence, the nature of season, i.e., slack season or busy season to which the inventory value belongs, should be duly considered.

Cash Turnover Ratio

This ratio relates the average cash and bank balances to the total cash and cheque payments. It will indicate whether the cash and bank balances are in tune with the actual payments.

Formula

$$\text{Cash Turnover Ratio} = \frac{\text{Total cash and cheque payments}}{\text{Average cash and bank balances}}$$

Significance: This ratio measures the efficiency of cash management. A high ratio may indicate that the cash and bank balances kept are unduly low, while a low ratio may indicate that the balances are unduly high, which signifies inefficiency of cash management. Establishing a standard is very difficult as it will be a matter for the management to decide about proper cash and bank balances, considering possible future requirements, which may vary from time to time, and from business to business.

8.9. Significance of Analysis of Profitability or Profitability Ratios

Profitability is a measure of efficiency and control. It indicates the efficiency or effectiveness with which the operations of the business are carried on. Poor operational performance may result in poor sales and, therefore, low profits. Low profitability may be due to lack of control over expenses resulting in low profits. Profitability Ratios are employed by management in order to assess how efficiently they carry on business operations. Profitability is the main base for liquidity as well as solvency. Creditors, banks, and financial institutions are interested in profitability ratios since they indicate liquidity or capacity of the business to meet interest obligations, and regular and improved profits to enhance the long-term solvency position of the business. Owners are interested in profitability for they indicate the growth of and also the rate of return on their investments. The amount and rate of profits earned depend on the quantum of investment committed. Hence, the profitability ratios are calculated relating the profits either to sales or to investments.

8.10. Principal Profitability Ratios

The profitability ratios are calculated by relating profits either to sales or investments. Profitability ratios based on sales are as follows:

Gross Profit Ratio (G.P.Ratio)

Meaning: G P Ratio is the ratio of gross profit to net sales expressed as a percentage. It expresses the relationship between gross profit margin and sales. The basic components are gross profit and sales. Net Sales means total sales minus sales returns. Gross profit would be the difference between net sales and cost of goods sold. Cost of goods sold in the case of a trading concern would be equal to opening stock plus purchases and all direct expenses relating to purchases (i.e., all expenses charged to trading a/c) minus closing stock. In the case of manufacturing concerns, it would be equal to opening stock plus cost of production minus closing stock.

Formula

$$\text{Gross Profit Ratio} = \frac{\text{Gross Profit}}{\text{Net Sales}} \times 100$$

Example 6

From the following particulars, calculate G P Ratio.

Opening Stock	Rs. 25,000
Purchases	80,000
Closing Stock	35,000
Purchase Returns	2,000
Sales	1,05,000
Sales Returns	5,000

Solution

Net sales = Sales-Sales Returns

= Rs.1,05,000 – 5,000 = 1,00,000

Coat of goods sold = Opening Stock + Purchases less returns– Closing Stock

= Rs.25,000 + 80,000 – 2,000 – 35,000 = Rs.68,000

Gross Profit = Net Sales - Cost of goods sold Rs.1,00,000 – 68,000 = Rs.32,000.

=

$$\text{Gross Profit Ratio} = \frac{\text{GrossProfit}}{\text{Net Sales}} \times 100$$

$$\text{Gross Profit} = \frac{\text{Rs.}32{,}000}{\text{Rs.}1{,}00{,}000} \times 100 = 32\%$$

Significance: G P Ratio may indicate as to what extent the selling prices of goods per unit may be reduced without incurring losses on operations. It is useful to ascertain whether the average of the mark up on the goods sold is maintained. There is no standard G P Ratio for evaluation. Trend observed may be used for the analysis. However, the gross profit earned should be sufficient to recover all operating expenses and to build up reserves after paying all fixed interest charges and dividends.

Enumerate the factors that influence the Gross Profit Ratio

It should be observed that an increase in G P ratio might be due to the following factors:

(a) Increase in the selling price of goods sold without any corresponding increase in the cost of goods sold.

(b) Decrease in cost of goods sold without corresponding decrease in selling price.

(c) Omission of purchase invoices from accounts.

(d) Under-valuation of opening stock or over-valuation of closing stock.

On the other hand, the decrease in the G P Ratio may be due to the following factors:

(a) Decrease in the selling price of goods sold without corresponding decrease in cost of goods sold.

(b) Increase in cost of goods sold without any increase in selling price.

(c) Unfavorable purchasing or mark-up policies

(d) Inability of management to improve sales volume, or omission of sales

(e) Over-valuation of opening stock or under-valuation of closing stock

Hence, an analysis of GP margin should be carried out in the light information relating to purchasing, mark-ups and markdowns, credit and collections as well as merchandising policies. However, these items of information may not be easily available to the external analyst.

Net Profit Ratio (N P Ratio)

This is the ratio of net income or profit after taxes to net sales. Net Profit as used here, is the balance of Profit and Loss Account, which is arrived at after considering all non-operating income such as interest on investments, dividends received, etc., and all non-operating expenses like loss on sale of investments, provision for contingent liabilities, etc.

Formula

$$\text{Net Profit Ratio} = \frac{\text{Net Profit}}{\text{Net Sales}} \times 100$$

This is used as a measure of overall profitability and is useful to the owners. It is both an index of efficiency as well as profitability when used along with GP Ratio and Operating Ratio.

Operating Ratio (O R Ratio)

This is the ratio of operating cost to net sales. The term 'operating cost' refers to cost of goods sold plus operating expenses. This is closely related to the ratio of operating profit to net sales. For example, if the operating ratio is 80%, then the operating profit ratio would be 20% (i.e., 1 - operating cost ratio).

Components: The main items are operating cost and net sales. Operating expenses normally include the following items:

(a) Office and administrative expenses;

(b) Selling and distribution expenses.

Financial charges such as interest, provision for taxation, etc., are generally excluded from operating expenses.

Formula

$$\text{Operating Ratio} = \frac{\text{Operating Cost}}{\text{Net Sales}} \times 100$$

An alternative form of this ratio may be expressed as follows:

$$\text{Operating Profit Ratio} = \frac{\text{Operating Profit (Net Sales} - \text{Operating Cost)}}{\text{Net Sales}} \times 100$$

Computation of any one of these two would be adequate, since the other one can be found out by deducting the first one from 100.

Example 7

Compute the Operating Ratio from the following particulars:

Total sales	Rs.2,65,000
Sales Returns	15,000
Gross Profit Ratio	30%
Administrative expenses	15,000
Selling & Distribution expenses	10,000

Solution

Cost of goods sold = Net Sales – Gross Profit

Net Sales = Total sales – Returns = Rs.2,65,000 – 15,000 = Rs.2,50,000

Gross Profit = Net sales × GP Ratio = Rs.2,50,000 × 30% = Rs.75,000

Cost of goods sold = Rs.2,50,000 – 75,000 = Rs.1,75,000

Operating Cost = Cost of goods sold plus operating expenses

= Rs.1,75,000 + 15,000 + 10,000 = Rs.2,00,000

$$\text{Operating Ratio} = \frac{\text{Operating Cost}}{\text{Net Sales}} \times 100$$

$$\text{Operating Ratio} = \frac{\text{Rs.2,00,000}}{\text{Rs.2,50,000}} \times 100 = 80\%$$

Significance: This ratio indicates the operational efficiency with which the business is being carried on. It shows the percentage of net sales that is absorbed by the cost of goods sold and operating expenses. Hence, the lower the operating ratio, the higher will be the operating profit. While the ratio serves as an index of overall efficiency, its usefulness is limited by a number of financial and extraordinary factors. While interpreting the ratio, it is important to note that changing management decisions may create possible variations in expenses from year to year, or company to company. An operating ratio ranging between 75% and 85% is generally considered as standard for manufacturing concerns.

It is not necessary that the management should be concerned only when the operating ratio rises. If the operating ratio falls, while the selling price per unit remains the same, it may be the sum total of efficiency in some departments, and inefficiency in others. A dynamic management should be interested in making a full analysis. It is therefore necessary to examine each of the individual components of the operating ratio into various expenses ratios.

Expenses Ratios

These ratios supplement the information given by the operating ratio. Some of the important expense ratios are as follows:

$$\text{Factory Expenses Ratio} = \frac{\text{Factory Expenses}}{\text{Net Sales}} \times 100$$

$$\text{Administrative Expenses Ratio} = \frac{\text{Administrative Expenses}}{\text{Net Sales}} \times 100$$

$$\text{Selling Expenses Ratio} = \frac{\text{Selling Expenses Ratio}}{\text{Net Sales}} \times 100$$

Return on Capital employed - Meaning

The prime objective of making investments in any business is to obtain satisfactory return on capital invested. Hence, the return on capital employed is used as a measure of success of a business in realizing this objective. This ratio is also known as Return on Investment (ROI). It is an overall profitability ratio. It indicates the percentage of return on the capital employed in the business and it can be used to show the efficiency of the business as a whole.

Formula

$$\text{Return on Capital employed} = \frac{\text{Operating Profit}}{\text{Average Capital employed}} \times 100$$

Components: Capital employed and operating profits are the main items. Capital employed may be defined in a number of ways. However, two widely accepted definitions are 'gross capital employed' and 'net capital employed'. Gross capital employed usually means the assets used in the business, while net capital employed refers to total assets minus current liabilities. On the other hand, it refers to the total of capital, capital reserves, revenue reserves (including Profit and Loss a/c balance), debentures and long-term loans.

Computation of Capital Employed

It may be computed from the asset side as well as from the liabilities side. If it is computed from the asset side, it will comprise

(a) **Fixed assets:** Land and Buildings, Plant and Machinery, Furniture and Fittings, and Motor Vehicles, etc.

(b) **Investments made in the business**

(c) **Current Assets:** Inventories, Book Debts less provision for bad and doubtful debts, Bills Receivable, Bank, and Cash, etc.

Less Current Liabilities: Sundry Creditors, Bills Payable, Bank overdraft, Outstanding expenses, etc.

Gross Capital employed = Fixed Assets + Investments+ CurrentAssets

Net Capital employed = Fixed Assets + Investments + Working Capital (Current Assets minus Current Liabilities)

Alternatively, if it is calculated from the liabilities side it will include the following items:

Share Capital: Equity and Preference Share Capital (issued capital)

Reserve and Surplus: Capital Reserve, General Reserves, P&L A/C balance

Debentures

Other Long-term loans

What precautions should be taken, while computing Capital employed?

(a) The valuation of fixed assets may be done at their replacement cost. The current market prices may be ascertained either by reference to reliable published index numbers, or on valuation of experts. At the same time the provision for depreciation should also be readjusted.

(b) All idle assets should be excluded from the computation. However, standby plant and equipment required for normal working may be included.

(c) All intangible assets like goodwill, patents and trademarks unless they have potential sales value and all fictitious assets like preliminary expenses, discount on issue of shares, etc., should be excluded.

(d) All investments made outside the business should be excluded.

(e) All current assets should be properly valued. Any excess bank balance, which is more than the normal requirements, should not be considered.

Some people suggest that average capital employed should be used in order to give effect to the capital investment throughout the year. It is argued that the profits earned remain in the business throughout the year and are distributed by way of dividends only at the end of the year. Average capital employed may be calculated by two methods. Under the first method, only the simple arithmetic mean of the total capital employed at the beginning and at the end of the year is found out. Under the second method, it is calculated by adding half of the profits after tax and interest to the opening capital employed. When net capital employed has been calculated either from the asset side or liabilities side, half of the profits earned during the year may be deducted from the figure so computed in order to arrive at 'average capital employed'.

Operating profit used for the computation of return on capital employed should be the profits earned by such capital. Hence, the net profit should be adjusted, if necessary, for obtaining the true operating profit with the following items:

(a) Any abnormal and non-recurring losses or gains,

(b) Income from investments made outside the business,

(c) Depreciation based on the replacement cost of the asset,

(d) Interest on long-term loans and debentures should be added back.

(e) Profits before the payment of income tax

Example 8

From the following financial statements, calculate Return on Capital employed.

Profit and Loss Account for the year ended 31-12-2002

	Rs.		Rs.
To Cost of goods sold	1,50,000	By Sales	2,50,000
To Interest on debentures	5,000	By Income from investment	5,000
To Provision for Taxation	50,000		
To Net Profit c/d	50,000		
	2,55,000		2,55,000

Balance Sheet as on 31-12-2002

Liabilities	Rs.	Assets	Rs.
Share Capital:		Fixed Assets	2,25,000
Preference	50,000	Investments in Govt. Bonds	50,000
Equity	1,00,000	Current Assts	75,000
Reserves	50,000		
P & L A/C	50,000		
10% Debentures	50,000		
Provision for Taxation	50,000		
	3,50,000		3,50,000

Solution

$$\text{Return on Capital employed} = \frac{\text{Operating Profit}}{\text{Average Capital employed}} \times 100$$

Operating

Profit = Net Profit before interest and tax minus income from investments

= Rs.50,000 + 5,000 + 50,000 − 5,000 = Rs.1,00,000

Capital employed = Fixed Assets + Current Assets − Provision for Taxation

= Rs.2,25,000 + 75,000 − 50,000 = Rs.2,50,000

OR

= Share capital + Reserves + P & L a/c + Debentures − Government Bonds

= Rs.1,50,000 + 50,000 + 50,000 + 50,000 −50,000

= Rs.2,50,000

Average Capital employed

= Capital employed − 1/2 (Profits earned during the year)

= Rs.2,50,000 − 25,000 = Rs.2,25,000

$$\text{Return On Capital employed} = \frac{\text{Rs.}1,00,000}{\text{Rs.}2,25,000} \times 100 = \frac{400}{9}$$

$$= 44.4\% \text{ (app.)}$$

OR

Return on Closing Capital employed

$$= \frac{\text{Rs.}1,00,000}{\text{Rs.}2,50,000} \times 100 = 40\%$$

Significance: Return on Capital employed is considered to be the best measure of profitability in order to assess the overall performance of the business satisfactorily. It is commonly used as a basis for various managerial decisions since it relates to the benefits obtained in the form of income with the sacrifice made in the form of capital invested.

A starting point in budgeting and management planning is the determination of a minimum rate of return on capital invested. All business decisions should result in a reasonable (minimum) return. Investments, which generate rates lower than this minimum rate of return, are rejected. However, it is very difficult to set a standard rate of return on capital employed as a number of factors such as business risk, the type of industry, inflation, changes in economic conditions, etc., may influence such a rate. Different views prevail with regard to standard rate. Bank rate, discount rates of gilt-edged securities or some opportunity rate are some of the suggested rates as the norm for this ratio. However, it is left to the discretion of management to set some rate against which they are to compare the actual result with a view to measuring their efficiency, or the overall performance of the business. This ratio could be supplemented with a number of ratios depending upon the purpose for which it is computed.

8.11. Enumerate the advantages of the concept of "Return on Capital employed".

(a) It is the only measure, which can be said to show satisfactorily the benefits being obtained for the sacrifice involved, the latter being represented by capital invested.

(b) It allows external comparisons to be made. The progress of one company or companies may be compared with that of other companies.

(c) It is an effective tool for making an internal comparison in respect of different divisions or departments of a company. It may be used as a instrument of control by comparing the relative profitability of different products.

(d) It enables the management to make efficient capital budgeting decisions. It can become an integral part of the budgetary control system.

(e) It gives ideas for analysis and decisions to bring about effective changes in the financial policies. For example, there should be no borrowing when the rate of interest is higher than the rate of return.

(f) If management ensures that an adequate return on capital invested is earned, then many direct benefits such as regular and satisfactory dividends to shareholders, adequate strength to face competition, etc., may accrue to the business concern.

Return on Shareholders' Investment

It is the ratio of net profit to shareholders' investment. It is also called 'Return on Proprietors' funds or capital employed. This ratio establishes the profitability from the shareholders' point of view.

Formula

$$\text{Return on Shareholders' Funds} = \frac{\text{Net Profit after interest and tax}}{\text{Shareholders' Funds}} \times 100$$

Components: The term 'Net Profit' as used here, means 'Net Income' available for distribution as dividends to shareholders, i.e., income after payment of interest and tax, including net non-operating income (non-operating income minus non-operating expenses). Shareholders' funds include both preference and equity share capital and all reserves and surplus belonging to shareholders.

Significance: This ratio is another effective measure of the profitability of a business. It is one of the most important relationships in financial statement analysis. It is an index to know whether the main objective of the business, i.e., realization of satisfactory net income, has been achieved. It is useful for inter-industry comparisons. But if the comparisons are made between two companies belonging to two different industries, the value of this ratio would be very much limited since the margins and operating costs among industries may vary widely.

Return on Equity capital

This ratio relates the net profits finally available to equity shareholders to the amount of capital invested by them. Alternatively, this ratio could be derived dividing the profits available to equity shareholders by the share capital held by them.

Formula

$$\text{Return on Equity Capital} = \frac{\text{Net Profit} - (\text{Income Tax} + \text{Preference Dividend})}{\text{Equity Share Capital}} \times 100$$

Or

$$\text{Earnings Per Share [EPS]} = \frac{\text{Net Profit} - (\text{Income Tax} + \text{Preference Dividend})}{\text{Number of Equity Shares}}$$

Components: As the profits used for the calculation are the final profits available to equity shareholders as dividends, the preference dividend and taxes are deducted in order to arrive at such profits. Equity share capital would be the total called up value of equity shares.

Example 9

Calculate the EPS or Return on Equity Capital from the following information.

Equity Share Capital (Rs.10 each):	Rs.10,00,000
9% Preference Share Capital (Rs.100 each):	Rs.5,00,000
Taxation rate:	50 percent
Net Profit before tax:	Rs.4,00,000

Solution

$$\text{Return on Equity Capital} = \frac{\text{Net Profit after Tax and Preference divided}}{\text{Equity Share Capital}} \times 100$$

$$= \frac{\text{Rs.}4{,}00{,}000 - (\text{Rs.}2{,}00{,}000 + 45{,}000)}{\text{Rs.}10{,}00{,}000} \times 100$$

$$= \frac{\text{Rs.}1{,}55{,}000}{\text{Rs.}10{,}00{,}000} \times 100 = 15.50\%$$

$$\text{Earnings per Share (EPS)} = \frac{\text{Net Profit after tax and preference dividend}}{\text{Number of Equity Shares}}$$

$$EPS = \frac{Rs.1,55,000}{1,00,000} = Rs.1.55 \text{ per share}$$

Significance: This ratio indicates what percentage of profits earned are enjoyed by equity shareholders. Return on equity capital or EPS helps to determine the market price of equity share of the company. By comparing the ratios of other companies, it will indicate whether the capital is effectively used or not.

Return on Total Resources or Total Assets

This ratio relates the net profit after tax and interest to the total productive assets used. This ratio is computed to find out the productivity of the total assets.

Formula

$$\text{Return on Total Assets} = \frac{\text{Net Profit after tax and interest}}{\text{Total Assets} - \text{Fictitious Assets}} \times 100$$

8.12. What is Du Pont Control Chart?

The Du Pont Control Chart is called as such because Du Pont Company of the USA first used it. The various factors affecting the Return on Investment (ROI) are illustrated through this chart. ROI represents the earning power of the business. It depends on two ratios: (a) Net Profit ratio and (b) Capital Turnover Ratio. A change in any one of the two ratios will change the business earning power (i.e., ROI), and they are affected by many factors. The chart shown below exhibits that ROI is affected by a number of factors.

Any change in these factors will affect the return on capital employed. For example, if the cost of goods sold decreases without any corresponding decrease in selling price, the net profit will increase and therefore, ROI will also increase. Similarly if there is decrease in working capital, the total capital employed will decrease and therefore, in the absence of any decrease in the net profit, ROI will decrease.

The Control Chart

RETURN ON INVESTMENT (ROI)

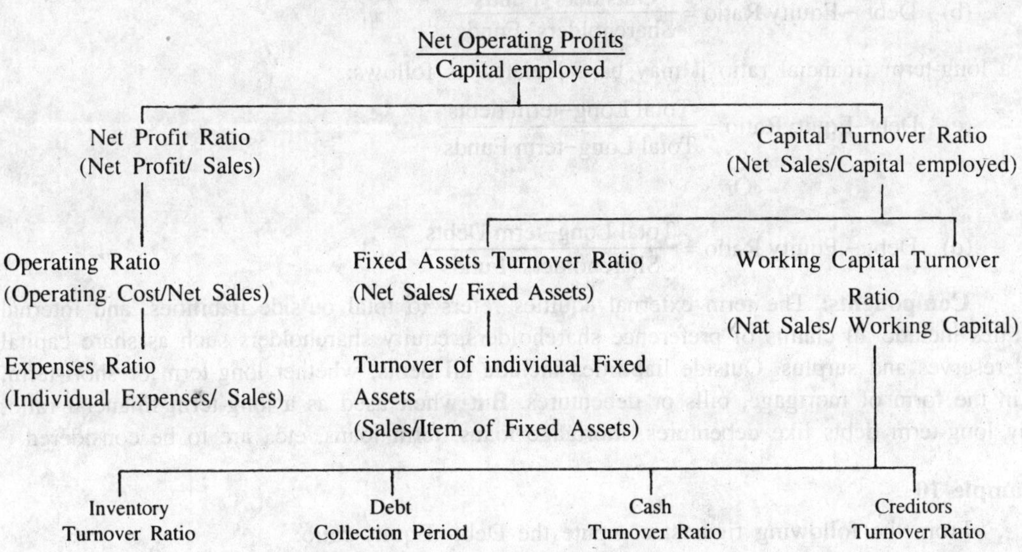

The Du Pont Chart helps management to identify the areas of problems, which affect profit. In other words, management can easily visualize the different forces affecting profits, and profits could be improved either by putting capital into effective use, which will result in higher turnover ratio, or by better sales efforts, which will result in higher profit ratio. The same rate of return could be obtained either by a higher net profit ratio but low turnover ratio, or by a higher turnover ratio but a low net profit ratio.

8.13. What is analysis for solvency? Or How can the solvency position of a business be measured?

Solvency generally refers to the capacity or ability of the business to meet its short-term and long-term obligations. The capacity to pay off the current debts of the company is represented by the liquidity ratios. Liquidity ratios will explain the short-term solvency or financial position of the business. Hence, the solvency refers to the ability to meet the long-term obligations of the business and the ratios used to assess the long-term solvency or financial position of the business is called as solvency ratios. Generally, shareholders, debenture holders, and long-term creditors like financial institutions are interested in these ratios. These ratios are also used to analyze the capital structure of the company. They indicate the pattern of financing, whether the long-term requirements have been met out of long-term funds or not. Some of the important solvency ratios are as follows: Debt- Equity Ratio, Proprietary Ratios, Debt Service Ratio or Interest coverage Ratio, etc.

8.14. Principal Solvency Ratios

Debt-Equity Ratio

Debt-equity Ratio relates all external liabilities to Owners recorded claims. It is also known as 'External-Internal Equity ratio. It is determined to measure the firm's obligations to creditors in relation to the funds invested by owners.

Formula

Generally it is calculated as follows:

(a) $$\text{Debt} - \text{Equity Ratio} = \frac{\text{External Equities}}{\text{Internal Equities}}$$

Or

(b) $$\text{Debt} - \text{Equity Ratio} = \frac{\text{Outsiders' Funds}}{\text{Shareholders' Funds}}$$

As a long-term financial ratio it may be calculated as follows:

(c) $$\text{Debt–EquityRatio} = \frac{\text{Total Long–term debts}}{\text{Total Long–term Funds}}$$

Or

(d) $$\text{Debt} - \text{Equity Ratio} = \frac{\text{Total Long–term Debts}}{\text{Shareholders' Funds}}$$

Components: The term external equities refers to total outside liabilities, and internal equities include all claims of preference shareholders, equity shareholders such as share capital and reserves and surplus. Outside liabilities include all debts, whether long-term or short-term, or in the form of mortgage, bills or debentures. But when used as a long-term financial ratio, only long-term debts like debentures, mortgage loans, term loans, etc., are to be considered.

Example 10

From the following figures, compute the Debt- Equity ratio:

Preference Share Capital	Rs.	3,00,000
Equity Share Capital		11,00,000
Capital Reserve		5,00,000
Profit and Loss account		2,00,000
6% Debentures		5,00,000
Sundry Creditors		2,40,000
Bills Payable		1,20,000
Provision for Taxation		1,80,000
Outstanding Creditors		1,60,000

Solution

Internal Equities = Shareholders' Funds = Rs.21,00,000(1st four items)

External Equities = Creditors' Funds = Rs.12,00,000(Remaining items)

$$\text{Debt} - \text{Equity Ratio} = \frac{\text{External Equities}}{\text{Internal Equities}}$$

$$= \frac{\text{Rs.}12{,}00{,}000}{\text{Rs.}21{,}00{,}000} = 0.57 \text{ or } 4:7$$

This means that the external debts are equal to about 57% of shareholders' funds. This indicates that even if the value of assets decreases by 43%, the creditors will be paid in full. Normally this ratio is expressed as a proportion. It means that for every four rupees worth of the creditors investment, the shareholders have invested seven rupees worth.

Significance: This ratio enables one to ascertain the proportion of shareholders' stake in the business. Excessive liabilities tend to cause insolvency. The ratio indicates the extent of assets 'cushion' available to creditors on liquidation. However, the interpretation of the ratio depends upon the financial and business policy of the company. While the owners try to gain the benefits of maintaining control with limited investment, the creditors would insist that the owners' investment is more in the business. Hence, an acceptable norm for this ratio is considered to be 1:1 (i.e., possessing equal interest in the business by both creditors and owners). Theoretically, if the owners' interest is greater than that of creditors, the financial position is highly solvent. In the analysis of the long-term financial position of business, it enjoys the same importance as the current ratio does in the short-term financial position.

Proprietary Ratio

This is a variant of the debt -equity ratio. This ratio relates the shareholders' funds to total assets. It is calculated by dividing the shareholders' funds by the total tangible assets. This ratio indicates the long-term or the future solvency position of the business.

Formula

$$\text{Proprietary Ratio} = \frac{\text{Shareholders' Funds}}{\text{Total Assets or Total Resources}}$$

Components: Shareholders' funds include preference and equity share capital plus all reserves and surplus items. Total assets include all assets including goodwill. Some authors exclude it from total assets. In that case, the total shareholders' funds are to be divided by total tangible assets. As the total assets are always equal to total liabilities, the total liabilities may also be used as the denominator in the above formula.

Example 11

Using the data given in Example 10, compute Proprietary Ratio.

Shareholders' Funds = Rs.21,00,000

Total Liabilities (Resources) = Rs.33,00,000

$$\text{Proprietary Ratio} = \frac{\text{Rs.21,00,000}}{\text{Rs.33,00,000}} = 0.64 \text{ or } 7:11$$

Interpretation: This ratio explains that out of every Re.1 employed in the business, shareholders' contribution is about 64 paise or 64% of total resources used. The difference between this ratio and 100 per cent represents the ratio of other liabilities to total assets or total liabilities. Accordingly, the creditors' contribution would be the remaining 36 paise.

Significance: This ratio throws light on the general financial strength of the company. It has come to be regarded as a test of the soundness of the capital structure. It is of great importance to creditors since it enables them to find out the proportion of shareholders' funds in the total assets used in the business. While a high proprietary ratio indicates a relatively secure position to the creditors in the event of liquidation, a low proprietary ratio will include greater risk to the creditors.

The Debt-Equity Ratio or Proprietary Ratio may be analyzed further into the following ratios:

(a) Ratio of Fixed Assets to Shareholders' Funds

(b) Ratio of Current Assets to Shareholders' Funds

Fixed Assets to Shareholders' Funds Ratio

This ratio establishes the relationship between fixed assets and shareholders' funds. The purpose of this ratio is to indicate the percentage of Owners' Funds invested in fixed assets. It is calculated as follows:

$$\text{Fixed Assets to Proprietors' Funds} = \frac{\text{Fixed Assets}}{\text{Proprietors' Funds}}$$

The fixed assets are considered at their depreciated book values and the proprietors' funds consist of all the items of internal equities such as preference shareholders' claims and equity shareholders' claims, viz., equity share capital and reserves and surplus. This ratio may be expressed as a percentage or as a proportion.

Example

Suppose the depreciated book value of fixed assets is Rs.36, 000 and proprietors' funds are Rs.48, 000, the relevant ratio will be as follows:

$$\text{Fixed Assets to Proprietors Funds} = \frac{\text{Rs.36,000}}{\text{Rs.48,000}} = 0.75 \text{ or } 0.75:1$$

From the above computation it can be ascertained that 75 percent of the shareholders' funds have been invested in Fixed Assets and 25 percent have been used for working capital purpose. The standard for this ratio may vary from business to business and it may be taken as standard at 65% for industrial undertakings. If the ratio is more than one, it may mean that creditors' obligations have been used to acquire a part of the fixed assets.

Current Assets to Proprietors' Funds Ratio

This ratio establishes the relationship between current assets and shareholders' funds. The purpose of the ratio is to indicate the percentage of shareholders' funds invested in current assets. This may be expressed as a percentage or as a proportion. It is calculated as follows:

$$\text{Current Assets to Shareholders' Funds Ratio} = \frac{\text{Current Assets}}{\text{Proprietors' Funds}}$$

Example: Suppose the value of current assets is Rs.36,000 and the proprietors' funds are Rs.1,80,000, the relevant ratio would be

$$= \frac{\text{Rs.}36{,}000}{1{,}80{,}000} = 0.20$$

This may also be expressed as 20% or 0.2:1. it means that 20% of proprietors' funds have been invested in current assets. Different industries have different norms and therefore, this ratio should be studied carefully taking the history of individual concern into consideration before relying too much on this ratio. For a meaningful analysis, this ratio should be read along with the results given by the Fixed Assets to Proprietors' Funds Ratio.

Debt Service Ratio

This ratio relates fixed interest charges to the income earned by the business. It is also known as Interest Coverage Ratio. It indicates whether the business has earned sufficient profits to pay periodically the interest charges. It is calculated as follows:

$$\text{Interest Coverage Ratio} = \frac{\text{Net Profit before Interest and Tax}}{\text{Fixed Interest Charges}}$$

Example: The operating profit of Excel Ltd. after charging interest and tax is a sum of Rs.1,24,000. The amount of interest charged is Rs.25,000 and the provision made for taxation has been Rs.1,24,000 being 50% of total profits. Calculate the Interest Coverage Ratio.

Solution

$$\text{Interest Coverage Ratio} = \frac{\text{Net Profit before charging interest and tax}}{\text{Fixed Interest charges}}$$

$$\text{Interest Coverage Ratio} = \frac{\text{Rs.}1{,}24{,}000 + 1{,}24{,}000 + 25{,}000}{\text{Rs.}25{,}000}$$

$$= \frac{\text{Rs.}2{,}73{,}000}{25{,}000} = 10.92$$

Sometimes, there may be need to calculate Fixed Charges Cover or Ratio. In that case, the ratio may be calculated as follows:

$$\text{Fixed Charges Cover} = \frac{\text{Net Profit before interest and tax}}{\text{Interest and Preference dividend}}$$

In case, if it is desired to calculate the fixed dividend cover, it may be calculated as follows:

$$\text{Fixed dividend cover} = \frac{\text{Net Profit after interest and tax}}{\text{Preference dividend}}$$

Significance: The Interest Coverage Ratio is very important from the lenders' point of view. It gives an idea of the number of times that the fixed interest charges are covered by earnings. It is an index of financial strength of an enterprise and indicates the margin of safety of the long-term creditors. The standard for this ratio for an industrial company is that the interest charges should be covered by six to seven times. A high ratio assures the lender a regular and periodical interest income. But the weakness of the ratio may create some problems to the financial manager in raising funds from debt sources.

Capital Gearing Ratio

This ratio is closely related to solvency ratios, which is mainly used to analyze the capital structure of a company. The term "capital gearing" or leverage normally refers to the proportion between the fixed interest or dividend bearing funds and non-fixed interest or dividend bearing funds. While the former includes funds supplied by debenture-holders and preference shareholders, the latter would include equity share capital and reserves and surplus. This ratio relates the equity share capital to debentures and preference share capital. It is calculated as follows:

$$\text{Capital Gearing Ratio} = \frac{\text{Equity Share Capital}}{\text{Fixed interest and dividend bearing funds}}$$

Equity Share Capital includes equity capital and all reserves and surplus that belong to equity shareholders. Fixed interest or dividend funds include debentures, preference shares and other long-term loans. It may be noted that the gearing is in inverse ratio to the equity share capital.

Highly geared - low equity share capital

Low geared - high equity share capital

Significance: This ratio reveals the suitability or other of company's capitalization. It is important not only to the company, but also to the prospective investors. It must be carefully planned since it affects the company's capacity to maintain an even distribution policy during difficult trading periods. Furthermore, its immediate effect may be to enable a company to pay higher equity dividends, when there is only narrow margin of profit. But its long-term effect on the efficiency of the company is far-reaching. Distribution policies and the building up of reserves, as well as an even dividend policy are all affected by the company's 'gearing ratio'.

In addition to capital gearing ratio, the following ratios may also be used to analyze the capital structure of the company. These ratios would also throw light to a certain extent on the financial strength of the company.

(a) Total Investments to long-term liabilities

This ratio compares share capital to loan capital. Generally a high proportion of long-term liabilities is risky to any company, which, this ratio enables one to find out.

(b) Current liabilities to Proprietors' Funds

This ratio compares current liabilities to proprietors' funds. This ratio is an index for measuring the amount of funds supplied by proprietors as against those supplied by short-term creditors in the financing of the company.

(c) Reserve to Equity Capital Ratio

This ratio compares reserves to equity capital. It may reveal the company's policy with regard to growth and distribution of dividends. It also indicates the effect of ploughing back of profits on share value.

Computation of Ratios from Financial Statement Information

Illustration 1

ABC Ltd., sells goods on cash and credit terms. The following particulars are extracted from their books of accounts for the calendar year 2002:

Total Gross Sales	Rs. 2,00,000
Cash sales (included as above)	44,000
Sales Returns	12,000
Book Debts as on 31-12- 2002	20,000
Bills Receivables as on 31-12-2002	4,000
Provision for bad debts on 31-12-2002	1,500
Sundry Creditors on 31-12-2002	12,000

Calculate Debtors Turnover Ratio and Average Collection Period.

Solution

Workings

(1) Calculation of Credit sales for 2002

Total sales	Rs.2,00,000
Less: Sales Returns	12,000
Net Sales	Rs.1,88,000
Less: Cash Sales	44,000
Total Credit sales	Rs.1,44,000

(2) Credit Sales per day

$$= \frac{\text{Rs.}1{,}44{,}000}{360} = \text{Rs.}400$$

(a) $$\text{Debtors Turnover Ratio} = \frac{\text{Total Credit Sales}}{\text{Average Receivables}}$$

$$= \frac{\text{Rs.}1{,}44{,}000}{24{,}000} = 6 \text{ times}$$

(b) $$\text{Average Collection Period} = \frac{\text{Total Number of days}}{\text{Debtors Turnover Ratio}}$$

$$= \frac{360}{6} = 60 \text{ days}$$

OR

$$\text{Average Collection Period} = \frac{\text{Total Accounts Receivables}}{(\text{Total Credit Sales}/360)}$$

$$= \frac{\text{Rs.}20000+4000}{(\text{Rs.}1{,}44{,}000/360)} = \frac{\text{Rs.}24000}{400} = 60 \text{ days}$$

Note: (1) It has been assumed that the number of working days in a year is 360.

(2) Information relating to Provision for bad debts and sundry creditors is not relevant for computation.

Illustration 2

From the following details, calculate the current ratio and acid test ratio:

Current assets	Rs.	Current liabilities	Rs.
Stock in trade	77,000	Sundry creditors	23,300
Sundry debtors	47,300	Acceptances	9,460
Cash in hand	6,700	Dividend warrants issued but not	190
Advances (short-term)	13,300	cashed	
Prepaid taxes	700	Provision for Taxation	10,150

Solution

$$\text{Current Ratio} = \frac{\text{Current Assets}}{\text{Current liabilities}}$$

$$= \frac{\text{Rs. } 1,45,000}{\text{Rs. } 43,100} = 3.36$$

$$\text{Acid Test Ratio} = \frac{\text{Liquid Assets}}{\text{Liquid liabilities}}$$

$$= \frac{\text{Rs. } 67,300}{\text{Rs. } 43,100} = 1.56$$

Note

Liquid assets = Current assets − stock and prepaid taxes = 1,45,000 − 77,700 = 67,300.

Liquid liabilities = Current liabilities − Bank overdraft and income received in advance

Illustration 3

The Balance Sheet of Sriram Ltd., as on 31.12.2002 is as follows:

Liabilities	Rs.	Assets	Rs.
Equity Share Capital (shares of Rs.10 each)	5,00,000	Land and Buildings	6,00,000
10% Preference Share Capital (Shares of Rs.00 each)	2,00,000	Plant and Furniture	5,00,000
Reserves and surplus	3,00,000	Stock in trade	2,40,000
12% Debentures (Rs.100 each)	4,00,000	Sundry Debtors	1,95,000
Sundry creditors	1,50,000	Cash in hand	60,000
Bank overdraft	50,000	Prepaid expenses	5,000
	16,00,000		16,00,000

Calculate: (a) Current Ratio (b) Liquid Ratio (c) Debt - Equity Ratio (d) Capital Gearing Ratio (e) Proprietary Ratio

Solution

(a) $$\text{Current Ratio} = \frac{\text{Current Assets}}{\text{Current Liabilities}}$$

$$= \frac{\text{Rs.5,00,000}}{\text{Rs.2,00,000}} = 2.5 \text{ or } 2.5:1$$

(b) $$\text{Liquid Ratio} = \frac{\text{Liquid Assets (Current Assets − Stock + Prepaid Expenses)}}{\text{Liquid Liabilities (Current Liabilities − Bank Overdraft)}}$$

$$= \frac{\text{Rs.}5{,}00{,}000 - (\text{Rs.}2{,}40{,}000 + 5{,}000)}{\text{Rs.}2{,}00{,}000 - \text{Rs.}50{,}000}$$

$$= \frac{\text{Rs.}2{,}55{,}000}{\text{Rs.}1{,}50{,}000} = 1.7 \text{ or } 1.7 : 1$$

(c) Debt – Equity Ratio $= \frac{\text{External Equities or Liabilities}}{\text{Internal Equities}}$

$$= \frac{\text{Rs.}6{,}00{,}000}{\text{Rs.}10{,}00{,}000} = 3 : 5$$

(d) Capital Gearing Ratio $= \frac{\text{Fixed interest/dividend bearing Funds}}{\text{Equity shareholders' Funds}}$

$$= \frac{\text{Rs.}6{,}00{,}000}{\text{Rs.}8{,}00{,}000} = 0.75 : 1$$

(e) Proprietary Ratio $= \frac{\text{Proprietors' Funds}}{\text{Total tangible assets}}$

$$= \frac{\text{Rs.}10{,}00{,}000}{\text{Rs.}16{,}00{,}000} = 5 : 8 \text{ or } 0.625 : 1$$

Illustration 4

From the following Income Statement of Excel Ltd., compute the Profitability Ratios.

Particulars	Rs.	Particulars	Rs.
To Opening Stock	2,00,000	By Sales	16,00,000
To Purchases	12,00,000	By Closing Stock	3,20,000
To Gross Profit c/d	5,20,000		
	19,20,000		19,20,000
To Administration Expenses	1,20,000	By Gross Profit b/d	5,20,000
To Selling Expenses	80,000	By Dividend	4,000
To Finance Expenses	40,000		

Solution

(a) Current Ratio $= \frac{\text{Current Assets}}{\text{Current Liabilities}} = \frac{1{,}34{,}000}{76{,}000} = 1.76$

Current Assets			Current Liabilities	
Drs	42,000		S.Crs	32,000
Less:			Provision for taxation	15,000
Provision	2,000		B/P	29,000
		40,000		
Cash		10,000		
Bank		8,000		
B/R		15,000		
Securities		8,000		
Stock		53,000		
		1,34,000		76,000

To Loss on sale of assets	5,000		
To Net Profit	2,79,000		
	5,24,000		5,24,000

Solution

Computation of Profitability Ratios

(a) $\text{Gross Profit Ratio} = \dfrac{\text{Gross Profit}}{\text{Net Sales}} \times 100$

$= \dfrac{\text{Rs.}5{,}20{,}000}{\text{Rs.}16{,}00{,}000} \times 100 = 32.5\%$

(b) $\text{Net Profit Ratio} = \dfrac{\text{Net Profit}}{\text{Net Sales}} \times 100$

$= \dfrac{\text{Rs.}2{,}79{,}000}{\text{Rs.}16{,}00{,}000} \times 100 = 17.44\%$

(c) $\text{Operating Ratio} = \dfrac{\text{Operating Cost}}{\text{Net Sales}} \times 100$

$= \dfrac{\text{Rs.}10{,}80{,}000 + 2{,}00{,}000}{\text{Rs.}16{,}00{,}000} \times 100 = 80\%$

Note: (1) Operating Cost = Cost of goods sold + operating expenses

(2) Cost of Goods sold = Opening Stock + Purchases – Closing tock

(3) Operating Expenses = Office and administration expenses + Selling & Distribution exps.

(d) Operating Profit Ratio = 1 – Operating Cost Ratio

$= 1 - 80\% = 20\%$

(e) $\text{Non–operating Expenses Ratio} = \dfrac{\text{Non – operating Expenses}}{\text{Net Sales}} \times 100$

$= \dfrac{\text{Rs.}5{,}000 + 40{,}000}{\text{Rs.}16{,}00{,}000} \times 100 = 2.81\%$

Non-operating expenses = Loss on sale of assets + Finance expenses.

Illustration 5

From the following particulars extracted from the financial statement of ABC & Co., compute (a) Current Ratio (b) Liquid Ratio (c) Inventory Turnover Ratio (d) Debtors Turnover Ratio and (e) creditors Turnover Ratio

	Rs.		Rs.
Opening stock	47,000	Sundry Debtors	42,000
Closing stock	53,000	Cash	10,000
Sales less returns	2,52,000	Bank	8,000
Provision for bad debts	2,000	Bills Receivable	15,000
Sundry Creditors	32,000	Provision for Taxation	15,000
Loose tools	4,000	Bills payable	29,000
Purchases	1,80,000	Marketable securities	8,000

(b) $\text{Liquid Ratio} = \dfrac{\text{Liquid Assets}}{\text{Liquid Liabilities}} = \dfrac{\text{Current Assets} - \text{Stock}}{\text{Liquid Liabilities}}$

$$\text{Liquid Ratio} = \frac{\text{Rs. } 1{,}34{,}000 - 53{,}000}{76{,}000}$$

$$= \frac{81{,}000}{76{,}000} = 1.07 \text{ (app.)}$$

(c) $\text{Inventory Turnover Ratio} = \dfrac{\text{Net Sales}}{\text{Average Inventory}}$

$$= \frac{\text{Rs. } 2{,}52{,}000}{\text{Rs. } 50{,}000} = 5.04 \text{ times}$$

$$\text{Average Inventory} = \frac{\text{Opening stock} + \text{closing stock}}{2}$$

$$= \frac{\text{Rs. } 47{,}000 + 53{,}000}{2} = 50{,}000$$

(d) $\text{Debtors Turnover Ratio} = \dfrac{\text{Total Receivables}}{\text{Credit sales per day}}$

$$\text{Credit sales per day} = \frac{\text{Total Sales}}{360} = \frac{\text{Rs. } 2{,}52{,}000}{360} = \text{Rs. } 700$$

$$\text{Debtors Turnover Ratio} = \frac{\text{Rs. } 42{,}000 + \text{Rs. } 15{,}000}{\text{Rs. } 700}$$

$$= \frac{57{,}000}{700} = 82 \text{ days}$$

Alternatively,

$$\text{Debtors Turnover Ratio} = \frac{\text{Total sales}}{\text{Average Receivables}}$$

$$= \frac{\text{Rs. } 2{,}52{,}000}{\text{Rs. } 57{,}000} = 4.42$$

$$\text{Average collection period} = \frac{360 \text{ days}}{4.42} = 82 \text{ days}$$

(e) $\text{Creditors Turnover Ratio} = \dfrac{\text{Total Accounts payable}}{\text{Credit purchases per day}}$

$$\text{Credit purchases per day} = \frac{\text{Total purchases}}{360 \text{ days}}$$

$$= \frac{\text{Rs. } 1{,}80{,}000}{360} = \text{Rs. } 500$$

$$\text{Creditors Turnover Ratio} = \frac{\text{Rs. } 32{,}000 + \text{Rs. } 29{,}000}{\text{Rs. } 500}$$

$$= \frac{\text{Rs. } 61{,}000}{500} = 122 \text{ days}$$

Illustration 6

The Balance Sheet Anish & Co., as on 31-12-2002 is as follows:

Balance Sheet

Liabilities	Rs.	Assets	Rs.	Rs.
Share capital		Fixed Assets		
10,000, 10% Preference share of Rs. 10 each	1,00,000	Land & Building		2,00,000
		Plant & Machinery	3,60,000	
20,000 Ordinary shares		*Less* depreciation	1,20,000	
of Rs. 10 each	2,00,000			2,40,000
Share premium	50,000	Motor Vehicles	50,000	
Reserves	1,70,000	*Less* depreciation	30,000	
Dividend Equalisation fund	25,000			20,000
10% Debentures	25,000	Investments		50,000
Creditors	50,000			
Bank Overdraft	20,000	*Current Assets:*		
Provision for taxation	30,000	Stock		70,000
		Debtors	80,000	
		Less provision	2,000	
				78,000
		Cash		2,000
		Deferred Advertisement expenditure		10,000
	6,70,000			6,70,000

Calculate the value of capital employed in the business, considering the following information:

(a) Freehold land and buildings are valued at Rs. 2,60,000

(b) Plant and Machinery has a replacement cost of Rs. 4,50,000

Depreciation on replacement cost would amount to Rs. 1,50,000

(c) Motor vehicles would cost Rs. 60,000 to replace. Depreciation on replacement cost would amount to Rs. 36,000.

(d) Investments have been analysed to show the following:

Investment outside the business: Rs. 40,000

Investment inside the business: Rs. 10,000

(e) Included in the stock valuation are items now considered obsolete, which amount to Rs. 2,000

Solution

Value of Capital Employed as on 31-12-2002

Fixed Assets	Rs.	Rs.
Land and Buildings		2,60,000
Plant & Machinery	4,50,000	

Less depreciation		1,50,000	3,00,000
Motor vehicles		60,000	
Less Depreciation		36,000	
			24,000
Investment made inside the business			10,000
Current Assets			
Stock		68,000	
Debtors		78,000	
Cash		2,000	
		1,48,000	
Less Current liabilities			
Creditors	50,000		
Overdraft	20,000		
Taxation	30,000	1,00,000	48,000
			6,42,000

Alternative Method

Value of Capital Employed as on 31-12-2000

Issued Capital-Preference	1,00,000		
Equity	2,00,000		3,00,000
Share premium A/c			50,000
Reserves			1,70,000
Dividend Equalisation Fund			25,000
10% Debentures			25,000
Difference on revaluation:			
Add: Land and Buildings		60,000	
Plant and Machinery		60,000	
Motor vehicles		4,000	
Stock		(2,000)	
Less: Assets not included in		1,22,000	
Capital employed:			
Investment outside the business		40,000	
Deferred advertising cost		10,000	72,000
			6,42,000

Illustration 7

Redraft the following financial statements for the purpose of analysis and then compute the following ratios:

(a) Gross Profit ratio
(b) Return on Capital Employed
(c) Operating Cost Ratio
(d) Net Profit Ratio
(e) Current Ratio
(f) Liquid Ratio
(g) Stock turnover Ratio

Profit and Loss Account

Dr. Cr.

	Rs.		Rs.
To Opening Stock:		By Sales	2,00,000
Raw Materials	10,000	Closing stock:	
Finished Goods	20,000	Raw Materials	30,000
To Purchase of		Finished goods	20,000
Raw Materials	60,000	Profit on sale,	
To Wages	40,000	Shares	10,000
To factory expenses	20,000		
To Administration expenses	10,000		
To Selling and distribution expenses	10,000		
To Interest on debentures	2,000		
To Loss on sale of plant	13,000		
To Net Profit	75,000		
	2,60,000		2,60,000

Balance Sheet

Liabilities	Rs.	Assets	Rs.
Share capital		Fixed Assets	50,000
Equity shares		Stock of raw	
(Rs. 10/- each)	20,000	Materials	30,000
Preference shares		Stock of finished,	
(Rs. 10/- each)	20,000	Goods	20,000
Reserves	20,000	Books debts	20,000
5% Debentures	40,000	Cash	15,000
Creditors	20,000		
Bills payable	10,000		
Bank overdraft	5,000		
	1,35,000		1,35,000

Solution

Income Statement

		Rs.	Rs.	Rs.
	Sales			2,00,000
Less:	Cost of goods sold			
	Raw materials consumed			
	Opening stock	10,000		
Add:	Purchases	60,000		
		70,000		
Less:	closing stock	30,000	40,000	
	Wages		40,000	
	Factory expenses		20,000	
	Cost of production		1,00,000	
Add:	Opening stock of finished goods		20,000	
			1,20,000	
Less:	Closing stock of finished goods		20,000	1,00,000
	Gross profit			1,00,000
Less:	Operating expenses:			
	Administration expenses	10,000		
	Selling and distribution, Expenses	10,000		20,000
	Net operating profit			80,000
Add:	Non-trading income:			
	Profit on sale of shares			10,000
Less:	Non-trading expenses or losses			90,000
	Loss on sale of plant			13,000
	Net profit before tax and Interest			77,000
Less:	Debenture interest			2,000
	Net profit before tax			75,000

Balance Sheet

Cash balance		15,000
Book debts		20,000
Liquid assets		35,000
Stock raw materials	30,000	
Finished goods	20,000	50,000
Current assets		85,000

Less current liabilities		
Sundry creditors	20,000	
B/P	10,000	
Liquid liabilities	30,000	
Bank overdraft	5,000	35,000
Working capital		50,000
Add fixed assets		50,000
Capital employed		1,00,000
Less 5% Debentures		40,000
Shareholders' funds		60,000
Less Preference share capital		20,000
Equity shareholders net worth		40,000
Represented by		
Equity share capital		20,000
Reserves		20,000

Calculation of Ratios

$$\text{Gross Profit Ratio} = \frac{\text{Gross Profit}}{\text{Sales}} \times 100$$

$$= \frac{\text{Rs. } 1,00,000}{\text{Rs. } 2,00,000} \times 100 = 50\%$$

$$\text{Net Profit Ratio} = \frac{\text{Net Profit}}{\text{Sales}} \times 100$$

$$= \frac{\text{Rs. } 75,000}{\text{Rs. } 2,00,000} \times 100 = 37.5\%$$

$$\text{Operating Ratio} = \frac{\text{Operating Cost}}{\text{Sales}} \times 100$$

$$= \frac{\text{Rs. } 1,00,000 + \text{Rs. } 20,000}{\text{Rs. } 2,00,000} \times 100$$

$$= \frac{\text{Rs. } 1,20,000}{\text{Rs. } 2,00,000} \times 100 = 60\%$$

Alternatively,

$$\text{Operating Profit Ratio} = \frac{\text{Operating Profit}}{\text{Sales}} \times 100$$

$$= \frac{\text{Rs. } 80,000}{\text{Rs. } 2,00,000} \times 100 = 40\%$$

$$\text{Return on Capital employed} = \frac{\text{Operating Profit}}{\text{Capital employed}} \times 100$$

$$= \frac{\text{Rs. } 80,000}{\text{Rs. } 1,00,000} \times 100 = 80\%$$

$$\text{Current Ratio} = \frac{\text{Current Assets}}{\text{Current Liabilities}}$$

$$= \frac{\text{Rs. } 85{,}000}{\text{Rs. } 35{,}000} = 2.43\ (\approx)$$

$$\text{Liquid Ratio} = \frac{\text{Liquid Assets}}{\text{Liquid Liabilities}}$$

$$= \frac{\text{Rs. } 35{,}000}{\text{Rs. } 30{,}000} = 1.17\ (\approx)$$

$$\text{Stock turnover Ratio} = \frac{\text{Cost of goods sold}}{\text{Average stock*}}$$

$$= \frac{\text{Rs. } 1{,}00{,}000}{\text{Rs. } 40{,}000} = 2.5 \text{ times}$$

* Average stock of raw materials and finished goods

$$\text{Raw Material Turnover Ratio} = \frac{\text{Materials consumed}}{\text{Average raw Materials inventory}}$$

$$= \frac{\text{Rs. } 40{,}000}{\text{Rs. } 20{,}000} = 2 \text{ times}$$

$$\text{Finished Goods Turnover Ratio} = \frac{\text{Cost of goods sold}}{\text{Average finished goods stock}}$$

$$= \frac{\text{Rs. } 1{,}00{,}000}{\text{Rs. } 20{,}000} = 5 \text{ times}$$

Illustration 8

The following are the summarised profit and Loss Account of Priya Ltd. for the year ended 31.12.2002 and the Balance Sheet as on that date:

Profit and Loss Account

	Rs.		Rs.
To Opening stock	99,500	By Sales	8,50,000
To Purchases	5,45,250	By Closing stock	1,49,000
To Incidental Expenses	14,250		
To Gross Profit	3,40,000		
	9,99,000		9,99,000
To Operating Expenses:			
Selling and Distribution		By Gross Profit	3,40,000
expenses	30,000	By Non-operating	
		income: Interest	3,000
Administrative expenses	1,50,000	By Profit on sale of shares	6,000
Finance charges	15,000		
To non-operating expenses:			
Loss on sale of Assets	4,000		
To Net Profit	1,50,000		
	3,49,000		3,49,000

Balance Sheet

Liabilities	Rs.	Assets	Rs.
Issued capital:		Land & Buildings	1,50,000
2000 Equity shares		Plant & Machinery	80,000
of Rs. 100 each	2,00,000	Stock	1,49,000
Reserve	90,000	Sundry Debtors	71,000
Current Liabilities	1,30,000	Cash and Bank	30,000
P & L A/c	60,000		
	4,80,000		4,80,000

From the above statement you are required to calculate the following ratios and state the purpose they serve.

(i) Current Ratio

(ii) Liquid Ratio

(iii) Operating Ratio

(iv) Stock Turnover Ratio

(v) Return on Total Resources and

(vi) Turnover of Fixed Assets

Solution

(i) Current Ratio $= \dfrac{\text{Current Assets}}{\text{Current Liabilities}}$

$$= \frac{\text{Rs. } 1{,}49{,}000 + \text{Rs. } 71{,}000 + \text{Rs. } 30{,}000}{\text{Rs. } 1{,}30{,}000}$$

$$= \frac{\text{Rs. } 2{,}50{,}000}{\text{Rs. } 1{,}30{,}000} = 1.923 \text{ (Approx)}$$

(ii) Liquid Ratio $= \dfrac{\text{Liquid Assets}}{\text{Liquid Liabilities}}$

$$= \frac{\text{Rs. } 71{,}000 + \text{Rs. } 30{,}000}{\text{Rs. } 1{,}30{,}000}$$

$$= \frac{\text{Rs. } 1{,}01{,}000}{\text{Rs. } 1{,}30{,}000} = 0.78 \text{ (Approx)}$$

$$= 0.78 : 1$$

Compared to the standard of 2:1 expected for the Current Ratio the actual ratio of 1.923 is very near. But the liquid ratio, which is 0.78:1 against the standard for 1:1, reveals that a large part of the Current Assets consists of stock. Hence, it may be inferred that the liquidity position is not satisfactory since the stock is not so easily convertible into cash.

(iii) Operating Ratio $= \dfrac{\text{Operation Cost}}{\text{Net Sales}} \times 100$

$$= \frac{\text{Rs. } 5{,}10{,}000 + \text{Rs. } 1{,}95{,}000}{\text{Rs. } 8{,}50{,}000} \times 100$$

$$= \frac{\text{Rs. } 7{,}05{,}000}{\text{Rs. } 8{,}50{,}000} \times 100 = 83\% \ (\approx)$$

Cost of goods sold $= \text{Opening stock} + \text{Purchases} + \text{Incidental}$

$= \text{Rs.}99{,}500 + \text{Rs. } 5{,}45{,}250 + 14250 - 1{,}49{,}000 = \text{Rs. } 5{,}10{,}000$

For every rupee worth of sales, the ratio indicates that 83 paise constitute cost of goods sold and operating expenses.

(iv) Stock Turnover Ratio $= \dfrac{\text{Cost of goods sold}}{\text{Average inventory at cost}}$

$= \dfrac{\text{Rs. } 5{,}10{,}000}{\text{Rs. } 1{,}24{,}250} = 4.1 \text{ (Approx)}$

Average inventory $= \dfrac{\text{Rs. } 99{,}500 + \text{Rs. } 1{,}49{,}000}{2} = \text{Rs.} 1{,}24{,}250$

During 2000, the stock turned over slightly more than 4 times. However, it should be compared with the previous years ratios for arriving at any conclusions.

(v) Return on Total Resources $= \dfrac{\text{Net Profit}}{\text{Total assets}}$

$= \dfrac{\text{Rs. } 1{,}50{,}000}{\text{Rs. } 4{,}80{,}000} = .31:1$

The business has earned a return of 31 paise for every one rupee of total resources employed. This ratio shows a favorable position.

(vi) Turnover of Fixed Assets $= \dfrac{\text{Net Sales}}{\text{Fixed assets}}$

$= \dfrac{\text{Rs. } 8{,}50{,}000}{\text{Rs. } 2{,}30{,}000} = 3.7:1$

This shows that ever rupee worth of fixed assets has been used to generate net sales of Rs. 3.70. This ratio may also be calculated using cost of goods sold, instead of net sales, as follows:

Turnover of Fixed Assets $= \dfrac{\text{Cost of goods sold}}{\text{Fixed Assets}}$

$= \dfrac{\text{Rs. } 5{,}10{,}000}{\text{Rs. } 2{,}30{,}000} = 2.22:1$

This means that every rupee invested in fixed assets results in the sale of goods costing Rs. 2.22.

Computation of Fiancial Statement Information from Ratios

Illustration 9

Debtors Velocity	3 months
Creditors Velocity	2 months
Stock Velocity	8 times
Bills payable	Rs. 10,000
Bills receivable	Rs. 4,000
Total Sales	Rs. 2,40,000

The closing stock is Rs.2,000 more than the opening stock. Gross profit on the above sales is Rs. 40,000. There are no cash sales and cash purchases, and the accounting year consists of 360 working days. Find out (a) Sundry Debtors, (b) Sundry Creditors, and (c) Closing Stock.

Solution:

(a) Calculation of Sundry Debtors

$$\text{Debtors velocity} = \frac{\text{Total Debtors}}{\text{Total Credit Sales}} \times 360$$

Let 'a' be the value of total Debtors

$$90 = \frac{a \times 360}{\text{Rs. } 2,40,000} \quad \text{Credit Sales per day} = \frac{\text{Credit Sales}}{360}$$

$$360\,a = \text{Rs. } 2,40,000 \times 90$$

$$a = \frac{\text{Rs. } 2,40,000}{360} \times 90 = \text{Rs. } 60,000$$

$$\text{Sundry Debtors} = \text{Total Debtors} - \text{Bills Receivable}$$

$$\text{Sundry Debtors} = \text{Rs. } 60,000 - \text{Rs. } 10,000 = \text{Rs. } 50,000$$

(b) Calculation of closing stock

$$\text{Stock velocity} = \frac{\text{Cost of goods sold}}{\text{Average stock}}$$

$$\text{Cost of goods sold} = \text{Sales} - \text{Gross Profit}$$

$$\text{Rs. } 2,00,000 = \text{Rs. } 2,40,000 - \text{Rs. } 40,000$$

$$8 = \frac{\text{Rs. } 2,00,000}{\text{Average Stock}}$$

$$8 \times \text{Average Stock} = \frac{\text{Rs. } 2,00,000}{8} = \text{Rs. } 25,000$$

$$\text{Average Stock} = \frac{\text{Opening Stock} + \text{Closing Stock}}{2}$$

$$2 \times \text{Average Stock} = \text{Opening stock} + \text{Closing Stock}$$

$$2 \times 25,000 = \text{Opening} + \text{closing stock}$$

$$\text{Closing stock} + \text{Opening stock} = \text{Rs. } 50,000 \text{–(1)}$$

$$\text{Closing Stock} - \text{Opening stock} = \text{Rs. } 2,000 \text{–(2)}$$

Adding both equations we get

$$2 \text{ closing stock} = \text{Rs. } 52,000$$

$$\text{Closing Stock} = \text{Rs. } 52,000/2 = 26,000$$

(c) Calculation of Sundry Creditors

$$\text{Creditors Velocity} = \frac{\text{Total creditors}}{\text{Credit purchases}} \times 360$$

$$\text{Cost of goods sold} = \text{Opening stock} + \text{Purchases} - \text{Closing Stock}$$

$$\text{Rs. } 2{,}00{,}000 = \text{Rs. } 24{,}000 + \text{Purchases} - \text{Rs. } 26{,}000$$

$$\text{Purchases} = \text{Rs. } 2{,}00{,}000 - \text{Rs. } 24{,}000 + \text{Rs. } 26{,}000$$

$$\text{Purchases} = \text{Rs. } 2{,}02{,}000$$

Let y be the total creditors

$$60 = \frac{y \times 360}{\text{Rs. } 2{,}02{,}000} \times 60 = 2{,}02{,}000$$

$$y = \frac{60 \times 2{,}02{,}000}{360} = \text{Rs. } 33{,}667\ (\approx)$$

Sundry creditors = Total creditors – Bills payable

= Rs. 33,667 – Rs. 4,000

= Rs. 29,667 (Approx)

Illustration 10

From the following information, find out (a) Sales (b) Closing stock, (c) Sundry Debtors, and (d) Sundry creditors

Gross Profit Ratio	25 percent
Debtors Turnover Ratio	4 months
Stock Turnover Ratio	4 times
Creditors Turnover Ratio	6 months

Closing stock is Rs.10,000 more than the opening stock. Bills receivables amount to Rs. 65,000, and Bills payable to Rs.80,000. Cost of goods sold for the year is Rs. 9,00,000.

Solution

Calculation of sales

Gross Profit Ratio = 25%

Cost of goods sold to sales = 75%

Sales = Cost of goods sold × 100/75

= Rs. 9,00,000 × 100/75

= Rs. 12,00,000

Calculation of closing stock:

$$\text{Stock turnover Ratio} = \frac{\text{Cost of goods sold}}{\text{Average stock}} = 4$$

$$4 = \frac{\text{Rs. } 9{,}00{,}000}{\text{Average stock}}$$

$$4 \times \text{Average stock} = \text{Rs. } 9{,}00{,}000$$

$$\text{Average stock} = \text{Rs. } 2{,}25{,}000$$

Closing stock= Average + 1/2 (Difference between opening and closing stocks)

Closing stock= Rs. 2,25,000 + (1/2 × Rs. 10,000)

= Rs. 2,30,000

Calculation of Sundry Debtors

Accounts Receivable = Sales × Debtors Turnover Ratio

= Rs. 12,00,000 × 4/12 = Rs. 4,00,000

Less Bills Receivable	= Rs. 65,000
Sundry Debtors	= Rs. 3,35,000

Calculation of Sundry Creditors

Purchases = Cost of goods sold + closing stock − opening stock

= Rs. 9,00,000 + Rs. 2,30,000 − Rs. 2,20,000

= Rs. 9,10,000

Accounts payable = Purchases × Creditors Turnover Ratio

= Rs. 9,10,000 × 6/12 = Rs. 4,55,000

Less Bills payable	= Rs. 80,000
Sundry Creditors	= Rs. 3,75,000

Illustration 11

Calculate current assets, current liability, stock turnover ratio from the following information:

Current ratio	:	2.5
Working capital	:	Rs. 60,000
Opening Stock	:	29,000
Closing stock	:	31,000
Sales	:	3,20,000
Gross profit ratio	:	25% on sales

(B.Com., Bharathidasan, April 1992)

Solution

$$\text{Current Ratio} = \frac{\text{Current assets}}{\text{Current liabilities}}$$

$$2.5 = \frac{\text{Current assets}}{\text{Current liabilities}}$$

Current assets = 2.5 current liabilities

Working capital = Current assets − Current liabilities

60,000 = 2.5 Current liabilities − Current liabilities

60,000 = 1.5 current liabilities

$$\text{Current liabilities} = \frac{60,000}{1.5}$$

$= \text{Rs. } 40{,}000$

Current assets $= 2.5$ currentliabilities

$= 2.5 \times 40{,}000$

$= \text{Rs. } 1{,}00{,}000$

Gross profit : 25% on sales, i.e., 25% of 3,20,000 = Rs. 80,000

Cost of goods sold = Sales – Gross profit

$= 3{,}20{,}000 - 80{,}000$

$= \text{Rs. } 2{,}40{,}000$

$$\text{Average Stock} = \frac{\text{Operating stock} + \text{Closing Stock}}{2}$$

$$= \frac{29{,}000 + 31{,}000}{2}$$

$= \text{Rs. } 30{,}000$

$$\text{Stock turnover} = \frac{\text{Cost of Goods Sold}}{\text{Average stock}}$$

$$= \frac{2{,}40{,}000}{30{,}000}$$

$= 8$ times

Illustration 12

From the following information, make out a statement of proprietor's funds with as much details as possible.

	Rs.
Current ratio	2.5
Liquidity ratio	1.5
Proprietary ratio	
(Fixed assets/proprietary funds)	0.75
Working capital	Rs. 60,000
Bank overdraft	10,000
Reserves and surplus	40,000

There are no long-term loans or fictitious assets.

(C.S. Inter, June 1994; B.Com., S.V. Univ. April 1992)
(M.B.A. Andhra, March 1992; B.Com., Bharathidasan, Nov.1994)

Solution

If current ratio is 2.5. It means that for every Re.1 current liability, current assets amount to Rs.2.5. Therefore, excess of current assets over current liabilities is 2.5 – 1 = 1.5. Working capital being excess of current assets over current liabilities. 1.5 should be working capital. The amount of working capital given in the problem is Rs.60,000. Hence, if working capital is 1.5... Current assets are 2.5

Working Capital is Rs. 60,000 then

$$\text{Current Assets} = \frac{2.5 \times 60{,}000}{1.5} = \text{Rs. } 1{,}00{,}000$$

If working capital is 1.5. ... Current liabilities 1

Working Capital is Rs. 60,000 then

$$\text{Current Liabilities} = \frac{\text{Rs. } 60{,}000}{1.5} = 40{,}000$$

$$\text{Liquid Ratio} = \frac{\text{Liquid assets}}{\text{Current Liabilities}}$$

$$1.5 = \frac{\text{Current assets} - \text{Stock} - \text{prepayments}}{40{,}000}$$

$$1.5 = \frac{1{,}00{,}000 - \text{Stock}}{40{,}000}$$

$$1{,}00{,}000 - \text{Stock} = 60{,}000$$

$$\text{Stock} = \text{Rs. } 40{,}000$$

$$\text{Proprietary Ratio} = \frac{\text{Fixed Assets}}{\text{Proprietor's funds}}$$

$$0.75 = \frac{\text{Fixed assets}}{\text{proprietor's funds}}$$

$$\text{Proprietor's funds} - \text{Fixed assets} = \text{Current assets} - \text{Current liabilities}$$

According to this relationship, if 0.75 were the proprietary ratio, 75% of the total capital covers fixed assets and the balance of 25% finances working capital. Accordingly,

$$25\% = 1{,}00{,}000 - 40{,}000$$

$$25\% \text{ or } 1/4 \rightleftarrows = 60{,}000$$

$$1 = 60{,}000 \times 4$$

$$= \text{Rs. } 2{,}40{,}000 \text{ (proprietor's funds)}$$

This amount should include retained earnings also.

Statement of Proprietor's Funds

			Rs.	Rs.
Share Capital			2,00,000	
Reserves and Surplus			40,000	
				2,40,000
Fixed Assets: 75% of proprietor's funds			1,80,000	
Current Assets:				
Stock	Rs. 40,000			
Liquid assets	60,000			
		1,00,000		
Current Liabilities:				
Bank overdrafts	10,000			
Others	30,000			

Working capital		40,000	60,000	2,40,000

Illustration 13

Following are the details of the trading activities of Murugan Traders Ltd.

Stock velocity	8 months
Debtors velocity	3 months
Creditors velocity	2 months
Gross profit ratio	25%

Gross profit for the year is Rs.4,00,000. Bills receivable Rs.25,000 and Bills payable Rs. 10,000. Closing stock for the year is Rs.10,000 more than the opening stock . Find out: (i) Sales, (ii) Debtors, (iii) closing stock, (iv) Creditors,

(B.Com., Bharathidasan, Nov. 1995; M.com., Kerala, April 1995)
(B.Com., Madras, Sept 1991)

Solution:

$$\text{Gross profit ratio} = \frac{\text{Gross profit}}{\text{Sales}} \times 100$$

$$\frac{25}{100} = \frac{4,00,000}{\text{Sales}}$$

$$25 \text{ sales} = 4,00,00,000$$

(i) Sales $= \text{Rs. } 16,00,000$

(ii) Debtors

Debtors velocity given as 3 months, indicates debt collection or average age of accounts receivable.

$$\text{Average age of debtors} = \frac{\text{Months or days in a year}}{\text{Debtors turnover}}$$

$$3 = \frac{12 \text{ months}}{\text{Debtors turnover}}$$

$$3 \text{ Debtors turnover} = 12$$

$$\text{Debtors turnover} = 4$$

$$\text{Debtors Turnover Ratio} = \frac{\text{Credit sales}}{\text{Debtors} + \text{Bills receivable}}$$

OR

$$\text{Debtors} + \text{Bills receivable} = \frac{\text{Credit Sales}}{\text{Debtors Turnover Ratio}}$$

$$= \frac{16,00,000}{4}$$

$$\text{Debtors} + \text{Bills receivable} = \text{Rs. } 4,00,000$$

$$\text{Bills receivable} = \underline{25{,}000}$$

$$\text{Debtors} = \text{Rs. } 3{,}75{,}000$$

(iii) Closing stock:

Stock velocity is 8 months, Hence, the turnover ratio is 12/8 = 1.5

$$\text{Stock Turnover Ratio} = \frac{\text{Cost of goods sold (Sales – Gross Profit)}}{\text{Average stock}}$$

$$1.5 = \frac{12{,}00{,}000}{\text{Average Stock}}$$

$$1.5 \text{ Average Stock} = 12{,}00{,}000$$

$$\text{Average stock} = \text{Rs. } 8{,}00{,}000$$

$$\text{Average stock} = \frac{\text{Opening stock} + \text{Closing Stock}}{2}$$

$$8{,}00{,}000 = \frac{\text{Opening stock} + \text{Closing Stock}}{2}$$

$$\text{Opening stock} + \text{Closing Stock} = 16{,}00{,}000$$

$$x + (x + 10{,}000) = 16{,}00{,}000$$

$$2x + 10{,}000 = 16{,}00{,}000$$

$$2x = 16{,}00{,}000 - 10{,}000$$

$$2x = 15{,}90{,}000$$

$$x = \text{Rs. } 7{,}95{,}000$$

Opening stock is Rs. 7,95,000 and closing stock Rs.8,05,000. With the figures of opening stock, closing stock, sales and gross profit, purchases may be ascertained as the balancing figure by preparing trading account.

The figure of purchases is Rs.12,10,000

Trading Account

To Opening stock	7,95,000	By Sales	16,00,000
To Purchases (Balancing figure)	12,10,000	By Closing stock	8,05,000
To Gross profit	4,00,000		
	24,05,000		24,05,000

Substituting the figures in the Creditors Turnover formula.

(iv) Creditors: Creditors velocity being 2 months, credit payment period is 2 months.

Accordingly, 12/2 = 6 is the creditors turnover Ratio.

$$\text{Creditors Turnover Ratio} = \frac{\text{Credit purchases}}{\text{Creditors} + \text{Bills payable}}$$

$$6 = \frac{12{,}10{,}000}{\text{Creditors} + \text{Bills Payable}}$$

$$\text{Creditors} + 10{,}000 = \frac{12{,}10{,}000}{6}$$

$$\text{Creditors} + 10{,}000 = 2{,}01{,}667$$

$$\text{Creditors} = 2{,}01{,}667 - 10{,}000$$

$$\text{Creditors} = \text{Rs. } 1{,}91{,}667$$

Illustration 14

From the following details, prepare the Balance Sheet of the firm concerned:

Stock velocity	6
Capital turnover ratio	2
Fixed assets turnover ratio	4
Gross profit ratio	20%
Debt collection period	2 months
Creditors payment period	73 days

The gross profit was Rs. 60,000. Closing stock was Rs. 5,000 in excess of the opening stock. *(B.Com., Punjab, April 1995)*

Solution

Gross profit ratio is 20% of turnover. If sales are 100, gross is 20, i.e. 1/5 of turnover. Accordingly, gross profit Rs. 60,000 is 1/5 of sales. Hence, sales are Rs.3,00,000.

$$\text{Sales} - \text{Gross profit} = \text{Cost of goods sold}$$

$$3{,}00{,}000 - 60{,}000 = \text{Rs. } 2{,}40{,}000$$

$$\text{Stock Turnover Ratio} = \frac{\text{Cost of goods sold}}{\text{Average Stock}}$$

$$6 = \frac{2{,}40{,}000}{\text{Average Stock}}$$

$$6 \text{ Average Stock} = \text{Rs. } 2{,}40{,}000$$

$$\text{Average Stock} = \text{Rs. } 40{,}000$$

$$\text{Average Stock} = \frac{\text{Opening stock} + \text{Closing Stock}}{2}$$

$$40{,}000 = \frac{\text{Opening Stock} + \text{Closing Stock}}{2}$$

$$\text{Opening stock} + \text{Closing stock} = 80{,}000$$

$$x + (x + 5{,}000) = 80{,}000$$

$$2x + 5{,}000 = 80{,}000$$

$$2x = 75{,}000$$

$$x = \text{Rs. } 37{,}500$$

Opening stock is Rs. 37,500 and closing stock Rs. 42,500

$$\text{Capital Turnover Ratio} = \frac{\text{Cost of goods sold}}{\text{Capital}}$$

$$2 = \frac{2,40,000}{\text{Capital}}$$

2 capital = 2,40,000

Capital = Rs. 1,20,000

$$\text{Fixed Assets Turnover Ratio} = \frac{\text{Cost of goods sold}}{\text{Fixed assets}}$$

$$4 = \frac{2,40,000}{\text{Fixed assets}}$$

4 Fixed assets = 2,40,000

Fixed assets = Rs. 60,000

$$\text{Debtors Turnover Ratio} = \frac{\text{12 months}}{\text{Debt collections period}}$$

$$= \frac{\text{12 months}}{2}$$

= 6 times

$$\text{Debtors Turnover Ratio} = \frac{\text{Credit sales}}{\text{Debtors}}$$

$$6 = \frac{3,00,000}{\text{Debtors}}$$

6 Debtors = 3,00,000

Debtors = Rs. 50,000

$$\text{Creditors Turnover Ratio} = \frac{\text{365 days}}{\text{Payment period}}$$

$$= \frac{\text{365 days}}{\text{73 days}}$$

= 5 times

$$\text{Creditors Turnover Ratio} = \frac{\text{Credit purchases}}{\text{Creditors}}$$

Purchases = Cost of goods sold + Closing stock − Opening stock

= 2,40,000 + 42,500 − 37,500

= 2,45,000

$$5 = \frac{2,45,000}{\text{Creditors}}$$

5 Creditors = 2,45,000

Creditors = Rs. 49,000

Balance Sheet as at ....

	Rs.		Rs.
Capital	1,20,000	Fixed assets	60,000

Creditors	49,000	Stock	42,500
		Debtors	50,000
		Cash (balancing figure)	16,500
	1,69,000		1,69,000

Illustration 15

The information relating to the business of XY company as at the end of March 1994:

(i)	Gross profit ratio	25%
(ii)	Net profit/Sales	20%
(iii)	Stock turnover ratio	10
(iv)	Net profit/Capital	1/5
(v)	Capital/Total liabilities	1/2
(vi)	Fixed assets/Capital	5/4
(vii)	Fixed assets/Current assets	5/7
(viii)	Fixed assets	Rs. 10,00,000
(ix)	Closing stock	1,00,000

From the above information, find out: (1) Cost of sales, (2) Gross profit, (3) Net profit, (4) Value of current assets, (5) Amount of capital, (6) Amount of liabilities.

Also prepare a Trading and Profit and Loss Account for the year ended 31st March 1994.

(B.A., Madras, March 1994; B.Com., Bangalore, Nov.1995)

Solution

Since sales-cost of goods sold = Gross profit, it is necessary, first of all, to find out the figure of sales.

Fixed assets/Capital ratio is 5/4, Accordingly.

For 5 fixed assets ... Capital is 4

10,00,000 ... ?

$$= \frac{4 \times 10,00,000}{5} = 8,00,000$$

Net profit/Capital ratio being 1/5,

For Rs. 5 capital ... Net profit is Re.1

8,00,000 ... ?

$$= \frac{8,00,000}{5} = \text{Rs. } 1,60,000$$

Net profit/sales ratio being 20%,

For Rs. 20 net profit ... Sales are Rs. 100

1,60,000 ... ?

$$= \frac{100 \times 1,60,000}{20} = \text{Rs. } 8,00,000$$

Cost of goods sold = Sales − Gross profit

$= 8,00,000 - 25\%$ of sales

$= 8,00,000 - 2,00,000$

= Rs. 6,00,000

(i) Cost of goods sold Rs. 6,00,000

(ii) Gross profit Rs. 2,00,000.

(iii) Net profit Rs. 1,60,000

Fixed assets/current assets ratio is 5/7, This means,

For 5 fixed assets — current assets 7

10,00,000 — ?

$$= \frac{7 \times 10,00,000}{5} = \text{Rs. } 14,00,000$$

(iv) Current assets Rs. 14,00,000

(v) Capital Rs. 8,00,000

(vi) Liabilities Rs. 16,00,000 (Capital/liabilities ratio being 1/2)

$$\text{Stock Turnover Ratio} = \frac{\text{Cost of goods sold}}{\text{Average inventory}}$$

$$10 = \frac{6,00,000}{\text{Average inventory}}$$

$$10 \text{ Average inventory} = 6,00,000$$

$$\text{Average inventory} = \text{Rs. } 60,000$$

$$\text{Average Stock} = \frac{\text{Opening stock} + \text{Closing stock}}{2}$$

$$60,000 = \frac{\text{Opening stock} + 1,00,000}{2}$$

$$\text{Opening stock} + 1,00,000 = 1,20,000$$

$$\text{Opening stock} = 1,20,000 - 1,00,000 = \text{Rs. } 20,000$$

Trading and profit and Loss Account for the year ended 31-3-1994

	Rs.		Rs.
To Opening stock	20,000	By Sales	8,00,000
To Purchases (balancing figure)	6,80,000	By Closing Stock	1,00,000
To Gross Profit	2,00,000		
	9,00,000		9,00,000
To Administration, Selling & Distribution expenses (balancing figure)	40,000	By Gross Profit b/d	2,00,000

To Net profit	1,60,000		
	2,00,000		2,00,000

Illustration 16

From the following data, prepare balance sheet:

Sales Rs.32,00,000

Sales to net worth 2.3 times

Current debt to net worth 42%

Total debt to net worth 75%

Current ratio 2.9 times

Net sales to inventory 4.7 times

Average collection period (assume 360 days) 64 days

Fixed assets to net worth 53.2% *(B.Com., Andhra, 1995)*

Solution:

$$\text{Sales to net worth} = \frac{\text{Sales}}{\text{Net worth}}$$

$$2.3 = \frac{32,00,000}{\text{Net worth}}$$

$$2.3 \text{ Net worth} = 32,00,000$$

$$\text{Net worth} = \frac{32,00,000}{2.3} = \text{Rs. } 13,91,304$$

Current debt is 42% of net worth, i.e. Rs. 5,84,348

Total debt is 75% of net worth. i.e. Rs. 10,43,478

The difference between total debt and current debt should be longterm debt. The same is Rs. 4.59,130.

$$\text{Current Ratio} = \frac{\text{Current assets}}{\text{Current Liabilities}}$$

$$2.9 = \frac{\text{Current assets}}{5,84,348}$$

$$\text{Current assets} = 5,84,384 \times 2.9 = \text{Rs. } 16,94,609$$

$$\text{Net sales inventory} = \frac{\text{Net sales}}{\text{Inventory}}$$

$$4.7 = \frac{32,00,000}{\text{Inventory}}$$

$$4.7 \text{ Inventory} = 32,00,000$$

$$\text{Inventory} = \frac{32,00,000}{4.7} = \text{Rs. } 6,80,851$$

$$\text{Debtors' Turnover Ratio} = \frac{\text{Net Sales}}{\text{Debtors}}$$

$$\frac{360}{64} = (5.6\text{times}) = \frac{32,00,000}{\text{Debtors}}$$

5.6 Debtors = 32,00,000

Debtors = Rs. 5,71,428

$$\text{Fixed assets to Net Worth} = \frac{\text{Fixed Assets}}{\text{Net Worth}}$$

$$53.2\% = \frac{\text{Fixed assets}}{13,91,304}$$

$$100 \text{ Fixed Assets} = 13,91,304 \times 53.2$$

$$\text{Fixed Assets} = \text{Rs. } 7,40,173$$

Balance Sheet

	Rs.		Rs.
Net Worth	13,91,304	Fixed Assets	7,40,173
Long-term Debt	4,59,130	Stock	6,80,851
Current Liabilities	5,84,348	Debtors	5,71,428
		Cash (balancing figure)	4,42,330
	24,34,782		24,34,782

REVIEW PROBLEMS

1. Balance Sheet of ABC Co. as at Dec. 2000 (Rs. in 000s)

Liabilities		Rs.	Assets	Rs.
Equity share capital		2,000	Goodwill	1,200
Capital reserves		400	Fixed assets	2,800
Loan (mortgage) 8%		1,600	Socks	600
Creditors		800	Debtors	600
Bank overdraft		200	Investments	200
Taxation: Current		200	Cash in hand	600
Future		200		
Profit after tax and fixed deposit Int.	1,200			
Less:				
Transfer to reserve	400			
Dividends	200			
		600		
		6,000		6,000

You are required to find out the long-term solvency ratios, and give your comments on the solvency on the basis of the information.

[**Ans:** Long-term solvency ratios: Debt-Equity Ratio=1 : 1; Fixed Assets Ratio [FA/LTFunds] = 0.77; Interest Coverage Ratio = 11.94.]

2. Balance Sheet of X Ltd., as on 31st December 2000:

Liabilities	Rs.	Assets	Rs.
Equity share capital	20,000	Goodwill	12,000
Capital reserves	4,000	Fixed assets	28,000

8% loan on mortgage	16,000	Stocks	6,000
Trade creditors	8,000	Debtors	6,000
Bank overdraft	2,000	Investments	2,000
Taxation: Current	2,000	Bank	6,000
Future	2,000		
Profit & Loss A/c			
Profit 1999 after tax and Int. on fixed deposits 12,000			
Less:			
Transfers to reserve 4,000			
Dividends 2,000	6,000		
	60,000		60,000

Sales amounted to Rs. 1,20,000.

You are required to calculate ratios for

(a) testing liquidity, (b) testing profitability, (c) testing solvency.

[**Ans:** Test of liquidity: Current Ratio = 1.67; Liquid Ratio = 1.17; both are satisfactory. Test of Profitability: NP ratio 10% Return on capital employed = 33.22%; both are satisfactory. Test of Solvency: Debt-equity ratio = 1 : 1; Fixed Assests Ratio = 0.77; Interest Coverage Ratio = 11.94; all are satisfactory.

3. (a) From the following details, calculate the current Ratio and Acid Test Ratio:

Current Asset loan and Advances		Current Liabilities	
Stock in trade	77,000	Sundry creditors	23,300
Sundry Debtors	47,300	Acceptances	9,460
Cash in hand	6,700	Dividend warrants issued but not cashed	190
Loans and advances (short term)	13,300	Provision for Taxation	10,150
Prepaid Taxes	700		

(b) Velan & Co., sell their goods on cash as well as credit. The following particulars are taken out from their records for the year 2002:

	Rs.
Total gross sales (including cash sales of Rs. 30,000)	1,60,000
Sales Returns	10,000
Total debtors for sales on 31.12.2002	15,000
Bills Receivable on 31.12.2002	3,000
Provision for doubtful debts 31,12.2002	2,000
Sundry creditors	18,000
Prepaid expenses	6,000

Calculate the average collection period.

[**Ans:** (a) Current Ratio = 3.37; Acid Test Ratio = 1.56.
(b) 54 days; assume 360 days in a year.]

4. Calculate the following ratios from the Balance Sheet given below:

(a) Debt-Equity Ratio; (b) Liquidity Ratio; (c) Fixed Assets to Current Assets; (d) Fixed Assets Turnover

Balance Sheet

Liabilities	Rs.	Assets	Rs.
Equity Shares of Rs. 10 each	1,00,000	Goodwill	60,000
Reserve	20,000	Fixed Assets (cost)	1,40,000
Profit and Loss Account	30,000	Stock	30,000
Secured Loans	80,000	Sundry Debtors	30,000
Sundry Creditors	50,000	Advances	10,000
Provision for Taxation	20,000	Cash balance	30,000
	3,00,000		3,00,000

The sales for the year were Rs. 5,60,000.

[**Ans:** (a) 1 : 1; (b) 1 : 1; (c) 1.4 : 1; (d) 4.]

5. From the data given below compute:

(a) Working Capital; (b) Net Capital Employed; (c) Current Ratio; (d) Debt/Equity Ratio.

A. Co Ltd. Balance Sheet as on 31.12.2000

	Rs.		Rs.
Equity share capital	25,000	Fixed Assets	30,000
Pre. share capital	5,000	Stores	2,000
Reserves & Surplus	4,000	Stock in Trade	4,000
Debentures	8,000	Sundry Debtors	3,000
Bank Loan	4,000	Cash in hand	500
Sundry creditors	1,000	Bal. with Sch. Bank	2,500
Proposed dividends	1,000	Preliminary exp.	8,000
Provision for taxation	2,000		
	50,000		50,000

Contingent liabilities 2,000. Comment on financial health of company.

[**Ans:** (a) Rs. 8000; (b) Rs. 38,000; (c) Rs. 3; (d) 0.57]

6. (a) A company has an inventory of Rs.7,20,000, debtors Rs. 4,30,000 and an inventory turnover ratio of 12. The gross profit margin is 10% and its credit sales are 20% of the total sales. Calculate the average collection period.

(b) Srinivasa cotton company's stock turnover is 5 times, stock at the end is Rs.20,000 more than that at the beginning. Sales (all credit) are Rs.8,00,000; rate of gross profit on cost is one fourth. Current liabilities Rs. 1,20,000. Quick ratio is 0.75. Calculate current assets.

[**Ans:** (a) 81 days; (b) Rs. 1,64,000]

7. Debtors velocity 3 months
Creditors velocity 2 months

Stock velocity	8 times
Capital-turnover ratio	2.5 times
Fixed Assets turnover	8 times
Gross Profit turnover ratio	25%

Gross profit in a year amounted to Rs. 80,000. There is no long-term loan or overdraft. Reserves and surplus amount to Rs. 28,000. Liquid assets are Rs. 97,333. Closing stock of the year is Rs. 2,000/- more than the opening stock. Bills Receivable amount to Rs. 5,000 and Bills payable to Rs. 2,000.

Find out:

(a) Sales; (b) Sundry debtors; (c) Sundry creditors

(d) Closing stock; (e) Fixed assets; (f) Capital.

[**Ans:** (a) Rs. 3,20,000; (b) Rs. 75,000; (c) Rs. 38,333; (d) Rs. 16,000 (e) 1,00,000]

8. From the following information prepare a summarised Balance Sheet as at 31st March 2000.

1.	Working capital	Rs. 1,20,000
2.	Reserves and surplus	80,000
3.	Bank overdraft	20,000
4.	Assets (fixed) Proprietary ratio	0.75
5.	Current ratio	2.5
6.	Liquid ratio	1.5

[**Ans:** Share capital Rs. 4,00,000; Creditors Rs. 60,000; Fixed Assets Rs. 3,60,000; Stock Rs. 1,10,000; Other Assets Rs, 90,000; Total of B/S Rs. 5,60,000.]

9. From the following details prepare statement of proprietary funds with as many details as possible:

   1. Stock velocity - 6
   2. Capital turnover ratio - 2
   3. Fixed asset turnover ratio - 4
   4. Gross profit turnover ratio - 20%
   5. Debtors' velocity - 2 months
   6. Creditor's velocity - 73 days

The gross profit was Rs. 60,000. Reserve and Surplus amounted to Rs. 20,000. Closing stock was Rs. 5,000 in excess opening stock.

[**Ans:** Share capital Rs. 1,00,000; Fixed Assets Rs. 60,000; Closing stock Rs. 42,500; Debtors Rs, 50,000; Creditors Rs. 49,000; Cash & Bank [Balancing figure] Rs. 16,500]

10. From the following information, you are required to prepare a Balance Sheet:

1.	Current Ratio	1.75
2.	Liquid Ratio	1.25
3.	Stock Turnover Ratio (Cost of Sales/Closing Stock)	9
4.	Gross Profit Ratio	25%

5.	Debt collection period	1½ months
6.	Reserves and Surplus to Capital	0.2
7.	Turnover to Fixed Assets	1.2
8.	Capital Gearing Ratio	0.6
9.	Fixed Assets to Net Worth	1.25
10.	Sales for the year	Rs. 12,00,000

[**Ans:** B/S total Rs. 11,00,000; Share capital Rs. 5,00,000; Reserve & Surplus Rs. 1,00,000; Long-term debt Rs. 3,00,000; Current liabilities Rs. 2,00,000; Fixed Assets Rs. 7,50,000; Stock Rs. 1,00,000; Debtors Rs. 1,50,000; Cash & Bank Rs. 1,00,000.]

11. What does Ratio Analysis mean?
12. How can Ratios be interpreted?
13. State the advantages and limitations of Ratio analysis.
14. Describe the various methods of classification of ratios.
15. Explain the significance of liquidity ratios.
16. Explain the meaning and significance of Current Ratio and Acid Test Ratio.
17. Describe Principal Profitability ratios.
18. Write a note on "Return on Capital employed".
19. What is Du Pont Control Chart?
20. How can the solvency position of a business be measured?
21. Explain the meaning and significance of Debt Equity Ratio and Proprietary Ratio.
22. Write Short notes on: (a) Capital Gearing Ratio (b) Return on Investment (c) Turnover Ratios.

9

FUNDS FLOW ANALYSIS

Learning Objectives

After completing this chapter, you should be able to:

— Discuss the need for and importance of Funds Flow Analysis.

— Define the various concepts in Funds Flow Analysis.

— Know the preparation of Funds Flow Statement.

— Work out problems in Funds Flow Analysis.

9.1 Need for Funds Flow Analysis

The traditional package of financial statements has as such limited role to play in financial analysis. The balance sheet is a statement of assets and liabilities on a particular date and portrays the financial position as on that particular date. Similarly the income statement will show in more detail only the profit or loss arising out of the productive and commercial activities of the enterprise during that period. However, they fail to throw light on those major financial transactions, which are behind the balance sheet changes. In order to ascertain such major financial transactions or movement of financial resources or funds, a separate statement is prepared by comparing the balance sheets of two periods. This statement is variously known as funds flow statement or statement of sources and uses of funds.

The funds statement aims to supplement the two conventional statements. It shows information that can only be obtained through analysis and interpretation of income statements and opening and closing balance sheets. This information relates to the overall investment and financial activities of the company, showing the principal sources and application of funds.

By recording these changes in the financial structure that have resulted from the company's trading activities, and at the same time indicating the reasons for those changes, the funds statement serves the dual role of an accounting report and an analytical tool. This is so because the funds statement can be used as part of budgetary process in forecasting the company's financial requirements for the future.

9.2 Significant Role or Importance of Funds Flow Analysis

Funds flow analysis is an invaluable analytical tool for a financial manager or a creditor for evaluating the employment of funds by a firm, and in determining the sources for such funds. In addition to studying the past flows, the analyst can evaluate the future flows by means of a funds statement based upon forecasts. Such a statement provides an efficient method for the finance manager to assess the growth of the firm and its resulting financial needs, and to determine the best way to finance those needs. In particular, funds flow analysis is very useful in planning intermediate and long-term financing.

By highlighting the changes in the distribution of resources of an undertaking, the fund flow statement enables the finance manager to have a clear perspective of the organization's financial questions as follows:

1. Where did the profits go?
2. Why were the dividends not larger?
3. How was the purchase or expansion of fixed assets financed?
4. What happened to the sale proceeds of assets?
5. How was repayment of debt achieved?
6. What became of the proceeds of the debenture issue?
7. How was it possible to distribute dividends in excess of current earnings?

9.3 Define the concepts of 'funds ' and 'flow of funds'.

Concept of Funds

Some define the term funds as cash and they concern themselves with the movements in the cash account. The statement showing the changes in cash balances is termed as cash flow statement. Though a record of cash inflows and outflows is invaluable in its own way, it would, however, fail to throw light on many important changes involving the disposition of resources. At the other end there are those who view funds in a broader sense as all assets to which the firm's resources stand committed and all liabilities from where the resources are obtained. This is known as all financial resources concept of funds. In between these two concepts, the third one is that funds mean net working capital i.e., excess of current assets over current liabilities. To conclude, funds may be defined in different ways depending upon the purpose of analysis. However, the following are most commonly used definitions:

(a) Funds mean cash,

(b) Funds mean net working capital, and

(c) Funds mean all financial resources.

The 'working capital' is considered the most appropriate expression since the wealth of an enterprise continuously revolving through the various current assets supplemented by current liabilities. The broad categories of current assets include such items as cash and bank (including short-term fixed deposits with banks), sundry debtors, bills receivable, marketable securities or short-term investments, inventories, advances recoverable and prepaid expenses. The broad categories of current liabilities include such items as sundry creditors, bills payables, outstanding expenses, bank overdraft, and other short-term loans and income received in advance. Long-term liabilities, if their maturity date falls within the accounting year or they are payable out of current assets or current liabilities, may be treated as current liabilities.

Concept of Flow of Funds

The term 'flow' refers to change or transfer, and therefore, the flow of funds means transfer of economic values from one asset to another, from one liability to another, from one asset to a liability or vice versa, or a combination of these. But as per the working capital concept of funds, it means 'changes in working capital' i.e., any increase or decrease in working capital. The change in funds (i.e., current assets and current liabilities_ occurs when changes occur in non-current assets (all assets other than current assets) and in non-current liabilities (all liabilities other than current liabilities). They are offset by corresponding changes in each other. If any transaction results in increase of funds (i.e., working capital item), it will be considered as a "source of funds". For example, issue of shares (non-current item) for cash (working capital item) will be taken as a source of fund. Similarly, a transaction, if it results decrease of funds, will be treated as 'application of funds'; example, purchase of assets for cash. Transactions, which do not affect the working capital items would be treated as non-fund transactions and be excluded from the funds flow analysis; purchase of machinery by issuing shares is a non-fund transaction.

Concept of Funds Flow Statement

Funds Flow Statement is a statement in summary form that indicates the changes in items of financial position between two different balance sheet dates showing clearly the sources and application of funds. The major purpose of the funds statement is to provide a detailed presentation of the results of financial management, as distinguished from operating management. It summarizes the financing and investing activities of the enterprise. The statement shows directly the information that the readers of financial reports could otherwise obtain only by making an analysis and interpretation of published balance sheets and statements of income and retained earnings.

	Principal Sources of Funds		Principal Uses of Funds
1.	Issue of shares and debentures	1.	Redemption of shares and debentures
2.	Long and medium-term borrowings	2.	Repayment of long and medium-term loans
3.	Sale of fixed assets and long-term investments	3.	Purchase of fixed assets and investments
4.	Funds from operations or trading income	4.	Funds lost in trading operations or trading losses
5.	Non-trading income	5.	Non-trading losses such as fine etc.

9.4 Distinction between Funds Flow Statement and Income Statement

(a) A funds flow statement deals with the financial resources required for running the business activities. It shows how the funds were obtained and how they were used. Whereas an Income statement shows the results of the business activities i.e., how much has been earned and how much has been spent.

(b) A funds flow statement matches the funds raised with funds used during a particular period. They may be of capital or revenue nature. But an income statement matches the income of a period with the expenditure of that period. Both the income and expenditure are of revenue nature.

(c) Besides funds from operations, sources of funds are many such as share capital, debentures, sale of fixed assets, etc. An income statement shows the results of operations. It cannot give accurately the funds from operations because of non-fund items such as writing off of depreciation, fictitious assets , etc. being included therein.

Thus both income statement and funds flow statement perform different functions. One cannot be a substitute for the other; rather they are complimentary to each other. Modern management needs both.

9.5 Distinctions Between Balance Sheet and Funds Statement

Balance sheet is a statement of financial position, whereas funds statement is obviously a statement of 'changes' in financial position.

Balance sheet shows the status of a business on a day. In contrast, funds statement, income statement and statement of retained earnings cover a period of time; they provide the explanation of why the balance sheet items have changed.

The conventional financial statements show mostly the position of accounting, rather than the financial condition in terms of flow of funds. But it becomes easy to unearth unusual trends and proportions by the use of analytical tools like the funds flow statement

Thus the funds flow statement is intended to supplement and not to supplant the conventional financial statements.

9.6 State the uses and limitations of Funds Flow Statement

Uses of Funds Flow Statement

By highlighting the changes in the distribution of the resources of an undertaking, the funds flow statement enables the financial manager to have a clear perspective of the organization's financial strengths and weaknesses. It provides answers to a number of difficult questions.

(a) It explains the financial consequences of business operations. For example, a business may be earning huge profits but its liquidity position would be highly unsatisfactory. The funds statement will explain the causes for such situation by showing what has become of the profits earned. Further, the statement would explain the direction of flow of funds into productive or non-productive activities. When a balance sheet presents a distorted picture of an undertaking because of a number of non-fund transactions, the funds statement would be an illuminating document.

(b) Debt capital is very essential for increased profitability of any enterprise. But the creditors may like to ascertain the credit worthiness and the funds generating capacity of the organization. They may like to know in what way the management has utilized the funds in the past and how the funds would be utilized in future. The funds flow statement would enable the finance manager to answer such questions in a befitting manner.

(c) It acts as an instrument for allocation of the company's scarce resources. A proposed funds statement will help to find out how the management is going to allocate the resources for meeting future productive programmes of the business. When the projected funds statement is tied to the capital budget, it will help management to maintain the financial health of the organization.

(d) It is a test for evaluating the effective use of working capital by the management. Information on the adequacy or inadequacy of working capital will enable the management to decide what possible steps it should take for effective use of surplus working capital, or in the case of inadequate working capital to make suitable arrangements to make up the deficiency.

Limitations of Funds Flow Statement

Despite its multiple managerial uses, the funds flow statements suffer from certain limitations.

1. As this statement ignores non-fund items, it becomes a crude device compared to the income statement and balance sheet.

2. The statement does not reveal shifts among the items making up the current assets and current liabilities. It does not tell whether any loss of working capital has unduly weakened the financial position. Only an examination of the balance sheet at the end of the period will show the end of these changes. Therefore, funds flow statement cannot supplant but only supplement the conventional financial statements, either in whole or in part.

3. The information used for the preparation of funds flow statement is essentially historical in nature, though attempts are made to project the funds statement for the future period.

Despite these limitations, the information supplied by the funds flow statement is really an invaluable aid to management in planning capital expenditure, devising dividend and other financial policies.

Preparation of Funds Flow Statement

Mainly two comparative balance sheets at the beginning and end of a period are used for preparing a funds flow statement. In addition, a summarised income statement and retained earning statement or, at least material information from these statements are required in order to obtain information relating to funds from operation and ownership transactions. These are the basic minima and not maxima. Additional information, if available, will sharpen the firm's financial profile as reveled by the statement.

The funds flow analysis involves the preparation of two statements, viz.

(a) Statement or schedule of changes in working capital; and

(b) Sources and uses of funds statement.

(a) Statement of Changes in Working Capital

Since a funds flow statement depicts changes in working capital, it will be better to prepare first the schedule of changes in working capital before preparing a Funds Flow Statement. The statement of changes in working capital or simply called "*working capital statement*" is prepared with the help of current assets and current liabilities. There is no effect of additional information given separately, and such information will affect only the funds flow statement. While preparing the statement of changes in working capital, the current assets may be shown either at their gross values, showing provisions as current liabilities, or at their net values after deducting such provisions. The usual items are: provision for doubtful debts, provision for loss of stock, provision for discount on debtors, etc. The purpose of this statement to find out the net change in working capital.

The format of the statement is as follows

Statement of Changes in Working Capital

	Previous Year Rs.	Current Year Rs.	Effect of Change on Working capital	
			Increase Rs.	Decrease Rs.
Current Assets				
Cash				
Bank				
B/R				
Debtors				

Stock Prepaid expenses				
Total (a)				
Current Liabilities:				
Outstanding expenses B/P Creditors				
Total (b)				
Working capital (a-b)				
Net increase/decrease in working capital				

Rules for preparing the statement of changes in working capital:

(i) Increase in a current asset, results in increase (+) in "working capital".

(ii) Decrease in a current asset, result in decreases (-) in "working capital".

(iii) Increase in a current liability, results in decrease (-) in "working capital".

(iv) Decrease in a current liability, results in increase (+) in "working capital".

Example 1

From the following two balance sheets on 31.12.2001 and 31.12.2002 prepare a Schedule of Changes in working capital.

Liabilities	2002 Rs.	2001 Rs.	Assets	2002 Rs.	2001 Rs.
Share Capital	3,25,000	3,00,000	Land &,		
P and L A/c	1,20,000	1,00,000	Buildings	5,00,000	4,00,000
9% Debentures	2,00,000	2,00,000	Machinery	1,00,000	1,60,000
Trade Creditors	98,000	75,000	Stock-in trade	1,10,000	80,000
Outstanding			Debtors	30,000	36,000
Creditors	2,000	5,000	Cash	5,000	4,000
	7,45,000	6,80,000		7,45,000	6,80,000

Solution

Schedule of Changes in Working Capital

	2001	2002	Effect on working Capital	
			Increase	Decrease
	Rs.	Rs.	(+) Rs.	(−) Rs.
Current assets:				

Stock-in-trade	80,000	1,10,000	30,000,	
Debtors	36,000	30,000		6,000
Cash	4,000	5,000	1,000	
(a) Total of current assets	1,20,000	1,45,000		
Current liabilities				
Trade creditors	75,000	98,000		23,000
Outstanding creditors	5,000	2,000	3,000	
(b) Total current liabilities	80,000	1,00,000,		
Working Capital $(a - b)$	40,000	45,000		
Net increase in working capital	5,000			5,000
	45,000	45,000	34,000	34,000

(b) Funds Flow Statement:

The total difference between the total sources and application will be shown as either increase or decrease in working capital or funds and this could be verified with the net increase/decrease in working capital as derived from the above statement. The change in working capital may also be verified by calculating working capital separately.

While preparing a Funds Flow Statement, current assets and current liabilities are to be ignored. Attention is to be given to changes in Fixed Assets and Fixed Liabilities.

Proforma of a Funds Flow Statement
Statement of sources and applications of funds

	Sources	Rs.
1.	Issue of shares at par/discount/premium	
2.	Issue of debentures at par/discount/premium	
3.	Long-and medium-term borrowing	
4.	Sales of investments	
5.	Sales of fixed assets	
6.	Funds from operation	
7.	Non-trading income	
	Total sources	
	Applications	**Rs.**
1.	Redemption of shares at par/discount/premium	
2.	Redemption of debentures at par/discount/premium	
3.	Repayment of loans	
4.	Purchase of investments	
5.	Purchase of fixed assets	
6.	Funds lost from operations	
7.	Non-trading payments - dividends paid	

	Total Uses Net increase/decrease in working capital Total Source - Total Uses	

Alternatively, it may be prepared as follow:

Statement of Sources and Applications of Funds

Sources	Rs.	Appellations	Rs.
Issue of Shares		Redemption of shares	
Issue of debentures		Redemption of debentures	
Long-term and medium-term loans taken		Repayment of loans	
		Purchase of investments	
Sales of investments		Purchase of fixed assets	
Sales of fixed assets		Payment of dividends	
Trading profits		(last year and interim)	
Non-trading income		Funds lost from operations	
		Non-trading payments	
Net decrease in working capital, as per schedule of changes in working capital		Net increase in working capital as per schedule of changes in working capital	
Total		Total	

The given balance sheet items should be classified into current accounts (i.e., current assets and current liabilities) and non-current accounts (i.e. non-current assets and non-current liabilities). The following extract from the balance sheet of a company will explain the above method of classification.

Liabilities	Rs.	Assets	Rs.
Share capital		**Fixed assets**	
Equity share capital	50,000	Goodwill	15,000
Preference share capital	40,000	Premises	60,000
		Plant	50,000
Reserves and surplus:		Furniture	10,000
Share premium	2,000	**Investments:**	
Reserve fund	10,000	6% Government bonds	20,000
Sinking fund	15,000	Miscellaneous	20,000
Compensation fund	5,000	Expenditure:	
P & L A/c	10,000	Preliminary Expenses	2,000
Secured loans:			
12% debentures	25,000	Discount of issue of debentures	3,000
Mortgage loans	20,000		
Unsecured loans Deposits	8,000		
Total non-current liabilities	1,85,000	Total non-current assets	1,60,000
Sundry creditors	12,000	Inventories	25,000

Bills payable	8,000	Debtors	21,000
Bank overdraft	15,000	Bills receivable	9,000
Outstanding expenses	5,000	Prepaid expenses	2,000
		Outstanding income	3,000
		Cash	5,000
Total current liabilities	40,000	Total current assets	65,000
Total liabilities	2,25,000	Total assets	2,25,000

Calculation of Funds from Operations or Trading Profits

The current operating profit is the main source of funds. The operating profits is the excess of operating or sales revenue over operating cost, which includes cost of goods sold and operating expenses. While sales result in inflow of funds in the form of cash, bills receivable and sundry debtors, the operating cost results in outflow of funds in the form of reduction in cash and bank balances and increase in sundry and expense creditors and acceptances. Thus, the net inflow would amount to source of funds, and the net outflow would be application of funds.

While calculating the funds from operations, only those transactions, which affect the movement of funds, should be considered. In other words, all non-fund transactions such as depreciation, write-off and write-up of fixed assets or fictitious assets, appropriation etc., should be readjusted to current net profit if they have already been charged to such profits. Similarly, if the profit and loss account has been credited with certain non-operating income, viz. dividends received, transfer back of excess provision for taxation, interest on investment, refund for tax, profit on sale of fixed assets, etc., then such items should be readjusted to the current profits and be shown separately as a source in the funds flow statement. For making such readjustments, an Adjusted profit and loss statement should be prepared in a statement form or account form as shown below:

Proforma of adjusted Profit & Loss A/c

Debit	Rs.	Credit	Rs.
To Depreciation written off	xxx	By Opening balance	xxx
To Provision for tax	xxx	By Dividends already credited to P & L a/c	xxx
To Proposed dividend	xxx		
To Preliminary expenses written off	xxx	By Over-provision for taxation written back	xxx
To Goodwill written-off	xxx	By Gain on sale of Fixed assets	xxx
To Discount on issue of shares and debentures	xxx	By Funds from trading operations (Balancing figure)	xxx
To Deferred revenue expenses already charged	xxx		
To Transfer to general reserve	xxx		
To Transfer to sinking fund, etc.	xxx		
To Loss on sale of fixed assets written-off	xxx		
To Closing balance	xxx		
	xxxx		xxxx

In the case of accumulated losses, the opening balance should be shown in the debit side of Adjusted Profit & Loss A/c, and the closing balance should be shown on the credit side.

Alternatively,

Calculation of Funds from Operations

		Rs.
	Net profit for the current year	xxx
Add:	Non-fund/Non-operating items charged to profit and loss account, Depreciation on fixed assets, Goodwill written-off, Preliminary expenses written-off, Loss on sale on -non-current assets	xxx
		xxx
Less:	Non-fund/Non-operating credits appearing in the P & L a/c, Dividends received, Interest on investments received Profit, on sales of non-current assets	xxx
	Funds from operations	xxx

Determination of Net Funds in case of Net Loss

If the Profit & Loss A/c for the year shows net loss, it does not necessarily mean that the funds have been lost in operations. If the total of items to be added back (expenses and loses written-off and transfers to reserve, etc.) exceeds the total of net loss plus items to be deducted (dividend, etc.) the difference would represent funds provided by operations.

On the other hand, if the total of items to be added back is less than the total of the net loss, plus items to be deducted, the difference would reflect funds lost in operations. The funds so lost may be shown under the heading "Application of Funds" in the Statement of Sources & Application of Funds.

Example 2

From the following, compute the funds from operations

Trading and Profit and Loss Account

	Rs.		Rs.
To Cash purchases	50,000	By Sales	60,000
To Gross profit c/d	10,000		
	60,000		60,000
To Salaries	8,000	By Gross Profit c/d	10,000
To Rent	7,000	By Dividends received	3000
To Depreciation	2,000	By Interest on Investments	3,000
To Goodwill written off	1,000		
To Preliminary exp. written off	500	By Net loss	4000
To Discount on issue of debentures	1,500		
	20,000		20,000

Solution

Computation of Funds from operation

			Rs.
	Reported Net loss		(4,000)
Add:	Items not affecting the funds:		
	Depreciation	2,000	
	Goodwill written off	1,000	
	Preliminary expenses written off	500	
	Discount on issue of debentures	1,500	5,000
	Funds from operations		1,000
Less:	Non Operating income:		
	Dividends received	3,000	
	Interest received	3,000	6,000
	Funds lost from operations		(5,000)

Alternatively an account may be prepared as follows:

Adjusted Profit and Loss A/c

	Rs.		Rs.
To Items not affecting Funds:		By Non-operating income:	
Depreciation	2,000	Dividends received	3,000
Goodwill written off	1,000	Interest on investments	3,000
Preliminary exp. written off	500	By Net loss	4,000
Discount on issue of debentures	1,500		
Funds lost from operations (Balancing figure)	5,000		
	10,000		10,000

Note: Non-operating incomes will be shown as separate items of source of funds in the funds flow statement.

Example 3

From the following P & L Account calculate the funds from operations:

Profit and Loss Account

	Rs.		Rs.
To Salaries	28,000	By Gross Profit	1,50,000
To Rent	12,000	By Profit on sale of furniture	12,000
To Printing and stationery	6,000		
To Depreciation on plant	25,000	By Interest on investment	8,000

To Goodwill written-off	10,000		
To Loss on sale of plant	5,000		
To Provision for taxation	15,000		
To Proposed dividend	14,000		
To Net profit taken to Balance Sheet	55,000		
	1,70,000		1,70,000

Solution

Calculation of Funds from Operations

		Rs.	Rs.
	Net profit as per P & L (approbation) a/c		55,000
Add:	Non-fund/Non-operating items appearing in P & L a/c:		
	Depreciation on plant	25,000	
	Goodwill written-off	10,000	
	Loss on sale of plant	5,000	
	Provision for taxation	15,000	
	Proposed dividends	14,000	69,000
			1,24,000
Less:	Non-fund/non-operating credits appearing in the P & L a/c:		
	Profit on sale furniture	12,000	
	Interest on investments	8,000	20,000
Funds from operation			1,04,000

TREATMENT OF PROVISION FOR TAXATION AND PROPOSED DIVIDENDS

Provision for Taxation

There are two ways of treating this item in the Funds Flow Statement:

(a) Provision for Taxation made during the year may be treated as current liability. If this is the treatment, then provision for taxation made during the year is not used for adjusting the net profit made during the year for calculating the funds from operations. As such, tax paid during the year is not treated as 'Application of Fund'.

(b) Provision for taxation may be treated as internal appropriation and thus a non-current liability. Then it will be used for adjusting the net profit made during the year, and tax paid during the year is treated as an 'Application of funds'.

Proposed Dividends

This item is also treated in two ways in the Funds Flow Statement:

(a) Proposed dividend may be treated as current liability. Then it will not be used for adjusting the net profit made during the year for calculating funds from operations.

(b) The proposed dividend may be treated as non current liability i.e., an appropriation of profits. In that case, dividends paid during the year are shown as application of funds. It may be noted that it is the payment of dividend (and not the declaration of dividend) which reduces the working capital. The declaration of dividend does not affect the working capital because, it is a mere appropriation of funds. In order to find out funds from operations, such proposed dividends should be added back to the current year's net profit.

Hidden Transactions

Sometimes, the information required for the funds flow statement may have to be found out. Difference in the values of fixed assets and investments in the comparative balance sheet would generally represent either sources, or application byway of sale or purchase thereof, subject to an amount written-off as depreciation. A separate fixed assets account may be prepared in order to find out the inflow and/or outflow of funds from fixed assets. In the same way, the inflow and/or outflow of funds from long-term liabilities could be found out by taking into consideration the differences in the values of such liabilities. A separated ledger account may be prepared to locate such differences. For example, if the balance sheets on two different dates show machinery account as Rs. 50,000 and Rs. 60,000 respectively, and it is given that Depreciation on Machinery has been provided to the extent of Rs. 10,000 the hidden information can be ascertained by preparing a Machinery Account as under:

Machinery Account

	Rs.		Rs.
To Opening balance	50,000	By Depreciation	10,000
To Cash (purchase of machinery during year)	20,000	By Closing balance	60,000
(Balancing figure-Application of funds)	70,000		70,000

Suppose the opening balance of the machinery in the above example is Rs. 80,000 then the Machinery Account would appear as follows:

Machinery Account

	Rs.		Rs.
To Opening balance	80,000	By Depreciation	10,000
		By Cash (sale of Machinery) (Balancing figure source of funds)	10,000
		By Closing balance	60,000
	80,000		80,000

It may be noted that while preparing the fixed assets account as shown above, the opening and closing balances of such assets should be shown at cost. If the balance of fixed assets and provision for depreciations are given separately in the balance sheets, then the fixed assets accounts are prepared at original cost and a separate provision for Deprecation Account is prepared in order to find out deprecation provided during the year. But, if the assets are shown at their written down values in the balance sheets, and the provision for depreciation in the adjustments, then such provisions should be added back to the concerned balances of fixed assets and be shown as balance in their respective account. These points are illustrated as follows:

Example 4

Opening and closing balances of the Machinery Account (at W.D.V.) appearing in the comparative balance sheet are Rs. 1,50,000 and Rs. 2,50,000 respectively. The opening and closing balances of accumulated Depreciation Account were Rs. 25,000 and 40,000 respectively. Further it is given that during the year (a) a machine costing Rs. 50,000 was purchased in exchange for fully paid up shares, and (b) an old machine costing Rs. 10,000 (accumulated depreciation Rs. 4,000) was sold for Rs. 4,500. Show the ledger accounts.

Solution

Machinery Account (at original cost)

	Rs.		Rs.
To Opening balance (Rs. 1,50,000 + Rs. 25,000)	1,75,000	By Cash (sale of old machine)	4,500
		By Accumulated depreciation a/c	4,000
To Share capital (I) Issue for the purchase of machinery	50,000	By Loss on sale (2) (P & L a/c)	1,500
To Cash (Purchase of new Machinery - Bal.fig.)	75,000	By Closing balance (Rs. 2,50,000 + Rs. 40,000)	2,90,000
	3,00,000		3,00,000

Accumulated Depreciation Account

	Rs.		Rs.
To Machinery a/c (depreciation on machine sold)	4,000	By Opening balance	25,000
		By P & L a/c (balancing figure - depreciation provided)	19,000
To Closing balance	40,000		
	44,000		44,000

Note: 1. Purchase of machinery by exchanging fully paid-up shares is non-fund item which will not affect working capital and therefore will not be shown in the funds flow statement.

2. Original cost minus Accumulated Depreciation minus amount sold (i.e., Rs. 10,000 – Rs. 4,000 – Rs. 4,500)

9.7 Is depreciation a Source of Funds?

Depreciation refers to the decrease in the value of assets, particularly fixed assets. Fixed assets may lose their values due to wear and tear, obsolescence, passage of time, exhaustion and accident. As this loss in value i.e., depreciation arises out of operations of fixed asset, in the business, it is treated as an operating expense to profit and loss account. The usual treatment of depreciation in final account is to debit the same to profit and loss account and credit the concerned fixed asset account (i.e., deducted from fixed assets in balance sheet). Since, profit and loss account and fixed asset account are non-current accounts, depreciation is treated as a non-fund item while preparing the fund flow statement. In other words, depreciation is added back to operating profit to find out funds from operations since it does not affect the flow of funds. Hence, it is neither a source nor an application of funds. If depreciation were really a source of funds by itself, then any business could improve its funds position by providing periodical depreciation charge.

However, depreciation may be considered as a source in a limited sense for the reasons given below:

(a) Depreciation reduces taxable income and therefore tax liability for example, a company is in 40% tax bracket and the amount of depreciation charged to its profit and loss account is, say Rs.40,000. The company reduces the taxable income by Rs.40,000 and the tax liability by Rs.16,000 (i.e. 40% on Rs.40,000). The opportunity saving of cash outflow may be taken as a source of funds.

(b) Depreciation may not generate funds but it definitely saves funds. For example, if a company has taken an asset on lease, it must pay lease rentals which are cash outflows. But it may avoid this situation by owning the same asset.

(c) Depreciation forms part of current asset when it is charged as overheads. For example, the value of closing stock may include depreciation as an element of cost and in that case, it becomes a fund item.

Practical Problems

Illustration 1

From the following information, calculate funds from operations:

Profit and Loss Account

	Rs.		Rs.
To Expenses:		By Gross profit b/d	2,00,000
Operation	1,00,000	By Gain on sale of buildings	20,000
Depreciation	40,000	By other income	2,000
To Loss on sale of machinery	10,000		
To Advertisement suspense a/c	5,000		
To Discount of debtors	500		
To Discount on issue of shares	500		
To Goodwill w/off	12,000		
To Preliminary expenses w/off	2,000		
To Net Profit	52,000		
	2,22,000		2,22,000

(Madras University, B.Com., March 1997)

Solution

Calculation of Funds from operations

	Rs.	Rs.
Reported current profit		52,000
Add: Items not affecting funds:		
Depreciation	40,000	
Loss on sale of machinery	10,000	
Advertisement suspense a/c	5,000	
Discount on issue of shares	500	
Goodwill written off	12,000	
Preliminary expenses written off	2,000	69,500
		1,21,500
Less: Non-operating income:		
Gain on sale of buildings	20,000	
Other income	2,000	22,000
Funds from operations		99,500

Note: Other income Rs.2000 should be shown as a separate source in the Funds Flow Statement.

Alternatively, an Adjusted Profit and Loss Account may be prepared as follows:

Adjusted Profit and Loss Account

	Rs.		Rs.
Items not affecting funds:		Non-operating income:	
Depreciation	40,000	Gain on sale of buildings	20,000
Loss on sale of machine	10,000	Other income	2,000
Advertisement suspense a/c	5,000	Funds from operations (Balancing figure)	99,500
Discount on issue of share	500		
Goodwill written off	12,000		
Preliminary expenses written off	2,000		
Reported current profit	52,000		
	1,21,500		1,21,500

Illustration 2

Calculate the funds from operations from the following:

Profit and loss Account

	Rs.		Rs.
To Salaries	15,000	By Gross Profit	20,000

To Rent	15,000	By Profit on sale of land	5,000
To Depreciation	10,000	By Net loss	35,000
To Printing expenses	5,000		
To Goodwill w/off	3,000		
To Provision for Tax	4,000		
To Loss on sale of plant	2,000		
To Proposed dividends	6,000		
	60,000		60,000

Solution

Calculation of Funds from Operations

	Rs.	Rs.
Reported Net loss		(-) 35 000
Add: Items not affecting funds:		
Depreciation	10,000	
Goodwill written off	3,000	
Provision for Taxation	4,000	
Loss on sale of plant	2,000	
Proposed dividends	6,000	25,000
		(-) 10,000
Less: Non-operating income:		
Profit on sale of land		(-) 5,000
Funds lost from operations		(-) 15,000

Alternatively it may be prepared in the form of an account as follows:

Adjusted Profit and Loss Account

	Rs.		Rs.
To Depreciation	10,000	By Net loss	35,000
To Goodwill written off	3,000	By Profit on sale of land	5,000
To Provision for Taxation	4,000		
To Loss on sale of plant	2,000		
To Proposed dividends	6,000		
To Funds lost from operations (Balancing figure)	15,000		
	40,000		40,000

Illustration 3

From the following particulars prepare a Funds Flow Statement for the year ended 31st December 2001.

	Rs.
(a) Net Profit before writing off goodwill	21,500
(b) Depreciation written off on fixed assets	3,500
(c) Goodwill written off from profits	5,000
(d) Dividends paid	7,000
(e) Shares issued for cash	10,000
(f) Purchase of machinery	20,000
(g) Increase in working capital	8,000

Solution

Working notes:

Computation of Funds from operations

Net Profit before writing off goodwill	Rs.21,500
Add: Depreciation	3,500
Funds from operations	25,000

Goodwill need not be adjusted, as it is not written off from profits.

Funds Flow Statement

Sources	Rs.	Applications	Rs.
Issue of Shares	10,000	Machinery purchased	20,000
Funds from operations	25,000	Dividends paid	7,000
		Increase in working capital	8,000
	35,000		35,000

Illustration 4

From the following figures, prepare a Funds Flow Statement.

Assets	31-12-2001 Rs.	31-12-2002 Rs.
Cash	1,30,000	40,000
Debtors	1,00,000	1,60,000
Stock	2,35,000	2,55,000
Land and buildings	5,40,000	10,20,000
Plant and machinery	28,04,000	35,44,000
Furniture	2,10,000	2,10,000
	40,19,000	52,29,000
Liabilities		
Creditors	3,19,000	3,65,000
Provision for dividend		2,00,000
Long-term loan		5,35,000

Net Worth		
Equity capital	36,00,000	40,00,000
Surplus	1,00,000	1,29,000
	40,19,000	52,29,000

Solution

Schedule of Changes in Working Capital

Particulars	2001	2002	Effect on Working capital	
Current assets:	Rs.	Rs.	Increase (Rs.)	Decrease (Rs.)
Cash	1,30,000	40,000		90,000
Debtors	1,00,000	1,60,000	60,000	
Stock	2,35,000	2,55,000	20,000	
	4,65,000	4,55,000		
Current liabilities:				
Creditors	3,19,000	3,65,000		46,000
	3,19,000	3,65,000		
Net decrease in working capital			56,000	
			1,36,000	1,36,000

Funds Flow Statement

Sources	Rs.	Applications	Rs.
Long-term loans	5,35,000	Purchase of land and buildings	4,80,000
Issue of shares	4,00,000	Purchase of plant and machinery	7,40,000
Funds from operations	2,29,000		
	11,64,000		
Decrease in working capital	56,000		
	12,20,000		12,20,000

Workings

	Rs.	
Increase in profit (1,29,000 - 1,00,000)		29,000
Add: Provision for dividends		2,00,000
Funds from operations		2,29,000

Illustration 5

From the following balance sheets prepare schedule of changes in working capital:

Liabilities	Dec. 1980 Rs.	Dec.1981 Rs.	Assets	Dec.1980 Rs.	Dec.1981 Rs.
Share capital	2,00,000	2,50,000	Cash	30,000	47,000
Creditors	70,000	45,000	Debtors	1,20,000	1,15,000
Retained Earnings	10,000	23,000	Stock	80,000	90,000
			Land	50,000	66,000
Total	2,80,000	3,18,000		2,80,000	3,18,000

(M.B.A., April 2002, Madras University)

Solution

Schedule of Changes in Working capital

Particulars	1980	1981	Effect on working capital	
			Increase	Decrease
	Rs.	Rs.	Rs.	Rs.
Current Assets:				
Cash	30,000	47,000	17,000	
Debtors	1,20,000	1,15,000	–	5,000
Stock	80,000	90,000	10,000	
	2,30,000	2,52,000		
Current liabilities:				
Creditors	70,000	45,000	25,000	
Working Capital	1,60,000	2,07,000		
Net increase in working capital	47,000			47,000
			52,000	52,000

Illustration 6

From the following information, work out the figure of (a) fixed assets purchased, and (b) the items to be shown in the Funds Flow statements:

	Rs.
Fixed Assets W.D.V. on 1.1.1997	7,60,000
Fixed Assets W.D.V. on 31.12.1997	7,20,000
Depreciation charged during the year	1,40,000
W.D.V. of Asset sold during the year	20,000
Sale proceeds of scrapped assets	15,000

Solution

Fixed Assets Account

Date	Particulars	Rs.	Date	Particulars	Rs.
1.1.97	To Balance B/d	7,60,000	31.12.97	By Depreciation[2]	1,40,000
	To Cash (Fixed (assets purchased)[1]	1,20,000		By Cash (Sale of assets)[3]	15,000
				By Loss on sale of assets[4]	5,000
				By Balance c/d	7,20,000
		8,80,000			8,80,000

1. Fixed assets purchased to be shown as application of funds 1,20,000
2. Depreciation to be adjusted to operating profit 1,40,000
3. Sale of asset to be shown as a source of funds 15,000

4. Loss on sale to be adjusted to operating profit 5,000

Illustration 7

The opening and closing balances of plant and machinery at cost) amounted to Rs.2,00,000 and Rs.3,00,000 respectively. Accumulated depreciation at the beginning and the end amounted to Rs.50,000 and Rs.80,000 respectively. A machine costing Rs.10,000 (W.D.V. Rs.6,000) was sold for Rs. 5,000 during the year. Prepare necessary accounts to show the sources and application of fund during the year relating to plant and machinery.

(Madras, B.Com., March 1995)

Solution

Plant and Machinery a/c

	Rs.		Rs.
To Balance b/d	2,00,000	By Machine sold	10,000
To Cash (purchased) (Bal.fig)	1,10,000	By Balance h/d	3,00,000
	3,10,000		3,10,000

Accumulated Depreciation A/c

	Rs.		Rs.
To Machine sold (Depreciation)	4,000	By Balance b/d	50,000
To Balance c/d	80,000	By Adjusted P & L a/c (Depreciation) (Bal.fig)	34,000
	84,000		84,000

Machine sold account

	Rs.		Rs.
To Plant and Machinery A/c	10,000	By Accumulated depreciation	4,000
		By Cash (sales)	5,000
		By Adjusted P & L A/c - loss (Balancing figure)	1,000
	10,000		10,000

1. Plant and Machinery purchased Rs. 1,10,000 should be shown as application of funds.

2. Depreciation Rs. 34,000 and loss on sale Rs. 1,000 should be debited to adjusted P & L A/C in order to add back these amount, to find out funds from operations.

3. Machine sold for Rs. 5,000 will be shown as a source of funds.

Funds Flow Statement

Source	Rs.	Application	Rs.
Sale of machinery	5,000	Purchase of Machinery	1,10,000

Illustration 8

The non-current assets and equities of Anish Limited at the end of 1996 and 1997 are given below:

	31.12.1996 Rs.	31.12.1997 Rs.
Plant at W.D.V	25,400	57,000
Investment in shares of subsidiary co.	52,800	1,16,000
Bonds payable	1,00,000	2,80,000
Share capital	1,60,000	1,60,000
Reserves and surplus	95,200	1,64,200

Additional information

(a) Dividends of Rs.15,000 were paid.

(b) An equipment costing Rs.11,600 with a net book value of Rs.7,600 was sold and the profit on sale of equipment of Rs.5,200 has been included in net income. The gross plant assets increased by Rs.37,200. Prepare a funds flow statement.

Solution

Workings

Adjusted P & L a/c

	Rs.		Rs.
To Dividends paid	15,000	By Opening balance	95,200
To Depreciation on plant	9,600	By Profit on sale of equipment	5,200
To Closing balance	1,64,200	By Funds from operations (Balancing figure)	88,400
	1,88,800		1,88,800

Plant Account

	Rs.		Rs.
To Opening Balance	25,400	By Cash (equipment sold)	12,800
To Adjusted P & L a/c (Profit)	5,200	By Depreciation (Bal. fig)	9,600
To Cash (purchases of Plant & equipment) 37,200 + 11,600)	48,800	By Closing balance	57,000
	79,400		79,400

It is assumed that the equipment purchased during the year for Rs.11,600 has been sold at a profit. Depreciation includes the depreciation on equipment sold also.

Funds Flow statement for the year ended 31.12.1997

Sources	Rs.	Applications	Rs.
Issue of bonds	1,80,000	Purchase of investments	63,200

Sale of equipment	12,800	Plant purchased	48,800
Funds from operations	88,400	Dividends paid	15,000
			1,27,000
		Increase in working capital (Balancing figure)	1,54,200
	2,81,200		2,81,200

Illustration 9

Following are the comparative balance sheets of a company for the year 1989 and 1990

Balance Sheet

Liabilities	1989 Rs.	1990 Rs.	Assets	1989 Rs.	1990 Rs.
Share capital	70,000	74,000	Cash	9,000	7,800
Debentures	12,000	6,000	Debtors	14,900	17,700
Creditors	10,360	11,840	Stock	49,200	42,700
Profit & Loss a/c	10,740	11,360	Goodwill	10,000	5,000
			Land	20,000	30,000
	1,03,100	1,03,200		1,03,100	1,03,200

Additional information

(a) Dividends were paid totalling Rs.4,000

(b) Land was purchased for Rs.15,000

You are required to prepare a statement showing changes in working capital and a Funds Flow Statement.

(Madras B.Com., March 1993)

Solution

Statement showing changes in working capital

	1989	1990	Effect on working capital	
			Increase	Decrease
	Rs.	Rs.	Rs.	Rs.
Current assets:				
Cash	9,000	7,800	–	12,00
Debtors	14,900	17,700	2,800	–
Stock	49,200	42,700		6,500
	73,100	68,200		
Current Liabilities:				
Creditors	10,360	11,840		1,480
Working Capital	62,740	56,360		
Net decrease in working capital		6,380	6,380	
	62,740	62,740	9,180	9,180

Funds flow statement for the year ended 31.12.1990

Sources	Rs.	Applications	Rs.
Issue of shares	4,000	Purchase of land	15,000
Funds from operations	14,620	Redemption of debentures	6,000
	18,620	Dividends paid	4,000
Net decrease in working capital	6,380		
	25,000		25,000

Workings

Adjusted P & L a/c

	Rs.		Rs.
To Goodwill written off	5,000	By Opening balance	10,740
To Dividend paid	4,000	By Funds from operations	14,620
To Depreciation on land	5,000	(balancing figure)	
To Closing balance	11,360		
	25,360		25,360

Land a/c

	Rs.		Rs.
To opening balance	20,000	By Depreciation (Bal. fig)	5,000
To Cash (purchase)	15,000	By Closing balance	30,000
	35,000		35,000

Illustration 10

From the following comparative Balance Sheet of Shri Ram Ltd as on June 30, 1996 and June 30, 1997, you are required to prepare

1. A statement of changes in working capital
2. Funds flow statement

Liabilities	1996	1997	Assets	1996	1997
	Rs.	Rs.		Rs.	Rs.
Share capital	1,80,000	2,00,000	Goodwill	24,000	20,000
Reserve fund	28,000	36,000	Buildings	80,000	72,000
P & L A/c	39,000	24,000	Machinery	74,000	72,000
Trade creditors	16,000	10,800	Investments	20,000	22,000
Bank overdraft	12,400	2,600	Inventories	60,000	50,800
			Debtors	40,000	44,400
Provision for taxation	32,000	34,000	Cash	13,200	30,400

Provision for doubtful debts	3,800	4,200			
	3,11,200	3,11,600		3,11,200	3,11,600

Additional information

(a) Depreciation charged on machinery was Rs.8,000, and on building, Rs.8,000.

(b) Interim dividend paid on January 1997 was Rs.15,000.

(c) Provision of Rs.10,000 was made for taxation during the year ending 30th June 1997.

Solution

Schedule of changes in Working Capital

	1996	1997	Effect on working capital	
			Increase	Decrease
	Rs.	Rs.	Rs.	Rs.
Current assets:				
Inventories	60,000	50,800	–	9,200
Debtors, less provision for doubtful debts	36,200	40,200	4,000	–
Cash	13,200	30,400	17,200	–
	1,09,400	1,21,400		
Current liabilities:				
Trade creditors	16,000	10,800	5,200	–
Bank overdraft	12,400	2,600	9,800	–
Provision for tax	32,000	34,000	–	2,000
	60,400	47,400		
Working capital	49,000	74,000		
Net increase in Working capital			–	25,000
			36,200	36,200

Funds flow statement

Sources	Rs.	Applications	Rs.
Issue of shares	20,000	Purchase of land	2,000
Funds from operations	28,000	Purchase of machinery	6,000
		Interim dividend paid	15,000
			23,000
		Net increase in working capital	25,000
	48,000		48,000

Adjusted P & L A/c

	Rs.		Rs.
To Good will written off	4,000	By Opening balance	39,000
To Depreciation on Machinery	8,000	By Funds from operations (Balancing figure)	28,000
To Building	8,000		

To Interim dividend paid	15,000		
To Reserve fund	8,000		
To Closing balance	24,000		
	67,000		67,000

Buildings A/c

	Rs.		Rs.
To Opening balance	80,000	By Depreciation	8,000
		By Closing balance	72,000
	80,000		80,000

Machinery A/c

	Rs.		Rs.
To Opening balance	74,000	By Depreciation	8,000
To Cash (Purchase of machinery balancing figure)	6,000	By Closing balance	72,000
	80,000		80,000

Note: Since the provision for Taxation has been treated as a current liability, the adjustment item relating to this provision is omitted.

Alternatively,. if the provision for taxation is treated as a non-current liability, it will appear as follows:

Provision for Taxation a/c

	Rs.		Rs.
To Cash (taxes paid-balancing figure)	8,000	By Opening balance	32,000
To Closing balance	34,000	By (Adjusted) P & L a/c (Taxation provided during the year)	10,000
	42,000		42,000

The net effect would be that (i) the net increase in working capital will increase by Rs.2,000 (ii) the funds from operations will increase by Rs.10,000 and (iii) Rs.8,000 will be shown as application of funds in the funds statement.

Illustration 11

The comparative balance sheets of M/s. Venkat and Subbu as on 31.12.1996 and 31.12.1997 were as follows:

Liabilities	1996 Rs.	1997 Rs.
Sundry creditors	80,000	85,000

	Loan from Prasanna	40,000	35,000
	Bank Loan	80,000	90,000
	Combined capital	1,25,000	1,50,000
		3,25,000	3,60,000
Assets:			
	Cash	20,000	15,000
	Receivables	50,000	90,000
	Inventories	70,000	60,000
	Plant and machinery	80,000	55,000
	Land and buildings	1,05,000	1,40,000
		3,25,000	3,60,000

During the year, a machine costing Rs.10,000 (accumulated depreciation Rs.4,000) was sold for Rs.7,000. The provision for depreciation against plant and machinery, as on 31-12-1996 was Rs.25,000 and on 31-12-1997 Rs.40,000. Net profit for the year 1997 amounted Rs.46,000

Prepare

1. Schedule of changes in working capital; and
2. Statement of sources and applications of funds

Solution

1. Schedule of Changes in Working Capital

	1996	1997	Effect on working capital	
			Increase	Decrease
	Rs.	Rs.	Rs.	Rs.
(a) **Current assets:**				
Cash	20,000	15,000	–	5,000
Receivables	50,000	90,000	40,000	–
Inventories	70,000	60,000	–	10,000
Total (a)	1,40,000	1,65,009		
(b) **Current Liabilities:**				
Sundry creditors	80,000	85,000		5,000
Total (b)	80,000	85,000		
Working capital (a – b)	60,000	80,000		
Net increase in working capital	20,000			20,000
	80,000	80,000	40,000	40,000

Working

Plant and Machinery a/c

	Rs.		Rs.
To Opening balance (Rs.80,000 + Rs.25,000)	1,05,000	By Provision for depn. a/c (Depn on machine sold)	4,000

To Adjusted P & L A/c (profit on sale)	1,000	By Cash (machine sold)	7,000
		By Closing balance (Rs.55,000 + Rs.40,000)	95,000
	1,06,000		1,06,000

Provision for Depreciation

	Rs.		Rs.
To Plant and machinery A/c	4,000	By Opening balance	25,000
To Closing balance	40,000	By Adjusted P & L A/c (Bal. fig depreciation charged)	19,000
	44,000		44,000

Combined Capital A/c

	Rs.		Rs.
To Combined drawings (balancing figure)	21,000	By Opening balance	1,25,000
		By Net profit	46,000
To Closing balance	1,50,000		
	1,71,000		1,71,000

Calculation of funds from operations:

Net profit for the year	46,000
Add: Depreciation charged	19,000
	65,000
Less: Profit on sale of machinery	1,000
Operating profits	64,000

Sources and Applications of Fund Statement

Sources	Rs.	Applications	Rs.
Funds from operations	64,000	Purchase of land and building	35,000
Sale of machinery	7,000	Loan paid	5,000
Bank loan	10,000	Drawings	21,000
		Net increase in working capital	20,000
	81,000		81,000

Illustration 12

A statement of retained earning of A Ltd is given below:

		Rs.
Balance of retained earning 1st July 1995		2,08,640

Add: Net income after taxes		4,16,330
tax refund		14,215
		6,39,185
Less: Dividends	2,92,605	
Cost of investment written-off	61,150	
Loss on sale of plant	6,670	3,60,425
Balance of retained earnings 30th June 1996		2,78,760

Depreciation of Rs.39,760 was deducted in arriving at net income for the accounting year.

Plant having a net book value of Rs.21,605 was sold in August 95. Plant and equipment were purchased during the accounting year at a cost of Rs.1,60,000 and this purchase was financed by the issue of debentures.

Preference shares were reduced for Rs.38,200

Prepare statement of sources and uses of net working capital for the year ending 30th June 1996.

Solution

Funds Flow Statement

Sources	Rs.	Uses	Rs.
Sale of Plant	14,935	Dividends paid	2,92,605
Tax Refund	14,215	Preference shares reduced	38,200
Funds from operation	4,56,090		
			3,30,805
		Net increase in working capital (balancing figure)	1,54,435
	4,85,240		4,85,240

Workings

Calculations of funds from operations

	Rs.
Net income after taxes	4,16,330
Add: Depreciation	39,760
	4,56,090

Illustration 13

Balance sheets and income statement of Greenwood Company Limited as on December 31, 1987 and 1988 are as follows:

Liabilities	1987	1988	Assets	1987	1988
	Rs.	Rs.		Rs.	Rs.
B/P	15,000	25,000	Cash	5,000	2,000
Bank Overdraft	13,000	10,000	B/R	10,000	8,000
Outstanding exp.	2,000	3,000	Investments		

Long-term loan	30,000	20,000	(Short-term)	5,000	–
Capital	30,000	30,000	Inventories	20,000	25,000
P & L A/c	10,000	12,000	Fixed assets (net)	60,000	65,000
	1,00,000	1,00,000		1,00,000	1,00,000

Income statement for the year 1988

Sales	2,00,000
Less: Cost of goods sold (including depreciation Rs.10,000)	1,70.000
Gross profit	30,000
Less: Other expenses	20,000
	10,000
Less: Income tax provision	5,000
Retained in business	5,000

Prepare a statement of source and uses of funds.

(Madras, B.Com., May 1996)

Solution

Schedule of Changes in working capital

	1987	1988	Effect on working capital	
			Increase	Decrease
	Rs.	Rs.	Rs.	Rs.
Current Assets:				
Cash	5,000	2,000		3,000
Bills receivable	10,000	8,000		2,000
Investment (Short-term)	5,000	–		5,000
Inventories	20,000	25,000	5,000	–
	40,000	35,000		
Current Liabilities:				
Bills payable	15,000	25,000		10,000
Bank overdraft	13,000	10,000	3,000	
Outstanding expenses	2,000	3,000		1,000
	30,000	38,000		
Working capital	10,000	(3,000)		
Net decrease in working capital		13,000	13,000	
	10,000	10,000	21,000	21,000

Funds Flow Statement for the year ended 31.12.1988

Sources	Rs.	Application	Rs.
Funds from operations	12,000	Repayment of loan	10,000
Net decrease in working capital	13,000	Purchase of fixed asset	15,000
	25,000		25,000

Workings

Adjusted profit and loss A/c

	Rs.		Rs.
To Depreciation	10,000	By Opening balance	10,000
To Closing balance	12,000	By Funds from operations (Bal.fig.)	12,000
	22,000		22,000

Fixed assets a/c

	Rs.		Rs.
To Opening balance	60,000	By Adjusted P & L A/c (Depreciation)	10,000
To Cash (Purchases) (Bal. fig)	15,000	By closing balance	65,000
	75,000		75,000

Statement of Changes in Financial Position [SCFP]

Preparation of funds statement on the aforesaid pattern, however, excludes all those transactions which do not affect working capital. Consequently, many important activities where fund flows take place between non-current assets to one another, or from one non-current liability to another, or from non-current assets to non-current liabilities and vice versa remain altogether unreported. But these transactions influence significantly the financial resources of the business enterprise, and also the flow of funds. To incorporate all these interfirm non-current exchange transactions, an all financial resources flow statement, termed the Statement of Changes in Financial Position (SCFP) is constructed.

Like the funds statement, it is also prepared from financial data generally identifiable in the income statement, balance sheet and related notes. There is no standard format for this statement. However, the International According Standard (IAS-71) states that the presentation of the SCFP should be informative. It also requires that SCFP should be (i) presented for each period for which the income statement is prepared, (ii) included as an integral part of the financial statements (iii) the funds gained or lost in operations should be presented in SCFP separately from other sources or uses of funds. Unusual items which are not part of the ordinary activities of the enterprise should be separately disclosed in the statement.

SCFP is thus designed to report the causes of changes in financial position (all financial resources, i.e. all assets and liabilities, including owner's equities) of a business during the period that result from its financing and investment activities with others. It thus improves the understanding of the operations and activities of an enterprise for the relative period.

Illustration 14

From the figures given below,prepare a statement showing application and sources of funds during the year 1995.

	Dec. 31 1994 Rs.	Dec. 31 1995 Rs.
Assets:		
Fixed assets (Net)	5,10,000	6,20,000
Investments	30,000	80,000
Current Assets	2,40,000	3,75,000
Discount on Debenture	10,000	5,000
	7,90,000	10,80,000
Liabilities and capital:		
Share Capital (Equity)	3,00,000	3,50,000
Share Capital (9% preference)	2,00,000	1,00,000
8% Debentures	1,00,000	2,00,000
Reserves	1,10,000	2,70,000
Provision for Doubtful debts	10,000	15,000
Current Liabilities	70,000	1,45,000
	7,90,000	10,80,000

The provision for depreciation stood at Rs.1,50,000 on 31 st December, 1994 and at Rs.1,90,000 on 31.12.1995. During the year:

(i) A machine costing Rs.70,000 (book value Rs.40,000) was disposed off for Rs.25,000;

(ii) Preference share redemption was carried out at a premium of 5% on 1.1.95 and

(iii) Dividend @ 15% was paid on equity shares for the year 1994.

Solution

Statement of Sources and Application of funds For the Year ended December 31, 1995

Sources		Rs.	Application		Rs.
Profit earned during 1995		2,34,000	Purchase of Fixed assets		2,20,000
			Purchase of Investment		50,000
Add: Non-cash charges			Redemption of preference shares		1,05,000
Depreciation	70,000				
Discount on debenture written-off	5,000	3,09,000	Payment of Dividend:		
			Preference	9,000	
Issue of shares		50,000	Equity	45,000	54,000
Issue of Debentures		1,00,000	Increase in Working capital		55,000

Sale of machine	25,000		
	4,84,000		4,84,000

Working Notes

	31.12.94 Rs.	31.12.95 Rs.
(i) Working Capital:		
Current Assets	2,40,000	3,75,000
Less: Provision for Doubtful Debts	10,000	15,000
	2,30,000	3,60,000
Current Liabilities	70,000	1,45,000
Working Capital	1,60,000	2,15,000
Increase in Working Capital	55,000	
	2,15,000	2,15,000

(ii) Depreciation provided during the year

Provision as on 31.12.1994	1,50,000
Less: Provision relating to the machine sold, during the year (cost Rs. 70,000; book value Rs. 40,000)	30,000
	1,20,000
Provision as on 31.12.1995	1,90,000
Fresh Provision made during the year	70,000

(iii) Profit earned during the year

	Rs.		Rs.
To Loss on sale of machine	15,000	By Balance b/d	1,10,000
To Premium on Redemption of Preference shares	5,000	By Profit earned during the year (Balancing figure)	2,34,000
To Preference Dividend	9,000		
To Equity Dividend	45,000		
To Balance c/d	2,70,000		
	3,44,000		3,44,000

(iv) Fixed Assets acquired

Book value of fixed assets on 31.12.94	5,10,000
Add: Provision for Depreciation on 31.12.94	1,50,000

Cost of Fixed Assets as on 31.12.94	6,60,000
Less: Cost of machine disposed off	70,000
	5,90,000
New assets acquired during 1995 (balancing figure)	2,20,000
Cost of fixed assets as on 31.12.95 (Rs. 6,20,000 + 1,90,000)	8,10,000

REVIEW QUESTIONS

1. Explain the terms 'funds', 'funds flow', and 'funds flow statement'.
2. What are the major sources and application of funds?
3. What are the advantages and limitations of funds flow statement?
4. Illustrate the preparation of Schedule of Changes in Working Capital.
5. Explain the procedure for the preparation of funds flow statement.
6. 'Depreciation is a big source of funds.' Comment.
7. Explain the various techniques of funds reporting.

REVIEW PROBLEMS

8. From the following Balance Sheet as on 31st December, 1993 and 1994 prepare a Schedule of Changes in Working Capital for 1994.

	December 31	
	1993 Rs.	1994 Rs.
Assets:		
Cash	36,000	47,000
Debtors	1,20,000	1,15,000
Stock-in-trade	80,000	90,000
Land	50,000	66,000
	2,86,000	3,18,000
Capital and liabilities:		
Share Capital	2,00,000	2,50,000
Trade creditors	76,000	45,000
Retained earnings	10,000	23,000
	2,86,000	3,18,000

(Ans: Increase in Working Capital - Rs.47.000)

9. Kumar Limited presents the following information and you are required to calculate funds from operations

Profit and Loss Account

Debt	Rs.	Credit	Rs.
To Expenses:			
Operation	50,000	By Gross Profit	1,00,000

Depreciation	20,000	By Gain on sale of plant	10,000
Loss on sale of land	5,000		
Advertisement Suspense A/c	2,500		
Discount	250		
Goodwill	6,000		
Net Profit	26,250		
	1,10,000		1,10,000

(Madras, B.Com, May 1993) [Ans.Rs.49,750]

10. The following is the comparative balance sheet of A Ltd. Prepare a funds flow statement:

Balance Sheet

Liabilities	31.12.76 Rs.	31.12.77 Rs.	Assets	31.12.76 Rs.	31.12.77 Rs.
Share capital	8,000	8,500	Land	5,000	5,000
P & L Appn. A/c	1,450	2,450	Plant	2,400	3,400
Creditors	900	500	Debtors	1,650	1,950
Mortgage Loan	–	500	Stock	900	700
			Cash at Bank	400	900
	10,350	11,950		10,350	11,950

(Madras, B.A. Corporate: March 1995)
(Ans: Increase in working capital Rs.1,000;
Total sources Rs.2,000; Total uses Rs.1,000)

11. From the following information, prepare a statement of sources and application of funds for the year ended 31st December 1992.

(a) Increase in working capital Rs.4,000
(b) Net profit of Rs.10,750 before writing off goodwill
(c) Depreciation on fixed assets Rs.1,750
(d) Dividends paid Rs.3,500
(e) Goodwill Rs.5,000 written off out of profits
(f) Shares issued for cash for Rs.5,000
(g) Machinery was purchased for Rs.10,000

(Madras. B.Com, May 1994)
(Ans: Funds from operations Rs.12,500;
Total sources of Rs.17,500; applications Rs.13,500]

12. The following transactions in fixed assets section of the balance sheet of company took place in 1997.

The fixed assets at cost amount to Rs.1,92,680 on 1.1.1997 and Rs.2,02,240 on 31.12.1997. The accumulated depreciation account increased from Rs.85,600 in 1996 to Rs.88,500 in 1997. A piece of asset sold in 1997 for Rs.5,000 was originally purchased at Rs.20,000. Accumulated depreciation on the asset sold was charged against profit on the year.

Find out the amount of fixed assets acquired during the year. How other items shown above should appear in the funds flow statement?

13. From the following balance sheet of Durga Ltd., prepare a statement of Sources and Applications of Funds and Schedule of changes in working capital for 1991.

Liabilities	1990	1991	Assets	1990	1991
	Rs.	Rs.		Rs.	Rs.
Share Capital	1,00,000	1,25,000	Land & Buildings	1,00,000	95,000
General reserve	25,000	30,000	Plant & machinery	75,000	84,500
Profit & Loss A/c	15,250	15,300	Stock	50,000	37,000
Bank loan	35,000	–	Debtors	40,000	32,000
Creditors	75,000	67,500	Cash	250	300
Provision for taxation	15,000	17,500	Bank	–	4,000
			Goodwill	–	2,500
	2,65,250	2,55,300		2,65,250	2,55,300

Additional Information:

(a) Dividend of Rs. 11,000 was paid during 1991.

(b) Depreciation on plant written off in the year 1991 Rs. 7,000.

(c) A provisions for income tax Rs. 16,500 was made during the year.

(Madras, B.Com., May 1993)

(Ans: Increase in Working Capital Rs.9,450;
Total sources Rs.67,050; Applications Rs.76,500)

Funds Flow analysis

14. Prepare Fund Flow Statement for ABC Company Ltd. from the following particulars for the year ended 31st December 2001 and 2002.

Comparative Balance Sheet of ABC Ltd., as on

	2002	2001
	Rs.	Rs.
Liabilities and Capital:	5,00,000	4,00,000
Share Capital	1,50,000	50,000
Reserves and Surplus	3,50,000	4,00,000
Current Liabilities	5,00,000	6,00,000
	15,00,000	14,50,000

Assets:		
Fixed Assets	3,10,000	3,00,000
Investments	15,000	---
Cash and Bank balances	7,50,000	7,87,500
Stocks	4,00,000	3,50,000
	15,00,000	14,50,000

(a) The net profit after adjustments in respect of provision for dividends, taxation was Rs. 10,000 for the year.

(b) There was addition to Fixed assets during the year amounting to Rs. 40,000 and Depreciation for the year was Rs. 30,000. **(ICWA Final Adapted)**

(Ans: Increase in Working Capital Rs. 1,25,000; Sources Rs. 2,30,000; Applications Rs. 1,05,000)

10

CASH FLOW ANALYSIS

Learning Objectives

After going through this chapter, you should be able to.

— Explain the meaning of cash flow statement,

— Distinguish between Funds Flow Analysis and Cash Flow Analysis,

— Discuss the managerial uses of Cash Flow Analysis,

— Know the preparation of Cash Flow Statement,

— Work out problems in Cash Flow Analysis.

Preparation of Cash Flow Statement

10.1 Meaning of Cash Flow Analysis

When the concept of funds is used to mean 'Cash' the funds flow analysis would be called cash flow analysis. It is an analysis based on the movement of cash and bank balances. Under cash flow analysis, all movements of cash, rather than the movement of working capital would be considered. Such movements of cash are depicted in a statement called Cash Flow Statement. It is a statement of changes in financial position prepared on cash basis. While preparing cash flow statement, two types of cash flows, viz., actual cash flows and notional cash flows are identified. Actual cash flows refer to the actual movements of cash into or out of business. Purchase of fixed assets for cash, borrowing from bank or financial institutions, redemption of debentures, etc., are a few examples of cash flows. But notional cash flows result only in the case of increase or decrease in current assets. Notional cash flows result in indirect cash movements into or out of business. For example, increase in debtors does not result in any actual cash out flows since it is part of credit sales. But at the same time, cash flows out of business take place in the form of material cost, labour cost, and overheads, etc., incurred on the goods sold on credit.

10.2 Principal sources and application of cash in a business

Principal sources of cash include:

1. Issue of shares and debentures for cash,
2. Sale of fixed assets and investments for cash,
3. Borrowing from banks and other financial institutions,
4. Cash from operations or trading profits,
5. Decrease in current assets [notional cash inflows]: For example, credit sale of goods involves creation of assets in the form of debtors and bills receivable. When payment is received

[cash inflow] from the customer, there will be reduction in [debtors and bills] current assets. Thus, decrease in current assets involves cash inflows.

6. Increase in current liabilities [notional cash inflows]: For example, purchase of goods on credit results in the creation of creditors and bills payable. Here, it is assumed that creditors have given a loan of cash, which has been used to acquire the goods supplied by them.

Applications of cash include:

1. Redemption of shares and debentures by cash,
2. Purchase of fixed assets and investments by cash,
3. Repayment of loans,
4. Cash lost in operations or trading losses,
5. Increase in current assets,
6. Decrease in current liabilities.

10.3 Format of a Cash Flow Statement

Format of a Cash Flow Statement

Cash Flow statement for the year ending...

	Rs.		Rs.
Balance as on 1.1.19xx		Cash outflows:	
Cash in hand	xxx	Redemption of shares and debentures	xxx
Cash at bank	xxx	Purchase of fixed assets and investments	xxx
Add: Cash inflows:			
Issue of shares	xxx	Repayment of loans	xxx
Issue of debentures	xxx		
Sales of fixed assets	xxx	Increase in current assets	xxx
Sale of investments	xxx	Decrease in current liabilities	xxx
	xxx		
Borrowing (Long. medium & short-term)	xxx	Payment of taxes and dividends	xxx
Cash from operations:			
Decrease in current assets	xxx	Outstanding expenses of previous year paid	xxx
Increase in current liabilities	xxx		
Outstanding income of Previous year collected	xxx	Expenses paid in advance	xxx
advance	xxx		
		Balance as on 31.12.19 xx	
		Cash in hand	
		Cash at bank	
Total	xxx	Total	xxx

Alternatively, it may be shown in the form of a statement as follows:

Cash Flow Statement for the year ended...

		Rs.
Balances as on 1.1.19xx		
Cash in hand		xxx
Cash at bank		xxx
Add Cash in flows	xxx	
	xxx	xxx
(Refer the first alternative for details)		

Total sources (a)	xxxx
Loss: Cash outflows	
(Refer the first alternative for details)	
Total applications (b)	xxxx
Balance as on 31-12-19xx	
Cash in hand	xxx
Cash at bank	xxx

Note: The total closing balance should tally with the balance as shown by (a) – (b)

10.4. Calculation of Cash from Operations

The ultimate result of all business operations would be either net profit or net loss. When net profit results in the cash inflows, the net loss would result in cash outflow. Further, when all transactions are cash transactions, the net profit or loss as shown by the income statement may be taken as the amount of cash from operations. However, in actual practice it does not happen. A number of credit transactions take place, such as credit purchases, credit sales, outstanding expenses, etc. In such cases, the profit or loss as shown by the Income Statement may be more or less than actual cash flow. There are possibilities for a business with net loss to have positive cash flow from operations. Such a situation may arise owing to charging of non-cash or non-fund items to profit and loss account.

The cash from operations can be calculated by preparing one **Adjusted profit and Loss Account**, as in the case of funds flow analysis. That is, all non-fund items such as depreciation, goodwill written-off etc., should be readjusted. In addition to non-fund items, all non-cash transactions, such as outstanding expenses, outstanding income etc., should be readjusted. The proforma of the Adjusted Profit and Loss Account would be as follows:

Adjusted P & L A/c

	Rs.		Rs.
To Depreciation	xxx	By Opening balance	xxx
To Goodwill written-off	xxx	By Dividends received	xxx
To General reserve	xxx	By Interest on investments	xxx
To Loss on sale of fixed assets and investments	xxx	By Profit on sale of assets	xxx
To current year's outstanding expenses	xxx	By Current year's outstanding income	xxx
To Expenses paid in advance during last year	xxx	By Income received in advance during last year	xxx
To Closing balance		By Cash profits from operations (Balancing figure)	
	xxx		xxx

It may be noted that adjustments relating to stock, debtors, creditors, bills receivable and bills payable in the forms of increase/decrease are shown in the cash flow statements. alternatively, increase or decreases in the above mentioned items may be adjusted to cash profit from operations as follows:

Adjusted P & L A/c

	Rs.		Rs.
To All debit items as shown in	xxx	By Opening balance	xxx
the preforma given previously	xxx	By all credit items as shown in the proforma given previously	xxx
To Decrease in Current Assets		By Increase in current assets	
To Increase in current liabilities	xxx		
To Closing balance		By Decrease in current liabilities	
		By Cash from operations (balancing figure)	
	xxxx		xxxx

10.5 How does Cash Flow Analysis differ from Funds Flow Analysis?

Distinctions between Cash Flow Analysis and Funds Flow analysis

1. The concept of fund refers to actual or notional 'cash' under Cash Flow Analysis. But it means either all financial resources or net working capital in Funds Flow Analysis.

2. Cash flow analysis deals with the movement of only actual or notional cash. But funds flow is concerned with all the items constituting funds i.e., net working capital. Cash is one of the components of working capital.

3. Cash flow statements show the causes for the change in cash and bank balances i.e., cash receipts and cash payments alone. Funds flow statement shows the causes for the change in net working capital. It is a flexible device designed to disclose and emphasize all significant changes in the current assets and current liabilities of the firm during the period under study.

4. Cash flow analysis is a tool of short-term financial analysis while the funds flow analysis is comparatively a long-term one.

5. Funds flow statement is in consonant with the actual basis of accounting. But in cash flow statement, the data obtained on accrued basis is converted into cash basis.

6. Funds flow statement tallies the funds generated from various sources with the various uses to which they are put. But cash flow statement starts with the opening cash balance and reaches to the closing cash balance by processing through various sources and uses.

7. In funds flow analysis, the changes in various current assets and current liabilities are shown in a separate statement or schedule of changes in working capital in order to ascertain the net increase or decrease in working capital. But in cash flow analysis, such changes are adjusted to funds from operations in order to ascertain the cash from operations.

10.6 Managerial uses or Advantages of Cash Flow Analysis

Uses or Advantages of Cash Flow Analysis

1. It is very helpful in understanding the cash position of a firm. Since cash is the basis for carrying on business operations, the cash flow statement is very useful in evaluating the current cash position.

2. It helps management to understand the past behavior of the cash cycle, and to control the uses of cash in future.

3. The repayment of loans, replacement of assets and other such programs can be planned on its basis.

4. It throws light on the factors contributing to the reduction of cash balance, in spite of increase in income or vice versa.

5. A comparison of the cash flow statement with the cash budget for the same period helps in comparing and controlling cash expenditure.

6. The cash flow statement is helpful in making short-term financial decisions relating to liquidity, and the ways and means position of the firm.

Illustration 1

From the following balances, you are required to calculate cash from operations:

	December 31	
	1996	1997
	Rs.	Rs.
Profit and Loss account balance	25,000	1,55,000
Debtors	45,000	42,000
Creditors	20,000	26,000
Bills receivable	12,000	15,000
Prepaid expenses	1,600	1,400
Bill Payable	18,000	16,000
Outstanding expenses	1,200	1,600
Outstanding income	800	900
Income received in advance	250	300

Solution

Calculation of Cash from Operations
Adjusted Profit and Loss Account

	Rs.		Rs.
To Decrease in debtors	3,000	By Opening balance	25,000
To increase in creditors	6,000	By Increase in B/R	3,000
To decrease in prepaid exp.	200	By Decrease in B/P	2,000
To Increase in outstanding exp.	400	By Increase in outstanding income	100

To Increase income received in advance	50	By Cash from operation	1,34,550
To Closing balance	1,55,000	(Balancing figure)	
	1,64,650		1,64,650

Illustration 2

From the following Profit and Loss Account, compute the cash from operations:

Profit & Loss Account for the year ended 30th June 1998

	Rs.		Rs.
To Salaries	10,000	By Gross Profit	50,000
To Rent	3,000	By Profit on sale of land	9,000
To Depreciation	5,000	By Income tax refund	7,000
To Discount	1,000		
To Loss on sale of plant	2,000		
To Goodwill written off	8,000		
To Proposed dividends	10,000		
To Provision for tax	10,000		
To Net Profit	17,000		
	66,000		66,000

Solution

Computation of cash from operations

	Rs.	Rs.,
Net profit as per P & L Account		17,000
Add: Non cash/ non-operating charges:		
Depreciation	5,000	
Loss on sale of plant	2,000	
Goodwill written off	8,000	
Proposed dividends	10,000	
Provision for tax	10,000	35,000
		52,000
Less: Non -cash/non-operating income:		
Profit on sale of land	9,000	
Income tax refund	7,000	16,000
Cash from operations		36,000

Illustration 3

Following are the condensed balance sheets of Subha Ltd.

	1997 Rs.	1998 Rs.
Equity Share Capital	4,00,000	4,00,000
Reserves and surplus	2,82,000	3,46,000

Depreciation Reserve	20,000	28,000
Secured Loans	40,000	60,000
Creditors for goods	1,29,000	1,06,000
Outstanding expenses	17,000	3,000
	8,88,000	9,43,000
Plant and Equipment (Cost)	5,70,000	6,00,000
Inventories	1,96,000	2,26,000
Debtors	79,000	57,000
Cash at bank	43,000	60,000
	8,88,000	9,43,000

You are required to work out the figures of funds from operation and cash from operations.

Solution

Computation of Funds from operations

	Rs.
Reserves and surplus in 1998	3,46,000
Less: Balance in 1997	2,82,000
Profit added during the year	64,000
Add: Depreciation	8,000
Funds from operations	72,000

Computation of cash from operations

		Rs.
Profit earned		64,000
Add: Depreciation	8,000	
Decrease in Debtors	22,000	30,000
		94,000
Less: Decrease in creditors	23,000	
Decrease in outstanding expenses	14,000	
Increase in inventories	30,000	67,000
Cash from operations		27,000

Illustration 4

A summary of the financial position of Mr. X for the year 1996 and 1997 is given as follows:

Liabilities	1989 Rs.	1990 Rs.	Assets	1989 Rs.	1990 Rs.
Capital	70,000	83,000	Cash	7,000	13,000
Creditors	10,000	12,000	Debtors	20,000	18,000
			Stock	40,000	52,000
			Fixed assets	13,000	12,000
	80,000	95,000		80,000	95,000

There were no drawings or sale of fixed assets during the year. Prepare a cash flow statement.

(Madras, M.Com, 1996)

Solution

Cash flow statement for the year ended 31-12-1997

Sources	Rs.	Uses	Rs.
Cash balance 1.1.97	7,000	Cash outflows:	
Add: Cash inflows:		Increase in stock	12,000
Decrease in debtors	2,000	Cash balance 31-12-97	13,000
Increase in creditors	2,000		
Cash from operations	14,000		
	25,000		25,000

Workings:

	Rs.
Capital at end	83,000
Less: Capital at the beginning	70,000
Profit	13,000
Add: Depreciation	1,000
	14,000

Illustration 5

The following are the summarised balance sheets of M/s Rahul Brothers Private Limited as on March 31, 1992 and 1993:

	1992 Rs.	1993 Rs.		1992 Rs.	1993 Rs.
7% Redeemable			Fixed assets	4,100	4,000
Preference shares		1000	**Less:** Depreciation	1,100	1,500
Equity shares	4,000	4,000			
General reserve	200	200		3,000	2,500
Profit & Loss A/c	100	120	Debtors	2,000	2,400
Debentures	600	700	Stock	3,000	3,500
Creditors	1,200	1,100	Prepaid expenses	30	50
Provision for taxation	300	420	Cash	120	350
Proposed dividend	500	580			
Bank overdraft	1,250	680			
	8,150	8,800		8,150	8,800

You are required to prepare a statement of cash flow

(Madras, B.Com., May 1996)

Solution

Workings:

Adjusted P & L A/c

	Rs.		Rs.
To Provision for tax	420	By Opening balance	100
To Proposed dividend	580	By Increase in debtors	400
To Depreciation	400	By Increase in stock	500
To Closing balance	120	By Increase in prepaid expenses	20
		By Decrease in creditors	100
		By Cash from operations	400
	1,520		1,520

Cash flow statement for the year ended 31-12-1993

		Rs.			Rs.
1.1.93	Cash balance	120	1.1.93	Bank overdraft	1,250
	Cash inflows:			Cash outflows;	
	Issue of preference shares	1,000		Tax paid (1992)	300
	Issue of debentures	100		Dividends paid (1992)	500
	Sale of fixed assets	100			2,050
	Cash from operations	400			
		1,720	31.12.93	Cash balance	350
31.12.93	Bank overdraft	680			
		2,400			2,400

Illustration 6

Following are the comparative balance sheets of Brown Company Ltd.

Liabilities	1989 Rs.	1990 Rs.	Assets	1989 Rs.	1990 Rs.
Share capital	70,000	74,000	Bank balance	9,000	
Debentures	12,000	6,000	Accounts receivable	14,900	17,700
Accounts payable	10,360	11,840			
Provision for doubtful debts	700	800	Stock-in trade	49,200	42,700
P& L A/c	10,040	10,560	Buildings	20,000	40,600
Bank overdraft	–	2,800	Goodwill	10,000	5,000
	1,03,100	1,06,000		1,03,100	1,06,000

Additional information

1. Buildings were acquired for Rs.20,600
2. Amount provided for the amortisation of good will totalled Rs.5,000
3. Dividends paid totalled Rs.3,500
4. Debenture loan repaid was Rs.6,000

Explain how the overdraft of Rs.2,800 as on 31st dec 1996 has arisen.

Solution

1. Calculation of Operating Profit made during the year. (An increase in the Profit and Loss A/c may be taken as profit made (10,560 – 10,040 = 520)

Profit		520
Add: Amortisation of good will	5,000	
Dividend paid	3,500	
Provision for doubtful debts	100	
Opening profit made during the year		8,600
		9,120

Brown & Co. Ltd.
Statement of Cash Flow for the year ended
31st December 1996

Cash inflows	Rs.	Cash outflows	Rs.
Bank balance as on 1.1.1996	9,000	**Cash outflows:**	
Add: Cash inflows		1. Increase in accounts receivable	2,800
1. Decrease in stock in trade	6,500	2. Payment of dividend	3,500
2. Increase in accounts payable	1,480	3. Acquisition of building	20,600
3. Issue of shares	4,000	4. Repayment of debenture	6,000
4. Operating profit	9,120		
	30,100		
Bank overdraft as on 31-12-1996	2,800		
	32,900		32,900

Illustration 7

Balance sheets of X and Y on 1-1-2001 and 31.12-2001 were as follows:

Balance Sheet

Liabilities	2000 Rs.	2001 Rs.	Assets	2000 Rs.	2001 Rs.
Creditors	40,000	44,000	Cash	10,000	7,000
Mrs X's loan	25,000	–	Debtors	30,000	50,000
Loan from bank	40,000	50,000	Stock	35,000	25,000
Capital	1,25,000	1,53,000	Machinery	80,000	55,000

			Land	40,000	50,000
			Building	35,000	60,000
	2,30,000	2,47,000		2,30,000	2,47,000

During the year, a machine costing Rs.10,000 (accumulated depreciation Rs.3,000) was sold for Rs.5,000. The provision for depreciation against machinery as on 1-1-2001, was Rs.25,000, and on 31-12-2001 it was Rs.40,000. Net profit for the year 2001 amounted to Rs.45,000. You are required to prepare cash flow statement.

Solution

Cash Flow Statement

	Rs.	Rs.
Cash balance as on 1-1-2001		10,000
Add: Cash inflows:		
Cash from operation	59,000	
Loan from bank	10,000	
Sale of machinery	5,000	74,000
		84,000
Less: Cash outflows:		
Purchase of land	10,000	
Purchase of building	25,000	
Mr. X's Loan repaid	25,000	
Drawings	17,000	77,000
Cash balance on 31-12-2001		7,000
Working Notes:		Rs.
Cash from operations		
Profit made during the year		45,000
Add: Depreciation on machinery	18,000	
Loss on sale of machinery	2,000	
Decrease in stock	10,000	
Increase in creditors	4,000	34,000
		79,000
Less: Increase in debtors		20,000
Cash from operations		59,000

Machinery Account

	Rs.		Rs.
To Balance b/d	1,05,000	By Bank	5,000
		By Loss on sale of machinery	2,000
		By Provision for depreciation	3,000
		By Balance C/d	95,000
	1,05,000		1,05,000

Provision for Depreciation A/c

	Rs.		Rs.
To Machinery a/c	3,000	By Balance b/d	25,000
To Balance c/d	40,000	By Added P & L a/c	18,000
	43,000		43,000

Note: It may be observed that the increase/decrease in current assets have been adjusted to cash from operations. Alternatively, those items may also be shown in the cash flow statement.

Accounting Standard [AS 3] - Revised Format

AS 3 revised in 1997 has recommended revised Cash Flow Statement [CFS] for listed companies and other industrial, commercial, and business undertakings in the private and public sector. It is at present recommendatory in character. According to revised AS 3, CFS should be prepared in such a way as to report the cash flows during the period separately for operating, investing, and financing activities.

1. Cash Flows from Operating Activities. Examples are as follows:

(a) Cash receipts from sale of goods and services;

(b) Cash receipts from royalties, fees, commission, and other revenue;

(c) Cash payments to suppliers of goods and services;

(d) Cash payments to employees;

(e) In the case of insurance companies, cash receipts and payments for premium received and claims and other benefits to policy holders;

(f) Payment and refund of income tax;

(g) Cash receipts and payments relating to futures and options contracts taken up for trading purposes.

2. Cash Flows from investing activities. Examples of such activities are as follows:

(a) Purchase of fixed assets including intangibles and payments relating to capitalized research and development cost and self-constructed fixed assets.

(b) Cash receipts from sale of fixed assets including intangibles.

(c) Purchase of securities for cash such as shares, warrants, and debt instruments of other enterprises.

(d) Sale of securities for cash

(e) Loans and advances given to third parties

(f) Loans and advances collected from third parties

(g) Cash receipts and payments relating to futures and options contracts entered into for investment purposes.

3. Cash Flows from financing activities. Examples of such activities are as follows:

(a) Cash receipts from the issue of shares and other similar instruments,

(b) Cash receipts from the issue of debentures, bonds, long or other short-term borrowing,

(c) Redemption of shares and repayment of amounts borrowed.

The following illustrations would make clear the preparation of CFS under AS 3 method and Traditional method.

Illustration 8

The same information given in Illustration 7 is used for the preparation of CFS under AS 3 [Revised] method.

Cash Flow Statement [AS - 3 [Revised] Method]

	Rs.	Rs.
I. Cash Flow from Operating Activities:		
Net Profit made during the year	45,000	
Adjustment for depreciation	18,000	
Loss on sale of machinery	2,000	
Operating Profit before working capital changes	65,000	
Decrease in stock	10,000	
Increase in creditors	4,000	
Increase in debtors	[20,000]	
Net Cash Flow from operating activities		59,000
II. Cash Flows from Investing Activities:		
Sale of machinery	5,000	
Purchase of land	(10,000)	
Purchase of building	(25,000)	
Net Cash Flow from investing activities		(30,000)
III. Cash Flows from Financing Activities:		
Loan from bank	10,000	
Mrs. X's loan repaid	(25,000)	
Drawings	(17,000)	
Net Cash Flow from financing activities		[32,000]
Net increase [decrease] in cash and cash equivalent		[3,000]
Cash and cash equivalents opening balance		10,000
Cash and cash equivalents closing balance		7,000

Notes: 1. Cash and cash equivalents include cash and bank balances and risk less short-term investments.

2. Cash flow from operations are computed in the statement itself instead of preparing a separate statement showing cash from operations as in the case of traditional method.

3. Figures given within brackets represent cash outflows.

Illustration 9

Prepare Cash Flow Statement from the following balance sheets of Excel Ltd.:

Liabilities	2000 Rs.	2001 Rs.	Assets	2000 Rs.	2001 Rs.
Share capital	17,00,000	18,35,000	Buildings	8,00,000	10,00,000

Reserves	40,000	83,700	Plant and machinery	2,50,000	3,70,000
P & L App. A/c	1,00,000	1,30,000	Furniture	5,000	6,000
Provision for dividends	70,000	50,000	Cash	2,000	2,200
Creditors	1,00,000	95,000	Debtors	1,00,000	45,000
Bank overdraft	8,000	18,000	Bills receivable	8,000	9,000
Bills Payable	14,000	13,000	Stock	4,00,000	3,43,700
Mortgage Loan	10,000	70,000	Prepaid expenses	3,000	3,100
			Investments	1,64,000	1,70,000
			Goodwill	3,00,000	3,43,700
			Preliminary expenses	10,000	2,000
	20,42,000	22,94,700		20,42,000	22,94,700

(a) Depreciation is charged on buildings at 3% of cost of Rs.9 00,000; on Plant and machinery at 8% of cost Rs.4 00,000; Furniture at 5% of cost Rs.8,000.

(b) Investments were purchased and interest received Rs.3,000 was used in writing down the book value of investments.

(c) The declared dividends for 70000 were paid and interim dividend for Rs.20,000 was paid out of P & L App. A/c.

Solution
Workings

Net Profit as per P&L a/c	
Closing balance of P&L App. A/c	Rs.1,30,000
Add: Transfer to Reserves	43,700
Provision for dividends for 2001	50,000
Interim dividend paid	20,000
	2,43,700
Less Opening balance of P&L App a/c	1,00,000
Net Profit before tax and extraordinary items	1,43,700

Investment Account

	Rs.		Rs.
To Balance b/d	1,64,000	By Bank [interest]	3,000
To Bank [Purchase of investments]	9,000	By Balance c/d	1,70,000
	1,73,000		1,73,000

Cash Flow Statement [Revised Method]

		Rs.	Rs.
I.	Cash Flows from Operating Activities:		
	Net Profit before tax and extraordinary items	1,43,700	
	Adjustments for depreciation for Furniture	400	
	Adjustments for depreciation on Plant and machinery	32,000	
	Adjustments for depreciation on Buildings	27,000	
	Preliminary expenses written off	8,000	
	Operating profit before working capital changes	2,11,100	
	Decrease in debtors	55,000	
	Decrease in stock	56 300	
	Decrease in creditors	(5,000)	
	Increase in bills receivable	(1,000)	
	Decrease in bills payable	(1,000)	
	Increase in prepaid expenses	(100)	
	Net cash flow from operating activities		3,15,300
II	Cash Flows from Investing Activities:		
	Interest on investments	3,000	
	Purchase of investments	(9,000)	
	Purchase of buildings	(2,27,000)	
	Purchase of machinery	(1,52,000)	
	Purchase of furniture	(1,400)	
	Purchase of goodwill	(43,700)	
	Net cash flow from investing activities		(4,30,100)
III	Cash Flows from Financing Activities:		
	Issue of shares	1,35,000	
	Mortgage Loan	60,000	
	Dividend paid for 2000	(70,000)	
	Interim dividend paid	(20,000)	
	Net Cash flows from financing activities		1,05,000
	Net increase [decrease] in cash and cash equivalents		(9,800)
	Cash and cash equivalents opening balance [Bank O/D - Cash]		(6,000)
	Cash and cash equivalents closing balance [Bank O/D - Cash]		(15,800)

Note: Figures given within brackets represent cash outflows.

Illustration 10

A company finds on 1st January 2002 that it is short of funds with which to implement its expansion program. On 1st January 2001 it had a credit balance of Rs.1,80,000. From the following information prepare a statement for the Board of Directors to show how the overdraft of Rs.68,750 as on 31st December has arisen.

Figures as per Balance Sheet (as on 31st December)

	2000 (Rs.)	2001 (Rs.)
Fixed Assets	7,50,000	11,20,000
Stock and stores	1,90,000	3,30,000
Debtors	3,80,000	3,35,000
Bank balance	1,80,000	68,750 [O/D]
Share capital [Shares of Rs.10 each]	2,50,000	3,00,000
Bills Receivable	87,500	95,000

The profit for the year ended 31 December 2001 before charging depreciation and taxation amounted to Rs.2,40,000. On 1st January 2001, 5000 shares were issued at a premium of Rs.5 per share. Rs.1,37,500 was paid in March 2001 by way of income tax. Dividends were paid as follows:

2000 [final] on the capital on 31st December 2000 at 10% less tax at 25%,

2001 [interim] 5 per cent free of tax.

Preparation of Cash Flow Statement [as per Traditional Method]

Solution

Cash Flow Statement
For the year ended 31st December 2001

Sources (Cash inflows)	Amount (Rs.)	Application (Cash outflows)	Amount (Rs.)
Bank balance as on 1-1-2001	1,80,000	Cash outflows:	
Add Cash inflows:		Purchase of fixed assets	3,70,000
Issue of shares	50,000	Increase in stock and stores	1,40,000
Share premium	25,000	Increase in bills receivable	7,500
Decrease in debtors	45,000	Income tax paid	1,37,500
Increase in creditors	80,000	Final dividend for 2000	18,750
Cash from operations	2,40,000	Interim dividend for 2001	15,000
	6,20,000		
Bank balance (O/D) on 31.12.01	68,750		
	6,88,750		6,88,750

Workings

1. Final dividend works out to Rs.2,50,000 × 10% = Rs.25,000
   Less Tax deducted at source at 25% on, Rs.25,000 = 6,250
   Net dividend amount paid = 18,750

2. Interim dividend at 5% on Rs. 3,00,000 = Rs. 15,000

3. Interim dividend is free of tax, hence nothing is deductible from Rs.15,000 on account of tax. However, a sum of Rs.5,000 i.e., Rs.15,000 × 25/75 is payable to the Government on account of tax.

4. It is assumed that the figure of income tax paid Rs.1,37,500 includes Rs.11,250 [Rs.6,250 + 5,000] in respect of final and interim dividends.

5. It is assumed that fixed assets are appearing at cost.

6. It is obvious that the profit for the year 2001 Rs.2,40,000 is before charging the final dividend and interim dividends.

The cash flow statement as per Revised Method is as follows:

Cash Flow Statement for the year ended 31-12-2001

		Rs.	Rs.
I.	Cash Flows from Operating Activities:		
	Net Profit before tax and extraordinary items	2,40,000	
	Add: Decrease in debtors	45,000	
	Increase in creditors	80,000	
	Increase in stock and stores	(1,40,000)	
	Increase in bills receivables	(7,500)	
	Income tax paid	(1,37,500)	
	Net cash flows from operating activities		80,000
II.	Cash Flows from Investing Activities:		
	Purchase of fixed assets	(3,70,000)	
	Net cash flows from investing activities		(3,70,000)
III.	Cash Flows from Financing Activities:		
	Issue of shares	50,000	
	Share Premium	25,000	
	Final dividend paid	(18,750)	
	Interim dividend paid	(15,000)	
	Net cash flows from financing activities		41,250
	Net increase [decrease] in cash and cash equivalent		(2,48,750)
	Cash and cash equivalents at the beginning of the year		1,80,000
	Cash and cash equivalents at the end of the year (O/D)		(68750)

Review Questions

1. From the following balances you are required to calculate cash from operations:

	December 31	
	1993	1994
	Rs.	Rs.
Debtors	1,00,000	94,000
Bills receivable	20,000	25,000
Creditors	40,000	50,000
Bills payable	16,000	12,000
Outstanding expenses	2,000	2,400,
Prepaid expenses	1,600	1,400
Accrued income	1,200	1,500

Income received in advance		600	500
Profit made during the year			2,60,000

(Ans: 2,67,200)

2. The Profit and Loss Account of an enterprise for the year ended 31st December 1996 was as follows:

		Rs.			Rs.
To Opening stock		0,000	By Sales		1,40,000
To Purchases		98,000	By Closing stock		12,000
To wages	15,000				
Add: Outstanding	3,000	18,000			
To G.P c/d		26,000			
		1,52,000			1,52,000
To Salaries			By G.P. b/d		26,000
paid	10,000		By Int. received	2,000	
Add: Outstanding	2,000	12,000	**Add:** Accrued	500	2,500
To Insurance	1,200		By Net Loss		8,500
Less: Prepaid	200	1,000			
To Selling exp.		8,000			
To Depreciation		10,000			
To Goodwill w/off		5,000			
To Preliminary expenses w/off		1,000			
		37,000			37,000

Calculate cash from operations

3. Statement of the financial position of Mr. Ram are given below.

	1.1.94 Rs.	31.12.94 Rs.		1.1.94 Rs.	31.12.94 Rs.
Accounts payable	2,900	2,500	Cash	4,000	3,000
Capital	73,900	61,500	Debtors	2,000	1,700
			Stock	800	1,300
			Buildings	10,000	8,000
			Other fixed assets	60,000	50,000
	76,800	64,000		76,800	64,000

Additional Information

(a) There were no drawings

(b) There were no purchases or sales of either buildings or other fixed assets.

Prepare a statement of cash flow.

(Ans: Cash lost from Operations Rs. 1000)

4. Statement of financial position of XYZ Limited is given below

	1997 Rs.	1998 Rs.		1987 Rs.	1988 Rs.

Share capital	18,000	19,000	Cash	6,000	4,000
Creditors	6,400	7,600	Debtors	15,500	19,000
P & L Account	2,900	3,500	Buildings	5,000	6,200
			Patent rights	800	900
	27,300	30,100		27,300	30,100

You are asked to prepare a statement of flow of cash.

(Madras B.Com., March 96)

(**Ans:** Cash lost from Operations Rs. 1700; Source Rs. 1000 uses Rs. 1300)

5. From the following figures compute cash from operations:

	1987 Rs.	1988 Rs.
Stock	7,500	12,000
Debtors	15,000	18,000
Bad debts reserve	1,500	1,800
Bills Receivable	6,000	4,500
Bills payable	7,500	9,000
Creditors	12,000	13,500
Marketable securities	15,000	18,000
Outstanding salaries	1,500	2,250
Unexpired insurance	3,000	1,500
Outstanding income	4,500	6,000
Income received in advance	3,000	1,500

Profit earned during 1988 is Rs.15,000 after providing for depreciation of Rs.3,000

(Madras, B.Com.,)

(Ans. Rs.11,500)

7. From the following balance sheet of A Ltd. as on December 31, 1993 and 1994, you are required to prepare a Statement of sources and uses of cash.

1. Depreciation of Rs.3,000 and Rs.6,000 have been charged on plant account and land & buildings account respectively.
2. Dividends paid totalled Rs.3,000.

Liabilities	1993 Rs.	1994 Rs.	Assets	1993 Rs.	1994 Rs.
Share capital	80,000	85,000	Land & Building	50,000	50,000
P & L appn. A/c	14,500	24,500	Plant	24,000	34,000
Creditors	9,000	5,000	Stock	9,000	7,000
Mortgage	–	5,000	Debtors	16,500	19,500
			Cash at bank	4,000	9,000
	1,03,500	1,19,500		1,03,500	1,19,500

(Ans: Operating Profit - Rs.22,000; Sources - Rs.34,000; Uses - Rs.29,000)

7. From the following Balance Sheets prepare a cash flow statement:

Liabilities	1993 Rs.	1994 Rs.	Assets	1993 Rs.	1994 Rs.
Capital	1,50,000	1,75,000	Land & Buildings	1,10,000	1,50,000
Loan from Bank	1,60,000	1,00,000	Machinery	2,00,000	1,40,000
Creditors	85,000	93,000	Stock	50,000	45,000
Bills payable	50,000	40,000	Debtors	70,000	80,000
Loan from IFC	–	25,000	Cash	15,000	22,000
Outstanding exp.	5,000	7,000	Prepaid expenses	5,000	3,000
	4,50,000	4,40,000		4,50,000	4,40,000

Additional information

(a) Net profit for year 1994 amounted to Rs.60,000

(b) During the year a machine costing Rs.25,000 (accumulated depreciation Rs.10,000) was sold for Rs.13,000

(c) The provision for depreciation against machinery on 31.12.93 was Rs.50,000 and 31.12.1994 was Rs.85,000

(Madras, B.Com, May 1995)

(Ans: Cash from operations Rs.1,04,000; Cash inflows Rs.1,42,000; Cash Outflow Rs.1,35,000)

8. The following details are available from a company.

Liabilities	31.12.85 Rs.	31.12.86 Rs.	Assets	31.12.85 Rs.	31.12.86 Rs.
Share capital	70,000	74,000	Cash	9,000	7,800
Debentures	12,000	6,000	Debtors	14,900	17,700
Reserve for Doubtful debts	700	800	Stock	49,200	42,700
Trade creditors	10,360	11,840	Land	20,000	30,000
P & L A/c	10,040	10,560	Goodwill	10,000	5,000
	1,03,100	1,03,200		1,03,100	1,03,200

(a) Dividend paid Rs.3,500

(b) Land was purchased for Rs.10,000

(c) Amount provided for amortisation of goodwill Rs.5,000

(d) Debentures paid off Rs.6,000. Prepare cash flow statement

(Madras, B.Com., Sep.96)

(Ans: Cash from operation Rs.14,300; Cash inflows Rs.18,300; Cash outflows Rs.19,500)

9. From the following particulars prepare a cash flow statement:

Liabilities	1987 Rs.	1988 Rs.	Assets	1987 Rs.	1988 Rs.
Share capital	3,00,000	3,50,000	Fixed assets	5,10,000	6,20,000

8% Debentures	1,00,000	2,00,000	Discount on debentures	10,000	5,000
Reserve	80,000	1,00,000			
Creditors	70,000	50,000	Debtors	40,000	75,000
Bills payable	50,000	60,000	Stock	30,000	1,00,000
Bank overdraft	–	40,000	Bank	10,000	–
	6,00,000	8,00,000		6,00,000	8,00,000

Other information

1. Provision for depreciation was on 31.12.87 Rs.1,50,000 and on 31.12.88 Rs.1,90,000

2. A machine costing Rs.70,000 (Depreciation written-off Rs.30,000) was sold for Rs.25,000

3. Dividend paid was Rs.30,000

(Madras, B.A. Corporate), 1992)

(**Ans:** Cash from operations Rs.25,000; Cash inflow Rs.2,00,000; Cash outflows Rs.2,50,000)

10. The Balance Sheets of AB Ltd. as on 31st December 1992 and 31st December 1993 respectively are given below:

Liabilities	1992 Rs.	1993 Rs.	Assets	1992 Rs.	1993 Rs.
Share capital	1,00,000	1,60,000	Fixed assets at cost	1,52,000	2,00,000
Retained earnings	70,250	85,300	Inventory	93,400	89,200
Accumulated Depreciation	60,000	40,000	Debtors	30,800	21,100
6% debentures	50,000	–	Prepaid exp.	3,950	3,000
Sundry Creditors	28,000	48,000	Bank	28,100	20,000
	3,08,250	3,33,300		3,08,250	3,33,300

The following additional information for the year 1993 are also available:

(a) Net profit Rs.27,050

(b) Depreciation charged Rs.10,000

(c) Cash dividend declared during the period Rs.12,000

(d) An addition to the building was made during the year at a cost of Rs. 78,000 and fully depreciated equipment costing Rs.30,000 was discarded, no salvage being realised.

Prepare a cash flow statement (under Revised method)

(**Ans:** Cash from operations Rs. 71,900; Sources Rs. 60000 and Uses Rs. 1,40,000)

11. The financial position of Mr. R as on 31st December 2001 and 2002 was as follows

Liabilities	2001 Rs.	2002 Rs.	Assets	2001 Rs.	2002 Rs.
Sundry Creditors	35,000	40,600	Cash	4,000	3,000
Mrs. R's Loan		20,000	Debtors	35,000	38,000
Loan from Bank	30,000	25,000	Stock	25,000	22,000
Hire Purchase Vendor		20,000	Land	20,000	30,000
Capital	1,48,000	1,54,000	Building	50,000	55,000
			Machinery	80,000	86,000
			Delivery Van		25,000
	2,14,000	2,59,600		2,14,000	2,59,600

The delivery van was purchased in December 2002 on hire purchase basis; a payment of Rs. 5,000 was made immediately and the balance of the amount is to be paid in 20 monthly installments of Rs. 1,000 each together with interest at 12% p.a. During the year the proprietor withdrew Rs. 2,600 for domestic expenditure. The provision for depreciation against machinery on 31-12-2001 was Rs. 27,000 and on 31-12-2002 Rs. 36,000. You are required to prepare the Cash Flow statement as per revised method.

(**Ans:** Net Cash Flow from operating activities Rs. 45,600;
Net Cash Flow from investing activities (Rs. 35,000);
Net Cash Flow from financing activities (Rs. 11,000);
Profit for the year Rs. 32,000)

12. What does Cash Flow Analysis mean?
13. List out various sources and applications of Cash.
14. Give a Format of a Cash Flow Statement.
15. Explain the method of Computation of Cash From Operations.
16. Distinguish between Cash Flow Analysis and Funds Flow Analysis.
17. What are the managerial uses of Cash Flow Analysis?
18. Describe the procedure for the preparation of a Cash Flow Statement.

11

CAPITAL EXPENDITURE EVALUATION

Learning Objectives

After completing this chapter, you should be able to

— Explain the concept of capital expenditure and capital budgeting.

— Discuss the importance of Capital Budgeting and types of projects.

— Describe the various project appraisal methods.

— Discuss the project risk and uncertainty analysis.

— Work out problems in capital budgeting.

11.1. Concept of Capital Expenditure Decision

Capital expenditure is one, which is intended for future periods and normally includes investment in fixed assets and other development projects. Every business concern has to face the problem of capital expenditure decisions some time or the other. Hence, planning for capital expenditure has become an integral part of policy-making management and budgetary control. It is essentially a long-term function and such for a decision to buy land, buildings or plant and machinery, etc., would influence the activity of business for a considerable period of time. Hence, it is essential to keep a close watch on capital expenditure at all times. Further, the mechanization and automation has resulted in management being confronted with ever more frequent and difficult problems. Despite the fact that various techniques have been developed to assist management in its task of decision-making more effectively, the ultimate decision depends on the availability of relevant information, which can be generated by a well-established capital expenditure budgeting system. The other commonly used nomenclatures for capital expenditure decision are "Capital Budgeting", or "Capital Investment Decision" or simply "Investment Decision".

11.2. Concept of Capital Budgeting

Capital budgeting normally refers to long-term planning for proposed capital outlays and their financing. It is the decision-making process by which firms evaluate the acquisition of major fixed assets whose benefits would spread over several time periods. Succinctly, it involves current investment in which the benefits are expected to be received beyond one year in future. The use of one year as a line of demarcation is, however, somewhat arbitrary. The main exercise in capital budgeting is to judge whether or not an investment proposal provides a reasonable return to business. Hence, capital budgeting involves generation of investment proposals, estimating costs and benefits [cash flows] for the investment proposals and estimation of net benefits and selection of projects based upon an acceptance criterion.

11.3. Importance of Capital Budgeting

1. Commitment of huge financial resources: The capital investment involved is usually very large. It will have several far-reaching implications on the activities of business and may seriously affect the very financial stability or flexibility of the business. It is these implications, which make capital budgeting so important.

2. Wrong decisions may lead to over or under-investment of financial resources. For example, wrong sales forecast may result in over or under-investment in fixed assets, i.e., excess production capacity or inadequate capacity. It also enables the cash forecast to be completed.

3. Better timing of assets: Capital budgeting may allow alternative forms of assets to be considered as replacements for assets, which are wearing out or in danger of becoming obsolete. In other words, it would lead to better timing of assets purchases and improvement in quality of assets purchased. It helps to match efficiently the need for capital goods and their availability. It also assists in formulating a sound depreciation and asset replacement policy.

4. It ensures the selection of right source of finance at the right time. Capital expenditure decision involves substantial funds, which may not be immediately, and automatically available. A well-established capital budgeting system would enable management to decide in advance the sources of finance and ensure their availability at the right time

11.4 Objectives of Capital budgeting

1. Selection of the right mix of profitable projects. The overall objective of capital budgeting is to allocate the available resources among the competing projects in order to maximize the total profitability. This is made possible by employing the various evaluation techniques for the selection of investment projects, which contribute the maximum towards the overall investment objective. In the case of public enterprises, capital budgeting may also assure fulfillment of other objectives such as promotion of employment, development of backward region, etc.

2. Capital expenditure control. Control of capital expenditure is the next important objective of capital budgeting. Forecasting the long-term financial requirements and thereby enabling the management to plan in advance to raise the funds at the right time achieve this. The objective of preparing capital budget is to plan and then compare the actual capital expenditure with the budgeted figure for controlling costs.

3. Determining the required quantum and the right source of funds for investments. The next important objective is to determine the funds required for long-term projects and to see that such estimates fall in line with the company' financial policies. It also aims to compromise between availability of funds and needs of the capital projects.

11.5 Types of Capital Investment Projects

Investment projects may be classified in a number of ways. Both private and public sector business units in their capital expenditure forecasts commonly use the following types of investment projects:

(a) Expansion of existing product lines,

(b) Expansion into new product lines,

(c) Replacement and Modernization Schemes,

(d) Projects for the utilization of scraps, and also of surplus installed capacity, and

(e) Cost Reduction Projects.

The projects listed above are generally profit-oriented and therefore, they may be evaluated on the basis of their cost and benefits. But there are investments, which are undertaken by all business units and on which it would be difficult to measure returns, such as the following:

(i) Safety Precautions: Provision of safety devices and equipment may be demanded by various legal requirements.

(ii) Welfare Projects: Provision of sport facilities for employees may boost employees' morale. This cannot be evaluated financially.

(iii) Service Projects: Provision of buildings and equipments for non-manufacturing departments may be essential, but the return from investment on them cannot be evaluated.

(iv) Research and Development: This may be initiated to improve the company

(v) Educational Projects: Provision of company training course may be instrumental in improving the efficiency of employees but the returns from investment on such programmes may be difficult to evaluate.

11.6 Relevant Costs for Capital Expenditure Decision

Generally, costs and benefits in the form of cash flows are more relevant for capital budgeting than the conventional accounting cost and benefits, because such costs and benefits normally encounter a number of measurement problems owing to factors such as method of depreciation, valuation of inventories, write off, etc. Different types of investment decisions call for different kinds of costs. Not all costs, which are used in conventional accounting system, are relevant for investment decision-making. A few items of relevant costs are:

Future Costs. Future costs are the projected or estimated costs. They are relevant for all types of investment decisions. Past costs, though not relevant for decision-making, are useful to the extent that they furnish a starting point for future cost projections. While calculating these costs, factors such as market conditions, economic conditions, political situations, general trend in the price levels, probabilities relating to future production and sales, economic life of the project, etc., are to be taken into account.

Opportunity Costs. In simple terms, opportunity cost refers to the benefits of the best alternative foregone. As the investment in project involves commitment of firm's investible funds, it becomes relevant to consider the opportunity of getting some benefits by employing the resources on some other alternative. For example, in an expansion program the economic value of space required rather than its book value is relevant. In a replacement decision, the realizable value rather than the book value of the old asset may be relevant as a reduction of the cost of replacement. This type of cost is relevant for al type of investment decisions. Imputed cost is a kind of opportunity cost. It is the cost, which is not actually incurred, but would be incurred in the absence of self-owned factors, e.g., cost of retained earnings, rent on company owned facilities, etc.

Incremental or Differential Cost. It is the additional cost due to a change in the volume of business or nature of business activity. Hence, it is useful for decisions such as adding new machinery, new product, changing a distribution channel, etc. Sometimes, this cost is considered synonymous with marginal cost. But, marginal cost has much limited meaning as it refers to the cost of an added unit of output.

Interest Cost. Accounting reports normally ignore the imputed interest on capital, which is relevant for decision-making purposes. Interest cost constitutes the minimum acceptance criterion for capital investment projects undertaken for profits. A firm must at least recover its money costs before it can realize a profit on its own investment.

Depreciation and Income tax. Depreciation is normally excluded while calculating cash flows for investment appraisal and evaluation. But it is included for calculating the accounting rate of return of the project. Payment of taxes results in cash flows and therefore, is an important element in capital investment decisions. Income tax has a number of effects on capital investment decisions. Hence, tax laws and applicable legal decisions emphasize the need for special skill in this area.

Secondary Costs and Benefits. These costs and benefits are particularly relevant for capital expenditure decisions in public enterprises. They are external to the project implementing body and therefore, are called external costs and benefits. These are the costs and benefits, which are imposed on other sector such as government, society, or the economy as a whole during the construction and operation of the project and for which nothing is paid or received.

Cash Flows as Costs and Benefits. Generally the resources committed to an investment proposal are referred to as its costs and income or gain derived from it over a future period as benefits. Since the conventional accounting costs and benefits normally encounter a number of measurement problems, cash flows are considered more relevant. Costs are cash outflows and benefits are cash inflows. They are calculated by making adjustments in accounting costs and benefits for such non-cash items as depreciation, write off, and write ups, etc.

11.7 Concept of Project Appraisal

Project appraisal is the analysis of costs and benefits of a proposed project with the goal of assuring a rational allocation of limited funds among alternative investment opportunities in view of achieving certain specified goals. Project appraisal is necessary as the number of projects to satisfy the identified needs always exceeds the availability of resources and a choice among alternative projects is to be made.

Project appraisal is ex-ante analysis. It identifies and values the expected costs and benefits of a project. Project evaluation is ex-post analysis of an executed project. It determines the real cost and benefits of the project. By comparing the real costs and benefits, the project's real profitability is ascertained at the evaluation stage. However, sometimes the concepts of project appraisal and evaluation are used interchangeably.

11.8 Project appraisal methods

Project appraisal is a process of transmitting information accumulated through feasibility studies into a comprehensive form in order to enable the decision-maker undertake a comparative appraisal of various projec l embark on a particular project or projects for allocating scarce resources. Keeping the l objective of the enterprise in view, the appraisal is carried out employing certain decision criteria, viz., profitability or social profitability. Commonly used appraisal methods are as follows:

(a) Payback Period

(b) Average Rate of Return

(c) Discounted Cash Flow Techniques:

  (i) Net Present Value

  (ii) Benefit Cost Ratio

  (iii) Internal Rate of Return

Apart from these, a public sector project may be appraised by employing Social Cost Benefit Analysis so as to highlight its significance to nation's economy or society.

11.9 'Payback Period' Method of Investment Appraisal

The payback [PB] period is the length of time required to recover the initial cash outlay incurred on the project. For example, if a project involves a cash outlay of Rs.200000 and the annual cash inflows are Rs.50000, Rs.80000, Rs.60000, and Rs.40000 during its economic life of four years, the payback period is 3.25 years. During 3 years and three months, the project cost can be recovered with the cash inflows. Hence, it is the payback period. If the above-mentioned project returns constant annual cash inflows of Rs.80000 for four years, then the payback period is 2.5 years [Rs.200000/Rs.80000]

Formula

$$\text{Payback period} = \frac{\text{Original cost of Investment}}{\text{Annual cash inflows or savings}}$$

Selection Criteria: Among the mutually exclusive or alternative projects, whose PB periods are lower than the cut off period, the project with the shortest PB period would be selected. In case, there is funds scarcity or budget constraints the procedure would be to rank the projects in the ascending order of PB periods and select the first 'x' number of projects, which the funds position permits. However, with a view to making the selection process more realistic, a cut-off period or minimum payback ratio could be set up and all investment proposals for which the PB is greater than the cut-off period be rejected. PB ratio is the inverse of the PB period. For a PB period of 4 years, the PB ratio is 1/4. Thus, the project with larger PB ratio would be a better project.

Suitability of PB method

1. The PB method is suitable when the project has shorter gestation period and the project cost is small.

2. When a firm suffers from shortage of cash and depends on internal generation of cash, this method will prove to be the best method of appraisal.

3. It is also suitable when the project belongs to high-risk category and is susceptible to rapid technological changes.

4. It is the most suitable method for deciding upon overseas investments, when there is political uncertainty in such countries.

Example 1

From the following information advise the management as to which project is preferable based on payback period. The standard cutoff period for the company is 5 years.

	Project A (Rs.)	Project B (Rs.)
Capital cost	15,000	15,000
Cash flows (savings before depreciation, but after taxes)		
I Year	5,000	4,000
II Year	5,000	4,000
III Year	5,000	4,000
IV Year	2,000	3,000
V Year	2,000	7,000
VI Year	2,000	9,000
	21,000	31,000

Solution

Payback period	3 years	4 years
	(Rs. 5000 + 5000 + 5000)	(Rs. 4000 + 4000 + 4000 +
	= Rs. 15000)	3000 = Rs. 15000)

The PBs of A and B are 3 years and 4 years respectively and thus project A is adjudged superior to project B in terms of PB criterion since it is also shorter than the cut-off period.

Example 2

Kumar Ltd. is producing articles mostly by manual labour and is considering to replace it by a new machine. There are two alternative models M and N of the new machine. Prepare a statement of profitability showing the pay-back period from the following information.

	Machine M	Machine N
Estimated life of machine	4 years	5 years
Cost of machine	Rs. 9000	Rs. 18,000
Estimated savings in scrap	500	800
Estimated savings in direct wages	6000	8000
Additional cost of maintenance	800	1000
Additional cost of supervision	1200	1800

Ignore taxation (M.Com., Madurai, April 1979; MCA Bharathiyar, 1991)

Solution

Statement showing Annual cash inflows

	Machine M	Machine N
Estimated savings in scrap	Rs. 500	Rs. 800
Estimated savings in direct wages	6000	8000
Total savings (i)	6500	8800
Additional cost of maintenance	800	1000
Additional cost of supervision	1200	1800
Total additional costs (ii)	2000	2800
Net cash inflow (i-ii)	4500	6000

$$\text{Pay–back period} = \frac{\text{Original Investment}}{\text{Annual Average cash inflow}}$$

$$= \frac{9000}{4500} = 2 \text{ years} \quad \frac{18,000}{6,000} = 3 \text{ years}$$

Machine M has a shorter pay-back, hence it should be preferred to Machine M.

11.10 Merits and demerits of Payback method

Merits of PB method

1. It is easy to operate and simple to understand.

2. This method is preferred on the ground that returns beyond three or four years are so uncertain that it is better to disregard them altogether in a planning decision.

3. It is appropriate for industries with high rate of technological obsolescence in which the receipts beyond PB are regarded as totally uncertain.

4. This method is also useful to a concern, which is short of cash and eager to get back the cash invested in project.

5. As the method considers the cash flows during the PB period of the project, the estimates would be reliable and the results may be comparatively more accurate.

Despite the simplicity and ease of operation, this method suffers from several drawbacks.

Demerits of PB method

1. The PB is more a liquidity concept. It is not a profitability concept as it is based on the recovery of cash outlays. And it stresses the importance of liquidity that is recovery, at the cost of profitability.

2. It does not consider the earnings beyond the payback period. This may lead to wrong selection of investment projects. Profitable projects with long gestation periods or projects, which generate high returns only after a certain period of time, may be rejected under this method.

3. The most serious limitation of this method is that it ignores time value of money. In other words, it provides only for the recovery of the original investment and not for the cost of funds committed to such investments. But in practice, the investible funds of a business are not free of cost.

11.11 Accounting or Average Rate of Return method

Average Rate of Return [ARR] method is considered an improvement over the PB method for it considers the earnings of a project during its entire economic life. It is also known as 'Return on Investment method'. Return on Investment is the ratio of earnings after depreciation to original cost of investment. It may be calculated using any of the following methods:

1. $$\text{ARR} = \frac{\text{Average Net annual Earnings}}{\text{Original Investment}} \times 100$$

2. $$\text{ARR} = \frac{\text{Average Net annual Earnings}}{\text{Average Investment}} \times 100$$

Note. The term average net annual earnings are the average of the net earnings after depreciation and tax over the entire economic life of the project.

3. $$\text{ARR} = \frac{\text{Increase in expected future annual net earnings}}{\text{Initial increase in required investment}} \times 100$$

The amount of 'average investment' can be calculated according to any of the following methods:

(a) $$= \frac{\text{Original Investment}}{2}$$

(b) $$= \frac{\text{Original Investment} - \text{scrap value of the asset}}{2}$$

(c) $$= \frac{\text{Original Investment} + \text{Scrap value of the asset}}{2}$$

(d) $$= \frac{\text{Original Investment} - \text{Scrap value}}{2} + \text{Additional Working capital}$$

Adding all the earnings after depreciation, and dividing them by the economic life of the project compute the average return. Average investment is the simple average of the values of asset at the beginning and at the end of the useful life of the asset, which in most cases is zero. Though sometimes-initial investment is used, average investment is more logical.

Selection Criteria. The decision rule is that a project with the highest rate of return on investment is selected on condition that such rate is above the standard rate set or the cut-off rate. In the case of replacement or expansion, the return on investment on additional investment should be above the cut-off or minimum required rate. The company's cost of capital or any other desired rate might be set as the cut-off rate. Adding certain percentage to the desired rate of return could provide for risk and inflation. In case of alternative projects, one with the highest ARR is to be selected.

Example 3

Calculate the average rate of return for project 'A' and 'B' from the following information.

	Project A	Project B
Investment (Rs)	25,000	37,500
Expected life (in years)	4	5
Net earnings (after depreciation and taxes)		
Years		
1	2,500	3,750
2	1,875	3,750
3	1,875	2,500
4	1,250	1,250
5	-	1,250
	7,500	12,500

If the desired rate of return is 12%, which project should be selected?

Solution

Average return	Rs. 7500/4	Rs. 12500/5
	= Rs. 1,875	Rs. 2,500
Average Investment	(25000 + 0)/2	(37500 + 0)/2
	= Rs. 12,500	= Rs. 18,750
Average rate or return	$\frac{\text{Rs. } 1875 \times 100}{\text{Rs. } 12500}$	$\frac{\text{Rs. } 2500 \times 100}{\text{Rs. } 18750}$
	= 15%	= 13.33 %

Both the projects satisfy the minimum required rate of return. However, if the projects are mutually exclusive or alternative i.e., only one project is to be selected, project A will be selected as its ARR is higher than that of project B. If they are not mutually exclusive and there are no budget constraints, both the projects will be selected.

Example 4

The directors of Anish Limited decide to purchase of a new machine to replace a machine which has been in operation in the factory for the last 5 years.

Ignore interest but considering tax at 50% of net earnings, suggest which of the two alternative should be preferred. The following are the details:

	Old Machine	New Machine
Purchase price	Rs. 40,000	60,000
Estimated life of machine	10 years	10 years
Machine running hours p.a.	2000	2000
Units per hour	24	36
Wages per running hour	3	5.25
Power p.a.	2000	4500
Consumable stores p.a.	6000	7500
All other charges p.a.	8000	9000
Material cost per unit	0.50	0.50
Selling price per unit	1.25	1.25

You may assume that the above information regarding sales and cost of sales will hold good throughout the economic life of each of the machines. Depreciation has to be charged according to straight-line method.

Solution

Profitability Statement

	Old Machine		New Machine	
Cost of the Machine (Rs)		40,000		60,000
Life of Machine (yrs)		10		10
Output (Units)		48,000		72,000
Sales value Rs.		60,000		90,000
Less: Cost of sales:				
Direct Material	24,000		36,000	
Wages	6000		10,500	
Power	2000		4,500	
Consumable Stores	6000		7,500	
Other charges	8000		9,000	
Depreciation	4000	50,000	6,000	73,500
Profit before tax		10,000		16,500
Tax at 50%		5,000		8,250
Profit after tax		5,000		8,250

Accounting Rate of Return

Old Machine | New Machine

(i) $\dfrac{\text{Average Net earnings}}{\text{Original investment}} \times 100$

$= \dfrac{5000}{40000} \times 100 = 12.5\ \%$ | $\dfrac{8250}{60000} \times 100 = 13.75\ \%$

(ii) $\dfrac{\text{Average Net Earnings}}{\text{Average Investment}} \times 100,$

$= \dfrac{5000}{20000} \times 100 = 25\ \%$ | $\dfrac{8250}{30,000} \times 100 = 27.50$

(iii) $\dfrac{\text{Incremental Earnings}}{\text{Incremental Investment}} \times 100$

$= \dfrac{3{,}250}{\text{Rs. } 60000 - 20{,}000} \times 100$ (Approx) $\qquad \dfrac{3250}{40{,}000} \times 100 = 8\ \%$

Thus, replacement of the old machine by a new machine (ignoring interest) is profitable.

Assuming that the old asset will be sold at book value ie. Rs. 20,000.

11.12 Merits and Demerits of ARR Method

Merits

1. ARR method is easy to understand and simple to operate.

2. This method takes into account the earnings over the entire economic life of the project even though estimates of the distant future may be subject to a wide margin of errors.

3. It is really a profitability concept since it considers net earnings after depreciation, i.e., excess of earnings over original cost of investment.

4. Another advantage is that projects, which differ widely in character, could be compared under this method. For example, investment in new projects could be compared with a Cost reduction project or a current investment proposal could be compared with a future project.

5. This method is in consistent with the conventional accounting system and easy to comprehend as it is based on percentages.

Demerits

1. The most severe criticism of this method is that it ignores the time value of money.

2. This method ignores the risk and uncertainty factors also.

3. This method, which is based on conventional accounting system, is subject to the limitations of that system.

4. Normally, a host of variants are to be resolved relating to its components, viz., earnings and investment cost. For example, it may be the gross, net, or average investment that should be considered for computation. This may produce different rates of return for any one investment proposal.

5. Another problem is with regard to a reasonable rate of return on investments. Some stipulate a minimum rate so that if projects do not satisfy this rate they may be summarily excluded from consideration.

Discounted Cash Flow Techniques [DCF]

11.13 What are DCF Techniques?

Investments are essentially current capital expenditures incurred at present in anticipation of future returns. Hence, the timing of expected future cash flows is important in the investment decision. In any economy, capital or funds invested have value and therefore, time value of money is an important concept. For example, investors place a higher value on recent returns than on future ones. Hence, the technique that discounts [or reduces] the future values into their present values at a specified time value [discount rate] is called as DCF technique. It is considered that DCF techniques provide a more objective basis for evaluating and selecting investment projects. Also they enable one to isolate differences in the timing of cash flows for various projects by discounting the cash flows to their present values. Because these techniques take account of both the magnitude and the timing of expected cash flows in each period of a project's life. Generally, these techniques consider the net cash flows as representing the recovery of original investment plus a return on capital invested. There are mainly two types of DCF techniques viz., Net Present Value [NPV] and Internal Rate of Return [IRR].

11.13 What is Discounting?

Discounting is reducing the values of future cash flows or returns to make it directly comparable to the values at present. It is the basic operation of any DCF method. The problem is that a rupee today is worth more than the same rupee in a year's time regardless of inflation, because the rupee one has invested can grow to a larger sum in the future. The rate at which the future cash flows are reduced to their present value is termed as discount rate. Discount rate, otherwise called as the time value of money, is some interest rate that expresses the time preference for a particular future cash flow. Realistic capital investment appraisal depends on two factors, viz., discounting period and a suitable discount rate.

Normally, the economic life of a project is used as the discounting period. However, the length of discounting period depends on factors such as the life of equipment with the largest life span, technological change, availability of raw materials, market stability, etc. The market rate of interest is normally considered for discounting. But the cost of capital computed based on the overall capital structure of the company or on the basis of financial pattern would be an appropriate discount rate.

11.14 Define Net Present Value Techniques [NPV]

Net Present Value may be defined as the excess of present value of project cash inflows [stream of benefits] over that of outflows [cash outlays]. The cash flows of a project are discounted at some desired rate of return, which is mostly equivalent to the cost of capital. For a conventional investment where all cash outflows take place in the base year, NPV may be represented as follows:

$$NPV = \frac{B_1}{[1+k]^1} + \frac{B_2}{[1+k]^2} + \frac{B_3}{[1+k]^3} + \cdot + \cdot + \frac{Bn}{[1+k]^n} - Co$$

$$NPV = \sum_{t=1}^{n} \frac{B_t}{(1+k)^t} - C_0$$

where Bt = B1, B2, B3, ... Bn represent s the cash inflows in periods 1, 2, 3, ... n.

Co represents the cash outlays in time period 0.

K represents the discount rate, which is equal to firm's cost of capital.

For a non-conventional investment where the cash outflows take place over more than one year.

$$NPV = \frac{B_0}{(1+r)^0} + \frac{B_1}{(1+r)^1} + \frac{B_2}{(1+r)^2} + \dots + \frac{B_n}{(1+r)^n} - C_0 + \frac{C_1}{(1+r)^1} + \frac{C_2}{(1+r)^2} + \dots + \frac{C_n}{(1+r)^n}$$

$$NPV = \sum_{t=0}^{n} \frac{B_t}{(1+r)^t} - \sum_{t=0}^{n} \frac{C_t}{(1+r)^t}$$

where 'B_t', represents the cash inflows in periods, 0, 1, 2,... n.

'C_t', represents the cash outlays in periods 0, 1, 2, 3,....n; 'r' represents the desired discount rate:

where 'r' is equal to firm's cost of capital, it may be replaced by 'K'.

Selection Criteria. In the case of mutually exclusive projects or alternative projects [where only one project is to be selected] accept a project that has the highest NPV. In the case of independent investment projects, accept a project if its NPV is grater than or equal to zero; reject if its NPV is negative.

In the case budget constraints or capital rationing, project selection could be done by ranking projects having positive NPV in the descending order of their NPVs and then choosing the first 'x' number of projects that the budget provision permits.

Example 5 [Independent Investment]

The Bata Co. Ltd., is considering the purchase of a new machine costing Rs. 80,000. Earnings after taxation are expected to be as follows:

Years	Cash flows
1	8,000
2	24,000
3	32,000
4	48,000
5	32,000

The company has a target of return on capital of 10 per cent. On this basis, find the profitability of the machine and state if it is financially preferable.

Solution

Profitability Statement

(at 10 percent discount factors)

Year	PV of Re. 1 at 10%	Cash Flows Rs.	PV of cash flows Rs.
1	0.909	8,000	7,272
2	0.826	24,000	19,824
3	0.751	32,000	24,032
4	0.683	48,000	32,784
5	0.621	32,000	19,872
Total:		1,44,000	1,03,784
Cost:		80,000	80,000
NPV:			23,784

From the above statement it is evident that the new machine would be profitable since the PV of cash inflows is greater than the PV of cash outflows.

Example 6 [Mutually exclusive or alternative investments]

Vignesh Ltd is considering the purchase of a new machine. Two alternative machines (A and B) have been suggested, each having an initial cost of Rs. 4,00,000 and requiring Rs. 20,000 as additional working capital at the end of 1st year.

Earnings after taxation are expected to be as follows:

Year	Cash Inflows	
	Machine A	Machine B
1	40,000	1,20,000
2	1,20,000	1,60,000
3	1,60,000	2,00,000
4	2,40,000	1,20,000
5	1,60,000	80,000

The company has a target of return on capital of 10% and on this basis you are required to compare the profitability of the machines and state which alternative you consider financially preferable.

Note: The following table gives the present value of Re. 1 due in 'n' number of years.

Year	Present value at 10%
1	0.91
2	0.83
3	0.75
4	0.68
5	0.62

Solution

Statement showing the profitability of the two machines

Year	Discount Factor	Machine A		Machine B	
		Cash inflow	Present Value	Cash inflow	Present Value
1	0.91	40,000	36,400	1,20,000	1,09,200
2	0.83	1,20,000	99,600	1,60,000	1,32,800
3	0.75	1,60,000	1,20,000	2,00,000	1,50,000
4	0.68	2,40,000	1,63,200	1,20,000	81,600
5	0.62	1,60,000	99,200	80,000	49,600
		7,20,000		6,80,000	
	Total present value of cash inflows		5,18,400		5,23,200
	Total present value of cash outflows Rs. $400000 + 20000 \times 0.91$		4,18,200		4,18,200
	Net present value		1,00,200		1,05,000

Recommendations

Machine B is preferable to machine A. Though total cash inflow of machine A is more than that of machine B by Rs. 40,000, the net present value of the cash inflows of machine B is more than that of Machine A. Moreover, in case of Machine B cash inflow in the earlier years is comparatively higher than that in case of Machine A.

11.15 Merits and Demerits of NPV method

Merits

1. The salient feature of NPV technique is that it indicates the value added to the total assets of the firm by taking up the proposed investment at a particular rate of discount.

2. The NPV criterion automatically allows for the recovery of the initial investment and the cost of funds invested in such investments. For example, if the gross PV of a project costing Rs.50000 is Rs.58 645 at 10% discount rate, it means that the value added to the total assets in present value terms is Rs.8 645 [i.e., NPV = Rs.58645 - 50000]. This is after providing for the initial investment of Rs.50000 and for interest cost at 10% p.a.

3. The most significant advantage of NPV method is that it recognizes the time value of money and considers all cash flows over the entire economic life of the project.

4. It is in consistent with the objective of maximizing the welfare of the owners of the firm.

Demerits

1. It is difficult to understand and use. Since it requires accurate cash flows, accurate life of the project and discount rate.

2. It may not give satisfactory answer when the projects being compared involve different amounts of investments. For example, a project with high NPV may not be desirable if it also requires a large investment.

3. Selection of an appropriate discount rate is very difficult.

4. This technique is based on compound interest principle. Under this method, it is assumed that the cash flows could be reinvested at the same rate of interest [discount rate], which is not practically feasible.

5. Under the NPV criterion, profitability is not related to the capital outlay required for it. A project may have a high NPV but it can still be unattractive, for it requires a very high capital outlay. For example, two projects X and Y costing Rs.50000 and Rs.80000 respectively generate NPVs of Rs.11 500 and Rs.12 500. Of these two, Project Y would be recommended by NPV criterion since its NPV is higher by Rs.1000. However, the profitability is not attractive compared to the additional investment required for Project Y.

11.16 What is Benefit/Cost Ratio [BCR]?

With a view to establishing the profitability of projects relating to the investment required, the NPV criterion is usually supplemented with an additional tool called 'Benefit/Cost Ratio' or 'Profitability Index'. BCR may be defined as the ratio of gross discounted benefits to gross discounted costs. It is expressed in coefficient, or in percentage. Symbolically this could be expressed as follows:

$$BCR = B/C \text{ or } B/C \times 100$$

Or Profitability Index [PI] $= [B - C] / C \times 100$

Where B = Gross discounted benefits, and

C = Gross discounted costs.

Example: suppose the gross discounted value of benefits is Rs.103 784 and gross discounted value of costs is Rs.80000, then the BCR and PI would be as follows:

BCR = Rs. 103784/80000 = 1.297 [app.]

PI = [Rs. 103784 – Rs. 80000]/Rs. 80000

= Rs. 23784/80000 = 0.297 [app.]

The salient feature of BCR is that it can also explain the NPV position of an investment. If BCR is equal to ONE then NPV will be equal to ZERO. If it is greater than ONE, then NPV will be positive; if it is lesser than ONE then NPV will be negative.

Decision Criteria. In the case of independent investments, accept a project if the BCR is greater than one and reject it otherwise. In the case mutually exclusive or alternative investments, accept the project with the largest BCR, provided it is greater than one; reject others. Under conditions of capital rationing or budget constraints, rank the projects in the descending order of their BCRs and choose the first 'x' number of projects that the budget provision permits.

BCR is particularly useful for ranking the projects on the basis of their profitability. However, it suffers from the same limitations as the NPV technique. In other words, all the merits and demerits of NPV technique are attributable to this technique also.

Example 7

Calculate the NPV and BCRs of Machine A and Machine B from the following information

		Machine A	Machine B
Initial investment (Rs.)		40,000	60,000
Expected life		5 years	5 years
Salvage value (Rs.)		2000	3000
Cash inflows: Year	1	10,000	40,000
(Rs.)	2	20,000	20,000
	3	20,000	10,000
	4	5000	6000
	5	5000	4000
		60,000	80,000

The management determines 10% as the desired rate of return for the proposed investment project. Discount factors at this rate are given below:

Year	1	2	3	4	5
PV	0.909	0.826	0.751	0.683	0.621

Solution:

Profitability Statement

Cashoutlays	Discount factor	Machines A Cash flow Rs.	Machines A PV of cash flow Rs.	Machines B Cash flow Rs.	Machines B PV of cash flow Rs.
Initial investment at the year 0	1	40,000	40,000	60,000	60,000
Cash in flows year					
1	0.909	10,000	9090	40,000	36360
2	0.826	20,000	16,520	20,000	16,520
3	0.751	20,000	15,020	10,000	7,510
4	0.683	5,000	3,415	6,000	4,098
5	0.621	5,000	3,105	4,000	2,484
5 (Salvage value)	0.621	2,000	1,242	3,000	1,863
Total present value			48,392		68,835
NPV			8,392		8,835

Machine A

$$BCR = \frac{\text{(Gross discounted cash inflows)}}{\text{(Gross discounted cash outflows)}} = \frac{48392}{40,000} = 1.21 \text{ (app)}$$

Machine B

$$\frac{68835}{60,000} = 1.15 \text{ (app.)}$$

11.17 Define Internal Rate of Return [IRR]

The Internal Rate of Return may be defined as that rate of interest when used to discount the cash flows of an investment, reduce its NPV to zero. Or it is the rate of discount, which equates the aggregate discounted benefits with aggregate discounted costs. IRR is also called as 'Discounted Cash Flow Method' or 'Yield Method' or 'Time Adjusted Rate of Return Method'. This method is used when the cost of investment and the annual cash inflows are known but the discount rate [rate of return] is not known and is to be calculated. Symbolically, the IRR may be expressed as follows:

For a conventional investment,

$$NPV = \sum_{t=1}^{n} \frac{Bt}{[1+r]} = Co = 0$$

[Aggregate discounted cash inflows] = [Aggregate initial investment]

Where the discount rate 'r' is the IRR. Bt represents cash inflows during the time period 1, 2, 3 , ... n, and Co is the initial cash outflows.

IRR indicates the maximum rate of return that a project can contribute and is mainly based on the internal cash inflows generated by it. In other words it is the 'break-even interest showing the highest interest rate consistent with the project not making any loss. However, in order to judge the profitability of the project, IRR should be compared with a cut off rate of return, which might be the company's cost of capital.

Decision Criteria. In the case of an independent project, accept the project if it's IRR is greater than the cut off rate; if lower, reject it. In the case of mutually exclusive projects, accept the project with the largest IRR, provided it is greater than the cut off rate; reject others. In case there are budget constraints, rank the projects in the descending order of their IRRs and choose the first 'x' number of projects, which the budget provision permits.

Method of calculating IRR

Trial and Error Yield Method: As the name suggests, the object is to find the expected yield from the investment. The procedure involved may be summarized as follows:

(a) List the annual sales and cost other than depreciation and reducing the latter from the former obtain the net cash flow.

(b) Obtain the capital investment cost. Often this will be at present value because the amount spent is invested in the base year.

(c) Calculate the present value of the net cash inflows by using an appropriate discount rate. This rate is found by trial and error method from the present value tables. The object is to make the present value of cash inflows equal to the capital investment cost.

(d) Carry out this procedure for each project being considered and then rank them in the order of preference.

Merits of IRR method

1. Like NPV method, IRR method also recognizes the time value of money and considers cash flows over the entire life of the project.

2. It has a psychological appeal to the user as it is expressed in percentage figure.

3. Unlike NPV method, it does not require any discount rate. IRR is itself a break-even rate [discount rate], which makes the present values of all cash inflows equal to those of cash outflows.

4. It is also in consistent with the firm's objective of maximizing owners' welfare.

Limitations of IRR method

1. It is very difficult to use in practice as it involves complicated computational problems.

2. It assumes that the reinvestment rate of cash flows is at IRR, but it may be different for different projects considered by a firm. Under NPV method, the reinvestment rate [discount rate] is assumed to be the same for all projects, which seems a more appropriate assumption.

3. The IRR method may yield multiple rates for a project when cash flows take place at different time periods. This will make the decision-making more complicated.

4. It may give inconsistent results with NPV if the proiects differ in their expected lives, or cash flows, or timing of cash flows.

Example 8

Govindan Ltd., is planning to increase its present capacity, and is considering purchase of a new machine. Machine X is available at a price of Rs. 40,000. Earnings before tax have been estimated as follows.

Year	Cash flows
1	11,000
2	15,000
3	20,000
4	16,000
5	8,000
	70,000

Compute the IRR and ascertain the profitability of the project.

Solution

Trial and Error Method

Profitability statement for Machine X

Year	Cash flows Rs.	Trial Discount factor (20 %)	No.1 PV of cash flows Rs.	Trial Discount factor (24 %)	No.2 PV of cash flows Rs.	Trial Discount factor (22 %)	No.3 PV of cash flows Rs.
0	(40000)	1.000	(40000)	1.000	(40000)	1.000	(40000)
1	11000	.833	9163	.806	8866	.820	9020
2	15000	.694	10410	.650	9750	.672	10080
3	20000	.579	11580	.524	10840	.551	11020
4	16000	.482	7712	.423	6768	.451	7216
5	8000	.402	3216	.341	2728	.370	2960
NPV	30000		2081		(1048)		296

From the above statement it is ascertained that in the first trial at 20% the present value of cash inflows exceeds the present value of cash outflows by Rs. 2,081. On the second trial at 24% the present value of cash inflows is less than the cash outflows. On the third trial at 22%, cash inflows are marginally greater than cash outflows. Thus, approximately 22% is the rate of return which equates the present value of inflows with outflows. If greater accuracy is required interpolation may be used to find the required discount rate, rather than making calculation of unlimited trials. To apply interpolation techniques, a simple method is given here based on the above example.

$$\text{IRR} = 22\% + (296/1704) \times 2\% = 22.34\%$$

The profitability statement shows that by using the IRR method, Machine X yields a rate of return of 22.34%.

Formula for Interpolation

$$\text{IRR} = A + (C/[C - D] \times (B - A))$$

where A = Discount factor of the low trial

B = Discount factor of the high trial

C = NPV of cash inflows of the low trial

D = NPV of cash inflows of the high trial

Establishing the Trial Rates

In the Trial and Error method, difficulty is often experienced in the selection of the first trial rate. Once the first rate is established, the second trial rate is determined by considering the value of NPV. If the NPV is negative, the second trial rate will be higher than the first rate. If the NPV is positive, the second rate should be lower than the first rate. However, the problem is to select the first trial rate. As an aid to this selection, a rough guide is as follows:

$$\text{1st Trial Rate} = \frac{\text{Average Earnings or Savings}}{\text{Investment}}$$

11.18 Advantages of DCF techniques

Advantages

1. DCF techniques are superior to other methods since they consider the earnings of a project over its entire economic life, and also the time value of money flows.

2. They are more objective, for their conclusions are not directly influenced by decisions regarding depreciation methods, capitalization versus expense decisions and consideration.

3. The DCF method automatically gives more weight to units of money, which are nearer than those, which are distant. But other methods treat distant units of money unrealistically with the same weight as present units.

4. The DCF method allows a ready comparison to be made between projects having different lives and different timings of each flow by facilitating comparison at the same point of time.

5. By comparing the rates of return of projects with the cost of capital ratios, decisions can be taken quickly and safely.

10.19 General criticisms against DCF techniques

1. DCF methods are considered difficult to understand and operate. However, compared to the complexities associated with some modern statistical and mathematical tools, which have gained acceptance in recent times, DCF techniques are simple to understand. Further with the development of mechanized accounting and computer technology it has become very easy to operate.

2. The second assumption is against the assumption of a fixed investment rate throughout the life of the project. This assumption arises mainly because of the use of compound interest principle as the basis of these methods.

3. The third criticism is that they fail to take account of risks and uncertainties. However, recent developments in risk analysis, which could be incorporated into DCF methods, have made this criticism somewhat irrelevant.

4. It is said that the IRR and NPV methods give rise to conflicting issues while decisions are taken. Recent theoretical refinements have mitigated most of the weaknesses of these methods.

11.20 Compare and Contrast NPV and IRR Methods

NPV and IRR are the species of the same genus, i.e., DCF technique. They are based on the fundamental concept that money has a time value. However, there are certain fundamental differences between these two techniques.

First, the NPV treats the discount rate as a known factor while the IRR treats it as an unknown factor. In most cases the business' known cost of capital is used for discounting under NPV method.

Secondly, the IRR method seeks to find the maximum rate of return at which funds invested in any given project could be repaid with earnings generated by the project. But the present value method arrives at the amount to be invested in a given project so that its anticipated earnings could recoup the amount with the interest at the market rate.

Thirdly, at a particular discount rate, there can be only one NPV, and not multiple net present values of a project. But in the case of unconventional investments, where capital outlays are incurred at different time periods, a project may have more than one IRR, which may lead to baffling contradictions.

Fourthly, the present value method explicitly recognizes availability of a market for funds and assumes that business will use the market rationally to enhance its earnings; but IRR method does not recognize the existence of a such a capital market. In other words, the NPV method assumes mostly the cost of capital, which is based on the market rate of interest, as the discount rate. But the IRR method tries to find out a discount rate, which has no direct bearing on the market rate of interest.

11.21 Control of Capital Expenditure

Capital expenditure control is the purpose of, and an integral part of capital expenditure planning. Capital expenditure projects are so important that many enlightened companies always have formal programmes for capital expenditure control. The programmes include measures for the control and follow up of capital expenditures. These measures may be classified as follows:

(a) Preparation of Capital Expenditure Budgets,

(b) Request for funds i.e., Appropriation requests,

(c) Variance Analysis i.e., Comparison of actual against Appropriation,

(d) Follow up or Post Completion Audit.

Capital Expenditure Budget: Planning is the first and most essential step for control. Hence, the first step in the capital expenditure control is the preparation of capital expenditure budget. This budget outlines the various types of projects such as new projects, expansion projects, modernization projects and diversification projects to be taken up and also explains how these projects should be financed over a given period. The request for capital expenditure projects emanate from different divisions of the organization. While submitting the their requests for capital expenditure projects, they provide the following information:

(a) Description of the proposal,

(b) Justification for making such a proposal,

(c) Cost estimates,

(d) Estimates of effective economic life, and

(e) Net benefits expected from the proposal.

The individual requests are submitted to the budget committee for preliminary review, screening, coordination, and final consolidation. While considering the individual requests, the committee mainly looks into the proposal for the following aspects: (a) that all requests fit well into the company's long-range planning and programmes, (b) they are financially feasible, and (c) individual request does not create any departmental imbalances. For example, the consideration of an expansion project may lead to departmental imbalance if the sales department is unable to sell the excess production. Once the proposals are found worthwhile, they are recommended to the higher-level management for final approval.

Request for Funds: Once the projects are approved, the concerned department should submit a detailed request for appropriation of funds. This request may be a request for (a) original capital budget, (b) additional funds, and (c) substituted new project. Owing to certain changed conditions or circumstances, if the approved project could not taken up, it may be abandoned by providing proper reasons for abandonment. When the abandonment is approved, the funds allotted and later on canceled are used for other projects based on priorities.

Variance Analysis: This is an important task in capital expenditure control. The actual performance is compared with estimates and variance or deviations are noted, analyzed and reported upon. As the project implementation work progresses the actual expenditures incurred are compared with the budget estimates. When it is expected that the actual cost may exceed the original estimates, a formal request for additional funds or for revision of plan will be made. To have a better control, a system of calling for monthly or weekly reports on individual projects or jobs is introduced. These reports may be in the form of Capital Project Expenditure, Summary of Current Capital projects, Periodic Capital Project Cost Statement, and Weekly Statement of Cost Details.

Follow Up: A follow up of the performance of capital projects is very essential. It enables the management to determine whether the expected savings have actually been realized or not. The follow up in the form post completion audit serves two purposes: 1. It indicates the areas of weaknesses to the management. 2. It creates confidence on the future capital expenditure control programme. However, the post completion audit is a difficult task. Many offsetting factors like volume and price changes and wage increase, etc. may conceal or mislead the actual results obtained from the project. Hence, a post completion audit committee is constituted with Chief Engineer, Plant Manager, Internal Auditor, etc., as members. The committee should prepare a report in the proforma laid down in the capital budget manual. The committee report should specifically indicate the causes for deficiency, if any, the corrective measures to be taken, and the period within which the measures be taken.

PROJECT APPRAISAL UNDER RISK AND UNCERTAINTY

11.22 Need for Risk Analysis

Project cost estimates, life of the project and the estimates of demand, production, sales and prices, etc., may contain errors because of uncertainty about the future. Project decisions underlie many political and social developments as well as changes in technology, prices, and productivity. Hence, while deciding about the desirability of a project, all these factors have to be taken into account in the form of foreseeable risk, which the project proposal either can or cannot carry. This is probably the most difficult decision to be made during the entire process of project preparation. The size of allowance provided for this purpose will have a decisive impact on the profitability of the project and may, in the case of marginal proposal tilt the balance against the implementation of the project. Hence, it is essential to incorporate measures at the appraisal stage to identify the risk factors and provide for the same.

11.23 Meaning of the Concepts of Risk and Uncertainty

The decision situations are generally classified into three types, viz., certainty, risk and uncertainty. Certainty situation is one where the future occurrence of a particular outcome such as future cash flow or discount rate could be expressed with certitude. But in practice, all investment decisions are undertaken under conditions of risk and uncertainty. Risk refers to a situation where the probability distribution of a particular outcome could be objectively known

11.26 Modern methods of Risk Analysis

Sensitivity Analysis. Sensitivity analysis is a simulation technique in which key variables are changed and the resulting change in the rate of return or [the NPV] is observed. Some of the key variables are cost, prices, project life, market share, etc. The most practical way to do this is to select those variables whose estimated values may contain some significant errors or an element of uncertainty, and then to calculate the effect of errors of different sizes on the present value of the project. The common operating mechanism would be to vary each strategic variable by certain fixed percentages in both positive as well as negative directions in turn, say plus or minus 10% or plus or minus 5% etc., and study the effect of change on the rate of return [or on NPV].

It is an effective tool to handle risk in project appraisal. However, there are certain limitations in using this tool. They are:

(a) Unless the combined effect of change in a set of Inter-correlated variables is examined, single variable sensitivity testing could be worse than useless. It may lead to wrong conclusions. Hence, it is a very difficult task.

(b) The second limitation lies in the fact that the values of the variables [components] are generally changed in an arbitrary manner by say 5% or 10% to examine the effect on the returns. Unless it is done in a meaningful manner, it might mislead the investor.

(c) The third one is that it ignores the chances associated with the different possible values of the components.

Probability Analysis. Probability may be defined as a measure of some one's opinion about the likelihood that an event [cash flow] will occur. The likelihood of occurrence normally ranges from 1 to 0 i.e., 100 per cent certainty to 100 per cent uncertainty. In this analysis, in the place of one single estimate a range of estimates and their associated probabilities are calculated. A probability distribution in its simplest form could be with a few estimates such as "optimistic", "pessimistic", and "most likely". The real problem, however, is how this probability distribution can be obtained. Two types of probabilities - objective and subjective - are normally used for decision-making under uncertainty. The objective probability is the probability estimate, which is based on a very large number of observations, say, for example, on the objective evidence of 100 trials conducted repeatedly under independent identical situations. Subjective probabilities are those probability measures, which are based on the state of belief of a person rather than the objective evidence of a large number of trials. As the capital expenditure decisions are mostly non-repetitive and not made under identical situations, only subjective probabilities are useful.

Expected Values [EV]: EV is the sum of products of estimated outcomes and their respective probabilities. For example, if three possible yields for an investment are 8%, 12%, and 16% and the probabilities that any one of these will be achieved is 0.25, 0.50, and 0.25 respectively, the EV of the yield is as follows:

in advance, while uncertainty refers to a situation where such probability distribution cannot be objectively known, but only guessed. However, in the case of investment decisions, such a theoretical distinction is hypothetical and may not serve much useful purpose in practice. Even the best estimates of the project manager regarding the probability of the expected cash flows materializing, and their magnitude are only subjective guesses. Hence, both risk and uncertainty are used interchangeably to mean the same thing.

Some of the factors, which add to the degree of risk or uncertainty of an investment are the possibilities of (a) the process or product becoming obsolete, (b) declining demand for the product, (c) change in government policy on business, (d) price fluctuations, (e) foreign exchange restrictions, and (f) inflationary tendencies, etc.

11.24 Modern Quantitative Techniques that may be used in Risk Management

Systems Analysis: Systems analysis refers to the set of techniques concerned with the analysis, procedures, and other methods of doing things, and with the design and implementation of new and superior systems. Its principal objective is to evaluate alternatives in a consistent unarbitrary manner. Growth in size and complexity of business operations need a systematic examination of a problem of choice in which each step of the analysis is made explicit. This enables business units derive the benefits of computer technology.

Marketing Research: Marketing Research is used to forecast objectively the demand potential for goods and services of the prospective project. Demand appraisal is, in fact, the starting of point of feasibility analysis. The objective is to assess the available opportunities and study the future trends of these opportunities so that the investment decision could be taken with a degree of confidence. This would help to reduce the degree of risk.

Operations Research [O.R]: O.R enables a decision-maker to be more objective in choosing among alternatives. It surrogates mathematical reasoning for verbal arguments. Some well known O.R techniques are: (a) Linear Programming or Integer Programming - under conditions of capital rationing, integer or linear programming models could be used to determine the right project mix to commit scarce resources; (b) Game theory, for instance, would be an effective tool to predict to a certain extent the strategies of competing firms and counteract them; and (c) Inventory control techniques such as ABC analysis, EOQ models, etc.

Network Analysis [PERT/CPM]: The gestation period is the time lag, which will elapse between the commencement of investment and the start of the return on investment - a vital determinant in establishing the acceptability of the project. The longer the gestation period is, higher would be the cost escalations and the risks associated with the project resulting in low returns. PERT and CPM provide the project formulation team with one of the most effective analytical aids. Network analysis is useful in (a) developing the project, (b) controlling the project implementation delays and project cost, and (c) determining the gestation period realistically.

Cost-Volume-Profit Analysis: This analysis indicates the operating characteristics of a project. Under this analysis, first the break-even point i.e., no profit-no loss sales volume, is determined in terms of the project and may even be expressed as a percentage of the project capacity. It helps to identify the operating sensitivity of the project in terms of changes in the cost of raw materials, wages, and other project inputs.

Ratio Analysis: While comparing two or more investment proposals for resource allocation, costs, benefits and profits measured in absolute figures do not give information clearly. Hence, ratio analysis could be used for better, easy and useful comparisons.

All these management aids, when used at the project formulation stage, would minimize the degree of risk involved in different types of investment decisions. However, these tools cannot eliminate risk completely. Hence, risk analysis becomes an integral part of any investment analysis.

Techniques of Risk Analysis

The techniques used to handle risk in project appraisal may be classified into two groups as follows:

(a) Conservative Methods - such as Shorter Payback Period, Risk-adjusted Discount Rate, and Conservative Forecasts or Certainty Equivalents, etc.

(b) Modern Methods - such as Sensitivity Analysis, Probability Analysis, Decision Tree Analysis, etc.

11.25 Conservative methods or tools of Risk analysis

Shorter Payback Period. According to this method, projects with shorter payback periods are normally preferred to those with longer payback periods. It would be more effective when it is combined with a 'cut off period'. Cut off period denotes the risk tolerance level in the firm. For example, a firm has three projects, A, B, C for consideration with different economic lives, say 15, 16 and 7 years respectively, and with payback periods of say 6, 7, and 5 years. Of these three, project C will be preferred because its payback period is the shortest. Suppose, the firm's cut off period is 4 years, then all the three projects will be rejected.

Risk-adjusted Discount Rate. Under this method, the cut off rate or minimum required rate of return [mostly the firm's cost of capital] is raised by adding what is called 'risk premium' to it. When the risk is greater, the premium to be added would be greater. For example, if the risk free discount rate [say, cost of capital] is 10%, and the project under consideration is a riskier one, then the premium of, say 5% is added to the above risk-free rate. The risk-adjusted discount rate would be 15%, which may be used either for discounting purposes under NPV, or as a cut off rate under IRR.

Merits of Risk-adjusted Discount Rate

1. It is easy to understand and simple to operate.
2. It has a great deal of intuitive appeal for risk averse decision-makers.
3. It incorporates an attitude towards uncertainty.

Demerits

1. There is no easy way to derive a risk-adjusted discount rate.
2. A uniform risk discount factor used for discounting all future returns is unscientific as the degree of risk may vary over the years in future.
3. It assumes that investors are risk averse. Though it is generally true, there do exist risk-seekers in real world situation that may demand premium for assuming risk.

Conservative Forecasts. Under this method, employing intuitive correction factor or certainty equivalent coefficient, which is calculated by the decision-maker subjectively or objectively, reduces the estimated risks from cash flows. Normally, this coefficient reflects the decision-maker's confidence in obtaining a particular cash flow in a particular period. For example, the decision-maker estimates a net cash flow of Rs.60000 next year but if he feels [subjectively] that only 60% of such cash flow is a definite sum, and then the said coefficient would be 0.6. This may also be determined [objectively] by relating the desirable cash flows with estimated cash flows as follows:

$$\text{Certainty Equivalent Coefficient} = \frac{\text{Desirable Cash Flows}}{\text{Estimated Cash Flows}}$$

For Example, if the estimated cash flow is Rs.80000 in period 't' and an equally desirable cash flow for the same period is Rs.60000, then the certainty equivalent is 0.75 [60000/80000]. Besides the computations of certain cash flows in order to provide for more risk, the economic life over which cash flows are estimated may be reduced simultaneously.

$$EV = [0.25 \times 8] + [0.50 \times 12] + [0.25 \times 16] = 12\%$$

In the case of alternative projects, one with the highest EV is considered for selection. EVs may be used for computation of IRR and NPV. However, EVs fail to articulate the degree of risk involved.

Decision Tree Analysis: A decision may be taken by comparing various alternative courses at present with the decision-maker, each alternative course being studied in the light of the future possible conditions followed by future alternative decisions. The group of all these decisions present as well as future, viewed in relation to one another is called a 'decision tree'. It is a graphic display of the relationship between a present decision and future events, and future decisions and their consequences. The sequence of events is normally represented over time in a format similar to the branches of a tree. The major steps in a decision tree process are:

(a) The investment decision is defined clearly.

(b) The decision alternatives are identified.

(c) The decision tree graph indicates decision points, chance events, and other data.

(d) It presents the relevant data such as the projected cash flow, probability distribution, expected present value, etc., on the decision tree branches.

(e) Choosing the best alternative by analysis from the results displayed.

Example 9

Laxmi ltd. is considering purchase of a new machine at a cost of Rs. 20,000. The cash inflows for the three years of its life are forecast as follows:

Year	Cash Flow (Rs)	Probability	Cash Flow (Rs)	Probability
1	8,000	0.4	12,000	0.6
2	16,000	0.2	20,000	0.8
3	6,000	0.7	8,000	0.3

The desired rate of return of NPV purposes is 20 percent. Calculate the probability of the machine. Also draw a decision tree diagram.

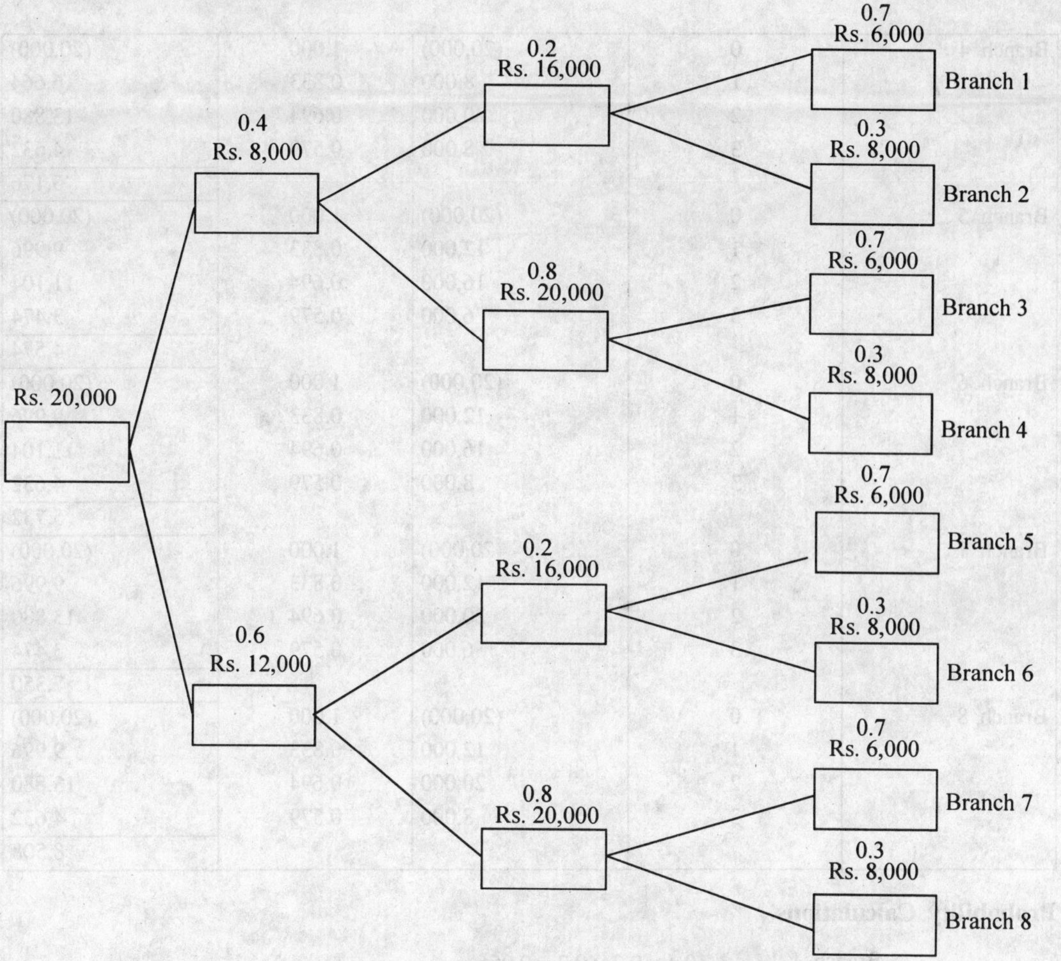

Net Present Values (at 20% Discount)

	Year	Cash Flow Rs.	Discount Factor Rs.	NPV Rs.
Branch 1	0	(20,000)	1.000	(20,000)
	1	8,000	0.833	6,664
	2	16,000	0.694	11,104
	3	6,000	0.579	3,474
				1,242
Branch 2		(20,000)	1.000	(20,000)
	1	8,000	0.833	6,664
	2	16,000	0.694	11,104
	3	8,000	0.579	4,632
				2,400
Branch 3	0	(20,000)	1.000	(20,000)
	1	8,000	0.833	6,664
	2	20,000	0.694	13,880
	3	6,000	0.579	3,474
				4,018

Branch 4	0	(20,000)	1.000	(20,000)
	1	8,000	0.833	6,664
	2	20,000	0.694	13,880
	3	8,000	0.579	4,632
				5,176
Branch 5	0	(20,000)	1.000	(20,000)
	1	12,000	0.833	9,996
	2	16,000	0.694	11,104
	3	6,000	0.579	3,474
				4,574
Branch 6	0	(20,000)	1.000	(20,000)
	1	12,000	0.833	9,996
	2	16,000	0.694	11,104
	3	8,000	0.579	4,632
				5,732
Branch 7	0	(20,000)	1.000	(20,000)
	1	12,000	0.833	9,996
	2	20,000	0.694	13,880
	3	6,000	0.579	3,474
				7,350
Branch 8	0	(20,000)	1.000	(20,000)
	1	12,000	0.833	9,996
	2	20,000	0.694	13,880
	3	8,000	0.579	4,632
				8,508

Probability Calculations

Branch 1 $0.4 \times 0.2 \times 0.7 = 0.056$

Branch 2 $0.4 \times 0.2 \times 0.3 = 0.024$

Branch 3 $0.4 \times 0.8 \times 0.7 = 0.224$

Branch 4 $0.4 \times 0.8 \times 0.3 = 0.096$

Branch 5 $0.6 \times 0.2 \times 0.7 = 0.084$

Branch 6 $0.6 \times 0.2 \times 0.3 = 0.036$

Branch 7 $0.6 \times 0.8 \times 0.7 = 0.336$

Branch 8 $0.6 \times 0.8 \times 0.3 = 0.144$

Branches	NPV (Rs.)	Probability	EV (Rs.)
1	1,242	0.056	70
2	2,400	0.024	58
3	4,018	0.224	900
4	5,176	0.096	497
5	4,574	0.084	384
6	5,732	0.036	206

7		7,350	0.336	2,470
8		8,508	0.144	1,225
Profitability (NPV of the Machine)				5,810

Alternatively, profitability can be calculated through EVs as follows:

Calculations of Net Present Value

Year		EV of cash flow (Rs.)	Discount Factor	NPV (Rs.)
0		(20,000)	1.000	(20,000)
1	3,200			
	7,200	10,400	0.833	8,662
2	3,200			
	16,000	19,200	0.694	13,324
3	4,200			
	2,400	6,600	0.579	3,824
				5,810

Illustration 1

Eskay Ltd is considering the purchase of a new machine. The two alternative models under consideration are 'Laxmi' and 'HMT'. From the following information, prepare a profitability statement for submission to the Board of Directors.

	Machine "Laxmi" Rs.	Machine "HMT" Rs.
Cost of machine	90,000	1,50,000
Estimated life (in years)	10	15
Estimated savings in scrap p.a.	6,000	9,000
Additional cost of supervision p.a.	7,200	9,600
Additional cost of maintenance p.a.	4,200	6,600
Cost of indirect material p.a.	3,600	4,800
Estimated savings in wages:		
Wages per worker p.a.	360	360
Workers not required	150	200

Assume the taxation rate to be 50 percent of profits. Suggest which model can be purchased, giving reasons for you answer.

Solution:

Profitability statement

	Machine 'Laxmi'		Machine 'HMT'	
	Rs.	Rs.	Rs.	Rs.
Estimated savings p.a.				
Scrap	6,000		9,000	

Wages	54,000	60,000	72,000	81,000
Less: Estimated Additional cost p.a.				
Cost of supervision	7,200		9,600	
Cost of Maintenance	4,200		6,600	
Indirect materials	3,600	15,000	4,800	21,000
Savings before depreciation		45,000		60,000
Less: Depreciation		9,000		10,000
Savings after depreciation		36,000		50,000
Less: Taxes at 50%		18,000		25,000
Net Savings p.a.	18,000		25,000	
Annual Cash flow:				
Net savings	18,000		25,000	
Depreciation	9,000		10,000	
		27,000		35,000

$$\text{Pay back period} = \frac{\text{Cost of machine}}{\text{Saving p.a.}}$$

Payback period:

	Machine 'Laxmi'		Machine 'HMT'	
Before Tax	$\frac{\text{Rs.}90{,}000}{\text{Rs.}45{,}000}$	= 2 years	$\frac{\text{Rs.}1{,}50{,}000}{\text{Rs.}60{,}000}$	=2 1/2 years
After tax	$\frac{\text{Rs.}90{,}000}{\text{Rs.}27{,}000}$	= 3 1/3 years	$\frac{\text{Rs.}1{,}50{,}000}{\text{Rs.}35{,}000}$	= 4 2/7 years

Thus machine 'Laxmi' clearly recommends itself for purchase. However, the information provided and conclusion derived may be supplemented with some additional calculations as regards profitability beyond pay back period.

	Machine 'Laxmi' Rs.	Machine 'HMT' Rs.
Profitability beyond pay back, Before tax		
Life beyond pay back period	8 years	12 1/2 years
Savings p.a.	45,000	60,000
Total savings	3,60,000	7,50,000
After tax:		
Life beyond pay back	6 2/3 years	10 5/7 years
Saving p.a.	Rs. 27,000	Rs. 35,000
Total savings	1,80,000	3,75,000

Illustration 2

Determine the average rate of return from the following data of two Machines A and B

	Machine A	Machine B
Original cost	56,125	56,125
Addl. Investment in net working capital	5,000	6,000
Estimated life in years	5	5
Estimated salvage value	3,000	3,000
Average income tax rate	55%	55%
Annual estimated income after depreciation and tax:		
1st year	3,375	11,375
2nd year	5,375	9,375
3rd year	7,375	7,375
4th year	9,375	5,375
5th year	11,375	3,375
	36,875	36,875

Depreciation has been charged on straight line basis.

(Delhi. M.Com., 1972 adapted)

Solution

$$\text{ARR} = \frac{\text{Average Earnings}}{\text{Average Investment}} \times 100$$

$$\text{Average Income} = \frac{\text{Total Income}}{\text{Number of years}}$$

$$\text{Machine A} = \frac{\text{Rs.}36{,}875}{5} = \text{Rs.}7{,}375$$

$$\text{Machine B} = \frac{\text{Rs.}36{,}875}{5} = \text{Rs.}7375$$

$$\text{Average Investment} = \frac{\text{Original Investment} - \text{Scrap value}}{2} + \text{Addl Net working capital} + \text{Scrap value}$$

$$\text{Machine A} = \frac{56{,}125 - 3{,}000}{2} + \text{Rs.}5{,}000 + \text{Rs.}3{,}000$$

$$= 26{,}562.50 + 8{,}000 = \text{Rs.}34{,}562.50$$

$$\text{Machine B} = 26{,}562.50 + 9{,}000 = \text{Rs.}35{,}562.50$$

$$\text{ARR for machine A} = \frac{\text{Rs.}7{,}375}{34{,}562.50} \times 100 = 21.34\%$$

$$\text{ARR for Machine B} = \frac{7{,}375}{35{,}562.50} \times 100 = 20.74\%$$

Illustration 3

A company is considering to expand its production. It can go in either for an automatic machine costing Rs. 2,24,000 with an estimated life of 5 1/2 years or an ordinary machine costing Rs. 60,000 having an estimated life of 8 years. The annual sales and costs are estimated as follows:

	Automatic Machine	Ordinary Machine
Sales	Rs. 1,50,000	1,50,000
Costs:		
Materials	50,000	50,000
Labour	12,000	60,000
Variable overheads	24,000	20,000

Compute the comparative profitability of the proposals under the 'pay-back period' and 'Return on Investment' methods. Explain the difference in the results obtained under the two methods.

Solution

Pay-back period

	Automatic Machine Rs.	Ordinary Machine Rs.
Investment Cost	2,24,000	60,000
Sales	1,50,000	1,50,000
Less: variable costs	86,000	1,30,000
Contribution	64,000	20,000

$$\text{Pay-back period} = \frac{\text{Original cost}}{\text{Cash inflow per annum}}$$

$$\text{Pay-back period} = \frac{2,24,000}{64,000} = 3.5 \text{ years} \quad \frac{60,000}{20,000} = 3 \text{ years}$$

The pay-back period in case of ordinary machine is shorter. Hence, ordinary machine is preferable.

Return on Investment:

Contribution p.a.	64,000	20,000
Less: Depreciation (according to Straight line method)	40,725	7,500
Net earnings	23,275	12,500

$$\text{Return on Investments} = \frac{\text{Net savings}}{\text{Average Investments}} \times 100$$

	Automatic Machine	Ordinary Machine
ROI	$\text{Rs.}\frac{23,275}{1,12,000} \times 100$	$\text{Rs.}\frac{12,500}{30,000} \times 100$
	20.8 %	41.67 %

Since the ROI is higher in the case of ordinary machine, it is preferable.

Illustration 4

A choice is to be made between two competing proposals which require an equal investment of Rs. 50,000 and are expected to generate net cash flows as under:

		Project I	*Project II*
End of year 1	Rs.	25,000	10,000
End of year 2		15,000	12,000
End of year 3		10,000	18,000
End of year 4		Nil	25,000
End of year 5		12,000	8,000
End of year 6		6,000	4,000

The cost of capital of the company is 10%. The following are the present value factors @ 10% p.a.

Year	P.v.Factors @ 10% p.a.
1	0.909
2	0.826
3	0.751
4	0.686
5	0.621
6	0.564

Which project proposal should be chosen and why? Evaluate the project proposals under:

(a) Pay-back period and

(b) Discounted cash flow methods, pointing out their relative merits and demerits.

(M.Com., Madras May, 1978.)

Solution

Pay-back period Method

	Net Cash Inflows	
	Project I	Project II
End of year 1	25,000	10,000
End of year 2	15,000	12,000
End of year 3	10,000	18,000
End of year 4	Nil	25,000
End of year 5	12,000	8,000
End of year 6	6,000	4,000

Project I has the pay back period of 3 years while project II has a pay-back period of 3.4 years (i.e. Rs. 40,000 in 3 years and Rs. 10,000 in the 4th year). Thus, project I has to be preferred because it has a shorter pay-back period.

Discounted cash flow method Project I

Year	Cash Inflow	Discount Factor at 10% p.a.	Present Value
1	25,000	0.909	22,725

2	15,000	0.826	12,390
3	10,000	0.751	7,510
4	Nil	0.683	
5	12,000	0.621	7,452
6	6,000	0.564	3,384
	Total present value of future cash inflows		53,461
	Initial investment		50,000
	Net present value (NPV)		3,461

Project II

Year	Cash inflow	Discount Factor at 10% p.a.	Present Value
1	10,000	0.909	9,090
2	12,000	0.826	9,912
3	18,000	0.751	13,518
4	25,000	.683	17,075
5	8,000	.621	4,968
6	4,000	0.564	2,256
	Total present value of future cash inflow		56,819
	Initial Investment		50,000
	Net Present value (NPV)		6,819

Project II is profitable since its NPV is high.

Illustration 5

K.N.P. Ltd is considering the purchase of a machine. Two machines are available, M. and N, each costing Rs. 50,000. In comparing the profitability of the machines, a discount rate of 10% is to be used. Earnings after tax are expected to be as follows:

Year	Cash flows	
	Machine 'M'	Machine 'N'
1	15,000	5,000
2	20,000	15,000
3	25,000	20,000
4	15,000	30,000
5	10,000	20,000

Indicate which machine would be profitable under the various methods of ranking investment proposals.

Solution

Profitability Statement

Year	Discount factor at 10%	Machine M		Machine N	
		Cash flow Rs.	PV of Cash flow Rs.	Cash flow Rs.	PV of Cash flow Rs.
1	0.909	15,000	13,635	5,000	4,545

2	0.826	20,000	16,520	15,000	12,390
3	0.751	25,000	18,775	20,000	15,020
4	0.683	15,000	10,245	30,000	20,490
5	0.621	10,000	6,210	20,000	12,420
		85,000	65,385	90,000	64,865
Less cost		50,000	50,000	50,000	50,000
NPV		35,000	15,385	40,000	14,865

According to this statement, Machine 'M' is more profitable as its NPV is greater than that of Machine N.

Comparison with Payback Period and Return in Investment

	Machine 'M'	Machine 'N'
Payback period	2 3/5 years	3 1/3 years
Post payback profitability	Rs. 35,000	Rs. 40,000
Return on investment (Average Return/Average Investment)	28% $\left[\frac{\text{Rs.}7{,}000}{\text{Rs.}25{,}000} \times 100\right]$	32% $\left[\frac{\text{Rs.}8{,}000}{\text{Rs.}25{,}000} \times 100\right]$
NPV	Rs.15,385	Rs.14,865

From the above figures it will be observed that Machine 'M' would be preferred under payback period and DCF method, while Machine 'N' would be preferred under post-payback profitability and return on investment method. These results are as can be expected. machine 'M' yields a high the payback period of DCF methods. But, as the total return on Machine 'N' is greater than Machine 'M', the post-payback profitability and Return on investment favour Machine 'N'.

Illustration 6

A B C Ltd. has Rs. 80,000 to invest. It has two attractive proposals at hand for consideration. The alternatives are:

		Proposal X Rs.	Proposal Y Rs.
Investment outlay		80,000	80,000
Cash inflows:	year		
	1	32,000	20,000
	2	32,000	20,000
	3	24,000	24,000
	4		32,000

Required:

(i) Which investment proposal would you recommend under the payback approach?

(ii) Would your decision be different if proposal Y has Rs.64,000 in the fourth year instead of Rs. 32,000 inflow?

Solution

Calculation of payback period.

Year	Estimated annual Cash flows Proposals		Cumulative Cash flow Proposals	
	X Rs.	Y Rs.	X Rs.	Y Rs.
1	32,000	20,000	32,000	20,000
2	32,000	20,000	64,000	40,000
3	24,000	24,000	88,000	64,000
4	-	32,000	-	96,000

Pay pack period

$$\text{Proposal X } = 2 + \frac{16,000}{24,000} = 2\frac{2}{3}\text{ years}$$

$$\text{Proposal Y } = 3 + \frac{16,000}{32,000} = 3\frac{1}{2}\text{ years}$$

(i) Proposal X will be reco mmended since its payback period is shorter than that Proposal Y.

(ii) Payback period of proposal Y when its fourth year cash flow is Rs.64,000 instead of Rs. 32,000.

$$3 + \frac{16,000}{64,000} = 3\frac{1}{4}\text{ years}$$

Even now the payback period is higher than that of proposal X. Hence, there is no change in the recommendation.

Illustration 7

Priya Industries Ltd. is contemplating to undertake a profit. Two alternative projects 'EX' and 'WYE' are available the details of which are given below:

		Projects	
		'Exe' Rs.	'WYE' Rs.
Investment outlay		40,000	60,000
Estimated economic life		4 years	5 years
Expected annual cash inflow:			
before tax year	1	18,000	24,000
	2	16,000	24,000
	3	16,000	20,000
	4	14,000	18,000
	5	-	16,000

The tax rate is 50 per cent. Calculate the average rate of return and advice management as to which project should be selected if the minimum required rate of return is 12 per cent.

Solution

Calculation of return after depreciation and tax

Project 'EX'

Year	Cash inflows Rs.	Depreciation Rs.	Tax 50% (2-3)	Net Income 2 − (3 + 4)
1	2	3	4	5
1	18,000	10,000	4,000	4,000
2	16,000	10,000	3,000	3,000
3	16,000	10,000	3,000	3,000
4	14,000	10,000	2,000	2,000
			Total income	12,000

Average return Rs. 12,000 ÷ 4 = Rs. 3,000

Average Rate of return on Original Investment

$$ARR = \frac{Rs.3{,}000 \times 100}{Rs.40{,}000} = 7.5\%$$

Average Rate of Return on Average Investment

$$ARR = \frac{Rs.3{,}000}{Rs.20{,}000} \times 100 = 15\%$$

Calculation of return after depreciation and tax.

Project 'WYE'

Year	Cash inflows Rs.	Depreciation Rs.	Tax 50% (2-3) Rs.	Net Income Rs.
1	2	3	4	5
1	24,000	12,000	6,000	6,000
2	24,000	12,000	6,000	6,000
3	20,000	12,000	4,000	4,000
4	18,000	12,000	3,000	3,000
5	16,000	12,000	2,000	2,000
			Total Income	21,000

Average Income = Rs.21,000 ÷ 5 = Rs.4,200

Average rate of return on Original Investment.

$$ARR = \frac{Rs.4{,}200}{Rs.60{,}000} \times 100 = 7\%$$

ARR on average Investment

$$ARR = \frac{Rs.4{,}200}{Rs.30{,}000} \times 100 = 14\%$$

The ARRs on Average Investment for both the projects are higher than the required rate of return, However, they are alternative projects and the company can adopt 'EXE' since it ARR higher than that of 'WYE'.

Illustration 8

Following data in respect of two machines namely 'A' and 'B; are detailed below. Depreciation has been charged on straight line basis and estimated life or both machines is five years.

(In Rupees)

Item	Machine 'A'	Machine 'B'
Cost	56,125	56,125
Net income after depreciation and taxes		
1st Year	3,375	11,375
2nd Year	5,375	9,375
3rd Year	7,375	7,375
4th Year	9,375	5,375
5th Year	11,375	3,375
	36,875	36,875

Find out

(a) average rate of return on 'A' and 'B' machines

(b) Which machine is better from the point of view of payback period and why ?

Solution

(a) Average Rate of Return (ARR)

$$\text{ARR} = \frac{\text{Average net income after taxes}}{\text{Average investment}}$$

$$\text{Average income of Machines 'A'} = \frac{36{,}875}{5}$$

$$= \text{Rs.}7{,}375$$

$$\text{Average income of Machine 'B'} = \frac{36575}{5}$$

$$= \text{Rs.}7{,}375$$

Average investment = 1/2(56.125)

= Rs.28,062.50

(Average investment of Machine A and Machine B is the same as the cost is same).

$$\text{ARR for Machine A} = \frac{7{,}375}{28{,}062.50} \times 100 = 26.28\%$$

$$\text{ARR for Machine B} = \frac{7375}{28062} \times 100 = 26.28\%$$

(b) From the point of view of payback period

From this point of view, machine B is better as the initial inflow is much higher compared to Machine A and hence, Machine B provides large liquidity of funds.

Computation of Payback period

Annual cash flow = Net income + depreciation

	Cash flow (Rs)	
	Machine A	Machine B
1st Year	14,600	22,600
2nd Year	16,600	20,600
3rd Year	18,600	18,600
4th Year	20,600	16,600
5th Year	22,600	14,600

Pay back period $= 3 + \frac{6,325}{20,660}$ $\quad 2 + \frac{12,925}{18,600}$

$= 3.31$ yrs app. $\quad$ 2.69 yrs (app)

B is better than A as it has shorter payback period.

Illustration 9

A company is considering to expand its production it can go in either for an automatic machine costing Rs. 2,20,000 with an estimated life of 5.5 years or an ordinary machine costing Rs. 60,000 having an estimated life of 8 years. The annual sales and costs are estimated as follows:

	Automatic Machine Rs.	Ordinary Machine Rs.
Sales	1,50,000	1,50,000
Costs:		
Material	50,000	50,000
Labour	12,000	60,000
Variable overheads	24,000	20,000

Compute the comparative profitability of the proposals under the Return on investment method.

Solution

Comparative Profitability Statement

	Automatic Machine Rs.		Ordinary Machine Rs.	
Sales		1,50,000		1,50,000
Less: *Costs:*				
Materials	50,000		50,000	
Labour	12,000		60,000	
Variable Overheads	24,000		20,000	
Depreciation	40,000		7,500	
		1,26,000		1,37,500
Profit		24,000		12,500

Return on Gross investment Automatic $= \frac{\text{Rs.}24,000}{\text{Rs.}2,20,000} \times 100$

$$= 10.9\%$$

$$\text{Ordinary} = \frac{\text{Rs.}12{,}500}{\text{Rs.}60{,}000} \times 100 = 20.8\%$$

$$\text{Return on Average Investment Automatic} = \frac{\text{Rs.}24{,}000}{\text{Rs.}1{,}10{,}000} \times 100 = 21.8\%$$

$$\text{Ordinary} = \frac{\text{Rs.}12{,}500}{\text{Rs.}30{,}000} \times 100 = 41.67\%$$

As the comparative profitability of ordinary machine is higher than that of automatic machine, the ordinary machine is preferable.

Illustration 10

Anish Ltd is evaluating two mutually exclusive proposals for new capital investment. The following information about the proposals are available:

	Proposal A Rs.	Proposal B Rs.
Investment Cost	80,000	1,00,000
Economic Life (years)	4 yrs	5 yrs.
Earnings before depreciation and taxes		
year		
1	24,000	28,000
2	28,000	32,000
3	32,000	36,000
4	44,000	44,000
5		40,000

The company's cost of capital is 10 percent and tax rate is 50%. Advice the company as to which proposal would be profitable using DCF techniques.

Solution

Calculation of cash inflows

Proposal A

Year	1	2	3	4
Earnings (Rs.)	24,000	28,000	32,000	44,000
Less: Depreciation (Rs.)	20,000	20,000	20,000	20,000
Earnings after Depreciation	4,000	8,000	12,000	24,000
Less: Tax @ 50%	2,000	4,000	6,000	12,000
Earnings after tax	2,000	4,000	6,000	12,000
Add: Depreciation	20,000	20,000	20,000	20,000
Net Cash inflows	22,000	24,000	26,000	32,000

Proposal B

Year	1	2	3	4	5
Earnings (Rs.)	28,000	32,000	36,000	44,000	40,000
Less: Depreciation (Rs.)	20,000	20,000	20,000	20,000	20,000
Earning after depreciation	8,000	12,000	16,000	24,000	20,000
Less: Tax (50%)	4,000	6,000	8,000	12,000	10,000
Earnings after tax	4,000	6,000	8,000	12,000	10,000

Add: Depreciation	20,000	20,000	20,000	20,000	20,000
Net Cash inflows	24,000	26,000	28,000	32,000	30,000

Profitability statement

Year	Cash flows A	Cash flows B	Discount factor at 10%	Present Values A	Present Values B
	Rs.	Rs.		Rs.	Rs.
0	(80,000)	(1,00,000)		(80,000)	(1,00,000)
1	22,000	24,000	0.909	19,998	21,816
2	24,000	26,000	0.826	19,824	21,476
3	26,000	28,000	0.751	17,526	21,028
4	32,000	32,000	0.683	21,856	21,856
5	-	30,000	0.621	-	18,630
		NPV		1,204	4,806

$$\text{Profitability index} = \frac{\text{PV of Cash inflow}}{\text{PV of Cash outflows}}$$

Proposal A

$$\frac{81204}{80000} = 1.015$$

Proposal B

$$\frac{104806}{100000} = 1.048$$

Calculation of Internal Rate of Return

The first trial rate can be taken as 10% since it has been used for the calculation of NPV. In both the cases the NPV is positive and therefore, a higher discount rate could be tried. Let us take 12% as the second trial rate.

Year	Cash flows A	Cash flows B	Discount factor at 12%	Present Values A	Present Values B
	Rs.	Rs.		Rs.	Rs.
0	(80,000)	(1,00,000)	1	(80,000)	(1,00,000)
1	22,000	24,000	0.893	19,646	21,432
2	24,000	26,000	0.797	19,128	20,722
3	26,000	28,000	0.712	18,512	19,936
4	32,000	32,000	0.636	20,352	20,352
5	-	30,000	0.567	-	17,010
		NPV		(2,362)	(548)

At 12% discount rate the NPVs of both the proposals are negative. Hence, the actual rate should be below 12% but above 10%. The correct rate could be ascertained by interpolation.

$$\text{I R R of proposal A} = 10 + \frac{1204 \times 2}{3566} = 10.66\%$$

$$\text{I R R proposal B} = 10 + \frac{4806 \times 2}{5354} = 11.80\%$$

Comparative Evaluation:	Proposal A	Proposal B
NPV	1204	4806
PI	1.015	1.048
IRR	10.66%	11.80%

Under all the three DCF methods, the proposal B shows better results, Hence it should be adopted.

Illustration 11

A Ltd., is considering a proposal to invest Rs.70000 in a project. The expected cash flows after taxes [CFAT] from the project for a period of three consecutive years are Rs.40000 each. The estimated salvage value of the project is Rs.2000. The company's cost of capital is 10% and a risk premium of 8% is considered necessary for undertaking the project. Advise the management as to the acceptance of the proposal. [P.V of annuity of Re.1 at 18% for three years 2.174 and PV of Re.1 at 10% for the third year 0.751].

Solution

Risk free rate = 10%

Risk premium = 8%

Risk adjusted discount rate = 18%

Profitability Statement

Year	CFAT [Rs.]	PV factor at 18%	PV of CFAT [Rs.]
1 - 3	40000	2.174	86960
3	2000	0.751	1502
	Total		88462
	Less: Capital Investment Outlay		70000
		NPV	18462

The company may undertake the investment proposal.

[As the salvage value is a certainty factor, the risk free rate is used for discounting.]

Illustration 12

B Ltd., is examining two mutually exclusive investment proposals. The management wants to use certainty equivalents [CE] for evaluation of new proposals. From the following information relating to these projects advise the management as to which project should be undertaken by it.

Year	Proposal A		Proposal B	
	Cash Flows	CE	Cash Flows	CE
0	[Rs.50000]	1.0	[Rs.50000]	1.0
1	30300	0.8	20000	0.9
2	35000	0.7	35000	0.8
3	30000	0.6	25000	0.7
4	25000	0.5	30000	0.5

The company's cost of capital is 12% and the risk free borrowing rate is 10%.

Solution

Profitability Statement

Proposal A

Year	Risky Cash Flows Rs.	CE	Risk Adjusted CF Rs.	PV factor @ 10% [Risk free rate]	Total PV Rs.
0	[50000]	1.00	[50000]	1.000	[50000]
1	30300	0.80	24240	0.909	22034
2	35000	0.70	24500	0.826	20237
3	30000	0.60	18000	0.751	13518
4	25000	0.50	12500	0.683	8538
				NPV	14327

Proposal B

Year	Risky Cash Flows Rs.	CE	Risk Adjusted CF Rs.	PV factor @ 10% [Risk free rate]	Total PV Rs.
0	[50000]	1.00	[50000]	1.000	[50000]
1	20000	0.90	18000	0.909	16362
2	35000	0.80	28000	0.826	23128
3	25000	0.70	17500	0.751	13143
4	30000	0.50	15000	0.683	10245
				NPV	12878

Recommendation: Project A should be accepted.

REVIEW QUESTIONS

1. Define the concept of Capital Expenditure Decision.
2. Define the concept of Capital Budgeting.
3. State the objectives of Capital Budgeting.
4. Discuss the importance of Capital Budgeting.
5. Mention the various types capital investment projects.
6. What are the relevant costs for capital expenditure decision?
7. Define the concept of project appraisal.
8. Describe the Payback Method and enumerate its merits and demerits.
9. Describe the Average Rate of Return Method. What are its merits and demerits?
10. What are DCF techniques? State the advantages and criticisms of DCF techniques.
11. Define Net Present Value technique.
12. What is Benefit-Cost ratio?
13. Explain the meaning, merits, and limitations of IRR method.
14. Explain the concepts of Risk and Uncertainty.
15. Describe the various modern Quantitative techniques used in Risk analysis.

16. Discuss the various conservative methods of risk analysis.
17. Describe a few modern methods of Risk Analysis.
18. Describe Decision Tree Analysis giving one illustration.

REVIEW PROBLEMS

1. A Ltd., is considering two projects Exe and Wye each costing Rs.20000. The net cash flows from the projects are as follows:

Year	1	2	3	4	5	6
Exe [Rs.]	10000	8000	6000	2000	-	-
Wye [Rs]	2000	4000	6000	8000	8000	9000

The company has fixed three years as the cut-off period. State which project should be accepted?

[Answer: PB for Exe 2 yrs 4 months and Wye 4 yrs. Project Exe should be accepted.]

2. Excel Ltd., is considering the purchase of a new machine, which would carry out some operations at present performed by Manual labour. Two models are available. Experts make the following estimates:

	Machine A	Machine B
Estimated working life [years]	5	6
	Rs.	Rs.
Cost of machine	100000	150000
Savings in scrap per annum	5000	6000
Indirect materials per annum	3000	3500
Savings in labour per annum	50000	60000
Cost of maintenance per annum	11500	7500

The tax rate may be regarded at 40 per cent of profits. Which model can be recommended for purchase? Use Payback Period and Average Rate of Return methods of projects appraisal.

[Answer: PB period A 3.1 yrs and B 3.49 yrs [app] and ARR [on average investment] A 24.6% and B 24%. Machine A can be recommended]

3. A ltd., is considering a project costing Rs.80000. The net income before depreciation and tax is estimated as follows:

Year:	1	2	3	4	5
Net Income [Rs.]	20000	24000	28000	32000	40000

Depreciation is charged at 20 per cent per annum. Corporate tax rate is 40%. Calculate the ARR on average investment.

[Answer: ARR = [Rs.7 680 / 40000] x 100 = 19.2%]

4. The initial cash outlay of a project is Rs.50000 and it generates cash inflows of Rs.20000, Rs.15000, Rs.25000, and Rs.10000 in four years. Using the net present value method appraise the profitability of the proposed investment using 10% rate of discount.
[Answer: NPV = Rs.6 175] [M.B.A., April 2002, Madras University]

5. NP ltd., is considering purchase of a machine, which will have a working life of 5 years. The machine is expected to earn Rs.15000 per annum, before taxes for the first three years, and Rs.12000 and Rs.8000 for the fourth and fifth years respectively. The company

considers a yield of 20% necessary before investment is made in a project. How much can be spent in purchasing the machine?

[Answer: Gross Present Value at 20% Rs.40590 would be amount that can be spent.]

6. Your company is considering investing in a project for which the investment data are as follows:
Capital outlay: Rs.200000; Depreciation charge: 20% per annum

Forecasted annual income before charging depreciation but all other charges was as follows:

Year:	1	2	3	4	5
Annual Income [Rs.]	100000	100000	80000	80000	40000

On the basis of figures given above, set out calculations illustrating and comparing the following methods of evaluating the return on capital employed:

(a) Payback Period (b) Average Rate of Return (c) NPV at 10% and (d) BCR

(Answer: (a) 2 years (b) 40% (c) Rs.125480 (d) 1.63 [app])

7. An investor who must have a minimum rate of return of 12% p.a., has two projects in view, both requiring initial outlay of Rs.30000. Project A gives an annual net income of Rs.6000 with a salvage value of Rs.10000 at the end of 10 years. Project B gives an annual net income of Rs.5000 with a salvage value of Rs.2000. at the end of 10 years. Which project should he prefer? [Note: PV of Re.1 at 12% received annually for 10 years = 5.65 and at the end of 10th year = 0.322]

[NPV of Project A = Rs.7 120 and NPV of B = Rs.4690]

8. An investment of Rs.600000 was made in a capital project two years ago. Following estimates were made at that time of investment:

(a) The effective life of the project was to be 5 years.

(b) The scrap value at the end of 5th year is to be Rs.20000.

(c) The expected cash inflows for 5 years were as follows: Year 1 Rs.300000; Year 2 Rs.250000; Year 3 Rs.200000; Year 4 Rs.150000; Year 5 Rs.100000

(d) The required rate was to be 10%. However, the past two years' results have not been promising. The net cash inflows for the last two years have been only Rs.2 50000 and Rs.1 50000 respectively. In view of the last two years' poor results, the cash inflows for the remaining three years are expected to be only Rs. 120000, Rs.90000, and Rs.40000 respectively. However, the investment has a present abandonment value of Rs.240000. Would you advise the management for abandoning the investment? Substantiate your answer.

[Answer: PV of new cash inflows is Rs.2 28 480, which is lower than the abandonment value. Hence, the management is advised to abandon the project.]

9. From the following data, state which project is better?

Year	Project A Cash Flows [Rs.]	Project B Cash Flows [Rs.]
0	[10000]	[10000]
1	4000	5000
2	4000	6000
3	2000	3000

Risk less discount rate is 5%. Project A is less rısky as compared to Project B. the management considers risk premium rates at 5% and 10% respectively appropriate for discounting the cash flows.

[Answer: Risk-adjusted discount rate, Project A 10%, and Project B 15%; NPV for A [Rs.1558], and that of B Rs.860, hence B is better.]

10. A project needs an investment of Rs.138500. The cost of capital is 12%. The net cash inflows are as under:

Year:	1	2	3	4	5
Cash inflows [Rs.]:	30000	40000	60000	30000	20000

Calculate the Internal Rate of Return and suggest whether the project should be accepted or not?

[Answer: IRR 10%, the project should not be accepted]

12

BUDGETING AND BUDGETARY CONTROL

Learning Objectives

After completing this chapter, you should be able to

— Explain the concepts of Budget and Budgetary Control.

— State the objectives, advantages, and limitations of Budgetary Control.

— Describe the Organization for Budgetary Control.

— Discuss the various methods of classification of budgets.

— Understand the methods of preparation of various budgets.

— Know the meaning of the concepts of Performance budgeting and Zero-base budgeting.

12.1. Need for Budgeting

The management is efficient if it is able to accomplish the objective of the enterprise. It is effective, when it accomplishes the objectives with minimum effort and cost. In order to attain long-range efficiency and effectiveness, management must chart out its course of action in advance. A systematic approach to facilitate effective management performance is profit **planning and control, or budgeting. Budgeting** is therefore an integral part of management. In a way, a budgetary control system has been described as a historical combination of a "goal-setting machine for increasing an enterprise's profits, and goal- achieving, machine for facilitating organizational coordination and planning while achieving the budgeted targets."

12.2. Concepts of Budget and Budgetary Control

The Institute of Cost and Management Accountants, London, gives the following definitions:

A **budget** is a "financial and quantitative statement, prepared and approved prior to a defined period of time, of the policy to be pursued during the period for the purpose of attaining a given objective. It may include income, expenditure and the employment of capital."

Budgetary Control is defined as "the establishment of departmental budgets relating the responsibilities of executives to the requirements of a policy, and the continuous comparison of actual with budgeted results, either to secure by individual action the objectives of that policy, or to provide a firm basis for its revision."

Thus a budget is a predetermined statement of management policy during a given period, which provides a standard for comparison with the results actually achieved. Budgetary control system is a system of controlling costs, which includes the preparation of budgets, coordinating the departments and establishing responsibilities, comparing actual performance with that of budgeted and acting upon results to achieve maximum profitability. Budgeting is essentially concerned with planning and can be broadly illustrated by comparison with the route a ship's captain follows on each voyage.

The following steps are involved in a budgetary control system:

1. Establish a plan or target of performance, which coordinates all the activities of the business.
2. Record the actual performance.
3. Compare the actual performance with that planned.
4. Calculate the differences, or variances and the reasons for them.
5. Act immediately, if necessary, to remedy the situation.

12.3. Objectives of Budgetary Control

Briefly, the main objectives of budgetary control are as follows:

1. To combine the ideas of all levels of management in the preparation of the budgets.
2. To coordinate all the activities of the business.
3. To centralize control.
4. To decentralize responsibility to each manager involved.
5. To act as a guide for management decision-making when unforeseeable conditions affect the business.
6. To plan and control income and expenditure so that maximum profitability is achieved
7. To direct the capital expenditures into the most profitability areas or direction.
8. To ensure that sufficient working capital is available for the efficient operation of the business.
9. To provide a yardstick against which actual results can be compared.
10. To show management where action is needed to remedy a situation.

12.4. Advantages of Budgetary Control

The following are some of the most significant advantages of budgeting:

1. Budgeting compels the management to plan for the future. The budgeting process forces management to look ahead and become more effective and efficient in administering business operations. It instills into managers the habit of evaluating carefully their problems and related variables before making any decisions.

2. Budgeting helps to coordinate, integrate, and balance the efforts of various departments in the light of the overall objectives of the enterprise. This results in goal congruency and harmony among the departments.

3. Budgeting facilitates control by providing definite expectations in the planning phase that can be used as a frame of reference for judging the subsequent performance. Undoubtedly, budgeted performance is a more relevant standard for comparison than past performance, since past performance is based on historical factors, which are constantly changing.

4. Budgeting improves the quality of communication. The enterprise's objectives, budget goals, plans, authority and responsibility and procedures to implement plans are clearly

written and communicated trough budgets to all individuals in the enterprise. This results in better understanding, and harmonious relations among managers and subordinates.

5. Budgeting helps to optimize the use of firm's resources, both human and capital. It aids in directing the total efforts of the firm into the most profitable channels.

6. Budgeting increases the morale and thereby the productivity of the employees by seeking their meaningful participation in the formulation of plans and policies, bringing about a harmony between individual goals and enterprise's objectives, and by providing incentives for better performance.

7. Budgeting develops profit-mindedness and cost consciousness.

8. Budgeting permits management to focus attention on significant matters through budgetary reports. Thus, it facilitates management by exception and thereby saves the management's time and energy.

9. Budgeting measures efficiency and thereby enables self evaluation by the management. It also indicates the progress made in attaining the enterprise's objectives.

12.5. Major problems involved in developing a budgeting system

The major problems involved in developing a budgeting system are as follows:

1. Getting the support and involvement of all levels of management.

2. Developing meaningful forecasts and plans, especially the sales plan.

3. Inducing all individuals to get involved in the budgeting process, and gaining their full participation.

4. Establishing realistic objectives, procedures, and standards of desired performance.

5. Applying the budgeting system in a flexible manner.

6. Maintaining effective follow-up procedures, and adapting the budgeting system to changing circumstances.

12.6. Limitations of Budgetary Control

Management must consider the following limitations in using the budgeting system as a device to solve managerial problems:

1. Budgeting is not an exact science; its success depends upon the precision of estimates. Estimates are based on facts and managerial judgment. Managerial judgment can suffer from subjectivity and personal biases. The efficacy of budgeting thus depends upon the quality of managerial judgment.

2. A perfect system of budgeting cannot be organized in a short period. Business condition change rapidly. Therefore, the budgeting system should be continuously adapted to changing circumstances. Budgeting has to be a continuous exercise; it is a dynamic process. Management should not lose patience; it should go on trying various techniques and procedures in developing and using the budgeting system.

3. A skillfully prepared budget system will not by itself improve the management of an enterprise unless it is properly implemented. For the success of the budgetary system, it is essential that it is understood by all, and that the managers and subordinates put in concerted efforts for accomplishing the budget goals. All persons in the enterprise must be fully involved in the preparation and execution of budgets, otherwise budgeting will not be effective.

4. Budgeting is a management tool, a way of managing, not the management itself. The presence of a budgetary system should not make management complacent. To get the best results, management should use budgeting with intelligence and foresight, along with other managerial techniques. Budgeting assists management; it cannot replace management.

5. Budgeting will be ineffective and expensive if it is unnecessarily detailed and complicated. A budget should be precise in format and simple to understand; it should be flexible in application.

6. The purpose of budgeting will be defeated if the budget goals are set carelessly. Budget goals are the definite targets to achieve the overall objectives of the enterprise. They must be in harmony with the aims of the enterprise.

7. Budgeting will hide inefficiencies instead of revealing them if there is no evaluation system. There should be continuous evaluation of actual performance. The standard should also be reexamined regularly.

8. Budgeting will lower the morale and productivity of the personnel if unrealistic targets are set and if it is used as pressure tool. To some extent, budgeting may be used as a pressure device but its extent must be carefully determined.

12.7. Organisation for Budgetary Control

It is essential that there should be an efficient organisation if budgetary control is to be operated effectively. Budgetary control is not only an accounting exercise, but also a tool of management at all levels. In organising a system, it is essential to obtain the full cooperation of each member of the management team. A number of preliminaries will be necessary if the staff are to have confidence in this system; these include:

1. Creation of budget centres or departments should be established for each of which budgets can be set with the help of the head of department concerned. A budget centre is a centre or department or a segment of an organisation for which budgets are prepared. Budgets should be set with the help of the heads of these centres so that these may be implemented more effectively.

2. Introduction of adequate accounting records: It is imperative that the accounting system should be able to record and analyse the information required.

3. All personnel should be trained in operating the system: Each person must know what a budget is, what it has to accomplish and how he fits into the plan. He must feel that he is capable of handling the budget centres.

4. Preparation of an organisation chart: This defines the functional responsibilities of each member of the management, and ensures that he knows his position in the company and his relationship with other members. The organisation chart will obviously depend upon the nature and size of the company, but a simplified specimen is given in figure I to show the general principles involved. Other budgets such as the raw materials or labour budgets may be prepared by heads of departments; for example by the accountant, in conjunction with the production management. It should be appreciated that in the preparation of each of these budgets the accountant will play a big part, especially those activities involving costs, such as the sales cost budgets will be prepared by heads of departments as shown below:

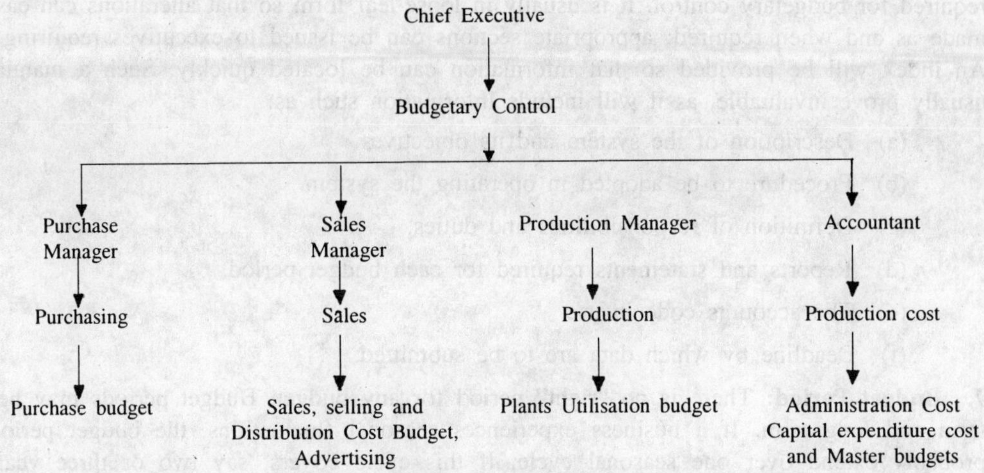

Fig.1. Organisation Chart for Budgetary Control

5. Establishment of a budget committee: In small companies, a budget officer or the accountant may coordinate all the work connected with budgets, but in large companies, a budget committee is often established to formulate a general program for preparing budgets and exercising overall control. 'The Chief Executive of the company may establish guiding principles but usually he delegates the responsibility for operating the system to the budget officer as secretary of the committee. This committee is composed of the chief executive, budget officer and heads of the main departments such as those shown in figures 1. Each member will prepare his own initial budget or budgets, which will then be considered by the committee, and all budgets will be coordinated. Usually, many changes are necessary before the budgets can be finally integrated and approved.

The Main Functions of the Committee are:

(a) To provide historical information to help managers in forecasting.

(b) To issue instructions regarding budget requirements, final dates for the receipt of budgets, etc.

(c) To define the general policies of management in relation to the budget.

(d) To advise in the preparation of budgets.

(e) To review budgets.

(f) To suggest revisions and amendments to budgets.

(g) To approve budgets.

(h) To ensure that budgets are submitted in due time.

(i) To prepare budget summaries wherever necessary.

(j) To prepare the master budget after functional budgets have been approved.

(k) To analyse comparison of budgeted and actual results, and to recommend corrective action wherever necessary.

(l) To coordinate the budget program.

6. Preparation of budget manual: This is defined (by the I.C.M.A.) as a document which sets out the responsibilities of the persons engaged in the routine of, and the forms and records required for budgetary control. It is usually in loose-leaf form so that alterations can easily be made as and when required; appropriate sections can be issued to executives requiring them. An index will be provided so that information can be located quickly. Such a manual will usually prove invaluable, as it will include information such as:

(a) Description of the system and its objectives.

(b) Procedure to be adopted in operating the system.

(c) Definition of responsibilities and duties.

(d) Reports and statements required for each budget period.

(e) The accounts code in use.

(f) Deadline by which data are to be submitted.

7. **Budget Period:** There is no "right" period for any budget. Budget periods may be short term and long term. If a business experiences seasonal fluctuations, the budget period will probably extend over one seasonal cycle. If this cycle covers, say two or three years, the long-term budget would cover that period, while the short-term budgets would perhaps be prepared on a monthly basis for control purposes. Short-term budgeting is usually costly to prepare and operate, while long-term budgeting may be considerably affected by unforeseen conditions. Budget periods frequently used in industry vary between one month and one year, the latter probably being the most commonly used as it fits in with the normally accepted accounting period. However, forecasts of much longer periods than a year may be used in the case of capital expenditure budgets, for example, which must be planned well in advance. A common practice in industry is to have a series of budget periods. Thus, the sales budget may cover the next five years, while production and cost budgets may cover only one year. These yearly budgets will be broken down into quarterly or even monthly periods. Where long-term budgets are operated it is usual to supplement them with short-term ones.

8. **The key factor:** This is the factor whose influence must first be assessed in order to ensure that functional budgets are reasonable capable of fulfillment. The key factor -known variously as the **"limiting"** or **"governing"** or **"principle budget"** factor-is of vital importance. It may not be the same for each budget period, as the circumstances may change. It determines priorities in functional budgets. Among the many key factors which may affect budgeting are the following:

(a) Materials

(i) Availability

(ii) Restrictions imposed by licenses, quotas, etc.

(b) Labour

(i) General Shortage

(ii) Shortage in certain key processes.

(c) Plant

(i) Insufficient capacity due to lack-of capital

(ii) or lack of space

(iii) or lack of markets.

(iv) Bottlenecks in certain key processes.

(d) Sales

(i) Low market demand

(ii) Shortages of experienced salesmen.

(iii) Insufficient advertising due to lack of money.

(e) Management

(i) Lack of capital, restricting policy.

(ii) Lack of know-how.

(iii) Inefficient executives.

(iv) Insufficient research into product design and methods.

The factor which is most often the key factor in industry is probably the sales demand. Very often the success or otherwise of budgetary control rests on the forecast of sales during the budget period. If the sales figures prove$ to be inaccurate, most of the budgets will be affected.

9. Level of activity: It will be necessary to establish the normal level of activity, that is the level the company can reasonably be expected to achieve. This level is important in forecasting, for example, material and labour requirements, and particularly production overhead budgets which are to be recovered on machine-hour rates.

12.8. Method Classification of Budgets

Though budgets can be classified according to various points of view the following bases of classification are generally in vogue:

(a) Classification according to time factor;

(b) Functional Classification;

(c) Classification according to flexibility factor.

(a) Classification according to Time Factor

In terms of time factor, budgets are broadly of the following three types:

1. Long-term Budgets: They are concerned with planning the operations of a firm over a perspective of five to ten years. They are usually in the form of physical quantities.

2. Short-term Budgets: They are usually for a period of a year or two and are in the form of production plan in monetary terms.

3. Current Budgets: They cover a period of a month or so and as short-term budgets, they get adjusted to prevailing circumstances. Sometimes, within the framework of a short-term budget, there are quarterly plans which are prepared by recasting the budget for a still shorter period on the basis of the performance of the immediate past. In a way, these quarterly budgets are meant to be an elaboration of the annual budget.

(b) Functional Classification

According to this basis of classification, budgets correspond, and are coterminous, with a particular function and are integrated with the master budget of the business. These are called functional budgets whose number depends on the size and nature of the business. The usual functional budgets of a business are:

1. Sales Budget: This is a forecast of total sales, classified according to groups of products, salesman and geographical locations.

2. Selling and Distribution Cost Budget: This is concerned with an estimate of the cost of selling and distribution of goods.

3. Production Budget: This is a forecast based on sales, productive capacity and requirements of inventories, etc.

4. Production Cost Budget: This is related to the cost of production, including direct material cost, direct labour cost and expenses -fixed, variable and semi-variable.

5. Purchase Budget: Correlated with sales forecast and production planning, it deals with purchases that are required for planned production. Purchase would include both direct and indirect materials and goods.

6. Personnel Budget: This has reference to the utilisation of men and would include labour employed in productive activity. This would be split up between direct and indirect labour.

7. Research Budget: This relates to improvement in the quality of the products or research for new products.

8. Cash Budget: This is a sum total of the requirements of cash in respect of various functional budgets as well as anticipated cash receipts.

9. Plant Utilisation Budget: This is intended to cover the plant and machinery requirements to meet the budgeted Production during the period. Schedules will be produced showing the available load in each department expressed in standard hours or units.

10. Office and Administration Budget: This budget represents cost of all administrative expenses, such as managing director's salary, staff salaries and expenses of office management like lighting and cleaning.

11. Capital Budget: This is a forecast of outlay on fixed assets as also of the sources of capital budget. It may differ from that of other budgets as, such expenditure is frequently planned a number of years in advance.

12. Master Budget: The ultimate integration of separate budgets by the accountant provides the. Master Budget which includes estimated profit and loss account for the future period, and an estimated Balance Sheet at the end thereof.

(c) Classification according to Flexibility

1. Fixed Budget: This is a budget in which targets are rigidly fixed. Such budgets are usually prepared from one to three months in advance of the fiscal year to which they are applicable. Thus, twelve months or more may elapse before figures forecast for the December budget are used to measure actual performance. Many things may happen during this intervening period and they may make the figures go widely out of line with the actual figures. Though it is true that a fixed, or static budget as it is sometimes called, can be revised whenever the necessity arises, it smacks of rigidity and artificially so far as control over costs and expenses are concerned. Such budgets are preferred only where sales can be forecast with the greatest of accuracy which means, in turn, that the cost and expenses in relation to sales can be quite accurately ascertained.

2. Flexible Budget: The figures used in this form of cost and expense budget are made adaptable to any month of the fiscal year. The figures range from the lowest to the highest probable percentages of operating activity in relation to the standard operating performance. From this point of view, a flexible budget prepared for an expenses group can be for the entire fiscal year, or as long as there is no need of material changes in the standards.

Thus, the flexible budget proposes a distinct advantage over the static budget particularly where it is difficult to forecast sales costs and expenses with any degree of accuracy.

PREPARATION OF BUDGET

12.9. Preparation of a Sales Budget

Sales Budget

This is a forecast of total sales expressed and incorporated in quantities and/or money. A sales budget may be prepared by expressing turnover under anyone or combination of the following:

1. Product or product group;
2. Territories, areas and countries;
3. Types of customers, e.g. national, government, export, home, wholesale or retail;
4. Salesman, agents or representatives, and
5. Period, such as quarters, months, weeks, etc.

A Sales budget may be prepared with the help of anyone or more of the following methods:

1. Analysis of past sales with adjustment for current conditions.
2. Field estimates by own sales staff.
3. Analysis of the potential market for the firm's products.
4. Studying the impact of other sundry factors affecting the sales budget.

1. Analysis of past sales: Analysis of past sales for a number of years, say 5 to 10 years, viz long-term trend, seasonal trend, cyclical trend, sundry other factors. The long-term trend represents the movement of the fortunes of a business over many years. The seasonal trend may affect many types of business and hence this factor must be taken into account when studying figures for consecutive months over a number of years. The cyclical trend represents the fluctuations in the business activity due to the effect of the trade cycle. In order to study the cyclical trend it is desirable to disregard the effects of the long-term and seasonal trends. Sundry factors include, such as a strike in the industry or a serious fire or flood. From such analysis, it will be possible to suggest future trends. In analysing such sales, considerable help can be obtained from statistical reports producted by the trade units and commercial intelligence units, government publication, etc.

2. Field estimates by own sales staff: The salesman in each area should have an intimate knowledge of the factors likely to affect his sales in the next few months or years. He can probably make a guess about the unsold stock in the shops of his customers. He is then in a position to make an estimate of future sales. When such estimates are available for a number of years, the actual sales for the year can be compared with the estimated sales and a correction factor calculated to allow for each salesman's tendency to over-estimate.

3. Analysis of the potential market: Market research people may report on the state of the market, population in area, fashion trends, the type of product design required by customers, purchasing power of people, activities of competitors and the prices the consumers are likely to pay.

4. Studying the impact of factors affecting sales: Any change in the company policy or methods should always be considered. **For example,** introduction of special discounts, special salesmen, a new design of the product, new or additional advertising campaigns, improved deliveries, after-sales service should have some market effect on a sales budget. While preparing such forecasts, the sales manager must consider the opinion of divisional managers and other sales staff, the budget officer and the accountant. It will be observed that the preparation of a sales budget involves many factors and calls for a high degree of knowledge of conditions, and of ability to deduce from the known facts and various estimates the probable course of sales over the budget period. If sales is the principal budget factor, then the sales budget is prepared first. If production is the key factor, the production budget should be built up first and the sales budget must be drawn up within the limits imposed by the production budget.

Example 1

AB Co. Ltd. manufactures two products A and B, and sells them through two divisions -North and South. For the purpose of submission of sales budget to the budget committee, the following information has been made available:

Product	North	South
A	4,000 at Rs. 9	6,000 at Rs. 9
B	3,000 at Rs. 21	5,000 at Rs. 21

Actual sales of the current year were:

Product	North	South
A	5,000 at Rs. 9	6,000 at Rs. 9
B	2,000 at Rs. 21	4,000 at Rs. 21

Market studies reveal that the product, A, is popular but under-priced. It is observed that if the price of A is increased by Re.l it will still find ready market. On the other hand, B is over-priced to customers and the market could absorb more if the sales price of B is reduced by Re.l. The management has agreed to give effect to the above price changes.

From the information relating to these price changes and reports from salesman, the following estimates have been prepared by divisional managers.

Percentage increase in sales over current budget is:

Product	North	South
A	+ 10%	+ 5%
B	+ 20%	+ 10%

With the help of an intensive advertisement campaign, the following additional sales over the estimated sales of divisional managers are possible: Additional sales above the estimated sales of divisional managers.

Solution

Sales Budget
A B Co. Ltd. For the Year : 20XX

Prepared by ....

Checked by ....

Submitted on ....

Division	Product	Budget for future period Unit Qty	Price Rs.	Value Rs.	Budget for current period Unit Qty	Price Rs.	Value Rs.	Actual sales for current period Unit Qty	Price Rs.	Value Rs.
North	A	5,000	10	50,000	4,000	9	36,000	5,000	9	45,000
	B	4,000	20	80,000	3,000	21	63,000	2,000	21	42,000
	Total	9,000		1,30,000	7,000		99,000	7,000		87,000
South	A	7,000	10	70,000	6,000	9	54,000	7,000	9	63,000
	B	6,000	20	1,20,000	5,000	21	1,05,000	4,000	21	84,000
	Total	13,000		1,90,000	11,000		1,59,000	11,000		1,47,000
	Total: A	12,000	10	1,20,000	10,000	9	90,000	12,000	9	1,08,000
	B	10,000	20	2,00,000	8,000	21	1,68,000	6,000	21	1,26,000
(Summary)	Total	22,000		3,20,000	18,000		2,58,000	18,000		2,34,000

Product	North (Units)	South (Units)
A	600	700
B	400	500

You are required to prepare a budget for sales incorporating the above estimates and also show the budgeted and actual sales of current year.

This budget may be modified according to salesmen, or period such as months, quarters, etc.

12.10. Preparation of Production Budget

Production Budget

Like the sales budget, the production budget is built up in terms of quantities and money. The quantities are entered at the beginning and, when the remainder of the budgets have been built up and the costs of production calculated, the costs are entered to compile a production cost budget. In preparing the production budget, consideration should be given to the following:

1. Principal budget factor, e.g., if sales be the budget factor then it should be the sales budget; otherwise other budgets.

2. Production planning and determination of optimum factory capacity.
3. The opening stocks, and stocks required to be carried at the end of the period.
4. The policy of the management regarding manufacture or purchase of components.

The production budget may be classified under the following heads: (a) Products (b) Manufacturing department (c) Months, Quarters, etc.

Example

Production budget of AB Co. Ltd. based on the sales budget of example I, and the following estimated stocks at the beginning and end of the future budget period:

Product	Estimated stock 1st January Units	Estimated stock 31st December Units	Sales as per sales budget Units
A	1,000	1,000	12,000
B	1,000	2,000	10,000

Solution

ABC Co. Ltd.
Production Budget (in units)

Items	A	B	For the year... Remarks
Sales during the period	12,000	10,000	
Required stock on 31st Dec.	1,000	2,000	
Total	13,000	12,000	
Less: Estimated opening stock	1,000	1,000	
Estimated production	12,000	11,000	

In case of normal loss on distribution, the quantity to be produced will be correspondingly increased. The total yearly production may be segregated to show monthly or quarterly production.

12.11. Preparation of: [a] Production Cost Budget [b] Materials Budget and [c] Purchase budget.

Production Cost Budget

A production cost budget summarises the materials budget, labour budget, and factory overhead budget, and may be expressed and analysed by departments and/or products. A production cost budget shows the estimated cost of carrying out the production plans and programs set out in production budget. It shows the following:

1. Material cost from materials budget.
2. Labour cost from labour budget.
3. Factory overhead - subdivided into fixed, variable and semi-variable costs, from factory overhead budget.

These costs are analysed by departments and/or products according to convenience.

ABC Co. Ltd.
Production Cost Budget

Items	For the year...		
	A Rs.	B Rs.	Total Rs.
Units to be produced Elements of cost Material cost (from material budget) Labour cost (from labour budget) Factory overhead (from factory overhead budget)			
Total			

Material Budget

A Materials Budget shows the estimated quantities as well as cost of raw materials and components required for producing goods as per production budget. At the first stage of preparation of the materials budget only quantities are incorporated. Later on the prices from the purchases budget are used to obtain the cost of each material consumed.

Example 4

Prepare a Materials Budget of XYZ Co., based on Production budget as given above. The production orders of the products show the following consumption.

Consumption for a batch of 1000 units of

Material No	Product A Kg	Product B Kg	Rate per Kg RS.
01	50	80	60
02	10	5	60
03	-	30	10
04	6	10	50
05	4	4	25
Total	70	129	205

Solution

XYZ Co. Ltd.
Materials Budget

Product	Qty. to be produced kg	For the year 1994				
		Mat 1 kg	Mat 2 kg	Mat 3 kg	Mat 4 kg	Mat 5
A	12,000	600	120	-	72	48

B	11,000	880	55	350	110	44
Total quantity		1,480	175	350	182	92
Rate per kg. from purchase budget		Rs. 60	Rs. 60	Rs. 10	Rs. 50	Rs. 25
		Rs.	Rs.	Rs.	Rs.	Rs.
Cost of each material		88,800	10,500	3,500	9,100	2,300

Note: Cost of Material = Quantity × Rate per kg.

Purchase Budget

A purchase budget gives the details of the purchase which must be made to meet the needs of the business. It includes all items of purchase, such as raw materials, indirect materials and other equipments. The purchase budget for raw materials is the most important and the following factors are required to be considered in preparing this budget:

1. Opening and closing stocks.
2. Unfulfilled orders at the beginning of the budget period.
3. Storage space, economic buying quantity, and financial resources.
4. The prices to be paid.

Example 5

The following information regarding the stocks of materials required for the production program of Ramesh Limited is available.

Materials	Estimated Consumption during 1993-94 (in kg)	Estimated Stocks (in kg)	
		On 1st July 1993	On 30th June 1994
AB	9,03,000	20,000	17,000
GH	6,90,000	10,000	20,000
XY	5,47,000	30,000	33,000

Collating the details given above with the information contained in the Materials Budget, prepare the Purchase Budget of Ramesh Limited.

Solution

Ramesh Limited
Purchase Budget (1993-94)

Particulars	AB kg	GH kg	XY kg
Estimated Consumption	9,03,000	6,90,000	5,47,000
Add: Stock required on 30-6-94	17,000	20,000	33,000
Total requirements	9,20,000	7,10,000	5,80,000
Less: Estimated stock on 1-7-93	20,000	10,000	30,000
Quantity to be purchased	9,00,000	7,00,000	5,50,000
Price per kg (Estimated)	Re. 1	50 P	40 P
Estimated cost of purchase of materials (Rs)	9,00,000	3,50,000	2,20,000

12.12. Preparation of Cash Budget

A complete system of budgetary control makes the construction of cash budget easy. It is one of the functional budgets which is prepared along with other budgets. There are three recognised methods of preparing a cash budget.

(a) The Receipts and Payments Method;

(b) The Adjusted Profit and Loss Method; and

(c) The Balance Sheet Method.

Receipts and Payments Method

Under this method, all actual possible items of cash receipts and payments for the budgeted period are considered. Sources of information are the various other budgets. For example, (a) Sales from the sales budget (b) Materials, labour, overhead expenditure and capital expenditure etc., from the concerned budgets.

Steps to be adopted

Cash Receipts Forecast: Cash receipts from sales, debtors, income from sales of assets and investments and.. probable borrowings should be forecast and brought into cash budget. Any lag in payment by debtors or by others shall be considered for ascertaining further cash inflows.

Cash requirements forecast : Total cash outflows are taken out from operating budgets for the elements of cost, and from capital expenditure budget for the purchase of fixed assets. Adjustments are to be made for any lag in payments.

Care must be taken to ensure that outstandings or accruals are excluded from the cash budget since this method is based on the concept of actual cash flows.

Example 6

A newly started company Quick Co. Ltd., wishes to prepare cash budget from January. Prepare a cash budget for the first six months from the following estimated revenue and expenditure:

Month 1999	Total Sales Rs.	Material Rs.	Wages Rs.	Production overheads Rs.	Selling and distribution overheads Rs.
January	20,000	20,000	4,000	3,200	800
February	22,000	14,000	4,400	3,300	900
March	24,000	14,000	4,600	3,300	800
April	26,000	12,000	4,600	3,400	900
May	28,000	12,000	4,800	3,500	900
June	30,000	16,000	4,800	3,600	1,000

Cash balance on 1st January 1999 was Rs. 10,000. A new machine is to be installed at Rs. 30,000 on credit, to be repaid by two equal installments in March and April.

Sales commission @ 5% on total sales is to be paid within the month following actual sales. Rs. 10,000 being the amount of 2nd call may be received in March. Share premium amounting to Rs.2,000 is also obtainable with 2nd call.

Period of credit allowed by suppliers	2 months
Period of credit allowed to customers	1 month
Delay in payment of overheads	1 month
Delay in payment of wages	1/2 month

Assume cash sales to be 50% of total sales.

Solution

Quick Co. Limited
Cash Budget

For the period January to June 1999

Details	Jan. Rs.	Feb. Rs.	Mar. Rs.	April Rs.	May Rs.	June Rs.
A Balance B/d	10,000	18,000	29,800	20,000	6,100	8,800
B Receipts:						
Cash sales (50%)	10,000	11,000	12,000	13,000	14,000	15,000
Debtors	-	10,000	11,000	12,000	13,000	14,000
Capital	-	-	10,000	-	-	-
Share premium	-	-	2,000	-	-	-
(A + B) Total	20,000	39,000	64,800	45,000	33,100	37,800
C Payments:						
Material	-	-	20,000	14,000	14,000	12,000
Wages	2,000	4,200	4,500	4,600	4,700	4,800
Production overheads	-	3,200	3,300	3,300	3,400	3,500
Selling and Distribution overheads	-	800	900	800	900	900
Commission	-	1,000	1,100	1,200	1,300	1,400
Machinery	-	-	15,000	15,000	-	-
(C) Total	2,000	9,200	44,800	38,900	24,300	22,600
Balance (A + B + C)	18,000	29,800	20,000	6,100	8,800	15,200

Sometimes, it is required to forecast cash or working capital and this can be computed in the usual way as described above. Further consideration is necessary in respect of lag in payment and lag in realisation.

Adjusted Profit and Loss Method

Compared with the previous method, this method is less detailed and more difficult to comprehend, It is particularly useful for the long-term forecasts, say for a period of over three years. It is called thus, because it transforms the profit and loss account into cash forecast.

The basic assumption in this method is that any increase or decrease in cash balance is due to profit or loss of the business. All non-cash items such as depreciation, write-offs or write-ups etc., are mainly adjusted to the net profit. The theory, under this method, is based on the assumption that profit is cash. If there were no credit transactions or transactions resulting in capital profits, the balance of profit on the Profit and Loss account should be equal to the balance of cash in the cash book. Such a situation however will never exist in practice in any business. Hence all adjustments with regard to the above items are to be made in the cash forecast. Sources of information are the firm's profit and loss account and balance sheet.

Example 7

From the following information prepare a cash budget under the adjusted profit and loss method:

Balance Sheet as on 1-1-1999

Liabilities	Rs.	Assets	Rs.
Share capital	50,000	Land and building	30,000
Capital reserve	5,000	Plant and machinery	20,000
Profit and loss a/c	9,000	Furniture and fixtures	5,000
Debentures	10,000	Closing stock	4,000
Creditors	28,800	Debtors	26,000
Accrued expenses	200	Bank	18,000
	1,03,000		1,03,000

Forecasting Trading, and Profit and Loss Account

For the year ending 31-12-1999

Particulars		Rs.	Particulars	Rs.
To Opening stock		4,000	By Sales	80,000
To Purchases		60,000	By Closing stock	10,000
To Gross Profit c/d		26,000		
		90,000		90,000
To Salary and wages	2,500		By Gross profit b/d	26,000
To Outstanding	500	3,000	By Interest received	100
To Depreciation:				
Plant and machinery		2,000		
Furniture and machinery		1,000		
To Administration expenses		3,500		
To Selling expenses		2,500		
To Net profit c/d		14,100		
		26,100		26,100
To Dividends paid		10,000	By Balance b/d	9,000
To Balance c/d		13,100	By Net profit b/d	14,100
		23,100		23,100

The following are the additional information for the year 1999: Shares were issued for Rs. 10,000, and debentures were issued for Rs. 2,000.

On 31-12-1999, the accured expenses were Rs. 500, debtors Rs. 20,000, creditors Rs. 30,000 and land and buildings, Rs. 40,000.

Solution

Cash Budget-Adjusted Profit and Loss Method

	Rs.	Rs.	Rs.
Cash balance on 1-1-1999			18,000
Additions to cash:			
Income-Net profit for the year		14,100	
Depreciation:			
Plant and machinery	2,000		
Furniture and fixture	1,000	3,000	
Accrued expenses (difference)	300		
Reduction in debtors	6,000		
Increase in creditors	1,200		
Issue of share capital	10,000		
Issue of debentures	2,000	19,500	36,600
Cash available			54,600
Deduction from cash:			
Dividends paid	10,000		
Increase of stock	6,000		
Purchase of land and building	10,000		26,000
Cash balance as on 31-12-1999			28,600

Balance Sheet Method

The same theoretical assumption of the adjusted profit and loss method holds good in this method also. Under this method, a budgeted balance sheet is prepared showing all items of assets and liabilities except cash balance. The balancing figure is considered to represent cash balance. If there is excess of liabilities over assets, the balance is ordinary cash balance; if there is excess of assets over liabilities, the balance is assumed to be bank overdraft. Of these three methods, the first method is mostly preferred because it is a short-term forecast and is much more detailed than the other two methods which are normally used as long-term forecasts.

Example 8

Using the data of Example 7, prepare a cash forecast showing cash at bank on 31-12-1999 under balance sheet method.

Solution

The balancing figure of Rs. 28,600 represents cash at bank on 31-12-1999. This is obtained by completing the balance sheet from the information obtained from example 7, as follows:

Forecast Balance Sheet as on 31-12-1999

Liabilities	Rs.	Assets	Rs.
Share capital	60,000	Land and building	40,000
Capital reserve	5,000	Plant and machinery	18,000
Profit and loss account	13,100	Furniture and fixture	4,000
Debentures	12,000	Closing stock	10,000
Creditors	30,000	Debtors	20,000
Arrued expenses	500	Bank (balancing figure)	28,600
	1,20,600		1,20,600

12.13. Preparation of Flexible Budget

In those industries where the pattern of demand is stable, a fixed budget may be adequate, especially where the budget period is comparatively short. In such businesses, it is possible to forecast sales with a considerable degree of accuracy. There are many undertakings where stable conditions are absent. In such concerns, it is usual to adopt the flexible budgetary technique. A flexible budget is a budget which is designed to change in accordance with the level of activity actually attained. If flexible budgeting is adopted, a series of budgets would be compiled to cover the range of levels of activity possible. In such budgets the division of costs and expenses into fixed and variable categories is very important.

The need for a flexible budget arises from the fact that some expenses are fixed in nature irrespective of the levels of activity, some are variable, which change with the levels of activity, and some expenses are partly variable and partly fixed in nature, which do not vary directly with the levels of activity. The underlying principle of a flexible budget is that for any given volume of business there should be some norm of expenditure and that norm should be known beforehand to provide a guideline to actual expenditure. To recognize this principle is to accept the fact that every business is dynamic, and ever changing. It is futile to expect a business to conform to a fixed and preconceived pattern. Preparation of flexible budget results in the construction of a series of formula, one for each department or cost center. The formula for each account indicates the fixed amount and/or a variable rate. The fixed amount remains constant regardless of activity and the variable potion is expressed in relation to a base such as direct labour hours, direct labour cost, or machine hours.

Originally, the flexible budget idea was applied principally to the control of departmental factory overheads. In recent years, the idea has, however, been applied to the entire budget so that production budgets as well as selling and administrative budgets are prepared on a flexible basis. The construction of a flexible budget is identical with that of a fixed budget, except that a budget is prepared for each volume ranging from a possible 60% to 100% of capacity. When actual figures are available, estimates previously determined for the level attained are compared with the actual results, and the differences are noted. The end-of-period comparison is used to measure the performance of each department head. It is this ready made method of comparison that makes the flexible budget a valuable instrument for cost control. The flexible budget assists in evaluating the effects of varying volumes of activity on profits and cash position.

Example 9

The following data are available in a manufacturing company for the half-year period ending 30th June, 1999.

	Rs. (lakhs)	
Fixed expenses:		
Wages and salaries	8.4	
Rent, rates, and taxes	5.6	
Depreciation	7.0	
Sundry administrative expenses	8.9	29.9
Semi-variable expenses: @ 50% of capacity -		
Maintenance and repairs	2.5	
Indirect labour	9.9	
Sales department salaries etc.,	2.9	
Sundry administrative expenses	2.6	17.9
Variable expenses: @ 50% of capacity -		
Material	24.0	
Labour	25.6	
Other expenses	3.8	53.4

It is assumed that fixed expenses remain constant for all levels of production; semi-variable expenses remain constant between 45% and 65% of capacity, increasing by 10% between 65% and 80% of capacity and 20% between 80% and 100% of capacity.

Sales at the various levels are:

60% capacity	Rs. 100.00 lakhs
75% capacity	120.00 lakhs
90% capacity	150.00 lakhs
100%capacity	170.00 lakhs

Prepare a flexible budget for the half-year and forecast the profits at 60%, 75%, 90% of capacity.

Solution

Flexible Budget for the Half-Year Ending 30th June 1999
(Showing the forecast of profit of different levels)

Elements of cost	Operating capacity				
	50%	60%	75%	90%	100% standard
A. Fixed expenses:					
Wages and salaries	8.4	8.4	8.4	8.4	8.4
Rent, rates and taxes	5.6	5.6	5.6	5.6	5.6
Depreciation	7.0	7. 0	7.0	7.0	7.0
Sundry Expenses	8.9	8.9	8.9	8.9	8.9
	29.9	29.9	29.9	29.9	29.9
B. Semi-variable expenses:					

Maintenance and repairs	2.5	2.5	2.75	3.00	3.00
Indirect labour	9.9	9.9	10.89	11.88	11.88
Sales Dept. salaries	2.9	2.9	3.19	3.48	3.48
Sundry adm. expenses	2.6	2.6	2.86	3.12	3.12
	17.9	17.9	19.69	21.48	21.48
C. Variables expenses:					
Material	24.0	28.80	36.00	43.20	48.0
Labour	25.6	30.72	38.47	46.08	51.2
Other expenses	3.8	4.56	5.70	6.84	7.6
	53.4	64.08	80.17	96.12	106.8
Total cost of production (i.e.) Total of A B and C	101.2	111.88	129.76	147.50	158.18
Profit (+) or Loss (–)	—	– 11.88	– 9.76	+ 2.50	+ 11.82
Sales		100.00	120.00	150.00	170.00

9.14. Construction of Master Budget or Consolidation of Budgets

A coordinating authority is necessary to resolve difficulties and disputes which arise between the departmental heads in relation to the budgets. The aim of budgeting is to produce a complete forecast of how all the various sections of the business should behave. Therefore, adjustments are often necessary. Decisions of this nature are the functions of the Managing Director. He will normally appoint a committee of the departmental heads to advise him. If, however, vital matters of policy are involved, the decision must be made by the Board of Directors. The Chief Accountant should prepare statement summarising the various budgets and bring out the points which need clarification and decision by the Managing Director.

Master Budget

When the necessary decisions have been taken by the Managing. Director to harmonise the different sectional budgets, a Master Budget will be prepared. This will set out, in considerable detail, the plan of operation for all departments for the budget period and will be placed before the Board of Directors, for its acceptance. After acceptance, the Master Budget becomes the authority for the necessary executive action to be taken to implement it. A Master Budget is basically a summary budget as it embodies the summarised figures, the details of which are incorporated in other principal budgets. It represents the overall plan of the enterprise. A specimen of a Master Budget is given below:

Example 10

Master Budget

1. Revenue budget for 3 months up to March 31, 1999.

Products	P Rs.	Q Rs.	R Rs.	Total Rs.
Sales	5,82,000	2,60,000	2,30,000	10,72,000
Materials	4,75,552	2,05,020	1,76,256	8,56,828
Labour	8,959	5,917	3,676	18,552
Factory overheads	26,015	18,900	8,580	53,495
	5,10,526	2,29,837	1,88,512	9,28,875

Administration		
Over heads:		
Fixed		20,000
Variable		10,000
Selling and Distribution:		
Fixed		11,000
Variable		18,000
		9,87,875
Budget profit on production c/d		84,125
		10,72,000
Budget profit on production b/d		84,125
Deduct Directors fees		2,000
Profit as per Capital Movements Budget, March 31, 1999 Budget (See Note 2)		82,125

2. Capital Movements Budget, 3 months to March 31, 1999

		Rs.
Capital expenditure		18,500
Increase in stock		50,000
Increase in debtors		36,000
Reduction in:		
Tax	2,00,000	
Dividends	60,000	2,60,000
		3,64,500
Proceeds of shares issue		1,00,000
Increase in provision for depreciation		8,110
Increase in creditors		32,915
Reduction in cash at bank		1,41,350
Budgeted profit		82,125
		3,64,500

12.15. Performance Budgeting (PB)

Meaning of PB

Performance budget may be defined as a budget based on functions, activities and projects. Performance budgeting may be described as a budgeting system, where under input costs are related to the end results, i.e., performance. According to the National Institute of Bank Management, Mumbai, the PB is the process of analyzing, identifying, simplifying, and crystallizing specific performance objectives of a job to be completed over a period, in the framework of the organizational objectives, the purpose and objectives of the job. It involves the evaluation of the performance of the organization in the context of both specific as well as overall objectives of the organization.

Purpose of PB

The performance budget is an instrument through which financial resources are allocated according to purposes and objectives. The cost of various programmes proposed for achieving these objectives are clearly indicated. It also presents data for measuring worth performance or the accomplishment of objectives set under each programme. The focus of attention is not only on expenditure but also on achievement. Both are integral parts of financial planning and expenditure authorization.

Process of PB

PB is a technique or a method employed by any agency/department. The first stage is to decide what its goal or objective should be, the next stage is to decide on a set of programmes in order to achieve the goal and then to implement the programme. Final stage is to evaluate the actual performance of each segment and its contribution towards achievement of its goal.

Operational Steps in PB

(a) Formulation of objectives of the agency/department

(b) Identification of various programmes or projects, which will help the agency to achieve its objective

(c) Evaluation of the programmes in terms of benefits that they produce compared to the resources that they consume

(d) Selection of the programmes on the basis of cost benefit analysis in order to utilize the funds in the optimal manner

(e) Development of performance criteria for the various programmes (suitable work measurement units, norms, yardsticks, standards, and other performance indicators)

(f) Preparation of long-term physical as well as financial plans

(g) Preparation of the annual budget

(h) Assessment of performance of each programme and by each responsibility unit and comparison of the same with the budget

(i) Undertaking periodical review of programmes with a view to assess the strengths and weaknesses and make modification, if necessary

Programme Budgeting

Programme budgeting was first evolved in United States. In Britain it is referred to as 'Output Budgeting'. It is mainly useful to government departments and non-profit organizations. In programme budgeting special emphasis is laid on formulation of different budgets for different programmes. It utilizes a planning and budgeting process in an output oriented programme format; which is oriented to its objectives to facilitate developing and evaluating alternatives. It leads to the allocation of resources over a planning period. Programme budgeting integrates all the organization's planning activities and budgeting into a total system.

Programme Budgeting Process

First, programmes are identified for achieving different goals of the organization. Then each programme is divided into different elements. Resources such as materials, men, machines, utilities, etc., are allocated to various programmes over the period. The emphasis is continuously placed on analysis of alternatives (including existing programmes) and estimating cost of accomplishing objectives and fulfilling purposes and needs. The steps involved in the programming budgeting may be listed as follows:

(a) Identification of programmes required fulfilling the mission

(b) Identification of programme elements

(c) Allocation of resources to programmes

(d) Utilizing forecast studies analysis-mostly multi-year forecasts are considered in programmed budgeting

(e) Measuring the actual performance of approved programmes and comparing with budget performance

In the case of non-profit organizations, output indicators are to be developed because output cannot be measured in monetary terms. For example, for training programmes the output indicator may be in terms of number of employees trained. For health programmes, output indicator may be reduction in disease. The programme budget, however, does not eliminate the need for traditional budget. It adds only a new dimension to planning and budgeting system. A traditional budget can be divided into a number of programme budgets.

Traditional Budgeting Vs. Programme Budgeting

Traditional budgeting involves establishment of functional budgets and their integration into a master budget. It works well in profit-oriented organizations. While it emphasizes the method and means used, the programme budgeting stresses the purpose and objectives of the programme. Programme budgeting is not only a linkage system for planning and budgeting but also a strategic decision-making tool for allocating resources. It provides the decision-makers with relevant data appropriately structured into object-oriented format and analysis into decision-making mode.

Performance Budgeting Vs. Programme Budgeting

1. Performance budgeting is a backward-looking approach and is based on past information and prior accomplishment whereas programme budgeting is a forward-looking approach. Programme budgeting is useful for review and decision-making at and above the departmental level. It is adapted to the requirement by overall budgetary planning.

2. Performance budget has drawn much of its form from cost accounting and scientific management. In contrast, programme budgeting has drawn its core of ideas from economic analysis and systems analysis.

3. A performance budget is normally considered as a work programme and as a tool of management. But, a programme budget is considered as a statement and allocation process among competitive claims.

Zero-Base Budgeting [ZBB]

Traditional budgeting starts with previous year expenditure level as a base and discussion is focused on certain 'additions' and 'cuts' to be made in the previous year spending. The top management finally gives its approval after hearing the arguments for and against the 'additions' and 'cuts'. In ZBB reference is not made to previous level of spending. A convincing case is made for each decision unit to justify the budget allotment for that unit during that period.

Meaning of ZBB

ZBB is anew approach to budgeting. it is defined by Peter A. Pyhor as an "operating planning and budgeting process, which requires each manager to justify his entire budget in detail from scratch (hence zero-base) and shifts the burden of proof to each manager to justify why he should spend any money at all."

This approach requires that all activities should be identified in 'decision packages', which should be evaluated by systematic analysis and ranked in order of importance. Leonard Mereunit and Stephen Sosmick define, "ZBB is a technique, which complements and links the existing planning, budgeting and review processes. it identifies alternative efficient methods of utilizing limited resources in effective attainment of selected benefits. It is a flexible management approach, which provides credible rationale for reallocating resources by focusing on the systematic review and justification of the funding and performance levels of current programmes or activities."

ZBB thus examines a programme or activity from scratch (i.e., zero-base). The manager proposing the activity should prove that the activity is essential and his budgeting request for funds is reasonable. Nothing can be taken for granted, for it was being done or allowed in the past. Hence, ZBB is a technique whereby each programmes, whether new or existing must be justified in its entirety each time a new budget is formulated.

Features of ZBB

The essential features of ZBB are as follows:

(a) The budget allotment to any decision unit should be first justified by the manager of that decision unit. He should justify his request without making any reference to previous level of spending in his decision unit.

(b) Activities are identified as decision packages and then the latter are ranked in order of priority.

(c) Decision packages are evaluated by systematic analysis linking them with clearly laid down corporate objectives.

(d) A frank relationship exists between superiors and subordinates.

(e) Available resources are directed towards alternatives in order of priority to ensure optimum results.

Process of ZBB

The following steps are implied in ZBB: The managers at all levels have to determine the objective of each programme of activity that they supervise and prepare alternative spending plans as 'decision packages'. There should be at least three, if not more, of such packages; one involving expenditure, or the minimum expenditure, which will permit the programme to continue meaningfully; another package indicating resources in men, materials and money, which will be needed to continue the present levels of performance and objectives; and a third package to indicate what more could be achieved if additional funds were available to the extent of [say] 10% or more.

The executives at the next higher level have then to consolidate these decision packages and rank them in order of priorities, keeping in view the cost benefit analysis and available funds.

ZBB differs from traditional budgeting on many points and following are a few points of difference between the two systems of budgeting:

Traditional Budgeting Vs. ZBB

1. Traditional budgeting is accounting-oriented and mainly lays its emphasis on previous year expenditure. ZBB is decision-oriented and makes all projects and programmes old and new programmes to compete for scarce resources.

2. In traditional budgeting, past expenditure forms the basis for future demand for inflation and new programmes. In ZBB, a decision unit is broken down into decision packages, which are ranked on priority basis.

3. In traditional budgeting, the top management takes decisions as regards the amount to be spent on a decision unit. But in ZBB this responsibility is shifted to the manager of a decision unit.

4. In traditional budgeting, deliberate manipulation of budget proposals is possible. But in ZBB, a rational analysis of budget proposals is made. Management approves only those carefully devised result-oriented decision packages.

5. Traditional budgeting makes a routine approach and is not clear and distinctive. ZBB makes each decision on budget proposals very distinctive and clear. It is a straightforward approach and highlights priority projects distinctively.

Advantages of ZBB

1. ZBB provides the organization with a systematic way to evaluate operations and programmes of activity, and allows management to allocate resources according to the priority of programmes.

2. It ensures through examination of every function. Managers are required to evaluate the need for every programme, and to consider different levels of effort and alternative ways of performing the operations.

3. It enables departmental budgets to be approved on the basis of cost-benefit comparison rather than be open to any arbitrary cuts or increases in budget estimates.

4. If decision packages are ranked in order of priority, subsequent budget cycles do not have to be based on a complete recycling of budget inputs.

5. If available resources vary from the budgeted estimates during the budget year, decision packages can be reduced or expanded on the basis of priority ranking of packages.

6. Long-range goals and plans can be linked with the annual budgets through the zero-bas budget. Not only does it facilitate quantification of costs and benefits of contemplated decisions, it also enables managers to communicate problems and opportunities to the higher management.

7. The performance of line managers can be judged against their commitments in terms of the approved decision packages and their budgets.

Limitations of ZBB

The limitations of ZBB, which arise due to certain operational problems, are as follows:

1. Implementation Problems: Successful implementation of ZBB may require wholehearted support from the top management, which may not readily be available owing to fear and problems in the minds of top management. The concerned managers should continue in the same decision units. If they are transferred frequently to other departments, it may lead to waste of time and resources in training and developing new managers.

2. Formulation Problems: Considerable problems may arise while formulating decision packages. For example, problems may arise in the fixation of minimum level of effort. Managers

may not like to fix the minimum level below the current levels. Similarly problems may arise in formulating meaningful performance evaluation measures.

3. Ranking Problems: Problems may arise in ranking of decision packages. General managers may like to continue their favourable projects for the reasons best known to them. Ranking may also become difficult when there are a large number of decision packages, particularly in a multi-product manufacturing firm.

PRACTICAL PROBLEMS

Illustration 1

The ABC Ltd. manufacturers two brands of pen - one sold under the name 'Writer' and another under the name 'Nice'. The sales department of the company has three departments in different areas of country.

The sales budgets for the year ending 31st December 1998 were Writer Department I - 3,00,000; Department II - 5,62,500; Department III - 1,80,000; and Nice - Department I - 4,00,000; Department II - 6,00,000 and Department III - 20,000. Sales price are Rs. 3 and Rs. 1.20 in all departments.

It is estimated that by forced sales promotion the sales in Nice in department I will increase by 1,75,000. It is also expected that by increasing production and arranging extensive advertisements Department III will be enabled to increase the sale of 'Nice' by 50,000.

It is recognized that the estimated sales by Department II represent an unsatisfactory target. It is agreed to increase both estimates by 20%.

Prepare a Sales Budget for the year 31st December, 1998.

Solution

Sales Budget for 1998

Selling Price	Writer Rs.3		Nice Rs. 1.20		Total
	Qty	Rs.	Qty.	Rs.	Rs.
Department I	3,00,000	9,00,000	5,75,000	6,90,000	15,90,000
Department II	6,75,000	20,25,000	7,20,000	8,64,000	28,89,000
Department III	1,80,000	5,40,000	70,000	84,000	6,24,000
Total	11,55,000	34,65,000	13,65,000	16,38,000	51,03,000

Illustration 2

The MNO company expects the following sales by month in units for the first six months of next year.

January	5,400	April	5,700
February	5,700	May	6,000
March	7,500	June	4,500

The company has a policy of maintaining an inventory equal to budgeted sales for the following two months. The beginning inventory reflects this policy. Each unit costs Rs. 10.

You are required to prepare purchase budget for as many months as you can both in units and rupees. Explain also why you had to stop where you did.

4. Cost Problems: ZBB needs properly trained managerial personnel to do the required job. This involves time as well as cost.

All these operational problems can, however, be overcome by consistent efforts. They may arise only in initial stages and once a system is created and methodology is clear, ZBB becomes a routine task for the managers. It may be time consuming at the beginning. But if it is done systematically it can help top management in solving a number of managerial, administrative and other problems.

Solution

Purchase Budget (January to April, next year) in units and rupees of MNO Company

Month	Sales (units)	Planned inventory in units		Estimated purchases in units	Estimated purchases in rupees
		Closing	Opening	(Col. 2 + 3 – 4)	(Col. 5 × Rs.10)
1	2	3	4	5	6
January	5,400	13,200	11,100	7,500	75,000
February	5,700	13,200	13,200	5,700	57,000
March	7,500	11,700	13,200	6,000	60,000
April	5,700	10,500	11,700	4,500	45,000

It was not possible to go beyond April because we must know budgeted sales for two months in advance. To budget purchases for May requires the sales forecast for July (information for which is not available).

Illustration 3

A Ltd manufacturers products X and Y. During January 1998 it expects to sell 10,000 kg. of X and 40,000 kg of Y at Rs.20 and Rs. 10 respectively. Direct materials P, Q and S, are mixed in equal proportions to produce X and materials Q, R and S are mixed in the ratio of 3:5:2 to produce Y. There is no loss of weight in production.

Actual and Budgeted stocks in quantities and costs for the month are as follows:

	Opening Stock (kg)	Desired Closing Stock (kg)	Anticipated Cost (per kg) Rs.
Material	P - 3,000	2,000	5.5
	Q - 2,000	4,000	5.0
	R - 20,000	6,000	1.0
	S - 10,000	12,000	3.5
Product	X - 2,000	1,000	–
	Y - 10,000	12,000	–

You are required to prepare (a) the Production Budget and (b) Materials Purchase Budget including the expenditure on raw materials for January.

Solution

(a) Production Budget for the Month of January, 1998

	Product X (kg)	Product Y (kg)
Sales Budget	10,000	40,000

Add: Closing stock	1,000	12,000
	11,000	52,000
Less: Opening stock	2,000	10,000
Production	9,000	42,000

(b) Materials Purchases Budget for the Month of January 1998.

	P (kg)	Q (kg)	R (kg)	S (kg)
Materials required for production	X: 3,000	3,000	-	3,000
	Y: -	12,600	21,000	8,400
	3,000	15,600	21,000	11,400
Add: Material required for closing stock	2,000	4,000	6,000	12,000
	5,000	19,600	27,000	23,400
Less: Opening stock	3,000	2,000	20,000	10,000
	2,000	17,600	7,000	13,400
Cost per kg (Rs)	5.5	5	1	3.5
Purchase price (Rs)	11,000	88,000	7,000	46,900

Illustration 4

The Fareal Company uses single raw material to make its product; for each unit of product three pounds of this material are required. The price of this material is Rs. 10 per pound - The Company follows a purchasing policy of placing orders on or before the 5th of each month to cover that month's requirements. It plans its inventory position in advance to cover expected situations.

The inventory of material at Dec. 31, 1998 was 9,000 pounds.

The inventory level planned for Jan. 1999 was 15,000 pounds.

The inventory level planned for Feb. 1999 was 30,000 pounds.

The inventory level planned for March 1999 was 20,000 pounds. Production scheduled for the three months period was :

During Jan. 1999 10,000 units

During Feb. 1999 12,000 units

During March 1999 14,000 units

Assume that this set of plans is carried out. Prepare Material Purchase Budget for the three months ending 31st March 1999.

Solution

Material Purchase Budget

Period : 3 Months ending March 31, 1999

	Jan. Rs.	Feb. Rs.	March Rs.
Estimated output (in units)	10,000	12,000	14,000

Production requirements (in lbs)	30,000	36,000	42,000
Add: end of inventory desired	15,000	30,000	20,000
	45,000	66,000	62,000
Less: inventory at the beginning of the month	9,000	15,000	30,000
Purchase required (in lbs)	36,000	51,000	32,000
Price per lb	10	10	10
Estimated cost of purchases (in Rs.)	3,60,000	5,10,000	3,20,000

Illustration 5

The Production manager of the ABC Company desires to maintain an inventory of raw material equal to the budgeted production needs for the next 2 months. Each unit of product takes 10 kg. of raw material. Inventory of finished goods is usually maintained at one and half times of the following month's sales; the forecast sales of 6 months of next year, in units are as follows:

January	3,600	April	4,800
February	4,200	May	5,600
March	3,200	June	3,800

On 31st December of last year, there were 80,000 kg. of raw material on hand and 5,600 units on finished goods.

You are required to prepare,

(i) budget for production and

(ii) budget for purchases of raw materials in units for as many months as possible.

Solution

(i) Production budget (January to May next year) in units, of ABC Company

	Sales (Units)	Desired Inventory		Desired production (Col. 2 + 3 – 4)
		Closing	Opening	
1	2	3	4	5
January	3,600	6,300	5,600	4,300
February	4,200	4,800	6,300	2,700
March	3,200	7,200	4,800	5,600
April	4,800	8,400	7,200	6,000
May	5,600	5,700	8,400	2,900

(ii) Purchase budget (January to March next year) in units

	Raw material required for (Production × 10)	Planned inventory		Desired purchases of raw material (Col. 2 + 3 – 4)
		Closing	Opening	
1	2	3	4	5
January	43,000	83,000	80,000	46,000
February	27,000	1,16,000	83,000	60,000
March	56,000	89,000	1,16,000	29,000

Illustration 6

Production costs of a factory for a year are as follows:

		Rs.
Direct wages		80,000
Direct materials		1,20,000
Product overheads:	Fixed	40,000
	Variable	60,000

During the forthcoming year it is anticipated that:

(a) The average rate for direct labour remuneration will fall from Re. 0.80 per hour to Re. 0.75 per hour.

(b) Production efficiency will be reduced by 5%.

(c) Price per unit of direct material and of other materials and services which comprise overheads will remain unchanged, and

(d) Production in the coming year will increase 33 1/3 %. Draw up a production cost budget.

Solution:

Production Cost Budget for the Next Year

	Rs.	(Amount Rs.)
Direct wages (1,40,000 hours × Re. 0.75)		1,05,000
Direct materials: Present	1,20,000	
Add: Additional expense (increase in 1/3 capacity)	40,000	1,60,000
Product overheads: Fixed		40,000
Variable (1,40,000Re. 0.60)		84,000
Total Production cost		3,89,000

Working notes

Determination of direct wages

Direct labour hours (last year)

(Total wage bill ÷ Labour rate per hour ÷ (Rs. 80,000 ÷ Re. 0.80) 1,00,000

Due to decline in efficiency labour hours to carry out the present volume of production will be more by 5% i.e., 1,05,000 hours. Since there is an increase in one-third capacity, total direct labour hours required during the year would be 1,05,000 + 33 ⅓% = 1,40,000 hours.

Determination of variable overheads

Existing variable overhead rate per hour

(Total variable overhead ÷ 1,00,000) = Re. 0.60 per hour.

Illustration 7

You are required to construct a selling overhead budget from the indication given below:

	Rs.
Establishment expenses of Sales Department	10,000
Other expenses of Sales department	4,000
Advertisement	3,000
Salaries to counter salemen	10,000

Commission to counter salemen @ 2% on their sales

Commission to Travelling salesmen @ 5% on their sales and out of pocket express @ 3% on their sales.

The following are the likely sales range for a year.

Sales at counter	Sales by Travelling Salesmen
Rs.	Rs.
1,50,000	15,000
2,00,000	20,000
2,50,000	25,000

Solution

Selling Overhead Budget

Particulars	Rs.	Rs.	Period Rs.
Counter Sales	1,50,000	2,00,000	2,50,000
Travelling salesman's sales	15,000	20,000	25,000
Total Estimated sales	1,65,000	2,20,000	2,75,000
Variable expenses:			
Commission to counter salesman @2% on their sales	3,000	4,000	5,000
Commission to travelling salesman @ 5% on their sales	750	1,000	1,250
Out of pocket expenses @ 3% on their sales	450	600	750
	4,200	5,600	7,000
Fixed Expenses:			

Establishment Expenses	10,000	10,000	10,000
Other expenses	4,000	4,000	4,000
Advertisement	3,000	3,000	3,000
Salaries to counter salesman	10,000	10,000	10,000
	27,000	27,000	27,000
Total	31,200	32,600	34,000

Illustration 8

From the following information and the assumption that the balance in hand on 1st Jan. 2000 is Rs. 72,500. Prepare a cash budget.

Month	Sales Rs.	Materials Rs.	Wages Rs.	Selling and Dis. cost Rs.	Production cost Rs.	Administr tion cost Rs.
Jan.	72,000	25,000	10,000	4,000	6,000	1,500
Feb.	97,000	31,000	12,100	5,000	6,300	1,700
March	86,000	25,500	10,600	5,500	6,000	2,000
April	88,600	30,600	25,000	6,700	6,500	2,200
May	1,02,500	37,000	22,000	8,500	8,000	2,500
June	1,08,700	38,800	23,000	9,000	8,200	2,500

Assume that 50% are cash sales. Assets are to be acquired in the month of February and April. Therefore, provision should be made for the payment of Rs. 8,000 and Rs. 25,000 for the same. An application has been made to the bank for the grant of a loan of Rs. 30,000 and it is hoped that it will be received in the month of May.

It is anticipated that a dividend of Rs.35,000 will be paid in June. Debtors are allowed one month's credit. Sales Commission @ 3% on sales is to be paid. Creditors (for goods or overheads) grant one month's credit.

Solution:

Cash Budget

	Jan. Rs.	Feb. Rs.	March Rs.	April Rs.	May Rs.	June Rs.	Total Rs.
Receipts:							
Cash sales	36,000	48,500	43,000	44,300	51,250	54,350	2,77,400
Debtors	--	36,000	48,500	43,000	44,300	51,250	2,23,050
Bank loan	--	--	--	--	30,000	--	30,000
Total	36,000	84,500	91,500	87,300	1,25,550	1,05,600	5,30,450
Payments:							
Materials	--	25,000	31,000	25,500	30,600	37,000	1,49,100
Wages	10,000	12,100	10,600	25,000	22,000	23,000	1,02,700

Selling overheads	--	4,000	5,000	5,500	6,700	8,500	29,700
Production overheads	--	6,000	6,300	6,000	6,500	8,000	32,800
Administration overheads	--	1,500	1,700	2,000	2,200	2,500	9,900
Capital expenditure	--	8,000	--	25,000	--	--	33,000
Dividend	--	--	--	--	--	35,000	35,000
Commission	2,160	2,910	2,580	2,658	3,075	3,261	16,644
Excess of receipts	23,840	24,990	34,320	--	54,475	--	1,21,606
Excess of payments				4358		11661	
Balance b/f	72,500	96,340	1,21,330	1,55,650	1,51,292	2,05,767	1,94,106
Balance c/f	96,340	1,21,330	1,55,650	1,51,292	2,05,767	1,94,106	3,15,712

Illustration 9

ABC Co. wishes to arrange overdraft facilities with its Bankers during the period April to June, 1999 when it will be manufacturing mostly for stock. Prepare Cash Budget for the above period from the following data, indicating the extent of bank facilities the company will require at the end of each month:

(a)

1999	Sales Rs.	Purchases Rs.	Wages Rs.
February	1,80,000	1,24,800	12,000
March	1,92,000	1,44,000	14,000
April	1,08,000	2,43,000	11,000
May	1,74,000	2,46,000	10,000
June	1,26,000	2,68,000	15,000

(b) 50 % of credit sales are realised in the month following the sales and the remaining 50 % in the second month following. Creditors are paid in the month following the month of purchase.

(c) Cash at bank on 1-4-99 (estimated) Rs. 25,000. **(I.C.W.A. Final)**

Solution:

Cash Budget

for April, May & June 1999

	April Rs.	May Rs.	June Rs.
Estimated Opening Balance	25,000	53,000	– 51,000
Receipts: From debtors			

(for sales)	1,86,000	1,50,000	1,41,000
Total Receipts	2,11,000	2,03,000	90,000
Estimated Payments:,			
Creditors for Purchase of Previous month	1,44,000	2,43,000	2,46,000
Wages of Previous month	14,000	11,000	10,000
Total Payments	1,58,000	2,54,000	2,56,000
Balance on Hand	53,000	--	--
Bank Overdraft	--	– 51,000	– 1,66,000

Note:

1. It is assumed that wages are paid on monthly basis on the first of very next month.
2. Debtors Realised as under:

For the month of April		For the month of May	
50 % of Feb. Sales =	Rs. 90,000	50 % of Mar. Sales =	Rs. 96,000
50 % of Mar. Sales =	Rs. 96,000	50 % of Apr. Sales =	Rs. 54,000
Total	Rs. 1,86,000	Total	Rs. 1,50,000

For the month of June	
50 % of April Sales =	Rs. 54,000
50 % of May Sales =	Rs. 87,000
Total	Rs. 1,41,000

Illustration 10

From the following information relating to Standard Engineering Co. Prepare a cash budget for the half year ending 30th September, 1998.

(a) Anticipated Sales and Costs

Month	Sales Rs.	Material Rs.	Wages Rs.	Overheads Rs.
March	1,50,000	90,000	18,000	31,000
April	1,40,000	1,20,000	28,000	35,400
May	1,54,000	84,000	20,800	36,500
June	1,68,000	1,36,000	22,200	36,500
July	1,82,000	1,28,000	30,000	37,000
August	2,04,000	1,51,000	28,000	37,500
September	2,40,000	1,62,000	25,000	38,000

(b) Other information

(i) Bank balance on 1-4-98 was Rs. 72,000.

(ii) The loan instalment of Rs. 25,000 per month was to be remitted from July up to December 1998.

(iii) Sales commission @ 5% on sales was to be remitted to the distributors in the month following the sales.

(iv) Rs. 50,000 was expected to be received as deposit from the distributors in the month of July.

(v) 50 % of the sales are on credit; the period of credit being 1 month.

(vi) 50 % of the material purchased can be paid for after a month.

(vii) 25 % of the overheads could be settled in the month following their incidence.

(viii) Wages are disbursed on the first working day of the following month.

Solution

Standard Engineering Co.

Cash Budget for the half year ending 30-9-1998

Item	April Rs.	May Rs.	June Rs.	July Rs.	August Rs.	September Rs.
A. Opening Balance	72,000	52,200	25,975	11,975	12,500	– 35,475
B. Receipts						
Cash Sales	70,000	77,000	84,000	91,000	1,02,000	1,20,000
Collection from Debtors	75,000	70,000	77,000	84,000	91,000	1,02,000
Capital receipts	--	--	--	50,000	--	--
Total (A + B)	2,17,000	1,99,200	1,86,975	2,36,975	2,05,500	1,86,525
C. Payments						
Materials	1,05,000	1,02,000	1,10,000	1,32,000	1,39,500	1,56,500
Wages	18,000	28,000	20,800	22,200	30,000	28,000
Overheads (others)	34,300	36,225	36,500	36,875	37,375	37,875
Sales commission	7,500	7,000	7,700	8,400	9,100	10,200
Capital Expen.	--	--	--	25,000	25,000	25,000
Total Payments	1,64,800	1,73,225	1,75,000	2,24,475	2,40,975	2,57,575
D. Cash Balance, (Surplus) (A + B – C),	52,200	25,975	11,975	12,500	--	--
E. Bank O.D. (Deficit)	--	--	--	--	– 35,475	– 71,050

Illustration 11

Premier Ltd has Rs. 50,000 share capital and Rs. 6,000 Reserve against Rs. 40,000 invested in Fixed Assets. Stock and debtors were Rs. 4,000 and 13,000 and Trade Creditors were Rs. 2,000. To sustain the increase in activity, stock level is proposed to be increased by 100% by the end of the year Machinery worth Rs. 2,000 is proposed to be acquired during the year as per Capital Expenditure budget. Estimated profit for the year is Rs. 7,000 after charging Rs. 4,000 depreciation and 50% of profit for taxation. Advance income tax payment is estimated at Rs. 6,000. Trade creditors are likely to be doubled. A 5% dividend is to be paid and provision for 10% dividend for next year is to be made. Debtors are estimated to be outstanding for 2 months. Sales budget shows Rs. 1,50,000 sales.

Make an estimate of cash position as at the end of the budget period.

Solution:

Budgeted Balance Sheet as at ....

Liability	Rs.	Rs.	Assets	Rs.	Rs.
Share Capital		50,000	Fixed Assets	40,000	
Reserves and Surplus:			Additions	2,000	
Reserves	6,000			42,000	
Profit for the year	7,000		Less: Depreciation	4,000	38,000
	13,000		Current Assets:		
Less: Last year loss	1,000		Stock		8,000
	12,000		Debtors		25,000
Less: Dividend	2,500		Advance Tax		6,000
Provision for dividend	5,000	4,500			
Current Liabilities					
Trade Creditors		4,000			
Provision for Tax		7,000			
Provision for Dividend		5,000			
Bank overdraft (Balancing figure)		6,500			
		77,000			77,000

Illustration 12

Prepare a Flexible Budget for the Year from the following data made available in respect of half-yearly period and forecast the results at 70%, 85% and 100% of capacity when the respective sales are Rs. 110 lakhs Rs. 134 lakhs and Rs. 150 lakhs. While fixed cost remain constant semi variable expenses are constant between 60% and 75% capacity, increasing by 10% between 75% and 90% capacity, and by 20% between 90% and 100% capacity. The expenses at 60% capacity are as follows:

		Rs. in lakhs
Variable	Materials	30.00
	Labour	18.00
	Other expenses	3.60
Semi-variable	Repairs & Maintenance	3.00
	Indirect labour	10.00
	Selling overheads	2.00
	Sundry other overheads	2.00
Fixed	Salaries & Wages	8.40
	Rent, Taxes & Rates	5.00
	Depreciation	6.00
	Sundry overheads	8.00
		96.00

Solution

Flexible Budget for the year

Capacity Utilisational Particulars	Existing 60% Rs./lakhs	Forecast at 70% Rs./lakhs	85% Rs./lakhs	100% Rs./lakhs
Variable Costs:				
Materials	30.00	35.00	42.50	50.00
Labour	18.00	21.00	25.50	30.00
Other expenses	3.60	4.20	5.10	6.00
Semi Variable Costs:				
Repairs & Maintenance	3.00	3.00	3.30	3.60
Indirect Labour	10.00	10.00	11.00	12.00
Selling overheads	2.00	2.00	2.20	2.40
Sundry other overheads	2.00	2.00	2.20	2.40
Fixed Cost:				
Salaries & Wages	8.40	8.40	8.40	8.40
Rent, rates & taxes	5.00	5.00	5.00	5.00
Depreciation	6.00	6.00	6.00	6.00
Sundry overheads	8.00	8.00	8.00	8.00
Total costs	96.00	104.60	119.20	133.80
Sales		110.00	134.00	150.00
Profit		5.40	14.80	16.20

Illustration 13

Prepare a flexible budget from the following data made available in respect of a half-yearly period and forecast the working results at 70%, 85% and 100% of capacity when the respective sales are Rs. 50 lakhs, Rs. 60 lakhs and Rs. 85 lakhs. While fixed expenses remain constant, semi-variable expenses are constant between 55% and 75% of capacity, increasing by 10% between 75% and 90% of capacity and by 20% between 90% and 100% of capacity. The expenses at 60% capacity are as follows:

		(Amount in lakhs) (Rs.)
Semi-variable	Maintenance and repairs	1.25
	Indirect labour	5.00
	Sales department expenses	1.50
	Sundry overheads	1.25
Variable:	Material	12.00
	Labour	13.00

	Other expenses	2.00
Fixed:	Wages and salaries	4.20
	Rent, rates and taxes	2.80
	Depreciation	3.50
	Sundry overheads	4.50
		51.00

Solution:

Flexible Budget

(Amount) in lakhs of rupees)

	Percentage of Capacity		
	70%	85%	100%
Sales revenue	50.00	60.00	85.00
Less: Variable expenses			
(A) Material	14.00	17.00	20.00
Labour	15.17	18.42	21.67
Other expenses	2.33	2.83	3.33
	31.50	38.25	45.00
(B) Semi-variable expenses			
Maintenance and repairs	1.25	1.38	1.50
Indirect labour	5.00	5.50	6.00
Sales department salaries	1.50	1.65	1.80
Administrative salaries	1.25	1.37	1.50
Total semi-variable expenses	9.00	9.90	10.80
(C) Fixed expenses			
Wages and salaries	4.20	4.20	4.20
Rent, rates and taxes	2.80	2.80	2.80
Depreciation	3.50	3.50	3.50
Sundry and other overheads	4.50	4.50	4.50
	15.00	15.00	15.00
(D) Total costs (A + B + C)	55.50	63.15	70.80
Budget Profit (loss)	(− 5.50)	(− 3.15)	14.20

Illustration 14

For Production of 10,000 Electrical Automatic Irons the following are budgeted expenses:

	Per Units Rs.
Direct Material	60

Direct Labour	30
Variable Overheads	25
Fixed Overheads (Rs. 1,50,000)	15
Variable Expenses (Direct)	5
Selling Price (10% Fixed)	15
Administration exp.	
(Rs. 50,000 rigid for all levels of production)	5
Distribution expenses (20% fixed)	5
Total cost of Sales per Unit	160

Prepare a budget for Production of 6,000; 7,000 and 8,000 Irons, showing distinctly Marginal cost and total cost.

[Bharathidasan, B.Com., Nov.97]

Solution:

Flexible Budget of Electrical Automatic Irons

Production	6,000 units		7,000 units		8,000 units	
	Total Rs.	Per unit Rs.	Total Rs.	Per unit Rs.	Total unit Rs.	Per unit Rs.
Direct Material	3,60,000	60.00	4,20,000	60.00	4,80,000	60.00
Direct Labour	1,80,000	30.00	2,10,000	30.00	2,40,000	30.00
Direct Variable expenses	30,000	5.00	35,000	5.00	40,000	5.00
Variable overheads:						
Production	1,50,000	25.00	1,75,000	25.00	2,00,000	25.00
Selling	81,000	13.50	94,500	13.50	1,08,000	13.50
Distribution	24,000	4.00	28,000	4.00	32,000	4.00
Marginal Cost	8,25,000	137.50	9,62,500	137.50	11,00,000	137.5
Fixed production overheads	1,50,000	25.00	1,50,000	21.43	1,50,000	18.75
Administration overheads	50,000	8.33	50,000	7.14	50,000	6.25
Selling overheads	15,000	2.50	15,000	2.14	15,000	1.88
Distribution overheads	10,000	1.67	10,000	1.43	10,000	1.25
Fixed costs	2,25,000	37.50	2,25,000	32.14	2,25,000	28.13
Total cost (Marginal cost + Fixed cost)	10,50,000	175.00	11,87,500	169.64	13,25,000	165.63

Notes: Variable Selling Expenses per Unit,

$$= \frac{1,50,000 \times 90/100}{10,000} = \text{Rs. } 13.50 \text{ per unit}$$

Distribution expenses have been computed on a similar basis.

REVIEW QUESTIONS

1. Define the following terms: [a] Budget, [b] Budgetary Control, and [c] Budgeting
2. What are the objectives of budgetary control?
3. Enumerate the advantages and limitations of budgetary control.
4. State the functions of a budget committee.
5. What is a budget manual?
6. Explain the meaning of a key factor.
7. Describe the various functional budgets.
8. How is Sales budget prepared? Illustrate your answer.
9. Explain the Receipts and Payments method of preparation of Cash budget.
10. Briefly explain the various types of budgets.
11. What is Flexible Budget? How is it prepared?
12. What is Master Budget?
13. State the points to be considered while preparing: [a] Purchase Budget [b] Production Budget.
14. Discuss the various steps involved in framing a budgetary control system.
15. What is Zero-base Budgeting? How does it differ from traditional budgeting?
16. Explain the meaning and process of Performance budgeting.
17. State the process, advantages and limitations of Zero-base Budgeting.

REVIEW PROBLEMS

1. Gohila Bros. sell two products which are manufactured in one plant. During the year 1999 they plan to sell the following quantities of each product:

Sales Budget (Units)

	First Quarter	Second Quarter	Third Quarter	Fourth Quarter	Total
Product 1	90,000	2,30,000	3,00,000	80,000	7,00,000
Product 2	85,000	75,000	55,000	85,000	3,00,000

Each of these two products is sold on a seasonal basis. Product 1 tends to sell better in the summer months, while product 2 sells better during the winter. Gohila Bros. plan to sell product 1 throughout the year at a price of Rs. 10 unit, and Product 2 at price of Rs. 20 unit.

A study of the past experience reveals that Gohila Bros. have lost about 3% of their billed revenue each year because of returns (constituting 2% of loss of revenue) allowances and bad debts (1% loss).

Prepare a budget incorporating the given information.

Ans:

Sales Budget

Quarter	I	II	III	IV
Net Sales [Rs.]	25,22,000	36,86,000	39,77,000	24,61,000

2. The Golden Company plans to sell 1,08,000 units of a certain product line in the first fiscal quarter, 1,20,000 units in the second quarter, 1,32,000 units in the third quarter, 1,56,000 units in the fourth quarter, and 1,38,000 units in the first quarter of the following year. At the beginning of the first quarter of the current year, there are 18,000 units of the product in stock. At the end of each quarter, the company plans to have an inventory equal to one-sixth of the sales for the next fiscal quarter.

   How many units must be manufactured in each quarter of the current year?

Ans:

Production Budget

Quarter	**I**	**II**	**III**	**IV**
Production [Units]	1,10,000	1,22,000	1,36,000	1,53,000

3. ABC Co., wished to arrange overdraft facilities with its bankers during the period April to June, 1999 when it will be manufacturing mostly for stock. Prepare a cash budget for the above period from the following data, including the extent of the bank facilities the company will require at the end of each month:

(a)

1999	Sales Rs.	Purchase Rs.	Wages Rs.
February	1,80,000	1,24,800	12,000
March	1,92,000	1,44,000	14,000
April	1,08,000	2,43,000	11,000
May	1,74,000	2,46,000	10,000
June	1,26,000	2,68,000	15,000

(b) 50 per cent of credit sales are realised in the month following the sales, and the remaining 50 per cent in the second month following. Creditors are paid in the month following the month of purchase.

(c) Cash at bank on 1.4.1999 (estimated) is Rs. 25,000.

Ans:

Cash Budget [O/D facilities required]

Months	**April**	**May**	**June**
Surplus/[O/D] Rs.	56,000	(47,000)	(1,67,000)

4. For production of 20,000 electrical automatic irons, the following are the budgeted expenses:

	Per Unit
Direct materials	60
Direct Labour	30
Variable overheads	25
Fixed overheads (Rs. 3,00,000)	15
Variable expenses (direct)	5

Selling expenses (10% fixed)	15
Administration expenses	
(Rs. 1,00,000 rigid for all levels of production)	5
Distribution expenses (20% fixed)	5
Total cost of sales per unit	160

Prepare a budget for production of 16,000, 17,000 and 18,000 irons showing distinctly marginal cost and total cost. (Refer illustration 14).

5. A glass manufacturing company requires you to calculate and present the budget for the next year from the following information:

Sales:

Bent toughened glass	Rs. 3,00,000
Toughened glass	Rs. 5,00,000
Direct material cost	60% of sales
Direct wages	20 workers @ Rs. 150 pm.
Factory overheads:	
Indirect labour:	
Works manager	Rs. 500 per month
Foreman	Rs. 400 per month
Stores and spares	2 1/2% on sales
Depreciation on machinery	Rs. 12,600
Light and power	Rs. 5,000
Repairs and maintenance	Rs.8,000
Other Sundries	10% on direct wages

Administration, selling and distribution expenses Rs.14,000 per year.

[**Ans:** Budgeted Net income Rs. 2,10,000]

6. The selling expenses of a business for a particular budget period are:

	Rs.
Sales Office Salaries	4,000
Fixed Expenses of sales office	3,000
Amount allocated for advertising	4,000
Fixed salaries and car allowances	12,000
Traveller's remuneration and	
Commission 1% on sales effected	
Outward carriage estimated @ 5% on sales	
Agent's commission 7 1/2 % on sales	

Prepare selling overheads budget for the following levels of sales for the period:

Rs. 2,80,000 including agent's sales	Rs. 30,000
Rs. 3,20,000 including agent's sales	Rs. 35,000
Rs. 3,60,000 including agent's sales	Rs. 35,000

[**Ans:** Rs. 41,750; 44,475; 46,875]

7. A manufacturing company submits the following figures for the first quarter of 1998:

	Product X	Product Y	Product Z
Sale (in units) January	25,000	30,000	10,000
February	20,000	25,000	10,000
March	30,000	35,000	10,000
Selling price per unit	Rs. 10	Rs. 20	Rs. 40
Targets for 1st Quarter 1999:			
Sales quantity increases	20%	10%	10%
Sales price increase	Nil	10%	25%
Stock position 1st Jan. 1999:,			
Percentage of Jan. 99 sales	50%	50%	50%
Stock position 31st March 1999:	20,000	25,000	5,000
Stock position-end Jan. and February			
Percentage of subsequent months sales	50%	50%	50%

You are required to prepare the sales and production budgets for the 1st quarter of 1999. Show working clearly.

[**Ans:** **Sales Budget**

	X Rs.	Y Rs.	Z Rs.
January	300000	726000	550000
February	240000	605000	550000
March	360000	847000	550000

Production Budget (Units)

	X	Y	Z
January	27000	30250	11000
February	30000	33000	11000
March	38000	44250	10500

8. Excellent Engineering works had prepared its budget for 2000, based on the production of 1 lakh units of their only product as follows:

		Rs. (in 000's)
(i)	Raw materials	252
(ii)	Direct labour	75
(iii)	Direct expenses	10
(iv)	Works overheads (60% fixed)	22.5
(v)	Administrative overheads	40
(vi)	Selling overheads (50% fixed)	20

For want of demand the actual production for that period was only 60,000 units.

Calculate the budgeted cost per unit under both the original plan and under actual performance.

[**Ans:** Original Plan Rs. 4.20; Actual Rs. 4.62 per unit]

9. Laxmi Enterprises Ltd., ended with the following profit/loss during the year 1999 (All figures in Rs. lakhs).

	Rs.	Rs.
Sales		35.58
Less: Expenses: Raw materials	7.42	
Stores	4.88	
Expenses	20.40	
Interest	2.00	
Depreciation	2.00	36.70
Loss for the year		1.12

The company had been working at 60% of capacity during the year and of the expenses of Rs. 20.40 lakhs 25% is variable.

Production/sale volume at 80% of capacity is expected to be achieved next year. Fixed cost is however expected to increase by Rs. 1.20 lakhs.

Draw up a budget for next year.

[**Ans:** Budgeted Profit Rs. 3,74,000]

10. A new company commences business on 1st July and deposits Rs. 10,000 in the bank. This sum will be insufficient to finance its operations over a period of six months, and you are asked to prepare a cash budget from July to December to determine the monthly overdraft limits to seek from the company bankers. Data supplied to you are:

(a) Sales are made to one distributor only on 30 days' terms, 3% discount, and cheques are received on the first day of the month following the due date.

(b) Plant purchases totalling Rs.5,000 are to be made in July.

(c) Budget figures are:

	July Rs.	Aug. Rs.	Sept. Rs.	Oct. Rs.	Nov. Rs.	Dec. Rs.
Purchases	5,000	4,000	3,000	4,000	4,000	5,000
Wages	4,000	5,000	4,000	4,000	5,000	4,000
Cash expenses	400	500	400	400	500	400
Sales	6,000	7,000	8,000	8,000	9,000	12,000

All purchases are made on 30 days terms and cheques are posted to creditors on the last day of the month due.

Ans:

Cash Budget

	July Rs.	Aug. Rs.	Sept. Rs.	Oct. Rs.	Nov. Rs.	Dec. Rs.

Surplus [O/D]	4,600	920	(1,690)	(1,330)	(2,070)	(2,740)

Notes: Wages paid by next month; cash expenses paid in the same month]

11. From the following information relating to the previous year and conditions expected to prevail in the next year, prepare a budget for the next year:

	Rs.
Last Year (Actuals):	
Sales	1,00,000 (40,000 units)
Raw Material	53,000
Wages	11,000
Variable overheads	16,000
Fixed overheads	10,000
Next Year (prospects):,	
Sales	1,50,000 (60,000 units)
Raw Material	5% price increase
Wages	10% increase in wages
	5% increase in Productivity

Additional plants:

One lathe Rs. 25,000 and one drill Rs. 12,000. Charge depreciation at the rate of 20% on additional plant.

[**Ans:** Budgeted Profit Rs. 9,082.50]

13

COST ACCOUNTING – ELEMENTS OF COST

Learning Objectives

After completing this Chapter, you should be able to

— Explain the concept of cost accounting and other cost concepts.

— Describe the various methods of costing.

— Discuss what the elements of cost are,

— Know how to prepare a Cost Sheet.

— Understand the meaning and methods of inventory valuation.

13.1 Concept of Cost Accounting

As the term itself suggests that cost accounting deals with cost. Cost is the amount of resources given up in exchange for some goods or services. The resources given up are money or money's worth expressed in monetary terms. The Chartered Institute of Management Accountants, London (CIMA) defines cost as "the amount of expenditure (actual or notional) incurred on, or attributable to a specified thing or activity." When the term is used as a verb it means 'to ascertain the cost of a specified thing or activity'.

However, the process or technique of ascertaining cost of activities, processes, products, or services is termed as costing. This technique consists of a body of principles and rules, which govern the procedure of ascertaining costs. The process of costing is the day-to-day routine of ascertaining costs, whatever the costs ascertained may be and by whatever means these costs are determined.

The official terminology of CIMA defines cost accounting as "the process of accounting for costs from the point at which the expenditure is incurred or committed to the establishment of its ultimate relationship with cost centers and cost units. In its widest usage, it embraces the preparation of statistical data, the application of cost control methods and the ascertainment of the profitability of activities carried out or planned." It is a formal mechanism by means of which costs of products or services are ascertained and controlled. It provides information to the management for taking all sorts of managerial decisions.

13.2 Objectives of cost accounting

The main objectives of cost accounting are as follows:

1. To record, analyze, and classify the cost of products and operations with a view to ascertain the cost per unit of production, also the cost of each element of expenditure and thereby to determine the selling price of such products or services.

2. To help management in its task of cost minimization by facilitating cost control through standard costing and budgetary control, etc. and enable management to measure the efficiency of the organization as a whole or departmentally and also devise means of increasing efficiency.

3. To provide information to enable management to make such tactical decisions as the closing down of or continuance of a department, a product mix, make or buy, etc., and also strategic investment decisions.

4. To enable management to have frequent review of production, sales and operating by supplying information at shorter intervals say, daily, weekly, or monthly about the volumes of units produced, accumulated costs together with appropriate analysis.

13.3 Functions of cost accounting

More specifically the following may be listed as the functions of cost accounting:

1. To ascertain the unit cost of product, service or department and estimate the net result i.e., cost, profit or loss, for each item of operation, production or service.

2. To help construction of budget and budgetary control and standard costing and develop control systems through analysis and exceptions.

3. To present and interpret data for managerial decision-making and control and suggest suitable criteria for choosing among alternative investments, products, market, etc.

13.4 Importance (advantages) of cost accounting

(a) Cost accounting is *an aid to management*. It enables management to maintain effective control over inventory, to maximize efficiency, and to minimize wastages and losses by providing detailed costing information. it facilitates delegation of responsibility for important tasks and rating of employees. It helps cost estimation and price fixation.

(b) *It is an aid to creditors*. Investors, banks and other financial institutions benefit immensely by the installation of an efficient costing system. They can rely on costing records to form their judgment about the profitability and future of the firm.

(c) *It is an aid to employees.* Employees are benefited in a number of ways by the installation of an efficient costing system. For example, they are benefited, through continuous employment and higher remuneration by way of incentives, bonus plans, etc.

(d) *It is an aid to nation.* Costing system boost up the government revenue by bringing prosperity to the business firms. Cost reduction, cost control, and elimination of wastes and inefficiencies lead to the progress of the nation as a whole.

13.5 Limitations of cost accounting

Despite its advantages to various parties such as management, employees, creditors, etc., cost accounting has certain inherent limitations or deficiencies, which pave the way for the emergence of management accounting.

Any costing system needs to conform to the nature and character of the business firm and this affects the uniformity and universality of any such system.

Costing data are essentially 'post facto' and historical in nature. However, different forms of predetermined cost systems such as estimating costing, standard costing, etc rectify this limitation. But they are also notional costs, which enhance the degree of approximation and therefore limit accuracy.

Cost accounting system is also based on conventional treatment certain items such as depreciation, capital and revenue expenditure, fixed costs, wastes, and intangible assets, etc. This necessarily introduces subjective elements into the whole process.

Cost accounting depends heavily on the interpretation rather than on the actuality of collected information. This is a part of its role in managerial assistance. However, this tends to make the system more interpretative than factual.

Installation of cost accounting system is costly, which small firms cannot afford to have. Such firms find it unnecessary, for the financial accounting system itself can take of costing information.

Some basic cost concepts explained

13.6 Cost Unit and Cost center

Cost unit: After the cost of various cost centers has been ascertained, it becomes necessary to express the cost of output (production, or service). Cost unit may be defined as the quantity upon which the cost can be conveniently allocated. The official terminology defines a cost unit a 'unit of quantity of product, service or time in relation to which costs are ascertained or expressed.' According to this definition, the choice of a cost unit depends on what is being produced, whether goods or services, and what is relevant to the purpose of cost ascertainment. The selected cost unit should be simple, unambiguous, and commonly used. A few examples of cost units are as follows:

Industry	Cost unit
Automobile	Number of vehicles
Brick works.	Per 1000 bricks made
Bridge Construction	Each contract
Chemical units	Litre, Gallon, kilogram, tonne
Cement, sugar, steel, etc	Tonne
Power	Kilowatt-hour
Transport	tonne kilometer or passenger kilometer

Cost center: The CIMA defines a cost center as 'a location, person or item of equipment (or group of these) for which costs may be ascertained and used for the purpose of cost control.' It is the smallest organizational sub-unit for which separate cost collection is attempted. For example, the production department of an oil milling industry may be divided into distinct parts such as crushing, refining, and finishing. Each of these production lines or process forms one cost center. Cost centers may classified as follows:

(a) Personal or Impersonal cost centers

(b) Production cost center or Service cost center

(c) Operation and Process cost centers

A personal cost center is one, which consists of a person or group of persons, while an impersonal cost center consists of a department, plant or item of equipment.

A production cost center is one, which is actually engaged in production activities, while service cost centers render services to production centers, e.g., repair shop, boiler plant, crane, etc.

A operation cost center is one, which consists of those machines and/or persons or group of persons and where the same operation is carried out. If a cost center consists of a continuous sequence of operations, it is called process cost center.

Profit Center: A profit center usually refers to a segment of an organization that generates revenue. It is a responsibility center, the manager of which is responsible for the amount of profits earned. The managers in the profit center are, therefore responsible for both revenue and costs. For example, the manager of a furniture department of a departmental store is responsible for earning a profit on the furniture sold.

Investment Center: It is a responsibility center whose manager is responsible for earning a rate of return on the assets used in his responsibility center. Major segments of companies are normally investment centers. For example, a segment in an automobile manufacturing company, individual departments of a departmental store, and individual branches of a multiple shop are investment centers.

An investment center differs from a profit center in that as investment center is evaluated on the basis of the rate of return earned on the assets invested in the segment, while a profit center is evaluated on the basis of excess of revenue over expenses for the period. However, it is better to designate a segment as an investment center rather than a profit center. A segment may earn greater profits than others not because of better performance but by using more assets to earn such profits.

13.7 Cost estimation and Cost ascertainment

Cost estimation means computation of future cost. It is the process of predetermining the costs of certain products, jobs, orders, or services. Cost estimation may be needed for several purposes such as budgeting, preparation of financial statements, fixation of selling prices, etc. But cost ascertainment means computation of historical costs based on actual data.

Both are interrelated and useful to the management. In an efficient costing system, cost ascertainment enables the management to make cost estimation more accurately with the help of ascertained historical costs. Further the comparison of ascertained costs with the estimated costs on a continuous basis assists management in identifying variances and controlling costs.

Cost allocation and Cost apportionment

Cost allocation and apportionment refer to the identification and allotment of costs to various cost centers and cost units. However, cost allocation refers to charging of direct expenditures fully and directly to cost centers or cost units, while cost apportionment refers to charging of indirect expenses proportionately to cost centers or cost units. For example the cost of labour incurred in a service department is charged (or allocated) to it fully and directly. But the canteen expenses of the factory are apportioned proportionately to the production and service departments based on the number of employees working in various departments.

Cost Control and Cost Reduction

Cost control is defined as the regulation of costs of operating an undertaking by executive action where such action is guided by cost accounting. The steps involved in cost control are: (a) To establish plans or targets in the form of standards, budgets, estimates, etc. (b) To communicate the plans and policy laid down by the management to all those responsible for carrying them out. (c) To observe and record the actual performance. (d) To compare the actual with the budget or standards and identify the variances. (e) To review the variances and take decisions in the form of corrective action, and remedial measures or revision of targets.

Common tools of cost control are budgetary control, standard costing, inventory control, quality control, etc.

Cost Reduction may be defined as the real and permanent reduction in the unit costs of goods and services without affecting their quality. Reduction should be permanent and real and not temporary or fortuitous. The aim of cost reduction is to bring about a saving in the costs incurred – materials, labour, overheads, etc. Real cost reduction comes through greater productivity and savings in cost such as obtaining more production from the same facilities, using materials of lower quality or price without sacrificing the quality of finished product, etc.

Distinctions between Cost Reduction and Cost Control

1. The objective of cost control is to achieve a target or goal, but the objective of cost reduction is to achieve real reduction in cost.

2. The cost control is to set up targets, ascertain actual, identify variances and take necessary remedial measures. But cost reduction does not depend on such control process.

3. Cost control works on scientifically established standards or norms, which are very rigid in nature. On the other hand cost reduction works on the assumptions of potential savings in standards or norms, which are challenged constantly to get or improve such savings in costs.

4. While cost control is a preventive action, cost reduction is a corrective function.

5. While cost control lacks dynamism and is a static approach, cost reduction is a continuous and dynamic analysis.

13.8 Methods of Cost Accounting

The methods used for the ascertainment of cost of production differ from industry to industry. It primarily depends on the manufacturing process and also on the methods of measuring departmental and finished products. Basically there are two methods of costing viz., (a) Job costing and (b) Process costing. Job costing is suitable for industries manufacturing different products or executing different jobs for different customers according to different specifications. Process costing is suitable for industries where production is continuous and units are identical. All other methods of costing are improvements, extensions, or combinations of the above two methods. However, the principles in every method of costing are the same but the methods of analyzing and presenting the costs differ with the nature of business.

Job Costing: Under this method costs are collected and accumulated for each job or work order or project separately. Each job can be identified separately and hence becomes essential to analyze the costs according to each job. Normally production consists of distinct jobs or lots so that order number can identify costs. A job card is prepared for each job for cost accumulation. This method is suitable for Printers, Machine tool manufacturers, Foundries, and general engineering workshops.

Contract Costing: Contract costing does not in principle differ from job costing. When the job is big and spread over long period of time, the method of contract costing is used. A separate account is kept for each individual contract. Civil engineering contractors, constructional and mechanical engineering firms, builders, etc use this method. In contracts, when it is agreed to pay an agreed sum or percentage to cover overheads and profit to the contractors, it will be termed as 'cost plus costing'. The term cost here refers to the prime cost. Usually government contracts are assigned in this basis.

Batch Costing: This is an extension of job costing. A batch may represent a number of small orders or group of identical products passed through the factory in batch. Each batch is treated as a cost unit and cost is ascertained separately. The cost per unit is determined by dividing the cost of the batch by the number of units produced in a batch. The manufacturers of biscuits, garments, spare parts and components mainly use this method.

Process Costing: A process refers here to a stage of production. If a product passes through different stages, each distinct and well defined, then in order to ascertain the cost at each stage or process, the process costing is used. Under this method, a separate process account is prepared and all costs incurred in that process are charged. Normally the finished product of one process becomes the raw material of the subsequent process and a final product is obtained in the last process. As the products are manufactured in continuous process, this is also known as Continuous costing. Process costing method is generally followed in textile units, chemical industries, refineries, tanneries, paper manufacture, etc.

Operation Costing: It is a further refinement of process costing. It is suitable to industries where mass or repetitive production is carried out or where the goods have to be stocked in semi-finished stage, to enable the execution of special orders, or for the convenient use in later operations. In this method, the cost unit is an operation. It is used in cycle manufacturing, automobile units, etc.

Unit Costing: This is also known as single or output costing. This method is suitable for industries where the manufacture is continuous and units are identical. This method is applied in industries like mines, quarries, cement works, brick works, etc. In all these industries there is natural or standard unit of cost, for example, tonne of coal in collieries, tonne of cement, one thousand of bricks, etc. The object of this method is to ascertain the cost per unit of output and the cost of each element of such cost. Here the cost account takes the form of cost sheet or statement prepared for a definite period. The cost per unit is determined by dividing the total expenditure incurred during a given period by the number of units produced during that period.

Operating Costing: This is suitable for industries, which render services as distinct from those, which manufacture goods. This is applied in transport undertakings, power supply companies, gas, water works, municipal services, hospitals, hotels, etc. It is used to ascertain the cost of services rendered. There is usually a compound unit in such undertakings, for example, tonne-kilometres or passanger-kilometres in transport companies, kilo-watt-hour in power supply, patient-day in hospitals, etc.

Multiple Costing: It is also called as composite costing. It represents the application of more than one method of costing in respect of the same product. This is suitable for industries where a number of component parts are separately produced and subsequently assembled into a final product. In such industries each component differs from others as to price, materials used, and manufacturing processes. So it will be necessary to ascertain the cost of each component. For this purpose process costing may be applied. To ascertain the cost of the final product batch costing may be applied. This method is used in factories manufacturing cycles, automobiles, engines, radios, typewriter, aeroplane and other complex products.

13.9 Techniques of costing

In order to produce useful information for managerial purposes, cost data are collected should be processed according to costing principles, using one or more costing techniques. They are used mainly to link or relate costs to cost units or cost centers. They are not independent methods of cost ascertainment such as job costing or process costing, but are basically costing techniques used along with the various methods of costing. Important costing techniques are as follows:

Absorption Costing: This is also known as orthodox costing, conventional costing, full costing, or total costing. It is a technique of cost ascertainment and presentation under which all costs are charged to the cost units or cost centers to be ultimately absorbed by the same. The CIMA terminology defines this technique as "the procedure, which charges fixed as well as variable overheads to cost units." Accordingly, although variable costs may be distinguished from fixed costs, both are treated as product costs. And the cost unit is made to bear the burden of the full cost by computing absorption rates, in spite of the fact that fixed costs are period costs and have no relevance to current operations.

Marginal Costing: This technique is used as an alternative to absorption costing and it demands the classification of costs according to behaviour or variability. It is an accounting system in which variable costs are charged to cost units and fixed costs of the period are written off in full against the aggregate contribution. According to this definition, the cost of a cost unit comprises only variable costs. Fixed costs are treated as period costs and written off to costing profit and loss account. Consequently, finished goods and work in process are valued at marginal cost i.e., prime cost plus variable overheads.

Differential Costing: The official terminology defines the differential costing as "the difference in total cost between alternatives calculated to assist decision-making." Although this technique distinguishes between variable costs and fixed costs, unlike marginal costing, it takes into consideration fixed costs also for decision-making under certain circumstances. As such the concept is much broader than marginal costing.

This technique considers all revenue and cost differences amongst the alternative courses of action to enable management to take appropriate decision. It is most suitable as a decision-making tool for situations in which fixed cost also change, and become relevant for both short as well as long-run decisions. But marginal costing is appropriate for short-run tactical decisions.

Uniform Costing: It is defined as 'the use by several undertakings of the same costing systems, i.e., the same costing methods, principles, and techniques.' With a view to promoting uniformity in the adoption of costing methods so that cost comparison can be made, several undertakings adopt the technique of uniform costing. This technique facilitates inter-firm comparisons, establishing of realistic pricing policies, etc.

13.10 Cost Accounting Systems

Costs are accumulated and recorded in an organized and orderly manner be setting up a formal mechanism known as the cost accounting system. According to Batty, 'a system of cost accounting implies that there is a planned and coordinated arrangement of all matters relating to costing.' The two systems of costing, which are referred to very frequently in the cost accounting literature are historical costing and standard costing.

Historical Costing: Costs may be ascertained either after they are incurred or before they are incurred. The process of accumulating costs after they are incurred in an orderly manner, costing of actual costs in a systematic manner is known as historical costing system. The official CIMA terminology defines historical cost as "the actual cost of acquiring assets, goods and services" and historical costing as "a system of accounting in which all values are based on the historical costs incurred. This is the basis prescribed in the companies Act for published accounts." According to Batty, historical costing is concerned with the ascertainment and recording of actual costs when or after they have been incurred and was one of the first stages in the growth of the cost accountant's work. Actual costs represent material cost, labour cost, and overheads, and they tell us what the costs are.

Limitations of historical costing are:

1. It is merely a post mortem examination of the actual costs.
2. It does not provide a yardstick for comparing and evaluating operating efficiency.
3. Cost comparison cannot be made under this method.
4. Costs cannot be calculated accurately.
5. Prices cannot be fixed scientifically.
6. Cost data cannot be interpreted properly.

Standard Costing: Standard costing is the technique of setting up of definite standards or targets of performance in advance of the costing period. This is done even before production begins. The standards are expressed in monetary terms. The establishment of standards provides management with goals to attain and the bases for comparison with actual results.

Standard cost represents the planned or predetermined cost of a product. It tells what the product should cost on the basis of a specification of all the factors affecting cost. Standard costing is a yardstick against which actual costs can be compared and operating efficiency be measured. It is a managerial tool of analysis of variances, fixation of responsibility, cost control and cost reduction. It facilitates the formulation of production and pricing policies with certainty before production takes place. It ensures accurate and prompt reporting of cost data to management.

13.11 Classification of Costs

Costs can be classified into different categories depending upon the purpose of classification. A suitable classification of costs is of vital importance in order to identify the cost with cost centers or cost units. The important ways of classification are:

By Nature or Element: According to this classification, the costs are divided into thee categories i.e., Material, Labour, and Expenses. There can be sub-classification of each element, for example material into indirect materials, components, and spar parts, consumable stores, packing material, etc. This classification is important as it helps to find out the total cost, how such total cost is constituted, and valuation of work in process.

By Functions: According to this classification, cost is divided based on purpose for which they are incurred. It leads to grouping of cost according to broad division of activity i.e., production, administration, selling, and distribution.

As Direct and Indirect Costs: According to this classification, total cost is divided into direct costs and indirect costs. Direct costs are those, which are incurred for and may be conveniently identified with a particular cost center or cost unit. Whereas indirect (residual) costs are those costs, which are incurred for the benefit of a number of cost centers or cost units and therefore, cannot be conveniently identified with a particular cost center or cost unit.

By Controllability: On this basis, the costs can be classified into controllable costs and uncontrollable costs. Controllable costs are those, which can be influenced by the action of a specified member of an undertaking, that is to say, costs are at least partly within the control of management. An organization is divided into a number of responsibility centers and controllable costs incurred in a particular cost center can be influenced by the action of the manager responsible for the center. Generally speaking, all direct costs including direct material, direct labour and some of the overhead expenses are controllable by lower level of management.

Uncontrollable costs are those costs, which cannot be influenced by the action of a specified member of an undertaking, that is to say, which are not within the control of management. Most of fixed costs are uncontrollable. For example, rent of the building and managerial salaries, etc are not controllable. Similarly, overhead costs, which are incurred by one service department and apportioned to another department, are not controllable by the other. For canteen expenses apportioned to other production and service departments are uncontrollable as regards other departments.

The distinction between controllable and uncontrollable is sometimes left to the individual judgment and is not sharply maintained. It is only in relation to a particular level of management or an individual manager that we may say whether a cost is controllable or uncontrollable. A particular item of cost, which may be controllable from the point of view of one level of management, may be uncontrollable from another point of view. Moreover, there may be an item of cost, which is controllable from long-term point of view and uncontrollable from short-term point of view. This is partly so in the case of fixed costs.

By Normality: Under this, costs may be classified into normal costs and abnormal costs. Normal cost is the cost, which is normally incurred at a given level of output in the conditions in which that level of output is normally attained. It is a part of cost of production.

Abnormal cost is the cost, which is not normally incurred at a given level of output in the conditions in which that level of output is normally attained. It is not a part of cost of production and is charged to costing profit and loss account.

Capital and Revenue: The cost, which is incurred in purchasing an asset either to earn income or increase the earning capacity of the business is called capital cost, for example, the cost of buildings, machineries, etc. If any expenditure is incurred in order to maintain the earning capacity of the business as cost of maintaining an asset or running a business is revenue expenditure. This distinction is important in costing as all items of revenue expenditure are considered for calculating the profit while capital items are normally ignored.

By Time: Under this, costs are classified as historical cost and predetermined cost. Historical cost is the cost ascertained after it is incurred or past cost. Such cost is available only when the production of a particular thing has already been done. Such cost is only of historical value and not at all helpful for cost control purposes. Predetermined costs are estimated costs, i.e., computed in advance of production taking into consideration the cost and the factors affecting the cost. A predetermined cost determined on scientific basis becomes standard cost. Such costs when compared with actual costs will give the reasons of variances and help the management to fix responsibilities and take remedial actions to avoid their recurrence in future.

By Variability: Under this category, costs are classified as fixed costs, variable costs, and semi-variable or semi-fixed costs.

Fixed or Period Costs: It is commonly described as those, which remain fixed or constant in total amount with increase or decreases in the volume of output or productive activity for a given period of time. Fixed cost per unit decreases as production increases and increases as production decreases. Examples are rent, insurance, manager's salary, etc. These fixed costs are constant in total amount but fluctuate per unit as production changes.

Variable or Product Costs: These costs vary in total in direct proportion with the volume of output. These costs per unit remain relatively constant with changes in production. Thus variable costs fluctuate in total amount but tend to remain constant per unit as production activity changes. Examples are direct material cost, direct labour cost, power, repairs, etc.

Semi-variable Costs: These costs are partly fixed and partly variable. For example, telephone charges include a fixed portion of annual charge plus variable charge according to calls; thus the telephone expenses are semi-variable cost. Other examples are depreciation, repairs and maintenance of buildings and plant, etc.

Advantages of making distinction between fixed and variable cost

1. Better control can be exercised over expenses if the estimate of expenses is properly made.

2. It enables the ascertainment of marginal cost i.e. that cost, which can be avoided or incurred additionally when a unit is given up or an additional unit is produced.

3. This helps in determining the level of output where all the expenses can be met i.e. determining the break-even point.

4. It also helps in determining the price during slump or a depression or in special markets.

5. It helps to take make or buy decisions by comparing the price demanded by outsiders with the marginal cost.

6. It helps to decide as to continue or close down a product or department or increase the capacity of another product etc.

7. In short, it enables to derive the advantages of marginal costing and budgetary control techniques.

For Managerial Decisions: Based on the relevance and irrelevance of costs for managerial decision-making the costs may be classified into the costs:

Marginal cost: It is the total of variable cost i.e., prime cost plus variable overheads. It is based on the distinction between fixed and variable costs. Fixed costs are ignored and only variable costs are taken into consideration for determining the cost of products, and value of work in progress and finished goods.

Out of Pocket costs: These are the costs, which involve the cash outflow due to a particular management decision. Depreciation will not form part of out of pocket cost because it does not entail cash outflows. Such costs are relevant for price fixation during recession or when make or buy decision is to be made.

Differential Costs: The change in costs due to change in level of activity or pattern or method of production is known as differential cost. if the change increases the cost, it will be called incremental cost. if there is decrease in costs resulting from decrease of output, the difference is known as decrement cost.

Sunk Costs: A sunk cost is an irrecoverable cost and is caused by complete abandonment of a plant. It is the written down value of the abandoned plant less its salvage value. Such costs are not relevant for decision-making and are not affected by increase or decrease in volume.

Imputed Cost /Notional Cost: It is the cost, which does not involve actual cash outlay. It is a hypothetical cost and does not appear in financial records. Interest on capital and notional rent charged for owned premises are common examples of imputed cost. When alternative investment projects are being evaluated, it is necessary to consider the imputed interest on capital before a decision is arrived at as to which is the most profitable project.

Opportunity Cost: It is the maximum alternative earning that might have been earned if the productive capacity or services had been put to some alternative use. In simple words it is the advantage, in measurable terms, which has been foregone due to not using the facility in the manner originally planned. For example, if the owned building is proposed to be used for a project, the likely rent of the building is the opportunity cost that should be taken into consideration for evaluating that project.

Replacement Cost: It is the cost at which there could be purchase of an asset or material identical to that, which is being replaced or revalued. It is the cost of replacement at current market price.

Avoidable and Unavoidable costs: Avoidable costs are those costs, which can be eliminated if a particular product or department, with which they are related, is discontinued. For example, salary of clerks employed in a particular department can be eliminated if it is discontinued. Unavoidable cost is that cost which cannot be eliminated with the discontinuation of a product or department. For example, salary of factory manager or factory rent cannot be eliminated even if a product is eliminated or discontinued.

13.12 What are the elements of cost?

The cost of making and selling a product mainly consists of three elements, namely material cost, labour cost, and expenses. The CIMA defines the elements of cost as "the primary classification of costs according to the factors upon which expenditure is incurred, viz., material cost, wages (labour cost), and expenses." There are, thus, three elements of cost. Material may be classified into direct material and indirect material.

Direct Material: CIMA defines material cost as "the cost of commodities supplied to an undertaking." All materials, which becomes an integral part of the finished product and which can be conveniently allocated to specific physical units is termed as direct material. Some of the examples are all material components or spare parts specifically purchased, produced or supplied from stores, primary packing materials, and purchased or partly produced components. It is also called as process material or production material.

Indirect Material: All material, which is used for secondary purposes and cannot be allocated conveniently to specified physical units, is called as indirect material. A few examples are consumable stores, oil and waste, printing and stationery material, and etc. Indirect material may be used at the factory, office or selling and distribution divisions.

Labour: Human effort required to convert materials into finished products is termed as labour. It may be classified into direct labour and indirect labour.

Direct Labour: Labour, which plays an active and direct part in the production of a particular product, is termed as direct labour. CIMA defines labour cost as "the cost of remuneration (wages, salaries, commission, bonus, etc.) of the employees of an undertaking." Direct labour cost can be conveniently and specifically charged to specific products.

Indirect labour: It is employed to carry out tasks incidental to goods produced or services rendered. Indirect labour cost cannot be practically traced to specific units of output. A few examples indirect labour costs are wages of storekeeper, salaries of office staff and salesmen, directors' fees, etc. It may be incurred in the factory, office, and selling and distribution divisions.

Expenses: CIMA defines expenses as "the cost of services provided to an undertaking and the notional cost of the use of owned assets." It may be classified into direct expenses and indirect expenses.

Direct Expenses: These are expenses, which can be directly allocated to a particular job, product or unit of service. They are also called as 'chargeable expenses.' Examples of such expenses are hire charges paid to some special machinery required for a particular contract, cost of designs or mould incurred in toy manufacturing, cost of blocks needed in book publishing, etc.

Indirect Expenses: These are expenses, which cannot be conveniently and directly allocated to a particular job, product or unit of service. They are incurred in common and can be apportioned to various cost centers or cost units proportionately on some basis. Examples of such expenses are factory rent, lighting, insurance, office and administration expenses, selling and distribution expenses, etc.

Overheads: The aggregate of indirect material cost, indirect labour cost, and indirect expenses is termed as overheads. Thus all indirect costs are overheads. They may be classified broadly into types:

(a) Factory or Works Overheads: These are indirect costs incurred inside a factory or works. Examples are factory supplies such as oil, consumable stores, lubricants, indirect labour such as factory manager's salary, timekeeper's salary, etc., and indirect expenses such as factory rent, factory lighting, factory insurance, etc.

(b) Office and Administration Overheads: These are indirect costs incurred in the general and administrative office. Examples are indirect materials such as stationery, brooms, dusters, etc, and indirect labour such as salaries of office staff, directors' fees, etc., and indirect expenses such as rent, insurance, lighting, etc., of the office.

(c) Selling and Distribution Overheads: These are indirect costs incurred in connection with the selling and distribution of goods and services. Examples are indirect materials such as packing materials, printing and stationery materials, etc., and indirect labour such as salaries of sales staff and sales manager, commission, etc., and indirect expenses such as advertising expenses, insurance, godown rent, etc.

Figure 1: Elements of Cost

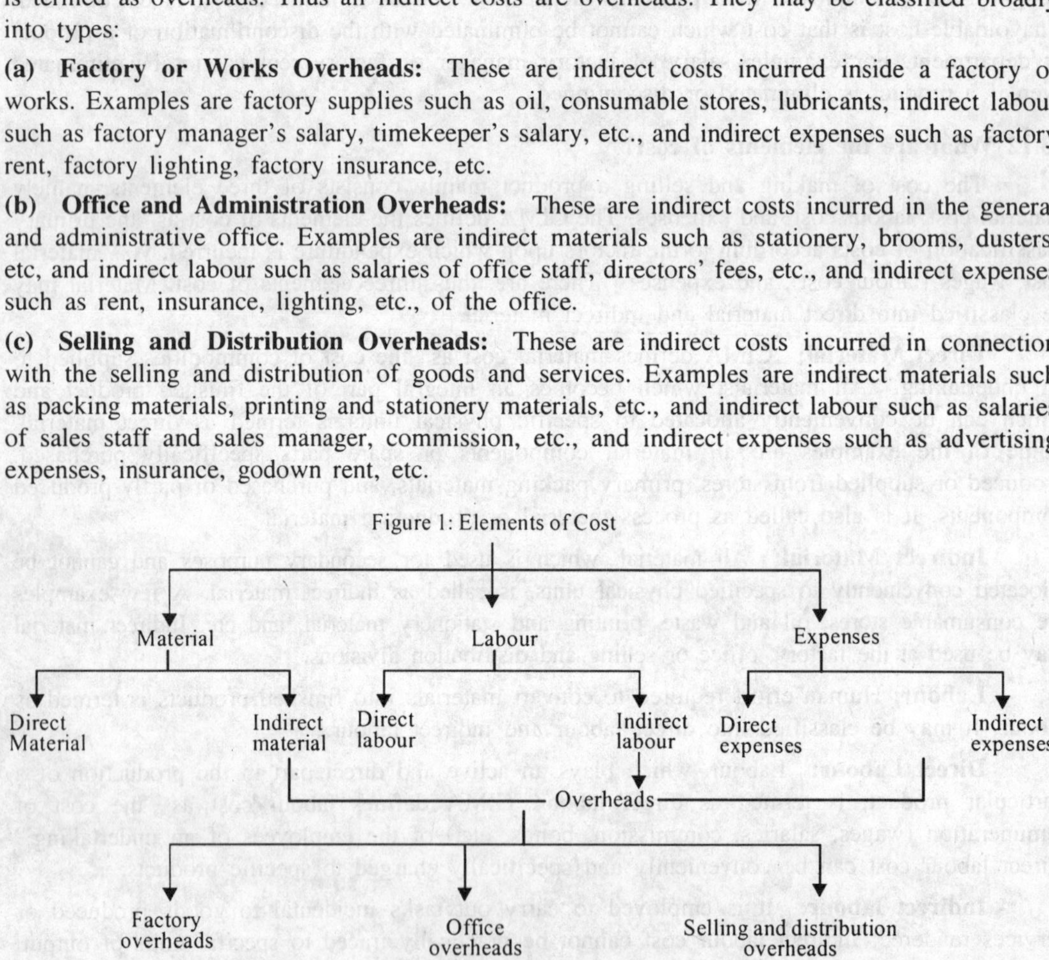

Figure 1: Elements of Cost

13.13 What is a Cost Sheet?

A statement, which is prepared at given intervals of time and provides information regarding the elements of cost incurred in production is known as a Cost Sheet. It is a statement of various cost items extracted from the financial records or estimated on the basis of a predetermined rate. The cost sheet is generally prepared at short intervals and presents the total as well as cost per unit of products manufactured during the period. It is more or less like a Manufacturing Account. The difference is in the form of presentation.

A Production Statement or Cost Statement is a statement, which shows all the costs incurred, selling price of goods and profits earned during a period. In deed a production statement may be regarded as an expanded form of cost sheet. When it is drawn in the form of a T- account (the conventional form of account) it is called Production Account. Production account or Statement consists of two parts. The first part shows the cost components and total cost of current production. The second part shows the cost of sales, selling price and the profit. The cost sheet can be drawn with as much details regarding costs as may be necessary. Often, it includes cost data of previous year for comparison. Moreover, costs estimates can be prepared with the help of cost sheets and tenders for supply and price quotations can be submitted with greater reliability and precision. The components of total cost normally presented in a cost sheet are as follows:

Prime cost: It is the aggregate of direct material cost, direct wages, and direct expenses.

Factory cost: It includes prime cost plus all factory or works overheads. It is also known as works cost, production cost or manufacturing cost.

Cost of Production or Production Cost: It is arrived at after adding office and administration overheads to factory cost.

Cost of sales or Total cost: It is arrived at after adding selling and distribution overheads to cost of production.

Chart showing the components of Total Cost

(A)	Direct Materials Direct Wages Direct Expenses	Prime Cost
(B)	Prime cost plus Factory Overheads	Factory or Works Cost (A) +(B)
(C)	Factory cost plus Office and Administration Overheads	Cost of Production (A) + (B) + (C)
(D)	Cost of Production plus Selling and Distribution Overheads	Cost of sales or Total cost (A) + (B) + (C) + (D)
(E)	Total cost plus Profit	Selling Price

Items not included in cost accounts

Items of expenses, which are apportionment or appropriation of profits, should normally be excluded from costs. These are: (i) Income tax, (ii) Dividends to shareholders, (iii) Commission to partners, managing agents, etc. (iv) Capital losses, (v) Interest on capital (under certain circumstances), (vi) Interest paid on debentures, (vii) and capital expenses, etc.

Treatment of stocks

Stocks are generally of three types (a) Raw Materials (b) Work in Progress and (c) Finished Goods.

Stocks of Raw materials should be adjusted in order to arrive at the cost of consumption of raw materials.

Raw Materials consumed = Opening stock of Raw Materials + Purchases less returns – Closing stock of Raw Materials

Work-in Progress is the value of semi- or partly finished goods at the time of preparation of cost sheet. The amount of work-in-progress should be adjusted to Factory Cost in order to arrive at Net Factory Cost.

Net Factory Cost = Opening Work in Progress + Gross Factory Cost (i.e., Prime cost plus Factory Overheads) – Closing Work in Progress

Stocks of Finished goods should be adjusted to Cost of Production in order to arrive at the Cost of Goods sold.

Cost of Goods sold = Opening stock of finished goods + Cost of Production – Closing stock of finished Goods

Absorption of Overheads: Absorption is the allotment of overheads to cost units. A very important task for the purpose of proper costing is the determination of the amount, which should be charged to each cost unit – each product and each job. The process of charging overheads to different cost units is known as overhead absorption. Factory overheads may be charged to production either on the basis of predetermined rates or on the basis of actual expenses incurred. An overhead absorption rate is usually applied to charging the amount of overhead expenses to respective cost units. It is a 'a ratio obtained by dividing the amount of overheads by some activity factor or base.'

Common Overhead Absorption Methods

Factory overheads Absorption Methods: (a) Direct Labour Hour Method; (b) Direct Labour Cost Method; (c) Direct Material Cost Method; (d) Prime Cost Method; (e) Production Unit Method; (f) Machine Hour Rate Method.

Office and Administration Overheads: (a) A Predetermined Rate; (b) A Percentage of Factory Cost.

Selling and Distribution Overheads: (a) Estimated Rate per unit; (b) Percentage on Factory Cost Method; (c) Percentage on Selling Price Method.

Among these absorption methods, suitable methods would be selected to allot the overheads to various cost units. Commonly used method for factory overhead is direct labour cost method and for office expenses percentage on works cost method and for selling expenses an estimated rate per article.

13.14 Installation of a Costing System

A costing system is an established set of procedures, rules, cost records, etc., for the purpose of achieving specified objective at minimum cost. It forms the basis for future operations. All types of concerns can adopt no one single system. Each concern may design and install a system of its own depending upon its requirements. It may establish the practice and procedure of making cost records. The need for installing a costing system should be justified by a cost-benefit analysis. The benefits expected from the costing system should more than compensate the expenses of installing and operating the system. When a decision to install a system is taken, it should be so designed as to serve the purpose of the particular concern. It should be useful in accordance with the objectives of costing and be flexible enough to adapt itself to changing conditions.

Basic Consideration or Requisites of a Good Costing System

1. The costing system should be simple and easy to operate. It must suit to the requirements of the concern.

2. The benefits derived from the system must more than compensate the expenses incurred in the installation and operation of the system in the organization. In short, the system should be highly economical.

3. The system should facilitate closer coordination among the various divisions in the organization.

4. The system should not disturb the existing organizational set up and if necessary, it should be introduced gradually.

5. The employees concerned should be able to understand the system without much difficulty. The purpose of costing records and reports should be clear to all.

6. There should be promptness and regularity in the preparation and presentation of cost reports.

Steps involved in the Installation

Before installing a costing system all care should be taken to study and analyze all aspects involved as otherwise, the system will be a misfit and its full advantage may not be derived. Special attention should be taken to collect information about the various aspects of the organization. The size of the firm, the nature of business, the nature, method, and stages of production, the number of varieties and quantities of each product and such other technical aspects should be examined carefully. The analysis of materials and wage payment systems should be done.

Forms and records of original entry should be so designed as to involve minimum clerical work and cost. There should be facility to exercise proper control over the system and adopt efficient reporting system. The management requirements and the policy adopted by them towards cost control should be kept in view.

Some formal steps such as codification and classification, establishment of cost centers, guidelines for allocation of indirect costs, introduction of formats and periodical reports, and post installation appraisal of costing system should also be taken to operate the system more effectively.

Difficulties in installing a costing System

Just as any system is opposed in the beginning, the costing system may have to encounter implementation problems. Some of the problems are as follows:

Lack of support from top management: Effective functioning of nay system requires wholehearted support from the management. Otherwise the system will fail or may not produce the desired results. Management has all responsibility to receive the reports and feed backs and take necessary actions on the reports. When management lacks interest in the system [i.e., may accept the system but may not encourage], the system will fail miserably.

Lack of cooperation from the staff: The tendency of the staff is to resist any new system at the beginning and may not extend full cooperation for the system to function effectively. If the tendency continues further and refuse to cooperate then problems may arise.

Different Authority Structure: The costing system may be based on formal authority structure, but in reality there may exist a different authority structure. For example, if trade unions have greater influence in the decision-making process, then the system may run into difficulties.

Changing Environment: Changing environment has greater influence on business operations. The market may change, the production process may change and the management ideas may change. If the costing system fails to take account of the changes, then the system will fail to deliver the desired results and may run into difficulties.

Lack of overall Control on the system: The system should be watched continuously. When some part of the system breaks down, it should be set right then and there. Otherwise the whole system will break down. For example, if inventory is not properly controlled, then the whole material control system may break down. Ultimately the whole cost accounting system may fail.

Lack of clarity on Objectives: The cost accounting department staff should be clear about the priorities and objectives of the system. They should know the purpose of information collected and its end use. If not, they may not collect correct information or may send wrong or inadequate information. In addition if the cost accountant is not given proper status in the organization, he may not be able to collect information from others without fear or favour. Well-trained and adequate staff should also assist him.

13.15 Inventory Valuation

Meaning of Inventory Valuation

Inventory generally refers to stock or stock in trade. In a trading concern, it refers to goods meant for resale or unsold goods. In a manufacturing concern, it includes items such as raw materials, semi-finished goods, and finished goods. The Institute of Chartered Accountants of India (ICAI) defines in Accounting Standard 2 inventories as tangible properties held:

(a) For sale in the ordinary course of business, or

(b) In the process of production for such sale; or

(c) For consumption in the production of goods or services for sale, including maintenance supplies and consumables other than machinery parts

The inventory valuation is done at the end of each financial year in order to assess the operating performance (i.e., to find out profit or loss) and the financial position of the business (along with others of the business through the balance sheet). Generally inventory is valued at cost or market price, whichever is lower. The basis of stock valuation adopted should be consistent over a period in order to make comparative evaluation meaningful.

Objectives of Inventory Valuation

(a) Determination of Trading Profit: Inventory is an important item for ascertaining the trading profit or gross profit. Gross profit is the excess of sales over cost of goods sold. Cost of goods sold is computed by adjusting the opening and closing stocks to purchases, as shown follows:

$$\text{Cost of goods sold} = \text{Opening stock} + \text{Purchases} - \text{Closing stock.}$$

From the above equation it may be understood that the values of stocks influence the cost and thereby affect the gross profit. For example, over valuation of closing stock will reduce the cost and increase the current profit and reduce profits of subsequent years and vice versa.

(b) Determination of Financial Position: Inventory plays an important role in the ascertainment of the financial position of a business. Closing stock is shown as a current asset in the balance sheet. Over and under valuation of stock will give a misleading picture about the working capital position and the overall financial position of the business.

Methods of Stocktaking

Stocktaking refers to the physical verification of the items of inventory in order to ascertain the value for accounting purposes. Either one or combination of the following two methods can make the physical verification: (a) Periodic Inventory System and (b) Perpetual Inventory System.

Periodic Inventory: It refers to a system where stocktaking is usually done periodically; say once or twice in a year. It is actually done holding up purchases and sales for a day or two or a week. Under this method, the items of inventory are physically counted, weighed and verified thoroughly depending upon the nature of items. Then they are listed out in a Stock Sheet and priced and values ascertained.

Perpetual Inventory System: This is a method of recording store balances after every receipt and issue to facilitate regular checking and to obviate to close down for stocktaking. A programme of continuous stocktaking follows a perpetual inventory. Perpetual inventory means the system of records, whereas continuous stocktaking means the physical checking of those records with actual stock. Under this method separate stock ledgers are prepared for each of the items of inventory e.g., stores ledger, work in progress ledger, finished goods ledger. The inventory purchases and issues are recorded in these ledgers on a continuous basis. Hence, these ledgers show the balances of the respective items of inventory at any point of time. The physical verification is done on a continuous basis by comparing the physical balance with book balance. Discrepancies, if any, are located, investigated and necessary actions taken immediately. It is commonly used in large business concerns.

Valuation of Inventory

The method of inventory valuation is very important because it determines the amount of firm's investment in inventory and it influences the firm's reported income. In Financial accounting, the inventory is traditionally valued at lower of the cost or market value. On the other hand, in Cost accounting it is valued at cost of production. Hence, the valuation of socks in two sets of books will be different and there will be difference in profits shown by financial and cost accounting records. This difference will be reconciled through a Reconciliation Statement.

Bases of Inventory Valuation

Historical Cost: The actual cost of raw materials, Work in Progress, and Finished Goods is the most logical method of valuing inventory. Cost Accounting (Records) Rules also provide that the inventory should be valued 'at cost'. Historical cost of inventories is the expenditure incurred for bringing inventory in a saleable condition. Accounting Standard 2 of the Institute of Chartered Accountants Of India states that historical cost represents an appropriate combination of cost of purchase, cost of conversion, and other costs incurred in the normal course of business bringing the inventory up to the present location and condition.

Lower of the Cost or Market Price (LCM): Under this method, the inventory is valued at cost or market price whichever is lower. The market price may be lower than the cost when the price levels of declining (during deflation) and the inventory may become obsolete because of technological and other changes. It is a conservative method. It shows a lower income than the income shown under the cost method. However, when prices fluctuate, this method switches to period by period from cost to market price and vice versa. This reduces the usefulness of cost data for managerial analysis. It expects only losses but not gains.

Net Realizable Value Method: This method is used for inventories, which are damaged or partly obsolete. Net realizable value means the estimated selling price less cost of completion. Normally the stock is valued at historical cost as the selling price will be less. The loss incurred by writing down the stock to the net realizable value is adjusted to the profit and loss account. The inventory value, under this method, should not exceed the expected realizable value.

Replacement Cost Method: Under this method, the inventories are valued at a price, which is equal to the current acquisition cost either by production or at a price that would have to be paid for those items at the inventory date. Or simply the replacement value may be taken as 'market value' or 'reproduction value'. This method is a conservative method since it takes into consideration all possible losses but not expected profits. Hence, the inventory is valued at the minimum of (a) historical cost; (b) replacement value; and (c) net realizable value. This method is not approved by Income Tax Authorities. Similarly the accountants also do not follow this method in practice.

Example 1

The following purchases and issues were made in a company:

1-8-2002	Purchases	300 units at Rs.15
6-8-2002	Issues	200 units
10-8-2002	Purchases	400 units at Rs.20
15-8-2002	Issues	450 units
22-8-2002	Purchases	400 units at Rs.25

What will be the value of stock on 22-8-2002 as per (a) FIFO; and (b) LIFO?

Solution (a) FIFO method

Stores Ledger Account

Date	Receipts			Issues			Balances		
	Qty.	Price Rs.	Amount Rs.	Qty.	Price Rs.	Amount Rs.	Qty.	Price Rs.	Amount Rs.
1-8-02	300	15	4 500	--	--	--	300	15	4,500
6-8-02	--	--	--	200	15	3,000	100	15	1,500
10-8-02	400	20	8,000	--	--	--	100	15	
							400	20	9,500
15-8-02	--	--	--	100	15	1,500			
				350	20	7,000	50	20	1,000
22-8-02	400	25	10,000	--	--	--	50	20	
							400	25	11,000

Value of Closing Inventory as on 22.8.2002 = Rs.11,000

Methods of determining Historical Cost of Inventories

Accounting Standard 2 of ICAI recommends the use of the following for determining the historical cost of inventories for valuation purposes.

First In First Out (FIFO) Method: Under this method, the stock received first (oldest stock) is issued first. In other words, the stock received last (latest stock) remains in the stock. Their relevant prices are used for pricing the issues as well as inventory. Accordingly the closing inventory is valued at latest purchase prices and issues of stocks are valued at oldest purchase prices.

Merits

1. This method is simple and easy to operate.
2. It is useful when there prevails deflationary conditions (i.e., falling prices).
3. Old stock is cleared first and closing stock is valued at latest cost.
4. The inventory valuation is close to current replacement cost.

Demerits

1. This method is not suitable when inflationary conditions prevail.
2. The cost of goods sold will be understated and profits and stock will be overstated.
3. Inventory cost may not reflect current price.
4. When there is many inventory prices the chances of committing clerical errors are more.

Last In First Out (LIFO) Method: Under this method the stock received last (latest purchases) is issued first. In other words, the stock received first (oldest stock) remains in stock. The relevant prices are used for pricing the issues as well as inventory. Accordingly the closing inventory is valued at oldest purchases and issues of stocks are valued at latest purchase prices.

Merits

1. This method is simple and easy to operate. It matches current costs with current revenues.
2. During inflation it minimizes distortions. Inventory is valued at lowest possible values and reduces income tax liability.
3. Inventories are charged to cost of production at current market prices.

Demerits

1. It is not a good method when prices fluctuate frequently.
2. During inflation, profits and inventory values are understated in the financial statements.
3. When there is too many inventory prices, the chances of committing clerical errors are more.

Weighted Average Price Method: Dividing the total cost of inventory (i.e., total quantity x price) by total quantity gives the weighted average price. Every time, whenever inventory is received, it is calculated before any issue is made. All issues of stocks to cost of production are charged at weighted average price. The closing inventory will remain at weighted average price.

Merits

1. When there are wide fluctuations in prices of different inventories, this would be highly suitable. It will even out such fluctuations.

2. Chances of clerical errors are less.

Demerits

1. When there are too many purchases at different prices, it becomes difficult to calculate issue rates.

2. It is used only with periodic inventory method.

3. There is variation between cost of production and actual cost.

Base Stock Method: Base Stock is the minimum stock, which a business concern should maintain in order to maintain production schedule uninterrupted. Usually the price at which first lot of stock was purchased will be used to value the base stock. Value will remain constant and any stock excess of base stock will be valued by any other method, say FIFO or LIFO etc. If the actual stock falls below the base stock, then the reduced actual stock will be treated as base stock in future. And future-closing stock will be valued based on revised base stock. Refineries, chemical and leather concerns, etc., use this method.

Standard Price Method: This method is not based on historical cost. It is usually adopted by manufacturing concerns using standard costing system. Under this method, standard price is set after considering various factors affecting the price. The actual purchase price has no relevance for valuation purpose. All issues and closing inventory are valued at standard price. At the end of a period the difference between standard price and actual price, called price variance, is adjusted to costing profit and loss account.

(b) LIFO method

Stores Ledger Account

Date	Receipts			Issues			Balances		
	Qty.	Price	Amount	Qty.	Price	Amount	Qty.	Price	Amount
		Rs.	Rs.		Rs.	Rs.		Rs.	Rs.
1.8.02	300	15	4,500	--	--	--	300	15	4,500
6.8.02	--	--	--	200	15	3,000	100	15	1,500
10.8.02	400	20	8,000	--	--	--	100	15	
							400	20	9,500
15.8-02	--	--	--	400	20	8,000			
				50	15	750	50	15	750
22.8.02	400	25	10,00')				50	15	
							400	25	10,750

Value of closing inventory as on 22.8.2002 = Rs.10,750

Example 2

Prepare a Stores Ledger Account and find out the value of stock as on 30.8.2002 using Weighted Average Price method of inventory pricing.

2002 August 1	Opening balance 50 units at Rs.3 per unit
4	Issued 2 units
8	Purchased 48 units at Rs.4 per unit
9	Issued 20 units
15	Purchased 76 units at Rs.3 per unit
22	Received back into stores 19 units out of 20 units issued on 9th August
30	Issued to production 10 units

Solution

Date	Receipts			Issues			Balances		
	Qty.	Price Rs.	Amount Rs.	Qty.	Price Rs.	Amount Rs.	Qty.	Price Rs.	Amount Rs.
Aug. 1	--	--	--	--	--	--	50	3.00	150.00
4				2	3.00	6.00	48	3.00	144.00
8	48	4.00	192	--	--	--	96	3.50	336.00
9	--	--	--	20	3.50	70.00	76	3.50	266.00
15	76	3.00	228	--	--	--	152	3.25	494.00
22	19	3.50	66.50	--	--	--	171	3.28	560.50
30	--	--	--	10	3.28	32.80	161	3.28	527.70

Working, notes:

1. Weighted Average on 8.8.02 $= \dfrac{(144 + 192)}{96} = 3.50$

2. Weighted Average on 15.8.02 $= \dfrac{(266 + 228)}{152} = 3.25$

3. Weighted Average on 22.8.02 $= \dfrac{(494 + 66.50)}{171} = 3.28$

PREPARATION OF COST SHEET

Illustration 1

From the following particulars of Product X, prepare a Production Statement (Cost Sheet) for the month of September 2002.

Raw Materials:	Rs.
Opening stock	40,000
Purchases	3,00,000
Closing stock	20,000
Direct labour	1,20,000
Factory overheads	45,000
Office and Administration overheads	55,000
Selling and distribution expenses	20,000
Finished stock:	
Opening stock 1,000 units at Rs.11.20 per unit	
Closing stock 3,000 units at current cost price	
Profit on sales at 20 per cent	
Units produced 50,000 units	

Solution

Production Statement of Product X for the month of September 2002

Particulars		Units	Total Cost Rs.	Cost per unit Rs.
Raw materials:				
Opening stock	40,000			
Add Purchases	3,00,000	50,000		
	3,40,000			
Less Closing stock	20,000		3,20,000	6.40
Direct labour			1,20,000	2.40
Prime cost			4,40,000	8.80
Factory overheads			45,000	0.90
Factory cost			4,85,000	9.70
Office and Admn. Overheads			55,000	1.10
Cost of Production			5,40,000	10.80
Add Opening stock at Rs.11.20		1,000	11,200	
		51,000	5,51,200	
Less Closing stock at Rs.10.80		3,000	32,400	
Cost of goods sold		48,000	5,18,800	10.81
Selling and Distribution expenses			40,000	0.83
Cost of sales		48,000	5,58,800	11.64
Profit at 25% on cost of sales		48,000	1,39,700	2.91
Sales		48,000	6,98,500	14.55

Profit on sales = 20%; If sales = 100then profit = 20 and cost = 80.

If cost is 80 then profit is 20 i.e., 25% on cost $\left(\frac{20}{80}\right) \times 100$.

Closing stock is valued at current price of Rs.10.80.

Illustration 2

The following extracts of costing information relate to product X for the year ending 31.3.2002.

	Rs.
Purchase of Raw materials	48,000
Direct wages	40,000
Stock of Raw material on 1.4.2001	8,000
Stock of finished goods on 1.4.2001 (1,600 units)	6,400
Stock of Raw material on 31.3.2002	8,800
Stock of finished goods (3,200 units) at current cost of production	
Works overheads	16,800
Work in progress on 1.4.2001	1,920
Work in progress on 31.3.2002	6,400
Office on cost	3,200
Sales (finished product)	1,20,000

Selling and distribution cost is 40 paise per unit. During the year 25 600 units were produced. Calculate the cost of production and extend the cost sheet to show the profit also.

Solution

Cost Sheet for the year ending 31.3.2002

Particulars		Total cost Rs.	Cost per unit Rs.
Raw materials consumed: Rs.			
Opening stock	8,000		
Add: Purchases	48,000		
	56,000		
Less: Closing stock	8,800	47,200	
Direct wages		40,000	
Prime cost		87,200	3.41
Factory overheads		16,800	
Gross factory cost		1,04,000	
Add: Opening work in progress		1,920	
		1,05,920	
Less: Closing work in progress		6,400	
Net factory cost		99,520	3.89
Office on cost		3,200	
Cost of production units	25,600	1,02,720	4.01
Add: Opening stock of finished goods	1,600	6,400	
	27,200	1,09,120	

Less: Closing stock of finished goods		3,200	12,840	
Cost of goods sold		24,000	96,280	4.01
Selling cost at 40 paise per unit sold			9,600	0.40
Cost of sales	units	24,000	1,05,880	4.41
Profit (balancing figure)			14,120	0.59
Sales	units	24,000	1,20,000	5.00

$$\text{Closing stock of finished goods} = \frac{1,02,720 \times 3,200}{25,600} = 12,840$$

Illustration 3

The following figures relate to the costing of a manufacturer of electric fans of one uniform size and quality for a period of three months:

	Rs.
Completed stock on 1.10.2002	Nil
Completed stock on 31.12 2002.	2,02,500
Stock of Raw materials on 1.10.2002	50,000
Stock of Raw materials on 31.12.2002	35,000
Factory wages	7,50,000
Indirect charges	1,25,000
Materials purchased	3,25,000
Sales (2500 fans)	11,25,000

The number of fans manufactures during the three months was 3,000.

Prepare a statement, showing the cost per fan and the price to be quoted for 750 fans to realize the same percentage of profit as was realized during the months referred to above, assuming identical costs.

Solution

Cost Sheet of Electric fans for the quarter ending 31.12.2002

	No of fan manufactured: 3,000	
	Per unit Rs.	Total Rs.
Stock of raw materials 1.10.2002		50,000
Add: Purchases		3,25,000
		3,75,000
Less: Closing stock of raw materials		35,000
Raw materials consumed	113.33	3,40,000
Factory wages	250.00	7,50,000
Prime cost	363.33	10,90,000
Indirect charges	41.67	1,25,000

Cost of production	405.00	12,15,000
Less: Closing stock of finished goods (500 units)		2,02,500
Cost of goods sold (2,500 units)	405.00	10,12,500
Profit (10% of sales)	45.00	1,12,500
Selling Price	450.00	11,25,000

Quotation for 750 fans	Rs.
Cost of production of 750 fans at Rs.405.00	3,03,750
Profit at Rs.45.00 per fan (10% on Sales)	33,750
Selling Price of 750 fans at Rs.450.00	3,37,500

Illustration 4

SF ltd., is manufacturing refrigerators and the following details are furnished in respect of its factory operations for the year ended 31st December 2001:

	Rs.	Rs.
Work in process 1.1.2001:		
At prime cost	51,000	
Manufacturing expenses	15,000	66,000
Work in process 31.12.2001:		
At prime cost	45,000	
Manufacturing expenses	9,000	54,000
Opening stock of Raw materials		2,25,000
Purchases of raw materials		4,77,000
Direct labour		1,71,000
Manufacturing expenses		84,000
Closing stock of Raw materials		2,04,000

On the basis of the above data, prepare a statement showing the cost of production. Also indicate separately the amount of manufacturing expenses, which enter into the cost of production.

Solution

Statement showing Cost of Production of Refrigerators for the year ended 31.12.2001

	Rs.	Rs.
Work in Process on 1.1.2001 (at prime cost)		51,000
Raw materials: opening stock	2,25,000	
Purchases	4,77,000	
	7,02,000	
Less Closing stock	2,04,000	4,98,000
Direct wages		1,71,000
		7,20,000
Less Closing work in process (at prime cost)		45,000
Prime cost		6,75,000

Manufacturing expenses:		
In opening work in process	15,000	
Add Expenses for the year	84,000	
	99,000	
Less in closing work in process	9,000	90,000
Cost of Production		7,65,000

Illustration 5

The following details are available from a company's books.

	Rs.
Stock of Raw materials on 1.1.2002	12,800
Stock of finished goods on 1.1.2002	28,000
Purchases during the year	2,92,000
Productive wages	1,98,800
Sale of finished goods	5,92,000
Stock of finished goods on 31.12.2002	30,000
Stock of Raw materials on 31.12.2002	13,600
Works overheads	43,736
Office and general expenses	35,524

The company is about to send a tender for a plant. The costing department estimates that the materials required would cost Rs.20,000 and wages for making the plant would cost Rs.12,000. Tender is to be made keeping a net profit of 20% on selling price. State what would be the amount of the tender, if based on the percentages. (B.Com., Madras University)

Solution

Cost Sheet for year ended 31st December 2002

	Rs.	Rs.
Opening Stock of Materials	12,800	
Add: Purchases during the year	2,92,000	
	3,04,800	
Less: Closing Stock of Materials	13,600	
Materials consumed		2,91,200
Productive wages		1,98,800
Prime Cost		4,90,000
Add: Works overheads		43,736
Factory Cost		5,33,736
Add: Office and General overheads		35,524
Cost of Production		5,69,260
Add: Opening Stock of Finished Goods		28,000
		5,97,260

Less: Closing Stock of Finished Goods		30,000
Cost of Goods sold		5,67,260
Profit		24,740
Sale of Finished Goods		5,92,000

Absorption of Overhead Rates:

(a) Percentage of Factory Overheads to Productive Wages $= \frac{\text{Rs.}43{,}736}{1{,}98{,}800} \times 100 = 22\%$

(b) Percentage of Office on cost to Factory cost $= \frac{\text{Rs.}35{,}524}{5{,}33{,}736} \times 100 = 6.66\%$

	Rs.
Materials	20,000
Productive wages	12,000
Prime Cost	32,000
Factory overheads (22% on Wages)	2,640
Factory Cost	34,640
Office on cost (6.66% on Factory Cost)	2,307
Total Cost	36,947
Profit (20% on selling price)	9,237
Tender Price	46,184

Illustration 6

The following data have been extracted from the books of a Paper Mill in December 2002. Prepare a Cost Sheet and find out the cost per ton of special paper.

Direct Materials:	Paper pulp.500 tons at Rs.500 per ton;
	Other Materials.100 tons at Rs.300 per ton.
Direct Wages:	80 skilled men at Rs.30 per day for 25 days
	40 unskilled men at Rs.20 per day for 25 days
Direct Expenses:	Special Equipment.Rs.30 000
	Special dyes -- Rs.1 000
Factory Expenses:	Variable at 100% and Fixed at 60% on direct wages.

Administration overheads at 10% and selling and distribution overheads at 15% on Factory cost

400 tons of special paper was manufactured and Rs.8 000 was realized by the sale of waste material during the course of manufacture. The scrap value of the special equipment after utilization in manufacture is nil. **(C.A. Inter adapted)**

Solution

Cost Sheet of Paper Mill for December 2002

Particulars	Cost per ton Rs.	Total Rs.
Direct Materials:		
Paper Pulp 500 tons at Rs.500 per ton	625.00	2,50,000
Other materials 100 tons at Rs. 300	75.00	30,000

Particulars	Cost per ton Rs.	Total Rs.
	700.0	2,80,000
Less: Sale of waste realized	20.00	8,000
	680.0	2,72,000
Direct wages:		
Skilled men. $80 \times 30 \times 25$	150.00	60,000
Unskilled men. $40 \times 20 \times 25$	50.00	20 000
Direct Expenses:		
Special Equipment	75.00	30,000
Special dyes	25.00	10,000
Prime Cost	980.00	3,92,000
Factory Expenses: Variable 100% on Wages	200.00	80,000
Fixed -- 60% on Wages	120.00	48,000
Factory Cost	1,300.00	5,20,000
Administration overheads. 10% on Factory cost	130.00	52,000
Cost of Production	1,430.00	5,72,000
Selling overheads.15% on Factory cost	195.00	78,000
Total Cost	1,625.00	6,50,000

Illustration 7

	Rs.		Rs.
To Cost of materials	80,000	By Sales (1,000 coolers)	4,00,000
To Direct Wages	120,000		
To Other manufacturing cost	50,000		
To Gross Profit C/D	1,50,000		
	4,00,000		4,00,000
To Office salaries	60,000	By Gross Profit b/d	1,50,000
To Rent and insurance	10,000		
To Selling expenses	30,000		
To General expenses	20,000		
To Net Profit	30,000		
Total	1,50,000		1,50,000

For the year ending 31st December 2003, it is estimated that

(a) Output and sales will be 1200 coolers.

(b) Prices of material will rise by 20% on the 2002 level.

(c) Wages will increase by 5%.

(d) Manufacturing cost will rise in proportion to the prime cost.

(e) Selling expenses per unit will remain unaffected.

(f) Other expenses will also remain constant.

You are required to prepare a Cost Sheet showing the price at which the coolers should be marketed in order to earn a profit of 10% on selling price.

Solution

Cost Sheet for the year ending 31th December 2002

	Output: 1,000 coolers	
	Per unit (Rs.)	Total (Rs.)
Cost of materials	80.00	80,000
Direct wages	120.00	1,20,000
Prime cost	200.00	2,00,000
Manufacturing expenses	50.00	50,000
Factory cost	250.00	2,50,000
Office salaries	60.00	60,000
Rent and insurance	10.00	10,000
General expenses	20.00	20,000
Cost of production	340.00	3,40,000
Selling expenses	30.00	30,000
Cost of sales or Total Cost	370.00	3,70,000
Profit	30.00	30,000
Sales	400.00	4,00,000

Estimated Cost Sheet for the year ending 31st December 2003

		Estimated output: 1,200 coolers	
	Rs.	Cost per unit (Rs.)	Total (Rs.)
Materials	80.00		
Add: 20% increase	16.00	96.00	1,15,200
Wages	120.00		
Add: 5% increase	6.00	126.00	1,51,200
Prime cost		222.00	2,66,400
Manufacturing expenses (25% on Prime cost)		55.50	66,600
Factory cost		277.50	3,33,000
Office salaries (Remain constant)		50.00	60,000
Rent and insurance (Constant)		8.33	10,000
Other expenses (Constant)		16.67	20,000
Cost of Production		352.50	4,23,000
Selling expenses (Constant per unit)		30.00	36,000
Cost of Sale or Total Cost		382.50	4,59,000
Profit (10% on selling price)		42.50	51,000
Selling Price		425.00	5,10,000

Computation of Profit: 10% on Selling Price

If selling price is Rs.100 then profit is Rs.10 and cost is Rs.90 (100 – 10)

If cost is Rs.90 then profit is Rs.10.

If cost is Rs.382.50 then profit is $= \left(\frac{382.50}{90}\right) \times 10 =$ Rs. 42.50.

Total Profit = Rs. 42.50 × 1200 = Rs. 51,000

Illustration 8

The cost structure of an Iron box, the selling price of which is Rs.500 is as follows:

Direct material -- 50% of Total cost

Direct wages -- 30% of Total cost

Overhead -- Balance

Due to anticipated increase in existing material price by 20% and in the labour rate by 10%, the existing profit would come down by 30% if the selling price remains unchanged. Prepare a Comparative Statement showing the cost, selling price and profit under the present conditions and with the increase expected for future, assuming the same percentage of profit on cost as at present is to be earned (calculations may be made to the nearest rupee).

(I.C.W.A. Final)

Solution

Since the total cost is not given, it may be assumed as C. Selling price (SP) = Rs. 500

Elements of cost	Existing	Anticipated
Material	0.50 C	0.60 C (20% increase)
Labour	0.30 C	0.33 C (10% increase)
Overhead	0.20 C	0.20 C (No change)
Total Cost	1.00 C	1.13 C
Profit (SP – C)	(Rs.500 – C)	(Rs.500 – 1.13 C)

The anticipated profit is less by 30% of existing profit. In other words the difference between the existing profit and anticipated is equal to 30% of current profit.

$$(500 - C) - (500 - 1 \cdot 13\ C) = 30\% \text{ of } (500 - C)$$

$$500 - C - 500 + 1.13\ C = 150 - 0.30\ C$$

$$0.43\ C = 150$$

$$C = \frac{150}{0.43} = 350 = \text{Total cost}$$

Comparative Statement showing Cost, Profit and Selling Price

Particulars	Present Condition	Anticipated Conditions	
		SP constant	SP changed
	Rs.	(Rs.)	(Rs.)
Selling Price	500	175	564
Direct Material	175	210	210
Direct Wages	105	115	115

Overheads	70	70	70
Total Cost	350	395	395
Profit	150	105	169
		(30% of Selling Price)	

Illustration 9

Oil India is a bulk distributor of high-octane petrol. A periodic inventory of petrol on hand is taken when the books are closed on at the end of each month. The following summary of information is available for the month of June 2002.

	Rs.
Sales	9,45,000
General administrative cost	25,000
Opening Stock: 10 000 liters at Rs.30 per liter	3,00,000
Purchases (including freight in)	

June 1, 20,000 liters at Rs.28.50 per liter

30, 10,000 liters at Rs.30.30 per liter

Closing Stock on 30th June 13,000 liters

Compute the following data by FIFO, LIFO, and Weighted Average Methods of Inventory costing:

(a) Value of inventory on 30th June

(b) Amount of cost of goods sold for June

(c) Profit or loss for June **(C.A. inter adapted)**

Solution

First In First Out Method: inventory will be valued at the latest purchase prices

(a) Value of Closing Stock

	Rs.
10,000 liters at Rs.30.30	3,03,000
3,000 liters at Rs.28.50	85,500
Value of Closing Stock	3,88,500

(b) Amount of the cost of goods sold for June (at oldest prices)

	Rs.
Opening Stock.10 000 @ Rs.30	3,00,000
Purchases: June 1.20 000 liters @ Rs.28.50	5,70,000
June 30.10 000 liters @ Rs.30.30	3,03,000
Cost of goods available for sale	11,73,000
Less: Closing Stock (as valued above)	3,88,500
Cost of goods sold	7,84,500

(c) Profit or Loss for June

	Rs.
Sales	9,45,000
Less: Cost of goods sold	7,84,500

Gross Profit	1,60,500
Less: General Administrative Cost	25,000
Net Profit	1,35,500

Last In First Out Method: inventory will be valued at the oldest prices

(a) Value of Closing Stock

3,000 liters at Rs.30.00	90,000
10 000 liters at Rs.30.30	3,03,000
Value of Closing Stock	3,93,000

(b) Amount of cost of goods sold for June (at latest prices)

	Rs.
Value of purchases plus opening stock	11,73,000
Less: Closing Stock (as valued above)	3,93,000
Cost of goods sold	7,80,000

(c) Profit for June

	Rs.
Sales	9,45,000
Less: Cost of goods sold	7,80,000
Gross Profit	1,65,000
Less: General Administrative Cost	25,000
Net Profit	1,40,000

Weighted Average Price Method: inventory will be valued at the last Weighted Average Price

(a) Value of Closing Stock

13,000 liters at Rs.30.00 Rs.3,90,000

The rate has been arrived at as follows:

Weighted Average after first purchase

$$= \frac{(10{,}000 \times \text{Rs. } 30.00) + (20{,}000 \times 28.50)}{(10{,}000 + 20{,}000)}$$

$$= \frac{8{,}70{,}000}{30{,}000} = \text{Rs. } 29.00$$

Balance after first issue at Rs.29.00 per liter = 3 000 liters

Weighted Average after last purchase

$$= \frac{(3{,}000 \times 29.00) + (10{,}000 \times 30.30)}{(3{,}000 + 10{,}000)}$$

$$= \frac{3{,}90{,}000}{13{,}000} = \text{Rs. } 30.00$$

(b) Amount of cost of goods sold

	Rs.
Value of purchases plus opening stock	11,73,000
Less: Closing Stock (as valued above)	3,90,000
Cost of goods sold	7,83,000

(c) Profit for June

	Rs.
Sales	9,45,000
Less: Cost of goods sold	7,83,000
Gross Profit	1,62,000
Less: General Administrative Cost	25,000
Net Profit	1,37,000

REVIEW QUESTIONS

1. Define Cost Accounting.
2. What are the objectives of Cost Accounting?
3. List out the functions of cost accounting.
4. What are the advantages and limitations of cost accounting?
5. Explain the following terms: (a) Cost Unit, (b) Cost Center, (c) Cost Estimation and Ascertainment, (d) Absorption of overheads.
6. Describe various methods of Cost Accounting.
7. What are the various techniques of costing?
8. Describe various costing systems.
9. How can costs be classified? Explain
10. What are the various elements of cost?
11. What is a Cost Sheet? Give format of a Cost Sheet.

REVIEW PROBLEMS

12. The following particulars relate the costing of a manufacturer of electric fans of one uniform size and quality for a period of six months:

	Rs.
Completed Stock on 1.1.2002	Nil
Completed Stock on 30.6.2002	40,500
Stock of Materials on 1.1.2002	10,000
Stock of Materials on 30.6.2002	7,000
Productive Wages	1,50,000
Overheads	25,000
Materials purchased	75,000
Sales	2,25,000

The number of fans manufactured during the three months was 6 000. Prepare Cost Sheet showing the cost per fan and the price to be quoted for 1500 fans to realize the same percentage of profit as was realized during the three months referred to above, assuming identical costs.

(**Answer:** refer illustration 3)

13. Following are the particulars obtained from the records of Excel Engineering Company for the year ended 31st December 2002:

	Rs.
Cost of materials	40,000
Wages paid	60,000

Factory overheads	25,000
Salaries	30,000
Rent and Insurance	5,000
Selling expenses	15,000
General expenses	10,000
Sales	2,00,000

During 2002 the company produced and sold 500 sewing machines and plans to produce and sell 600 machines during 2003. you are required to prepare a statement showing the price at which machines should be sold so as to show a profit of 10% on the selling price. The following additional information is supplied to you:

(a) The price of materials will rise by 20% on previous year's level.

(b) Wage rates will rise by 5%.

(c) Factory overheads will rise in proportion to the combined cost of materials and wages.

(d) Selling expenses per unit will remain constant.

(e) Other expenses will remain unaffected by the rise in output.

(**Answer:** Refer illustration 7)

14. The following particulars have been taken out from the books of Engineering Company for the year ended 31st December 2002:

	Rs.
Opening Stock of materials	50,000
Purchase of raw materials	12,00,000
Carriage on purchases	60,000
Manufacturing wages	7,00,000
Factory on cost	1,96,000
Establishment and general charges	1,49,170
Closing Stock of materials	75,000

Find out the Works Cost and Total Cost, the percentage of works expenses on manufacturing wages, and the percentage of establishment charges on Works cost.

The company produced during the year 100 units of 5 HP motors. Work out the price that the company should quote for a motor, which, it is estimated, will require an expenditure of Rs.5,500 in materials and Rs.4,000 in wages, so that it would yield a profit of 331/3 % on selling price.

(**Answer:** 28%, 7%, Production cost Rs.22,80,170, Quotation Price Rs.17,045.10)

15. From the following particulars relating to the manufacture of a standard product during the month of January 2003, prepare a statement showing the cost and profit per unit.

	Rs.
Raw materials consumed	4,00,000
Direct wages	2,40,000
Machine Hours worked	9,500
Machine hour rate	Rs.40 per hour
Office on cost	20% on Works cost

Selling overheads	Rs.10 per unit
Units produced	20,000
Units sold at Rs.10 per unit	18,000

(**Answer:** Total cost Rs.12 81 600, Rs.71.20; Profit Rs.28.80 per unit)

16. A Ltd produces two types of products X and Y. the total expenditure during the period is shown by the books for assembly of 600 units of X and 800 units of Y are as under:

	Rs.
Materials	39,600
Wages	2,400
Stores overheads	3,960
Running expenses of machine	880
Depreciation	440
Labour amenities	300
Factory expenses	6,000
Administration expenses	5,360
Other information	X: Y
Material cost ratio per unit	1: 2
Wages cost per unit	2: 3
Machine utilization	1: 2

Calculate the cost of each product giving reasons for the basis of apportionment adopted by you.

(I.C.W.A. Inter adapted)

(Answer: Total cost of X: Rs.16 655, of Y Rs.42 285)

Hints. Apportionment Ratios: Material cost (1 x 600) : (2 x 800); Wages $(2 \times 600) : (3 \times 800)$; Stores overheads: as a percentage of material cost i.e., $\frac{3960}{39600} = 10\%$; Running expenses and depreciation: (Machine ratio x No of units) $(1 \times 600) : (2 \times 800)$; Works overheads and Labour amenities as percentage on wages.250% and 12.5%; Administration expenses as percentage on works cost)

17. The ABC Co. produces a fan that sells for Rs.600. an increase of 15% in cost of materials and 10% in cost of labour is anticipated. If the only figures available are given below, what must be selling price to give the same percentage of gross profit as before?

(a) Material cost 45% of Total cost

(b) Labour cost 40% of Total cost

(c) Overhead cost 15% of Total cost

(d) The anticipated increased costs in relation to the present selling price would cause a 35% decrease in the amount of the present gross profit.

(B.Com. Madras University, adapted)

(**Answer:** Selling price Rs.664.50; Rate of GP 10.24%; Anticipated cost Rs.596.48)

(Hints: Refer illustration 8)

18. The following information is available on the purchase and issue of a material during the month of January 2003:

Purchased Issued

Purchased	Issued
January 2 -- 200 units at Rs.2 per unit	January 15 -- 250 units
Jan. 10 300 units at Rs.2.40 per unit	20 -- 200 units
Jan. 18 250 units at Rs.2.60 per unit	

Prepare a Statement showing Base stock method of inventory valuation along with LIFO method of pricing material issues. The normal base quantity is 100 units.

(**Answer:** The value of closing inventory is comprised of the following:

100 units (base stock) at Rs.2 per unit =Rs.200
50 units at Rs.2.60 per unit = 130
50 units at Rs.2.40 per unit = 120
100 units at Rs,2 per unit = 200
300 units valued at =Rs.650

14

PRODUCT COSTING METHODS

Learning Objectives

After completing this chapter you should be able to

— Explain the concepts of Job costing, Process costing and their accounting procedures,

— Discuss their advantages, limitations, distinctions, etc.,

— Work out problems in job costing, process costing,

— Explain the concepts of joint products and by-products,

— Describe the accounting methods for joint products and by-products.

Basically there are two methods of costing, viz., Job Order costing and Process Costing. Job order costing is a system of costing, which is applied to non-repetitive, job order type of activities. It is adopted by different types of enterprises in different forms such as batch costing, departmental costing and contract costing. Process costing is a system of costing, which is applied in the case of continuous manufacture and the product passes through distinct stages of processing.

Job Costing or Job Order Costing

14.1 Definition

Job costing may be defined as a system of costing in which the elements of cost are accumulated separately for each job or work order undertaken by an organization. The ICMA terminology defines job costing as "that form of specific order costing which applies where work is undertaken to customers' requirements and each order is of comparatively short duration. The work is usually carried out within a factory or work shop and moves through processes or operations as a continuously identifiable unit." This system is usually adopted by concerns engaged in job order type of production or servicing where a specific job is done for a stipulated price, e.g., job printing, manufacture of special type of equipments, design engineering, repairing, etc. In these cases work may be carried out within the factory or in private households as in plumbing or electrical repairs. Job orders are often undertaken along with the manufacture of goods for sale in open market.

Purpose: The primary purpose of job costing is to bring together all the costs incurred for completing the job. It also ensures that there is proper control over costs incurred, that jobs are completed in time, and that information is available at regular intervals about the jobs completed and progress made with works in process.

Features

1. Every order in job costing is separate. However, it is not essential that the same manufacturing operations are carried out or the same materials be used in respect of each.

2. The job order may be for a number of identical orders or identical products together to form lots or batches as job orders. Each job order or lot or batch may be taken as a cost unit i.e., a job.

3. The cost ascertainment and analysis of various elements of cost of a job is done always relating to a specific order.

4. A job order may relate to several accounting periods and therefore, the job costs are not related to particular periods.

14.2 Advantages

1. Job costing helps management to detect, which jobs are profitable and which is not by enabling the same to know the trend of costs.

2. Future cost estimates for similar works may be made on the basis of accurate record of job costs.

3. Comparing the actual costs against the estimates made while submitting tender for jobs or giving quotations can control efficiency of operation.

4. Wastes, spoilage and defective work can be easily identified with specific jobs or products and responsibility be fixed on departments or individuals.

5. In the case of cost plus contracts, the selling price is dependent upon the actual cost incurred. Job costing provides accurate data for such purposes.

6. The actual overhead costs are compared with the overheads applied at predetermined rates; thus at the end of an accounting period, overhead variances can be analyzed.

7. By adopting predetermined overhead rates in job costing all advantages of budgetary control can be obtained.

14.3 Limitations

1. Job costing is comparatively more expensive as a great deal of clerical work is involved in connection with the estimation of costs, designing and scheduling of production, etc.

2. With the increase in clerical processes, chances of committing errors are more.

3. If major economic changes take place, comparison of cost of a job for one period with that of another becomes meaningless.

4. As the costs ascertained are historical in nature, they may not be useful for future planning and control.

5. It cannot be operated effectively without having a highly developed production control system. It requires an intricate factory organization system.

14.4 Job Cost Accounting Procedure

On receipt of an order from the customer or an indication from the sales department for manufacturing a particular product, a suitable design for the product or job is prepared. The requirements of materials for the product is worked out and a list of operations to be carried out and the departments or individuals to be entrusted with the operations are also prepared.

Job order number: Job costing emphasizes accumulation of cost by specific job or work orders. Hence, it is essential to assign a number for each job.

Production order: A production order is a written order issued to the shops to proceed with the manufacture of a product. It is an important control document and constitutes the authority for work. Usually it contains all relevant information regarding production such as the particulars of the product or job, the quantity to be manufactured, date of start and completion of production, materials required, the operations and various shops involved etc. Production orders may be of two types: production orders for stock and production orders for supply.

Bill of materials: It is a list of all materials and parts required for a job. It is sent along with the production order to the foreman to call for the materials and other parts in order to complete the job. A separate tool list is also prepared for special tools, which may be necessary for a job.

Job Card or Job Cost Sheet: Separate job cost sheets are maintained for each job and all costs relating to the job are recorded there. Cost of raw materials used and direct wages are entered in the job card directly from the cost records, and manufacturing overheads are added on the basis of a predetermined rate. The total factory cost accumulated in the job card is debited to work-in process account at periodic intervals, say a week or month. When the production order is completed, the total cost incurred on completion is credited to work-in-process account. Thus the balance of the work-in-process account at the end of the period represents the incomplete job, i.e., inventory of work-in-process. The job cost sheet serves as a control document by facilitating the comparison of actual cost against estimated cost of a job. It also serves as a guide to pricing and indicates the relative profitability of different jobs.

Specimen job card or job cost sheet

Sources of cost information for Job Order

Material Cost: The bill of material or stores requisitions provides the required cost information as regards materials issued to specific jobs. The particular job order number is indicated in each requisition. Material return notes are used to return excess, surplus or incorrect materials to stores. Scrap and waste arising in the course of manufacture are returned in a similar manner. A periodical analysis of material requisitions, material return notes, and bill of materials is made and cost is totaled daily or weekly. For recording material consumption on a specific job, work-in-process account is debited and stores ledger control account is credited. When the number of issues to jobs is large, a material analysis sheet is prepared. The total of individual jobs is booked to job account and total of material analysis sheet is debited to work-in-process account.

Labour Cost: The information regarding direct labour working on particular jobs can be drawn from the time cards issued to each workman. The time card will indicate the time spent by the worker on each job as well as his time spent for indirect work. Wages paid for indirect work will be treated as works overheads.

Direct Expenses: These expenses are chargeable to particular jobs. They are analyzed and posted in the same way as direct materials or direct wages. The job cost sheet will specifically show the direct expenses relating to a particular job.

Manufacturing Overheads: For accounting manufacturing overheads, the entire factory is treated as one cost center. In that case, one overhead recovery rate is used; say percentage on direct wages or machine hour rate, etc., for charging manufacturing overheads. Or it may be possible to set up two or more cost centers (departments, operations, machines) for overhead cost accounting. In that case, different overhead recovery rates are determined for the respective cost centers. Example: Direct labour hour rate or percentage on direct wages for one, Percentage on material cost for another, Machine hour rate for the third one and so on. The factory overhead costs are charged to various jobs on the basis of one or more predetermined rates.

Administrative Overheads: Office and administrative overheads may be charged to jobs on the basis of a predetermined rate. The basis of percentage on works cost is commonly used for charging the administrative overheads.

Selling and distribution Overheads: These overheads are added to the cost of production to ascertain the total cost of sales. The commonly used method of recovery rate is certain percentage on cost of production, or cost per unit sold. By adding certain percentage of profit to total cost, the selling price is arrived at.

Valuation of Work-in-process (WIP): The WIP account is periodically debited with the direct and indirect manufacturing costs and credited with the total cost of completed jobs as shown in the job cost sheets. The balance of the WIP account represents the cost of incomplete jobs. The balance of WIP account, which is maintained in the cost ledger, shows the value of WIP.

Practical Problems

Illustration 1

The following direct costs were incurred on Job No. 0686 of Beta Engineering Works:

Materials	Rs. 68 300
Wages: Department I	– 800 hours at Rs.5 per hour
Department II	– 600 hours at Rs.8 per hour

Overhead expenses were estimated as follows:

Variable overheads: Department I -- Rs.10 000 for 4000 direct labour hours

Department II – Rs.12 000 for 3000 direct labour hours

Fixed overheads: Estimated at Rs.15 000 for 10 000 hours normal working time.

Prepare a simple job cost sheet for Job No.0686 and estimate the percentage of profit earned if the price quoted was Rs.91 960.

Solution

Job Cost Sheet for Job No. 0686

	Rs.	Rs.
Direct materials		68,300
Direct wages:		
Department I – 800 hrs @ Rs.5.00	4,000	
Department II – 600 hrs @ Rs.8.00	4,800	8,800
Prime cost		77,100

Variable overheads:		
Department I – 800 hrs @ Rs.2.50	2,000	
Department II – 600 hrs @ Rs.4.00	2,400	4,400
Fixed overheads: 1 400 hrs @ Rs.1.50		2,100
Total cost		83,600
Profit at 10% on cost		8,360
Selling price		91,960

Working Notes: Overheads recovery rates

Department I – Rs.10 000/ 4 000 = Rs2.50 per hour

Department II – Rs.12 000/ 3 000 = Rs.4.00 per hour

Fixed overhead rate – Rs.15 000/ 10 000 hours = Rs.1.50

Percentage of profit on cost = Rs.8 360/ 83 600 x 100 = 10%

Illustration 2

A has undertaken a job No.4604. As per cost ledger, the following expenses have been debited to this job. Prepare a job cost sheet and calculate the total amount to be charged to the customer in order to obtain 20% profit on sales. Following are additional information based on normal capacity.

Particulars	Department A	Department B	Total for factory
Budgeted Production in terms of			
Direct labour hours	9,000	13,500	30,000
Budgeted variable overheads	13,500	16,200	

Job cost details:

Direct materials:	(I)	Cast Iron 150 kg at Rs.2 per kg.
	(ii)	Gun metal 50 kg at Rs.10 per kg.
Direct labour:	(I)	Department A 200 hours at Re.1 per hour
	(ii)	Department B 150 hours at Re.0.60 per hour
Direct expenses	--	Special tools Rs.310 (to be paid by the customer)

Solution

Job Cost Sheet for Job No.4604

	Quantity	Rate (Rs.)	Details (Rs.)	Total Cost (Rs.)
Direct materials: Cast Iron	150 kg	2.00	300	
Gun metal	50 kg	10.00	500	

	Quantity (Rs.)	Rate	Details (Rs.)	Total Cost (Rs.)
Direct labour: Dept. A	200 hours	1.00	200	
Dept. B	150 hours	0.60	90	
Direct Expenses				
Prime cost				1,400
Add Variable overheads				
Dept. A (13 500/9000)	200 hours	1.50	300	
Dept. B (16 200/ 13 500)	150 hours	1.20	180	
Fixed overheads (30 000/ 30 000)	350 hours	1.00	350	830
Total cost				2,230
Add Profit (20% 0n sales or 25% on cost)				557.50
Total amount to be charged				2,787.50

Illustration 3

From the following particulars taken out from the books of engineering works in respect of Job No.99, prepare a job cost sheet and calculate the price to give profit of 25% on selling price.

Materials		Rs. 4 010
Wages:	Department A	-- 60 hours at Rs.3 per hour
	Department B	-- 40 hours at Rs.2 per hour
	Department C	-- 20 hours at Rs.5 per hour

Overhead expenses for these departments were estimated as follows:

Variable overheads: Department A Rs. 5 000 for 5 000 hours

Department B Rs.3 000 for 1 500 hours

Department C Rs.2 000 for 500 hours

Fixed overheads: Estimated at Rs.20 000 for 10 000 normal working hours.

Solution

			Amount (Rs.)	
Direct materials			-	4,010
Wages:	Department A	60 hours at Rs.3 per hour	180	
	Department B	–40 hours at Rs.2 per hour	80	

	Department C	– 20 hours at Rs.5 per hour	100	360
Variable Overheads:	Department A	– 60 hours at Re.1	60	
	Department B	– 40 hours at Rs.2	80	
	Department C	– 20 hours at Rs.4	80	220
Fixed overheads: 120 hours at Rs.2 per hour				240
		Total cost		4830
		Profit 25% on S.P or 331/3 % on cost		1,610
		Selling Price		6,440

Workings

Variable overheads recovery rate:

Department A = Rs.5 000/5000 hours = Re. 1 per hour

Department B = Rs.3 000/ 1 500 hours = Rs. 2 per hour

Department C = Rs.2 000/ 500 hours = Rs. 4 per hour

Fixed overheads recovery rate:

Rs.20 000/ 10 000 hours = Rs.2 per hour

Profit percentage on cost:

If selling price is 100, profit is 25 and cost is 75.

If cost is 75, then profit is 25 and profit on cost is 25/75 x 100 = $33\frac{1}{3}\%$

Illustration 4

From the following particulars taken out from the books of a factory for the year ended 31st December 2002, prepare (a) Consolidated completed job account showing the profit or loss; and (b) Consolidated work in progress account.

	Completed Jobs	Work in Progress
	Rs.	Rs.
Raw materials supplied from stores	9,000	3,000
Chargeable expenses	1,000	400
Direct wages	10,000	4,000
Materials transferred to work in progress	200	200
Materials returned to stroes	100	

Factory overheads are charged at 80% of wages and office overheads at 25% of factory cost.

The value of executed jobs during the year ended 31st December 2002 was Rs.41 000.

Solution

Consolidated completed Job Account

	Rs	Rs		Rs
To Materials	9,000		By sales (amount of jobs finished)	41,000
Less transfer to WIP	– 200			
Less Returns	– 100	8,700		
To Wages		10,000		
To Chargeable expenses		1,000		
To Factory overheads (80% of wages)		8,000		
Factory Cost		27,700		
To Office overheads (25% of factory cost)		6,925		
To Net Profit Rs.		6,375		
		41,000		41,000

Consolidated work in progress

To Raw materials	3,000			
Add: Transferred from completed Jobs	200	3,200	By Balance c/d	13,500
To Wages		4,000		
To Chargeable expenses		400		
To Factory overheads (80% of wages)		3,200		
Factory cost		10,800		
To Office overheads (25% of factory cost)		2,700		
		13,500		13,500

Illustration 5

A shop-floor supervisor of a small factory presented the following cost for Job No. 277 to determine the selling price.

	Per unit (Rs.)
Material	70
Direct wages 18 hours at Rs.2.50 (Dept. X 8 hrs; Dept. Y 6 hrs; Dept. Z 4 hrs.)	45
Chargeable expenses (special stores item)	5
	120
Add 331/3% for expenses	40
Total cost	160

		Rs.		Rs.
Materials used		1,50 000	Sales less returns	2,50,000
Direct wages: Department X	10,000			
Y	12,000			
Z	8,000	30,000		
Special stores item		4,000		
Over heads: Department X	5,000			
Y	9,000			
Z	2,000	16,000		
Gross Profit c/d		50,000		
		2,50,000		2,50,000
Selling expenses		20,000	Gross Profit b/d	50,000
Net Profit		30,000		
		50,000		50,000

It is also noted that average hourly rates for the three department X, Y, and Z are similar

You are required to: (a) draw up a Job cost sheet and (b) claculate and enter revised cost using 2002 actual figures as basis; and (c) add 20% to total costs to determine selling price.

(I.C.W.A inter adapted)

Solution

Job Cost Sheet for Job No. 277

Particulars	Rate	Hours	Amount (Rs.)
Materials			70.00
Direct wages: Department X	2.50	8	20.00
Y	2.50	6	15.00
Z	2.50	4	10.00
Chargeable expenses			5.00
Prime Cost			120.00
Overheads Department X	1.250	8	10.00
Y	1.875	6	11.25
Z	0.625	4	2.50
Total Cost			143.75
Profit (20% of total cost)			28.75
Selling Price			172.50

Note: Overhead rates have been computed on the basis of previous year's figures as follows:

Overheads recovery rate $\frac{\text{Overhead}}{\text{No. of Hours}}$

Department X = Rs. $\frac{5000}{4000}$ = Rs. 1.250 per hour

Y = Rs. $\frac{9000}{4800}$ = Rs. 1.875

Z = Rs. $\frac{2000}{3200}$ = Re. 0.625 per Hour

Illustration 6

The following figures have been extracted from the records of ABC Ltd., for the year 2002.

Cost of materials	Rs. 60,000
Labour cost	50,000
Factory overheads	30,000
Distribution expenses	14,000
Administration expenses	33,600
Selling expenses	22,400
Sales	2,52,000

A work order has been accepted in 2003 and the following expenses have been estimated:

Cost of materials	Rs. 8,000
Labour cost	5,000

Assuming that in 2003 the rate for factory overheads will go up by 20%, distribution expenses will go down by 10%, and selling and administration charges will go up by 12.5%, at what price the product of the job should be quoted so as to earn the same percentage of profit on the selling price as in 2002? Distribution, administration and selling expenses are based on factory cost.

Solution

	Rs.
Direct materials	60,000
Direct labour	50,000
Prime cost	1,10,000
Factory overheads	30,000
Factory cost	1,40,000
Add: Administration expenses	33,600
Cost of production	1,73,600
Add: Distribution expenses	14,000
Selling expenses	22,400
Cost of sales	2,10,000
Add: Profit	42,000
Sales	2,52,000

Cost relations in 2002

(a) Percentage of profit on selling price

$$\frac{\text{Rs. } 42.000}{\text{Rs.} 2{,}52{,}000} \times 100 = 16.67\%$$

If the selling price is 100 then profit is 16.67 and cost is 83.33.

Percentage of profit on cost = $16.67/83.33 \times 100 = 20\%$ or Rs. $42{,}000/2{,}10{,}000 \times 100 = 20\%$

(b) Percentage of factory overheads on Direct wages

$$\frac{\text{Rs. } 30{,}000}{\text{Rs. } 50{,}000} \times 100 = 60\%$$

(c) Percentage of administration expenses on factory cost

$$\frac{\text{Rs. } 33{,}600}{\text{Rs. } 1{,}40{,}000} \times 100 = 24\%$$

(d) Percentage of selling expenses on factory cost

$$\frac{\text{Rs. } 22{,}400}{\text{Rs. } 1{,}40{,}000} \times 100 = 16\%$$

(e) Percentage of distribution expenses on factory cost

$$\frac{\text{Rs. } 14{,}000}{\text{Rs. } 1{,}40{,}000} \times 100 = 10\%$$

Cost relations in 2003

(a) Factory overheads = (60% + 20%) of direct wages = 80% of wages

(b) Distribution expenses = (10% -- 10% of 10%) of factory cost = 9% of factory cost

(c) Selling expenses = (16% + 12.5% of 16%) of factory cost = 18% of factory cost

(d) Administration expenses = (24% + 12.5% of 24%) of factory cost = 27% of factory cost

	Rs.
Direct materials	8,000
Direct wages	5,000
Prime cost	13,000
Factory overheads (80% of wages)	4,000
Factory cost	17,000
Administration expenses (27% of factory cost)	4,590
Cost of production	21,590
Selling expenses (18% of factory cost)	3,060
Distribution expenses (9% of factory cost)	1,530
Cost of sales	26,180
Profit (20% on cost of sales)	5,236
Selling price	31,416

Note: The factory overheads have not increased by 20% but the ratio of factory overheads to wages has increased by 20%.

14.5 Batch Costing

Batch costing is a kind of job costing. In this method, the cost of a batch (group) of products is ascertained. The batch or a group of identical products is used as a cost unit. It is used in engineering works, which produces components or spare parts in economical batches for subsequent assembly purposes or manufacture on mass scale comparatively small items of products. The batch costing procedure is similar to that of job costing. Separate batch cost sheets are maintained for each batch of components and for the assembly of finished products.

Essential Features of Batch costing

1. This method is used where small components such as machine tools, machine parts, etc. are produced on mass scale.

2. Each batch constitutes a separate unit consisting of specified number of small components produced.

3. The entire production is divided into economic batches or groups and suitable costing method is applied to each batch.

4. The profit or loss of each batch is ascertained separately.

14.6 Contract Costing

Contract costing is a variant of job costing system. Contracts are big jobs, which require comparatively more time to complete and include activities outside the factory premises. Under this system costs are accumulated for each contract separately. It may be regarded as the application of job costing system to relatively large cost units. It is adopted in the case of companies engaged in building construction, road construction, shipbuilding, civil engineering works and similar activities.

14.7 Contract cost accounting procedure

For costing purposes a separate 'Contract Account' is prepared for each contract and all costs relating to a particular contract are charged to the same. As the contract is carried out at the customer's place, all expenses incurred for the execution of that contract become direct costs. All direct costs such as material cost, wages, cost of special plant and equipment, cost of special services like architect's fees, etc., are debited to the Contract account. And all indirect expenses such as office and administrative expenses, repairs and storeroom expenses are charged to contract account on an equitable basis.

The balance of materials at site and plant and equipment at depreciated value are credited to contract account. Any abnormal loss such as materials lost and plant damaged during transit is credited to contract account by debiting Profit and loss account. On completion of the contract, the agreed price for the work done is credited to contract account. The balance of the contract account represents profit or loss (actual or notional) and is transferred to Profit and loss account.

Specimen format of Contract Account

	Rs.		Rs.
To Materials issued from stores To Materials purchased		By Work in Progress: Work completed and certified	

To Direct wages		Work completed but uncertified	
To Direct expenses		Materials at site	
To Plant and machinery (actual value)		Plant at site (depreciated value)	
To Overheads		By Materials returned to stores	
To Balance c/d (Notional Profit)		By Plant returned to stores	
		By Profit and loss account (abnormal loss)	
To Work in Progress (Reserve)			
To Profit and loss account		By Balance b/d (Notional Profit)	

Treatment of Plant and Equipment used for the contract

(a) If the plant and machinery is used for the contract for a long period of time, then the particular contract should be debited with the original cost of the plant and the same be credited with the depreciated value at the end of the accounting period.

(b) When a plant and machinery is used for different contracts, the cost of operation (depreciation) of such plant should be determined and be charged to individual contracts based on certain predetermined hourly rate during the period of use.

Progress Payment (Advance Payment)

When a contract extends beyond one accounting year, an architect will certify the value of work completed. This certificate is produced to the contractee as evidence in support of the work done. The progress payment is paid on the basis of work certified.

Retention Money

When a contract provides for progress payment, it is laid down that a proportion (certain percentage) of the contract price or value certified will be withheld for a specified period of time as retention money. This money will be paid only on the satisfactory completion of the contract and all defects in the work are set right fully. It will vary from 10 to 20 per cent depending upon the reputation or reliability of the contractor.

Profits on incomplete Contracts

When a contractor has a number of contracts at different stages of completion at the end of an accounting period, the normal practice is to carry forward the work in progress valued at cost and no profit is taken into account before the completion of contracts. However in order to even out the profits over the period of contract, the practice is to calculate some notional profit every year on incomplete contracts and transfer to profit and loss account proportionately depending upon the ratio of work completed to total contract price. Notional profit is equal to total value of completed work minus net actual cost incurred in completing that work. Depending upon the degree of completion and cash advance received from the contractee, proportionate notional profit is transferred to profit and loss account and the balance is kept as reserve for future contingencies.

Profit transferred to P&L a/c =

$$\text{Notional Profit} \times \frac{\text{Work certified}}{\text{Total contract Price}} \times \frac{\text{Cash received}}{\text{Work certified}}$$

Guidelines for transferring profits to P&L a/c

(1) In case the contract is ¼ but less than ½ complete, one-third of the profit disclosed (i.e., notional profit) as reduced to the percentage of cash received to work certified should be transferred to P&L a/c, the balance being treated as provision.

(2) In case the contract is one-half or more complete, two-thirds of notional profit as reduced by the percentage of cash received should be transferred to P&L a/c. the remaining profit being treated as provision.

(3) In case of loss, the whole of loss should be transferred to P&L a/c.

Cost Plus Contract

Cost plus contract refers to a contract between the contractor and contractee whereby the contract price is determined on the basis of the actual cost of the product or services plus an agreed profit margin. When the actual cost cannot be estimated in advance, an agreement may be made whereby the contractee undertakes to reimburse the actual cost of the work plus a reasonable percentage to cover overheads and profit of the contractor. The profit margin may be certain percentage on costs incurred or otherwise related to costs. In that case the admissible costs are agreed upon and included in the text of the agreement. There is also a stipulation of cost audit before claims are admitted.

Escalation Clause

The escalation clause refers to a clause in any contractual agreement whereby the contract price is to be adjusted upward or downward in accordance with the rise or fall in the costs incurred by the contractor beyond a certain percentage of the original estimates submitted at the time of submitting the tender or quotation. This clause generally stipulates that the contractee will compensate the contractor for rise in the material prices or wages beyond certain percentage. It may also provide for a rebate on the contract price, if the material prices or wage rates decline below an agreed level. Sometimes, the clause may also provide for certain additional costs arising from the excess use of materials or labour time beyond certain limit.

Illustration 7

From the following information given below relating to an unfinished contract, ascertain:

(a) Profit in work certified;

(b) Cost of Work in Progress at the end of year.

	Rs.
Materials sent to site	86 000
Direct wages	70,000
Plant issued to site	80,000
Direct expenses	3,000
Establishment charges	4,000
Materials returned to stores	600
Work certified by architect	1,90,000
Work completed but uncertified	7,700

Materials at site as at the end of period	2,000
Wages accrued as at the end of period	300
Cash received against on account bills	1,61,500
Depreciation on plant	7,000
Total contract price	3,00,000

Solution

Contract Account for the year ending -------

		Rs.		Rs.
To Materials issued to site		86,000	By Work in Progress:	
To Wages	70,000		Work completed and certified	1,90,000
Add Outstanding	300	70,300	Work completed but uncertified	7,700
To Direct expenses		3000	Materials in hand at site	2,000
To Establishment charges		4,000	Plant at site less depreciation	73,000
To Plant issued		80,000		2,72,700
To Balance c/d (Notional Profit)		30,000	By Stores a/c (materials returned)	600
		2,73,300		2,73,300
To P & L a/c (profit transferred)		17,000	By Balance b/d	30,000
To Work in Progress (reserve)		13,000		
		30,000		30,000

Cost of Work in Progress	Rs. 2,72,700
Less Reserve for contingencies	13,000
	2,59,700

Workings:

$$\text{Profit transferred P and L a/c} = \text{Notional Profit} \times \frac{2}{3} \times \frac{\text{Cash received}}{\text{Work certified}}$$

$$= \text{Rs.}30{,}000 \times \frac{2}{3} \times \frac{1{,}61{,}500}{1{,}90{,}000} = \text{Rs.}17{,}000$$

Illustration 8

A & Co., obtained a contract for building a factory for Rs.10 00 000. Building operation started on 1-1-1999, and at the end of December 1999, they received from the contractee a sum of

Rs.3.90 lakhs being 75% of the amount due on the surveyor's certificate. The following additional information is given from the books of the company:

	Rs.
Stores issued to contract	2,00,000
Stores on hand 31-12-1999	10,000
Wages paid	1,80,000
Plant purchased for the contract	2,00,000
Direct expenses	25,000
Overheads allocated to the contract	12,000
Work completed but not certified	12,000

Plant to be depreciated at 10 per cent

Prepare a Contract Account showing the profit or loss on contract as on 31-12-1999. State whether the company would be justified in taking the full amount of the profit to its profit and loss account.

Solution

Contract Account for the year ended 31-12-1999

	Rs.		Rs.
To Stores issued	2,00,000	By Work in Progress:	
To Wages paid	1,80,000	Work certified	5,20,000
To Direct expenses	25,000	Work uncertified	12,000
To Plant purchased	2,00,000	Plant at site less depreciation	1,80,000
To Overheads allocated	12,000	Stores on hand	10,000
To Balance c/d (Notional Profit)	1,05,000		
	7,22,000		7,22,000
To Profit transferred to P&L a/c	52,500	By Balance b/d	1,05,000
To Work in Progress (reserve)	52,500		
	1,05,000		1,05,000

Workings: The value of work certified is estimated on the basis of the cash received. 75% of the certified value is Rs.3.90 lakhs. Hence, the value of work certified

$= \text{Rs. } 3{,}90{,}000 \times \frac{100}{75} = \text{Rs. } 5{,}20{,}000.$

The company is not justified in taking credit of full amount of profit without making provision for contingencies, since only half of the work has been completed. Hence the profit transferred would be calculated as follows:

Profit transferredo P & L a/c = Notional Profit $\times$ 2/3

$$\times \text{cash received/work certified}$$

$$= \text{Rs. } 1{,}05{,}000 \times 2/3 \times \text{Rs. } 3{,}90{,}000/5{,}20{,}000 = \text{Rs.}52{,}500$$

Illustration 9

Builders ltd., obtained a contract for constructing a bridge. The value of the contract is Rs.12 50,000 subject to retention of 20% until one year after the certified completion of the contract. The following details are obtained from the books of the company on 30th June 2002:

	Rs.
Labour on site	4,05,000
Direct Materials to site less returns	3,20,000
Materials from stores	81,200
Hire and use of plant-plant upkeep account	12,100
Direct expenses	23,000
Overheads allocated to the contract	37,100
Materials on hand on 30th June 2002	6,300
Wages accrued on 30th June 2002	7,800
Direct expenses accrued on 30th June 2002	1,600
Works uncertified at cost	16,500
Cash received on account	8,80,000
(Being 80% of work certified)	

Prepare (a) Contract Account and (b) show how it would appear in the balance sheet.

Solution

Contract Account for the year ended 30th June 2002

Particulars		Amount (Rs.)	Particulars	Amount (Rs.)
To Materials direct to site		4,20,000	By Work in Progress:	
To Materials from stores		81,200	Work certified	11,00,000
To Direct wages	4,05,000		Work uncertified	16,500
Add: Wages accrued	7,800	4,12,800	By Materials on hand	6,300
To Direct expenses	23,000			
Add: Accrued	1,600	24,600		
To Hire and use of plant		12,100		
To Overheads allocated		37,100		
To Profit and Loss a/c		72,000		

To Work in Progress - Reserve	63,000		
	11,22,800		11,22,800

Balance Sheet as on 30th June 2002

Liabilities	Amount (Rs.)	Assets		Amount (Rs.)
Wages accrued	7,800	Materials hand		6,300
Direct expenses accrued	1,600	Work in Progress:		
		Work certified	11,00,000	
		Work uncertified	16,500	
			11,16,500	
		Less Profit in reserve	63,000	
			10,53,500	
		Less Cash received	8,80,000	1,73,500

Workings: Cash received 80% of work certified. If cash received is 80, then work certified is 100.

If cash received is Rs.8,80,000, then work certified is

$$(8,80,000/80) \times 100 = 11,00,000$$

Profit transferred to P&L a/c

$$= \text{Rs. } 1,35,000 \times 2/3 \times 80\% = \text{Rs. } 72,000$$

Illustration 10

The following particulars have been taken out from the books of a firm of building contractors on 1st January 2002 relating to a contract for Rs.4 50,000:

	Rs.
Materials issued to the contract	76,500
Plant used for contract	22,500
Wages	1,21,500
Other expenses	7,500

Cash received on account to 31st December 2002 amounted to Rs.1 92,000 being 80% of the work certified.

Of the plant and materials charged to the contract, plant costing Rs.4,500 and materials costing Rs.3,750 were lost. On 31st December 2002 plant costing Rs.3,000 was returned to stores; the cost of work done but uncertified was Rs.1 500 and materials costing Rs.3 450 were in hand. Charge 15% depreciation on plant, reserve 1/3rd profits earned and prepare Contract Account from the above particulars.

Solution

Contract Account for the year ending 31st December 2002

Particulars	Amount (Rs.)	Particulars		Amount (Rs.)
To Materials	76,500	By Work in Progress:		
To Wages	1,21,500	Work certified		2,40,000
To Plant	22,500	Work uncertified		1,500
To Other expenses	7,500	Materials on site		3,450
To Profit and loss a/c (transfer)		Plant at site less depreciation		12,750
$40{,}500 \times 2/3 \times 80\%$ 21,600		By Costing P & L A/c:		
To Work in Progress		Plant lost	4,500	
(reserve) 18,900	40,500	Material lost	3,750	8,250
		By Plant returned	3,000	
		Less Depreciation (@ 15%)		2,550
			450	
	2,68,500			2,68,500

Workings:

Value of Plant at the end of the year

Cost of Plant		22,500
Less Plant lost	4,500	
Plant returned (Rs.3000 less 15% dep.)	2,550	7,050
		15,450
Less depreciation on Rs.18,000 @ 15%		2,700
Closing value of plant at site		12,750

Plant at site + Plant returned = 12,750 + 2,550 = 15,300

Illustration 11

A limited obtained a contract for the building of an office for Rs.3,00,000. Building operations started on 1st April 2001, and at the end of the financial year 31st March 2002, they received from the party a sum of Rs.1 20,000 being 80% of the amount on the surveyor's certificate. The following additional information is given from the books of A ltd.:

	Rs.
Stores issued to contract	60,000
Stores on hand (31-3-2002)	2,500
Wages paid	80,000
Plant purchased for the contract	60,000
Direct expenses	11,000
Overheads allocated to this contract	5,500
Works completed but uncertified	5,000

Plant to be depreciated at 10 per cent

You are required to prepare an account showing the profit on contract as on 31-3-2002.

Discuss whether A ltd., would be justified in taking the full amount of this profit to the credit of their Profit and Loss Account.

Solution

Contract Account for the year ending 31-3-2002

Particulars	Amount (Rs.)	Particulars	Amount (Rs.)
To Materials	60,000	By Work in progress:	
To Wages	80,000	Work certified	1,50,000
To Direct expenses	11,000	Work uncertified	5,000
To General overheads	5,500	By Materials on hand	2,500
To Plant	60,000	By Plant less depreciation	54,000
		By Profit and Loss a/c	5,000
	2,16,500		2,16,500

Notes: Work certified = 1,20,000 × 100/80 = 1,50,000

Normally when there is profit, the proportion of the profit to be taken to the credit of P & L a/c is

= Notional Profit × 2/3 × 80%.

As it is a case of loss in the present problem, the full amount of loss should be taken to the debit of Profit and Loss account.

PROCESS COSTING

14.8 Meaning

A process is an organizational entity or section of the firm, in which a separate or repetitive work is done. A few other terms used to describe a process are department, cost center, responsibility center, function, operation or stage of manufacture. It is a specifically defined sub-unit of an organization created for cost accumulation.

Process costing is a method of costing used to ascertain the costs of each process or operation or stage of manufacture. Kohler defines process costing as " a method of accounting whereby costs are charged to processes or operations and averaged over units produced; it is employed principally where a finished product is the result of a more or less continuous operation, as in paper mills, refineries, canneries and chemical plants; distinguished from job costing, where costs are assigned to specific orders, lots or units.

Process costing is useful or found to be most suitable for industries engaged in continuous manufacture of products in bulk in which the units of products are uniform and cannot be differentiated. It may be adopted in organizations producing a single commodity in bulk, or a group of products of different types. It is suitable for the following industries: chemical works, sugar mills, oil refining, textiles, breweries, rubber and tanning works, bottling companies, packing, mining, gas manufacturing, electric supply undertakings, food processing and fruit canning, etc.

Features: The distinctive feature of process costing is that the unit costs of products are determined for the respective process through which the units pass. All costs relating to a process are charged to a separate account and then averaged out to determine the cost per unit. When a product pass through several processes the total cost of one process is transferred to next process. To this costs are added the additional cost of materials, labour, and overheads, and the total cost transferred until production is completed and finished products turned out.

14.9 Distinctions between Job Costing and Process Costing

	Job costing		Process costing
1.	Production is carried on by specific job order and costs are determined by jobs or batches of products.	1.	Production is continuous and products are homogenous. Costs are accumulated on time basis i.e., for a particular process over a period of time.
2.	Various jobs are separate and independent.	2.	Processes are related to each other and products also lose their individual identity.
3.	Costs are calculated when a job is completed and unit cost is calculated by dividing the total cost by units produced in the lot or batch.	3.	Costs are calculated at the end of period under each process. The unit cost of a process is calculated by dividing the total cost of the process for the period by the number of units of output of the process.
4.	There may not be opening or closing Work in Progress in an accounting period.	4.	As the production is continuous, there is normally work in progress at the beginning and closing.
5.	There is normally no transfer of costs from one job to another. It will take place only when there is surplus or excess production.	5.	Transfer of costs from one process to another is a usual feature.
6.	Each production unit is different and therefore more managerial control is needed for proper functioning of the system.	6.	Production is standardized and stable and therefore, control is easier.

14.10 Advantages of Process Costing

1. Process costing helps determination of cost in each process and of the final product at short intervals. If overhead rates are predetermined, unit costs can be computed very promptly even at weekly or monthly.

2. The average cost can be easily determined when the methods of production are standardized. Price quotations can be submitted more promptly with standardization of processes.

3. It involves less clerical work and cost than job costing. Cost finding is simpler and less expensive.

4. Allocation of expenses can be easily made and the costs in each process accurately determined.

5. Use of standard costing system is very effective in process costing.

6. The performance analysis and managerial control is facilitated to a greater extent because of the availability of cost data in the form of prompt and accurate cost reports.

14.11 Limitations of Process costing

1. Process costing is based on historical cost. The available cost information may not be useful for future managerial decision-making.

2. Unfinished units (work in process) at the end of the period are expressed in equivalent production units. This introduces subjective element in scientific cost determination.

3. The whole concept of process costing system is based on average costs. Average costs do not always reflect the true costs. If there is an error in cost determination in one process, it will affect the cost estimation in subsequent processes as well as the cost of work in process and finished products.

4. When two or more products are produced in the same process, the joint costs are prorated to the various products using some weightage say in terms of points. Giving weightage in terms of points is a subjective decision, which will give rise to approximate costs and cannot be taken as fully reliable. Absence of scientific base makes the process costing inadequate for managerial purposes.

5. Process costing system presumes that production activity of a factory is divided according to processes. A process is an organizational entity or section of a firm, in which specific and repetitive work is done. Thus a process becomes a practical unit for purpose of supervision of production and often it is an unsatisfactory unit for cost accounting purposes.

14.12 Process Cost accounting Procedure

1. Separate account is opened for each process or department. All costs (both direct and indirect) are charged to each such process or department.

2. The physical units (quantity) of output in each process are recorded in the respective process accounts.

3. The cost per unit of output is determined by dividing the total cost of each process by total production at the end of each period.

4. The total cost of one process is transferred to the next process as an initial cost till the production is completed. The cumulative costs of different processes determine the total cost and per unit cost at the final stage.

5. When there is work in progress at the end of the period, the stage of completion of the incomplete work is determined, and the computation of inventory is in terms of equivalent

production units. For example, if 100 units are 40% complete, they are taken as equivalent to 40 completed units. The total number of completed units divides the total cost and the unit cost is obtained for the process.

6. In case of any normal loss in the process, the units produced in that process bear that loss. Accordingly the average cost of that process is increased. In case of any abnormal loss, it is treated as general business loss and transferred to costing profit and loss account.

Illustration 12

A chemical product requires three distinct processes and after the third process the product is transferred to finished stock. From the following particulars, prepare various process accounts:

	P I	P II	P III
	Rs.	Rs.	Rs.
Direct materials	8,000	1,200	800
Direct wages	3,000	3,200	1,800
Direct expenses	1,000	600	–

Total production overheads Rs.12,000.

Production overheads are to be allocated to different processes on the basis of 150% of direct wages. Production during the period was 400 units. Assume there is no opening or closing stock.

Solution

Process I Account

Particulars	Per unit Rs.	Total Rs.	Particulars	Per unit Rs.	Total Rs.
To Direct materials	20.00	8,000	By Transfer to Process II account	41.25	16,500
To Direct wages	7.50	3,000			
To Direct expenses	2.50	1,000			
To Production overheads	11.25	4,500			
	41.25	16,500		41.25	16,500

Process II Account

Particulars	Per unit Rs.	Total Rs.	Particulars	Per unit Rs.	Total Rs.
To Transfer from Process I	41.25	16,500	By Transfer to Process III	65.75	26,300
To Direct materials	3.00	1,200			
To Direct wages	8.00	3,200			

To Direct expenses	1.50	600			
To Production overheads	12.00	4,800			
	65.75	26,300		65.75	26,300

Process III Account

Particulars	Per unit Rs.	Total Rs.	Particulars	Per unit Rs.	Total Rs.
To Transfer from Process II	65,75	26,300	By Transfer to Finished Stock A/c	79.00	31,600
To Direct materials	2.00	800			
To Direct wages	4.50	1,800			
To Production overheads	6.75	2,700			
	79.00	31,600		79.00	31,600

Process losses

Process loss refers to the loss in quantity of output during the normal course of manufacture due to various reasons. The process may take the form of wastage, spoilage, defectives, or scrap. It may be due to the nature of operations involved and to that extent inevitable. If the loss of quantity occurs in the normal course of work and inherent in the nature of work, it is known as 'normal loss'. Normal loss is an expected loss and uncontrollable. Management can provide for such loss based on past experience or technical data. Besides this, the loss of quantity may arise due to certain unexpected or abnormal factors or inefficiency of operations. Such loss is known as 'abnormal loss'. It cannot be accurately estimated in advance. However, to a larger extent, it is controllable. Abnormal loss is estimated by fixing due allowance for normal loss. For example, if the management decides to allow 10% of input as normal loss, and the actual loss is more than 10%, then the excess loss will be treated as abnormal loss.

Sometimes, it may happen that the actual loss in a process is less than the estimated normal loss or actual output is more than the expected normal output. The difference is regarded as abnormal gain. As the normal loss is the expected loss of the concerned process, it should form part of the cost of the process. But abnormal loss or abnormal gain does not affect the cost of production of the concerned process. Hence, it should be transferred to costing profit and loss account. Abnormal loss is credited to process account and debited to abnormal loss account. Abnormal gain is debited to process account and credited to abnormal gain account. Following examples will explain the above points clearly.

Illustration 13

From the following particulars prepare Process Account and calculate abnormal loss. Input of raw materials 1 200 units at Rs. 60 per unit:

Direct labour	Rs.48,000
Factory expenses	Rs.56,100
Scrap value of process loss	Rs.5 per unit

Net production 1,060 units
Normal loss 10% of input

Solution

Process Account

Particulars	Units	Rs.	Particulars	Units	Rs.
To Raw materials at Rs.60 Per unit	1,200	72,000	By Normal loss: 10% At Rs.5 per unit	120	600
To Direct wages		48,000	By Abnormal loss	20	3,250
To Factory expenses		56,100	By Transfer to next process	1,060	1,72,250
	1,200	1,76,100		1,200	1,76,100

Abnormal loss

	Rs.		Rs.
To Process Account	3,250	By Sundry debtors or Cash/ac (Sale of scrap at Rs.5 per unit)	100
		By Costing P & L a/c	3,150

Workings: Input put into Process = 1200 units

Normal loss 10% on 1200 = 120 units

Expected output = 1080

Less: Actual output = 1060

Abnormal loss = 20 units

Illustration 14

A product passes through two distinct processes A and B and then to Finished Stock. The output of A passes direct to B and that of B passes to finished stock. From the following information you are required to prepare the Process Accounts:

	Rs.	Rs.
Materials consumed	12,000	6,000
Direct labour	14,000	8,000
Manufacturing expenses	4,000	4,000
Input in Process A (10,000 units)	10,000	
Output (units)	9,400	8,300
Normal wastage (on input)	5%	10%
Value of normal wastage (per 100 units)	8	10

No opening or closing stock is held in process.

Solution

Process A Account

Particulars	Units	Rs.	Particulars	Units	Rs.
To Inputs	10,000	10,000	By Normal loss @ 5%	500	40
To Materials		12,000	By Abnormal loss	100	420
To Direct wages		14,000	By Transfer to process B a/c	9,400	39,540
To Manufacturing expenses		4,000			
	10,000	40,000		10,000	40,000

Note: Normal output = 10,000 less normal loss @ 5% on 10,000 units = 9,500 units

Actual output = 9,400

Abnormal loss = 100

Normal cost of Normal output = Rs.40,000 − 40 = 39,960

Cost of abnormal loss = (Normal Cost/Normal Output) × Abnormal loss

= (Rs.39,960/9,500) × 100 = 420 (approx)

Process B Account

Particulars	Units	Rs.	Particulars	Units	Rs.
To Input from Process A	9,400	39,540	By Normal loss @ 10%	940	94
To Materials		6,000	By Abnormal loss	160	1,087
To Direct wages		8,000	By Financial Stock	8,300	56,359
To Manufacturing exps.		4,000			
	9,400	57,540		9,400	57,540

Note: Normal output = 9,400 less 10% on 9,400 = 8,460 units

Actual output= 8,300

Abnormal loss = 160 units

Cost of abnormal loss = (57,740 − 94)/8,460 × 160 = Rs. 1,087

Cost of finished stock = 57,446 − 1087 = Rs.56,359

Illustration 15

The following particulars are given for Process B:

	Units	Rs.
Transfer from Process A	4000	9,000
Direct materials		3,000
Direct wages		2,000
Transfer to Finished Stock	3240	

Factory overheads in process are absorbed at the rate of 400% of direct materials.

Allowance to normal loss is 20% of units worked. Scrap value is Rs.5 per unit.

Prepare Process B Account and Abnormal Loss or Gain Account.

Solution

Process B Account

Particulars	Units	Rs.	Particulars	Units	Rs.
To Transfer from Process A	4,000	9,000	By Normal loss @Rs. 5	800	4,000
To Direct materials		3,000	(20% of 4,000 units)		
To Direct wages		2,000	By Transfer to Next Process	3,240	22,275
			(@ Rs. 6.88 per unit)		
To Factory overheads		12,000			
(400% of materials)					
To abnormal gain a/c	40	275			
	4,040	26,275		4,040	26,275

Abnormal Gain account

Particulars	Units	Rs.	Particulars	Units	Rs.
To Process B A/c	40	200	By Process B A/c	40	275
(Units not lost)					
To Costing P&L A/c		75			
	40	275		40	275

Note: In Process B 4000 units have been worked. The normal loss is 20% i.e., 800 units. The normal output should be 3 200 units (4,000-800). But the actual output is 3 240 units. Hence, the excess 40 units is abnormal gain and is valued as follows:

$$\text{Cost of abnormal gain} = (\text{Normal Cost}/\text{Normal Output}) \times \text{Units of Abnormal Gain}$$

$$= (\text{Rs.}26{,}000 - 4{,}000)/(4{,}000 - 800) \times 40$$

$$= (\text{Rs. } 22{,}000/3{,}200) \times 40 = \text{Rs.}275$$

Illustration 16

A product passes through distinct processes before completion. The following information is obtained from the accounts for the month of January 2002.

	Process I	Process II	Process III
	Rs.	Rs.	Rs.
Direct materials	2,600	1,980	2,962
Direct wages	2,000	3,000	4,000

Factory overheads	2,000	3,000	4,000

1000 units at Rs.3 each were introduced to Process I. There was no stock of materials or work in progress at the beginning or end of the period. The following additional information is obtained:

	Output during the month Units	Normal loss % on input	Value of scrap per unit Rs.
Process I	950	5%	2
Process II	840	10%	4
Process III	750	15%	5

Prepare Process Accounts and Abnormal loss or Gain Accounts.

Solution

Process I Account

Particulars	Units	Rs.	Particulars	Units	Rs.
To Units introduced @ Rs. 3 per unit	1,000	3,000	By Normal (5% of 1000 units; Value @ Rs. 2 per unit)	50	100
To Direct materials		2,600	By Transfer to Process II (cost per unit unit Rs.10)	950	9,500
To Direct wages		2,000			
To factory overheads		2,000			
	1,000	9,600		1,000	9,600

Process II Account

Particulars	Units	Rs.	Particulars	Units	Rs.
To Transfer from Process I	950	9,500	By Normal loss (10% on 950; value @ Rs. 4, per unit)	95	380
To Direct materials		1,980			
To Direct wages		3,000	By Abnormal loss a.c	15	300
To Factory overheads		3,000	By Transfer to Process II (cost per unit Rs. 20)	840	16,800
	950	17,480		950	17,480

Process III Account

Particulars	Units	Rs.	Particulars	Units	Rs.
To Transfer from Process III	840	16,800	By Normal loss (15% of 840; value Rs.5 per unit)	126	630
To Direct materials		2,962			
To Direct wages		4,000	By Transfer to Finished stock	750	28,500

To Factory overheads		4,000	(cost per unit Rs.38)		
To Abnormal Gain a/c	36	1,368			
	876	29,130		876	29,130

Abnormal Wastage or Loss Account

Particulars	Units	Rs.	Particulars	Units	Rs.
To Process II Account	15	300	By sale of scrap @ Rs.4	15	60
			By Costing P&L A/c		240
	15	300		15	300

Abnormal Effectiveness or Gain Account

Particulars	Units	Rs.	Particulars	Units	Rs.
By Process III a/c (Units not lost) at Rs 5	36	180	By Process III a/c	36	1368
By Costing P&L A/c		1188			
	36	1368		36	1368

Equivalent Production Units (EPU)

When production is incomplete or in partly finished stage at the end of the period, it is shown as work in process. And it must bear a proportion of total cost of the process. For this purpose, the work in process is expressed in terms of completed units of production before the total cost is spread over all the units. In other words, partly completed units are converted into equivalent fully completed units in order to ascertain the cost per unit. This is done based on the percentage of completion of the work in process. For example, when 500 units are 50% complete, the work in process is taken as equivalent to 250 units of fully completed production or 250 equivalent production units. Hence, equivalent production refers to the production of a process of manufacture in terms of fully completed units.

EPU = Actual number of units in the process of manufacture $\times$ Percentage of completion

Computation of Equivalent Production Units

The EPU should be calculated taking into account the stage of completion of opening and closing work in process and the number of units put into process and finished during the period. The steps involved are as follows:

1. The opening WIP should be converted into equivalent completed units. Considering the percentage of work to be completed during the current period may do this. For example opening WIP is 400 units, which is 60% complete, therefore only 40% to be completed now. In terms of completed units, it is equivalent to 160 units, i.e., $400 \times 40\% = 160$.

2. To the above units, add the number of units introduced and completed during the period. This may be found by deducting the closing WIP from the number of units put into process.

3. Then add to the above, the equivalent units of closing WIP. This can be obtained based on the percentage of completion of the closing inventory at the end of the period. For

example, if the number of units of closing inventory is 500 units, which is 30% complete, then the equivalent completed units will be 150 i.e., $500 \times 30\% = 150$.

The total of all these will be the equivalent production units. When the stages of completion is same for all elements of cost (i.e., materials, labour, and overheads), then the above procedure shall be adopted. If they are different for each element of cost, then the EPU shall be calculated separately for each element. The following examples explain the above points clearly.

Example 1

Calculate the equivalent production relating to a process from the production data of March 2002 given below:

	Units
Work In Progress on 1st March 2002, 40% complete	900
Put into the process during March	12,000
Transferred to the next process	10,500
Work In Progress on 31st March, 40 complete	1,000

Solution

	Equivalent Production Units
Opening inventory of WIP (60% incomplete	
Completed during the month) $900 \times 60\% =$	540
Number of units completed during the month	
Units put into process 12,000	
Less: Units not yet completed 1,000	11,000
Closing WIP (40% completed during the month)	
$1000 \times 40\% =$	400
Equivalent Production =	11,940

Example 2

In process A 2,000 units were introduced during the month. The normal loss was estimated at 5% of input. At the end of month 460 units were incomplete. The stage of completion is as follows:

Materials	75%	complete
Labour	50%	complete
Overheads	60%	complete

Calculate the Equivalent Production.

Solution

Statement of Production

Input Units	Output	Units	Equivalent Production		
			Materials	Labour	Overheads
2000	Normal loss	100	–	–	–

	Finished Product	1440	1440	100%	1440	100%	1440	100%
	Work in Progress	460	345	75%	230	50%	276	60%
2000		2000	1785		1670		1716	

EPU as regards materials 1785 units

EPU as regards labour 1670 units

EPU as regards overheads 1716 units

Note: It should be assumed that the equivalent production as regards normal loss is always zero.

In the case of abnormal loss, the equivalent production should be assumed as 100%.

Example 3

In Process A 2000 units were introduced during the month. The normal loss was estimated at 5% of input. Finished products were 1400 units. At the end of month work in progress were 460 units and the stage of completion was: Materials 75% complete; Labour 50% complete; and Overheads 60% complete. Prepare a Statement of EPU.

Solution

Statement of Equivalent Production

Input Units	Output	Units	Materials		Labour		Overheads	
			Qty.	%	Qty.	%	Qty.	%
2000	Normal loss	100	–	–	–	–	–	–
	Abnormal loss	40	40	100	40	100	40	100
	Finished Product	1400	1400	100	1400	100	1400	100
	Work in Progress	460	345	75	230	50	276	60
		2000	1785		1670		1716	

Example 4

In Process A 2000 units were introduced during one month. The normal loss was estimated at 5% of input. At the end of the month the finished output was 1500 units, and closing work in progress was 460 units with the stage of completion as follows: Material 75% complete; Labour 50% complete; and overheads 60% complete. Calculate Equivalent Production.

Solution

Statement of Equivalent Production

Input Units	Output	Units	Materials		Labour		Overheads	
			Qty.	%	Qty.	%	Qty.	%
2000	Normal loss	100	–	–	–	–	–	–
	Finished Product	1500	1500	100	1500	100	1500	100
	Work in Progress	460	375	75	230	50	276	60
		2060	1875		1730		1776	

	Abnormal Gain	60	60	100	60	100	60	100
2000		2000	1785		1670		1716	

Note: The abnormal gain is also assumed as 100 per cent complete and deducted from the gross equivalent production.

Illustration 17

From the following particulars prepare (a) Statement of EPU, (b) Statement of Apportionment of Cost, and (c) Prepare Process Account.

Opening Work in Progress: 200 units at Rs.4 per unit and stage of completion – Materials 100%, Labour and overheads 40%.

Units introduced 1050 and units transferred to next process 1100.

Closing Work in Progress: 150 units and stage of completion – Materials 100%, Labour and overheads 70%.

Other Information: Material cost Rs.1050, labour Rs.2250, and overheads Rs.1125.

Solution

Statement of Equivalent Production Units

Input Units	Output	Units	Material		Labour		Overheads	
			Qty.	%	Qty.	%	Qty.	%
200	Opening WIP	200	–	–	120	60	120	60
1050	Completely processed	900	900	100	900	100	900	100
	Closing WIP	150	150	100	105	70	105	70
1250		1250	1050		1125		1125	

Calculation of each element of cost per EPU

	Amount (Rs.)	EPU	Cost per EPU (Rs)
Material	1050	1050	1.00
Labour	2250	1125	2.00
Overheads	1125	1125	1.00

Statement of Apportionment of Process cost incurred during the period

Particulars	Elements	EPU	Cost per EPU (Rs.)	Amount (Rs.)	Total cost (Rs.)
Opening WIP	Materials	–	1.00	–	–
	Labour	20	2.00	240	
	Overheads	120	1.00	120	360
Completely Processed	Materials	900	1.00	900	–
	Labour	900	2.00	1800	–
	Overheads	900	1.00	900	3600

Closing WIP	Materials	150	1.00	150	–
	Labour	105	2.00	210	–
Overheads		105	1.00	105	465
Total					4425

Value of Production transferred to next Process	Rs.
Opening WIP 200 units at Rs.4.00	800
Additional processing cost of opening WIP	360
Completely processed units 900	3600
Total 1100 units transferred to next process	4760

Process Account

Particulars	Units	Amount (Rs.)	Particulars	Units	Amount (Rs.)
Opening WIP @ Rs.4 per unit	200	800	Transferred to next Process	1100	4760
Material	1050	1050	Closing WIP	150	465
Labour		2250			
Overheads		1125			
	1250	5225		1250	5225

Joint Products and By-products

While processing certain input factors into a process, two or more products may be manufactured. Same raw materials and same operations may result in the production of multiple products. These multiple products are referred to as main products, joint products and by-products. Based on the commercial value of these products and the management objective and policies, they are classified as joint products and by-products.

14.13 Meaning of Joint Products

Joint products may be defined as two or more products produced simultaneously in a process, each having a sufficiently high saleable value to merit recognition as a main product. They cannot be produced separately. The processing of a particular material may result in the production of two or more products. If all the products are of equal economic importance and none of them can be termed as major products, then these will be referred to as joint products. A few examples of joint products are as follows:

In petroleum industry	Petrol, diesel, gas, and kerosene
In dairy industry	Skimmed milk, butter and cream
In saw mill	Several grades of lumber and slabs

14.14 Meaning of By-products

By-product is a secondary product. By-products are minor products obtained incidentally in the process of manufacturing the main product. They possess some saleable value. A by-product is of minor commercial importance and often requires further processing before sale. The commercial or economic importance of the products classifies as main or joint products and by-products. The relationship between main product and by-product changes with changes in economic or industrial conditions or with advancement of science. In the manufacture of sugar baggasse, press mud, and molasses are obtained as by-products along with the main product sugar. In dairy industry, buttermilk (a by-product) is produced along with butter and cheese (main products).

14.15 Distinction between Joint Product and By-product

Generally the difference between joint product and by-product is based on the relative commercial value of the products. Joint products have more or less same commercial value and importance while by-products have minor commercial importance. However, the consideration of whether the products are joint products or by-products depends primarily upon management objectives and policies. It has an important effect on income. It is possible for a by-product at one point of time to become a joint product at another point of time and vice versa. For example, in soap making, soap is the main product and glycerin is a by-product. But in wartime, glycerin, which was in great demand, became the main product and soap was reduced to a by-product. Sometimes, factors like business objective, profit pattern desired, the need for further processing before sale and certainty of market, etc, may influence the classification of products as joint products and by-products. However, definite criteria for distinguishing between the two types of products do not exist.

Split-off point. This is a point up to which input factors are commonly used for the production of joint products and by-products. This is a point of separation where these products gain individual identity. The costs incurred up to this point are joint costs common to all products identified at this point. In order to ascertain the profitability of the joint products and by-products these joint costs are to be apportioned appropriately to various products.

Distinction between Joint cost and Common cost

Joint costs are those costs that are common to the processing of joint products or by-products up to the split-off point. They are pre-separation costs and are incurred as a lump-sum for the combination and not separately for the individual products. After the point of separation, the products can be separately identified and further processing costs can be attributed to individual products. These preseparation costs should be appropriately apportioned for correct determination of product costs and managerial analysis for decision-making. For example, in dairy farming the cost of milk will be the joint cost.

Common cost is the cost of facilities or services incurred for the manufacture of multiple products or services simultaneously. It is the cost of indirect material, indirect labour, and indirect expenses incurred in a factory during the course of manufacture of multiple products or services. It is also referred to as 'overheads'. Common cost will not include elements of prime cost whereas joint costs do include prime cost. Though for a layman joint cost may appear to be a special type of common cost, but they are distinct in nature, scope and treatment.

14.16 Accounting for Joint Products

Apportionment of joint cost among the joint products is essential for determining the share of individual joint products correctly. Ascertainment of share of cost is required for pricing the products, valuing the closing inventory and ascertaining the profit or loss on sale of different products. Following methods are commonly used for apportioning the joint costs among the joint products.

(a) Physical Units Method: Under this method the joint costs are apportioned among the joint products in the ratio of physical units of output produced at the point of separation.

For example, the physical base like raw material weight in physical quantity is used as the base for apportioning the joint costs. This method is very simple and easy to use. It is also technically a sound method. However this method cannot be used when output consists of different types of units such as liquids, solids, etc. It is also illogical to assume that all joint products are equally desirable and valuable since this method assigns same unit to high quality and low quality joint products.

Example 5

The following data have been taken out from the books of Mass Coke ltd.

Joint products	Yield in lbs. of recovered Products per tonne of coal
Coke	1,420
Coal tar	120
Benzol	22
Sulphate of Ammonia	26
Gas	412
	2,000

The price of coal is Rs.800 per tonne; the direct wages and overhead costs to the point of separation are Rs.400 and Rs.600 respectively per tonne of coal. Calculate the material, labour, overheads and total cost of each product on the basis of weight.

Solution

Statement of Apportionment of Joint Cost

Joint products	Yield in Lbs.	% of total	Apportioned cost			
			Coal	Wages	Overheads	Total
Coke	1,420	71.0	568.00	284.00	426.00	1,278.00
Coal tar	120	6.0	48.00	24.00	36.00	108.00
Benzol	22	1.1	8.80	4.40	6.60	19.80
Sulphate Ammonia	26	1.3	10.40	5.20	7.80	23.40
Gas	412	20.6	164.80	82.40	123.60	370.80
	2,000	100.0	800.00	400.00	600.00	1,800.00

(b) Average Unit Cost Method: Under this method, the total units produced at that point divide the total cost incurred up to the split-off point to get average cot per unit of production. All joint products are valued at the average cost. This method can be used when all products are expressed in terms of same units. It cannot be used when the units are not comparable.

Advantages

(a) It is very simple and easy to adopt.

(b) It is logical to use this method as all joint products are produced from the same raw material and same process.

(c) When this method is used all joint products will have uniform cost.

Disadvantages

(a) The apportioned costs cannot be used for setting prices particularly in a competitive market.

(b) It is not useful for scientific decision-making.

(c) This method fails to recognize the fact that all joint products are not equally costly and to give due weightage to this factor.

Example 6

Total production 25 000 units and total cost (up to split-off point) is Rs.6,00,000. average cost per unit = 6,00,000/25,000 = Rs.24 per unit. If the joint products produced are A – 10,000 units, B – 6,000 units, and C – 9,000 units, then the joint cost will be apportioned as follows:

Joint Products	Quantity produced		Average cost	Value of Joint Product
A	10,000 units	×	Rs.24	Rs.2,40,000
B	6,000 units	×	Rs.24	1,44,000
C	9,000 units	×	Rs.24	2,16,000
Total Joint Cost				6,00,000

This method cannot be used when the units are not comparable. It is used in tobacco industry, timber industry, and glue making industry.

(c) Survey Method: This method assumes that the difference in costs of joint products arises due to certain qualitative and quantitative factors like raw materials used, labour operations performed, time consumed for production and technical difficulties in manufacture. Based on technical evaluation, weights are assigned to each product in the form of points. Apportionment of joint costs is made on the basis of these point values.

Advantages

(a) This method enables accurate allocation of joint costs.

(b) It is considered more equitable than other methods, for it takes into consideration all related factors and assigns due weightage in the form of point values.

(c) Usage of weight factors results in the fair allocation of joint costs based on the benefits received by each product.

Disadvantages

(a) Assignment of weights is based on intuitive judgment and therefore arbitrary in nature.

(b) The weights used may be inappropriate in the first place and may become useless with the passage of time.

Example 7

In a company the following joint costs are incurred: Materials Rs.10,000, Wages Rs.5,000, and Overheads Rs.5,000. The output of three joint products X, Y, and Z is: X – 100 units, Y – 600 units, and Z – 400 units. On the basis of technical evaluation the following weights were assigned to the products: X – 8, Y – 5, and Z – 3. Apportion the joint costs to the joint products on a suitable method.

Solution

The suitable method for apportioning the joint cost would be Survey method.

Statement of Apportionment of Joint Costs

X	100	8	800	16	3,200	32.00
Y	600	5	3,000	60	12,000	20.00
Z	400	3	1,200	24	4,800	12.00
Total	1,100		5,000	100	20,000	

Note: The total joint cost is as follows:

Materials	Rs.10,000
Wages	5,000
Overheads	5,000
Total	20,000

Apportioned cost of X = Rs.20,000 × 16% = Rs.3,200

Y = Rs.20,000 × 60% = Rs.12,000

Z = Rs.20,000 × 24% = Rs.4,800

(d) Standard Cost Method: This method can be used only when there is standard costing system in operation. Standard costs are set for each of the joint products and joint costs are apportioned among the joint products on the basis of standards set. This method has the advantage of measuring the efficiency and exercising control in producing joint products.

(e) Contribution Margin Method: This method employs marginal costing technique for apportioning joint costs among the joint products. Under this method the total joint cost is divided into two categories viz., variable and fixed costs. The variable cost is allocated on the basis of physical quantities produced and fixed cost is allocated on the basis of contribution margin ratio. Contribution means excess of sales over variable costs.

Example 8

From the following information, apportion the joint cost on a suitable method: A company produces three grades X, Y, and Z of jam at a total cost of Rs.15,000 of which fixed costs are Rs.6,000. The quantity produced and sold are 50 kgs, 30 kgs, and 70 kgs and their selling prices respectively are Rs.200, Rs.150 and Rs.120 per kg.

Solution

Total joint cost	Rs.15,000
Less: Fixed costs	6,000
Joint variable cost	9,000
Total production	= 50 kgs + 30 kgs + 70 kgs = 150 kgs.
Variable cost per kg	= Rs.9,000/150 kgs = Rs.60

Statement showing apportionment of joint cost

Product Grade	Sales value Rs.	Variable cost Rs.	Contribution Rs.	Fixed cost	Profit Rs.
X	50 × 200 = 10,000	50 × 60 = 3,000	7,000	3,158	3,842
Y	30 × 150 = 4,500	30 × 60 = 1,800	2,700	1,218	1,482
Z	60 × 120 = 7,200	60 × 60 = 3,600	3,600	1,624	1,976
Total	21,700	8,400	13,300	6,000	7,300

Note: Fixed cost has been distributed in the ratio of contribution.

(f) Market Value Method

Under this method the market values (sales values) of the joint products are used to apportion the joint costs incurred up to the point of separation. This method is considered logical since product with high sales value bears a larger portion of joint costs and one with low sales value bears smaller portion of joint costs. In other words, the joint costs are apportioned on the basis of their ability to absorb joint costs. This ability is measured by sales value or selling price. The justification for this method is that the joint products should generate enough revenues to cover all costs plus a reasonable return. However, this method may not be appropriate when the selling prices of joint products are highly fluctuating. Also determination of relative selling prices a difficult and time consuming exercise. The variants of this method are as follows:

(a) Market Value at the point of separation

(b) Market Value after further processing

(c) Market Value less completion cost of individual products

(d) Net Value method

(a) Market Value at the Split-off point: Under this method the sales value of individual products at the split-off point is ascertained and the joint cost is apportioned among the products in the ratio of total sales value of individual products to total sales value of all products. Some authors have suggested the market price of the products at the split-off point as the basis for apportioning the joint costs. However, the use of market price may lead to invalid apportionment of joint costs and present a number of problems in determining relative selling prices.

Example 9

The following cost data are given below: Joint costs of producing three joint products X, Y, and Z are Rs.9,000. Number of units produced at the split-off point is: X – 100; Y – 200; and Z – 300. The products did not require any further processing after the split-of point. The selling prices of the products per unit are given below: X – Rs.10; Y – Rs.15; and Z – Rs.20. Apportion the joint cost among the joint products using the Market Value at the point of separation.

Solution

Sales values of Joint Products

X – 100 units at Rs.10 per unit = Rs.1,000

Y – 200 units at Rs.15 per unit = Rs.3,000

Z – 300 units at Rs.20 per unit = Rs.6,000

Total sale value = 10,000

Sales Value Ratio = 1:3:6

Apportionment of Joint Cost of Rs.9,000

$X = Rs.9{,}000 \frac{1}{10} = Rs.900$

$Y = Rs.9{,}000 \frac{3}{10} = Rs.2{,}700$

$Z = Rs.9{,}000 \frac{6}{10} = Rs.5{,}400$

(b) Market Value after further processing: Determination of sales value at the point of separation may be difficult. In order to overcome this difficulty, the ratio of market values of individual products after further processing to their total sales value may be used to apportion the joint costs. It is easy to ascertain the sales value at the final stage (i.e., completion of products after processing). This method would be a convenient one when the output of the joint products are in different types of units such as pounds, litres, kilograms, etc. However, it may not be called a fair method since the cost of further processing costs to complete the products may not be same in all cases. Hence, the market values of the products at the final stage cannot be an accurate base for apportioning the joint costs at the split-off point.

Example 10

From the following particulars, prepare a Statement of Appropriation of Joint Costs:

Joint costs details: Materials Rs. 680; Wages Rs. 180; and Overheads Rs. 140. Three joint products A, B and C are produced at the split-off point. These products are further processed and sold as follows:

Joint Products	Quantity Units	Selling price per unit Rs.	Total sales value Rs.
A	60 kgs	12 per kg	720
B	120 kgs	8 per kg	960
C	40 litres	6 per litre	240
			1,920

Solution

Total joint costs Rs.680 + 180 + 140 = Rs.1,000

Apportionment Ratio based on total sales value of individual products =720 : 960 : 240 = 3 : 4 : 1

Statement of apportionment of Joint costs

Joint Products	Quantity	Sales value ratio	Apportioned joint costs Rs.	Joint cost per unit Rs.
A	60 kgs	3	375	6.25 per kg
B	120 kgs	4	500	4.17 per kg
C	40 litres	1	125	3.13 per litre
		Total	1,000	

(c) Market value less further processing costs: This method is used when sales values of joint products are not readily available at the split-off point. Joint products are further processed and the sales values at the final stage are ascertained. From these values of joint products, the further processing costs are deducted and net sales value at the point of separation is ascertained. These net sales values are used as the basis for apportioning the joint costs to individual products. It is a good method for product pricing but not for planning and control.

Example 11

From the data given below, prepare a Statement of Apportionment of joint costs to individual joint products A and B:

Total joint cost is Rs.9,000. After the split-off point, an amount of Rs.6,000 is incurred to complete 1,000 units product A and an amount of Rs.1,000 is incurred to complete 500 units product B. the completed units of products A and B are sold at Rs.20 and Rs.10 per unit respectively. Use Market value less further processing costs Method.

Solution

Statement of Apportionment of Joint Costs

Joint Products	Quantity Units	Selling price Rs.	Sales value Rs.	Less further processing	Sales value at split-off	Apportionment ratio	Apportioned joint cost Rs.
A	1,000 × 20		20,000	6,000	14,000	7	7,000
B	500 × 10		5,000	1,000	4,000	2	2,000
			25,000	7,000	18,000		9,000

(d) Net Value Method: Under this method, the following reduces the sales values of completed joint products: (i) Estimated profit margin, (ii) Selling and distribution expenses, if any, (iii) Further processing costs. The resultant net realizable values will be used as the basis for apportioning the joint costs among the joint products. This method is very difficult to use in practice since it requires detailed cost information and therefore very costly to operate.

Example 12

Excel ltd. manufactures three joint products X, Y, and Z. The joint cost of manufacture for the period was Rs.65,000. The estimated profit margin on each product as percentage of sales would be 30%, 25%, and 15% respectively. Additional information is as follows:

	Joint Products		
	X	Y	Z
	Rs.	Rs.	Rs.
Sales	60,000	40,000	25,000
Selling and distribution expenses	1,500	2,750	1,750
Subsequent processing costs	4,500	3,250	1,500

Prepare a Statement of Apportionment of joint costs using Net Value Method.

Solution

Statement of Apportionment of Joint costs

Particulars	Product X Rs.	Product Y Rs.	Product Z Rs.
Sales	60,000	40,000	25,000
Less: Estimated profit	18,000	10,000	3,750
	42,000	30,000	21,250
Less: Selling expenses	1,500	2,750	1,750
	40,500	27,250	19,500
Less: Further processing cost	4,500	3,250	1,500
Net Sales Value	36,000	24,000	18,000
Apportioning Ratio	6	4	3
Apportioned joint cost (Total cost Rs.65,000)	30,000	20,000	15,000

14.17 Accounting for By-products

By-products are secondary products and have very low commercial value. They are produced jointly with the main product and mostly in continuous process industries like oil refining, sugar manufacturing, chemical, meatpacking and coal. However, in order to ascertain the true cost and profit of main product the value of by-products should be dealt with in cost accounting. Various methods are used to deal with the cost and sales value of by-products. They are classified into two categories as Non-cost or Sales Value Method and Cost Method.

Non-cost methods include the following: (a) Other income or Miscellaneous Method, (b) Total Sales less Total Cost, (c) Total cost less sales value of by-product, (d) Total cost less net value of by-products, (e) Total cost less net yield of by-products, (f) Reverse cost method.

Cost Methods include the following: (a) Replacement or Opportunity Cost Method, (b) Standard Cost Method, (c) Joint cost proration.

Non-cost methods

(a) Miscellaneous Income Method: This method is used when the by-product has very low sales value and low commercial importance. Under this method the sales value of by-product is treated as other income or miscellaneous income and credited to profit and loss account. It is also used when the management's interest is in net results rather than close analysis.

(b) Total sales less Total cost: Under this method the sales value of by-product is added to sales value of main product. Then the combined total cost of main product is deducted from the total sales value.

(c) Total cost less sales value of by-products: Under this method the sales value of by-products like waste and scrap is reduced from the combined total cost of production. However the main disadvantage of this method is that the cost of main product fluctuates from time to time with the changing prices of by-product. If there is any inventory of by-product, it is valued at the market price.

(d) Total cost less net sales value of by-products: Under this method, net sales value (i.e., sales value minus selling and distribution expenses) of the by-product is deducted from the total cost of production. Selling and distribution expenses are charged only against by-products actually sold.

(e) Total cost less net yield of by-products: Under this method, costs incurred after the split-off point and selling and distribution expenses are deducted from the sales value of by-products. The net realized value is then deducted from the total cost of main product.

(f) Reverse cost method: This method assumes that the sales volume of by-product includes certain element of profit and therefore, it should not be charged to process account. Hence, the cost of by-product is arrived at working backwards. Estimated profit margin, then selling and distribution expenses first reduce the sales value of by-product and finally the cost incurred after split-off point.

Example 13

A manufacturing company produces one main product A and two by-products X and Y. Apportion the joint costs among the products using the Reverse Cost Method and also prepare a Comparative Profit and Loss Statement from the following data:

Products	A	X	Y
Sales (Rs.)	1,50,000	15,000	30,000
Further processing costs (Rs.)		4,500	9,000
Estimated profit margin (% on sales value)		20%	30%
Estimated selling expenses (% on sales) 20%		20%	20%
Total joint costs Rs.90,000			

Solution

Statement of Apportionment of Joint costs

Total cost at the point of separation					Rs. 90,000
Less: Cost of by-products working backward:			X	Y	
Sales value of by-products			Rs.15000	Rs.30,000	
Less: Profit margin	Rs.3,000	Rs.9,000			
Selling expenses	3,000	6,000			
Cost after separation	4,500	9,000	10,500	24,000	
Share of joint costs			4,500	6,000	10,500

Share of joint cost apportioned to main product	79,500

Comparative Profit and Loss Account

Products	A	X	Y	Total
	Rs.	Rs.	Rs.	Rs.
1. Sales	1,50,000	15,000	30,000	1,95,000
2. Cost of sales:				
Cost up to split-off point	79,500	4,500	6,000	90,000
Post separation cost		4,500	9,000	13 500
Cost of production	79,500	9,000	15,000	1,03,500
Selling expenses	30,000	3,000	6,000	39,000
Total cost of sales	1,09,500	12,000	21,000	1,42,500
3. Profit (1 - 2)	40,500	3,000	9,000	52,500
4. Percentage of profit on sales	27%	20%	30%	26.9%

Cost Methods

Standard Cost Method: This method can be used only when there is standard costing system in operation. Under this method the standards are set for each product based on technical assessment. The by-product is valued at standard rate and the standard cost of by-product is credited to the process account of the main product. As the standards set remain stable, the cost of main product would reflect changes, if any, due to operational factors. This is a good method to exercise control over the cost of main product effectively.

Replacement Cost Method: This method can be used when the by-product could be used as a raw material in the same undertaking. Under this method, the by-product is valued at the opportunity cost or replacement cost. The opportunity cost refers to savings in the cost of raw materials that need not be purchased from outside. For example in coke manufacturing, coal gas is obtained as a by-product. This coal gas may be used as fuel within the organization for heating purposes instead of buying gas from outside. The cost of gas so saved would be the opportunity cost or replacement cost of the by-product used for internal purposes. This cost is credited to the cost of production of main product (i.e., coke).

Proration of Joint Cost: This method is used when the by-product gains some economic significance or commercial value. In that case, the joint cost is apportioned between main product and by-products on some suitable basis. This method does not differentiate between joint products and by-products. For example, in oil refining, cooking gas was considered as a by-product. Now it has assumed greater economic significance like diesel, petrol, etc. and it is being treated as joint product. When a by-product is treated as a joint product, the joint costs are prorated (apportioned) between main product and by-products on a suitable basis.

Illustration 18

The following data have been taken out from the books of Indian Coke Company Ltd.

Joint Products	Yield per tonne of coal (kgs.)
Coke	665
Tar	57

Benzol	19
Sulphate of Ammonia	19
Gas	190
Water (waste)	50
Total	1,000

The price of coal is Rs.400 per ton. Direct wages and overhead costs to the point of split-off are Rs.600 and Rs.800 respectively per ton of coal. Apportion and ascertin the elements of cost and total cost of each product on the basis of weight.

Solution

Statement of Apportionment of joint costs

Joint products	Yield per ton kgs.	% to total coal	Apportionment of cost			
			Coal Rs.	Wages Rs.	Overheads Rs.	Total cost Rs.
Coke	665	70	280	420	560	1,260
Tar	57	6	24	36	48	108
Benzol	19	2	8	12	16	36
Sulphate of Ammonia	19	2	8	12	16	36
Gas	190	20	80	120	160	360
Total	950	100	400	600	800	1,800

Note: Percentage to total weight for distributing the elements of cost has been calculated ignoring the waste. In other words the loss in output (weight) due to waste has been distributed to other joint products.

Illustration 19

In a concern engaged in process industry four products emerge from a particular process of operation. The total cost of input for the period ended 30th September 1989 is Rs.2 53 500. The details of output, additional cost after split-off point and sales value of the product are given below:

Products Output		Additional processing cost after split-off point	Sales value at the split-off point	Sales value after processing
	Kgs.	Rs.	Rs	Rs.
A	8,000	60,000	1,15,000	1,68,000
B	5,000	10,000	90,000	1,10,000
C	3,000	--	55,000	60,000
D	4,000	20,000	80,000	90,000

You are required to prepare a statement of profitability based on the product being sold: (a) At the split-off point and (b) After further processing. (c) Advise the management as to what strategy should followed to improve the profits.

Solution

(a) Statement showing Profitability at the Split-off point

Joint Products	Sales value at the split-off point	Joint cost apportioned	Profit
	Rs.	Rs.	Rs.
A	1,15,000	85,743	29,257
B	90,000	67,103	22,897
C	55,000	41,007	13,993
D	80,000	59,647	20,353
Total	3,40,000	2,53,500	86,500

Note: Joint cost is apportioned in the ratio of sales value at the split-off point.

$$A = \text{Rs.}2{,}53{,}500 = \frac{1{,}15{,}000}{3{,}40{,}000}\ 85{,}743 \text{ and so on}$$

(b) Statement showing Profitability after further processing

Joint Products	Sales value after Further processing cost	Additional Processing	Net sales value	Joint cost	Profit
	(Rs.)	Rs.	Rs.	Rs.	Rs.
A	1,68,000	60,000	1,08,000	85,743	22,257
B	1,10,000	10,000	1,00,000	67,103	32,897
C	60,000	--	60,000	41,007	18,993
D	90,000	20,000	70,000	59,647	10,353
Total	4,28,000	90,000	3,38,000	2,53,500	84,500

Since the overall profit has decreased by Rs.2,000, the company should adopt a different strategy to improve the profits.

(c) Comparative Additional Cost and Incremental Revenue Statement

Joint Products	Additional processing Cost	Incremental Revenue
	(Rs.)	(Rs.)
A	60,000	1,68,000 – 1,15,000 = 53,000
B	10,000	1,10,000 – 90,000 = 20,000

C		–	60,000 – 55,000 = 5,000
D		20,000	90,000 – 80,000 = 10,000

Recommendation: Comparing the additional processing costs with incremental revenue, it is ascertained that in the case of B and C, the incremental revenue is greater than additional processing cost. Hence, they may sold after further processing. In the case of A and D, the additional processing cost is greater than incremental revenue. Hence, it is better to sell these two products at the split-off point.

Revised Profitability Statement

Joint Product	Profit (Rs.)	When to be sold
A	29,257	To be sold at the split-of point
B	32,897	To be sold after further processing
C	18,993	To be sold after further processing
D	20,353	To be sold at the split-off point
Total	1,01,500	Maximum Profit

Illustration 20

The yield of a certain process is 75% as to the main product, 20% as to the by-product and 5% as to the process loss. The material put into process 10,000 units at a cost of Rs.47.50 per unit all other charges are Rs.28 500, of which power cost accounted for one-third of the total. It is ascertained that power is chargeable as to the main product and by-product in the ratio of 10: 9. Draw up a statement showing the cost of the by-product.

Solution

Workings

Materials introduced 10,000 units at Rs.47.50 = Rs.475,000

Materials		4,75,000	
Power Charges (1/3 of Rs.28500)	9,500		
Other charges (28,500 – 9500)	19,000	28,500	
Joint costs		Rs.5,03,500	
Main product 75% of 10,000 units			7 500 units
By-product 20% of 10,000 units			2,000 units
Process loss 5% of 10,000 units			500 units

Joint cost apportioning ratio = 7,500: 2,000 = 15:4

Statement showing the cost of By-product

Particulars	Ratio	Total	Main Product	By-product
		Rs.	Rs.	Rs.
Production-units		9,500	7,500	2,000
Materials	15:4	4,75,000	3,75,000	1,00,000
Power	10:9	9,500	5,000	4,500
Other charges	15:4	19,000	10,000	9,000
Total cost		5,03,500	3,90,000	1,13,500

Illustration 21

A company manufacturing a product A also produces a by-product B, which is further processed into a finished product. The joint cost of manufacture is: Materials Rs.10,000, Wages Rs.6,000, and Overheads Rs.4,000. Further processing costs for A and B are Rs.10,000 and Rs.6,000 respectively. Sales values are: A - Rs.32,000 and B - Rs.16,000. Estimated profits on sales are 25% for A and 20% for B. Assume that the selling expenses are in proportion of selling price. Prepare a Statement of Apportionment of joint cost and a Statement showing cost of production of A and B.

Solution

Working notes: Computation of selling expenses

	Rs.	Rs.
Total sales value of A and B		48,000
Less: Profit: A – (25% on sales)	8,000	
B – (20% on sales)	3,200	11,200
Cost of sales or Total cost		36,800
Less: Production cost:,		
Joint cost-Materials	10,000	
Wages	6,000	
Overheads	4,000	
Separate expenses-A	10,000	
B	6,000	36,000
Selling expenses		800

Share of product A – $2/3 \times 800$ = Rs.533

Share of product B – $1/3 \times 800$ = Rs.267

Statement of Apportionment of joint cost

Particulars	Product A	By-product B
	Rs.	Rs.
Selling price	32,000	16,000
Less: Estimated profit	8,000	3,200

Cost of sales	24,000	12,800
Less: Selling expenses	533	267
Cost of production	23,467	12,533
Less: Further processing cost	10,000	6,000
Share of joint cost	13,467	6,533

Statement showing Cost of Production of A and B

Particulars	Product A	Product B
	Rs.	Rs.
Joint cost: Materials	6,734	3 266
Wages	4,040	1,960
Overheads	2,693	1,307
Total	13,467	6,533
Further processing cost	10,000	6,000
Cost of production	23,467	12,533

Note: Joint cost has been distributed to individual products in the ratio of their share of joint cost i.e., 13467: 6533. Selling expenses are distributed in the ratio of selling price i.e., 2: 1.

Illustration 22

A factory is engaged in the production of a Chemical Alpha and in the course of manufacture a by-product Beta is produced, which after a separate process has a commercial value. Following are the information for the month January 2003.

	Joint expenses	Separate expenses	
		Alpha Rs	Beta Rs.
Materials	20,000	4,000	5,600
Labour	8,000	5,000	5,000
Overheads	5,000	2,800	2,000

The output for the month was 300 kgs., of Alpha and 100 kgs. of Beta. The selling price of product Beta is Rs.200 per kg., on which the profit earned was 331/3% on cost price. Prepare an account to show the cost of Product Alpha per kg.

Solution

Joint Expenses Account

Particulars	Amount (Rs.)	Particulars	Amount (Rs.)
To Materials	20,000	By Product Beta a/c*	2,400

To Wages	8,000	By Product Alpha a/c**	30,600
To Overheads	5,000	(Balancing figure),	
	33,000		33,000

Product Beta Account
(Output: 100 kgs.)

Particulars	Amount (Rs.)	Particulars	Amount (Rs.)
To Joint Expenses A/c* (Balancing figure),	2,400	By Cost of Production	15,000
To Material	5,600		
To Wages	5,000		
To Overheads	2,000		
	15,000		15,000

$$\text{Rs. } 20000 \times \frac{100}{133\frac{1}{3}} = \text{Rs. } 15,000$$

Product Alpha Account
(Output: 300 kgs.)

Particulars	Amount (Rs.)	Particulars	Amount (Rs.)
To Joint expenses a/c**	30,600	By Cost of production	42,400
To Materials	4,000	At (42,400/300) = Rs.141.33	
To Wages	5,000		
To Overheads	2,800		
	42,400		42,400

Illustration 23

Calculate the estimated cost of production of by-products A and B at the split-off point from the main product.

	By-Product A	By-Product B
Selling price per unit	Rs. 60	Rs. 120
Cost per unit after separation from the main product	Rs. 15	Rs. 25
Units produced	2,500	1,000

Selling expenses amount to 25% of total factory cost i.e., including pre-as well as post-separation works cost. Selling price is arrived at by adding 20% of total cost i.e., cost of sales.

Solution

Statement of Apportionment of Joint Costs

Particulars	By Product A 2,500 units		By Product b 1,000 units	
	Per unit Rs.	Total Rs.	Per unit Rs.	Total Rs.
Selling Price	60	1,50,000	120	1,20,000
Less: Profit (1/6 of selling price)	10	25,000	20	20,000
Total cost	50	1,25,000	100	1,00,000
Less: Selling expenses (1/4 of works cost or 1/5 of total cot)	10	25,000	20	20,000
Cost of production	40	1,00,000	80	80,000
Less: After separation cost	15	37,500	25	25,000
Cost of production at the split off point	25	62,500	55	55,000

Note: 1/5 of total cost = 1/6 of selling price.

Illustration 24

B ltd produces four joint products A, B, C, and D all of which emerge from the processing of one raw material. The following are the relevant data:

Joint Products	Number of units	Selling price per unit
A	5,000	18.00
B	9,000	8.00
C	4,000	4.00
D	2,000	11.00

The company budgets for a profit of 10% of sales value. The other estimated costs are:

Carriage inwards	Rs.10,000
Direct wages	30,000
Manufacturing overheads	20,000
Administration overheads 10% on sales value	

You are required to (a) calculate the maximum price that may be paid for the new material. (b) Prepare a Comprehensive cost statement for each of the products allocating the materials and other costs based upon (i) number of units; (ii) sales value.

Solution

Computation of Joint Costs

Joint Products	No.of units	Selling price per unit	Sales value
A	5,000	Rs.18.00	Rs.90,000
B	9,000	8.00	72,000
C	4,000	4.00	16,000
D	2,000	11.00	22,000
Total sales value			2,00,000
Less:Budgeted profit (10%)			20,000
Total joint costs			1,80,000

(a) Maximum Price paid for raw materials

Total joint costs		Rs.1,80,000
Less: Other costs:		
Carriage inwards	Rs.10,000	
Direct wages	30,000	
Manufacturing expenses	20,000	
Administration overheads	20,000	80,000
Maximum price to be paid for raw materials		1,00,000

(b) (i) Comprehensive Cost Statement (based on number units)

Products No.of units	A	B	C	D	Total
Raw materials at Rs.5	25,000	45,000	20,000	10,000	1,00,000
Carriage at Re.0.50	2,500	4,500	2,000	1,000	10,000
Direct wages at Rs.1.50	7,500	13,500	6,000	3,000	30,000
Manufacturing expenses Re. 1	5,000	9,000	4,000	2,000	20,000
Admn.Overheads at Re.1	5,000	9,000	4,000	2,000	20,000
Total cost	45,000	81,000	36,000	18,000	1,80,000

(b) (ii) Comprehensive Cost Statement (based on sales value)

Products Sales Value (Rs.)	A	B	C	D	Total
Sales Value (Rs.)	90,000	72,000	16,000	22,000	2,00,000
Raw materials	45,000	36,000	8,000	11,000	1,00,000
Carriage	4,500	3,600	800	1,100	10,000
Direct wages	13,500	10,800	2,400	3,300	30,000
Manufacturing expenses	9,000	7,200	1,600	2,200	20,000
Administration overheads	9,000	7,200	1,600	2,200	20,000
Total Cost	81,000	64,800	14,400	19,800	1,80,000

14.18 Process Costing-Inter process Profits

In process costing, the usual practice is to transfer the output of one process to another and finally to finished stock at cost price. In this method of transfer, process accounts will not reveal any profit or loss. But sometimes, the transfer is made at transfer price or market price. This method is adopted in order to measure the efficiency or inefficiency of individuals process. When market price cannot be ascertained, certain percentage of profit margin is added to the cost of processing in order to arrive at the transfer price. Consequently, each process account reveals a profit and this profit is known as 'inter process profit'.

Advantages of accounting for inter process profits

(a) Inter process profits enable to measure the efficiency of each process.

(b) Comparison of costs with market price at each stage assist management to take 'make or buy' decisions.

(c) The efficiency of or inefficiency of one process. In other words, each process can be assessed separately on that account.

Adjustment for Inter process Profits

When the output of one process is transferred to another and finally to finished stock account at transfer price (cost plus estimated profit margin), the closing inventories, if any, will be valued at transfer price. Such inventories will include unrealized profits. Such profits should be adjusted for purposes of year-end financial reporting. Otherwise, it will amount to earning profit by trading within the organization. Hence, necessary adjustments are made in the values of closing inventories by means of creating reserves or provision for unrealized profits. Total profit less provision for unrealized profits would amount to profits earned on sale of finished stock. The closing inventories will be shown in the balance sheet at cost i.e., values of inventory at transfer price less provision for unrealized profits.

Computation of provision for unrealized profits

$$\text{Formula Cost of inventory} = \frac{\text{Cost}}{\text{Total}} \times \text{Closing inventory}$$

$$\text{Provision for unrealized profits} = \text{Value of closing inventory} - \text{Cost}$$

Illustration 25

A product passes through two process A and B. Output of A is transferred to B at cost plus 25% profit and from B to finished stock at cost plus 25% profit. There were no work in progress in both processes and opening stock of finished goods at the end of the period. Additional information available is as follows:

Particulars	Process A Rs.	Process B Rs.
Direct materials	20,000	60,000
Direct wages	30,000	40,000
Closing stock	10,000	30,000

Closing stock of finished goods was valued at Rs.45,000 and the balance was sold for Rs.1,50,000.

Prepare Process Accounts and Finished Stock Account.

Solution

Process A Account

Particulars	Total Rs.	Cost Rs.	Profit Rs.	Particulars	Total Rs.	Cost Rs.	Profit Rs.
To Materials	20,000	20,000	–	By Transfer to Process B	50,000	40,000	10,000
To wages	30,000	30,000	–				
	50,000	50,000					
Less: Closing Stock	10,000	10,000	–				
	40,000	40,000					
Add: Profit (25% on cost)	10,000	–	10,000				
	50,000	40,000	10,000		50,000	40,000	10,000

Process B Account

Particulars	Total Rs.	Cost Rs.	Profit Rs.	Particulars	Total Rs.	Cost Rs.	Profit Rs.
To Transfer from Process A	50,000	40,000	10,000	By Transfer to Finished Stock	1,50,000	1,12,000	38,000
To Materials	60,000	60,000					
To Wages	40,000	40,000					
	1,50,000	1,40,000	10,000				

Less: Closing stock	30,000	28,000	2,000				
	1,20,000	1,12,000	8,000				
To Profit (25% on cost)	30,000	–	30,000				
	1,50,000	1,12,000	38,000		1,50,000	1,12,000	38,000

Finished Stock Account

Particulars	Total Rs.	Cost Rs.	Profit Rs.	Particulars	Total Rs.	Cost Rs.	Profit Rs.
To Transfer from Process B	1,50,000	1,12,000	38,000	By Sales	1,50,000	78,400	71,600
Less: Closing Stock	45,000	33,600	11,400,				
	95,000	78,400	26,600				
To Profit	45,000	–	45,000				
	1,50,000	78,400	71,600		1,50,000	78,400	71,600

Working Notes: The stock in Process A is valued at cost and therefore there is no unrealized profit.

Computation of cost stock

$$\text{Formula} = \text{Cost of stock } \frac{\text{Cost}}{\text{Total}} \times \text{Closing Stock}$$

Unrealized Profit = Value of stock – Cost of Stock

Cost of stock in Process B = 1,40,000/1,50,000 × 30,000 = Rs. 28,000

Unrealized Profit = Rs. 30,000 – 28,000 = Rs. 2,000

Cost of Finished Stock = 1,10,000/1,50,000 × 45,000 = Rs. 33,000

Unrealized Profit = Rs. 45,000 – 33,000 = Rs. 12,000

Total unrealized Profit = Rs. 2,000 + 11,400 = Rs. 13,400

In Balance sheet the Stocks will be shown at cost as follows:

Stock in Process A = Rs. 10,000

Stock in B (Rs. 30,000 – 2,000) = 28,000

Finished stock (45,000 – 11400) = 33,600

Total (85,000 – 13,400) = 71,600

Illustration 26

From the following information prepare Process Accounts and calculate the actual profits earned by a company for the month of January 2003:

Particulars	Process A Rs.	Process B Rs.	Process C Rs.	Finished Stock Rs.
Opening Stock	4,000	4,800	3,200	12,000
Direct Material	8,000	8,400	12,000	
Direct Wages	6,000	6,000	6,400	
Overheads	5,600	2,400	16,000	
Closing Stock	2,000	2,400	1,600	6,000
Profit on cost	33⅓%	25%	25%	
Inter process profit for Opening stock	–	800	8000	4,400

Stocks in process are valued at prime cost and finished stock has been valued at price at which it received from Process C. Sales during the period were Rs.1,40,000.

Solution

Process A Account

Particulars	Total Rs.	Cost Rs.	Profit Rs.	Particulars	Total Rs.	Cost Rs.	Profit Rs.
To Opening Stock	4,000	4,000	–	By TRansfer to Process B	28,800	21,600	7,200
To Materials	8,000	8,000	–				
To Wages	6,000	6,000	–				
	18,000	18,000	–				
Less closing stock	2,000	2,000	–				
Prime cost	16,000	16,000	–				
Add: overheads	5,600	5,600	–				
	21,600	21,600	–				
Profit (33⅓% on cost)	7,200	–					
	28,800	21,600	7,200		28,800	21,600	7,200

Process B Account

Particulars	Total Rs.	Cost Rs.	Profit Rs.	Particulars	Total Rs.	Cost Rs.	Profit Rs.
Opening stock	4,800	4,000	800	Transferred to Process C	60,000	40,400	19,600
Transfer from A	28,800	21,600	7,200				
Materials	8,400	8,400					
Wages	6,000	6,000					
Prime cost	48,000	40,000	8,000				
Less closing stock	2,400	2,000	400				
	45,600	38,000	7,600				
Add overheads	2,400	2,400					
	48,000	40,400					
Profit (25% on cost)	12,000		12,000				
	60,000	40,400	19,600		60,000	40,400	19,600

Process C Account

Particulars	Total Rs.	Cost Rs.	Profit Rs.	Particulars	Total Rs.	Cost Rs.	Profit Rs.
Opening stock	3,200	2,400	800	Transferred to Finished Stock	1,20,000	76,000	44,000
Transfer from B	60,000	40,400	19,600				
Materials	12,000	12,000	–				
Wages	6,400	6,400					
	81,600	61,200	20,400				
Less closing stock	1,600	1,200	400				
Prime cost	80,000	60,000	20,000				
Overheads	16,000	16,000,					
	96,000	76,000,					
Profit (25% on cost)	24,000	–	24,000				
	1,20,000	76,000	44,000		1,20,000	76,000	44,000

Finished Stock Account

Particulars	Total Rs.	Cost Rs.	Profit Rs.	Particulars	Total Rs.	Cost Rs.	Profit Rs.
Opening stock	12,000	7,600	4,400	By Sales	1,40,000	79,800	60,200
Transfer from C	1,20,000	76,000	44,000				
	1,32,000	83,600	48,400				
Less closing stock	6,000						
		3,800	2,200				
	1,26,000	79,800	46,200				
Profit	14,000	–	14,000				
	1,40,000	79,800	60,200		1,40,000	79,800	60,200

Working Notes: Computation of unrealized profit

$$\text{Process B} = \frac{4{,}000}{4{,}800} \times 2{,}400 = \text{Rs. } 2{,}000$$

Unrealized profit = Rs. 2,400 − 2,000 = Rs. 400

$$\text{Process B} = \frac{71{,}200}{81{,}600} \times 1{,}600 = \text{Rs. } 1{,}200$$

Unrealized profit = Rs. 1,600 = 1,200 = Rs. 400

$$\text{Finished stock} = \frac{76{,}000}{1{,}20{,}000} \times 6{,}000 = \text{Rs. } 3{,}800$$

Unrealized profit = Rs. 6,000 − 3,800 = Rs. 2,200

Computation of Actual Profits

Process	Profits Rs.	Opening Reserve Rs.	Closing Reserve Rs.	Difference Actual Profits Rs.	Rs.
A	7,200	–	–	–	7,200
B	12,000	800	400	400	12,400
C	24,000	800	400	400	24,400
Finished Stock	14,000	4,400	2,200	2,200	16,200
Total	57,200	+ 6,000	− 3,000		60,200

Opening Reserve will be treated as realized profit and therefore added to process profits. Closing reserve will be treated as unrealized profit and therefore deducted from the process profits.

Illustration 27

There are two processes in a factory manufacturing a single product. Following are the particulars of expenses incurred in different processes:

	Process I	Process II
	Rs.	Rs.
Raw material	30,000	–
Transfer from Process I	–	88,000
Wages	26,000	20,000
Overheads	29,000	28,000

After crediting the Process I with Rs.5,000 being the estimated realizable value of waste and by-product and Rs.8,000 against process profits the balance is transferred to process II. There is no wastage of by-product in Process II and the output is transferred to Finished Stock Account with a margin of 25% on total cost. The Finished Stock inventories at the end of period showed a balance of Rs. 21,000.

Prepare Process Accounts and show what figure should be adopted for Balance Sheet purpose?

Solution

Process I Account

Particulars	Total Rs.	Cost Rs.	Profit Rs.	Particulars	Total Rs.	Cost Rs.	Profit Rs.
To Material	30,000	30,000	–	By Sale of by-product	5,000	5,000	–
To Wages	26,000	26,000	–				
To Overheads	29,000	29,000	–	By Transfer to Process II	88,000	80,000	8,000
To Profit (10% on cost)	8,000		8,000				
	93,000	85,000	8,000		93,000	85,000	8,000

Process II Account

Particulars	Total Rs.	Cost Rs.	Profit Rs.	Particulars	Total Rs.	Cost Rs.	Profit Rs.
To Transfer from I	88,000	80,000	8,000	By Transfer to			
To wages	20,000	20,000		Finished Stock	1,70,000	1,28,000	42,000
To Overheads	28,000	28,000					

Particulars	Total Rs.	Cost Rs.	Profit Rs.	Particulars	Total Rs.	Cost Rs.	Profit Rs.
	1,36,000	1,28,000	8,000				
To Profit (25% on cost)	34,000		34,000				
	1,70,000	1,28,000	42,000		1,70,000	1,28,000	42,000

Finished Stock Account

Particulars	Total Rs.	Cost Rs.	Profit Rs.	Particulars	Total Rs.	Cost Rs.	Profit Rs.
To Transfer from II Account	1,70,000	1,28,000	42,000				

Computation of Cost of Finished stock:

$$\text{Formula} = \frac{\text{Cost}}{\text{Total}} \times \text{Value of closing stock}$$

$$\text{Cost of stock} = \frac{1{,}28{,}000}{1{,}70{,}000} \times 21{,}000 = \text{Rs. } 15{,}812$$

The value of stock of finished goods should be shown at cost of Rs.15,812.

REVIEW QUESTIONS

1. Define Job costing. What are its purpose and features?
2. Enumerate the advantages and limitations of Job costing?
3. Describe the Job Cost accounting procedure.
4. What is Contract costing? Give a specimen format of a Contract Account.
5. Write short notes on: (a) Coat Plus Contract, (b) Escalation Clause, (c) Profit on Incomplete Contract, and (d) Treatment of Plant and Equipment used for the contract.
6. What is Batch Costing? What are its essential features?
7. State the meaning and features of Process Costing.
8. Distinguish between Job Costing and Process Costing.
9. List out the advantages and limitations of Process Costing.
10. Describe briefly the Process Cost Accounting procedure.
11. Explain the following concepts: (a) Equivalent Production Units, (b) Process Losses, and (c) Inter Process Profits.
12. Explain the concepts of Joint Products and By-products.
13. How can a By-product be differentiated from a Joint Product?
14. Describe the various methods of accounting for Joint products.
15. Describe how the joint costs may be apportioned among the joint products.
16. How can the Market Value Method be used for apportioning the joint costs?

17. Describe the various methods of accounting for By-products.
18. Describe the following methods of accounting for By-products: (a) Reserve Cost Method, (b) Standard Cost Method, and (c) Opportunity Cost Method.

REVIEW PROBLEMS

1. The following direct costs were incurred on JOb No.621 of Beta Engineering Works:

   Materials Rs.6,830

   Wages: Department I-160 Hours at Rs.2.50 per hour

   Department II-120 Hours at Rs.4 per hour

   Overhead expenses were estimated as follows:

   Variable Overheads - Department I: Rs.10,000 for 8000 hours

   Department II Rs. 12,000 for 6,000 hours

   Fixed overheads - Rs.15,000 for 20,000 normal working time of the factory

   You are required to calculate the cost of Job No.621 and estimate the percentage of profit earned if the price quoted was Rs.9,500.

   (Answer: Refer illustration 1. Profit Rs. 1,140 and 13.6%)

2. The following information for the year ended 31th December 2002 is obtained from the books of a factory:

Particulars	Completed Jobs Rs.	Work in Progress Rs.
Raw materials supplied from stores	90,000	30,000
Wages	1,00,000	40,000
Chargeable expenses	10,000	4,000
Materials transferred to Work in progress	2,000	2,000
Materials returned to stores	1,000	

   Factory overhead is 80% of wages and office overhead 25% of factory cost.

   The value of executed jobs during the year was Rs.4,10,000. Prepare (a) consolidated Completed Job account and (b) Consolidated Work in progress account.

   (Answer: Profit on Completed Jobs Rs. 63,750) (C.A. Adapted)

3. A ltd. accepted a contract for the construction of a building for Rs.20,00,000. The Contractee agreed to pay 90% of the work certified as completed by the architect. During the first year the amounts spent were: Materials Rs. 2,40,000; Labour Rs.3,00,000; Machinery Rs. 60,000; and other expenses Rs. 1,80,000.

   At the end of the year, machinery was considered to be of Rs. 40,000, and materials at site of the value of Rs. 10,000. Work certified during the year totaled Rs. 8,00,000 in addition work in progress but not certified at the end of the year had cost Rs. 30,000. Prepare Contract account in books of the company. Also show the amount that can reasonably be transferred to Profit and Loss account.

   (Answer: Total Profit Rs. 50,000; Transfer to P & L a/c Rs.15,000)

4. A firm of building contractors commenced to trade on 1st April 2000, the following was the expenditure on a contract for Rs. 3 lakhs;

	Rs.
Materials issued to contract	51,000
Plant used for contract	15,000
Wages incurred	81,000
Other expenses incurred	5,000

Cash received on account to 31th March 2001 amounted to Rs. 1,28,000, being 80% of the work certified. Of the plant and materials charged to the contract, plant that cost Rs.3,000 and materials, which cost Rs. 2,500, were lost. On 31th March, plant which cost Rs.2,000 was returned to stores, the cost of work done but uncertified was Rs. 1,000 and materials costing Rs. 2,300 were in hand at site. Charge 15% depreciation on plant, reserve 1/3rd of profit received and prepare a contract account from the above particulars.

(Answer: Total Profit Rs.26,000; transfer to P & L a/c Rs. 14,400)

5. A product passes through two processes A and B then to Finished Stock. It is ascertained that in each process normally 5% of the total weight is lost and 10% is scrap, which from Process A and B realizes Rs. 80 per ton and Rs. 200 per ton respectively. The following are the figures relating to both the process:

	Process A Rs.	Process B Rs.
Materials in tons	1,000	70
Material cost per ton	125	200
Wages in rupees	28,000	10,000
Manufacturing expenses	8,000	5,250
Output in tons	830	780

Prepare Process Accounts showing cost per ton of each process. There was no stock or work in progress in any process.

(Answer: Transfer to B Rs. 1,49,400 and Abnormal loss Rs. 3,600; Cost per ton Rs. 180; Transfer to Finished stock Rs. 1,63,800 and Cost per ton Rs. 210.)

6. The output from Process X totaled 2,500 units. It was considered that 200 units were an abnormal loss. Normal loss allowed was 10%. The other information are given below:

Material at	Rs.5 per unit
Labour	Rs. 4,000
Overheads	Rs. 3,350
Wastage realized	Rs. 2.50 per unit

Prepare Process Account and Abnormal loss Account.

(Answer: Input in Process 3,000 units; Transfer Rs. 20,000; abnormal loss Rs.1,600 and transfer to Costing P & L a/c Rs.1,100.)

7. An Oil company gives following data. Purchase of 1,000 quintals of copra is at Rs.500 per quintal.

	Crushing Rs.	Refining Rs.	Finishing Rs.
Cost of labour	6,600	3,000	3,000
Electric power	1,000	500	400
Sundry material	700	200	–
Repairs to Machinery	500	400	400
Steam	250	150	100

Other factory expenses Rs.9,450 to be charged at 75% of wages. Cost of casks Rs.580

Normal loss in 1st Process was 30% of input and actual output was 690 quintals.

Process II By-products 90 quintals value Rs.6,200

Process III Normal loss 5%, Actual output 580 quintals

Scrap of 1st Process realized Rs.10 per quintal.

Prepare various Process Accounts.

(Answer: Process I - Transfer Rs.5,03,700, Abnormal loss 10 quintals Rs.7,300; Process II - Transfer 600 quintals Rs.5,04,000; Process III - Transfer Rs.5,19,100, abnormal gain 10 quintals Rs.8,950. Finished stock - 580 quintals Rs.5,19,680 including cost of casks Rs.580)

8. From the following data prepare Process Account for a single product for December 2002:

	Process I	Process II
	Rs.	Rs.
(A) Cost incurred during the period:		
Direct materials	60,000	–
Direct wages	12,000	16,000
Factory overheads	24,000	20,000
(B) Units of Production	Units	Units
Received in Process	40,000	36,000
Completed and transferred	36,000	32,000
Closing Work in Process	2,000	2,500
Opening Work in Process	Nil	Nil
Loss in process (Normal loss)	2,000	1,500

(C) Closing Work in Process should be valued at Materials 100% and Labour and overheads 50%.

(Answer: Process I - EPU Material 38,000 units, Labour and overheads 37,000 units. Transfer 36,000 units at Rs.91,869;
Process II - EPU Material 34,500 units, Lab & overheads 33,250 units, Transfer 32,000 units at Rs.1,19,860; WIP-I-Rs.4131 & II - Rs.8009.)

9. A product passes through two processes I and II; the centre material being placed in Process I. From the following production and cost data relating to Process I work out the value of closing inventory and the value of the materials transferred to Process II.

Process I	Rs.
Opening inventory	10,000
Material	27,500
Labour	50,000
Manufacturing overheads	40,000
	Kg.
Opening inventory (25% complete)	4,000
Put into Process	12,000
Transferred to Process II	10,000
Closing inventory (20% complete)	5,000
Spoilage during process	1,000

(Answer EPU Material, Labour and Overheads 10,000 units; Closing inventory Rs.11,750, and transferred to II Rs.1,15,750)

10. From the following information, prepare process accounts:

	Process A	Process B	Process C
Direct material	60,000	15,000	15,000
Direct Labour	45,000	30,000	30,000
Closing Stock	15,000	17,500	42,600

Finished goods sold for Rs.2,60,000. Value of closing finished stock is Rs.11,224. It is the policy of the company to charge 20% on transfer price while transferring the goods from Process A to B and 20% on cost price from B to C and from C to Finished Stock.

(Answer: Total Profit Rs.1,34,600; Unrealized Profit - B -Rs.2,500, C-Rs.9,600; Profit-A-Rs.22,500, B-Rs.28,000, C-Rs.34080)

11. Z ltd. manufactures product X, which yields two by-products B1 and B2. The actual joint cost of manufacturing for the month of December 2002 were Rs.24,600. The profits on each product as a percentage of sales are 331/3%, 25% and 15% respectively. Further processing costs were as follows:

	X	B1	B2,
Direct material	300	225	75
Direct wages	600	375	150
Overheads	450	375	225
	1,350	975	225
Sales	18,000	12,000	7,500

(Answer: Share of Joint cost - X Rs.10,650, B1 Rs.8,025, B2 Rs.5,925)

12. A certain chemical process yields 75% of the material introduced as main product, 20% as a by-product, and 5% being lost. The ratio of material consumed by main product and by-product is 4:1. Time taken to produce one unit of by-product is half the time taken by main product. Overheads have been allocated two times of wages of each product.

Cost data: Raw material 4,000 units Rs.	20,000
Direct Wages	17,000
Factory overheads	34,000
Total	71,000

(Answer: Cost per unit: Main Product Rs.20.33; By-product Rs.12.50)

13. A ltd. manufacture a product M that yields two by-products B1 and B2. During a period the amount spent up to the point of separation was Rs.20,600. Subsequent expenses were:

	M	B1	B2
	Rs.	Rs.	Rs.
Direct materials	300	200	150
Direct wages	400	300	200
Manufacturing overheads	300	270	280
	1000	770	630

Sales value of products M, B1, and B2 was Rs.15,000, Rs.10,000, Rs.5,000 respectively. It was estimated that the net profit as percentage of sales in case of B1 and B2 would be 25% and 20% respectively. Ascertain the profit earned on Product M.
(Answer: Share of joint costs: M - Rs.10,500; B1 - Rs.6730; B2 - Rs.3370. Profit of M Rs.3,500)

15

STANDARD COSTING AND VARIANCE ANALYSIS

Learning Objectives

After completing this Chapter, you should be able to

— Define Standard costing and differentiate it with other systems.

— Explain the mening and types of variances

— Compute different kinds of variances.

— Analyse the causes and disposition of variances.

15.1 Defintion of Standard Costing

The word 'standard' means a benchmark or yardstick. The standard cost is a predetermined or expected cost, which determines what each product or service should cost under given conditions. In other words it is the expected cost of producing one unit. It is, in effect, a budget for one unit. Standard costing may be defined basically as a technique of cost accounting, which compares the standard cost of each product or service with the actual cost to determine the efficiency of operation so that remedial action may be taken immediately.

The Institute of Cost and Management Accountants, England defines standard costing as "the preparation and use of standard costs, and the analysis of variances of their causes and the points of incidence." Variance is the difference between a budgeted or standard amount and the actual amount during a given period. The following steps are thus involved in standard costing:

(a) Preparation and use of standards;

(b) Comparison of actual costs with standards to determine the variance; and

(c) Investigating the variance and taking appropriate actions where necessary.

15.2 Compare and Contrast Budgetary Control and Standard Costing

Similarities: Budgetary control and standard costing are comparable systems of cost accounting in that they are both predetermined and forward-looking. The common objective is of controlling business operations by establishing pre-determined targets. The modus operandi is also the same for both the systems where the actual performance is compared with the pre-determined targets (standards or budgets) in order to ascertain variance. The causes of such variances are then investigated and appropriate actions taken wherever necessary. However, there are few distinctions between these two systems.

Distinctions between Budgetary Control and Standard Costing

	Standard Costing System		Budgetary Control System
1.	Standard costing is related to production and production costs. Hence, it is more rigorous and intensive.	1.	Budgetary control is related to all types of items of revenue and expenditure. whether they belong to the product or not. i.e, to all types of business activities. Hence, it is more extensive.
2.	Standard is established on the basis of technical estimates. It is a projection of cost accounts.	2.	Budget is based on past experience and in most cases, it is a projection of financial accounts.
3.	Standards are very rigid and 'ought to be' estimates. They fix targets.	3.	Budgets are comparatively less rigid and 'should be' estimates. They fix limits.
4.	Standard costing system cannot operate well without a budgetary control system. It is also not possible to operate the system in parts.	4.	Budgetary control can be operated without a standard costing system. It can also be adopted in part.
5.	Variance analysis is a subject of special study of standard costing.	5.	The study of variances is not a subject of special study as in the case of standard costing.
6.	Standards are the minimum targets, which are to be attained at specific efficiency levels.	6.	Budgets determine the maximum limits of expenses above which actual expenditure should not go.

Historical costing: It is a system of costing where the costs are ascertained after they have been incurred. This costing is based on recorded data and the costs arrived at are verifiable by past events. The historical costs are actual costs and therefore, the question of exercising control over them does not arise at all. It is simply an analysis of costs after they have been incurred and therefore pertain to past data.

15.3 How does Standard Costing Differ from Estimated Costing?

Estimated costing refers to the system of costing where the costs are estimated in advance, which means that costs, likely to be incurred during a given period of time, are estimated well before their being incurred. This is done with reference to historical costs and the prevailing conditions of business. It is thus an estimation of actual or historical costs of a business in anticipation.

Standard costing refers to the system of costing where the costs, which ought to be there and should be attained, are determined in advance. It strives to make the actual costs equal or approximate to the predetermined costs. Thus the term 'standard costs' does not refer to what the costs are or what the costs shall be, but refers to what the costs should be or ought to be.

The main points of difference between Estimated costing and Standard costing are as follows:

	Estimated costing		Standard costing
1.	It can be used in any business, which is running under historical costing system.	1.	It can be applied in a business operating under standard costing system.
2.	Calculation of estimated costs may be made at any time for any specific purpose. These costs may reflect approximations or less accuracy.	2.	Scientific basis of calculation is made for arriving at standard costs.
3.	The use of estimated cost is as statistical data only.	3.	Standard costs are used as a regular system of accounts from which variances are found out.
4.	The main emphasis under estimation is on the ascertainment of costs and such costs depend on expected actual or average of past performances.	4.	Under this system the main aspect involved is the cost control. It serves as yardstick for measurement of performance.
5.	It can be ascertainment for a part of the business also and for a particular purpose.	5.	Standard costs are to be fixed in respect of every element of cost and therefore, it incorporates whole of the manufacturing process.

15.4 Type of Industries where Standard Costing is More Suitable

Standard costing is a system or technique of cost accounting, which can be used in conjunction with process, job or operating costing without any difficulty, whatsoever. Industries where standard costing is more suitable and used can be listed as under:

1. Process industries where the method of production and nature of output are the same.

Examples: Chemical works, Paper mills, Oil refineries, etc.

2. Industries where the methods of manufacture are repetitive and products are homogeneous.

Examples: Agricultural and food products.

3. Service industries where operating or operation costing system is also applicable.

Examples: Transport, Water, Gas, and Electricity, etc.

4. Engineering and textile industries where a large range of products are produced.
5. Extraction industries such as coal, oil, and timber, etc.

15.5 Utility of Standard Costing as a Management Tool

Standard costing aids management in making correct predictions and provides a framework for judging business performance. The utility of standard costing to management is as follows:

1. It acts as a valuable guide to management in the formulation of price and production policies. For example, it assists management in the field of inventory pricing, product pricing and profit planning, etc.

2. It provides a stable and sound basis for comparison of actual costs with standard costs according to different elements of costs separately. It also shows places where remedial action is necessary and how far improvement is possible in the long run.

3. It creates an atmosphere of cost consciousness among the office and managerial staff and workmen of the business. It also provides incentives to workers, middle and top-level executives for efficiency.

4. It helps to formulate tighter, more accurate and effective budget for the coming years.

5. Standard costing assists management in the delegation of authority and responsibility to control the affairs of various departments.

6. With the use of standard costing, the principle of 'management by exception' can be practiced with ease and more effectively.

7. It assists management to put the men, machines and materials more effectively and reap the benefits of better economy, efficiency, and higher productivity.

8. Budgetary control system becomes far more effective when used in conjunction with the standard costing system. Standard costs being scientifically determined are very much useful for better planning and control.

15.6 Advantages of Standard Costing

The main advantages of standard costing are:

1. Compiling standard costs more carefully can eliminate the weakness of the traditional costing system.

2. Standard costs can be used as a yardstick against which actual costs can be compared. It is an effective tool for planning production costs. Hence, cost control is greatly facilitated.

3. Variance analysis helps management to have regular as well as better checks over costs incurred. It makes the application of the principle of management by exception more easy. That is, the management can concentrate its attention on variances only, leaving the other aspects of cost control to be taken care of at the lower level.

4. It is a valuable guide to management in the formulation of production and price policies in advance with certainty. It also assists management in the areas of profit planning, product pricing, and inventory pricing, etc.

5. Standard costing makes the reporting of operating data more meaningful and also fast. This makes the interpretation of management reports easy.

6. As the emphasis of standard costing is more on cost variations, it makes the entire organization cost conscious. It makes the employees to recognize the importance of efficient operations so that costs can be reduced by joint efforts.

7. Men, machines and materials can be effectively used, and economies can be effected in addition to increased productivity. Standards may also be used as the basis for introducing incentive schemes. Wastage and inefficiency are curtailed, eliminated and reduced in all aspects of manufacturing process over a period of time if standard costing is in continuous operation.

8. Management can easily fix up responsibility through variance analysis. Variance analysis can determine the persons responsible for each variance; shifting or evading responsibility is not so easy under this system.

15.7 Limitations of Standard Costing

The important limitations of standard costing are as follows:

1. Setting of standards is a very difficult task. It requires a lot of scientific studies such as time-study, motion- study, fatigue study etc., and therefore it is very costly. Small firms may find it very difficult to operate such system.

2. Standards are very rigid estimates and once set, are not changed for a considerable time. This makes the standards highly unrealistic in certain industries, which face fluctuations in prices of products due to frequent changes in material and labour costs. Revision of standards is also not easy; in case of revision, costs would be high.

3. The utility of variance analysis depends much more on the standards set. While a loosely set standard may be ridiculed, the very high standards may create frustration in the minds of workers. At the same time setting of correct standards is also very difficult.

4. It is not suitable for industries producing non-standardized products. It is of little value in job or contract costing. Also it is difficult to apply this system when production takes more than one accounting period.

5. Fixation of responsibility to a particular person, process or production becomes very difficult as it may not be possible to identify the controllable and non-controllable factors easily.

6. Normally the system is strongly opposed by managers and others as they see it as a threat to their freedom of action. Standards may sometimes create adverse psychological effects on managers and workers, who are operating the system.

15.8 Procedure for Establishing a Standard Costing System

The procedure for establishing a standard costing system is as follows:

1. Establishment of cost centers: A cost center is a location, person or item of equipment (or a group of these) for which costs may be ascertained and used for the purpose of cost control. The cost center may be classified into a personal cost center, which relates to persons, or impersonal cost center, which relates to equipment or location. Cost centers are set up for cost ascertainment and cost control. In many cases, the department or functions will form natural cost centers, but it may happen that there are a number of cost centers in a department. For example, if there are five machine groups in a production department, each group may be taken as a cost center. Cost centers are essential for establishing standards and analyzing the variances.

2. Classification and codification of accounts: The accounts are classified for the purpose of collection and analysis. Codes and symbols are used to facilitate this purpose. For example, the codes for elements of cost may be as follows:

Direct materials	001 – 010
Direct labour	011 – 020
Indirect materials	021 – 030
Indirect labour	031 – 040 and so on.

3. Determination of Type of Standard: The standard is the level of attainment accepted by the management as the basis upon which standard costs are determined. The standards are classified mainly into four types. They are as follows:

Ideal standard: This is one, which is set up under ideal conditions. The ideal conditions may be such as maximum output and sales, best possible prices for materials and most satisfactory rates for labour and overhead costs. As these conditions do not continue to remain ideal, this standard is of little practical value. It also calls for efficiency of a high order in the task of working out the standard.

Expected standard: This is the level, which is actually expected. Standards are set normally on a short-term basis and frequent revisions may be necessary. This standard is more realistic than the ideal standard.

Normal Standard: This represents an average figure, which it is hoped will smooth out fluctuations caused by seasonal and cyclical changes. This should be attainable and it provides a challenge to the staff.

Basic Standard: This is the level fixed in relation to a base year. The principle used in setting the basic standard is similar to that used in statistics, while calculating an index number. Thus, if 1990 is the base year and the standard wage rate then is Rs.5 per hour, and in 1995 the rate is Rs.6 per hour, the basic standard must be adjusted by 20%. This standard is set on a long-term basis and seldom revised.

Organization for Standard Costing

The success of the standard costing system depends upon the reliability of standards. Hence, the responsibility for setting standards should be entrusted to a specific person or a committee. The persons involved in the setting of standards in a large concern are as follows:

(a) **Purchase Manager:** He will give details of prices of materials and the trend of market prices.

(b) **Personnel Manager:** He will give details of wage rates and possible future changes in rates.

(c) **Production Manager:** He will give details of production requirements in terms of materials, labour and overheads.

(d) **Time and Motion Study Engineer:** He will give details of standard time for the different operations in the production process.

(e) **Cost Accountant:** He will furnish all necessary cost data such as overheads absorption rates. He will also coordinate the activities of the committee. His duty is to present standard cost statements in the most satisfactory manner.

4. Setting of Standards: The standards are set mainly for the elements of cost, viz., Direct Materials, Direct Labour, and Overheads. Details of the elements of cost must be ascertained. Briefly, standard costs will be established as shown below.

Direct Material

Quantity: Material specifications will be produced showing the standard quantity of each type of material required. Normal loss in process must also be estimated before the standard cost can be ascertained.

Price: A standard price will be calculated for each type of material.

Direct Labour

Standard Time: Standard time, based on the best way of performing the job will be computed for each grade of labour for each operation involved.

Rate: The standard rate for the job will be determined.

Variable Overhead

This is defined by the I.C.M.A as 'a cost, which intends to vary directly with the volume of output.' It is assumed that the overhead rate per unit is constant, irrespective of the quantity produced, so it is necessary to calculate only a standard cost per unit or per hour.

Fixed Overhead

This is defined by I.C.M.A. as 'a cost, which intends to be unaffected by variations in volume of output.' The standards will be ascertained for the 'budgeted expenditure' for the period and also for the 'budgeted output' in units or standard hours will be used to calculate the overhead recovery rate.

The Standard Hour

In the system of standard costing, the introduction of standard hours can be very valuable. The I.C.M.A. defines a standard hour as "a hypothetical hour, which represents the amount of work that should be performed in one hour under standard conditions." Time and motion study engineers can calculate what the output of each process in one hour should be. For example, if 20 units of product A should be produced in one hour, then an output of 100 units would represent five standard hours.

VARIANCE ANALYSIS

15.9 What does Variance Analysis mean?

The main advantage of standard costing system is variance analysis. The principle of management by exception is practiced easily with the help of variances. Variance may be defined as the difference between standard and actual for each element of cost and sometimes for sales. And variance analysis may be defined as the process of analyzing variance by subdividing the total variance in such a way that management can assign responsibility for off-standard performance. When the actual results are better than standard, a favorable variance arises; when they are not up to the standard, an adverse variance occurs.

Variance helps to fix the responsibilities so that management can ascertain the person responsible for the poor results. For example, an adverse material usage variance would indicate that excess material cost was due to inefficient use of materials. This would enable management to fix the responsibility on the supervisor in charge of a particular operation in which the inefficiency occurred. It may be discovered that that the variance was caused by (say) inefficient handling, purchase of poor quality materials or employment of trainees. The important point is that the reason for the variance must be found, explained and wherever necessary, corrective measures taken.

15.10 Classification Variances

Different variances are used in different industries. However, the following are the most commonly used variances:

1. Direct Material variances
2. Direct Labour variances
3. Variable Overhead variances
4. Fixed Overhead variances: (a) Based on units (b) Based on standard hours
5. Sales variances:(a) Based on value and (b) Based on profit

Basically, there are two types of variances: (a) Price variance and (b) Volume variance. Price variance refers to variation in the prices of materials, labour rates, and expenditure on overheads or selling prices of products. Volume variance refers to variance in the quantity of units in terms of raw materials consumed, number hours worked, utilization of plant and number of units sold. The total of price variance and volume variance for each element of cost is known as the cost variance and the same for sales is known as the value variance.

Thus, the basic variances may be listed as follows:

1. Direct material cost variance: (a) Material price variance and (b) Material usage variance
2. Direct labour cost variance: (a) Labour rate variance (b) Labour efficiency variance
3. Variable overhead cost variance: (a) Variable expenditure variance (b) Variable overhead efficiency variance.
4. Fixed overhead cost variance: (a) Fixed overhead expenditure variance (b) Fixed overhead volume variance
5. Sales value variance: (a) Sales price variance (b) Sales volume variance

Advanced Variances

Basic variances, though useful, do not meet all the needs of the management. Further, they are useful only when one type of material is used in the manufacture of a product. When more than one type of materials are used, the simple basic variance may not serve the required purpose fully. Particularly, the volume variance is not enough to know that the volume has changed since the important point to know is the cause of change. From this point of view, the basic variance analysis may be extended further and the list of advanced variances may be shown as follows:

1. Material cost variance
   (a) Material price variance
   (b) Material usage variance:
   Material revised usage variance
   Material yield variance
   Material mix variance
2. Labour cost variance
   (a) Labour rate variance
   (b) Labour efficiency variance:
   Labour revised efficiency variance
   Or Idle time variance
   Labour mix variance
3. Variable overhead cost variance
   (a) Variable expenditure variance
   (b) Variable overhead efficiency variance
4. Fixed overhead cost variance
   (a) Fixed overhead expenditure variance
   (b) Fixed overhead volume variance
   Efficiency variance
   Capacity variance
   Calendar variance

5. Sales value variance

Based on value

(a) Sales value price variance

(b) Sales value volume variance
Sales value mix variance
Sales value quantity variance

Based on margin

(a) Sales margin price variance

(b) Sales margin volume variance
Sales margin mix variance
Sales margin quantity variance

Note: An adverse variance will be denoted by the symbol 'A' and favorable variance by 'F'.

15.11 Computation of Variances

Material Cost Variance (MCV)

Material cost variance is the difference between the standard cost of materials specified for the actual output achieved, and the actual cost of materials consumed. Symbolically, the material cost variance is calculated as follows:

MCV = Standard cost - Actual cost

Standard cost = Standard price (SP) per unit x Standard quantity (SQ) for actual output achieved

Actual cost = Actual price (AP) per unit × Actual quantity (AQ) used

MCV has two components viz., Material price variance and Material usage variance. In other words, the Material cost variance = Material price variance + Material usage variance

Material price variance (MPV) represents the difference between the actual price and standard price of materials consumed. It is calculated as follows:

MPV = AQ (SP – AP)

The cause for material price variance may be a combination of factors such as changes in prices, uneconomical size of purchase orders, poor purchasing procedures, excessive freight charges and failure to avail of discounts allowed, etc. For example, the adverse material price variance may show that unfavorable prices were paid for materials consumed during the period. The buyer would be asked to explain the position.

Material Usage Variance (MUV) represents the difference between the actual quantity consumed and the standard quantity, which should have been consumed for actual output achieved, expressed in terms of money.

MUV = Standard Price (Standard Quantity – Actual Quantity)

Or = SP (SQ – AQ)

This variance will be considered favorable when the standard quantity is more than actual quantity and vice versa. The supervisor would be asked to explain this variance.

Example 1

It is estimated that a product required 100 kgs of material at the rate of Rs.5 per kg. The actual consumption of material for manufacturing the same product came to 120 kgs. at the rate of Rs.4.75 per kg. Calculate material cost variances.

Solution

	Standard	Actual
Price	Rs.5 per kg.	Rs.4.75 per kg.
Quantity	100 kgs.	120 kgs.

$$MCV = (SQ \times SP) - (AQ \times AP)$$

$$MCV = (100 \times Rs.5) - (120 \times Rs.4.75)$$

$$= Rs.500 - Rs.570 = Rs.70\ (A)$$

(Adverse variance, since the actual cost is more than the standard cost)

$$MPV = AQ\ (SP - AP)$$

$$= 120\ (Rs.5 - Rs.4.75)$$

$$= 120\ (Re.0.25) = Rs.30\ (F)$$

Favorable, since the actual price is less than the standard price)

$$MUV = SP\ (SQ - AQ)$$

$$= Rs.5\ (100 - 120) = Rs.100\ (A)$$

(Adverse, since the actual quantity consumed is more than the standard quantity set)

Check

$$MCV = MPV + MUV$$

$$Rs.70\ (A) = Rs.30\ (F) + Rs.100\ (A)$$

Example 2

From the following particulars, calculate (a) Material price variance, (b) Material usage variance, and (c) Material cost variance.

Materials purchased: 3000 kgs., at Rs.3 per kg. Standard quantity of material fixed for one unit of finished product is 25 kgs. at Rs.2 per kg.

Opening stock of material	=	Nil
Closing stock of material	=	500 kgs.
Actual Output during the period	=	80 units

Solution

$$MPV = AQ\ (SP - AP)$$

$$= 2500\ (Rs.2 - Rs.3) = Rs.2{,}500\ (A)$$

$$MUV = SP\ (SQ - AQ)$$

$$= Rs.2\ (2000 - 2500) = Rs.1{,}000\ (A)$$

$$MCV = MPV + MUV$$

= Rs.2,500 (A) + Rs.1,000 (A) = Rs.3,500 (A)

Or MCV = Standard cost of actual output – Actual cost

= (SQ × SP) – (AQ × AP)

= (2000 × Rs.2) – (2,500 × Rs.3)

= Rs.4,000 – Rs.7,500 = Rs.3,500 (A)

SQ = SQ per unit of output × Actual output achieved

= 25 kgs. × 80 units = 2000 kgs

AQ = Opening stock +Purchases – Closing stock

= 0 + 3,000 kgs – 500 kgs = 2,500 kgs

The student should note that the variances should be calculated always for the actual output achieved.

Advanced Variances

When more than one type of material is used, the total usage variance will be classified into material mix variance, material revised usage variance or yield variance.

Material Mix Variance (MMV): It is that portion of total usage variance, which is due to the difference between the standard proportion or mix of materials fixed and actual proportion or mix of materials used. If the standard mix or proportion of materials fixed and the actual mix or proportion of materials used are the same, then the MMV will be zero. It is calculated as follows:

MMV = SP (Revised standard quantity - Actual quantity)

$$\text{Revised standard quantity (RSQ)} = \frac{\text{SQ for each material}}{\text{Total SQ}} \text{ x Total AQ}$$

or = Total AQ × (Standard mix ratio)

If the AQ is more than RSQ, an adverse variance will occur and vice versa.

Material Revised usage variance (MRUV): This is that portion of total usage variance, which is due to the difference between the total standard quantity for actual output and total actual quantity. Both the standard and actual quantities will be compared at standard proportion. If the total standard quantity for actual output and total actual quantity are the same, then the MRUV will be zero.

MRUV = SP (SQ – RSQ)

SQ refers to total standard quantity of materials for actual output at standard proportion. If the RSQ were more than the SQ, then the variance would be termed as 'Adverse', and vice versa.

Material Yield Variance (MYV): While the other variances are calculated on the basis of input, MYV is calculated on the basis of output. It represents that portion of total usage variance, which is due to the difference between the standard output and the actual output. If the actual output is greater than the standard output, then the variance would be favorable, and vice versa. The MYV variance may be caused by such factors as defective method of operation, substandard quality of materials purchased, lack of due care in handling, and lack of proper supervision, etc. It is calculated as follows:

MYV = SC per unit of output × (Standard yield - Actual yield)

Where several types of materials are used, MRUV and MYV imply the same thing, they are computed using different formulae. The numerical results would work out to the same.

Example 3

From the following information, calculate material cost variance:

	Standard kg		Actual kg	
Material X	100	at Rs.3 per kg	120	at Rs.3.25 per kg
Material Y	80	at Rs.4 per kg	70	at Rs.4.50 per kg
Material Z	60	at Rs.5 per kg	50	at Rs.6.00 per kg
	240		240	

Solution

Material cost variance	=	(SQ × SP) − (AQ × AP)		
Material X	=	(100 × 3) − (120 × 3.25)		
	=	300 − 390	=	90 (A)
Material Y	=	(80 × 4) − (70 × 4.50)		
	=	320 − 315	=	5 (F)
Material Z	=	(60 × 5) − (50 × 6)		
	=	300 − 300	=	0
Total material cost variance				85 (A)
Material price variance	=	AQ (SP − AP)		Rs.
Material X	=	120 (3 − 3.25)	=	30 (A)
Material Y	=	70 (4–4.50)	=	35 (A)
Material Z	=	50 (5 − 6)	=	50 (A)
Total				115 (A)
Material usage variance	=	SP (SQ − AQ)		
Material X	=	3 (100 − 120)	=	60 (A)
Material Y	=	4 (80 − 70)	=	40 (F)
Material Z	=	5 (60 − 50)	=	50 (F)
Total				30 (F)
MCV	=	MPV + MUV		
MCV	=	Rs.115(A) + Rs.30 (F)	=	85 (A)
Material mix variance	=	SP (RSQ − AQ)		
Material X	=	3 (100 − 120)	=	60 (A)
Material Y	=	4 (80 − 70)	=	40 (F)
Material Z	=	5 (60 − 50)	=	50 (F)
Total				30 (F)

RSQ = Total Quantity × Standard Ratio

Material	=	240 × (5 : 4 : 3)
X	=	240 × 5/12 = 100
Y	=	240 × 4/12 = 80
Z	=	240 × 3/12 = 60

Note: As the total quantity used is the same as the total standard quantity established, there is no material revised usage variance. Also the number of units of output is not given. Hence, there is no yield variance.

Example 4

From the following data, calculate material cost variances:

	Standard Mix	Actual Mix
Material X:	60 kgs at Rs.20	72 kgs at Rs.20
Material Y:	40 kgs at Rs.10	31 kgs at Rs.11
	100	103

Solution

MCV = (SQ × SP) – (AQ × AP)

Standard cost – Actual cost

Material X	= (60 × 20)	= 1,200	72 × 20 =	1,440
Mateiral Y	= (60 × 10)	= 400	31 × 11 =	341
		1,600		1,781

		Rs.
MCV	= 1,600 – 1,781	= 181 (A)
MPV	= AQ (SP – AP)	
Material X	= 72 (20 – 20)	= 0
Material Y	= 31 (10 – 11)	= 31 (A)
Total		31 (A)
MUV	= SP (SQ – AQ)	
Material X	= 20 (60 – 72)	= 240 (A)
Material Y	= 10 (40 – 31)	= 90 (F)
Total		150 (A)
MMV	= SP (RSQ – AQ)	
Material X	= 20 (309/5 – 72)	= 204 (A)
Material Y	= 10 (206/5–31)	= 102 (F)
Total		102 (A)
Calculation of RSQ		
Material X	= 103 × 3/5	= 309/5
Material Y	= 103 × 2/5	= 206/5
MRUV	= SP (SQ – RSQ)	

Material X	=	20 (60 – 309/5)	= Rs.36 (A)
Material Y	=	10 (40 – 206/5)	= Rs.12 (A)
Total			Rs.48 (A)
MUV	=	MMV + MRUV	
	=	Rs.102 (A) + Rs.48 (A) = Rs.150 (A)	
MCV	=	MPV + MMV + MRUV	
	=	Rs.31 (A) + Rs.102 (A) + Rs.48 (A)	
	=	Rs.181 (A)	

Example 5

ABC Limited manufactures a simple product, the standard mix of which is

Material A	60% at Rs.20
Material B	40% at Rs.10

Normal loss in production is 20% of input. Due to shortage of material A, the standard mix was changed. Actual results for April 1985 were:

Material A	105	kg at Rs.20
Material B	95	kg at Rs.9
Input	200	
Loss	35	kg
Output	165	kg

Calculate material cost variances

Solution

Material price variance	=	AQ (SP – AP)	
Material A	=	105 (20 – 20)	= 0
Material B	=	95 (10 – 9)	= 95 (F)
Material usage variance	=	SP (SQ – AQ)	
Material A	=	Rs.20 (495/4 – 105)	= Rs.375 (F)
Material B	=	Rs.10 (165/2 – 95)	= Rs.125 (A)
Total			Rs.250 (F)

Standard quantity for acutal production

Material A	=	$60 \times 165/80$	= 495/(4)
Material B	=	$40 \times 165/80$	= 165/2 kg
MMV	=	SP (RSQ – AQ)	
Material A	=	20 (120 – 105)	= 300 (F)
Mateiral B	=	10 (80 – 95)	= 150 (A)
Total			150 (F)

Calculation of RSQ

Material A	=	$200 \times 3/5$	= 120 kg
Material B	=	$200 \times 2/5$	= 80 kg

MRUV	=	SP (SQ – RSQ)	
			Rs.
Mateiral A	=	20 (495/4 – 120)	= 75 (F)
Mateiral B	=	10 (165/2 – 80)	= 25 (F)
Total			100 (F)

Calculation of SQ

Material A	=	$120/160 \times 165$	= 495/4
Material B	=	$80/160 \times 165$	= 165/2

MYV = Standard cost per unit of output (Standard output × Actual output)

= Rs.20 (160 – 165) = Rs.100 (F)

Calculation of Standard Cost per Unit of Output

Mateiral A	=	60×20	= Rs.1200
Material B	=	40×10	= 400
		100	1,600
20% Less		20	
Output		80	

$$\text{Cost per unit} = \frac{\text{Rs.}180}{80} = \text{Rs.}20$$

Note:

MYV and MRUV have the same value. They are two sides of the same coin. While the MRUV is calculated from the input angle, the MYV is calculated from the output angle. MRUV is the difference between the standard quantity of input and actual quantity (at standar proportion) for the actual output. MYV is the difference between the standard output for the actual input and the acutla output for the actual input.

Labour Cost Variance (LCV)

LCV is the difference between the standard direct wages specified for the activity attained, and the actual direct wages paid. As the wages of labour is determined by labour rate and labour time, the LCV consists of either or both of two variances, relating to rate and time, viz., Labour rate variance and Labour (Time) efficiency variance.

Symbolically,

LCV = SC – AC

= (Standard time in hours × Standard Rate) – (Actual time in hours × Actual rate)

(or)

(SHrs × SR) – (AHrs × AR)

If the actual cost is less than standard cost, the variance is favorable and vice versa.

Labour Rate Variance (LRV)

This is the difference between the standard rate of payment specified and the actual rate paid.

LRV = Actual Hours (Standard rate – Actual rate)

= AH (SR – AR)

If the actual rate paid is less, the variance is favorable, and the vice versa. The LRV may reveal one or more of the following reasons:

(a) Changes in the basic wage rates; this may be caused by an award of the labour tribunal in fulfillment of union's demands subsequent to the setting of standard rates;

(b) Employment of one or more workers of different graders than the standard grade;

(c) Overtime work in excess of that provided in the standard rate; and

(d) Faculty recruitment and placement of workers.

Labour Efficiency Variances (LEV)

This is the difference between the standard labour hours specified for the activity attained (i.e., for actual output) and the actual hours paid for. It provides a key to the control of workers' efficiency and labour cost. LEV may reveal one or more of these reasons:

(a) Defective machinery and equipment;

(b) Lack of proper supervision;

(c) Low employee morale due to inefficient organisation and poor working conditions; and

(d) Inadequate training of workers, and strained Industrial relations.

LEV = Standard rate (Standard hours – Actual hours)

= SR (SH – AH)

If the actual hours taken is less the standard, than the variance is favorable and vice versa.

Example 6

From the following data, calculate labour cost variances:

Standard rate of wage per hour	Rs. 5
Standard time set	500 hours
Actual rate of wages per hour	Rs. 6
Actual time taken	490 hours

Solution

		Rs.
LCV	= (SH × SR) – (AH × AR)	
	= (500 × 5) – (490 × 6)	
	= Rs. 2,500 – 2,940	= 440 (A)
LRV	= AH (SR – AR)	
	= 490 (5 – 6)	= 490 (A)
LEV	= SR (SH – AH)	
	= 5 (500 – 490)	= 50 (F)
LCV		= 440 (A)

Advanced Variances

When more than one type or grade of labour is used for a job, standards are set for the labour mix as well total labour hours used. In such cases, advanced variances such as labour mix variance and labour revised efficiency variance may arise.

Labour Revised Efficiency Variance [LREV]

This variance arises due to the difference between the total actual hours taken, and the total standard hours specified for the actual activity achieved. They are compared at standard ratio. The formula is follows:

LREV = SR (SH – RSH)

If the RSH is less than standard, the variance is favorable, and vice versa.

LMV and LREV are sub-variances of LEV.

Example 7

	Standard	
Grade A	40	Workers at Rs. 5 per hour
Grade B	60	Workers at Rs. 3 per hour
	100	
	Actual	
Grade A	50	Workers at Rs. 6 per hour
Grade B	40	Workers at Rs. 2 per hour
	90	

Calculate the labour mix variance and Labour Reviled Efficiency Variance.

Solution

Calculation of RSH (Revised Standard hours)

Grade A	= 90 × 2/5	=	36
Grade B	= 90 × 3/5	=	54
LMV	= SR (RSH – AH)		
Grade A	= 5 (36 – 50)	=	Rs. 70 (A)
Grade B	= 3 (54 – 40)	=	Rs. 42 (F)
Total			Rs. 28 (A)

LEV	=	SR (SH – AH)		
Grade A	=	5 (40 – 50)	=	Rs.50 (A)
Grade B	=	3 (60 – 40)	=	Rs. 60 (F)
Total			=	Rs. 10 (F)
Check				
LEV		LMV + LREV		
	=	Rs.28 (A) + Rs. 38 (F)	=	Rs. 10 (F)
LREV		SR (SH – RSH)		

Labour Mix Variance (LMV)

This is similar to Material Mix Variance. LMV is the difference in labour cost due to changes in the composition of the labour force (ie., difference between standard composition mix, and actual labour mix). In order to calculate this variance, the total actual hours spent is compared with the revised standard hours. The revised standard hours are calculated as follows:

Actual hours (Total) × Standard ratio

LMV = SR (RSH – AH)

If the actual hours taken are lesser than the revised standard hours, the variance is favorable, and vice versa.

Grade A	=	5 (40 – 36)	=	Rs. 20 (F)
Grade B	=	3 (60 – 54)	=	Rs. 18 (F)
		Total	=	Rs. 38 (F)

Idle Time Variance

The standard wage payable during the idle hours due to abnormal circumstances like strike, lockout, breakdown of machinery, power-cut, etc. is termed as idle time variance. This abnormal idle time is shown separately and not normally concealed in the LEV as it is due to reasons beyond their control. This variance will always be adverse. The formula is as follows:

Idle time variance = Idle hours × Standard rate

Example 8

100 workers are employed in a factory and the average rate of wage is Re.1 per hour. Standard working time per week is 48 hours. During the week in May, wages paid for 50 workers were at the rate of Rs. 1.10 per hour, 20 workers at Re.1.00 per hour and 30 workers at Re. 0.90 per hour. The factory did not work for 8 hours due to power failure.

Calculate suitable labour variances:

Solution

LRV	=	AH (SR – AR)		Rs.
Category I (50 workers)	=	2,400 (1–1.10)	=	240 (A)
Category II (20 workers)	=	960 (1 – 1.0)	=	0
Category III (30 workers)	=	1,440 (1–0.90)	=	144 (F)
		Total		96 (A)

Workings

Actual hours paid	=	50 × 48	=	2,400
	=	20 × 48	=	960
	=	30 × 48	=	1,440
	=		=	4,800

LEV		SR (SH – AH)		
Category I (50 workers)		1 (2000 – 2400)		400 (A)
Category II (20 workers)		1 (800 – 960)		160 (A)
Category III (30 workers)	=	1 (1200 – 1440)	=	240 (A)
		Total		800 (A)

Workings

	Standard hours per week	100 × 48	=	4,800 hours
Less:	Idle hours	100 × 8	=	800 hours
	Actual hours worked			4,000

Idle time Variance = Standard rate per Gang hour × Idle hours

= Rs. 100 × 8 Rs. 800 (A)

Standard rate per gang hour = No. of workers × Rate per hour

Category I	= 50 × 1	= Rs. 50
Category II	= 20 × 1	Rs. 20
Category III	= 30 × 1	= Rs. 30

Note: In this example, the main component of LEV is idle time variance. Suppose the actual hours worked is, say 4,200 hours, then the LEV will have labour revised efficiency variance and Idle time variance.

REV	= SR (SH – AH)	Rs.
	= Re.1 (4,000 – 4,200)	200 (F)
Idle time variance	= Rs. 100 × 8	= 800 (A)
LEV		600 (A)

Example 9

Calculate the labour variance from the following information:

Standard wages

Grade A = 90 workers at Rs. 2 per hour

Grade B = 60 workers at Rs. 3 per hour

Actual wages

Grade A = 80 workers at Rs. 2.50 per hour

Grade B = 70 workers at Rs. 2.00 per hour

Budgeted hours: 1,000; Actual hours: 900

Solution

LRV	=	AH (SR – AR).	=	Rs.
Grade A	=	72,000 (2–2.5)	=	36,000 (A)
Grade B	=	63,000 (3-2.0)	=	63,000 (F)
Total	=			27,000 (F)
LEV	=	(SR-AH)	=	Rs.
Grade A	=	2 (90,000 – 72,000)	=	36,000 (F)
Grade B	=	3 (60,000 – 63,000)	=	9,000 (A)
Total				27,000 (F)
LMV	=	SR (RSH-AH)	=	Rs.
Grade A	=	Rs. 2 (81,000 – 72,000)	=	18,000 (F)
Grade B	=	Rs 3 (54,000 – 63,000)	=	27,000 (A)
Total				9,000 (A)

Workings

	Standard hours		Actual hours	
Grade A	$90 \times 1000 =$	90,000	$80 \times 900 =$	72,000
Grade B	$60 \times 1000 =$	60,000	$70 \times 900 =$	63,000
		1,50,000		1,35,000

Revised Standard hours

$1{,}35{,}000 \times 9/15 =$	81,000
$1{,}35{,}000 \times 6/15 =$	54,000
	1,35,000

LREV = SR (SH-RSH)

		Rs.
Grade A	= Rs. 2 (90,000 − 81,000)	= 18,000 (F)
Grade B	= Rs. 3 (60,000 − 54,000)	= 18,000 (F)
Total		36,000 (F)
LEV	= LMV + LREV	
	= Rs. 9,000 (A) + 36,000(F)	= 45,000 (F)

Overhead Cost Variances

Variable Overhead Cost Variance (VOHV)

This is the difference between standard variable overheads for actual production and the actual variable overheads.

Symbolically,

$$VOHV = SC - AC$$

It can be subdivided into VOH expenditure variance, and VOH efficiency variance.

VOH expenditure variance is the difference between the standard variable overheads for the actual hours worked, and the actual variable overheads incurred. The formula is as follows:

VOH Exp. Variance = AVOH − SVOH for actual hours worked.

VOH efficiency variance arises when the actual output produced differs from the standard output for actual hours worked. It is a measure of extra overhead (for saving) incurred solely because of the efficiency shown during the actual hours worked. The formula is as follows:

VOH efficiency variance

= (SVOH for actual hours worked) − (SVOH for actual output)

VOH = VOH exp. variance + VOH efficiency variance.

Example 10

From the following information calculate VOH cost variances:

Budgeted output	5,000 units
Budgeted hours	10,000
Budgeted variable overheads	Rs. 2,000

Actual variable overheads	Rs. 3,000
Actual output	4,000 units
Actual hours	12,000

Solution

VOH cost variance	= AVOH – SVOH for actual production		
VOH expenditure variance	= AVOH – SVOH for actual hours worked.		
VOH efficiency variance	= SVOH for Ahrs-SVOH for actual output		
VOH cost variance	= Rs.3,000 – (4,000 × 0.40)	Rs.	
	= Rs. 3,000 – Rs. 1,600 =	1,400 (A)	
VOH Expenditure variance	= 3,000 – (12,000 × 0.20) =	600 (A)	
VOH efficiency variance	= Rs. 2,400 – Rs. 1,600 =	800 (A)	
		1,400 (A)	

Workings

SVOH per hour Rs. $\frac{2,000}{10,000} = 0.20$ perhour

SVOH per unit of output $=$ Rs. $\frac{2,000}{5,000} =$ Re. 0.40 per unit

Fixed Overheads Cost Variance (FOHCV)

This is the difference between the standard fixed overheads for actual output and actual fixed overheads. The reasons for the variance are over absorption or under-absorption of overheads for the actual production. The budgeted production may be different from the actual production for the actual overheads incurred. The major sub-divisions of FOHCV are FOH expenditure variance and FOH volume variance. The formula for FOHCV is as follows:

FOHCV = AFOH – SFOH for actual production

If the AFOH is less than the SFOH, the variance is favorable, and vice versa.

FOH Expenditure Variance (FOHEV)

This is the difference between AFOH and BFOH.

FOHEV = AFOH – BFOH

If the actual is grater than the budgeted, the variance is adverse, and vice versa.

FOH Volume Variance (FOHVV)

This is the difference between the budgeted fixed overheads and the standard fixed overheads absorbed on actual production. The formula is as follows:

FOHVV = BFOH – SFOH on actual production. If the BFOH is greater than the SFOH on actual production, the variance is adverse and vice versa.

Example 11

From the following data, calculate FOH cost variances:

Budgeted hours: 10,000; Budgeted Output: 5,000 units

Budgeted FOH: Rs. 3,000

Actual hours: 12,000; Actual Output: 4,800 units; Actual FOH: Rs. 3,600

Solution

SFOH per hour $= \dfrac{3,000}{10,000} =$ Re. 0.30 per hour

SFOH per unit $= \dfrac{3,000}{5,000} =$ Re. 0.60 per unit

FOHCV = AFOH – SFOH on actual output

= Rs. 3,600 – (0.60 × 4,800)

= Rs. 3,600 – 2,880 = Rs. 720 (A)

FOHEV = AFOH – BFOH

= Rs. 3,600 – 3,000 = Rs, 600 (A)

FOHVV = BFOH – SFOH on actual output

= Rs. 3,000 – (0.60 × 4,800)

= Rs. 3,000 – 2,880 = Rs. 120 (A)

FOHCV = FOHEV + FOHVV

Rs. 600 (A) + Rs. 120 (A) = Rs. 720(A)

Advanced Variances

FOHV may be classified into the sub-variances as follows:

(a) Calendar Variance, (b) Capacity variance and (c) Efficiency variance.

Calendar variance: This is a part of capacity variance. It arises only when the actual number of working days differs from the budgeted working days. It is an indicator of variations in overhead recovery of different months due to changes in number of working days. The formula is as follows:

Calendar variance = BFOH – SFOH for revised budgeted hours.

Revised budgeted hours are equivalent to the standard hours for actual working days. If BFOH is greater than the SFOH, the variance is adverse, and vice versa.

Capacity variance: This is the difference between the SFOH for revised budgeted hours and SFOH for actual hours worked. This may arise due to strikes, lockouts, breakdown of machinery, short supply of labour, absenteeism, etc. Overtime, change in number of shifts etc., may also contribute towards this variance. It is an indicator of the degree of utilization of available capacity. The formula is as follows:

Capacity variance

= SFOH for RBH – SFOH for AH = SFOH (RBH – AH)

If the SFOH for RBH is greater than for AH, the variance is adverse, and vice versa.

Efficiency variance: This variance arises when the actual production differs from the standard output for actual hours worked. It is the difference between the SFOH recovered on actual output and SFOH for actual hours worked. The major causes for this variance are lack of proper supervision and inspection, improper handling of materials and machines, variation in production methods and changes in efficiency of machine operations, etc. The formula is as follows:

Efficiency variance = SFOH for AH worked – SFOH for actual output.

If the SFOH for actual output is greater, the variance is favorable and vice versa.

FOHVV = Calendarvariance + Capacityvariance + Efficiency variance.

Example 12

From the following data calculate FOH cost variances:

	For the month of July 2002	
	Budget	Actual
Fixed overheads in Rs.	30,000	31,000
Output in units	20,000	22,000
No.of working days	25	27

Budgeted fixed overhead rate is Re. 1 per hour. In July 2002, the actual hours worked were 31,500.

Solution

SFOH per unit $= \text{Rs. } \dfrac{30,000}{20,000} = \text{Rs. } 1.50$

SFOH per hour = Re. 1

FOHCV = AFOH − SFOH on actual output
= 31,000 − (1.50 × 22,000)
= 31,000 − 33,000 = Rs. 2,000 (F)

FOHCV = FOHEV + FOHVV

Rs. 2,000 (F) = Rs. 1,000 (A) + Rs. 3,000 (F)

FOHEV = AFOH − BFOH
= 31,000 − 30,000
= Rs. 1,000 (A)

Calendar variance = BFOH − SFOH for RBH
= 30,000 − Re. 1 × 32,400
= Rs.2,400 (F)

Calculation of RBH = Standard hours per day × Actual working days

$= \dfrac{30,000}{25} \times 27 = 32,400 \text{ hours}$

Since the budgeted fixed overhead rate is Re 1 per hour, and the total budgeted fixed overhead is Rs. 30,000, the number of budgeted hours is 30,000. $\left(\dfrac{\text{i.e } 30.000}{1}\right)$

Capacity Variance = SFOH for RBH-SFOH for AH
= Rs. 32,400 − 31,500 = Rs.900(A)

Efficiency Variance = SFOH for AH-SFOH for actual output
= (Re.1 × 31,500) − (Rs. 1.5 × 22,000)
= Rs. 31,500 − 33,000 = Rs. 1,500 (F)

FOHVV = Calendar variance + Capacity variance + Efficiency variance
= Rs. 2,400 (F) + Rs. 900 (A) + Rs. 1,500 (F)

FOHVV = Rs. 3,000 (F)

FOHCV = FOHEV + Calendar variance + Capacity variance + Efficiency variance
= Rs. 1,000 (A) + Rs. 2,400 (F)
Rs.900 (A) + Rs.1,500 (F)

= Rs. 2,000(F)

Sales Variances

The standard costing system is complete only when sales variances are dovetailed with it as part of comprehensive information presented to management. Sales variances are calculated by two methods. viz., sales value method, and sales margin or profit method. Basically, changes in price and changes in sales volume give rise to sales variances. A change in value may, in its own turn, result due to a change in quantity, or a change in sales mix.

The value method is used to denote variances arising to change in sales price, quantity mix etc., or the sales value. The sales variances may be classified as follows:

(a) Sales price variance and

(b) Sales volume variance.

Sales volume variance may be further divided into sales mix variance and sales quantity or sub-volume variance.

Sales value variance (SVV) is the difference between standard sales and the actual sales.

$$SVV = (SS - AS) = (SP \times SQ) - (AP \times AQ)$$

Sales price variance (SPV) is the difference between standard price of actual quantity and actual price of the actual quantity of goods sold.

$$SPV = AQ\ (SP - AP)$$

If the actual price is greater than the standard price, the variance is favorable, and vice versa.

Sales Volume Variance (SVLV) is the difference between the actual quantity of volume and the standard quantity of volume of sales. It shows the effect of a change in volume of total sales.

$$SVLV = SP\ (SQ - AQ)$$

If the actual quantity sold is greater than the standard, the variance is favorable, and vice versa.

Sales Mix Variance

Where two or more items are used in the composition of sales, the difference between the standard composition of sales and the actual composition or mix is called the Sales Mix Variance. It is a part of the value variance arising due to change in the mix. It highlights the fact that the actual mix of sales has not been in the same ratio as budgeted.

$$SMV = SP\ (\text{Revised standard sales} - \text{Actual Sales})$$

The revised standard sales is calculated by dividing the total actual sales quantity in the standard proposition. If the actual sales quantity is greater than the revised standard quantity, the variance is favorable, and vice versa.

Sales Quantity Variance: This is the difference between the revised standard quantity of sales and the standard quantity budgeted. This variance shows the position of actual quantity of sales, as distinct from the mix of sales, in comparison with budgeted or expected sales.

$$SQV = SP\ (SQ - RSQ)$$

If the RSQ is greater than the SQ, the variance is favorable, and vice versa.

$$SVLV = SMV + SQV$$

Example 13

Calculate (i) Sales value variance, (ii) Sales price variance, (iii) Sales volume variance, (iv) Sales mix variance and (v) Sales quantity variance from the following:

Product	Standard		Actual	
	Qty (units)	Price (Rs)	Qty (units)	Price (Rs)
A	5,000	5.00	5,000	5.00
B	4,000	6.00	6,000	6.25
C	3,000	7.00	4,000	6.75
	12,000		15,000	

Solution

Sales Value Variance	=	SS – AS
	=	(SQ × SP) – (AQ × AP)
Product A = (5,000 × 5) – (5,000 × 5)	=	0
Product B = (4,000 × 6) – (6,000 × 6.25)	=	Rs. 13,500 (F)
Product C = (3,000 × 7) – (4,000 × 6.75)	=	Rs. 6,000 (F)
Total		Rs. 19,500 (F)
Sales price variance	=	AQ (SP – AP)
		Rs.
Product A = 5,000 (5–5)	=	0
Product B = 6,000 (6–6.25)	=	1,500 (F)
Product C = 4,000 (7–6.75)	=	1,000 (A)
Total		500 (F)
Sales Volume Variance	=	SP (SQ – AQ)
		Rs.
Product A = Rs.5 (5,000 – 5,000)	=	0
Product B = Rs. 6 (4,000 – 6,000)	=	12,000 (F)
Product C = Rs. 7 (3,000 – 4,000)	=	7,000 (F)
Total		19,000 (F)

Sales Value Variance

= Sales price variance + Sales Volume Variance

= 500 (F) + Rs. 19,000 (F) = 19,500 (F)

Sales mix variance = SP (RSQ – AQ)	=	Rs.
Product A = Rs.5 (6,250 – 5,000)	=	6,250 (A)
Product B = Rs.6 (5,000 – 6,000)	=	6,000 (F)
Product C = Rs.7 (3,750 – 4,000)	=	1,750 (F)
	Total	1,500 (F)

Calculation of RSQ: Total AQ × Standard ratio
= 15,000 units × (5:4:3)

Product A = 15,000 × 5/12	=	6,250 units
Product B 15,000 × 4/12	=	5,000 units
Product C = 15,000 × 3/12	=	3,750 units
Total	=	15,000 units

Sales Quantity Variance = SP (SQ – RSQ)

		Rs.
Product A = Rs.5 (5,000 – 6,250)	=	6,250 (F)
Product B = Rs.6 (4,000 – 5,000)	=	6,000 (F)
Product B = Rs. 7 (3,000 – 3,750)	=	5,250 (F)
Total		17,500

Sales Volume Variance

= Sales mix variance + Sales Quantity variance

19,000 (F) = Rs.1,500 (F) + Rs.17,500 (F)

Sales Margin Method or Profit Method

Sales margin variance: This is the difference between the standard margin appropriate to the quantity of sales budgeted for a period, and the margin between standard cost and the actual selling price of the sales effected. This variance is similar to the price variance calculated under value method, and the formula is as follows:

Margin price variance = AQ (Standard profit – Actual Profit)

If the actual profit is greater than the standard profit, the variance is favorable, and vice versa.

Sales margin volume variance: This is that portion of total margin variance which is due to the difference between the budgeted and actual quantities of each product of which the sales mixture is composed, valuing sales at the standard net selling prices and cost of sales at standard. That is, the difference between the revised standard profit is the mix variance.

Margin Mix Variance: Standard profit (RSQ-AQ)

If the actual quantity is greater than the revised standard quantity the variance is favorable, and vice versa.

Example 14

ABC Ltd., had budgeted the following sales for December 1996

Product A	9,000 units at	Rs. 5 per unit
Product B	6,500 units at	Rs. 10 per unit
Product C	12,000 units at	Rs. 7.5 per unit

As against this the actual sales were:

Product A	10,000 units at	Rs. 5.5 per unit
Product B	7,000 units at	Rs. 9.5 per unit
Product C	11,000 units at	Rs. 7.8 per unit

The cost per unit of A, B and C was Rs.4.5 Rs. 8.5 and Rs. 6.5 respectively. Compute the different variance to explain the difference between budgeted profit and actual profit.

Solution

Sales margin variance = (SM × SQ) – (AM × AQ)

Product A	= (0.5 × 9,000) – (1 × 10,000)	= Rs. 5,500 (F)
Product B	= (1.5 × 6,500) – (1 × 7,000)	= Rs. 2,750 (A)
Product C	= (1 × 12,000) – (1.3 × 11,000)	= Rs. 2,300 (F)
Total		Rs. 5,050 (F)

Sales margin price variance = AQ (SM – AM)

Product A	= 10,000 (0.5–1.00)	= Rs. 5,000 (F)
Product B	= 7,000 (1.5–1.0)	= Rs. 3,500 (A)
Product C	= 11,000 (1.0–1.3)	= Rs. 3,300 (F)
Total		Rs. 4,800 (F)

Sales margin volume variance = SM (SQ – AQ)

Product A	= 0.5 (9,000 – 10,000)	= Rs. 500 (F)
Product B	= 1.5 (6,500 – 7,000)	= Rs. 750 (F)
Product C	= 1.0 (12,000 – 11,000)	= Rs. 1,000 (A)
Total		= Rs. 250 (F)

SMV = SMPV + SMVV

Rs. 5,050 (F) = Rs. 4,800 (F) + Rs. 250 (F)

Sales margin mix variance = SM (RSQ – AQ)

Product A	= 0.5 (9.164 – 10,000)	= Rs. 418 (F)
Product B	= 1.5 (6.618 – 7,000)	= Rs. 573 (F)
Product C	= 1.0 (12,218 – 11,000)	= Rs. 1,218 (A)
Total		= Rs. 227 (A)

Workings

BUDGET

Product	SQ Rs.	SP Rs.	Total Sales Rs.	Cost per unit Rs.	Total Cost Rs.	Profit per unit Rs.	Total Profit Rs.
A	9,000	5	45,000	4.5	40,500	0.5	4,500
B	6,500	10	65,000	8.5	55,250	1.5	9,750
C	12,000	7.5	90,000	6.5	78,000	1.0	12,000
	27,500		2,00,000		1,73,750		26,250

			Actual				
A	10,000	5.5	55,000	4.5	45,000	1.0	10,000
B	7,000	9.5	66,500	8.5	59,500	1.0	7,000
C	11,000	7.8	85,000	6.5	71,500	1.3	14,300
	28,000		2,07,300		1,76,500		31,300

Workings

$$RSQ = AQ \times (\text{Standard ratio})$$

$$= 28{,}000 \times (18{:}13{:}24)$$

Product A	$= 28{,}000 \times 18/55$	=	Rs. 9,164
Product B	$= 28{,}000 \times 13/55$	=	Rs. 6,618
Product C	$= 28{,}000 \times 24/55$	=	Rs. 12,218

Sales margin quantity variance = SM(SQ − RSQ)

Causes and Disposition of Variances

In order to make the analysis a control instrument, the management should investigate the causes of variances and take the necessary corrective measures. Another method is to carry forward the variances to the next financial year by crediting the same to a reserve account to be set off in the subsequent year or years. The favorable and adverse variances may cancel each other in the course of reasonable time and thus be disposed off.

1. Materials Price variance

(a) Causes: Change in market price, delivery costs; purchase of non-standard materials, emergency purchases, incorrect shipping instruction, loss of discount, etc.

(b) Disposition: If all or a portion of the price variance is the result of inefficiencies or a saving has resulted from efficient purchasing, the amount may be adjusted to P&L account. If it is due to incorrect standards or change in market price the amount may be adjusted to inventories and cost of goods sold. It may be mentioned that under Method I, such adjustment must be made for inventories under materials control, work-in-progress, finished goods, and cost of goods sold. Under Methods II and III, such adjustments are required for inventories under work-in-progress, finished goods and cost of goods sold.

2. Materials usage variance

(a) Causes: Poor quality of materials; change in material mix, product or production methods; careless handling; excessive waste or scrap; incorrect setting of standards.

(b) Disposition: The amount of usage variance resulting in inefficiency in handling and processing materials is transferred to profit and loss account. The amount of usage variance due to incorrect standards is apportioned to work in progress, finished goods and cost of goods sold.

3. Direct wages rate variances

(a) Causes: General rise due to award or agreement, non-standard grade, abnormal overtime or payment above or below standard rates during seasonal or emergency operations.

(b) Disposition: The amount of variance arising out of inefficiency can be controlled if transferred to profit and loss account. The amount of variance resulting from the use of out-of-date standards or from conditions beyond the control of management is adjusted to work-in-progress, finished goods and cost of goods sold, on the basis of wages or time.

4. Direct labour efficiency variance

(a) Causes: Poor working conditions, abnormal idle time i.e., power failure, breakdown, go-slow technique, quality of supervision, non-standard grade of material, or employees' non-co-operation in service departments.

Product A = 0.5 (9,000 – 9,164) = Rs. 82 (F)

Product B = 1.5 (6,500 – 6,618) = Rs. 177 (F)

Product C = 1.0 (12,000 – 12,218) = Rs. 218 (F)

Total Rs. 477 (F)

SM Volume variance = SMMV + SMQV

= Rs.227 (A) + Rs. 477 (F)

= Rs. 250 (F)

(b) Disposition: The amount of variance attributed to various forms of inefficiency which are controllable is transferred to profit and loss account. The amount of variance resulting from improperly prepared standards and from conditions beyond the control of management may be adjusted to work-in-progress, finished goods and cost of goods sold.

5. Overhead expenditure variance

(a) Causes: Under or over utilisation of a service; seasonal conditions; inefficiency in the use of a service (e.g. electricity in lieu of gas).

(b) Disposition: The amount of variance due to seasonal conditions should be treated as a deferred item. The amount arising out of inefficiency which is controllable is transferred to profit and loss account. The amount resulting from incorrectly prepared standard and from conditions beyond control is adjusted to work-in-progress, finished goods and cost of goods sold.

6. Overhead cost of capacity variance:

(a) Causes: Calendar variations, abnormal idle time such as strikes, breakdowns absenteeism, labour shortage, etc.

(b) Dispostition: The amount of seasonal variations is reasonably a deferred item. The amount arising from inefficient operations controllable by management is transferred to profit and loss account. The amount of variance arising out of abnormal idle time and beyond control of management is transferred to profit and loss account.

15.12 Explain the conditions required for effective Reporting of Variances

In order to make the variance analysis more effective the following conditions should be fulfilled:

(a) The variance arising out of each factor should be correctly separated. If it is not done properly or one merged with another, the reporting would be misleading or wrong inferences may be drawn.

(b) Variance, particularly the controllable variances should be reported immediately. This would enable remedial measures being taken on time.

(c) Analysis of uncontrollable variances should be made with the same case as for controllable variances since it may reveal far-reaching effects on the operating results of the company.

(d) The forms of reports for the different types of variances should be designed taking into consideration the needs of the management, size of the company.

It is better to present the profit figures by way of reconcillation of budgeted or standard and actual profits on the basis of variances:

PRACTICAL PROBLEMS

Illustration 1

From the following information calculate material cost variances:

Material	Standard Qty Kg	Standard Qty Rs.	Actual Qty Kg	Actual Price Rs.
X	10	4	12	3.75
Y	15	5	18	4.50
	25		30	

Solution

Material cost variance $= (SQ \times SP) - (AQ \times AP)$

Material X $= (10 \times 4) - (12 \times 3.75)$

$=$ Rs.40 – Rs.45 $=$ Rs.5 (A)

Material Y $= (15 \times 5) - (18 \times 4.50)$

$=$ Rs. 75 – Rs. 81 $=$ Rs. 6 (A)

Total $=$ Rs.11 (A)

Material price variance $=$ AQ (SP – AP)

Material X:12 (4-3.75) $=$ Rs. 3.00 (F)

Material Y:18 (5-4.50) $=$ Rs. 9.00 (F)

Total $=$ Rs.12.00 (F)

Material usage variance $=$ SP (SQ – AP)

Material X $=$ Rs.4 (10–12) $=$ Rs.8 (A)

Material Y $=$ Rs. 5 (15–18) $=$ Rs.15 (A)

Total $=$ Rs.23 (A)

MCV $=$ MPV + MUV

MCV $=$ Rs 12 (F) + Rs 23 (A) $=$ Rs.11 (A)

Material mix variance $=$ SP (RSQ – AQ)

Material mix variance is nil, since the actual mix is the same as the standard mix.

Material sub-usage variance $=$ SP (SQ – RSQ)

This is the same as the material usage variance.

Illustration 2

From the following information calculate material cost variances:

	Standard		Actual	
	Quantity Tons	Price per ton Rs	Quantity Tons	Price per ton Rs
Material X	20	20	10	30
Material Y	40	30	20	40
Material Z	40	50	30	45

Solution:

Material cost variance = (SQ × SP) − (AQ × AP)

Material X = (20 × 20) − (10 × 30) = Rs.100 (F)

Material Y = (40 × 30) − (20 × 40) = Rs.400 (F)

Material Z = (40 × 50) − (30 × 45) = Rs.650 (F)

Total = Rs.1,150 (F)

Material price variance = AQ (SP − AP)

Material X = 10 (20 − 30) = Rs.100 (A)

Material Y = 20 (30 − 40) = Rs.200 (A)

Material Z = 30 (50 − 45) = Rs.150 (F)

Total = Rs.150 (A)

Material usage variance = SP (SQ − AQ)

Material X = 20 (20 − 10) = Rs. 200 (F)

Material Y = 30 (40 − 20) = Rs. 600 (F)

Material Z = 50 (40 − 30) = Rs. 500 (F)

Total = Rs. 1,300 (F)

MCV = MPV + MUV

MCV = Rs.150 (A) + Rs.1,300 (F) = Rs.1,150 (F)

Material mix variance = SP (RSQ − AQ)

Calculation of RSQ = AQ × Standard Ratio = 60 × (1:2:2)

Material X, Y, Z, 12, 24, 24 respectively

Material X = 20 (12 − 10) = Rs. 40 (F)

Material Y = 30 (24 − 20) = Rs. 120 (F)

Material Z = 50 (24 − 30) = Rs. 300 (A)

Total = Rs. 140 (A)

Material revised usage variance = SP (SQ − RSQ)

Material X = 20 (20 − 12) = Rs. 160 (F)

Material Y = 30 (40 − 24) = Rs. 480 (F)

Material Z = 50 (40 − 24) = Rs. 800 (F)

Total = Rs. 1.440 (F)

MUV = MMV + MRUV = MUV

= Rs.140 (A) + Rs.1,440 (F) = Rs.1,300 (F)

Illustration 3

The following standard and actual data relate to a manufacturing concern:

	Standard	Rs.
Material X	40 Kgs at Rs. 6 =	240
Material Y	60 Kgs at Rs. 4 =	240

Standard output is 80% of input i.e., 800 units. Process loss is 20%.

	Actual
Material X	600 kgs at Rs.4
Material Y	400 kgs at Rs.6

Actual output is 70% of input i.e., 700 units. Process loss is 30%. You are required to calculate material cost variances.

Solution

Calculation of standard quantity for actual output:

For 80 units SQ of materials is 100 units

For 700 units SQ of materials is $100/80 \times 700 = 875$ units

SQ for material X $= 875 \text{ units} \times 4/10 = 350$ units

SQ for material Y $= 875 \text{ units} \times 6/10 = 525$ units

Material cost variance = SC for actual output – AC

Material X $= (350 \times \text{Rs.}6) - (600 \times \text{Rs.}4) =$ Rs. 300 (A)

Material Y $= (525 \times \text{Rs.}4) - (400 \times \text{Rs.}6) =$ Rs. 300 (A)

Total = Rs. 600 (A)

Material price variance = AQ (SP – AP)

Material X = 600 (6 – 4) = Rs. 1,200 (F)

Material Y = 400 (4 – 6) = Rs. 800 (A)

Total = Rs. 400 (F)

Material usage variance = SP (SQ – AQ)

Material X = Rs 6 (350 – 600) = Rs. 1,500 (A)

Material Y = Rs.4 (525 – 400) = Rs. 500 (F)

Total = Rs. 1,000 (A)

Verification MCV = MPV + MUV

MCV = Rs.400 (F) + Rs.1000 (A) = Rs.600 (A)

Calculation of RSQ = AQ × Standard ratio

Material X $= 1000 \times 4/10 = 400$ units

Material Y $= 1000 \times 6/10 = 600$ units

Material mix variance = SP (RSQ – AQ)

Material X = Rs 6 (400 – 600) = Rs. 1,200 (A)

Material Y = Rs 4 (600 – 400) = Rs. 800 (F)

Total = Rs. 400 (A)

Material revised usage variance = SP (SQ – RSQ)

Material X = Rs 6 (350 – 400) = Rs. 300 (A)

Material Y = Rs 4 (525 – 600) = Rs 300 (A)

Total = Rs.600 (A)

Material yield variance = SC per unit of output × (Standard yield – Actual yield)

$$\text{Calculation of SC per unit of output} = \frac{\text{Total material cost}}{\text{Total standard output}}$$

$$= \frac{(40 \times \text{Rs } 6) + (60 \times \text{Rs.}4)}{80 \text{ units}} = \text{Rs.}6$$

Standard yield for actual input = 1,000 less 20% loss = 800 units

Material yield variance = Rs.6 (800 – 700) = Rs.600 (A)

MYV will always be same as MRUV

Illustration 4

From the following particulars ascertain the actual consumption of materials, actual price and material usage variance:

Material cost variance Rs. 700 (Adverse)

Standard Quantity 1,000 kgs

Material price variance Rs. 300 (Favourable)

Standard price Rs. 5 per kg.

Solution

MCV = MPV + MUV

MUV = MCV – MPV

MUV = – 700 – 300 = 1,000 (Adverse is indicated by minus)

MUV = SP (SQ – AQ)

– 1,000 = Rs.5 (1,000 – AQ)

– 1,000 = 5,000 – 5AQ = 6,000

AQ = 1,200 kg

MPV = AQ (SP – AP)

300 = 1,200 (5 – AP)

300 = 6,000 – 1,200 AP

1,200 AP = 6,000 – 300 = 5,700

AP = Rs.4.75

Illustration 5

From the following information calculate

(a) the material cost variance

(b) standard quantity of materials

(c) standard price fixed for the materials.

Material usage variance Rs. 1,000 (A)

Actual consumption of materials 2,500 kgs.

Actual price per kg. Rs. 2

Material price variance = 0

Solution

MCV = MPV + MUV

Since the MPV is zero the MCV will be equal to MUV (i.e.,) Rs.1,000 (A)

MUV = SP (SQ – AQ) = Rs.1,000 (A)

Since the MPV is zero the standard price and the actual price will be same i.e., there is no price variation. Hence, the standard price per kg is Rs.2

$$2\,(SQ - 2{,}500) = -\,1{,}000$$

$$2\,(SQ) - 5{,}000) = -\,1{,}000$$

$$2\,SQ = 5{,}000 - 1{,}000 = 4{,}000$$

$$SQ = 2{,}000 \text{ kgs.}$$

Illustration 6

You are given the following information relating to the manufacture of a product:

Standard mix of materials

Material A 60 kgs at Rs. 20 per kg.

Material B 40 kgs at Rs. 10 per kg.

Total quantity of materials 105 kgs.

Material mix variance Rs. 100 (A)

Ascertain the actual quantities of materials A and B used in the production.

Solution

MMV = SP (Revised standard mix – Actual mix)

Revised standard mix

Material A = 105 × 3/5 = 63

Material B = 105 × 2/5 = 42

Actual mix

Material A = x

Material B = 105 – x

MMV

Material A = 20 (63 – x)

Material B = 10 [(42 – (105 – x)]

Total variance 100 (A)

$20(63-x)+10[42-(105-x)]=-100$

$1{,}260-20x+420-1{,}050+10x=-100$

$20x-10x=1260+420+100-1{,}050$

$10x=730$

$x=73$

Material A $= 73$ kgs

Material B $= 105-73=32$ kgs

Illustration 7

	Standard		Actual	
	Hours	Rates (Rs)	Hours	Rates (Rs)
Workman A	20	3	30	2.90
Workman B	25	4	15	4.50

Calculate the labour cost variance

Solution

Labour cost variance $=(SH-SR)-(AH\times AR)$

Workman A $=20\times3-30\times2.9$ = Rs. 27 (A)

Workman B $=25\times4-15\times4.5$ = Rs. 32.5 (F)

Total = Rs. 5.5 (F)

Labour rate variance $=AH(SR-AR)$

Workman A $=30\times(3-2.90)$ = Rs. 3 (F)

Workman B $=15\times(4-4.5)$ = Rs. 7.5 (F)

Total = Rs. 4.5 (A)

Labour efficiency variance $=SR(SH-AH)$

Workman A = Rs 3 (20 − 30) = Rs. 30 (A)

Workman B = Rs 4 (25 − 15) = Rs. 40 (F)

Total = Rs. 10 (F)

Labour cost variance = Labour price variance + Labour rate variance

= Rs.4.50 (A) + Rs.10 (F) = Rs.5.5 (F)

Illustration 8

The data obtained from a manufacturing concern are as follows:

	Standard	Actual
Number in the gang	Men 20; Women 10	Men 16; Women 18
Wage rate per hour	Rs.0.90; Rs.0.80	Re.1; Rs.0.50
Output per gang hour	50 units	Total output 2,400 units

Actual gang hours paid	40
Actual gang hours worked	30

Abnormal idle time is one gang hour

Compute the labour cost variances

Solution

Labour cost variance $= SC - AC$

$= Rs.1,248 - Rs.1,000 = Rs.248$ (F)

Workings

Actual output in gang hours $= \frac{2,400}{50} = 48$ standard gang hours.

Standard cost per gang hour $= (20 \times 0.90) + (10 \times 0.80) = Rs.26$

Hence, standard cost $48 \times Rs.26 = Rs.1,248$

Actual cost $= (16 \times 40 \times 1) + (18 \times 40 \times 0.50) = Rs.\ 1,000$

Labour rate variance $= AH\ (SR - AR)$

Men $= (40 \times 16) \times (Re.\ 0.90 - Re.\ 1) = Rs.64$ (A)

Women $= (40 \times 18) \times (Re.\ 0.80 - Re.\ 0.50) = Rs.\ 216$ (F)

Total $= Rs.152$ (F)

Labour efficiency variance $= SR\ (SH - AH)$

Men $= 0.90\ (960 - 640) = Rs.\ 288$ (F)

Women $= 0.80\ (480 - 720) = Rs.\ 192$ (A)

Total $= Rs.\ 96$ (F)

Workings

Standard hours for men $= 48 \times 20 = 960$

Standard hours for women $= 48 \times 10 = 480$

Total 1,440 hours

Now, the sub-variances of total efficiency variance may be calculated thus:

Idle time variance

Standard rate $\times$ idlehours

Men $0.90 \times 16 = Rs.\ 14.40$ (A)

Women $0.80 \times 18 = Rs.\ 14.40$ (A)

Total $= Rs.\ 28.80$ (A)

Mix variance

Standard rate (revised standard hours-actual hours)

Men Rs. 0.90 $(884 - 624) = Rs.\ 234.00$ (F)

Women Rs. 0.80 $(442 - 702) = Rs.\ 208.00$ (A)

Total $= Rs.\ 26.00$ (F)

Workings

Actial hours worked = Hours paid for – Idle hours

For men:	640 – 16 = 624
For women :	720 – 18 = 702
Total	1326

Revised standard hours = Actual hours worked expressed in standard ratio

For men $\frac{960}{1440} = \times 1326 = 884$

For women $\frac{480}{1440} = \times 1326 = 442$

Total = 1,326

Efficiency variance

Standard rate (Standardhous – Revised standard hous)

Men: Rs.0.90 (960 – 884) = Rs. 68.40 (F)

Women: 0.80 (480 – 442) = Rs. 30.40 (F)

Total = Rs. 98.80 (F)

Yield Variance

Standard cost of standard gang per hour (Standardyield* – Actual yield*)

Rs.26 (44.24 – 48) = 98.80 (F)

*Both have been expressed in standard gang hours.

Workings

(a) Standard yield expressed in standard gang hours

= yield (in terms of standard gang hours) which should have resulted from actual hours.

$= \frac{\text{Actual hours worked}}{\text{Hours in one standard gang hour}}$

$= \frac{1,326}{30} = 44.20$ standard gang hour

(b) 50 units of output = one standard gang hour

2400 units (actual output) $= \frac{2,400}{50} = 48$ standard gang hours

Alternatively, yield variance can be calculated thus:

Standard labour cost per unit output (SY* – AY*)

Rs. 26/50 (2,210 – 2,400) or (26/ 50) × 190 = Rs.98.80 (F)

* Both expressed in units of output

Workings

Standard yield = Actual hours × Yield per standard hour

$= 1,326 \times 50 / 30 = 2,210$ units

Verification

Total efficiency variance = idle time variane + mix variance +

Either efficiency or yield variance

or 96 (F) = Rs.28.80 (A) + Rs.26 (F) + Rs.98.80 (F)

or 96 (F) = 96 (F)

Illustration 9

The standard labour mix for producing 100 units of a product is:

10 men of Grade I for 6 hours at Rs. 2 per hour

10 men of Grade II for 8 hours at Re. 1 per hour

Actual production is 1,000 units. But due to shortage of grade I labour, the standard mix had to be revised as 50 hours of Grade I and 90 hours of Grade II for producing 100 units.

Actual hours paid for were:

Grade I - 480 hours at Rs. 2.20 per hour

Grade II - 940 hours at Rs. 1.10 per hour

Calculate the labour cost variances.

Solution

Labour rate variance = A hrs (SR – AR)

Grade I = 480 (2–2.2) = Rs. 96 (A)

Grade II = 940 (1–1.1) = Rs. 94 (A)

Total = Rs. 190 (A)

Labour effieciency variance = SR (S Hrs – A Hrs)

Grade I = Rs.2 (500 – 480) = Rs. 40 (F)

Grade II = Re.1 (900 – 940) = Rs. 40 (A)

Total = Nil

Labour efficiency variance may be divided into labour mix variance and labour revised efficiency variance.

Labour mix variance = SR (RSM – AM)

Grade I = 2 (3,550 / 7–480) = Rs. 54.30 (F)

Grade II = 1 (6,390 / 7–940) = Rs. 27.10 (A)

Total = Rs. 27.20 (F)

Revised standard mix of A Hrs (RSM)

Grade I = $1,420 \times 50 / 140 = 3550/7$

Grade II = 1,420 – 90 /140 = 6390/7

Illustration 10

Your are given the following information:

Standard rate of wage per hour Rs.5

Standard time set 500 hours

Labour cost variance Rs. 440 (A)

Labour rate variance Rs. 490 (A)

Find out the actual time taken and actual rate of wage paid and also compute labour efficiency variance.

Solution

LCV = LRV + LEV = (SR × S Hrs) − (AR × A Hrs)

LRV = A Hrs (SR − AR)

LEV = SR (S Hrs − A Hrs) (Adverse is denoted by negative sign)

LEV = LCV − LRV

= 440 (A) − 490 (A)

= − 440 (A) − (490) = 50 (F)

LEV = SR (SHRs − A Hrs)

= 5 (500 − A Hrs) = 50

= 2,500 − 5 A Hrs = 50

5 A Hrs = 2,450

A Hrs = 490

LRV = A Hrs (SR − AR)

490 (A) = 490 (5 − AR)

− 490 = 2,450 − 490 AR

490 AR = 2,940

AR = Rs. 6

Illustration 11

Following information is obtained from the records of a manufacturing concern relating to the manufacture a product:

	Standard wages
Grade A	900 hours at Rs. 2 per hour
Grade B	600 hours at Rs. 3 per hour

Total time taken 1,600 hours

Actual wage rate paid for grade B workers is Rs. 2 per hour

Labour mix variance 60 (Adverse)

Labour rate variance 250 (Favoruable)

Calculate

(a) Labour cost variance

(b) Labour efficiency variance

(c) Labour revised efficiency variance

(e) Actual wage rate paid for grade A workers.

Solution

Labour mix variance = SR (RSM − AM)

Revised standard mix

Grade A = 1,600 × 900 / 1,500 = 960 hrs

Grade B = 1,600 × 600 / 1,500 = 640 hrs

Rs.2 (960 − x) + Rs.3 [(640 − (1,600 − x)] = − 60

Let x be actual hours taken by grade A

1,920 − 2x + 1,920 − 4,800 + 3x = − 60

x = 4,800 − 1,920 − 1,920 − 60 = 900 hrs

Actual hours taken by grade B = 1,600 − 900 = 700 hrs

Actual wage rate paid for Grade A workers be x

LRV = AHrs (SR − AR)

900 (2 − x) + 700 (3 − 2) = 250 (F)

1,800 − 900x + 700 = 250

900x = 2,250

x = Rs.2.5

Labour revised efficiency variance = SR (S hrs − RS hrs)

Grade A = 2 (900 − 960) = 120 (A)

Grade B = 3 (600 − 640) = 120 (A)

240 (A)

LEV = LMV + LREV
= 60 (A) + 240 (A) = 300 (A)

Alternatively,

LEV = SR (S Hrs − A Hrs)

Grade A = 2 (900 − 900) = 0

Grade B = 3 (600 − 700) = 300 (A)

= 300 (A)

Labour cost variance = LRV + LEV

= 250 (F) + 300 (A) = 50 (A)

Alternatively

LCV = (SR × SHrs) − (AR × AHrs)

Grade A = (2 × 900) − (2.5 × 900) = 450 (A)

Grade B $= (3 \times 600) - (2 \times 700) = 400$ (F)

$= 50$ (A)

Illustration 12

The standard time and rate for unit component A are given below:

Standard hours	15
Standard rate	Rs. 4 per hour

The actual data and related information are as under:

Actual production	1,000 units
Actual hours	15,300 hours
Actual rate	Rs.3.90 per hour

Calculate (i) Labour Cost variance (ii) Labour efficiency variance (iii) labour rate variance

Solution

(i) Labour cost variance

(Standard hours for actual production $\times$ SP) $-$ (AH $\times$ AP)

$= (15{,}000 \times 4) - (15{,}300 \times 3.90)$

$=$ Rs.60,000 $-$ 59,670 $=$ Rs.330 (F)

(ii) Labour efficiency variance

(AH $-$ SH) $\times$ Standard rate $= (15{,}300 - 15{,}000) \times$ Rs. 4

$= 300 \times 4 =$ Rs.1,200 (A)

(iii) Labour rate variance

(SR $-$ AR) $\times$ Actual hours $= (4 - 3.90) \times 15{,}300$

$= 0.10 \times 15{,}300 =$ Rs.1,530 (F)

Check:

Labour efficiency variance + Labour rate variance = Labour cost variance

Rs.1,200 (A) + Rs.1,530 (F) = Rs.330 (F)

Working Note:

Standard hours for actual production

For 1 unit standard hours $= 15$

1,000 units standard hous $= 15 \times 1{,}000 = 15{,}000$ hours

Illustration 13

From the following data calculate (i) Labour Cost Variance (ii) Labour Rate Variance and (iii) Labour Efficiency variance for each department.

	Departments	
	Polishing	Painting
Standard Hours	8,640	6,015

Standard Rate per hour (Rs)	2	1.70
Actual Hours worked	8,200	6,295
Actual Wages (Rs)	18,090	9685

Solution

LCV = SC – AC = (SR × S.Hrs) – (AR × A.Hrs)

LRV = A Hrs (SR – AR)

LEV = SR (S Hrs – A H rs)

Polishing Department

LCV = (8,640 × 2) – (18,090)

Rs.17,280 – Rs.18,090 = Rs. 810 (A)

LRV = 8,200 × 2) – 18,090

Rs.16,400 – 18,090 = Rs. 1,690 (A)

LEV = 2 × (8,640 × 8,200) = Rs. 880 (F)

Painting Department

LCV = Rs. (6,015 × 1.7) – Rs.9,685

Rs. 10,225.5–9,685 = Rs.540.5 (F)

LRV= (6,295 × 1.7) – 9,685 = Rs.1,016.5 (F)

LEV = Rs.1.70 (6,015 – 6,295) = Rs.476 (A)

Illustration 14

The standard time and rate for a product are given below:

Standard time perunit 10 hours

Standard rate Rs. 3 per hour

The actual data and related information are given below:

Actual output 1,000 units

Actual time 10,200 hours

Actual rate Rs. 2.90 per hour

Calculate (i) Labour Cost variance (ii) Labour efficiency variance (iii) Labour rate variance.

Solution

Labour Cost Variance = Standard Cost – Actual Cost

= (SR × S Hrs.) – (AR × A Hrs)

= (Rs.3 × 10,000) – (Rs2.9 × 10,200)

= Rs.30,000 – Rs.29,580

= Rs.420 (F)

Labour rate variance = A Hrs (SR – AR)

= 10,200 (Rs.3 − Rs.2.9)

= Rs.1,020 (F)

Labour efficiency variance = SR (S Hrs − A Hrs)

= Rs.3 (10,000 − 10,200)

= Rs. 600 (A)

Check

LCV = L R V + L E V

Rs. 420 (F) = Rs.1,020 (F) + Rs. 600 (A)

Illustration 15

Using the following information calculate each of three labour variance for each department

	Department X	Department Y
Gross wages direct (Rs)	2,080	19,370
Standard hours produced	8,640	6,015
Standard rate per hour (Rs)	3	3.40
Actual hours worked	8,200	6,345

Solution

(i) Labour Cost variance

(Standard hours × Standard Rate − (Actual hours × Actual rate)

Department X (8,640 × 3) − 28,080

Rs. 25,920 − 28,080 = Rs. 2,160 (A)

Department Y (6,015 × 3.40) − 19,370

Rs. 20,451 − 19,370 = Rs1,081 (F)

(ii) Labour rate variance

(SR − AR) × Actual hours

Department X (3 × 8,200) − 28,080

Rs. 24.600 − 28,080 = Rs. 3,480 (A)

Department Y (3.40 × 6,345) − 19,370

Rs. 21,573 − 19,370 = Rs. 2,203 (F)

(iii) Labour Efficiency variance

(SH − AH) × SR

Department X (8,640 − 8,200) × 3

440 × 3 = Rs1,320 (F)

Department Y (6,015 − 6,345) × 3.40

330 × 3.40 = Rs1,122 (A)

Illustration 16

From the following information calculate the variances:

Standard direct cost per unit:

Material cost 10 kg	Rs. 100
Labour cost: 40 hours	20
Total	120

For the production of 250 units materials consumption amounted to Rs. 25,625 against 2,600 kgs. Wages payment was Rs 5,950 for 10,900 hous including 10 hours idle time due to power failure.

Solution

Material variance

M C V $= SC - AC = (SQ \times SP) - (AQ \times AP)$

$= (2{,}500 \times 10) - \text{Rs}25{,}625$

$= \text{Rs. } 25{,}000 - \text{Rs. } 25{,}625$

$= \text{Rs. } 625 \text{ (A)}$

M P V $= AQ\,(SP - AP) = (AQ \times SP) - (AQ \times AP)$

$= (2{,}600 \times \text{Rs } 10) - \text{Rs } 25{,}625$

$= \text{Rs. } 26{,}000 - \text{Rs. } 25{,}625$

$= \text{Rs. } 375 \text{ (F)}$

M U V $= SP\,(SQ - AQ)$

$= \text{Rs. } 10\,(2{,}500 - 2{,}600) = \text{Rs. } 1{,}000 \text{ (A)}$

Check:

M C V = M P V + M U V

Rs. 625 (A) = Rs. 375 (F) + Rs. 1,000 (A)

Labour variance:

L C V $= (SR \times SH) - (AR \times AH)$

$= (\text{Rs. } 0.50 \times 10{,}000) - \text{Rs. } 5{,}950$

$= \text{Rs. } 5{,}000 - \text{Rs. } 5{,}950 = \text{Rs. } 950 \text{ (A)}$

L R V $= AH\,(SR - AR)$

$= (AH \times SR) - (AH \times AR)$

$= (10{,}900 \times 0.5) - \text{Rs } 5{,}950$

$= \text{Rs. } 5{,}450 - \text{Rs. } 5{,}950 = \text{Rs. } 500 \text{ (A)}$

L E V $= SR\,(SH - AH)$

$= 0.5\,(10{,}000 - 10{,}900)$

$= \text{Rs. } 450 \text{ (A)}$

Check:

L C V = L R V + L E V

Rs 950 (A) = Rs 500 (A) + Rs 450(A)

Illustraiton 17

Find out variable overhead variances from the following:

Budgeted variable overhead for January	Rs.8,000
Budgeted production for the month	500 units
Standard time for one unit of production	10 hours
Actual variable overhead	Rs. 6,600
Actual production for the month	400 units
Actual hous worked	3,800

Solution

Standard variable overhead rate per unit $\frac{8,000}{500}$ = Rs 16

Standard variable rate per hour $\frac{8,000}{500 \times 10}$ = Rs 1.60

Computation of variable overhead variance

		Rs.
(a)	Actual variable O.H. during the period	6,600
(b)	Actual hours worked× standardvariable overheadrateperhour 3,800 hrs × Rs 1.60	6,080
(c)	Actual production × standard variable overhead rate per unit 400 units × Rs 16	6,400

Variable overhead variance:

(i)	Expenditure variance (a – b)	Rs 520 (A)
(ii)	Efficiency variance (b – c)	Rs 320 (F)
(iii)	Total variable Overhead variance (a – c)	Rs 200 (A)

By application of formulae:

Variable overhead variance = (SVO – AVO)

= (Rs 6,400 – 6,600) = Rs 200 (A)

(i) Expenditure variance = (AH × SR) – AVO

= (3,800 Hrs. × Rs 1.60) = Rs 6,600

= Rs (6,080 – Rs 6,600) = Rs 520 (A)

(ii) Efficiency variance = Standard overhead rate (Actual Hrs – Standard hous for actual production)

= Rs 1.60 (3,800 hrs – 4,000 hrs) = Rs 320 (F)

Illustration 18

A factory has estimated its overheads for the next year at Rs.48,999. The factory works 300 days in a year. It works for 8 hours a day. The total budgeted production for the year is 24,000 units.

Actual data for the month of April are given us under:

Actual Overheads	Rs 4,250
Actual Output	2,100 units
Idle time	4 hours

Calculate

(i) Overhead cost variance

(ii) Overhead expenditure variance

(iii) Overhead efficiency variance

(iv) Idle time variance.

Solution

Overhead cost variance

$$= \left(\begin{array}{c}\text{Standard Overhead for}\\ \text{actual output}\end{array}\right) - \left(\begin{array}{c}\text{Actual Overhead Cost}\\ \text{for actual Output}\end{array}\right)$$

$$= \text{Rs. } (2{,}100 \times 2) - (\text{Rs. } 4{,}250) = \text{Rs. } 50 \text{ (A)}$$

Overhead expenditure = Budgeted overheads – Actual overheads

Variance = Rs. 4,000 – Rs. 4,250

= Rs. 250 (A)

Overhead efficiency = (Standard Overheads for actual hours worked)

– Standard overheads for actual production

$$= \text{Rs. } (20 \times 196) - \text{Rs } (2 \times 2{,}100)$$

$$= \text{Rs } 3{,}920 - \text{Rs } 4{,}200 = \text{Rs } 280 \text{ (F)}$$

Idle time variance $= 4 \times \text{Rs } 20 = \text{Rs } 80 \text{ (A)}$

Check

Overhead Cost Variance = Overhead expenditure variance

+ Overhead efficience variance + Idle time variance

Rs: 50 (A) = Rs.250 (A) + Rs 280 (F) + Rs 80 (A)

Standard overhead rate perunit $= \dfrac{\text{Rs.}48{,}000}{24{,}000} = \text{Rs } 2.$

Standard Overhead rate per hour $= \dfrac{\text{Rs } 48{,}000}{300 \times 8} = \text{Rs } 20$

Illustration 20

Item	Budget	Actual
No.of working days	20	22

Man-hour per day	8,000	8,400
Output per man-hour in unit	1	0.9
Overhead cost (Rs)	80,000	84,000

Calcualte overhead variances:

Solution

Overhead cost variance

= Actual overhead – Standard overhead for actual production

= Rs 84,000 – (0.50 × 1,66,320)

= Rs 84,000 – 83,160 = Rs 840 (A)

Overhead expenditure = Actual overheads – Budgeted overheads

Variance = Rs 84,000 – 80,000 = Rs 4,000 (A)

Overhead volume variance

= Budgeted overheads – Standard overheads for actual production

= Rs 80,000 – Rs 83,160 = Rs 3,160 (F)

Overhead calendar variance

= Revised Budgeted overheads – standard overheads for actual man hours

= Rs 88,000 – (Re. 0.5 × 184800)

= Rs 88,000 – Rs 92,400 = Rs 4,400 (F)

Overhead efficiency variance

= (Standard overheads for actual man–hours–standard overheads for actual output)

= (0.5 × 1,84,800) – (0.50 × 1,66,320)

= Rs. 9240 (A)

Capacity Variance = (Budgeted Overheads – Revised Budgeted overheads)

= Rs. 80,000 – 88,000 = Rs. 8,000 (F)

Workings

Standard overhead per hour $= \frac{80,000}{1,60,000} =$ Re. 0.50

Standard overhead per unit = 0.50

Budgeted man hours = 20 × 8,000 = 1,60,000 hours

Budgeted output = 1,60,000 × 1 = 1,60,000 units

Budgeted man hours for actual working days = 22 × 8000 = 1,76,000 hours

Actual man hours for acutal working days = 8,400 × 22 = 1,84,800 hours

Actual output for actual hours = 1,84,000 × 0.9

= 1,66,320 units

Revised budgeted overheads $= \frac{80,000}{20} \times 22 = \text{Rs } 88,000$

Volume variance

= Calendar variance + Capacity variance + Efficiency variance

Rs 3,160 (F) = 4,400 (F) + 8,000 (F) + Rs 9,240 (A)

Illustration 20

From the following basic data calculate

(a) Overhead cost variance (b) Overhead expenditure variance
(c) Overhead volume variance (d) Overhead capacity variance and
(e) Efficiency variance

Standard output for 40 hours	1,400 units
Standard fixed overheads (Rs)	1,400
Actual output	1,200 units
Actual hours worked	32
Actual fixed overheads (Rs)	1,500

Solution

Overhead cost variance = AC − SC for actual output

= Rs. 1,500 − Rs. 1,200

= Rs. 300 (A)

Overhead expenditure variance = AFOH − BFOH

= Rs 1,500 − Rs 1,400

= Rs 100 (A)

Overhead volume variance = BFOH − SFOH for actual output

= Rs 1,400 − Rs 1,200

= Rs 200 (A)

Cost Variance = Expenditure variance + Volume variance

Rs 300 (A) = Rs 100 (A) + Rs 200 (A)

Capacity variance = SFOH for SHrs − SFOH for A Hrs

$= \frac{1,400}{40} \times (40 - 32)$

$= \frac{1,400}{40} \times 8 = \text{Rs } 280 \text{ (A)}$

Efficiency variance = SFOH for A Hrs − SFOH for actual output

= (Rs 1,120 − Rs 1,200) = 80 (F)

Check:

Volume variance $=$ Capacity + Efficiency

Rs. 200 (A) $=$ Rs 280 (A) + Rs 80 (F)

Workings

SFOH for actual hours $= \frac{1,400}{40} \times 32 =$ Rs 1,120

Illustration 21

From the following data calculate,

(a) Overhead cost variance; (b) Overhead expenditure variance; (c) Overhead efficiency variance; (d) Overhead capacity variance; (e) Calendar variance; (f) Volume variance

For the month of March, 1996.

Items	Budget	Actual
No.of working days	24	22
No.of hours worked	2,200	1,950
Overhead cost (Rs)	1,100	1,200
Production units	1,100	1,000

Solution

(a) Overhead cost variance

= Actual overheads − Standard overheads for actual production

= Rs 1,200 − Rs 1,000 = Rs 200 (A)

(f) Overhead capacity variance

= (Standard overhead for actual working days −

(Standard overhead for actual hours worked)

$= \frac{1,100}{24} \times 22 - (1,950 \times 0.50)$

= Rs 10,08.33 − Rs 975

= Rs 33.33 (A)

Check

Volume variance = Capacity + Calender + Efficiency

Rs 100 (A) = Rs 33.33 (A) + Rs 91.67 (A) + Rs 25 (F)

Illustration 22

From the following data, calculate:

(a) Expense variance (b) Efficiency Variance (c) Capacity variance

Budgeted direct labour hours	4,000
Standard direct labour hours for actual production	4,200

(b) Overheads Expenditure variance

= Budgeted overheads − Actual overheads

= Rs 1,100 − Rs 1,200 = Rs 100 (A)

(c) Overhead volume variance

= Budgeted overheads − Standard overheads for actual production

= Rs 1,100 − 1,000 = Rs 100 (A)

(d) Overheads efficiency variance

= (Standard overheads for actual worked) − (Standard overheads for actual production).

$= (1{,}950 \times 0.5) - (1000 \times 1)$

= Rs 975 − 1000 = Rs 25 (F)

(e) Overhead Calender variance

= (Standard overheads for budgeted working days) −

(Standard overhead for actual working day)

$= \text{Rs. } 1{,}100 - \frac{1{,}100}{24} \times 22$

= Rs 91.67 (A)

Actual direct labour hours	4,300
Actual overhead expenses incurred:	
Variable	Rs 4,500
Fixed	Rs 8,500

Applied overhead rate: Rs 3.00 per direct labour hour (of which are Rs 2.00 per hour being fixed overheads) *(Adapted from ICWAI, Inter)*

Solution

(a) Budget or expenses variance:

Fixed: Actual expenses	Rs.	8,500	
Budgeted hours× Standard rate			
4,000 hours× Rs 2.00/hour	Rs.	8,000	
	Rs.	500	Adverse
Variable: Actual expenses	Rs.	4,500	
Actualhours× Standardrate			
4,300 hours× Re1.00/hour	Rs.	4,300	
	Rs.	200	Adverse

(b) Efficiency variance:

Fixed: (Standard hours − Actual hours) × Standard rate

(4,200 − 4,300) Rs 2.00/hour Rs. 200 Adverse

Variable: Same formula as above

(4,200 – 4,300) Re 1.00 /hour Rs. 100 Adverse

(c) Capacity variance:

Fixed: (Actualhours – Budgeted hours) × Standard rate

(4,300 – 4,000) Rs 2.00/hour Rs 600 Favorable

Reconciliation

Overheads recovered through production

Standard hours for actual production × Standard rate

4200 hours × Rs 3.00 / hour	Rs. 12,600	
Actual overheads	Rs. 13,000	
	Rs. 400	Adverse
(a) Budget or expense variance	Rs. 700	Adverse
(b) Efficiency variance	Rs. 300	Adverse
(c) Capacity variance	Rs. 600	Favorable
Total	Rs. 400	Adverse

Illustration 23

The following are the standard and actual cost figures for the month of January 1998.

	Standard	Actual
	20,000	20,000
	Rs.	Rs.
Material at Re 1 per kg.	20,000	@ Re 1.10 23,100
Labour @ Re 0.5 per hour	15,000	@ Re 0.52 15,340
Fixed expenses	30,000	33,000

Compute the variance for January 1998

Solution

Computation of variance for January 1998

Material Variances

Price	= AQ (SP – AP)	
	21,000 units (1.00–1,10)	= Rs2,100 (A)
Usage	= SP (SQ – AQ)	
	= Re.1(20,000 – 21,000)	= Rs 1,000 (A)
Cost	= (Price + Usage)	= Rs 3,100 (A)

Labour variances

Rate	= A Hrs (SR – AR)	
	= 29,500 (0.50 – 0.52)	= Rs 590 (A)
Efficiency	= SR (S Hrs – A Hrs)	
	= Re0.50 (30,000 – 29,500)	= Rs 250 (F)

Cost	= (Rate + Efficiency)	= Rs 340 (A)
Fixed overheads variances		
Expenditure	= (AFOH − BFOH)	
	= (Rs 33,000 − Rs 30,000)	= Rs 3,000 (A)
Volume	= (BFOH − SFOH)	
	= (Rs 30,000 − Rs 30,000)	= Nil
Cost	= (AFOH − SFOH)	Rs 3,000 (A)

Workings

AQ of material used $= \text{Rs.}\ \dfrac{23{,}100}{1.10} = \text{Rs.}\ 21{,}000$ kgs

A Hrs of labour $= \dfrac{15{,}340}{0.52} = \text{Rs.}\ 29{,}500$ hrs

Illustration 24

Reconcile the standard sales with actual sales and the standard profit with the actual on the basis of variances from the information given below:

Product Standard	Qty Sold units	Selling price Per unit (Rs)	Cost per Unit (Rs)
A	3,000	50	35
B	2,000	60	40
Actual			
A	3,250	55	36
B	2,750	58	37

Solution

Reconciliation of standard Sales and Profit with Actual Sales and profit

	Sales Rs.	Profit Rs.
Standard	2,70,000	85,000
variances		
Price	10,750 (F)	10,750 (F)
Quantity	54,000 (F)	17,000 (F)
Mix	3,500 (F)	1,750 (F)
Cost -	--	5,000 (F)
Actual	3,38,250	1,19,500

Workings

Sales		Rs.	Profit variances	Rs.
Price variances	= AQ (SP − AQ)		AQ (SM − AM)	

Product A	= 3,250 (50 – 55)	= 16,250 (F)	3,250 (15-20)	= 16,250 (F)
B	= 2,750 (60 – 58)	= 5,500 (A)	2750 (20-18)	= 5,500 (A)
Total		10,750 (F)		10,750 (F)
Mix variance	= SP (RSQ – AQ)		SM (RSQ – AQ)	
Product A	= 50 (3,600 – 3,250)	= 17,500 (A)	15 (3,600 – 3,250)	= 5,250 (A)
B	= 60 (2,400 – 2,750)	= 21,000 (F)	20 (2,400 – 2,750)	= 7,000 (F)
		3,500 (F)		1,750 (F)
Quantity Variance	= SP (SQ – RSQ)		SM (SQ – RSQ)	
A	= 50 (3,000 – 3,600)	= 30,000 (F)	15 (3,000 – 3,600)	= 9,000 (F)
B	= 60 (2,000 – 2,400)	= 24,000 (F)	20 (2,000 – 2,400)	= 8,000 (F)
		54,000 (F)		17,000 (F)
Cost variance	= AQ (SC – AC)			
A	= 3,250 (33 – 36)	= 3,250 (A)		
B	= 2,750 (40 – 37)	= 8,250 (F)		
		5,000 (F)		

Revised Standard Quantity (RSQ)

Product A $= 6,000 \times 3/5 = 3,600$

Product B $= 6,000 \times 2/5 = 2,400$

Illustration 25

The following information relate to the variable overhead expenses incurred by a manufacturing concern for the month of April 1998.

Actual variable overheads incurred Rs.6,600

Budgeted Production for the month 500 units

Standard time for one unit of production 10 hours

Variable overhead expenditure variance Rs.520 (A)

Variable overhead efficiency variance Rs.320 (F)

Actual hours worked 3,800 hours

Calculate the variable overhead cost variance, the value of budgeted overheads and the actual production for the month.

Solution

VOH expenditure variance = SVOH worked on A hrs – AVOH

Let the SVOH rate be x

$$-520 = 3,800x - 6,600$$

$$3,800x = 6,600 - 520 = 6,080$$

$$x = 1.60$$

Budgeted variable overheads $= 500 \times 10 \times 1.6 = $ Rs.8,000

VOH Efficiency variance = SVOH on actual output – SVOH on A hrs worked

Let the actual output be y

$$320\ (F) = 16y - 1.6 \times 3{,}800$$

$$320 = 16y - 6{,}080$$

$$16y = 6{,}080 + 320 = 6{,}400$$

$$y = 400 \text{ units}$$

VOH cost variance = SVOH on actual output – AVOH

= Rs.16 × 400 – Rs.6,600

= Rs.200 (A)

Check:

VOH cost variance = VOH expenditure variance + VOH efficiency variance

200 (A) = 520 (A) + 320 (F)

Illustration 26

A factory has estimated its overheads for the next year at Rs.48,000. The factory works 300 days in a year. It works for 8 hours a day. The total budgeted production for the year is 24,000 units. The overheads cost variance for the month of April is 50 (A). Actual output for the month is 2,100 units. Calculate the overhead expenditure variance and overhead efficiency variance.

Solution:

Overhead cost variance

= Standard overhead for actual output – Actual overhead

50(A) = (2 × 2,100) – Actual overheads

– 50 = 4,200 – Actual overheads

Actual overheads = Rs. 4,250

Overhead expenditure variance, = Budgeted overheads – Actual overheads

= Rs. 4,000 – 4,250 = 250 (A)

Workings

Total annual overheads, = Rs.48,000

Total working hours, $= 300 \times 8 = 2{,}400$ hours

Annual production, = 24,000 units

Standard overheads per hour, $= \dfrac{48{,}000}{2{,}400} =$ Rs.20

Standard overheads per unit, $= \dfrac{48{,}000}{24{,}000} =$ Rs. 2

Overheads efficiency variance = Standard overhead for actual hours worked – Standard for actual output

= (Rs.20 × 200) – (Rs. 2 × 2,100)

= Rs. 4,000 – Rs. 4,200

= Rs. 200 (F)

As the recovery of overheads based on actual production is more than based on actual hours worked, the efficiency variance is considered as favorable.

Illustration 27

You are given the following information for the month of January 1998.

Budgeted fixed overheads Rs.3,000

Actual output is 4,800 units

Budgeted overhead rate Re.0.60 per unit.

Fixed overhead cost variance Rs.720 (A)

Calculate the FOH expenditure variance and FOH volume variance.

Solution:

FOH cost variance = SFOH for actual output – AFOH

720 (A) = (0.6 × 4,800) – AFOH

– 720 = 2880 – AFOH

AFOH = 2,880 + 720 = Rs.3,600

FOH expenditure variance = BFOH – AFOH

= Rs.3,000 – Rs.3,600 = – 600

= 600 (A)

FOH Volume variance = SFOH – BFOH

= 2,880 – 3,000 = – 120

= 120 (A)

Illustration 28

From the following data calculate sales value variances:

	Standard		Actual	
	Qty	SP (Rs.)	Qty	AP (Rs.)
Product X	500	5	500	5
Product Y	400	6	600	6.25
Product Z	300	7	400	6.75

Solution

Sales value variance = (SQ × SP) – (AQ × AP)

Product X = (500 × 5) – (500 × 5) = nil

Product Y = (400 × 6) – (600 × 6.25) = 1,350 (F)

Product Z = (300 × 7) – (400 × 6.75) = Rs. 600 (F)

Total Rs. 1,950 (F)

Sales price variance = AQ (SP – AP)

Product X = 200 (5 – 5) = nil

Product Y = 600 (6 – 6.25) = Rs. 150 (F)

Product Z = 400 (7 – 6.75) = Rs. 100 (A)

		Total	Rs. 50 (F)
Sales Mix variance	=	SP (RSQ – AQ)	
Product X	=	5 (625 – 500)	= Rs. 625 (A)
Product Y	=	6 (500 – 600)	= Rs. 600 (F)
Product Z	=	7 (375 – 400)	= Rs. 175(F)
		Total	Rs. 150 (F)
RSQ	=	Total AQ × Standard ratio	
	=	1,500 × (5:4:3)	
Product X	=	1,500 × 5/12	= 625 units
Product Y	=	1,500 × 4/12	= 500 units
Product Z	=	1,500 × 3/12	= 375 units
Sales quantity variance	=	SP (SQ – RSQ)	
Product X	=	5 (500 – 625)	= Rs. 625 (F)
Product Y	=	6 (400 – 500)	= Rs. 600 (F)
Product Z	=	7 (300 – 375)	= Rs. 525 (F)
		Total	Rs. 1,750 (F)

Illustration 29

From the following figures calculate the variances on sales margin basis:

Budget

Sales 2,000 units at Rs 15 each	= Rs. 30,000
Cost of sales at Rs 12 each	= Rs. 24,000
Profit	= Rs. 6,000

Actual

Sales 1,900 units at Rs 14 each	= Rs. 26,600
Cost of sales at Rs 10 each	= Rs. 19,000
Profit	Rs. 7,600

Solution

Standard margin	= Rs 15 – Rs 12	= Rs 3 per unit
Actual margin	= Rs 14 – Rs 10	= Rs 4 per unit

Sales margin quantity variance = SM (SQ – AQ)
= Rs 3 (2,000 – 1,900)
= Rs 300 (A)

Sales margin price variance = AQ (SM – AM)
= 1,900 (3 – 4) = Rs. 1,900 (F)

Sales margin variance = Rs 300 (A) + Rs 1,900 (F)
= Rs. 1,600 (F)
= **Total actual margin – Total budgeted margin**

= Rs.7,600 – Rs6,000 = Rs 1,600 (F)

Illustration 30

From the following data calculate

(a) Sales value variance (b) Sales price variance and

(c) Sales volume variance.

Budget : 10,000 units at Rs. 5 per unit

Actual : 5,000 units at Rs. 5 per unit

8,000 units at Rs. 4.50 per unit

Solution

Sales = Standard sales – Actual sales

= (10,000× 5) – (5000 × 5) + (8,000 × 4.5)

= 50,000 – (25,000 + 36,000)

= 50,000 – 61,000

= Rs.11,000 (F)

Sales price variance = AQ (SP – AP)

= 5,000 (5 – 5) = 0

= 8,000 (5–4.5)

= Rs. 4,000 (A)

Sales volume variance = SP (SQ – AQ)

= Rs 5 (10,000 – 13,000)

= Rs. 15,000 (F)

Check:

Sales value variance = Pricevariance+ Volume variance

Rs. 11,000 (F) = Rs. 4,000 (A) + Rs. 15,000 (F)

Illustration 31

From the following data calculate sales variances:

Product	Standard		Actual	
	Qty	Price per unit Rs.	Qty	Price per unit Rs.
X	200	15	220	12.5
Y	120	20	100	22.5
Z	80	10	120	15.0
	400		440	

Solution

Sales value variance = Standard Sales – Actual Sales

(SP × SQ) (AP × AQ)

X = 3,000 – 2,750 = Rs 250 (A)

Y	=	2,400 – 2,250	=	150 (A)
Z	=	800 – 1,800	=	1,000 (F)
				600 (F)
Sales volume variance	=	SP (SQ – AQ)		
X	=	Rs 15 (200 – 220)	=	Rs 300 (F)
Y	=	Rs 20 (120 – 100)	=	Rs 400 (A)
Z	=	Rs 10 (80 – 120)	=	Rs 400 (F)
				Rs 300 (F)

***Check*:**

Sales value variance	=	Pricevariance + Volumevariance		
Rs 600 (F)	=	Rs. 300 (F) + Rs. 300 (F)		
Sales mix variance	=	SP (AQ – RSQ)		
X	=	Rs 15 (220 – 220)	=	0
Y	=	Rs 20 (100 – 132)	=	Rs 640 (A)
Z	=	Rs 10 (120 – 88)	=	Rs 320 (F)
				Rs 320 (A)
Sales quantity variance	=	SP (RSQ – SQ)		
X	=	Rs 15 (220 – 200)	=	Rs 300 (F)
Y	=	Rs 20 (132 – 120)	=	Rs 240 (F)
Z	=	Rs 10 (88 – 80)	=	Rs 80 (F)
				Rs 620 (F)

Volume variance = Mix variance + Quantity variance

Rs. 300 (F) = Rs 320 (A) + Rs 620 (F)

Calculation of revised standard quantity:

RSQ = Standard proportion of actual quantity

X	= 440 × 5/10	= 220 units
Y	= 440 × 3/10	= 132 units
Z	= 440 × 2/10	= 88 units

Illustration 32

Following sales data taken out from the books of a company for the month of March 1998.

Budget for the month of 10,000 units at Rs. 5 per unit

Sales volume variance Rs. 15,000 (F)

Actual selling price Rs. 4.50 per unit

Calculated the actual quantity sold and sales value variance and price variance.

Solution:

Sales volume variance	= SP (AQ – SQ)
15,000	= 5 (AQ – 10,000)

5 AQ = 50,000 + 15,000

5 AQ = 65,000

AQ = 13,000 units

Sales price variance = AQ (AP – SP)

= 13,000 (4.5–5)

= Rs. 6,500 (A)

Sales value variance (SVV) = Volume variance + Price variance

= Rs 15,000 (F) + Rs. 6,500 (A)

= Rs. 8,500 (F)

Check:

SVV (Sales value variance) = Actual Sales + Standard Sales

= (58,500 – 50,000) = Rs. 8,500 (F)

REVIEW QUESTIONS

1. Define the following terms:
   Standard cost, Standard Costing, Estimating costing.
2. What is Standard costing? State its main objectives.
3. Describe the various types of standards.
4. Distinguish between Standard costing and Budgetary control.
5. What is Estimating costing, and how does it differ from Standard costing?
6. What is meant by historical costing?
7. Explain the following:
   Material mix variance, Labour efficiency variance, Overhead expenditure variance, Sales quantity variance.
8. Distinguish between Current Standard and Basic Standard.
9. State to which type of industries Standard Costing may be applied.
10. Explain the major advantages of Standard Costing.
11. How are standards fixed? Explain.
12. Discuss the causes for material price and usage variances.
13. List out the reasons for labour efficiency variance.
14. State the preliminaries to be considered while setting production standards.
15. "Proper managerial control of manufacturing operations depends upon standard costing". Do you agree? Explain the above statements.
16. Explain the limitations of standard costing.
17. Explain the term 'Variance' under standard costing, and discuss its significance.
18. What do you mean by variance analysis? What are its advantages?

REVIEW PROBLEMS

1. From the following particulalrs calculate material cost variance:
   Material purchased: 3,000 kgs at Rs 3 per kg.
   Standard quantity of materials required per unit of output: 30 kgs.
   Standard rate of materials: Rs. 2.50 per kg.
   Opening stock of materials: 250 kgs
   Closing stock of materials: 500 kgs

Production during the period: 80 units

[Ans: MCV= Rs. **2,250(A);** *MPV= Rs.* **1375 (A);** *MUV= Rs.* **875 (A)]**

2. It is estimated that in the manufacture of a product, for each tonne of material used, 100 pieces should be produced. The standard price per tonne of material is Rs. 10. During the second week of June 1988, 100 tones of material were used for the production. The issue price was Rs. 10.50 per tonne. The actual output for the period was 10,250 pieces. Calculate the material cost variances.

[Ans: MCV= Rs. **25 (A);** *MPV= Rs.* **50 (A);** *MYV= Rs.* **25 (F)]**

3. The standard and actual mix of materials used in the manufacturing of a product are as under:

Material	Standard	actual
A	60 tons @ Rs 5 per ton	80 tons @ Rs 4 per ton
B	40 tons @ Rs 10 per ton	70 tons @ Rs 8 per ton

Reconcile actual material cost with standard material cost.

[Ans: MPV Rs. 220 (F) MUV RS. 400 (A); MMV Rs. 100 (A); MRUV Rs. 300 (A) MCV= Rs **180 (A)]**

4. From the following information, calculate
(i) MCV, (ii) MPV, (iii) MUV, (iv) MMV, (v) MYV and (vi) MRUV.

Material	Standard		Actual	
	Qty. (kg.)	Price (Rs)	Qty. (Rs)	Price (Rs)
X	50	6	40	6
Y	40	3.75	50	3.60
Z	30	3.00	40	2.80
Total	120		130	
Less:				
10% Normal loss	120		130	
Actual loss	12		22	
	108		108	

[Ans: **MCV = Rs 8 (F); MPV = Rs 15.5 (F); MUV = Rs. 7.5 (A);MMV = Rs 37.5 (F); MYV & MRUV RS 45 (A)]**

5. The standard cost of a certain chemical mixture is as follows:

60% of Material X at Rs 300 per ton.

40% of Material Y at Rs 200 per ton.

A standard loss of 10% is expected in production. During a period the following quantity is used.

110 tons of material X at the cost of Rs. 340 per ton.

90 tons of material Y at the cost of Rs. 180 per ton.

The weight produced is 182 tons of good production.

Calculate

(i) Material price variance, (ii) Material usage variance

(ii) Material mix variance and (iv) Material yield variance

[Ans:] MPV= Rs **2,600** *(A); MUV= Rs* **577.77** *(F); MMV= Rs* **1,000** *(F);*
MYV = Rs 577.77 (F)]

6. Calculate the labour cost variances.

		Standard	Actual
Output		1,000 units	1,200 units
Rate of payment:	Rs.6 per unit	Wages paid with bonus: Rs. 8,000	
Time Taken:	50 hrs	Time Taken	40 hrs

[Ans:] LCV= Rs **800** *(A), LRVRs* **3,200(A)**, *LEVRs* **2,400** *(F)]*

7. The production of a certain unit is assumed to require 18 hours labour at a rate of Rs. 1.25 per hour. On completion of the production of a unit it was found that the time taken was 16 hours, the wage rate being Rs. 1.50 per hour.
Calculate the labour variances.

[Ans: LCV] = *Rs* **1.5** *(A); LRV= Rs* **4** *(A); LEV= Rs* **2.5** *(F)]*

8. Details regarding the composition and the weekly wage rates of a labour force engaged on a job scheduled to be completed in 30 weeks are as follows:

Category of workers	Standard		Actual	
	No.of labourers	Weekly wage rate per labourer	No.of Labourers	Weekly wage rate per labourer
		Rs.		Rs.
Skilled	75	60	70	70
Semi-skilled	45	40	30	50
Unskilled	60	30	80	20

The work is actually completely in 32 weeks. Calculate the various labour variances.

[Ans: LCV] **= Rs. 13,000 (A); LRV= Rs, 6,400 (A); LEV= Rs. 6,600 (A)]**

9. The following figures have been extracted from the cost books of a factory for the month of March 1998.

	Standard	Actual
No. of units produced	15,000	16,000
Capacity	100%	100%
No. of days worked	25	26
Variable overheads	Rs. 30,000	Rs. 31,500
Fixed overheads	Rs. 45,000	Rs. 46,500

Analyse the total overhead variance into

(a) Expenditure

(b) Capacity

(c) Calendar

(d) Efficiency variance

[Ans: (a) Rs. 300 (F); (b) Rs. 1,800 (F); (c) Rs. 1,800 (F); (d) 1,200 (F)]

10. The budgeted output of a product is 5,00,000 units per annum. Fixed overheads for the same period are Rs. 2,25,000. Each year the factory closes for two weeks annual holiday.

During the first week in January, the actual output was 10,250 units while the actual expenditure was Rs. 4,750.

Standard performance is 250 units per hour on a 40 hours week basis. One hour a week was lost due to abnormal idle time.

Calculate various fixed overhead variances.

[Ans: FOH Exp. V Rs. 250 (A); Vol V Rs. 112.5 (F); Eff. V Rs. 225 (F); Capacity Rs. 112.5 (A)]

11. The standard overhead rate of a product is developed as follows:

Variable	Rs. 4.00
Fixed (Budgeted production 10,000 units)	Rs. 6.00

Standard time allowed for production of each unit of product is 5 hours. The following actual data are available for month:

Production 9,600 units

Time taken	47,900 hours
Overhead: Variable	Rs. 38,500
Fixed	Rs. 60,500

Compute overhead variances

FOH Exp. V Rs. 180 (A); Eff. V Rs. 80 (F); VOH Cost V Rs. 100 (A); FOH Exp. V Rs. 500 (A); Vol Rs. 2,400 (A); Efficiency V Rs. 120 (F); Capacity Rs. 2,520 (A); FOH Cost Rs. 2,900 (A)]

12. For one unit of product A, the standard data are given below:

	Rs.
Material	
5 Kgs @ Rs. 40 per kg	200
Labour	
40 hours @ Rs. 1.00 per hour	40
	240

Actual data

Actual production: 100 units

Total

Material 490 Kg. @ Rs. 42 each	20,580
Labour 3,960 hrs @ Rs. 1.10 per hour	24,936

Calculate variances

[Answer: MCV = Rs. 580 (A); MPV = Rs. 980 (A); MUV =Rs. 400 (F); LCV Rs. 356 (A); LRV = Rs. 396 (A); LEV = Rs. 40 (F)]

13. Following is the sales data of a manufacturing concern:

The budget is based on 1,000 standard units of production

	Standard data			Actual data		
	Qty Units	S.P. Rs.	Total Rs.	Qty. Units	S.P. Rs.	Total Rs.
Product A	500	5.00	2,500	625	5.40	3.375
Product B	700	8.00	5,600	875	8.20	7.175
			8,100			10,500

Calculate

(i) Sales Value Variance, (ii) Sales price variance, (iii) Sales volume variance.

[Ans: (i) Rs. 2,450 (F); (i) 425 (F); (iii) 2,025 (F)]

16

MARGINAL COSTING AND BREAK EVEN ANALYSIS

Learning Objectives

After completing this chapter, you should be able to

— Explain the concepts of Marginal Cost and Marginal Costing.

— Differentiate Marginal Costing from Direct Costing and Differential Costing

— Discuss the practical applications of Marginal Costing

— Discuss CVP Analysis and BEP Analysis.

— Illustrate the practical applications of Marginal Costing and BEP Analysis.

16.1. Concepts of 'Marginal Cost' and 'Marginal Costing'

The concept of marginal cost has been borrowed from economic theory. In economics, marginal cost is an incremental cost; it is considered as the addition to the total cost , which results from the production of one more unit of output. That is, it does not arise if the additional unit is not produced. The Institute of Cost and Management Accountants, London defines marginal cost as "the amount at any given volume of output by which aggregate costs are changed if the volume of output is increased or decreased by one unit." As referred to here, an unit may indicate a single article, a batch of articles, an order, a stage of production capacity, a process or a department, i.e., it relates to the change in output in the particular circumstances under consideration.

The Institute of Chartered Accountants of England defines marginal cost as "every expense [whether of production, selling or distribution] incurred by taking of a particular decision." In the short - term period, marginal cost will be equal to prime cost plus all overheads that vary with volume.

According to the Institute of Cost and Management Accountants, London, "Marginal Costing is the ascertainment, by differentiating between fixed costs and variable costs, of marginal cost and of the effect of profit of changes in the volume or type of output."

An understanding of the concept of marginal cost requires a thorough understanding of the various classes of costs and their relation with the change in the level of activity. Under marginal costing, costs are mainly classified into fixed costs and variable costs. The essential feature of marginal costing is that the product or marginal costs i.e., those costs that are dependent on the volume of activity are separated from the period or fixed costs i.e., costs that remain unchanged with a change in the volume of activity. Variability with the volume of output is the main criterion for the classification of costs into product and period categories. Even semi-variable costs have to be bifurcated into their fixed and variable components based on the variability criterion.

16.2 Distinctions between Marginal Costing and Absorption Costing

Absorption costing generally refers to the practice of charging all costs, both variable and fixed costs, to operations, processes or products and treats all costs as product costs. And as such, the product is made to bear the burden of full costs even though these costs have no relevance to current operations. But under the marginal costing technique, only variable costs are regarded as product costs and the fixed costs are transferred to the Profit and Loss Account.

Absorption costing also differs from marginal costing with regard to inventory valuation. While under marginal costing, closing stocks are valued at the marginal costs, under absorption costing; they are valued at full costs. Such a method of valuation has the effect of carrying over fixed costs from one period to another. This procedure would normally affect the trading results and vitiate cost comparison also.

In absorption costing, fixed overheads can never be absorbed exactly because of the difficulty in forecasting costs and volume of output. But the exclusion of fixed costs from product costs in the case of marginal costing does not give rise to the problem of over or under- absorption of the fixed overheads.

In the case of absorption costing, profit is the difference between sales revenue and total cost. But under the marginal costing, the excess of sales over marginal cost of sales is known as contribution. It is the contribution that is the guiding principle for decision-making under marginal costing technique. In order to ascertain net profits, fixed costs are absorbed from total contribution.

The following example would illustrate the various points explained above.

Example 1

Anish Ltd. supplies the following particulars for preparing the income statements for the year ended 31.12.2000

Sales	-	2,000 units at Rs.50 per unit
Manufacturing cost:		
Fixed	-	Rs.22,000
Variable	-	2,200 units at Rs.31 per unit
Closing stock	-	200 units
Selling and administrative expenses		
Fixed	-	Rs.6,000
Variable	-	Rs.4,400

Solution

Income statement of Anish Ltd. for the year ended 31.12.2000

(i) Under Absorption Costing Method

	Rs.	Rs.
Sales (2,000) units at Rs.50 units)		1,00.000
Less: Cost of Sales		
Manufacturing cost-Fixed	22,000	
Variable 2,200 × Rs.31)	68,200	
	90,200	
Less: Closing stock (200 units at Rs.41 unit)	8,200*	82,000
Gross profit		18,000
Less: Selling and administrative expenses		
Fixed	6,000	
Variable	4,400	10,400
Net Profit		7,600

***Working**

Total cost for 2,200 units Rs.90,200

$$\text{Cost of closing stock} = \frac{\text{Rs.}90{,}200 \times 200}{2{,}200} = \text{Rs.}8{,}200$$

(ii) Under Marginal Costing Method

	Rs.	Rs.
Sales (2,000 units at Rs.50 each)		1,00,000
Less: Variable cost of sales		
Variable manufacturing cost	68,200	
Less: Closing Stock	6,200	62,000
Variable gross margin		38,000
Less: Variable selling and administrative expenses		4,400
Contribution margin		33,600
Less: Fixed cost		
Manufacturing cost	22,000	
Selling and Administration	6,000	28,000
Net Profit		5,600

Workings

Closing stock is valued on the basis of variable manufacturing cost.

$$= \frac{\text{Rs.}68{,}200 \times 200}{2{,}200} = 6{,}200$$

The difference in profits is due to the difference in the valuation of closing stocks.

Alternatively, the closing stock may be valued on the basis of total variable cost, as follows:

$$= \frac{\text{Rs.}68{,}200 + \text{Rs.}4{,}400}{2{,}200} \times 200 = 6{,}600$$

In that case, profit will be more by Rs.400.

16.3. Advantages of Marginal Costing

The important advantages of Marginal Costing are:

(a) Marginal costing is easy to understand. It can be combined with standard costing and budgetary control and thereby makes the control mechanism more effective.

(b) Eliminating of fixed overheads from the cost of production prevents the effect of varying charges per unit, and also prevents the carrying forward of a portion of the fixed overheads of the current period to the subsequent period. As such, costs and profits are not vitiated and cost comparisons become more meaningful.

(c) The problem of over or under absorption of overheads is avoided.

(d) A clear - cut division of costs into fixed and variable elements makes the flexible budgetary control system easy and effective and thereby facilitates greater practical cost control.

(e) It helps profit planning through break-even charts and profit graphs. Comparative profitability can easily be assessed and brought to the notice of the management for decision-making.

(f) It is an effective tool for determining efficient sales or production policies, or for taking pricing and tendering decisions, particularly when the business is at a low ebb.

16.4. Managerial uses of Marginal Costing

From the advantages stated above. The following may be listed as specific managerial uses:

(a) Cost Ascertainment: Marginal costing technique facilitates not only the recording of costs but their reporting also. The classification of costs into fixed and variable components makes the job of cost ascertainment more easy. The main problem in this regard is only the segregation of the semi-variable cost into fixed and variable elements. However, this may be overcome by adopting any of the methods in this regard.

(b) Cost Control: Marginal cost statements can be understood easily by the management than those presented under absorption costing. Bifurcation of costs into fixed and variable enables management to exercise control over production cost and thereby effect efficiency. In fact, while variable costs are controllable at the lower levels of management, fixed costs can be controlled at the top level. Under this technique, management can study the behaviour of costs at varying conditions of output and sales and thereby exercise better control over costs.

(c) Decision-making: Modern management are faced with a number of decision-making problems every day. Profitability is the main criterion for selecting the best course of action. Marginal costing through 'contribution' assists management in solving problems. Some of the decision-making problems that can be solved by marginal costing are: (a) Profit planning (b) Pricing of products (c) Make or buy decisions (d) Product mix etc.

16.5. Limitations of Marginal Costing

Despite its superiority over absorption costing, the marginal costing technique has its own limitations.

(a) Segregation of all costs into fixed and variable costs is very difficult. In practice, a major technical difficulty arises in drawing a sharp line of demarcation between fixed and variable costs.The distinction between them hold good only in the short run. In the long run, however, all costs are variable.

(b) In marginal costing, greater importance is attached to the sales function thereby relegating the production function largely to a secondary position. But, the real efficiency of a business is to be assessed only by considering the selling and production functions together.

(c) The elimination of fixed costs from the valuation of inventories is illogical since costs are also incurred in the manufacture of goods. Further, it results in the understatement of the value of stock, which is neither the cost nor the market price.

(d) Pricing decision cannot be based on contribution alone. Sometimes, the contribution will be unrealistic when increased production and sales are effected, either through extensive use of existing machinery or by replacing manual labour by machines. Another possibility is that there is danger of too many sales being effected at marginal cost, resulting in denial to the business of inadequate profits.

(e) Although the problem of over or under absorption of fixed overheads can be overcome to a certain extent, the same problems still persists with regard to variable overheads.

(f) The application of the technique is limited in the case of industries in which, according to the nature of business, large stocks have to be carried by way of work-in-progress (e.g. contracting firms).

16.6. Specimen Marginal Cost Sheet or Statement

The following is the specimen marginal cost statement, which may be used by a concern producing and selling single or multiple products.

MARGINAL COST STATEMENT

Particulars	Products						
	A		B		C		Total
	Per Unit	Total	Per Unit	Total	Per Unit	Total	
	Rs.	Rs.	Rs.	Rs.	Rs.	Rs.	Rs.
Net Sales	x	xx	x	xx	x	xx	xxx
Less: Marginal Cost:	x	xx	x	xx	x	xx	xxx
Prime Cost + all Variable Overheads i.e.,, Manufacturing selling and distribution overheads							
Contribution	x	xx	x	xx	x	xx	xx
Less: Specific fixed costs		x		x		x	xx
(Specific fixed costs that can be identified with individual products)							
Net contribution		xx		xx		xx	xx
Less: General Fixed Cost							xx
Net Profit							

This presentation would be useful in order to ascertain the contribution made by each towards general fixed costs and profit.

Special Note for the Students:

From the marginal cost statement the following equations may be derived, which would be useful for the students to solve various problems in marginal costing.

Sales [S] – Marginal Cost [M] = Contribution [C]

Fixed Cost [F] + Profit [P] = Contribution

Combining these two equations, the following fundamental marginal cost equation may be derived:

Sales – Marginal Cost = Fixed Cost + Profit

Symbolically:

$S - M = F + P = C$

$S - C = M$

$M + C = S$

$C - F = P$

$C - P = F$

$F + P = C$

$F - C = L$ (Loss)

$F - L = C$

$C + L = F$

These equations may be used for solving problems of different types involving cost-volume-profit relationships.

Example 2

The following information has been obtained from the accounts section of a store having three departments:

	Departments		
	Q Rs.	R Rs.	S Rs.
Sales	50,000	75,000	1,25,000
Marginal costs	45,000	50,000	75,000
Fixed costs (apportioned on the basis of sales)	10,000	15,000	25,000
Total costs	55,000	65,000	1,00,000
Profit (loss)	(5,000)	10,000	25,000

On the basis of the above information, management wants to discard Department Q immediately as it shows a loss. Also, it requests you to give your opinion on the comparative profitability of different departments if specific fixed costs are ascertained to be Rs.2,000 for Department Q; Rs.28,000 for Department R; and Rs.15,000 for Department S; the remaining Rs.5,000 being general fixed costs.

Prepare appropriate statements and also give your comments explaining the position presented in the statement.

Solution

(a) When all fixed costs are regarded as general fixed costs:

Marginal Cost Statement

	Department			Total
	Q	R	S	
	Rs.	Rs.	Rs.	Rs.
Sales	50,000	75,000	1,25,000	2,50,000
Less: Marginal cost	45,000	50,000	75,000	1,70,000
Contribution	5,000	25,000	50,000	80,000
Less: Fixed cost	–	–	–	50,000
Profit				30,000

Comments

The loss in Department Q of Rs.5,000 is due to the arbitrary basis of apportioning fixed costs to different departments. If Department Q is closed, the total contribution as well as profit will be reduced by Rs.5,000. Hence, it is not advisable to close Department Q.

(b) When there are specific as well as general fixed costs:

Marginal Cost Statement

	Departments			Total
	Q	R	S	
	Rs.	Rs.	Rs.	Rs.
Sales	50,000	75,000	1,25,000	2,50,000
Less: Marginal cost	45,000	50,000	75,000	1,70,000
Contribution	5,000	25,000	50,000	80,000
Less: Specific fixed cost	2,000	28,000	15,000	45,000
Net contribution	3,000	(3,000)	35,000	35,000
Less: General fixed cost	–	–	–	5,000
Profit				30,000

Comments

According to the statement, it is Department R which is to be closed since it shows a loss of Rs.3,000 after apportioning the specific fixed costs. If Department R is closed. the total contribution as well as profit would increase by Rs.3,000. Hence, it is always better to close Department R if its working cannot be improved, or if the price of the products cannot be increased. The position recommending closure of Department R can be shown as below.

Statement of Comparative Profitability

	Department		Total
	Q	S	
	Rs.	Rs.	Rs.
Sales	50,000	1,25,000	1,75,000

Less: Marginal costs	45,000	75,000	1,20,000
Contribution	5,000	50,000	55,000
Less: Specific fixed costs	2,000	15,000	17,000
Net contribution	3,000	35,000	38,000
Less: General fixed costs	–	–	5,000
Profit			33,000

It is clear from the above statement that the profit would increase by Rs.3,000 on the closure of Department R, which is exactly equal to the loss incurred by that Department before closure.

16.7. Significance of 'Contribution' in marginal Costing

Contribution is the difference between sales and marginal cost, and it is used to recover the fixed costs first. Any excess of contribution over fixed costs would be profits. When a business manufactures more than one product, the computation of profit realized on individual products may be difficult due to the problem of apportionment of fixed costs to different products. The rationale of contribution lies in the fact that fixed costs are done away with under marginal costing. The concept of contribution helps to determine the break-even point, profitability of products, departments, etc., to select product mix for profit maximization, and to fix selling prices under different circumstances such as trade depression, export sales, price discrimination, etc. Contribution is the definite test to ascertain whether a product or process is worthwhile to continue among different products or processes.

Measurement of Profitability: The contribution could be used as a measure to solve the problem of key factor. A key factor, otherwise called 'limiting factor' or 'principal budget' or 'scarce factor' may be defined as the factor, which over a period will limit the volume of output, or puts a limit on the efforts of the management to produce as many units of the selected products as it would like to. When manufacture and sale of a product are confronted by the problem of key factor, the profitability of that particular product is ascertained by relating the key factor used for the manufacture of the product and its resulting contribution. Generally, sales would be the limiting factor, but sometimes, materials, labour, plant capacity, etc., may be the limiting factors. When the key factor and contribution are given, the relative profitability may be calculated by employing the formula given below:

$$\text{Profitability} = \frac{\text{Contribution}}{\text{Key Factor}}$$

For example, when material is in short supply, profitability is determined by dividing the contribution per unit by the quantity of materials used per unit. When sales is the key factor, profitability is measured by Contribution/ Sales Ratio, and so on.

Example 3

Comment on the relative profitability of the two products 'Alpha' and 'Beta', which are produced from the same raw material. The total quantity of materials available is 26,000 kgs only.

	Alpha	Beta
Contribution per unit	Rs.120	Rs.100
Material required per unit	15 kgs.	10 kgs.

Assume that the maximum production otherwise possible for each of the products., Alpha and Beta, is 2,000 units, and the fixed overheads are Rs.1,60,000

Solution

$$\text{Profitability} = \frac{\text{Contribution per unit}}{\text{Materials required per unit (key factor)}}$$

Since the quantity of materials available is limited, it is assumed to be the key factor.

Profitability of products

$$\text{Alpha} = \frac{\text{Rs.}120}{15} = \text{Rs.}8 \text{ per kg}$$

$$\text{Beta} = \frac{\text{Rs.}100}{10} = \text{Rs.}10 \text{ per kg}$$

In the absence of the key factor, product 'Alpha' is profitable. But during shortage of materials, product 'Beta' is more profitable as its contribution per kilogram of materials is higher. Total profits can be calculated as follows:

Using the available material, 2,000 units of Beta which will consume (2,000 × 10) 20,000 kgs of material and 400 units of Alpha (which is the maximum possible production from the balance of material (i.e., 6,000/15) can be produced.

Profitability Statement

	Rs.
Contribution from 2,000 units of Beta	
= Rs.100 × 2,000 =	2,00,000
Contribution from 400 units of Alpha = Rs.120 × 400 =	48,000
Total Contribution	2,48,000
Less: Fixed cost	1,60,000
Profit	88,000

16.8. Practical applications of marginal Costing

Marginal costing technique may be applied for the following purposes:

(a) Profit Planning: A business concern exists with the objective of making profits, and profits are the yardstick of its success. Profit planning is therefore a part of operations planning. It is the basis of planning cash, capital expenditure, and pricing. If growth and survival of a business are to be ensured, planning becomes an absolute necessity. Marginal costing assists profit planning through computation of contribution ratio. It enables planning of future operations in such a way as to either maximize profits or maintain specified levels of profits. Normally, profits are affected by several factors such as the volume of sales, marginal cost per unit, total fixed costs, selling price, sales mix, etc. Hence, management can achieve their profit goals by varying one or more of the above variables.

Basic marginal costing equations, which are useful in profit planning, are as follows:

Profit/Volume Ratio [P/V Ratio]: This is the ratio of contribution to sales. Symbolically, it is expressed as follows:

$$\text{P/V Ratio} = \frac{\text{Contribution (C)}}{\text{Sales (S)}} \times 100$$

From the above equation, we may derive the following equations:

$$\text{Contribution} = \text{Sales} \times \text{P/V ratio}$$

$$\text{Sales} = \frac{\text{Contribution}}{\text{P/V ratio}}$$

Break-even Point [BEP]: BEP may be defined as that level or point of sales volume at which the total revenue is equal to total costs. It is a no-profit, no-loss point. It may be expressed as follows:

$$\text{BEP (in rupees)} = \frac{\text{Fixed Cost}}{\text{P/V Ratio}}$$

$$\text{BEP (in units)} = \frac{\text{Fixed cost}}{\text{Contribution per unit}}$$

Margin of Safety [MS]: MS may be defined as the excess of actual sales or production at the selected activity over break-even sales or production.

Margin of Safety = Actual sales − Break–even sales or point

It may be calculated as follows:

$$\text{Margin of Safety (in rupees)} = \frac{\text{Profit (P)}}{\text{P/V Ratio}}$$

$$\text{Margin of Safety (in units)} = \frac{\text{Profit}}{\text{Contribution per unit}}$$

Margin of safety may also be expressed as a percentage on actual sales as follows:

$$\text{Margin of Safety Sales Ratio} = \frac{\text{Margin of Safety (Sales)}}{\text{Actual Sales at Selected activity}} \times 100$$

Example 4

From the following information, calculate BEP and determine the net profit if sales are 25% above BEP.

		Rs.
Selling price per unit	:	50
Direct material cost per unit	:	20
Direct wages per unit	:	10
Variable overheads per unit	:	7.5
Fixed overheads (total)	:	50,000

Solution

Marginal Cost Statement

	Rs.	Rs.
Selling price per unit:		50.00
Less: Marginal cost per unit		
Materials	20.00	
Wages	10.00	
Variable overheads	7.50	37.50
Contribution		12.50

$$\text{P/V ratio} = \frac{C}{S} \times 100 = \frac{12.50}{50} \times 100 = 25\%$$

$$\text{BEP} = \frac{F}{\text{P/V ratio}} = \frac{\text{Rs.}50{,}000}{25} \times 100 = \text{Rs.}2{,}00{,}000$$

BEP	=	Rs.2,00,000
25% of BEP	=	Rs.50,000
Total Sales	=	Rs.2,50,000
Contribution	=	Sales × P/V ratio
Contribution at Rs.2,50,000 sales	=	Rs.2,50,000 × 25%
Contribution	=	Rs.62,500
Less: Fixed cost	=	Rs.50,000
Net Profit	=	Rs.12,500

(b) Level of Activity Planning

Business concerns may have plans to expand or contract the level of activities depending upon the conditions prevailing in the market. Such planning is to be considered before the events overtake the business. Marginal costing is very useful for taking such decisions by enabling management to compare the contribution at different levels of activities.

Example 5

Following is the Cost Structure of JB Limited

	Level of Activity		
	60%	70%	80%
Output (in unit)	2,400	2,800	3,200
Costs (Rs.)			
Materials	48,000	56,000	64,000
Wages	14,400	16,800	19,200
Factory overheads	25,600	27,200	28,800
Factory cost	88,000	1,00,000	1,12,000

The factory is considering an increase of production to 90% level of activity. No increase in fixed overheads is expected at this level. The management requires a statement showing all details of factory costs at 90% level of activity.

Solution

Marginal Cost Statement

	Level of activity output	90% 3,600 units
	Total cost Rs.	Per unit Rs.
Material	72,000	20.00
Wages	21.600	6.00
Variable overheads	14,400	4.00
Marginal cost	1,08,000	30.00
Fixed overheads	16,000	
Total factory cost	1,24,000	

Note: Factory overheads increase by Rs.1,600 at each level of activity. Therefore, variable overheads must be Rs.1,600/400 units = Rs. 4 per unit. At 80% level of activity, factory overheads are Rs.28,000, of which variable cost are Rs.12,800 (Rs.4 × 3,200), resulting in fixed overheads of Rs.16,000 (Rs.28,800 - 12,800)

(c) Profitable Mix of Sales

A company, which has a variety of product lines, can employ marginal costing in order to determine the most profitable sales mix from a number of selected alternatives.

Example 6

The directors of AB Ltd. are considering the sales budget for the next budget period. The following information has been made available from the cost records:

	Product Z (per unit)	Product Y (per unit)
Direct materials	Rs.40	Rs.50
Selling price	Rs.120	Rs.200
Direct wages @ Rs.2 per hour	10 hours	15 hours

Variable overheads: 100% of direct wages.

Fixed overheads: Rs.20,000 p.a.

You are required to present to the management a statement showing the marginal cost of each product, and to recommend which of the following sales mix should be adopted:

(a) 450 units of Z and 300 units of Y

(b) 900 units of Z only

(c) 600 units of Y only

(d) 600 units of Z and 200 units of Y

Solution:

Marginal cost Statement

	Per unit			
	Product Z		Product Y	
	Rs.	Rs.	Rs.	Rs.
Selling Price		120		200
Less: Marginal cost				
Direct Materials	40		50	
Direct wages	20		30	
Variable overheads	20	80	30	110
Contribution		40		90

Selection of Sales Alternatives

	Products		
	Z Rs.	Y Rs.	Total Rs.
(a) 450 units of Z and 300 units of Y contribution (450 × Rs.40) + (300 × Rs.90)	18,000	27,000	45,000
Less: Fixed overheads			20,000
Profit			25,000
(b) 900 units of Z only			
contribution (900 × Rs.40)	36,000		36,000

Less: Fixed cost			20,000
Profit:			16,000
(c) 600 units of Y only contribution (600 × Rs.90)	-	54,000	54,000
Less: Fixed cost			20,000
Profit			34,000
(d) 600 units of Z and 200 units of Y Contribution (600 × Rs.40) + (200 × Rs.90)	24,000	18,000	42,000
Less: Fixed cost			20,000
Profit			22,000

Thus, alternative (c) is the one recommended.

(d) Marginal Costing and Pricing

Pricing is a very difficult problem and the basic problem involved in pricing is the matching of demand and supply. Marginal costing is sometimes used to determine prices, a simple and familiar example being the railway ticket. The normal fare will usually be more than the charge collected for excursion fare [concession fare], for the normal fare is calculated to cover all the railway costs including fixed overheads, which is a considerable item; whereas the excursion fare will probably cover only marginal cost (which is relatively small) and some contribution towards profit. The marginal costing technique can help management in fixing prices in such special circumstances as

1. A trade depression in the industry;
2. Spare capacity in the factory;
3. A seasonal fluctuation in demand; and
4. When it is desired to obtain a special contract.

Example 7

M. Ltd manufactures and sells light engineering goods. Due to competitions, the company proposes to reduce its selling price. If the present level of profit is to be maintained, indicate the number of units to be sold if the proposed reduction in selling price is 5%, 10% and 15%

The following additional information is available:

	Rs.	**Rs.**
Present sales (60,000 units)	-	1,50,000
Variable cost (60,000 units)	90,000	
Fixed cost	35,000	1,25,000
Net Profit		25,000

Solution:

Marginal Cost Statement

	Present price	No.of units: 60,000 Price Reductions		
		5%	10%	15%
	Rs.	Rs.	Rs.	Rs.
Sales	1,50,000	1,42,500	1,35,000	1,27,500
Less: Marginal cost	90,000	90,000	90,000	90,000
Contribution	60,000	52,500	45,000	37,500
Less: Fixed cost	35,000	35,000	35,000	35,000
Profit	25,000	17,500	10,000	2,500
Contribution per unit	Re.1.00	Re.0.875	Re 0.75	Re.0.625

Profit to be maintained = Rs.25,000

Contribution to be earned = Profit to be earned + Fixed cost

= Rs.25,000 + Rs.35,000 = Rs.60,000

The number of units required to be sold at different levels of price reduction $= \frac{\text{Total contribution to be earned}}{\text{Contribution per unit}}$

Hence,

At 5% Reduction $= \frac{\text{Rs.60,000}}{\text{Rs.0.875}}$ = 68,572 units (app)

At 10% Reduction $= \frac{\text{Rs.60,000}}{\text{Rs.0.75}}$ = 80,000 units

At 15% Reduction $= \frac{\text{Rs.60,000}}{\text{Rs.0.625}}$ = 96,000 units

16.9. Cost-Volume-Profit Analysis

Cost-Volume-Profit [CVP] analysis is an analytical tool for studying the relationship between volume, cost, prices, and profits. It is very much an extension, or even a part of marginal costing. It is an integral part of the profit planning process of the firm. However, formal profit planning and control involves the use of budgets and other forecasts, and the CVP analysis provides only an overview of the profit planning process. Besides it helps to evaluate the purpose and reasonableness of such budgets and forecasts. Generally, CVP analysis provides answers to questions such as:

(a) What will be the effect of changes in prices, costs, and volume on profits?

(b) What minimum sales volume need be effected to avoid losses?

(c) Which product is the most profitable one and which product or operation of a plant should be discontinued? Etc.

16.10 Importance of CVP Analysis

The CVP analysis is very much useful to management as it provides an insight into the effects and inter-relationship of factors, which influence the profits of the firm. The relationship between cost, volume and profit makes up the profit structure of an enterprise. Hence, the CVP relationship becomes essential for budgeting and profit planning. As a starting point in profit planning, it helps to determine the maximum sales volume to avoid losses, and the sales volume at which the profit goal of the firm will be achieved. As an ultimate objective it helps management to find the most profitable combination of costs and volume. A dynamic management, therefore, uses CVP analysis to predict and evaluate the implications of its short run decisions about fixed costs, marginal costs, sales volume and selling price for its profit plans on a continuous basis.

16.11 Concept of Break-even Analysis

The break-even analysis is the most widely known form of the CVP analysis. The study of CVP relationship is frequently referred to as beak-even analysis. However, some state that up to the point of activity where the total revenue equals total costs, the study can be called as break-even analysis and, beyond that point, it is the application of CVP relationship.

Thus a narrow interpretation of break-even analysis refers to a system of determining that level of activity where total revenue equals total costs i.e., the point of zero profit or zero loss. The broader interpretation denotes a system of analysis that can be used to determine the probable profit at any level of activity.

Computation of Break-even point (BEP): BEP refers to that volume of sales where the profit or loss is zero or the total sales is equal to total costs (fixed as well as marginal costs), or total contribution is equal to total fixed costs. It is calculated as follows:

$$\underset{\text{(in Rs.)}}{\text{Break - even Point}} = \frac{\text{Fixed costs}}{\text{P/V Ratio}} \quad \text{or} \quad \frac{\text{Fixed costs}}{1 - \dfrac{\text{Marginal cost per unit}}{\text{Selling price per unit}}}$$

$$\text{BEP (in units)} = \frac{\text{Fixed costs}}{\text{Contribution per unit}}$$

16.12. Assumptions of Break-even Analysis

Break-even analysis can be carried out in two ways: (a) Algebraic method and (b) Graphical method. Both the methods are based on certain assumptions, which are rarely found in practice. Some of the assumptions are as follows:

(a) All costs can be classified into fixed and variable elements.

(b) While variable costs vary proportionately with volume, the fixed costs remain constant.

(c) Selling price remains constant despite volume changes.

(d) In the case of multiple products, sales mix also remains constant.

(e) Productivity per worker, and efficiency of plant, etc., remain mostly unchanged.

Any change in any one of the above factors will alter the break-even point and the profits will be affected by factors other than volume. Hence, the results of the break-even analysis should be interpreted subject to the limitations of the above assumptions.

Example 8

The fixed costs for the year are Rs.40,000. Variable cost per unit for the single product being made is Rs.6. Estimated sales for the period are valued at Rs.1,60,000. The number of units involved coincides with the expected volume of output. Each unit sells at Rs.10 each. Calculate the break-even point.

Solution

$$\text{Break-even point (in Rs.)} = \frac{\text{Fixed costs}}{\text{P/V ratio}} \text{ (or) } \frac{\text{Fixed costs}}{1 - \dfrac{\text{Marginal cost per unit}}{\text{Selling price per unit}}}$$

$$= \frac{\text{Rs.4,00,000}}{1 - 6/10} = \frac{\text{Rs.40,000} \times 10}{4} = \text{Rs.1,00,000}$$

Alternatively

$$\text{BEP} = \frac{\text{Fixed costs}}{\text{P/V ratio}}$$

$$= \frac{\text{Rs.40,000} \times 100}{40} = \text{Rs.1,00,000}$$

$$\text{BEP (in units)} = \frac{\text{Fixed costs}}{\text{Contribution per unit}}$$

$$= \frac{\text{Rs. 40,000}}{\text{Rs.4}} = \text{Rs.10,000 units}$$

16.13. What is P/V Ratio? What are its uses?

The ratio that shows the relationship between the value of sales and contribution is called as P/V Ratio. A more appropriate term might be the **Contribution/Sales Ratio.** This is often expressed as a percentage and calculated as follows:

$$\text{Profit/Volume Ratio} = \frac{\text{Contribution}}{\text{Sales}} \times 100$$

When total sales and total costs [without break up for fixed and variable components] are given for two periods of activity, the following formula may be used to calculate the P/V Ratio:

$$\text{Profit/Volume Ratio} = \frac{\text{Change in Profit}}{\text{Change in Sales}} \times 100$$

Where, Sales – Total Costs = Profits

A few uses of P/V Ratio are as follows:

(a) Determination of marginal costs for any volume of sales: Deducting P/V Ratio from 100 can arrive at Marginal cost percentage. For example, if P/V Ratio is 25%, then the marginal cost percentage would be 75% (100 – 25).

(b) It may be used for the calculation of the desired volume of output, profit or other essential facts

(c) Comparisons can be made by calculating the P/V Ratio for each of the factors to be compared, viz.,

(i) Line of product, (ii) Sales area, (iii) Method of sales (e.g., sales through wholesalers or retailers). (iv) Individual factories, (v) Separate companies, etc.

Example 9

The following products are manufactured and sold by Rashmi Limited. Variable costs and prices are shown below:

Product	Price (Rs.)	Variable cost (Rs.)
A	10,000	5,000
B	20,000	15,000
C	40,000	25,000

Show the P/V Ratio and Marginal Cost Ratio for each line of product.

Solution

$$\text{P/V Ratio} = \frac{\text{Contribution}}{\text{Sales}} \times 100$$

Marginal cost Ratio = 1 – P/V Ratio

Marginal Cost Sheet

Particulars	Product A Rs.	Product B Rs.	Product C Rs.
Sales	10,000	20,000	40,000
Less: Marginal cost	5,000	15,000	25,000
Contribution	5,000	5,000	15,000

$$\text{P/V Ratio} = \frac{5{,}000}{10{,}000} \times 100 \quad \frac{5{,}000}{20{,}000} \times 100 \quad \frac{15{,}000}{40{,}000} \times 100$$

$$= \quad 50\% \qquad 25\% \qquad 37.5\%$$

$$\left.\begin{array}{c}\text{Marginal Cost}\\ \text{Ratio}\end{array}\right\} = 1 - 50\% = 50\% \quad 1 - 25\% = 75\% \quad 1 - 37.5\% = 62.5\%$$

Example 10

Assuming the cost structure and selling prices remain the same in periods I and II, find out the P/V Ratio and Break-even Point.

Periods	Sales (Rs.)	Total Cost (Rs)
I	1,20,000	1,08,000
II	1,40,000	1,24,000

Solution

Periods	Sales (Rs)	Total Cost (Rs)	Profit (Rs)
I	1,20,000	1,08,000	12,000
II	1,40,000	1,24,000	16 000

$$\text{P/V Ratio} = \frac{\text{Change in Profit}}{\text{Change in Sales}}$$

$$= \frac{\text{Rs. } 16{,}000 - 12{,}000}{\text{Rs. } 1{,}40{,}000 - 1{,}20{,}000} \times 100$$

$$= \frac{\text{Rs. } 4{,}000}{\text{Rs. } 20{,}000} \times 100 = 20\%$$

Applying the P/V Ratio on Sales, we may get contribution.

Contribution = Sales × P/V Ratio

Contribution for Period I = Rs.1,20,000 × 20% = Rs. 24,000

Less: Profit for Period I = 12,000

$$\text{Break-even Point} = \frac{\text{Fixed cost}}{\text{P/V Ratio}}$$

$$\text{Break-even Point} = \frac{\text{Rs.}12{,}000}{20} \times 100 = \text{Rs.}60{,}000$$

16.14 What is Margin of Safety?

The margin of safety is the difference between the total sales and break-even sales. It may be expressed in monetary terms or as a percentage, i.e., the margin of safety in relation to total sales. It is an extremely valuable guide and indicates the financial strength of the business. It is calculated as follows:

(a) Margin of Safety = Actual Sales − Break–even Sales

(b) $\text{Margin of Safety (in Rs.)} = \frac{\text{Profit}}{\text{P/V Ratio}}$

(c) $\text{Margin of Safety (in units)} = \frac{\text{Profit}}{\text{Contribution per unit}}$

(d) $\text{Margin of Safety Ratio} = \frac{\text{Margin of Safety Sales}}{\text{Actual Sales}} \times 100$

Example 11

Current sales are 20,000 units p.a.

Selling price is Rs.6 per unit.

Prime costs are Rs.3 per unit.

Variable overheads Re. 1 per unit

Fixed costs are Rs.30,000.

Calculate (i) P/V ratio (ii) Break-even point, and (iii) Margin of safety

Solution

Marginal Cost Statement

	Output: 20000 units	
	Per Unit Rs.	Total Rs.
Sales	6	1,20,000
Less: Marginal cost		
Prime cost	3	
Variable overheads	1	80,000
	4	
Contribution	2	40,000
Less: Fixed Cost		30,000
Profit		10,000

$$\text{P/V ratio} = \frac{C}{S} \times 100 = \frac{\text{Rs.}40{,}000}{\text{Rs.}1{,}20{,}000} \times 100 = 33\ 1/3\%$$

or Rs. $2/6 \times 100 = 33\ 1/3\%$

$$\text{BEP} = \frac{F}{\text{P/V ratio}} = \frac{\text{Rs.}30{,}000}{33\ 1/3} \times 100$$

BEP = Rs.90,000

$$\text{BEP (in units)} = \frac{F}{\text{C per unit}} = \frac{\text{Rs.}30{,}000}{\text{Rs.}2} = 15{,}000 \text{ units}$$

MS = Actual sales − BEP

= Rs.1,20,000 − Rs.90,000 = Rs.30,000

or MS = 20,000 units − 15,000 units = 5,000 units

$$\text{or MS} = \frac{\text{Profit}}{\text{P/V ratio}} = \frac{\text{Rs.}10{,}000}{33\ 1/3} \times 100 = \text{Rs.}30{,}000$$

$$\text{or MS} = \frac{\text{Profit}}{\text{C per unit}} = \frac{\text{Rs.}10{,}000}{\text{Rs.}2} = 5{,}000 \text{ units}$$

16.15. What is a Break-even Chart? How is it constructed?

The break-even chart is a graphical representation of break-even point. It portrays a pictorial view of the relationship between costs, volume, and profit. The break-even point indicated in the chart will be one of which the total cost line and the total sales line intersect. It is an important aid to profit planning.

Construction of Break-even Chart

(a) Select a scale for sales or production in units on the horizontal axis.

(b) Select a scale for costs and revenue on the vertical axis.

(c) Draw the fixed cost line parallel to the horizontal axis.

(d) Draw the variable cost line starting from the point on the vertical axis, which represents fixed costs.

(e) Draw the sales line starting from the point of origin (zero) and finishing at point of maximum scale.

Example 12

From the following data compute the break-even point by means of a Break-even Chart.

	Volume of Sales (units)			
Sales at Rs. 10	5,000	10,000	15,000	20,000
Fixed cost (Rs.)	60,000	60,000	60,000	60,000
Variable costs:		Rs.6 per unit		
Current sales:		20000 units		

Solution

Output units	Variable costs Rs.	Fixed costs Rs.	Total cost Rs.	Sales Rs.
5,000	30,000	60,000	90,000	50,000
10,000	60,000	60,000	1,20,000	1,00,000

15,000	90,000	60,000	1,50,000	1,50,000
20,000	1,20,000	60,000	1,80,000	2,00,000

The data can now be shown graphically as follows:

From figure 1 given below it can be noticed that the break-even point occurs when sales are 15,000 units, valued at Rs.1,50,000.

This can be verified algebrically

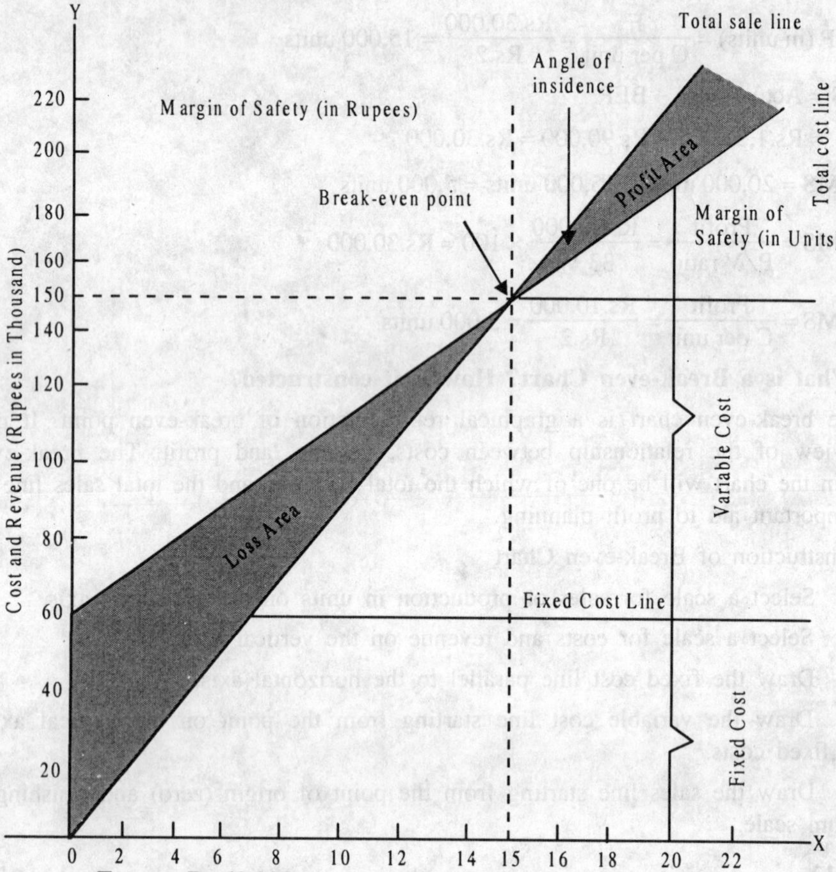

$$\text{BEP} = \frac{F}{C \text{ per unit}} = \frac{\text{Rs.}60{,}000}{\text{Rs.}4} = 15{,}000 \text{ units}$$

16.16. What is Angle of Incidence?

This is an angle formed between the total sales line and total cost line at (above) the break-even point (refer break-even chart). It indicates the rate of profit earned by the business. A large angle of incidence indicates a high rate of profit while a narrow angle would show a relatively low rate of profit. It is important in boom periods when sales are expanding. Once the break-even point is reached, additional sales show a good profit.

16.17. What is Profit Volume Graph or Chart? How is it Constructed?

Profit Volume Graph is a graphical representation of the relationship between profit and volume. It is based on the same information and assumptions as are necessary for a break-even chart. It also suffers from the same limitations.

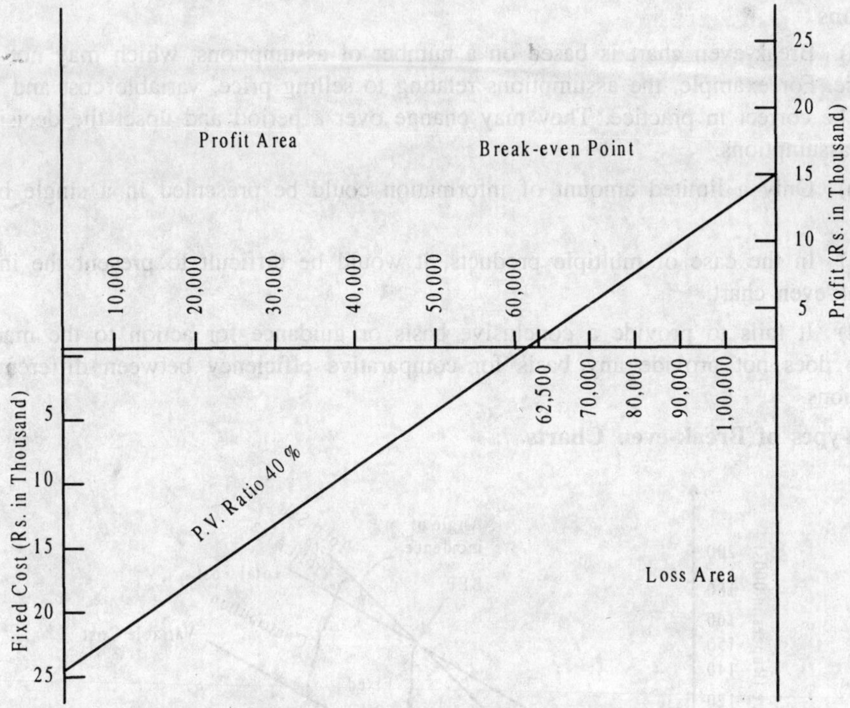

Construction of a Profit Volume Graph

(a) Select a scale for sales on the horizontal axis.

(b) Select a scale for profit and fixed costs on the vertical axis.

(c) Divide the graph into two areas, one representing profit and the other representing loss. The sales line that divides the graph horizontally forks these areas.

(d) On the vertical axis, the area below the sales line represents fixed costs and that above the sales line represents profits

(e) Points are plotted for the required fixed costs and for profit, and a line is drawn to connect the two points.

16.18. Advantages and Limitations of Break-even Charts.

Advantages

(a) The break-even chart visualizes the information very clearly and at a glance it provides a vivid picture of the whole affair of the business in a detailed and easily understandable form.

(b) It portrays clearly the effect of changes in costs and selling price,

(c) Besides clearly showing the break-even point , it enables to know the profitability of different products.

(d) It is a managerial tool for control and reduction of costs, elimination of wastage, and achieving better efficiency.

(e) It is very useful for forecasting, long-term planning, and growth.

Limitations

(a) Break-even chart is based on a number of assumptions, which may not hold well in practice. For example, the assumptions relating to selling price, variable cost and fixed cost may not be correct in practice. They may change over a period and upset the decisions taken on such assumptions.

(b) Only a limited amount of information could be presented in a single break-even chart.

(c) In the case of multiple products, it would be difficult to present the information in a break-even chart.

(d) It fails to provide a conclusive basis or guidance for action to the management. And also does not provide any basis for comparative efficiency between different units or organizations.

16.19. Types of Break-even Charts

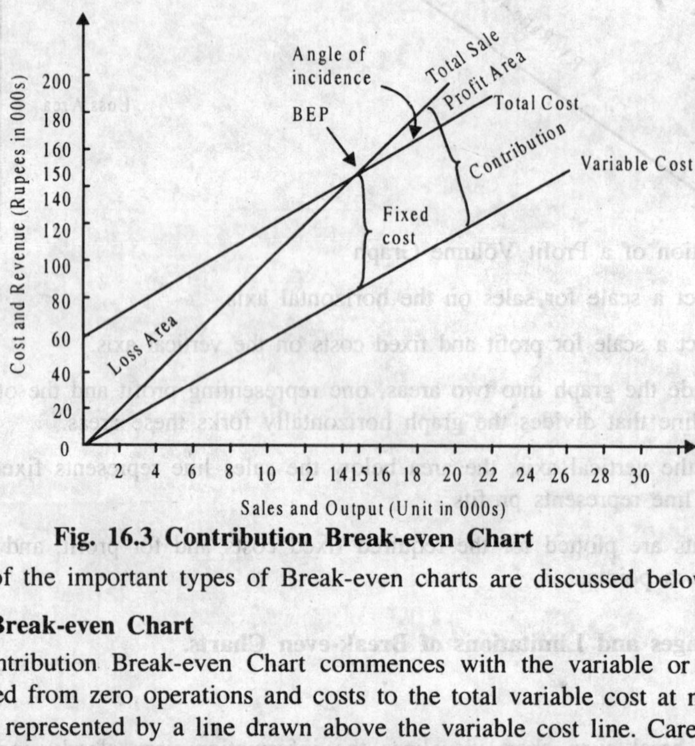

Fig. 16.3 Contribution Break-even Chart

A few of the important types of Break-even charts are discussed below:

Contribution Break-even Chart

The Contribution Break-even Chart commences with the variable or mariginal costs. These are plotted from zero operations and costs to the total variable cost at maximum output. Fixed costs are represented by a line drawn above the variable cost line. Care has to be taken to ensure that the line slopes upwards from left to right; it is not a horizontal line. The same may be explained with the following:

Variable costs: Rs.6 per unit, Fixed costs: Rs.60,000

Sales at 100% capacity: Rs.2,00,000 (20,000 units at Rs.10 each)

From the chart one can easily note that the contribution at maximum capacity is Rs.80,000. Also, the contribution at different levels of activity canbe seen quite easily from the chart.

Cash Break-even Chart

The Cash Break-even Chart follows the conventional form, except that fixed costs are divided into two groups:

1. Fixed costs requiring immediate cash, e.g. rent, rates, insurances, salaries, "immediate" means during the course of the period covered by the chart.

2. Fixed costs not required immediate cash; e.g., depreciation and other deferred expenses such as advertising and research and development written-off over a period.

Control Break-even Chart

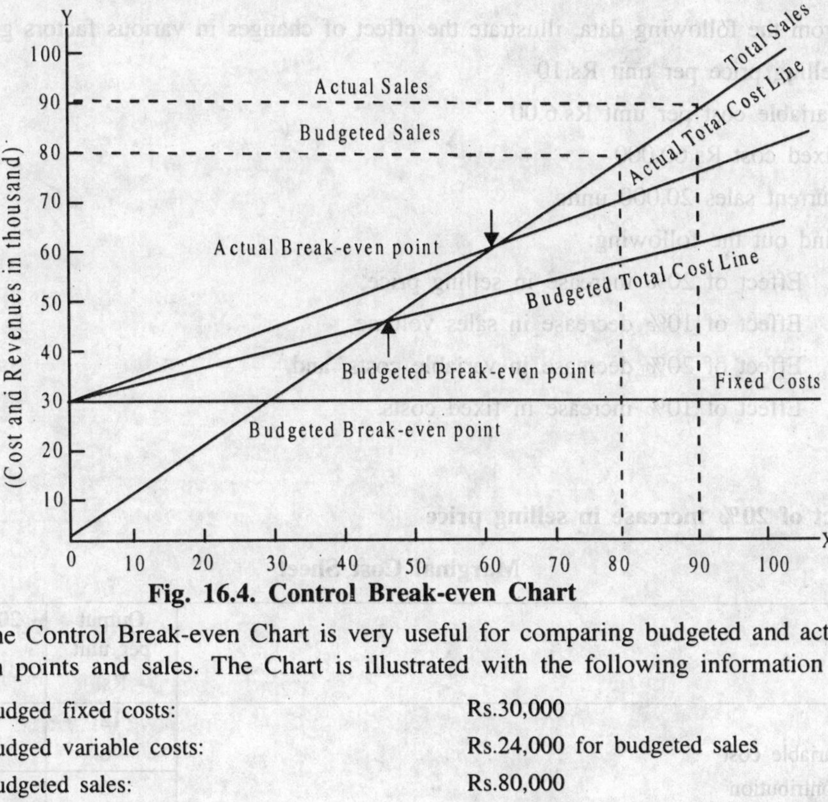

Fig. 16.4. Control Break-even Chart

The Control Break-even Chart is very useful for comparing budgeted and actual profits, breakeven points and sales. The Chart is illustrated with the following information

Budged fixed costs:	Rs.30,000
Budged variable costs:	Rs.24,000 for budgeted sales
Budgeted sales:	Rs.80,000
Actual fixed costs:	Rs.30,000
Actual variable costs:	Rs.32,400
Acual sales:	Rs.90,000

Significant facts brought to light by the chart are indicated on and below the chart. Special care should be taken to study the relationship between sales and costs. The fact that a larger volume of sales has been obtained is, obviously, a mark in favour of the sales force. However, the budgeted variable cost for the increased sales should be Rs.27,000 not Rs.32,400. This apparently disproprtionate increase in costs should be explained as management would want to know why the additional costs are incurred. If budgeting or standard costing is employed then an appropriate variance analysis should give the details required. Note carefully that variable costs are extended to cover sales of Rs.1,00,000.

16.20. Illustrate the practical utility of Break-even Analysis

Break-even analysis can be used to show the effect of a change in any of the following profit factors:

1. Change in selling prices,
2. Change in volume of sales'
3. Change in variable costs, and
4. Change in fixed costs.

Example 13

From the following data, illustrate the effect of changes in various factors given below:

Selling price per unit Rs.10

Variable cost per unit Rs.6.00

Fixed cost Rs.60,000

Current sales 20,000 units

Find out the following:

1. Effect of 20% increase in selling price,
2. Effect of 10% decrease in sales volume,
3. Effect of 20% decrease in variable costs, and
4. Effect of 10% increase in fixed costs.

Solution

1. Effect of 20% increase in selling price

Marginal Cost Sheet

	Output per unit Rs.	20,000 units Total Rs.
Sales	12	2,40,000
Less: Variable cost	6	1,20,000
Contribution	6	1,20,000
Less: Fixed cost		60,000
Profit		60,000

$$\text{Break-even point} = \frac{\text{Rs.}60{,}000}{\text{Rs.}6} = 10{,}000 \text{ units}$$

Margin of safety = 20,000 – 10,000 = 10,000 units

MS (as a percentage on total sales)

$$= \frac{\text{Rs.}1{,}20{,}000}{\text{Rs.}2{,}40{,}000} \times 100 = 50\%$$

– It can be observed that due to 20% increase in selling prices, the profit has increased by Rs.40,000, and BEP has decreased to 10,000 units or Rs.1,20,000. The same effects maybe illustrated through the Break-even Chart.

2. Effect of 10% decrease in sales volume

Marginal Cost Sheet

	Output per unit Rs.	18,000 units Total Rs.
Sales	10	1,80,000
Less: Variable costs	6	1,08,000
Contribution	4	72,000
Less: Fixed costs		60,000
Profit		12,000

$$\text{P/V ratio} = \text{Rs.}4/\text{ Rs.}10 \times 100 = 40\%$$

$$\text{BEP} = \frac{\text{Rs.}60{,}000}{\text{Rs.}4} = 15{,}000 \text{ units}$$

$$\text{MS} = \frac{\text{Profit}}{\text{C per unit}} = \frac{\text{Rs.}12{,}000}{\text{Rs.}4} = 3{,}000 \text{ units}$$

It may be observed 10% reduction in sales volume has affected only the Margin of Safety. There is no change in BEP since the P/V ratio and fixed cost are the same.

3. Effect of 20% decrease in variable costs.

Marginal Cost Sheet

	Output per unit Rs.	20,000 units Total Rs.
Sales	10.00	2,00,000
Less: Variable costs (Rs.6 less 20%)	4.80	96,000
Contribution	5.20	1,04,000
Less: Fixed costs		60,000
Profit		44,000

$$\text{P/V ratio} = \frac{\text{Rs.}5.20}{\text{Rs.}10} \times 100 = 52\%$$

$$\text{BEP} = \frac{\text{Rs.}60{,}000}{\text{Rs.}5.2} = 11{,}539 \text{ units}$$

$$= (\text{Rs.}10 \times 11.539) = \text{Rs.}1{,}15{,}390$$

$$\text{MS} = 20{,}000 - 11{,}539 = 8{,}461 \text{ units (Approx)}$$

Reducation in variable cost will improve the P/V ratio and reduce BEP. Ultimately, the MS will also increase.

4. Effect of 10% increase in fixed costs.

Marginal Cost Sheet

	Output per unit Rs.	20,000 units Total Rs.
Sales	10	2,00,000
Less: Variable costs	6	1,20,000

Contribution	4	80,000
Less: Fixed costs (Rs.60,000 + 10%)		66,000
Profit		14,000

$$P/V \text{ ratio} = \frac{Rs.4}{Rs.10} \times 100 = 40\%$$

$$BEP = \frac{Rs.66,000}{Rs.40} \times 100 = Rs.1,65,000 \left[BEP = \frac{F}{P/V\ Ratio} \right]$$

$$\text{or } \frac{Rs.1,65,000}{Rs.10} = 16,500 \text{ units}$$

$$MS = \frac{Rs.14,000}{40} \times 100 = Rs.35,000\ MS = \frac{P}{P/V\ Ratio}$$

Or MS = (Rs.2,00,000 – Rs.1,65,000) = Rs.35,000

Increase in fixed cost will increase BEP and thereby reduces MS.

Example 14

Polestar Electronics decides to effect a 10% reduction in the price of its product because it is felt that such a step may lead to a greater volume of sales. It is anticipated that there are no prospects of a change in total fixed costs and variable cost per unit. The directors wish to maintain net profits at the present level.

The following information has been obtained from its books:

Sales - 10 000 units	Rs. 2,00,000
Variable cost - Rs.15 per unit Fixed Cost	Rs. 40,000

How does the management proceed to implement this decision?

[MCA May 1998, Madras University]

Solution

Marginal Cost Statement

	Per unit Rs.	Total Rs.
Sales - 10 000 units	20.00	2,00,000
Less Variable Cost	15.00	1,50,000
Contribution	5.00	50,000
Less Fixed Cost		40,000
Profit		10,000

$$P/V\ Ratio = \frac{Contribution}{Sales} \times 10 = \frac{Rs.\ 5}{Rs.\ 20} \times 100 = 25\%$$

BEP = Fixed Cost/P/V Ratio = Rs. 40000/25% = Rs. 160000

Effect of change of 10% reduction in Selling Price

Marginal Cost Statement

	Per unit Rs.
Sales (10% less)	18.00

Less: Variable cost 15.00

Contribution 3.00

$$P/V \text{ Ratio} = \frac{C}{S} \times 100 = \text{Rs.} \frac{3}{18} \times 100 = 16.67$$

New BEP = F/ New P/V Ratio = Rs.40 000/ 16.67% = Rs.2 40 000.

Sales to earn present level of Profit i.e., Rs.10 000

$$\text{Sales} = \frac{\text{Fixed Cost} + \text{Desired Profit}}{\text{New P/V Ratio}}$$

$$\text{Sales} = \frac{\text{Rs. } 40000 + \text{Rs. } 10000}{16.67\%} = \text{Rs. } 300000$$

Comments: The management should proceed to implement this decision if it can affect sales above the new BEP i.e., Rs.2,40,000. If it wants to earn profit at the present level i.e., Rs.10,000, then it should make sales amounting to Rs.3,00,000.

16.21 Meaning of Direct Costing

The term 'direct costing' is used in USA, while it is used as marginal costing in UK. Direct costing and Marginal costing are used more or less synonymously. However, direct costing may be differentiated from marginal costing for academic purposes. Direct costing may be defined as a technique where only direct costs, which are attributable to a product directly, are considered for the computation of cost of the product. Indirect costs are charged against the total margin that is excess selling price over direct costs. A direct cost is a cost, which can be identified readily with a unit of a product. Hence, it may be said that all variable costs are direct costs, but all direct costs may not be variable costs. There may be some fixed costs, which may be identified with a product and classified as direct costs. Under direct costing the inventory is valued at direct costs. Marginal costing is a technique where only variable costs are considered relevant. The inventory is also valued at marginal costs. Hence, the most appropriate term to marginal costing would be 'variable costing' as compared to 'direct costing'.

16.22 Meaning of Differential Cost Analysis

Differential costing is a technique where mainly differential costs are considered relevant. Differential cost is the difference in total costs between two acceptable alternative courses of action. The alternative actions may arise due to change in sales volume, price, product mix, or such actions as make or buy or continue or stop production, etc. The key emphasis in differential costing is on change in total costs associated with alternative decisions. When the change in costs occurs due to change in the activity from one level to another, it may result in incremental cost [i.e., increase in costs] or decremental cost [i.e., decrease in costs]. Differential costing is a broader term that includes both incremental costing and decremental costing.

The differential cost analysis is a useful tool for the management to know the results of any proposed changes in the level or nature of activity. Under this method, the differential costs are ascertained for each proposal and compared with the expected changes in revenue associated with each proposal. When there is net excess revenue, the proposal will be accepted; otherwise it will be rejected. The determination of differential cost is simple. It represents the difference in the relevant costs for the alternative proposal under consideration. When two levels of activities are being considered, the differential cost is obtained by deducting the cost at one level from another level.

The following example will illustrate the computation of differential cost:

	Alternative I	Alternative II	Differential Cost
Sales	Rs. 50,000	80,000	Rs. 30,000
Direct Material	7,500	12,000	4,500
Direct wages	10,000	16,000	6,000
Semi-variable overheads	7,500	9,000	1,500
Fixed overheads	10,000	10,000	
Total cost	35,000	47,000	12,000
Profit	15,000	33,000	18,000

In the above analysis, it is ascertained that the fixed overheads and a portion of semi-variable overheads remain constant for both the alternatives. Hence, they will be considered irrelevant for decision-making, as they are not affected by increase in sales volume. However, if some additional fixed costs are incurred for increased sales volume that will be considered for computation.

Practical Applications of Differential Cost Analysis

Differential cost analysis may be used for problems where capital investment is involved and also for those where which does not involve capital investments. Some of the problems where it may be applied are as follows:

(a) Determination of the most profitable levels of production and price

(b) Acceptance of special orders - offer at a lower price or offering a quotation at lower selling price in order to increase the capacity.

(c) Sell a product as it is or after further processing

(d) Determination of right price at which materials may be purchased

(e) Decisions regarding alternative capital investment and plant replacement

(f) Decisions such as changing the product mix, method of production, make or buy, adding new product, etc.

Distinctions between Differential Cost Analysis and Marginal Costing

1. Differential cost analysis can be used in the case of marginal costing as well as absorption costing. Marginal costing is different from absorption costing.

2. Differential cost analysis take into account all relevant variable as well as fixed costs. But marginal costing excludes the entire fixed costs.

3. Marginal costs may be embodied in the cost accounting system, but differential costs are worked out separately as analytical statement.

4. In differential cost analysis the net incremental revenue over differential costs are used for decision-making. But in marginal costing contribution margin and profit volume ratio are used as decision criteria.

Example 15

In a light engineering company, Kitchen mixer machines are manufactured. Prepare a schedule showing the total differential costs and increments in revenue from the following data. At what volume the company should set its level of production?

Output [Nos. in lakhs]	Selling price per machine [Rs.]	Total semi-fixed costs [Rs. In lakh]	Total variable cost [Rs. In lakhs]	Total fixed cost [Rs. In lakhs]
0.60	240	30.00	83.60	28.40
1.20	220	30.00	163.60	28.40
1.80	200	34.00	255.60	28.40
2.40	180	34.00	315.60	28.40
3.00	160	40.00	355.60	28.40
3.60	140	40.00	380.40	28.40

[ICWA. Final]

Solution

Comparative Statement of Incremental Revenue and Differential Cost

Output in lakhs	Total Sales [Rs. In lakhs]	Incremental Revenue [Rs. In lakhs]	Total cost [Rs. In lakhs]	Differential cost [Rs. In lakhs]
0.60	144	–	142.00	–
1.20	264	120	222.00	80.00
1.80	360	96	318.00	96.00
2.40	432	72	378.00	60.00
3.00	480	48	424.00	46.00
3.60	504	24	448.80	24.80

Analysis

In the above case, the output level should be fixed at Rs.3 lakhs where the selling price is at Rs.160 per machine. Under differential cost method, the decision criterion is that it would be profitable to increase the output as long as the incremental revenue equals or exceeds the differential cost. Up to Rs.3 Lakhs level the incremental revenue is more than differential cost thereby adding to the profit figure. After that level the differential cost is more than the incremental revenue thus resulting in a loss on additional output.

Illustration 3

The present sales of a company are Rs.15,000 and marginal costs are Rs.9,550. Calculate marginal costs of proposed sales of Rs.18,000.

(i) assuming no change in the rate of variable costs and

(ii) assuming 10% increase in variable costs.

Solution

(i) Present Sales:

Present sales = Rs.15,000

Marginal cost = Rs.9,550

$$\text{Marginal cost ratio} = \frac{\text{MarginalCost}}{\text{Sales}} \times 100$$

$$= \frac{9.550}{15,000} \times 100 = \frac{191}{3} = 63\ ^2\!/\!_3\%$$

Proposed Sales = 18,000

PRACTICAL PROBLEMS

Illustration 1

From the following data you are required to calculate the break-even point and the net sales values at this point

	Rs.
Selling price per unit	25
Direct material cost per unit	8
Direct labour cost per unit	5
Fixed overheads	24,000
Variable overhead @60% on direct labour	
Trade discount 4%	

If sales are 15% and 20% above the break-evenvolume determine the net profit.

(*MCA Nov'97, Madras University*)

Solution

Marginal Cost Statement

		Per unit (Rs.)
Sales		25
Less: Marginal cost		
Trade discount	1	
Direct materials	8	
Direct labour	5	
Variable overheads	3	17
Contribution		8

$$\text{P/V Ratio} = \frac{8 \times 100}{25} = 32\%$$

$$\text{Break} - \text{even point} = \frac{\text{Fixed Costs}}{\text{Contribution per unit}}$$

$$= \frac{\text{Rs.24,000}}{\text{Rs.8}} = 3{,}000 \text{ Units}$$

$$\text{Sales value} = 3{,}000 \times \text{Rs.25} = \text{Rs.75,000}$$

When the sales volume is 15% above break-even volume:	Rs.
Sales = Rs.75,000 + 15% = 86,250	
Contribution = Rs.86,250 × 32/100	27,600
Less: Fixed Cost	24,000
Profit	3,600

When the sales volume is 20% above break-even point.

Sales Rs.75,000 + 20% = 90,000	
Contribution = Rs.90,000 × 32/100	28,800
Less: Fixed Cost	24,000
Profit	4,800

Illustration 2

The projected capacity of a plant, when sold, would return Rs.70,000 in sales income to the company. The variable costs for this production volume were determined to be Rs.30,000. The fixed costs are Rs.20,000. Determine the following:

(a) the break-even point of the business

(b) the profit or loss to the business on sales of Rs.49,000; Rs.28,000

(c) the amount of sales that will enable the business to earn a net profit of Rs.26,000

Solution

Marginal Cost Shett

	Rs.
Sales	70,000
Less: Marginal cost	30,000
Contribution	40,000
Less: Fixed cost	20,000
Profit	20,000

$$\text{P/V Ratio} = \frac{40{,}000}{70{,}000} \times 100 = \frac{400}{7} = 57\ 1/7\%$$

(a) $\text{BEP} = \dfrac{\text{FC}}{\text{P/V Ratio}} = \dfrac{\text{Rs.}20{,}000 \times 7 \times 100}{400}$ 35,000

(b) (i) Sales Rs. 49,000

Contribution $\dfrac{\text{Rs.}49{,}000}{7 \times 100} \times 400$	28,000
Less: Fixed Cost	20,000
Profit	8,000

(ii) Sales Rs. 28,000

Contribution $\dfrac{\text{Rs.}28{,}000}{7 \times 100} \times 400$	16,000
Less: Fixed Cost	20,000
Loss	4,000

(c) Profit tobe earned	26,000
Add: Fixed cost	20,000
Contribution	46,000

$$\text{Sales} = \frac{\text{C}}{\text{P/V Ratio}} = \frac{46{,}000}{400} \times 7 \times 100 = \text{Rs.}80{,}500$$

$$\text{Marginal cost} = \frac{\text{Rs.}18{,}000 \times 191}{3 \times 100} = \text{Rs.}11{,}460$$

(ii) When there is 10% increase in marginal cost:

$$\text{New Marginal cost} = \frac{191}{300} \times \frac{110}{100} = \frac{2{,}101}{3{,}000}$$

Increase in marginal cost:

Proposed Sales = Rs.18,000

$$\text{Marginal Cost} = \text{Rs.}18{,}000 \times \frac{2{,}101}{3{,}000} = \text{Rs.}12{,}606$$

Illustration 4

A company estimates that next year it will earn a profit of Rs.50,000. The budgeted fixed costs and sales are Rs.2,50,000 and Rs.9,93,000 respectively. Find out the break even point for the Company.

Solution

$$\text{BEP} = \frac{F}{\text{P/V Ratio}} \text{ or } \frac{F}{C} \times S$$

C	=		F + P
S	=	Rs.	9,93,000
F	=	Rs.	2,50,000
P	=	Rs.	50,000
C	=	Rs.	3,00,000

$$\text{BEP} = \frac{2{,}50{,}000}{3{,}00{,}000} \times 9{,}93{,}000 = \text{Rs. } 8{,}27{,}500$$

Illustration 5

Mr. X has a Rs.1,50,000 investment in a business. He wants a 15% return on his money. From an analysis of recent cost figure he finds that his variable cost of operating is 60% of sales; his fixed costs are Rs.75,000 per year. Show supporting computations for each answer.

(a) What sales volume must be obtained to break-even?

(b) What sales volume must be obtained to get his 15% return on investment.

(c) Mr. X estimates that even if he closed the doors of his business he would incur Rs.25,000 expenses per year. At which sales would he be better off by locking his sales up?

Solution

(a) $\text{BEP} = \frac{\text{Fixed Costs}}{\text{Contribution Ratio}} = \frac{75{,}000}{0.40} = 1{,}87{,}500$

(b) Sales volume to earn Rs.22,500 profit (15% of Rs.1,50,000).

$$= \frac{\text{Fixed Costs + Desired Profit}}{\text{Contribution Ratio}}$$

$$= \frac{75{,}000 + 22{,}500}{.40} = \frac{97{,}500}{.40} = \text{Rs.}2{,}43{,}750$$

(c) Shut-down point

$$= \frac{\text{Fixed Costs} - \text{Shut} - \text{down costs}}{\text{Contribution Ratio}}$$

$$= \frac{75{,}000 - 25{,}000}{0.40} = \text{Rs.}1{,}25{,}000$$

Illustration 6

A Ltd has a P/V Ratio of 30%. By what percentage must sales be increased to offset 10% reduction in selling price?

Solution

If sales is	Rs. 100
Contribution (30%)	30
Variable Cost	70
If SP is reduced by 10%	
Sales (Rs.100 - Rs.10)	90
Variable Cost	70
New Contribution	20

In order to maintain the same contribution, the value of sales should be

$$\frac{90 \times 30}{20} = \text{Rs.}135$$

If selling price is reduced by 10%, the volume of sales will have to be increased by 35%.

Illustration 7

Calculate from the following information the break-even point and the net profit if the sales volume is Rs.8,00,000

P/V Ratio is 40% and Margin of safety is 25%

Solution

Contribution = Sales × $^P/_V$ Ratio

Break-even point = Actual sales - Margin of safety

Given P/V Ratio and MS = 40% and 25%

Contribution at a sales volume of Rs.8,00,000

= $\text{Rs.}8{,}00{,}000 \times 40\% = \text{Rs.}3{,}20{,}000$

Calculation of fixed costs and BEP

$$\text{MS (as a percentage)} = \frac{\text{MS}}{\text{AS}} \times 100 = 25\%$$

(i.e.) MS is 25, then AS would be 100 and BEP is 75 (AS-MS)

BEP = 75% of AS

BEP = $\text{Rs.}8{,}00{,}000 \times 75/100 = \text{Rs.}6{,}00{,}000$

Contribution at BEP (which is always equal to fixed costs)

= BEP × P/V Ratio

Fixed cost = $\text{Rs.}6{,}00{,}000 \times 40\% = \text{Rs.}2{,}40{,}000$

Calculation of profit at a sales volume of Rs.8,00,000

Contribution	=	Rs.3,20,000
Less: Fixed Costs	=	Rs.2,40,000
Profit	=	Rs.80,000

Illustration 8

If P/V Ratio is 50% and Margin of Safety 40%. Work out the net profit and break even point if sales volume is Rs.5,00,000

Solution

	Rs.
Sales	5,00,000
Less: MS (40%)	2,00,000
BEP (AS-MS)	3,00,000
Fixed Cost = BEP× P/V Ratio	
Fixed cost = Rs.3,00,000 × 50% = 1,50,000	
Contribution (Rs.5,00,000 × 50%)	2,50,000
Less: Fixed Cost	1,50,000
Net Profit	1,00,000

Alternatively,,

Profit = MS × P/V Ratio

2,00,000 × 50% = Rs.1,00,000

Illustration 9

P/V Ratio is 30% and Margin of Safety is 40%. Find out the current Fixed Cost and net profit if the actual sales is Rs.5,00,000.

Solution

		Rs.
If Actual Sales is	100	5,00,000
Margin of Safety	40	2,00,000
BEP	60	3,00,000

$$FC = BEP \times P/V\ Ratio = \frac{3,00,000 \times 30}{100} = Rs.90.000$$

$$Net\ Profit = MS \times P/V\ Ratio = \frac{Rs.\ 2,00,000}{100} \times 30 = Rs.60,000$$

illustration 10

The income statement of C Ltd. is summarised as follows:

	Rs.
Net revenue	2,00,000
Less: Expenses, (including Rs.1,00,000 of fixed expenses)	2,20,000
Net loss	20,000

The Sales Manager believes that an increase of Rs.50,000 in advertising outlays will increase sales substantially. His plan was approved by the Chairman of the Board.

Show: (a) at what sales volume will the company break-even? (b) What sales volume will result in a net profit of Rs.10,000?

Solution

Marginal Cost Statement

	Rs.	Rs.
Sales		2,00,000
Less: Variable expenses:	2,20,000	
Less: Fixed expenses:	1,00,000	1,20,000
Contribution		80,000
Less: Fixed expenses		1,00,000
Net loss		20,000

$$\text{P/V Ratio} = \frac{80{,}000 \times 100}{2{,}00{,}000} = 40\%$$

When the proposed advertising expenditure is incurred and treated as fixed expenses, the total fixed expenses would be Rs.1,50,000.

(i.e. Rs.1,00,000 + Rs.50,000)

$$\text{Break-even point} = \frac{F}{\text{P/V Ratio}} = \frac{\text{Rs.}1{,}50{,}000}{40\%}$$

$$= \frac{\text{Rs.}1{,}50{,}000}{40} \times 100 = \text{Rs.}3{,}75{,}000$$

Required sales to earn a profit of Rs.10,000

$$= \frac{\text{Fixed expenses + Required Profit}}{\text{P/V Ratio}}$$

$$= \frac{\text{Rs.}1{,}50{,}000 + \text{Rs.}10{,}000}{40\%}$$

$$= \frac{\text{Rs.}1{,}60{,}000 \times 100}{40} = \text{Rs.}4{,}00{,}000$$

Illustration 11

The following figures relate to a company manufacturing a varied range of products:

Period	Total sales Rs.	Total Cost Rs.
Year ended 31 st Dec., 2000	22,23,000	19,83,600
Year ended 31 st Dec., 2001	24,51,000	21,43,200

Assuming stability in prices, with variable costs carefully controlled to reflect predetermined relationship, and an unvarying figure for fixed costs, calculate:

(a) The profit/volume ratio, to reflect the rates of growth for profit and sales; and

(b) Any other cost figures to be deduced from the data.

Solution

Year ended	Sales Rs.	Cost Rs.
2000	22,23,000	19,83,600
2001	24,51,000	21,43,200
Difference or change	2,28,000	1,59,600

Variable cost (% of sales)

$$= \frac{1,59,600}{2,28,000} \times 100 = 70\%$$

(or in other wounds, variable cost is 70 paise per Re.1,00 of sales) Variable cost for the year 2000

$$= 22,23,000 \times \frac{70}{100} = \text{Rs.}15,56,100$$

Variable cost for the year 2001

$$= 24,51,000 \times \frac{70}{100} = 17,15,700$$

(a) $^P\!/_V$ ratio $= \frac{(S - V)}{S} \times 100$

$$^P\!/_V \text{ Ratio for 2000} = \frac{6,66,900 \times 100}{22,23,000} = 30\%$$

$$2001 = \frac{7,35,300 \times 100}{24,51,000} = 30\%$$

(b) Other cost figures:

(i) Fixed Cost (Total cost - Variable cost):

2000 = Rs.19,83,600 − 15,56,100 = Rs.4,27,500

2001 = Rs.21,43,200 − 17,15,700 = Rs.4,27,500

(ii) Fixed cost % of sales:

$$2000 = \frac{4,27,500 \times 100}{22,23,000} = 19\% \text{ (approx)}$$

$$2001 = \frac{4,27,500 \times 100}{24,51,000} = 17\% \text{ (approx)}$$

(iii) Break-even point

$$\frac{F}{P/V} = \frac{\text{Rs.}4,27,500}{30\%} = \text{Rs.}14,25,000$$

(iv) Margin of safety

2000 = Rs.22,23,000 − 14,25,000 = 7,98,000

2001 = Rs.24,51,000 − 14,25,000 = Rs.10,26,000

Illustration 12

From the following data calculate break-even point

	Rs.
Selling price per unit	10.00
Trade discount	5%
Direct material cost per unit	3.00

Direct labour cost per unit	2.00
Fixed overheads	10,000.00
Variable overheads on direct labour cost	100%

It sales are 10% and 15% above the break-even volume, determine the net profits.

Solution

(a)	Rs.	Rs.
Selling price per unit		10.00
Less: Trade discount 5% of Rs.10	0.50	
Direct material cost per unit	3.00	
Direct labour cost per unit	2.00	
Variable overhead 100% on direct labour	2.00	
Total variable cost per unit		7.50
Contribution per unit		2.50

$$BEP = \frac{\text{Fixed costs}}{\text{Contribution per unit}} = \frac{10,000}{2.50} = 4,000 \text{ units}$$

Note: Trade discount has been considered as variable cost in the sense that it will be provided on the sale of every unit.

(b) 10% increase in break even sales means the sale of 4,400 units.

$(4,000 + 4,000 \times 10/100)$

Contribution $4,400 \times 2.50 =$	Rs.	11,000
Fixed costs		10,000
Profit		1,000

(c) 15% increase in break-even sale means the sale of 4,600 units $(4,000 + 4,000 \times 15\%)$

Contribution $4,600 \times 2.50$	Rs.	11,500
Fixed costs		10,000
Profit		1,500

or

If the trade discount is not considered as variable cost, the computations will be done as follows:

	Rs.
(a) Selling price	10.00
Less: Trade discount	0.50
Net revenue per unit	9.50
Variable costs	7.00
Contribution	2.50

$$BEP = \frac{10,000}{2.50} = 4,000 \text{ units}$$

Net sales revenue at BEP $= 4,000 \times 9.50 =$ Rs.38,000

(b) 10% increase in BEP sales = 4,400 units

Sales revenue (4400×9.5)	41,800
Variable cost (4.400×7)	30,800
Contribution	11,000
Fixed costs	10,000

	Profit	1,000
(c)	15% increase in BEP sales = 4,600 units	
	Sales revenue (4,600 × 9.50)	43,700
	Variable costs (4,600 × 7)	32,200
	Contribution	11,500
	Fixed costs	10,000
	Profit	1,500

Illustration 13

The budgeted analysis of A Co., Ltd., include

Product	Sales value Rs.	P/V ratio Rs.
A	50,000	50%
B	80,000	40%
C	1,20,000	30%

Fixed overhead for the period is Rs.1,00,000.

The directors are worried about the results of the company. They have requested you to prepare a statement showing the amount of loss expected and recommend a change in the sales of each product or in the total mix which will eliminate the expected loss.

Solution

Statement of Loss and Additional Sales

Product	Sales Rs.	P/V ratio %	Contribution Rs.	Additional Sales required Rs.
A	50,000	50	25,000	14,000
B	80,000	40	32,000	17,500
C	1,20,000	30	36,000	23,333
	2,50,000	37.2	93,000	18,817
Fixed overheads			1,00,000	
Loss			(7,000)	

Notes:

1. Contribution = Sales × P/V ratio. The total contribution of all products comes to Rs.93,000 which could not recover fixed overhead of Rs.1,00,000 and such loss is Rs.7,000. The overall P/V ratio of the budgeted sales mix is

$$\left(\frac{\text{Rs.}93{,}000}{\text{Rs.}2{,}50{,}000}\right) \times 100 = 37.2\%$$

2. In order to recoup the loss of Rs.7,000 it is necessary to increase the sales of any of the following products to the extent as shown in the table. That is computed as follows:

Loss to be recouped for product A (7,000/– 50%) = Rs.14,000 and so on. Alternatively the same sales mix may be increased by Rs.18,817 keeping the P/V ratio same as before (7,000/37.2%)

3. Care should be taken to increase the sales of more profitable products. Thus, if the total volume of sales is constant, but the mix is as follows:

Product	Sales Rs.	P/V ratio	Contribution Rs.
A	1,20,000	50%	60,000
B	80,000	40%	32,000
C	50,000	30%	15,000
	2,50,000	42.8%	1,07,000
Less: Fixed overheads			1,00,000
Profit			7,000

Illustration 14

The following particulars are taken from records of a company engaged in manufacturing two products, AD and BI, from a certain raw material

	Product AD (per unit) Rs.	Product BI (per unit) Rs.
Sales	125.00	250.00
Material cost (Rs.2.5 per kg.)	25.00	62.50
Direct labour (Rs.1.5 per hour)	37.50	75.00
Variable overhead	12.50	25.00
Total fixed overheads Rs.50,000		

Comment on the profitability of each product when (i) total sales in value is limited

(ii) raw material is in short supply,

(iii) Production capacity is the key factor, and

(iv) When total availability of raw material is 20,000 kgs., and maximum sales potential of each product is 1,000 units, find the product mix to yield maximum profit. Determine the maximum profit

Solution

Statement Showing Comparative Profitability

	Product AD (per unit)		Product BI (per unit)	
	Rs.	Rs.	Rs.	Rs.
Sales		125.00		250.00
Less: Marginal cost				
Materials	25.00		62.50	
Direct wages	37.50		75.00	
Variable overheads	12.50	75.00	25.00	162.50
		50.00		87.50

(i) When total sales in value is limited, the profitability is measured by

$$\text{P/V ratio} = \frac{\text{Rs.}50 \times 100}{\text{Rs.}125} = 40\%; \frac{87.50}{250} \times 100 = 35\%$$

Since the P/v ratio of AD is higher, it is more profitable.

Note: When the total sales in units is limited, the product BI is more profitable since its contribution per unit is higher.

(ii) Contribution per kg of material $\text{AD} = \frac{\text{Rs.}50}{10 \text{ kg}} = \text{Rs.}5$ per kg

$$\text{BI} = \frac{\text{Rs.}87.5}{25 \text{ kg}} = \text{Rs.}3.5 \text{ per kg}$$

When raw material is in short supply, contribution per kg. of raw material for product AD is more, and therefore more profitable.

(iii) It is a case of two key factors. When raw material is in short supply, product AD is more profitable. So maximum, i.e., 1,000 units of AD could be produced consuming 10,000 kg. of raw material. And with the balance quantity, i.e 20,000 kg-10,000 kgs = 10,000 kgs 400 units (10,000 ÷ 25 kgs) of product BI will be made. Hence, for maximum profit, the product mix would be:

Product AD 1,000 units	10,000 kgs.
Product BI 400 units	10,000 kgs
Total quantity of materials available	20,000 kgs.

	Rs.
Maximum contribution from	
1,000 units of product AD (1,000 × Rs.50)	50,000
400 units of product BI (400 × Rs.87.5)	35,000
Total Contribution	85,000
Less: Fixed overheads	50,000
Maximum profit	35,000

Illustration 15

A toy manufacturer earns an average net profit of Rs.6 per unit at a selling price of Rs.30 by producing and selling 30,000 units at 60% of the potential capacity. The composition of his cost of sales is:

Direct material:	Rs.8.00
Direct wages:	Rs.2,00
Work overheads:	Rs.12.00 (50% variable)
Sales overhead:	Rs.2.00 (75% fixed)

During the current year, he intends to produce the same number but anticipates that:

(a) his fixed charges will go up by 10%

(b) rates of direct labour will increase by 20%

(c) rates of material will increase by 5%

(d) selling price cannot be increased.

Under these circumstances he obtains an order for a further 20% of his capacity. What minimum price will you recommend for accepting the order to give the manufacturer an overall profit of Rs.1,80,000?

Solution:

Marginal cost statement for current year

		Number of units: Capacity: Per unit	30,000 60% Total
	Rs.	Rs.	Rs.
Sales		30.00	9,00,000
Less: Marginal cost			
Materials	8.40		
Wages	2.40		
Variable works overheads	6.00		
Variable sales overheads	0.50	17.30	5,19,000
		12.70	3,81,000
Less: fixed cost: Works overheads	1,80,000		
Add: 10% increase	18,000	1,98,000	
Sales overhead	45,000		
Add: 10% increase	4,500	49,500	2,47,500
Net profit			1,33,500

Calculation of minimum price for special order

(10,000 units at 20 capacity)

	Rs.
Planned profit	1,80,000
Actual profit	1,33,500
Increase in profit to be earned from the order	46,500

(a) Minimum Price		Rs.
Marginal cost to be recovered - $10,000 \times 17.3$	=	1,73,000
Increase in profit to be earned	=	46,500
Minimum selling price for 10,000 units	=	2,19,500
Minimum selling price per unit	=	21.95

Illustration 16

A firm has Rs.5,00,000 invested in its plant, and 20% as minimum required rate of return on investment.

Fixed costs in the factory presently amount to Rs.2,50,000 per annum, and variable costs amount to Rs.15 per unit produced. In the past year, the firm produced and sold 30,000 units at Rs.25 each and earned a profit of Rs.50,000. How can management achieve its target profit goal by varying different variable like variable costs, fixed costs quantity sold, or increasing the selling price per unit?

Solution

$$\text{Target profit to be earned} = \frac{\text{Rs.}5,00,000 \times 20}{100} = \text{Rs.}1,00,000$$

Profit equation

Profit = Sales - Marginal Cost - Fixed Cost

Profit = (Qty. sold × SP per unit) – (Qty.sold × $^{V}/_{C}$ per unit) – Fixed cost

(a) Achievement of target profit by varying variable costs

Let variable cost unit be Rs.V

Rs.1,00,000 = (30,000 × Rs.25) – (30,000 × V) – Rs.2,50,000

Rs.1,00,000 = 7,50,000 – 30,000 V – Rs.2,50,000

30,000 V = Rs.4,00,000

$$V = \frac{\text{Rs.}4,00,000}{30,000} = \text{Rs.}13\tfrac{1}{3}$$

The target profit can be achieved by decreasing the variable cost by Rs.1 ⅔ (i.e., Rs.15 – 13 ⅓)

(b) Achievement of target profit by varying fixed costs

Let fixed costs be F

Rs.1,00,000 = (30,000 × Rs.25) – (30,000 × Rs.15) – Rs.F

Rs.1,00,000 = Rs.7,50,000 – Rs.4,50,000 – F

F = Rs.2,00,000

The target profit can be achieved by reducing the fixed costs by Rs. 50,000 (i.e., Rs.2,50,000 - Rs.2,00,000)

c) Achievement of target profit by varying quantity sold

Let the quantity sold be Q units

Rs.1,00,000	=	(Q × Rs.25) – (Q × Rs. 15) – Rs.2,50,000
Rs.1,00,000	=	25Q – 15Q – Rs.2,50,000
10 Q	=	Rs.3,50,000
Q	=	35,000 units

The target profit can be achieved by increasing the volume of sales by 5000 units.

(d) Achievement of target profit by varying selling price

Let the selling price be S

Rs.1,00,000	=	(30,000 × Rs.S) – (30,000 × Rs.15) – Rs.2,50,000
Rs.1,00,000	=	30,000 S – Rs.4,50,000 – Rs.2,50,000
30,000 S	=	Rs.8,00,000

$$S = \frac{\text{Rs.}8,00,000}{30,000} = 26\tfrac{2}{3}$$

The target profit can be achieved by increasing the selling price by Rs.1 2/3.

Illustration 17 [Differential cost analysis]

A company is at present working at 90% capacity producing 13 500 units per annum. It operates a flexible budgetary control system. The following figures are obtained from its records budget:

	90%	100%
	Rs.	Rs.
Sales	15,00,000	16,00,000
Fixed Expenses	3,00,500	3,00,600
Semi-fixed expenses	97,500	1,00,500
Variable expenses	1,45,000	1,49,500
Units produced	13,500	15,000

Labour and material costs per unit are constant under present conditions. Profit margin is 10%.

(a) You are required to determine the differential cost of producing 1500 units by increasing capacity to 100%.

(b) What would you recommend for an export order the minimum price taking into account that overseas prices are much lower than indigenous prices? **(I C W A Final)**

Solution

Differential Cost Statement

	90% capacity	100% capacity	Differential Cost
Production in units	13,500	15,000	1,500
	Rs.	Rs.	Rs.
Material and Labour	8,07,000	8,96,667	89,667
Variable expenses	1,45,000	1,49,500	4,500
Semi-variable expenses	97,500	1,00,500	3,000
Fixed expenses	3,00,500	3,00,600	100
Total	13,50,000	14,47,267	97,267

(a) Total differential cost = Rs.97 267

(b) Minimum price for export = Rs.97 267/1500 = Rs.64.84 per

This price is the minimum that should be charged to avoid any loss. Hence, any price above Rs.64.84 may be acceptable. Working Notes:

	Rs.
Sales at 90% capacity	15,00,000
Less: Profit at 10%	1,50,000
Total cost	13,50,000
Less: All other expenses	5,43,000
Cost of labour and material at 90%	8,07,000

Cost of labour and material at 100% $= [Rs.\ 807000/90] \times 100 = 896667$

REVIEW QUESTIONS

1. Define Marginal Costing. What are its advantages and disadvantages?
2. Distinguish between (a) Marginal Costing and Absorption Costing
   (b) Marginal Costing and Direct Costing
   (c) Marginal Costing and Differential Costing
3. Discuss the managerial uses of marginal costing.
4. What is the significance of contribution in marginal costing?
5. State the various practical applications of marginal costing.
6. What is P/V Ratio? How can it be improved?
7. What are the uses of P/V Ratio?
8. Write a brief note on: (a) Margin of Safety and (b) Angle of Incidence
9. What is Break-even Chart? How is it constructed?
10. State the assumptions of Break-even analysis.
11. What are the advantages and limitations of Break-even analysis?
12. Define differential cost analysis. List out the practical applications of differential cost analysis.
13. Distinguish between differential costing , direct costing and marginal costing.

REVIEW PROBLEMS

1. On the basis of the following data, prepare a marginal cost statement:
   Direct materials - Rs.9,000; Direct labour - Rs.5,000; Factory over heads (60% variable) - Rs.3,000; Administration, selling and distribution (50% fixed) Rs.4,500; Sales Rs.30,000. Also ascertain the profit

   (Answer: Contribution - Rs.11,950, Profit - Rs.8,500)

2. From the following data prepare statements of cost according to both absorption costing and marginal costing methods:

	Product X Rs.	Product Y Rs.	Product Z Rs.
Sales	30,000	60,000	80,000
Direct materials	13,500	22,500	35,000
Direct labour	6,500	12,500	15,000
Fixed factory overheads	6,000	8,000	6,000
Variable factory overheads	2,000	3,000	4,500
Fixed administration expenses	1,500	2,500	3,000
Selling overheads (fixed)	1,500	2,500	3,000

3. Calculate the break-even point for the following data:
   The fixed costs for the year are Rs.1,50,000; variable cost per unit for the single product being produced is Rs.8. Estimated sales for the period are valued at Rs.2,00,000. Each unit sell at Rs.40.

   (Ans. Rs.1,87,500)

4. From the following data. Calculate break-even point.

	Rs.
Budgeted output (units)	70,000
Fixed cost	4,00,000
Variable cost per unit	12
Selling price per unit	22

If the selling price is reduced to Rs.20 per unit what will be the revised break-even point?

(Adopted form ICWAI, Inter)

(Ans. BEP - Rs.8,80,000 or 40,000 units; Revised: BEP - Rs.10,00,000 or 50,000 units)

5. Rajes Ltd. decides to effect a 10% reduction in the price of its product because it is through that such a step would increase the sales volume. It is expected that there are no prospects of a change in total fixed costs and variable costs per unit.
   The directors wish to maintain net profit at the present level.
   The following information has been obtained from its books:

Sales: 20,000 units	Rs.	2,00,000
Variables costs	Rs.	7.50 per unit
Fixed costs	Rs.	40,000

How would management proceed to implement this decision?

(Answer: Profit - Rs.10,000; units to be sold 33,334.
Management must be able to increase the sales volume by 13,334 units if it wants to reduce selling price by 10%)

6. From the following data, find out the break-even point, profit/volume ratio, and margin of safety ratio. Also draw a break-even chart indicating the marginal contribution.

	Rs.	
Fixed costs	60,000	30%
Variable costs	1,20,000	60%
Net profit	20,000	10%
Sales	2,00,000	100%

(Answer: P/V ratio - 40%; BEP - Rs.1,50,000; MS Ratio - 25%)

7. Two businesses, A Ltd. sell the same type of product in the same type of market. Their budgeted profit and loss account for year ending 30th June 2000 is as follows:

	A.Ltd	B.Ltd.
	Rs.	Rs.
Variable cost	2,40,000	2,00,000
Fixed cost	30,000	70,000
Total cost	2,70,000	2,70,000
Sales	3,00,000	3,00,000
Net budgeted profit	30,000	30,000

You are required to: (a) Calculate the break-even points of each business and (b) state which business is likely to earn greater profits in conditions of (i) heavy demand for the product (ii) low demand for the product.

(Answer (a) A Ltd. - Rs.1,50,000, B Ltd - Rs.2,10,000
(b) (i) B Ltd (ii) A Ltd)

8. The sales turnover and profit during two periods were as follows:

Period	Sales (Rs.)	profit (Rs.)
I	60,000	6,000
II	90,000	12,000

What would be the trading results with sales of Rs.54,000? What amount of sales will yield a profit of Rs.15,000?

(Ans. P/V ratio - 20% Rs.4,800, Rs.1,05,000)

9. A Ltd. sold in two successive years 21,000 and 27,000 units, and incurred a loss of Rs.30,000 and earned a profit of Rs.30,000 respectively. The selling price per unit is Rs.100

Calculate: (i) The amount of fixed cost (ii) The number of units to break-even (iii) The number of units to earn a profit of Rs.1,20,000

(Answer (i) Rs.2,40,000; (ii) 24,000; (iii) 36,000

10. X Ltd plans to earn Rs.49,500 after income taxes in 2001. The tax rate is to be assumed to be 55% of net income before taxes. The fixed costs for the year are estimated at Rs.90,000. The contribution margin is estimated at 25% of sale revenue.
You are required to compute the sales revenue needed to earn a net income after income tax of Rs.49,500. If the contribution margin can be increased to 30 percent, how much sales revenue will be required to earn a net income after income tax. of Rs.49,500?

(Answer: Rs.8,00,000; Rs.6,66,667 app.)

11. The following figure related to a company manufacturing multi products:

	Sales (Rs.)	Cost (Rs.)
Year ending Dec. 2000	39,00,000	34,80,000
Year ending Dec. 2001	43,00,000	37,00,000

Assuming stability in prices with variable costs carefully controlled and unchanging fixed costs., calculate:

(a) The profit volume ratio to reflect their rate of growth for profit and for sales, and

(b) Any other cost figure to be computed from the data.

How the profit volume ratio may be improved without increasing the selling prices or reducing costs?

(adapted from ICMA, London)

(Answers: P/V Ratio - 30%; variable cost - 70%)
Fixed cost- Rs.7,50,000; BEP - Rs.25,00,000)

12. A company with a sale of Rs.4,00,000 earned a profit of Rs.40,000 in one period, fixed cost being Rs.80,000 and in the next period the company incurred a loss of Rs.20,000 Calculate the amount of sales and establish your calculations. Verify the profit of Rs.40,000 of the earlier period. Calculate the break-even sales. (Adapted from ICWA/Inter)

(Answer: P/V Ratio - 30%; Sales - Rs.2,00,000;
BEP - Rs.2,66,667)

13. Any change in fixed costs, variable costs or selling price has the effect of shifting the break-even point although the impact of each such change on the BEP and the profit is different. Illustrate this with the help of the figure given below assuming a 10% increase individually in each of the three elements stated. Also show how the profit figure is affected if all the elements increase collectively, each by 10%

		Rs.
Sales (20,000 units)		1,20,000
Variable cost	40,000	
Fixed cost	50,000	90,000
Profit		30,000

(ICWAI final)

(Hint: Refer Example 13)

14. In a certain factory Type A and Type B machine have been designed to produce the same product, but Type A is less automatic than Type B and requires somewhat more labour to operate. Pertinent costs are as follow:

	Type A	Type B
Set up cost	Rs.400	Rs.600
Variable cost per unit	Rs.9.90	Rs.9.40

Which type of machine should be used for various sized orders?

(Ans: Below 400 units Type A and above 400 units Type B: BEP 400 units)

(ICWAI, Dec. 1984 Adapted.)

15. Rupail & Co is a large retailer in equipment. The company's profit and loss A/c for year ended 31st March 1999 is as follow:

	Rs.	Rs.
Sales		24,00,000
Less: Cost of sales		15,00,000
Gross Margin		9,00,000
Less: Operating expenses:		
Selling Expenses	3,00,000	
Administration Expenses	1,50,000	4,50,000
Net profit		4,50,000

The selling expenses are 90% Variable and administrative expenses are 20% variable. You are required to rewrite the profit and loss account in the contribution format and also calculate break even sales. (P/V Ratio 25% BEP Rs.6,00,000)

(ICWA Inter)

Books for Reference

Management Accounting by N.P. Srinivasan, Sterling Publisher, New Delhi.

17

REPORTING TO MANAGEMENT

Learning Objectives

— After going through this chapter, you should be able to:

— Explain the need for and meaning of a good reporting system.

— Enumerate the essentials of a good system.

— Describe the various modes of reporting.

— Explain the basic requisites of a good report.

— Discuss the steps involved in the preparation of report.

17.1Need for a good Reporting System in an Organization

Information is the basis for decision-making in an organization. The efficiency of management depends upon the availability of regular and relevant information to those who exercise the managerial functions. No planning and control procedure is complete without prompt and accurate feed back of operating results and availability of other information. For example, the management must know how the actual profit performance compares with that of budgeted or standard or with past performance. And to what extent, the variations have been caused by various influencing factors. A regular system of reporting is considered essential as a better guarantee of efficiency and operation than reliance on personal qualities. Hence, it is essential that an effective and efficient reporting system be developed as part of accounting methods in an organization. Reporting system enables management at all levels to keep itself abreast of past performance as well as developments and it facilitates a check on the individual operating levels. Based on reports, management takes crucial decisions.

17.2 What does Management Reporting Mean?

The term “reporting” mean different things as follows:

(a) Narrating some facts,

(b) Reviewing certain matter with its merits and demerits and offering comments,

(c) Furnishing data at regular intervals in standardized forms,

(d) Submitting specific information for particular purpose upon specific request instruction.

Management reporting refers to the formal system whereby relevant required information is furnished to management by means of reports constantly. Thus 'report' is the essence of any management reporting system. The term ‘Report’ normally refers to a formal communication, which moves upwards, i.e., for factual communication by a lower level to a higher level of authority in response to orders received from higher level. Reports provide the means of checking the performance. A person, who is issued with orders or instructions to do certain things, should report back what he has done in compliance thereof. Reports may be oral or written and also routine or special.

17.3 Objects of Reporting

The primary object of management reporting is to obtain the required information about the operating results of the organization regularly in order to use them for further planning and control. Another object is to secure understanding and approval of the judgment by the people engaged in various aspects of work of enterprise. The second object is closely related to the first one and is important in terms of efficiency, morale, and motivation.

17.4 Essentials of a good Reporting System

A good reporting system is a better guide and effective tool for efficient managerial decision-making. Hence, the essentials of a good reporting system are as follows:

1. Proper Form. In order to facilitate decision-making the information supplied should be in proper form. The style and layout of a report depend upon the needs of the individual who will use the same. The report may be submitted in the form of narration [written statement of facts], statistical tabulations, graphs, charts, etc.

2. Proper Time. Promptness is very important because information delayed is information denied. Reports are meant for action and when adverse tendencies or events are noticed, actions should follow forthwith. The sooner the report is made, the quicker the corrective action be taken.

3. Proper flow of Information. The information should flow from the right level of authority to the level of authority where the decisions are to be made. Further complete and consistent information should flow in a systematic manner.

4. Flexibility. The system should be capable of being adjusted according to the requirements of the user. For example, production manager should be provided with information relating to his division or area of control only.

5. Facilitation of evaluation. The system should distinctively report deviations from standards or estimates. Controllable factors should be distinguished from non-controllable factors and reported separately. A good reporting system should give information required for the evaluation of each manager's area of responsibility in relation to the goals of the organization.

6. Economy. There is a cost for rendering information and such cost should be compared with benefits derived from the report or loss sustained by not having the report. Economy is an information aspect to be considered while developing reporting system.

17.5 Various Modes of Reporting

Reports may be presented in the form of written statements, graphs, and/or oral.

1. Written Statements (a). Formal Financial Statements: These statements may deal with any one or more of the following: (i)Actual against the budgeted figures; (ii)Comparative statements over a period of time.

(b) Tabulated Statistics: This statement may deal with statistical analysis of a particular type of expenditure over a period of time or sales of a product over a period in different regions, etc.

(c) Accounting Ratios: The ratios may either form part of the formal financial statements or be given in the form of separate statements. Information is also given to throw light on certain aspects of the operations of business especially the following (i)Return on Capital employed; (ii)Profit/Volume ratio; (c)Break-even point, etc.

2. Graphic Reports: The information may be presented by means of graphic reports, which give a better visual view of the data than the long array of figures given in statements. Charts, diagrams and pictures are the usual form of graphic reports. They have the advantage of facilitating quick grasp of significant trends by receivers of information.

3. Oral Reports: Oral reports are mostly presented at group meetings and conferences with individuals. However, the written reports are always considered as the most appropriate basis for important managerial decisions.

17.6 Basic requisites of a Good Report

A report is a vehicle carrying information to different levels of administration. Quality of decision-making depends to a large extent on the quality of information supplied and on the promptness and consistency of reporting. Good reporting is necessary for effective communication. Hence, a good report should possess the following basic requisites.

1. Promptness: It means that report must be prepared and presented on time. Reports are meant for action. Business executives may need quick reports for day-to-day decision-making. In such cases accuracy may be sacrificed for speed and timely need. In order to achieve promptness accounting executives may improve the methods of collecting data, and employ modern mechanical accounting devices.

2. Form and Consent: A good report should have a suggestive title, headings and sub-headings, paragraph divisions, statistical figures, facts, data, etc. Further the contents should follow a logical sequence: (a) the summary of present position; [b] the course and expected results; and (c) recommendation and reasons for their submission.

3. Comparability: Reports are also meant for comparison. Hence, the information is placed in some perspective. Comparisons are generally effected over time as well as with a norm of performance. Figures should be given for some previous period such as 'last month' or 'same month for the last year', etc. Actual figures may also be placed side by side with corresponding budgets, standards or estimates. The object is to highlight significant variations.

4. Consistency: Consistency envisages the presentation of the same type of information as between different reporting periods. Uniform procedure should be followed over a period of time for collection, classification, and presentation of the accounting information. It is also important to present information in a consistent manner to the various operating levels of management.

5. Simplicity: The report should be in a simple unambiguous and concise form. In other words, the report should avoid technical jargons and be presented in simple style. Use of suitable units of measurement such as quantity, value, weight, machine hours, man hours, percentages, ratio, index numbers, etc., would greatly enhance the utility of the report.

6. Controllability: It is necessary that every report should be addressed to a responsibility center and present controllable and uncontrollable factors separately. So that while reporting performance against plans and targets, variances, which are controllable could be analyzed in depth, and details are interpreted in an objective manner to help the manager for taking corrective action.

7. Appropriateness: Reports are sent to different levels of management and the forms should be designed to suit the respective levels. While reporting to top management, broad trends and significant exceptions are to be presented in a summarized form with brevity, clarity, and should have comprehensive coverage. Reports to departmental managers are to be more detailed covering all aspects about their departments. Reports to sectional supervisors must still be more detailed with full information about their sections.

8. Cost considerations: The cost of maintaining the reporting system should commensurate with the benefits derived there from. Hence, it may not be an unnecessary burden on the resources of the enterprise.

9. Accuracy: The report should be reasonably accurate. This means that the report should be correct within the margin of error allowed; otherwise the management may lose faith in the reports.

15.7 Describe the Methods of Classification of Reports?

Reports may be classified in a number of ways. Some of the important ways are as follows:

According to object - (a) External Reports, (b) Internal Reports

According to period - (a) Routine Reports (b) Special reports

According to function (a) Operating Reports (b) Financial Reports

Different types of Reports

External Reports. These reports are meant for external parties such as government, shareholders, bankers, financial institutions, etc., for example, published financial statements of companies. Copies of such reports are also to be filed with the Registrar of Joint Stock companies and with the stock exchange. In the interest of general understanding, these reports are expected to conform to certain minimum standards of disclosure and disclose certain basic details under the Companies Act, 1956.

Internal Reports. These reports are meant for internal uses of different levels of management such as top level, middle level, and junior level of managements. Hence, the approach to the reporting problem would vary according to the reporting level. These reports do not have to conform to any statutory standards. While the reports meant for top management have to be comprehensive and concise, the reports to operating supervisors should be specific and detailed.

Routine Reports. These reports cover routine matters and are submitted at periodical intervals on regular basis. Example, variance analysis, financial statements, budgetary control statements are routine reports. They are submitted to different levels of management as per a fixed time schedule. Routine reports are usually printed or cyclostyled forms with blank spaces to be filled in. most of the internal reports are of the nature of the routine reports.

Special Reports. Reports, which are submitted on particular occasions on specific requests or instructions, are special reports. When problems arise in a business, they are to be investigative. The results of investigations and the recommendations are submitted by way of special reports. The form and contents of special reports will vary according to the nature of problem investigated. Usually a special report contains the terms of reference i.e., the problem to be studied, investigations made, findings and observations and finally conclusions and recommendations. Examples of some of the special reports are 1.Reports of information about competitive products, 2.Reports by the Cost Accountants on the implication of price changes on the cost of products, 3.Reports regarding choice of products or selection of a production method, etc.

Operating Reports: These reports may be classified into Control report and Information Report.

Control Report. It is an important ingredient of control process and helps in controlling different activities of an enterprise. It provides information properly collected and analyzed to different levels of management. The framework of this report is determined by the needs of the undertaking. It is based on the company's developed budgets and standards. It is related to responsibility centers and it observes decision needs. This report may be prepared on weekly, fortnightly, monthly, or yearly basis depending upon the urgency of the matter reported. Most of the internal reports are examples of control reports. They are also sort of routine reports.

Information Report. These reports provide information, which are very much useful for future planning and policy formulation. They may take the form of trend reports or analytical reports. Trend reports provide information in a comparative form over a period of time. On the other hand, analytical reports provide information n a classified manner. Sometimes these reports provide information in a summarized form the results of operation of a specific venture or of the organization as a whole for a specific period. In such cases they may be called as venture measurement reports.

Financial Reports: These reports contain information about the financial position of the business. They may be classified into Static Reports and Dynamic Reports. Static report reveals the financial position on a particular date e.g., balance sheet of a company. On the other hand, the dynamic report reveals the movement of funds during a specified period, e.g., funds flow statement, cash flow statement.

17.8 Informational Needs of Different Levels of Management

Generally the reporting levels in the internal management fall into three broad categories. They are top level, middle level, and junior level managements. They need different kinds of reports depending upon the nature of functions they do.

Top Management Level: The top management is primarily concerned with the policy formulation, planning and organizing. Hence, their function is to evolve proper plans, to carry out proper delegation of authority to subordinates with a view to obtain an effective and efficient utilization of resources and to promote appropriate development schemes. For the purpose they should rather be supplied with information in summary form covering all aspects of operating performance together with a comparison of actual with budgeted performance.

Generally, the top management should receive the following reports at different intervals:

Board of Directors — Quarterly statements on production costs, machine and labour utilization, quarterly cash flow statements, and quarterly income statement and balance sheet

Finance Director — monthly abstract of receipts and payments and monthly cash flow statements.

Production Director — production cost statement, department-wise machine and labour utilization statements, and material scrap statements, overhead cost and production statements. All these statements are to be presented to him on a monthly basis.

Sales Director — He is to receive the following reports on monthly basis: Reports on orders received, orders executed, orders kept pending - division-wise; Reports on selling and distribution cost - division-wise; Reports on credit collections, balances, and bad debts - division wise."

Middle Management Level: The departmental managers such as production, sales etc., are concerned with the execution of plans formulated by top management. They act mainly as coordinating executives to administer policies, direct operating supervisors, and evaluate their performance. Hence the reports submitted to them should enable to exercise these functions more effectively. They may require reports at shorter intervals, say weekly, fortnightly basis. For example, the works manager requires weekly reports on idle time, idle capacity, scrap production costs, quantity produced, etc. The sales manager needs fortnightly reports on budgeted and actual sales, credit collection, orders booked, executed and pending, and stock position-product-wise and area-wise.

Junior Management: Foremen, Supervisors, etc., constitute this level of management. They are interested in reports, which will apprise them of progress of jobs under their control. Some of these reports are almost in the form of scrap of paper having no proper format. They may need reports on daily or weekly basis. For example, the shop foreman requires daily report of idle time and machine utilization, daily scrap reports and daily report of production - actual and budgeted. Sales area supervisor needs weekly reports on sales - salesman-wise, orders booked, executed and outstanding, credit collections and outstanding, etc.

17.9 Steps Involved in the Preparation of Reports

Management reporting is a difficult task and therefore, the report writer must possess special skill for this job. He must be a financial analyst and in that capacity must be well trained in the areas of accounting, finance, and management. He must be able to make the analysis objectively putting his ideas cogently and clearly and communicate the results in a readable form for effective action.

Effective and efficient reporting requires the following steps to be followed:

(a) Reporting requires detailed planning of flow of paper work and its analysis. It should be the logical outcome of accounting operations.

(b) Duplication of work should be avoided. Accounting records should be designed in such a way as to obtain 'control data' without additional analysis.

(c) Codification and mechanization should be used for processing accounting data. They will help in speeding up of reports.

(d) Accounting records should be closed before time. This will facilitate the preparation of reports in time.

(e) When actual data are not readily available, certain estimates may be used in their place in order to avoid unnecessary delays. However, the actual may be compared with the estimate of a later date and deviations, if any, may be found out and analyzed. Such analysis of deviations will help for making better estimates in future.

17.10 Discuss the Usefulness of Reporting to Management

The reporting system enables the management to understand the functioning of the undertaking. When a particular reporting system fails to meet the requirements, it is either scrapped or readjusted to the needs. Hence, it is in a state of continuous development.

A good reporting system is a handy instrument of management to identify the areas of weaknesses and any untoward or unusual occurrences. Employees are put under constant control and management is free to devote fully on policy formulation and future development.

Reports deal with forecast of conditions under which planned operations would be carried out. This applies to budget estimates on product lines and forecast of business conditions in general.

Reports also provide a useful basis for deciding operating policy, volume of sales or production, stock policy, quality production, product design, etc.

Current reports enable management at different levels to keep itself abreast of past performance as well as development and it can keep a check on individual operating levels.

The reports and reporting methods provide executives with factual information for the execution of their duties. This forms the basis for developing policies by operating executives.

REVIEW QUESTIONS

1. What is meant by Management Reporting?
2. What is reporting? Explain the various types of reports submitted to management.
3. What are the essentials of a good reporting system?
4. Distinguish between Routine report and Special report.
5. Distinguish between Operating reports and Financial reports.
6. Explain the basic requisites of a good report.
7. Explain the various types of reports that are used for internal management of an enterprise.
8. Discuss the importance of a proper system of reporting.
9. Describe briefly the informational needs of different levels of management.
10. How can reports be classified? Explain giving suitable examples.
11. What are the objects of reporting ?
12. Explain the different methods of reporting.
13. Explain the managerial utility of reporting.
14. Describe the steps involved in the preparation of Reports

18
INFLATION ACCOUNTING

Learning Objectives

After going through this chapter, you should be able to

- Understand the relevant concepts in Inflation Accounting.
- Explain the various techniques of Inflation accounting.
- Work out problems incorporating the price level changes.

Concept of Inflation Accounting

Inflation normally refers to the increasing trend in general price levels. In economic sense it refers to a state in which the purchasing power of money goes down or conversely there is more money in circulation than is justified by goods and services. Inflation has come to stay as a standing feature in the economy of almost all countries of the would. The general weakness of the traditional accounting system is that is fails to reflect the price level changes in the financial statements as it is based on historical cost. The American Institute of Certified Public Accountants defines the Inflation accounting as a system of accounting, which purports to record as a built-in mechanism, all economic events in terms of current cost. It is a system of accounting like traditional accounting. It is method designed to show the effect of changing costs and prices on affairs of a business unit during the course of relative accounting period. But the difference lies in the process of matching cost against revenue. While the cost in the traditional accounting refers to historical cost, in inflation accounting it represents the cost the prevails at the time of reporting. The inflation accounting has an inbuilt and automatic mechanism to match the cost and revenue at current values.

Salient Features: From the above definition, the salient features of Inflation accounting may be listed as follows:

The inflation accounting has an inbuilt and automatic recording procedure.

The unit of measurement is not stable like traditional or historical accounting.

It takes into consideration all the elements of financial statements for reporting.

The realization principle is not rigidly followed, particularly in case of recording fixed assets and long-term loans.

Need for Inflation Accounting

In the traditional accounting, assets are shown in the financial statements year after year on the basis of acquisition prices or at historical cost. During the inflationary period, historical-cost based depreciation would be highly insufficient to replace the existing assets at current costs. Items like depreciation, cost of goods sold, and inventory are understated and the profit figure and financial position of the business units are highly distorted. Current revenues for the period are not properly matched with current cost of operation. Hence, the problems created by price changes in the histori-cal-cost based accounts necessitate some methods to take care of inflation into the accounting system.

Methods of Accounting for changing prices

International accounting bodies have suggested a number of methods for measuring the impact of changing prices on the profitability and financial position of the business units. However, no single method has gained universal acceptance. Noteworthy among the various methods the following are the generally accepted methods of accounting for price level changes:

Current Purchasing Power Method [CPP method]

Current Cost Accounting Method [CCA method]

Hybrid method [a Mixture of CPP and CCA methods]

CURRENT PURCHASING POWER METHOD

The CPP method [also termed as Constant rupee method] attempts to restate all items in the financial statements in terms of units of equal purchasing power. It seeks to eliminate the effects of changes in the general price levels or in the value of money itself. Money as a measuring rod is somewhat defective, because its value keeps on changing due to inflation or deflation. The CPP method basically attempts to remove the distortions in financial statements, which arise due to change in the value of rupee. For this purpose, any approved price index depicting the changes in the purchasing power of rupee is used to convert the various items of the financial statements. For example, an asset purchased in 2000 for Rs. 5,000 would be valued in 2005 based on the change in the general price index in 2005 as compared to that in 2000. Suppose the general price index was 200 in 2000 and it was 300 in 2005. The asset would be valued at Rs. 7,500 [*i.e.*, Rs. 5,000 × 300/200]. It implies that the current purchasing power of a sum of Rs. 5,000 spent in 2000 is equivalent to Rs. 7,500 in 2005. That is, the purchasing power of rupee in 2005 is 1.5 times [300/200] more than that in 2000. It is important to note that under CPP method only the changes in the general purchasing power of money is relevant and not the value of individual asset. For example a particular asset has become cheaper over the period of time as against the increase in the general price index. In such a case, the value of such an asset will be raised in accordance with the general price index.

Steps involved in CPP method

Conversion Factor: For converting historical rupees into equivalent uniform rupees [current purchasing prices] as at the date of balance sheet an index depicting the changes in the power of rupee is required. This is done through a conversion factor, which is calculated as follows:

$$\text{Conversion Factor} = \frac{\text{Price Index at the date of conversion}}{\text{Price at the date of transaction}}$$

For this purpose most broad-based retail or consumer price is used. And in case of transactions occurring throughout a period, an average price index of the period is used. Such transactions include items like sales, purchase of goods, payment of expenses, etc. The average price index may be calculated by taking the average of the opening and end of the period price index numbers.

Example 1.

A company purchased a plant on 1–1–2005 for a sum of Rs. 45,000. The consumer price index on that date was 125 and it was 250 at the end of the year. Restate the value of the plant as per CPP method as on 31st December 2005.

Solution

$$\text{Conversion Factor} = \frac{\text{Price index as on 31-12-2005}}{\text{Price as on 1-1-2005}} = \frac{250}{125} = 2$$

Value of the Plant on 31st December 2005 after conversion = Value of the plant on 1 – 1 – 2005 × Conversion Factor = Rs. 45 000 × 2 = Rs. 90 000.

Distinction between Monetary and Non-monetary items

The CPP method distinguishes between monetary items and non-monetary items for converting the figures.

Monetary items are those items whose amounts are fixed by contract or otherwise they remain constant in terms of monetary units [rupees, dollars, etc.]. The changes in price levels do not affect their values. Examples of monetary assets and liabilities are cash, debtors, creditors, debentures, outstanding expenses, preference share capital, etc. During the period of inflation, the holder of monetary assets lose general purchasing power since their claims against the firm remain fixed irrespective of any changes in the general price levels. Conversely the holder of monetary liabilities gains since he is to pay the same amount due in rupees of lower purchasing power. The CPP method suggests the computations of purchasing power gains or loss made by a firm on holding the net monetary items.

Non-monetary items are those items that cannot be stated in fixed monetary amounts. They include tangible assets such as buildings, plant and machinery, inventories for sale, etc. In other words non-monetary items do not carry a fixed value like monetary items. Under CPP method all such items are to be restated to represent the current purchasing power. For example, a machinery costing Rs.25 000 in 1996 may sell for Rs.35 000 today though it has been used. This may be due to change in the general price level. The equity capital is a non-monetary item since the equity shareholders have residual claim on the company's net assets.

Computation of Monetary Gain or Loss

The changes in purchasing power affect both monetary and non-monetary items of the financial statements. In case of monetary assets and monetary liabilities, the firm receives or pays the amounts fixed as per the terms of contract, but it loses or gains in terms of real purchasing power. Such monetary gain or loss should be computed separately and shown as a separate item in the restated income statement in order to find out the overall profit or loss under CPP method.

Example 2.

From the following data, compute the net monetary gain or loss as per CPP method:

Monetary Items	1 – 1 – 2005	31 – 12 – 2005
Cash	Rs. 5,000	Rs.10,000
Debtors	20,000	25,000
Creditors	15,000	20,000
Public Deposits	20,000	20,000
Consumer price index numbers are:		
On 1 – 1 – 2005 —	100	
On 31 – 12 – 2005 —	150	
Average for the year —	120	

Solution :

[A] Impact of changes of general price levels on liabilities:		Rs.
Monetary liabilities on 1 – 1 – 2005	Rs.35 000	
Value of liabilities at current prices [Rs.35 000 × 150/100]		52,500
Value of additional liabilities at current prices [Rs.40 000 – 35 000] x 150/120		6,250
		58,750
Less: Value as per closing balance sheet		40,000
Resultant monetary gain on holding liabilities		18,750

[B] Impact of changes of general price levels on monetary assets:

	Rs.	
Value of monetary assets on 1–1–2005	25,000	
Value at current prices on 31–12–2005 [Rs. 25,000 × 150/100]	37,500	
Additions at current prices [Rs. 35,000 – 25,000] × [150/120]		12,500
	50,000	
Value of assets as per closing balance sheet	35,000	
Resultant monetary loss on holding monetary assets	15,000	
Net monetary gain [A – B] [Rs. 18,750 – 15,000]	3,750	

Note: The conversion factors for the opening balances of assets and liabilities have been computed by dividing the year-end price index by opening price index, [i.e., 150/100]. And for additions made during the year, it has been calculated by dividing the year-end price index by average price index, [i.e., 150/120].

Adjustment for Cost of Sales and Inventories

For the purpose of restatement of the Cost of sales and Inventories under CPP method, the cost flow pattern of [i.e., First in First Out or Last in First Out] should be kept in mind. Under the First in First Out assumption, the inventories purchased first are issued to production or to customers. Later purchases remain in stock. Similarly under the last in First out assumption, the inventories purchased are issued first and the earlier purchases remain in stock. These cost flow pattern should be kept in mind while using the index numbers for computing conversion factors. Under FIFO method, the cost of sales normally includes the entire opening stock and current purchases less closing stock. Closing stock comprises entirely current purchases and sometimes part of opening stock. In case of LIFO, the cost of sales includes current purchases only and closing stock comprises opening stock and sometimes part of current purchases.

For the purpose of restatement of historical figures in terms of current values, the following price indices are used:

[i] Purchases of the previous year: Average indices for the relevant years.

[ii] Current Purchases: Average index of the year.

[iii] Opening stock: Index at the beginning of the year.

Example 3

From the following particulars, ascertain the values of Cost of Sales and Closing stock as per CPP method:

	Rs.		
Opening Stock on 31st December 2004	20,000	Price index on 31st December 2004	150
Purchases during 2005	1,20,000	Average index for 2005	180
Closing stock on 31st December 2005	24,000	Price index on 31st December 2005	240

Assume [a] FIFO method [b] LIFO method

Solution

FIFO Method

Values of Cost of Sales and Inventories

	Historical Cost Basis Rs.	Conversion Factor	CPP Method Rs.
Opening Stock	20,000	1.6 [240/150]	32,000
Add: Purchases	60,000	1.33 [240/180]	80,000
	80,000		1,12,000
Less: Closing Stock	24000	1.33 [240/180]	32,000
Cost of Sales	56,000		80,000

LIFO Method

Values of Cost of Sales and Inventories

	Historical Cost Basis		Conversion Factor	CPP Method	
		Rs.			Rs.
Opening Stock		20,000	1.6 [240/150]	32,000	
Add: Purchases		60,000	1.33 [240/180]	80,000	
		80,000			1,12 000
Less: Closing Stock:					
Opening stock	20,000		1.6 [240/150]	32,000	
Current Purchases	4,000	24,000	1.33 [240/180]	5,333	37,333
Cost of Sales		56,000			74, 667

Determination of Profit

There are two approaches to determine the profit under CPP method. They are [a] Net Change Method and [b] Restatement of Income Method.

Net Change Method: This approach is based on normal accounting concept that profit is equal to change in equity during an accounting period. Opening balance sheet based on historical cost is converted into CPP balance sheet by using index numbers. Monetary items should be converted and the net monetary gain or loss is shown. Equity capital is also converted. The difference in the balance sheet is taken as reserves. When equity is not converted, then the difference in the balance sheet is taken as equity.

Income Method: Under this method the historical profit and loss account is restated in CPP terms. All the items of Income Statement are converted into CPP values on the following basis:

[a] Sales and operating expenses are restated at the average index applicable for the year.

[b] Cost of sales is converted as per the cost flow assumption as explained above.

[c] Net gain or loss on monetary items will have to determined and shown separately in the restated income statement.

[d] Fixed assets and their depreciation are converted on the basis of the indices prevailing at the dates of purchase of such assets.

[e] Taxes and dividends paid are converted on the basis of indices prevailing at the dates of payment.

Limitations of CPP Method

The index numbers are statistical averages and the CPP method is based on indices. Hence, it would be very difficult to apply with precision to individual firms.

There are various price indices, which characterize different price situations. Hence, it would be a difficult task to select a suitable price index.

The method deals with changes in the general price level and not with the changes in prices of individual firms. However, the only relationship is that the individual prices move with the general price index to some extent.

Hence, a large number of accountants, economists, and Government authorities do not favor this method.

Current Cost Accounting [CCA] Method

Because of the limitations of CPP method, the Sandilands Committee recommended the current cost accounting system as a method for correcting the deficiencies of historical cost accounting. The Accounting Committee of U.K has issued a Statement of Standard Accounting Practice 16 [SSAP – 16] relating to CCA method.

Main Features of CCA method

Money remains to be the unit of measurement. The items of the financial statements are restated in terms of current value of that item and in terms of general purchasing power of money. Assets and liabilities are at their current value to the business. Similarly the profits are computed on the basis of current values of the various items to the business. This requires carrying out the following adjustments:

Revaluation Adjustment,
Depreciation Adjustment,
Cost of Sales Adjustment [COSA] and
Monetary Working Capital Adjustment

Methodology

Revaluation Adjustment: Fixed assets are shown in the balance sheet at their values to the business. The value to the business of an asset refers to the opportunity loss to the business if were deprived of such assets. In this context, it is pertinent to understand the gross and net replacement costs. The gross replacement cost of an asset is the cost to be incurred at the date of valuation to obtain a similar asset for replacement. For example, if an asset purchased on 1–1–2005 for Rs. 50,000 costs Rs. 80,000 on 31–12–2005, then the gross replacement cost on 31–12–2005 would be Rs. 80,000. Net replacement cost refers to the unexpired service potential of that part of gross current replacement cost. For example, a machine costing Rs. 80,000 has a life of eight years with zero scrap value and it has been used for three years. If the machine can be purchased now for Rs. 80,000 then the net replacement cost of the asset would be Rs. 70,000 i.e., the current price of the machine less depreciation for three years.

Plant and machinery, Motor vehicles, Officer equipment, Fixtures and fittings, Ships and Aircrafts, etc., are normally valued at their net current replacement cost. Land and buildings occupied by the owner himself should be shown in the balance sheet at their value to the business, which will comprise the market value for existing use plus estimated acquisition cost. If the open market is not available, then the net replacement cost of the buildings and open market value of land for its existing use plus the estimated acquisition cost should be taken as their value to the business. Long-term investments should also be shown in the balance sheet at their value to the business. Quoted investments should be valued at their unit market value and unquoted investments are valued on the basis of the current cost net worth of the company. Inventories should be valued at power of the current replacement cost as on the date of the balance sheet and the net realizable value.

Depreciation Adjustment: The profit and loss account should be charged for depreciation with an amount equal to the value of fixed assets consumed during the period. When the fixed assets are valued on the basis of their net current replacement cost, the depreciation charge should be based on such cost. The depreciation charge may be computed either on the basis of total replacement cost of the asset or on average net current cost of assets. Average current cost may be computed as follows:

$$\frac{\text{Current cost at the beginning of the year + Current cost at the end of the year}}{2}$$

The current depreciation charge is obtained by apportioning the average net replacement cost over the expected remaining useful life of the fixed assets as at the beginning of the period. When the fixed assets are revalued every year there will also be shortfall of depreciation representing the effect of price rise during the period. This shortfall is called backlog depreciation, which should be charged either to general reserves or against the related revaluation surplus on the fixed assets. The need for adjustment of backlog depreciation will arise whenever a depreciating asset is revalued.

Example 4

Vicky ltd. purchased new equipment on 1–1–2002 for Rs. 80,000 and its expected life was 10 years without any scrap value. On 1–1–2005 a similar new equipment costed Rs. 30,000 and on 31–12–2005 Rs. 40,000. What would be the depreciation charge for the year 2005 assuming that there is no change in the estimated life of the equipment.

Solution

Depreciation charge under CCA method

$$= \frac{\text{Current value at the beginning + Current value at the end}}{2 \times \text{Expected life}}$$

$$= \frac{\text{Rs.}30{,}000 + \text{Rs.}40{,}000}{2 \times 10} = \text{Rs. } 3{,}500$$

Example 5

On 1 – 1 – 2002 firm purchased equipment for a sum of Rs.5 00 000 and its expected life was 10 years without any scrap value. The price indices for the asset were as follows:

1 – 1 – 2002	100
1 – 1 – 2005	150
31 – 12 – 2005	180

Compute the depreciation adjustment for the year 2005 under CCA method charging depreciation on straight-line basis.

Solution

Statement showing the value and depreciation of the Equipment

Particulars	1 – 1 – 2005 Historical Cost [Rs.]	1 – 1 – 2005 Current Cost [Rs.]	31 – 12 – 2005 Historical Cost [Rs.]	31 – 12 – 2005 Current Cost [Rs.]
Cost	5,00,000	7,50,000	5,00,000	9,00,000
Less: Depreciation [3/4 yrs.]	1,50,000	2,25,000	2,00,000	3,60,000
Net Cost	3,50,000	5,25,000	3,00,000	5,40,000

Depreciation adjustment for 2005 based on Current Replacement value

Depreciation at 10% on Current Cost Rs.9 00 000		Rs.90,000
Less: Depreciation charged for 2005 as per HCA	50,000	
Depreciation Adjustment	40,000	

Cost of Sales Adjustment [COSA]

This adjustment is made in order to determine the current cost operating profit. COSA represents the difference between value to the business and the historical cost of stock consumed in the period. The amount of sales is the current revenue and requires no adjustment in its figure. Such as raw materials consumed or finished goods sold items. Which enter into the calculation of cost of sales, have to be taken at the present value at which they would be replaced or consumed or sold. The difference in values is called as COSA, which is debited to the Profit and loss account and credited to Current Cost Account Reserve.

Example 6

Determine the value of Cost of Sales Adjustment from the data given below:

Opening stock on 1 – 1 – 2005	Rs.12 000
Closing stock on 31 – 12 – 2005	16 000
Index number on 1 – 1 – 2005 [Io]	160
Index number on 31 – 12 – 2005 [Ic]	200
Average index number for the year [Ia]	190

Solution

Cost of Sales Adjustment = Closing stock [CS] – Opening stock [OS] – Ia [CS/ Ic – OS/ Io]

= [Rs.16,000 – 12,000] – 190 [16,000/200 – 12,000/160]

= Rs. 4,000 – 190 [80–75]
= Rs. 3,050

Monetary Working Capital Adjustment [MWCA]

The rising prices create the need for the additional working capital for efficient and profitable operation of the firm. The concept of monetary working capital refers to the excess of accounts receivables and unexpired expenses over accounts payables and accruals. Current cost accounting ensures that the impact of changing prices on working capital is taken care of through MWCA. This adjustment is to be carried out while computing current cost of operating profit by charging profit and loss account with any increase in net additional working capital owing to changing price levels and crediting the CCA Reserve. This adjustment is required only for price level changes and not for any increase in volume of business. The following formula may be used for calculating MWCA.

MWCA = C – O – Ia [C/Ic – O/Io]

Where C = Closing monetary working capital
O = Opening monetary working capital
Ia = Average price index
Io = Opening price index
Ic = Closing price index

Example 7

From the following information as per historical cost accounting, carry out Monetary Working Capital Adjustment under CCA method:

	Opening balance Rs.		Closing balance Rs.
Accounts Receivables	18,000		21,000
Accounts Payables	10,000		12,000
Price Index	175		205
Average Price Index		190	

Solution

MWCA = C – O – Ia [C/Ic – O/Io]
Opening monetary working capital [O] = Rs. 18,000 – 10,000 = Rs. 8,000
Closing monetary working capital [C] = Rs. 21,000 – 12,000 = Rs. 9,000
MWCA = Rs. 9,000 – 8,000 – 190 [9000/205 – 8000/175]
= Rs. 1,000 – 190 [43.9 – 45.7]
= Rs. 1,000 + 342 = Rs. 1,342

Gearing Adjustment: Gearing is the ratio of debt capital to shareholder's funds. When fixed assets and working capital are partially financed by debt capital the amount of debt remains the same because of repayment agreement. The price level changes do not affect this liability of the business. Thus, the shareholders enjoy the benefits in the period of rising prices. During the declining prices the reverse experience takes place. The entire net income goes to shareholders. However, in the calculation of operating profit, the existence of borrowing is ignored. Hence, the profits attributable to shareholders would be understated [or where prices fall overstated] if the whole of depreciation, COSA, and MWCA were charged or credited to profit and loss account. The total of these adjustments [Depreciation, COSA, and MWCA] are proportionately abated through gearing adjustment [gearing ratio]. The gearing adjustment is calculated by the application of the following formula:

$$\textbf{Gearing Adjustment [Gearing ratio]} = \frac{\mathbf{D}}{\mathbf{D+S}} \times \mathbf{S}$$

where D = average net debt S = average shareholders interest

In the calculation of net borrowing, cash or any other monetary asset not included in MWCA should be deducted from the total borrowing. It would be apt to use average gearing ratio for gearing adjustment. The calculated amount of gearing adjustment will be debited to Current Cost account Reserve and credited to Profit and Loss Account. In other words the shareholders' share will be charged to profit and loss account and credited to current cost account reserve.

Example 8

Following information relate to Rashmi & Co., Ltd.	Opening [Rs.]	Closing [Rs.]
[a] The net borrowing debentures and deferred taxation	2,80,000	2,80,000
Creditors	40,000	28,000
Bank Overdraft	1,20,000	92,000
Taxation	30,000	28,000
Cash	[80,000]	[1,20,000]
Total	3,90,000	3,08,000
[b] Share capital and Reserves from Current Cost Balance Sheet	7,41,600	9,41,000
Proposed dividend	10,000	12,000
Total Shareholders interest	7,51,600	9,53,000
[c] Current cost adjustment:		
Depreciation		34,000
Fixed assets disposal		36,000
COSA		32,400
MWCA		22,400
		1,24,800

Calculate the Gearing Adjustment Ratio and the Current Cost Adjustment after abating for gearing adjustment.

Solution

$$\text{Gearing Adjustment Ratio} = \frac{D}{D+S} \times 100$$

Average net borrowing [D] = [Rs.3 90 000 + Rs.3 08 000]/2 = Rs.3 49 000

Average Shareholders funds [S] = [Rs.7 51 600 + Rs.9 53 000]/2 = Rs.8 52 300

Average total funds employed [D + S] = [Rs.3 49 000 + Rs.8 52 300] = Rs.12 01 300

$$\text{Gearing Adjustment Ratio} = \frac{D}{D+S} \times 100 = \frac{\text{Rs. }3{,}49{,}000}{\text{Rs. }12{,}01{,}300} \times 100 = 29.05\%$$

Total current cost adjustment	Rs.1,24,800
Less: Gearing adjustment [29.05% of the above]	36,254
Current cost reserve after adjustment	88,546

Advantages of CCA Method

1. Computation of depreciation based on the fixed assets current value [or value to the business] provides a realistic measure of the resources used in a period.
2. Assets are shown at their current values in the balance sheet.
3. It clearly differentiates the gains from operations from the gains from holding assets.
4. Cost of sales adjustment enables the entity to maintain its value in real terms.
5. Computation of monetary gains and losses highlights the effect of holding monetary items.

6. The introduction of appropriation account brings together revaluation surplus and current cost profit together. It helps management in devising dividend policies realistically.
7. Both management and users of accounts are provided with realistic information relating to value of assets, costs and profit.

Deficiencies in CCA Method

1. Treatment of backlog depreciation is not proper. Charging against the current cost accounting reserve, which is a capital reserve, provides for backlog depreciation. The proper method would be to charge against revenue reserve available for dividend. This will enable the management to make available the funds for replacement of assets. Further it fails to provide adequate funds for replacements of new types of assets.

2. This method ignores materiality factor. If a particular adjustment is not necessary for a company, it cannot ignore such adjustment. Further the valuation process is subject to the discretion and personal judgment of the managers than the ascertainment of historical cost.

3. This method ignores purchasing power gains and losses on the monetary items of the firm. It takes into account such gains and losses in nature of cost of holding monetary assets and liabilities during a period of changing price levels. In fact such companies would gain or lose very much in terms of purchasing power on the items during the inflationary periods.

4. This method is based on uniform accounting practices, which are not true in actual practice. The accounting practices and maintaining of books differ from firm to firm. Hence, the information available for valuation purposes may not be adequate and real. Because of these deficiencies, many accountants feel that this method may not have adequate capacity to depict the true financial position of the business during the periods of price level changes.

5. The CCA method fails to provide for the gearing adjustment with regard to fixed assets and inventories. The are also financed partly by borrowings. Hence, it is pertinent to subject these assets to gearing adjustment.

Hybrid Method

Hybrid method combines some of the features of CPP method and CCA method. According to this method, the relevant adjustments are made with reference to specific indices in the place of general index as in the case of CPP method. In addition, the purchasing power gains and losses on monetary items are also taken into consideration. Combining of the two methods as a compromise formula brings both the benefits and limitations of both CPP and CCA methods. It is still in the evolutionary stage and not suitable for practical application.

Practical Problems

Illustration 1: On 1–1–2005 a company purchased equipment for Rs. 45,000. The price index on that date was at 150. Restate the value of the equipment as per CPP method on 31–12–2005 when the price index was at 200.

Solution

$$\text{Conversion Factor} = \frac{\text{Price index at the date of conversion}}{\text{Price index at the date of purchase}} = \frac{200}{150} = \frac{4}{3}$$

Value of equipment on 31–12–2005 as per CPP method
= Existing value × Conversion Factor
= Rs. 45,000 × [4/3] = Rs. 60,000

Illustration 2: Mr. Ram purchased shares in HLL Ltd., for Rs. 10,000 in 1991 when the index of the general price levels stood at 110. At the end of 1994 the market price of the shares was Rs. 8,000 and the index was 132. In 1995, the market price of the shares was Rs. 9,000 and the index was 145.2.

[i] Calculate the CPP value of the shares in 1994 and in 1995.

[ii] Under CPP accounting, what gain or loss would be shown in respect of shares?

[iii] What was the real gain or loss in purchasing power in respect of the shares during 1995?

Solution

[i] CPP value of the shares at the end of 1994 = $\frac{\text{Rs.10 000} \times 132}{110}$ = Rs.12,000

CPP value at the end of 1995 = $\frac{\text{Rs.10,000} \times 145.2}{110}$ = Rs.13,200

[ii] Determination of accounting gain or loss

	1994	1995
CPP value	Rs. 12,000	13,200
Less: Purchase price	10,000	10,000
Accounting loss	2,000	3,200

[iii] Determination of actual loss in purchasing power

	1994	1995
CPP value	Rs.12,000	13,200
Less: Market price	8,000	9,000
Loss in purchasing power	4,000	4,200

Illustration 3: From the data given below, compute the net monetary gain or loss as at 31 – 12 – 2005:

	1 – 1 – 2005	31 – 12 – 2005
Cash	Rs. 10,000	Rs. 20,000
Accounts Receivables	40,000	50,000
Sundry creditors	30,000	40,000
Debentures	40,000	40,000
Retail price index numbers	200	300

Average price index for the year 240

Solution

Statement showing monetary gain/loss on account of Price level changes

CPP value of Monetary liabilities on 1 – 1 – 2005 [Rs.70 000 × 1.5]	Rs. 1,05,000	
CPP value of increase in monetary liabilities during 2005 [Rs.10 000 × 1.25]	12,500	
CPP value of monetary liabilities on 31 – 12 – 2005	1,17,500	
Less: Monetary liabilities on 31 – 12 – 2005 as per balance sheet	80,000	
Gain on holding Monetary liabilities		Rs. 37,500
CPP value of monetary assets as on 1 – 1 – 2005 [Rs.50 000 × 1.5]		Rs. 75,000
CPP value of increase in monetary assets during 2005 [Rs.20 000 × 1.25]	25,000	
CPP value of monetary assets on 31 – 12 – 2005		1,00,000
Less: Book value as on 31 – 12 – 2005		70,000
Loss on holding monetary assets		Rs. 30,000
Net gain on monetary items		7,500

Working Notes:

Computation of conversion factors:

For monetary items as on 1–1–2005: 300/200 = 1.5

For monetary items as on 31–12–2005: 300/240 = 1.25

Increase in monetary items:	as on 1–1–2005	as on 31–12–2005	Increase during 2005
	Rs.	Rs.	Rs.
Monetary Assets	50,000	70,000	20,000
Monetary Liabilities	70,000	80,000	10,000

Illustration 4: Following information has been extracted from the books of a Limited Company: Monetary assets Rs. 30,000; Monetary liabilities Rs. 16,500

The price index at the time of monetary item were created was 200 and now it stands at 260. Assuming that thee has been no change in amount of assets and liabilities, ascertain the general purchasing power gain or loss.

Solution

		Rs.
	CPP value of monetary assets = [Rs. 30,000 × 260]/200 =	39,000
	Less: Actual book value	30,000
[A]	Loss on holding monetary assets	9,000
	CPP value of monetary liabilities = [Rs. 16,500 × 260]/200 =	21,450
	Less: Actual book value	16,500
[B]	Gain on holding monetary liabilities	4,950
	Net general purchasing power loss [A – B]	4,050

Illustration 5: On 1–1–2005 a firm had cash at bank balance of Rs. 40,000. On that date the consumer price index was 200. During the period ended 31–12–2005 the receipts and payments were as follows:

Receipts	Rs.	Price Index	Payments	Rs.	Price index
1–1–2005 Sales	21,000	210	10–6–2005 Costs	43,000	215
18–9–2005 Sales	69,000	230	1–8–2005 Plant	40,000	225
			15–12–2005 Costs	30,000	240

Ascertain the profit or loss on account of price changes at the year-end when the price index was 240.

Solution

Statement showing the profit or loss on account of price level changes during the year ended 31–12–2005

	Historical Cost	Conversion Factor	CPP Value
	Rs.		Rs.
1–1–2005 Bank balance	40,000	240/200	48,000
Receipts:			
1–5–2005 Sales	21,000	240/210	24,000
18–9–2005 Sales	69,000	240/230	72,000
Total bank balance [A]	1,30,000		1,44,000
Payments:			
10–6–2005 Costs	43,000	240/215	48,000
1–8–2005 Plant	42,750	240/225	45,600
15–12–2005 Costs	30,000	240/240	30,000
Total Payments [B]	1,15,750		1,23,600
31–12–2005 Bank balance [A–B]	14,250		20,400

The constant rupee [CPP] value of the closing bank balance should have been Rs.20 400 whereas the actual balance is only Rs.17 000. Hence, the difference in value of Rs.6 150 [Rs.20 400 – 14 250] represents the loss on account of price changes.

Illustration 6: Mr. Ram purchased shares at a cost of Rs.1 80 000 on 9th February 2005 when the price index stood at 300. On 31st December 2005 the index had moved to 345 and the market value of the investment was Rs.1 96 000. Find out the profit or loss on the investment as per CPP basis.

Solution

31 – 12 – 2005 Cost of shares as per CPP basis [Rs. 1,80,000 × 345/300] =Rs. 2 07,000	
Less: Market value of the shares	1,96,000
Loss on the value of the investment	11,000

Illustration 7: From the following information given on historical cost basis, restate the cost of goods sold according to HCA and CPP methods assuming that the firm is using LIFO method for pricing its inventories:

	Rs.
Inventories on 1 – 1 – 2005	2,400
Purchases during the year 2005	28,000
Inventories on 31 – 12 – 2005	6,800

The price index in the beginning of the year was 200 while at the end of 2005 it was 360. The closing inventory consists of purchases of purchases made when the price index was 330. The purchases were made uniformly during the year.

Solution

	HCA method	Conversion Factor		CPP method
	Rs.			Rs.
1 – 1 – 2005 Inventory	2,400	360/200 [1.8]		4,320
Purchases during 2005	28,000	360/280		36,000
Goods available for sale	30,400			40,320
31 – 12 – 2005 Inventory	6,800	2,400 × 1.8	4,320	
		4 400 × 360/330	4 800	9,120
Cost of goods sold during 2005	23,600			31,200

Note: Purchases have been converted into constant rupees using average price index, 280 [i.e., 200 + 360 /2]. Closing inventory includes the balance of the opening inventory.

Illustration 8: From the following information given on historical cost basis, compute the cost of goods sold under HCA and CPP methods assuming that the firm follows FIFO method for pricing its inventories:

Inventories on 1 – 1 – 2005	Rs. 4,800
Purchases during the year 2005	Rs. 42,000
Inventories on 31 – 12 – 2005	Rs. 11,400

The general price index was 200 on 1 – 1 – 2005 and at the end of 2005 it was 360. The closing inventory consists of purchases made when the price index was 228. The purchases were made uniformly throughout the year.

Solution

	HCA method	Conversion Factor	CPP method
	Rs.		**Rs.**
Inventory on 1 – 1 – 2005	4,800	360/200	8,640
Purchases made during 2005	42,000	360/280	54,000

Goods available for sales	46,800		62,640
Less: Inventory on 31–12–2005	11,400	360/228	18,000
Cost of goods sold during 2005	35,400		44,640

Note: Purchases have been converted into constant rupees using the average price index of 280.

Illustration 9: A firm purchased a plant for Rs. 5,00,000 on 1–1–2002. It has an expected life of 10 years with zero scrap value. The price indices for the asset were as follows:

1–1–2002	200
1–1–2005	320
31–12–2005	350

The firm charged depreciation on straight-line basis. Ascertain the values of machinery on 1st January and 31st December 2005 as per HCA and CCA methods. Also calculate the amount of depreciation adjustment to be made in the account of 2005.

Solution

Statement showing the value and depreciation of the Equipment

	1–1–2005		31–12–2005	
	Historical Cost	Current Cost	Historical Cost	Current Cost
	Rs.	Rs.	Rs.	Rs.
Cost	5,00,000	8,00,000	5,00,000	8,75,000
Less: Depreciation [3/4 yrs.]	1,50,000	2,40,000	2,00,000	3,50,000
Net Cost	3,50,000	5,60,000	3,00,000	5,25,000

Depreciation adjustment for 2005 based on Current Replacement value

	Rs.
Depreciation at 10% on Current Cost Rs. 8,75,000	87,500
Less: Depreciation charged for 2005 as per HCA	50,000
Depreciation Adjustment	37,500

Illustration 10: Following information have been taken out from the books of Mac Ltd., for the year 31st December 2005:

	Rs.
Materials consumed	5,00,000
Manufacturing wages and expenses	4,00,000
Inventories as on 1–1–2005 at cost:	
Raw materials	40,000
Finished goods	1,00,000
Inventories as on 31–12–2005 at cost:	
Raw materials	60,000
Finished goods	90,000

The value of inventories to business was ascertained	1–1–2005	31–12–2005
	Rs.	Rs.
Raw materials	48,000	70,000
Finished goods	1,10,000	1,00,000

Price of materials rose during the year steadily by 20% and manufacturing wages and expenses by 16%. Ascertain the adjustments required for the above under CCA method.

Solution

Statement showing adjustment for value of inventories to business and Cost of Sales adjustment for the year ended 31–12–2005

Adjustment for value of inventories to business:

Value of inventories to business on 31st December 2005:		Rs.
Raw materials		70,000
Finished goods		1,00,000
Total		1,70,000
Book value of inventories: Raw materials	Rs. 60,000	
Finished goods	90,000	1,50,000
Increase in value [credit to CCA Reserve]		20,000
Cost of sales Adjustment:		
Purchases as per books of account		5,20,000
Add: 10% being half the increase in raw material prices		52,000
		5,72,000
Add: Raw material stock on 1 – 1 – 2005 [value to business]		48,000
		6,20,000
Less: Closing stock of Raw materials [adjusted for price changes] [Rs.60 000 x 110/120]		55,000
Materials consumed at prices when consumed		5,65,000
Manufacturing wages and expenses	4,00,000	
Add: 8% being half the increase in rate during 2005	32,000	4,32,000
		9,97,000
Less: book value of materials, wages and expenses		9,00,000
Cost of Sales Adjustment		97,000

Debit to Profit and loss account and Credit to CCA Reserve

Notes: Computation of purchases = Materials consumed + Closing stock – Opening Stock

Purchases = Rs.5 00 000 + 60 000 – 40 000 = Rs. 5,20,000

Illustration 11: From the following particulars calculate the Monetary Working Capital Adjustment:

	1 – 1 – 2005	31 – 12 – 2005
Inventories	Rs. 2,20,000	Rs. 2,44,000
Accounts Receivables	1,80,000	2 20,000
Cash at bank	24,000	32,000
Advances for supplies of materials	40,000	50,600
Due to suppliers	1,00,000	1,28,800

During the year 2005 the material prices increase by 15% and those of finished goods by 10%.

Solution

Statement of Monetary Working Capital

	As On 1 – 1 – 2005	As on 31 – 12 – 2005
	Rs.	Rs.
Accounts Receivables	1,80,000	2,20,000
Advances for supply of materials	40,000	50,600
	2,20,000	2,70,600
Less: Accounts Payables	1,00,000	1,28,800
Monetary Working capital [MWC]	1,20,000	1,41,800
Increase in MWC during 2005	21 800	

Restatement showing increase in amounts due to change in volume in terms of mid-year prices

	As on 1–1–2005 Rs.	As on 31–12–2005 Rs.
Accounts Receivables Rs. 1,80,000 × 105/100	1,89,000	
Rs. 2,20,000 × 105/110		2,10,000
Advances for supply of materials Rs. 40,000 × 107.5/100	43,000	
Rs. 50,600 × 107.5/115		47,300
	2,32,000	2,57,300
Less: Due to suppliers Rs. 1,00,000 × 107.5/100	1,07,500	
Rs. 1,28,800 × 107.5/115		1,20,400
	1,24,500	1,36,900
Increase due to change in prices	12,400	
Increase in Monetary Working Capital – actual	21,800	
Less: Due to increase in volume in terms of mid-year prices	12,400	
Increase due to change in prices – MWCA	9,400	

Note: Accounts Receivables have been adjusted by change in prices of finished goods and the other two items by the change in prices of material.

Illustration 12: From the following comparative balance of Sri Ram Limited as prepared according to Current Cost Accounting Method, calculate the Gearing ratio.

Comparative Balance sheet

Liabilities	2004 Rs.	2005 Rs.	Assets	2004 Rs.	2005 Rs.
Share Capital	1,00,000	1,00,000	Fixed Assets [net]	2,40,000	2,80,000
Revenue Reserve	50,000	60,000	Inventories	1,00,000	1,30,000
CCA Reserve	1,00,000	1,20,000	Book debts	1,60,000	1,80,000
Secured Debts	1,16,000	1,76,000	Prepaid expenses	2,000	2,000
Creditors	1,00,000	92,000	Cash	10,000	14,000
Provision for Taxation	31,000	40,000			
Proposed dividend	15,000	18,000			
	5,12,000	6,06,000		5,12,000	6,06,000

Solution

Statement of Equity and Net Borrowings

	As on 31–12–2004 Equity Rs.	Net Borrowings Rs.	Total Rs.	As on 31–12–2005 Equity Rs.	Net Borrowings Rs.	Total Rs.
Share capital	1,00,000		1,00,000	1,00,000	1,00,000	
Revenue Reserve	50,000		50,000	60,000	60,000	
CCA Reserve	1,00,000		1,00,000	1,20,000	1,20,000	
Proposed dividend	15,000		15,000	18,000	18,000	
Secured debts	1,16,000		1,16,000	1,76,000	1,76,000	
Provision for taxation	31,000		31,000	40,000	40,000	
Cash	[10,000]		[10,000]	[14,000]	[14,000]	
Total 2,65,000	1,37,000		4,02,000	2,98,000	2,02,000	5,00,000

$$\text{Gearing Ratio} = \frac{\text{Net Borrowings [D]}}{\text{Equity [S] + Net Borrowings [D]}} \times 100$$

$$\text{Gearing Ratio for 2004} = \frac{\text{Rs. 1,37,000}}{\text{Rs. 4,02,000}} \times 100 = 34.08\%$$

$$\text{Gearing Ratio for 2005} = \frac{\text{Rs. 2,02,000}}{\text{Rs. 5,00,000}} \times 100 = 40.4\%$$

Average Gearing ratio = [34.08% + 40.4%]/2 = 37.24%

Illustration 13: From the following information, compute the values of cost of sales as per HCA and CCA methods:

Opening stock of materials on 1.1.2005 [500 tons at Rs. 60 per ton.] Rs. 30,000	
Materials consumed during 2005	400 tons
Purchases during 2005	Nil
Price of materials on 1.1.2005	Rs. 70 per ton
Price of materials on 31.12.2005	Rs. 90 per ton

Solution

Historical Cost Accounting method

Cost of sales [400 tons × 60]	Rs. 24,000
Closing stock [100 × 60]	Rs. 6,000

Current Cost Accounting method

Cost of Sales [400 tons × 80]	Rs. 32,000
Closing Stock [100 tons × 90]	Rs. 9,000

Cost of sales is calculated based on average price index [70 + 90/2] Rs. 80. The difference in the value of closing stock will be credited to CCA Reserve. The value of closing stock will appear at Rs. 9,000 in the balance sheet. The cost of sales adjustment of Rs. 8,000 [i.e., Rs. 32,000 – 24,000] will be charged to Profit and loss account and credited to CCA Reserve.

REVIEW QUESTIONS

1. Explain the term Inflation accounting.
2. Describe briefly the various types of Inflation accounting.
3. Explain the need for Inflation accounting.
4. What is Current Purchasing Power accounting?
5. Describe the various steps involved in CPP method?
6. What are monetary items and non-monetary items in CPP method?
7. How is monetary gain or loss computed? Illustrate.
8. What are the limitations of CPP method?
9. What are the advantages and deficiencies of CCA method?
10. Discuss the steps involved in Current Cost Accounting method.
11. Write Short notes on: (a) Monetary Working Capital (b) Gearing Adjustment (c) Cost of Sales Adjustment (d) Backlog Depreciation.
12. Describe the adjustments to be carried out while preparing financial statements under CCA method.

REVIEW PROBLEMS

1. On 1.4.2005 a firm had Rs. 2,00,000 as cash at bank. The retail price index on that date stood at 200. During the year ended 31.3.2006, the receipts and payments were stated below:

Receipts	Rs.	Index	Payments	Rs.	Index
June 1 Sales	1,05,000	210	September 15 Costs	2,15,000	215
Nov. Sales	3,45,000	230	December 1 Plant	2,00,000	225
			March 20 Costs	1,50,000	240

The year-end index was 240. Ascertain the profit or loss on account of price changes.

[Answer. Loss Rs. 31,667]

2. From the data given below, compute the net monetary gain or loss as at 31–12–2005:

	1–1–2005	31–12–2005
	Rs.	Rs.
Cash	10,000	20,000
Accounts Receivables	40,000	50,000
Sundry creditors	30,000	40,000
Debentures	40,000	40,000
Retail price index numbers	100	150

Average price index for the year 120

[Refer illustration no. 3]

3. The following particulars have been extracted from the books of Vicky Ltd. for the year ended 31–12–2005.

Inventories at cost	As on 1–1–2005	As on 31–12–2005
	Rs.	Rs.
Raw materials	80,000	1,20,000
Finished goods	2,00,000	1,80,000
Value of inventories to business:		
Raw materials	96,000	1,40,000
Finished goods	2,20,000	2,00,000
Materials consumed during 2005	10,00,000	
Manufacturing wages and expenses	8,00,000	

Price of raw materials rose during the year steadily by 20% and wages and expenses by 16%. Ascertain the adjustments that would be required in respect of the above under the Current Cost Accounting.

[Answer. COSA Rs. 1,94,000; credit to CCA Reserve for change in values Rs. 40,000]

4. From the following information, compute the amount of gearing adjustment to be made in case of a company with a capital mix of 45% debt and 55% equity. Explain how this amount will be treated in accounts.

	Rs.
Depreciation adjustment	2,00,000
COSA	1,00,000
MWCA	1,00,000
Total	4,00,000

[Answer. 45% of Rs. 4,00,000 = Rs. 1,80,000; Debit to CCA Reserve and Credit to P & L A/c]

5. From the following particulars calculate the general purchasing power gain or loss:

	Rs.
Monetary assets	50,000
Monetary liabilities	27,500

At the time the monetary assets were acquired and monetary liabilities were created was 200. It stands now at 260. Assume that there has been no change in the amount of assets and liabilities.

[Answer. General Purchasing Power Loss Rs. 6,750]

6. From the following particulars calculate the cost of goods sold under HCA and CPP methods assuming that the firm follows [a] FIFO and [b] LIFO methods for pricing its inventories:

Inventories on 1.1.2005	Rs. 24,000
Purchases during 2005	Rs. 2,10,000
Inventories on 31.12.2005	Rs. 57,000

The general price index was 100 when the beginning inventory was acquired. The ending inventory consists of purchases made when the price index was 110. The price index at the end of 2005 was 180. The purchases were made uniformly throughout the year.

[Refer illustration No. 7 and 8]

7. Following information have been taken out from the balance sheet of Karthik Ltd. prepared according to CCA method. Compute the gearing adjustment.

	1.1.2005 (Rs.)	31.12.2005 (Rs.)
Secure Debt	5,00,000	6,00,000
Bank Overdraft	3,00,000	4,00,000
Cash	50,000	1,00,000
Share capital	7,50,000	10,00,000
Reserve Fund	1,50,000	2,50,000

Additional information regarding different adjustments made is:

	(Rs.)
Cost of sales adjustment	1,00,000
Monetary Working Capital adjustment	75,000
Depreciation adjustment	25,000

[Answer. Gearing ratio 43.5%. Amount of gearing adjustments Rs. 87,000]

19

HUMAN RESOURCE ACCOUNTING (HRA)

1. Definition

Flamholtz, who has done considerable work in the area of human resource accounting, has defined it as follows:

"Human resource accounting is accounting for people as an organizational resource. It involves measuring the costs incurred by business firms and other organizations to recruit, select, hire, train, and develop human assets. It also involves measuring the economic value of people to the organization."[1]

American Accounting Association has defined human resource accounting as follows:

"Human resource accounting is the process of identifying and measuring data about human resource and communicating this information to interested parties".[2]

2. Concept

Thus, human resource accounting is primarily involved in measuring the various aspects related to human asses. Its basic purpose is to facilitate the effective management of human resources by providing information to acquiring, develop, retain, utilize, and evaluate human resources. The more specific objectives of human resource accounting are as follows:

1. To provide cost value date for managerial decisions regarding acquiring, developing, allocating and maintaining human resource so as to attain cost effective organizational objectives.
2. To provide information for effectiveness of human resource utilization.
3. To provide information for determining the status of human asset whether it is conserved properly; it is appreciating or depleting.
4. To assist in the development of effective human resource Management practices by classifying the financial consequences of these practices.

3. Methods of Valuation of Human Assets

There are a number of methods suggested for the valuation of human assets. Many of these methods are based on the valuation of physical and financial assets while others take into account human consideration. Major methods of valuation of human assets are historical cost, replacement cost, standard cost, present value of future earnings, and expected realizable value.

Historical Cost: Historical cost is based on actual cost incurred on human resources. Such a cost may be of two types – acquisition cost and learning cost. Acquisition cost is the expense incurred on recruitment, selection, and placement. While calculating the cost of recruitment and selection, entire cost is taken into consideration including those who are not selected. Learning cost involves expenses incurred on training and development. This method is very simple in its application but it does not reflect the true value of human assets. For example, an experienced employee may not require much training and, therefore, his value may appear to below though his real value is much mode than what is suggested by historical cost method.

Replacement Cost. As against historical cost method which takes into account the actual cost incurred on employees, replacement cost takes into account the national cost that may be required to acquire a new employee to replace the present one. In calculating the replacement cost, different types of expenses are taken into account which may be in the form of acquisition and learning cost. Replacement cost is generally much higher than the historical cost. For example, Friedman has estimated that the replacement cost of an executive in middle management level is about 1.5 to 2 times the current salary paid in that position.[3] Replacement cost is much better indicator of value of human assets though it may present certain operational problems. For example, true replacement of a person may not be found easily with whose cost the valuation is done.

Standard Cost: Instead of using historical or replacement cost, many companies use standard cost for the valuation of human assets just as its used for physical and financial assets. For using standard cost, employees of an organization are categorized into different groups based on their hierarchical positions. Standard cost is fixed for each category of employees and their value is calculated. This method is simple but does not take into account differences in employees put in the same group. In many cases, these differences may be quite vital.

Present value of future earnings:

In this method, the future earnings of various groups of employees are estimated up to the age of their retirement and are discounted at a predetermined rate to obtain the present value of such earnings. This method is similar to the present value of future earnings used in the case of financial assets. However, this method does not give correct value of human assets as it does not measure their contributions to achieving organizational effectiveness.

ACQUISITION COST METHOD:

Under this method the costs of acquisition, namely, the costs incurred in recruitment. Hiring and induction of employees are taken into account. The process involves capitalization of historic costs. The cost so capitalized has to be written off over a period of time for which the employee remains with the firm. If fir some reason the employee leaves the organization prematurely, the unamortized cost remaining in the books has to be written off against the profit and loss account of the particular year.

REPLACEMENT COST METHOD:

While in the case of acquisition cost past costs are considered, under this approach one takes in to account how much it costs to replace a firm's existing resources and thus represents a current value approach. So this is a method resource and thus represents a current market conditions. This exercise may be redundant unless the management desires to replace its present resources. It is also difficult exercise as in many cases the replacement may not be exactly similar.

PRESENT VALUE OF FUTURE EARNINGS METHOD:

This model is developed by Lev and Schwartz and is popular in India. This is also known as capitalization of salary method. Under this method the future earnings of an employee or grades of employees are estimated up to the age of retirement and are discounted at a rate appropriate to the person or the group in order to obtain the present value. The model may be expresses as follows:

V = the human capital value of a person y years old

I (t) = the person's annual earnings up to retirement

R = discount rate specific to the person

T= retirement age.

The above formula does not take into account the probability of a person dying before retirement or leaving the organization.

Expected realizable value:

The above methods discussed so far are based on cost consideration. Therefore these methods may provide information for record purpose but do not reflect the true value of human assets. As against these methods. Expected realizable value is based on the assumption. And this is true also. That there is no direct relationship between cost incurred on an individual and his value to organization can be defined as the present worth of the set of future services that he is expected to provide during the period he remains in the organization. Flamholtz has given the variables affecting an individual's expected realizable value (IERV): individual conditional values and his like hood of remaining in the organization. The former is a function of the individual's abilities and activation level. While the later is a function of such variables as job satisfaction, commitment, motivation, and other factors.

ECONOMIC VALUE METHOD:

The economist's concept of the value of an asset is equal to the present worth of its estimated future economic benefits. This approach has a strong theoretical appeal. But this method involves the following steps:

(a) Estimation of the future benefits, and

(b) Ascertaining the resent value of such benefits by using an appropriate interest (discount) rate.

COMPETITIVE BIDDING METHOD:

This is also known as the opportunity cost method. Opportunity cost is defined as the measurable value of benefits that could be obtained by choosing an alternative course of action. In the case of HRA. Opportunity costs is determined by a process of competitive bidding in which various divisions and departments bid for he services of various officers. The amount of bid is added to the capital employed of the successful bidder for determining the return on investment.

Advantages of human resource accounting:

Many organizations, particularly in the USA, are following the human resource accounting approach. In our country, too, there is a need for establishing systems which can generate monetary and non – monetary information about human beings in the organizations, particularly about managerial talents whose dearth is felt by business organization. This is due to the fact that human resource accounting offers following advantages:

1. It helps in giving valuable information to the management for effective planning and managing human resources.
2. It helps in measurement of standard cost of recruiting, selecting, hiring and training people and organization can select a person with highest expected realizable values.
3. Human resource accounting can change the attitude of managers completely, thereby, they would try to maximize the expected value of human resources and effective use of human resources in the organization.
4. It also provides necessary data to devise suitable promotion policy congenial work environment and job satisfaction to the people.
5. Problems in Human Resource Accounting.

There are certain operational problems in human accounting because it attempts to measure intangibles. Therefore, subjective factors may play crucial role. Thus, the major operational problems involved in human resource accounting are of the following types:

1. There is no well-set standard accounting practice for measuring the Value of human resources. In the case of financial accounting, there are certain specified standards which every organization follows. However, in the case of human resource accounting, there are no such standards.

Therefore, various organizations that adopt human asset valuation use their own models. With the result, value of human assets of two organizations may not be comparable.

2. The valuation of human assets is based on the assumption that the Employees may remain with the organization for certain specified period. However, this assumption may not hold true in today's context because of increased human resource mobility.
3. There is a possibility that human resource accounting may leas to the dehumanization in the organization if the valuation is not done correctly or results of the valuation are not utilized properly.
4. There is also a possibility that trade unions may oppose the use of human resource accounting. They may want parity of wages/ salaries and value of employees.

However many of these problems are of operational nature or of attitudinal nature. These may be overcome by developing suitable organizational climate and culture.

Illustration:

The dichotomy in accounting between human and nonHuman capital is fundamental. The latter is recognized as an asset and is therefore recorded in the books and reported in the financial statement, whereas, the former is totally ignored by accountants. The definition of wealth as a source of income inevitably leads to the recognition of human capital as one of several forms of wealth such as money, securities and physical capital.

The Lev & Schwartz model has been used to compute the latest value of the Human Resources.

Human resource accounting under the Lev & Schwartz Model.

The Lev & Schwartz Model belongs to the category of the present Value based models, which is salary based. The basic assumption of Lev & Schwartz Model is that the employee will not leave the organization till retirement.

The Lev & Schwartz Model attempts to value the Organization's Human Resources using the economic concept of human capital. The Model uses the employee's future earnings as a surrogate of his economic value of Human Capital embodied in a person of age "T' is the present value of remaining future earnings from employment.

Further the model assumes that the employee will sick to the same position, which is being currently occupied thus ruling out the possibility of change in role because of promotion or demotion.

The model requires the division of the whole labor force of an organization in to certain homogeneous group such as unskilled, semi skilled, skilled, technical, managerial staff etc., and in accordance with different classes and age groups are prepared for each group separately and the present value for human capital is computed by using the cost of capital as the discount rate. The aggregate present value of different groups represent the capitalized future earnings of the firm as a whole.

The Value of Human Resources of the Company and its subsidiaries is Rs. 19278 million. For the purpose of the valuation non-technical employees have been excluded.

The valuation is based on the following assumptions:

1. Employee compensation includes all direct and indirect benefits earned both in India and abroad.
2. The average annual increment is based on the increment paid during the last 3 years.
3. Retirement age is as per company policy.
4. Future earnings have been discounted at the weighted average cost of capital of the company.

HUMAN RESOURCES VALUATION

	1999	2000	2001
Total value of Human Resources (a)	11996	14201	19278
Total Revenue of the Company	1775	2532	3008
Net Profit After Tax of the Company	771	934	1055
Total Revenues / Total Value of Human Resources (b/a = c)	0.15	0.18	0.16
Revenues per employee	1.17	1.52	1.71
Value of Human Resources per employee	7.89	8.50	10.96
Net Profit per employee	0.51	0.56	0.60

(Source: Annual Report of 2001 – Rolta India ltd)

HRA IN INDIA:

Under sec.217 (2A) of the companies act, 1956 the report of the directors should include a statement showing the name of every employee of company who is employed throughout the financial year was in receipt of remuneration for that year which, in the aggregate, was not less than such sum as may be prescribed. With effect from 12-3-1999 the sum specified as per Companies (particulars of Employees) Rules, 1975 is Rs.6 lakhs. Expect for this requirement, Companies Act does not call for any disclosure regarding the human resources of an enterprise.

HRA information, if properly developed, will be useful to managers at all levels regarding costs of turnover and inefficient utilization of human resources. Such information will help managers to make better d3ecisions regarding personnel. Such information also helps these organizations to understand the costs involved in fulfilling social responsibilities such as training to the unemployed and retrenched personnel. Data could also be useful to investors to judge the future performances of the enterprise.

REVIEW QUESTIONS

1. What is HRA ?
2. What is the need for HRA ?
3. What are the advantages of HRA ?
4. What are the difficulties involved in preparation of HRA ?
5. Discuss the methods of preparation of HRA.

20

RESPONSIBILITY ACCOUNTING

After going through this chapter, you should be able to :

- Understand the concept of Responsibility Accounting.
- Explain the meaning and various types of Responsibility Centers.
- Describe the measurement of segment performance.
- Know the meaning and various methods of Transfer Pricing.

Concept of Responsibility Accounting

Responsibility accounting is a system under which managers are given decision-making authority and responsibility for each activity occurring within their organizational divisions or departments. Robert N. Antony defines responsibility accounting as that type of management accounting that collects and reports both planned and actual accounting information in terms of responsibility center. Another definition is that responsibility accounting is a system of accounting, which is tailored to an organization so that costs are accumulated and reported by levels of responsibility within the organization. Each supervisory area is charged with the cost for which it is responsible and over which it has control. According to Horngren, responsibility accounting is a system that recognizes various decision or responsibility centers throughout the organization and traces costs [and revenue, assets and liabilities where pertinent] to the individual managers who are primarily responsible for making decisions about the costs in question.

Pre-requisites for Responsibility Accounting

From the above definitions it is clear that the organization should be classified into suitable responsibility centers. The authority and responsibility of each individual should be defined clearly. Each manager should know about his task and his present level of performance. For this purpose the reporting system should be so designed as to obtain the required information by the managers. The budget system should make the manager to feel his responsibility to achieve the budgeted targets. There should be a continuous appraisal system for evaluating actual performance with the budget estimates. The variances are reported to the top management and corrective measures taken are communicated to the concerned responsibility center. In short, the communication system should be effective and the manager should participate in the system wholeheartedly.

Concept of Responsibility Centers

Any organizational or functional unit headed by a manager who is responsible for the activities of that unit is called a responsible center. The manager is responsible or accountable for the accomplishments of the tasks set in his unit. The total organizational task is divided into sub-tasks, which are performed by different departments. In this sense, all departments in an organization are responsibility centers. All responsibility centers use resources [inputs or costs] to produce something [output or revenues]. Typically responsibility is assigned to a revenue, expense, profit and/or investment center. The decision usually will depend on the activity performed by the organizational unit and on the manner in which inputs and outputs are measured by organizational control system.

The organizational chart shows the sub-tasks being performed by different departments and also the tasks to be performed by each responsibility center. The size of the responsibility center will, however, be determined by the nature of the task, technology, people and the level in the organization hierarchy. From the top management point of view, a division is a responsibility center, from the divisional management's point of view; the market department of that division is a responsibility center. And from the marketing manager's point of view, the sales, distribution, and advertising departments are responsibility centers.

Types of Responsibility Centers

The following are the types of responsibility centers: [a] Revenue Center, [b] Expense center, [c] Profit center, and [d] Investment Center. They are described below:

Revenue Centers: Revenue centers are those organizational units or segments in which outputs are measured in monetary terms but are not directly compared to input costs. The main focus of management's efforts will be on revenue generated by it. A sales department is an example for a revenue center. The effectiveness of the center is not judged by how much sales revenue exceeds the cost cf the center. Rather budgets [in the form of sales quotas] are prepared for the revenue center and the budgeted figures are compared with the actual sales. Generally the costs are not related to output. However, this does not mean that efforts are not taken to control costs in revenue centers. Though the management's main focus is more on revenues, necessary attempts are made to control costs.

Expense Centers: In expense centers, inputs [cost and expenses] are measured in monetary terms but outputs are not. The main focus of the management will be on the control of the expenses or costs incurred by the responsibility center. So budgets will be devised only for the input portion of these centers' operations. Organizational units commonly considered expense centers include administration service, and research departments.

There are two types of expense centers namely engineered expense/costs center and discretionary expenses/costs center. Engineered costs are those for which costs can be estimated with high reliability based on the engineering or technical relationship that exists between costs and output; for example the cost of direct materials or direct labour. Discretionary costs are those for which costs cannot be reliably estimated before hand and must depend to a large extent on the manager's discretion. In other words, it is not possible to determine the optimum relationship between costs and outputs and the choice of relationship is quite often highly subjective and is left to the discretion of the manager. For example, the amount spent on advertising, welfare schemes, management training, etc., cannot be determined objectively. The management has to make a judgment as to the right amount of such costs in a given situation subjectively. The discretionary costs can be varied at the discretion of the manager of the responsibility center. There is no scientific way of determining the right amount. Other examples of discretionary costs centers are the accounting department, personnel department, research and product development, and so on.

In the case of engineering costs center the objective is to reduce costs as far as possible consistent with quality and safety standards. The budgeted costs are calculated using the technical relationship for the actual level of output. Hence, the performance can be evaluated by comprising the actual costs incurred with the budgeted costs. The manger in charge of the center is responsible for both levels of budgeted output as well as cost efficiency. The costs should be reduced without sacrificing the quality. Traditionally, the focus of cost accounting has been on developing suitable systems for measurement of performance of engineered cost centers.

The performance of a discretionary cost center is also evaluated by comparing the actual expenses with budgeted expenses. However, the performance evaluation is on the basis of the manager's ability to spend on the amount agreed upon. The actual should not exceed budget commitment without the knowledge of the manager. This system motivates managers to keep expenses within the budgeted level. However, difficulties may arise in the measurement of efficiency or effectiveness since the output cannot be measured in monetary terms. Further it is difficult to set cost standards and measure financial performance against these standards. In an attempt to reduce costs, the divisional manager may cut costs by ignoring maintenance or avoiding training. But it may not be good for the company. Similarly, the marketing manager may cut costs by reducing sales promotional and advertising expenses. But this may affect the sales and profitability of the concern in the long run. Thus, the conflict between short-run goal [cutting costs] and long-run goal [improving profitability] assumes particular importance in the evaluation of the performance of discretionary cost centers.

Profit Centers: A profit center generally refers to a segment of an organization that generates revenue. It is a responsibility center, the manager of which is responsible for the amount of profits earned. In a profit center, performance is measured by the numerical difference between revenues [outputs] and expenditures [inputs]. The managers in the profit center are therefore, responsible for both revenues and costs. Such a measure is useful to determine the economic efficiency of the center and individual efficiency of the manager in charge of the center.

A profit center is created whenever an organizational segment [division/department] is given responsibility for earning a profit. In departmentalized organization in which each of the number of segments is completely responsible for its own product line, the separate divisions are considered profit centers. Each division's performance can be evaluated in terms of profits. Since divisional managers take all decisions relating to technology, product mixes strategies, and personnel, they may influence both revenues and expenses. The expenditure of a department's sub-units are added and then deducted from the revenues derived from that division's all products and services. The net result is the measure of that division's profitability. In non-divisionalized organizations, or within a division, individual departments may also be made into profit centers by crediting them for revenue and charging them for expenses. A manufacturing department, for example, would normally be considered as a cost center. Allowing the manufacturing department to 'sell' its products at an agreed rate [called transfer price] to the sale department would be a method of making it a profit center. The difference between the transfer price and the manufacturing costs per unit would represent the manufacturing department's profits.

Investment center: An investment center is a responsibility center whose manager is responsible for earning a rate of return on the assets used in his responsibility center. In an investment center, the control system again measures the monetary value of inputs and outputs, but it also assesses how those outputs compare with the assets employed in producing them. For example, divisions in an automobile manufacturing company, individual departments in a departmental store and individual branches of a multiple shop are investment centers.

It is important to realize that any profit center can also be considered an investment center, because its activities require some form of capital investment. In other words, an investment center can be considered as a special type of profit center, in which focus is also on assets employed. However, a center's capital investment insignificant [as a consultancy firm] or its managers have no control over capital investment, it may be more appropriately treated as a profit center. The distinguishing feature of an investment center that it is evaluated on the basis of the rate of return earned on the assets invested in that center, while a profit center is evaluated on the basis of excess revenue over expenses for the period. Hence, it is better to designate a segment as an investment center rather than a profit center in order to enhance the utility of responsibility accounting. A segment may earn greater profits than others not because of better performance but by using more assets to earn such profits.

Responsibility Centers Vs Cost Centers

A cost center as used in cost accounting is different from a responsibility center in many respects. A cost center is a location, person, or a piece of equipment [or a group of these] for which cost may be ascertained and used for cost control purposes. Thus, it is used as a means of assembling items of cost that can be assigned to goods and services. As in case of cost centers the emphasis is more on the product, job or process whose costs are to be ascertained rather on persons who may be managing them. On the other hand, responsibility centers are formed on the basis of responsibility delegated to the members of the organization in order to identify cost, which can be controlled by each one of them for facilitating the operation of management control process. However, cost centers are also used as responsibility centers but they are mainly expenses centers whose managers are responsible for costs incurred by the center.

Measurement of Segment Performance

Profit Centers: Profit is the most widely used measure of performance for a business firm. Hence, profit centers are more common in large decentralized organizations. Evaluating the performance of decentralized units with the same measure with which the firm as a whole is evaluated facilities goal congruence between decentralized units and the firm. A profit center is a unit for which the manager has the authority to make decisions on sources on supply and choice of markets. In general, a profit center will be selling a majority of its output to outside customers and is free to choose sources of supply for a majority of inputs. In this sense, the manufacturing and marketing divisions will not be profit centers, even though some firms may evaluate these units using a profit figure. Many managers of profit centers are evaluated not just on profit but on the level of profit related to the assets for their units. In that case, it may be referred to as investment center. Return on investment and residual income is typical performance measures for investment centers. However, profit center is an appropriate structure for an organizational unit if the fixed investments are stable from year to year and are not controllable by the manager of profit center.

Measures of Performance: Despite the weakness of the financial accounting system, the accounting profit is considered n effective measure of performance. The financial accounting process provides a formal discipline comes from the necessity for systematically accounting for all cash transactions. Since almost any activity of the firm will ultimately result in a cash transaction, the accounting system is comprehensive and pervasive. It is also mandatory in order to meet financial reporting and tax requirements. Fir these reasons business firms relay much on financial measures of performance, of which profit is the most common and comprehensive. However, two problems are encountered in measuring profit, they are: [a] choosing a profit index, and [b] pricing the transfer of goods between profit centers.

Choosing a Profit Index: Problems may arise in choosing a profit index and in the allocation of costs and revenues to the center. The following data relating to a division of a limited company would explain the point.

Sales revenue from the division	Rs. 4,50,000
Variable costs of goods sold	3,00,000
Fixed cost of the division [controllable Rs. 25,000 and non-controllable Rs.35,000]	60,000
Allocated administrative overheads of the company	30,000

From the data, a structured divisional income statement may be prepared as follows:

Divisional Income Statement

Sales revenue	Rs. 4,50,000
Less: Variable costs	3,00,000
[a] Variable contribution margin	1,50,000
Less: Controllable fixed costs	25,000

[b] Controllable contribution	1,25,000
Less: Non-controllable fixed costs	35,000
[c] Divisional contribution	90,000
Less: Allocated company expenses	30,000
[d] Divisional profit before taxes	60,000

There are at least four indicated measures to evaluate the divisional performance.

Variable Contribution Margin: The variable contribution margin is important for understanding the cost-volume-profit relationships within the division. But it is not much useful for performance evaluation. As the division manager has control over, at least, some of the fixed costs, he can have the option of trading between fixed and variable costs. Hence, the performance evaluation should include minimum controllable-fixed costs.

Controllable Margin: The controllable contribution is the total division revenues less all the costs that are directly traceable to the division and controllable by the division manager. It includes fixed costs that may arise from the use of indirect labour, indirect materials and utilities. The division manager has the option of reducing these fixed costs. Since they are fixed only with respect to changes in activity levels. Controllable contribution is perhaps the best performance measure of division manager. Since it reflects his ability to use effectively the resources under his control and authority. However, the main limitation of this measure is that it may be difficult to distinguish between controllable and non-controllable fixed costs. For example, depreciation, insurance, etc. on fixed costs would be controllable if the division manager had the authority to dispose of these assets but would be non-controllable if he did not have this discretion. Also salary levels of employees may be set centrally but the division manager may have the discretion to decide about the number to be employed at the division.

Divisional Contribution: The divisional contribution represents the contribution that the division is making to corporate profit and overheads. It evaluates more the performance of the division than that of the division manager. Some of the division overheads [e.g., cost of fixed assets] may result from past investment decisions by top management. Also, central management may set the salaries of division executives. The divisional contribution is clearly an important indicator for evaluating the division's profitability, but unless the division manger is given authority to restructure the investment or key personnel of the division, these costs are not controllable and hence they may not be relevant in evaluating the manager's performance.

Divisional Profits before Taxes: Many companies allocate all central, general, and administrative expenses to their divisions. The division managers are motivated to generate enough contribution margins to cover a fair share of these expenses. A company will be profitable when profits generated by divisions exceed centrally incurred costs. However, it doesn't seem proper to include these costs while evaluating the performance of a division or a divisional manager for the following reasons:

1. These costs are not controllable at the divisional level. Hence, an adverse profit variance due to unexpected large allocation corporate expenses cannot be attributed to divisional manager who have no control over such expenses.
2. The basis of allocation of corporate expenses to divisions is usually arbitrary having no causal relation to the way in which divisional activities influence the level of corporate expenses. Hence, the argument is that the division managers can concentrate only increasing the revenues and reducing costs that are under control and need not be concerned with analyzing costs that are non-controllable and that are allocated arbitrarily. However, there are two counter arguments to this. The first is that the divisions should be charged for increments in central corporate expenses caused by divisional activities. The second argument is that the allocation of central overhead expenses to divisions will make the division managers more aware of these costs, so that they will exert pressure to keep down the cost of central

staff departments. If the central management were willing to allow division managers participate in decisions on the level of corporate staff activities, it would be reasonable to allocate these expenses back to the divisions.

Common Revenues: Occasionally a conflict may arise on the allocation of revenue between profit centers. This can occur when a salesman of one division promotes the sale of products of other divisions during his call on customers. Unless some credit is given for selling the products of other divisions there will not be any motivation for attempting to make such sales. A similar problem arises when branch banks are evaluated as profit centers. A customer may open an account in a branch near his residence but majority of banking transactions may be conducted in branch near his place of work. Conflicts between these two branches may arise in the allocation of all revenues earned from his account and the cost of supplying the banking services to him. In such instances it would be reasonable to construct a fee schedule to debit or credit revenue earning and cost incurring divisions/branches for rendering services to customers. Of course, such arrangements are complicated. However, they illustrate the problems that arise from decentralized profit directed operations.

Transfer Pricing

Conflicts may arise when decentralized organizational units interact with each other. Potential for such conflicts will be more when goods produces in one unit are transferred to another. If both units are organized as profit centers, a price must be placed on such transfers; this price represents revenue to the producing division and a cost to the purchasing division. Therefore, the transfer price affects the profitability of both divisions, so that the managers of both divisions have to keep interest in how this is determined.

Meaning of Transfer Prices: Transfer prices are the amounts charged by one sub-unit of an organization for a product or service supplied to another sub-unit of the organization. Most often, the term is associated with materials, parts, or finished goods. The transfer price serves two roles. First as a price, it is a guide to local decision-making; it helps the producing division decide how much of the product it wants to sell, and for the purchasing division, how much to acquire. Second, the prices and subsequent profit measurement help the top management to evaluate the profit centers as separate entities. But a set of transfer prices by providing motivations and maximization of profits to the firm may cause a division to operate at a loss. This may lead the divisions to make sub-optimal decisions. Additional problem may arise if managers emphasize short-term performance in their transfer pricing negotiations at the expense of long-run profitability of their division and the firm.

Transfer Price Methods

Transfer price is typically based on cost, market price, marginal cost, or a negotiated price. To some extent, transfer price determination is based on the type of segment, the type of product, the type of firm, and the degree of decentralization within the firm. The transfer pricing methods may be broadly classified into cost-based transfer pricing, market prices and negotiated prices. Some of the cost-based transfer pricing are discussed below:

Cost: Transfers between cost centers are typically based on cost. When the transfer price is some form of cost, such transfer pricing is indistinguishable from the 'cost allocation' of interdepartmental services. Normally this should be standard cost and include both variable and fixed costs. Since the managers of cost centers are evaluated on their conformity to standard cost. Transfer price based on such cost does not normally present any problem. If a firm transfers at actual cost rather than standard cost, problems may develop. The transfer at actual costs provides no incentive for efficiency in the transferring division, since all actual costs, even excess costs, is transferred to the transfere division. In addition, the receiving division is unfairly charged with the cost of inefficiencies of the transferring division. If the receiving unit is an investment center then the rate of return is affected by the inefficiency of the cost center. For this reason, the use of standard cost as the base is considered appropriate.

Cost-Plus Profit: if the selling division is a profit or investment center, it would like to sell/transfer its products to the buying division at some price greater than cost, i.e., cost plus some mark up for profits. It will add some profit, which is the required rate of return or adequate profit for the division. In certain cases, the transfer price and rate of profit may be based on some outside market price. If no outside market price exists, it would, and then be difficult to determine the rate of profit to be charged. However, if the selling division sells other products, it may calculate its profits on internal transfer in the same way as it calculates on other products, say, and a percentage of cost. Or it may also be based on negotiations between the buying and selling divisions.

Variable Cost: The price equal to variable cost will be very attractive to the buying division but not to the selling division. However, when the objective is to measure the overall profitability of the company but not purely to measure the profit performance of each division, this method is useful. This method is particularly useful in the selling division when there is idle capacity.

Opportunity Cost: Horngren has suggested that for decision-making purposes a transfer should be one, which is based on marginal [incremental] cost plus any opportunity cost to the firm as a whole [for not being able to use them in the best possible way]. The effect of this will be different in different situations.

(*i*) In a perfectly competitive market, i.e., all products sold internally, can be sold externally, transfer pricing will be: Standard marginal cost + Lost contribution margin = Prevailing market price.

(*ii*) In a slightly imperfect market, the transfer pricing technique will be: Standard marginal cost + Lost contribution = Adjusted market price, i.e., prevailing market price benefits derived by selling internally.

(*iii*) In a perfectly competitive or slightly imperfect market, i.e., most products sold externally. Products sold internally do not have a market price. Production capacity used to produce internally sold products can be used to externally sold products. Transfer pricing techniques will be: Standard marginal cost + Lost contribution = Phantom market price. This reflects the opportunity cost of producing the product for the internal user.

Standard Cost: Under this method, the transfer pricing is based on standard cost. The variances form the standard cost are normally absorbed by the selling division. In certain cases, variances are transferred to buying division, and therefore both the selling and buying divisions at standard cost carry inventories. Once the standards are properly set, operation of this system is simple. Here, the responsibility of profit performance is centralized. Profit performance of each division cannot be measured.

Market Prices

When an organization has profit centers and investment centers, market price would be the ideal base for setting the transfer prices. If there were an outside market for the products being transferred between the divisions of a firm, then the market price would serve as the basis for the transfer price. Many times the outside market price is the ideal transfer price for it is considered to objectively determine the amount that was arrived at by factors outside the firm and therefore no one within the firm was able to influence it.

A competitive market being considered efficient provides incentive for efficient production because excessive costs cannot be passed on to the buyers. Since market prices are, by and large, determined by the free play demand and supply forces, it is considered that profits, which result under market price method, will provide a good indicator of the overall efficiency of the various divisions.

Frequently, internal transfers are made at market price-minus. That is, the selling division may avoid some marketing or transport costs by transferring goods internally instead of selling them to outside customers. These savings are often deducted when the transfer price is fixed. When market prices non-existent or impossible to determine, the cost-plus-profit method may be used. It is supposed to provide a fair or equitable substitute for regular market prices. Some of the limitations of market price method are:

[1] Collection of market prices may present a lot of difficulties, particularly when goods are manufactured for captive consumption; there may not any market price at all.

[2] When prices are highly fluctuating, it would be very difficult to use market price method, since price may become obsolete in short span of time.

[3] Market price includes cost elements like packing, selling and distribution expenses. Because of this, market price as such may not be used.

[4] When market price method is used the closing inventory is valued at market prices. Hence, it is essential to eliminate unrealized profit from inventory value.

Negotiated Price

Under this method, each decentralized unit is considered as an independent unit and competitive price is arrived at by negotiation or bargaining. The negotiating process typically begins when the producing division offers a price quotation plus all relevant delivery conditions [say, timeliness, quality, and so on]. The buying division may accept the deal or bargain to obtain a lower price or better conditions. In a different sequence, the buying division may make an offer to the producing division for a portion of its current output or an increment to current output. The producing division can then bargains with the purchasing division over terms or decide not to accept the offer. In either case, the divisional managers have full freedom to accept or reject a price at any stage of the negotiation.

The negotiated transfer pricing will be successful [effective] under the following conditions:

[a] Prices of all inter-division transfers should be determined by negotiation between producing and buying divisions.

[b] Negotiators should have easy access to full data on alternative sources or markets.

[c] Negotiators should have full freedom to buy or sell outside the company.

Limitations of Negotiated Price Method

1. It is time-consuming for the managers involved.
2. It may lead to conflicts between divisions.
3. It makes the measurement of divisional profitability sensitive to the negotiating skills of managers.
4. It requires the time of top management to oversee the negotiating process and mediate disputes.
5. It may lead reduced level of output if the negotiating price is above the opportunity cost of supplying the transferred goods.

   Despite these limitations, a negotiated transfer price system seem to offer desirable mechanisms for permitting divisional managers to exploit the specialized information they possess about the local opportunities.

Non-profit Measures of Performance

Profit as the sole measure of performance for divisional managers has certain limitations. The most serious concern about the periodic profit reports is that managers will take actions that sacrifice long-term profitability for short-term reported profits. They would attempt to glorify their short-term position by resorting to a number of ways such as lowering of quality controls, inadequate maintenance, insufficient allocation to R&D and employee training and lack of attention to customer relations and employee morale. To balance of such situations some companies have developed performance appraisal systems in which profitability is only one component. For example, a division manager may be given objectives to meet in human resources, distribution, technology, product quality, or new products depending upon which of these key areas are most crucial to the long-tern success of the division and which are susceptible to the greatest improvement. The manager would then be evaluated on whether targeted objectives were achieved in these key areas.

An evaluation programme developed by General Electric in USA is based on eight key result areas, which are as follows:

1. Profitability – based on residual income measure is still a profitability measure.
2. Productivity – This variable represents the value of output to input.
3. Market Position – It is measured as market share in the appropriately defined market category.
4. Product Leadership – It is the appraisal of each of the division's main products to assess its superiority or otherwise with those of competitors and their place of development, etc.
5. Personnel Development – Evaluating the output of the employee development programmes. Measuring the job satisfaction among the employees.
6. Employee Attitude – this area is measured by periodic surveys of employee attitude towards factors such as job satisfaction, pay policies, and promotion chances.
7. Public Responsibility – This is ensuring compliance with antimonopoly and fair trade practices and avoiding conflicts of interest.
8. Balance between short and long range Goals – The results in each of the previous seven key areas are evaluated in terms of both of their short-term and long-term consequences.

When performance is evaluated on more than one dimension, the problem of weighing the various dimensions into an overall measure may arise. The managers should not be allowed to trade off performance along one dimension against performance on another. All dimensions should be given equal importance in order to avoid negative performance review. The management should remain constantly vigilant to ensure that long-run profitability is not sacrificed by actions that maximize short-term reported profits.

Investment Centers, Return on Investment, and Residual Income

Investment centers are decentralized divisions or sub-units for which the manager has maximum discretion in determining not only short-term operating decisions on product mix, pricing and production methods, but also level and type of investment. An investment extends the profit center concept in that the measured profit is related to the center's investment. It may be described as a special form of profit center since a profitability measure is being developed for the center. The concept relating profits to assets employed have an intuitive appeal for it indicates whether the profits generated give sufficiently high return for the capital invested in the division. Capital is always a scarce resource, and it is important that an evaluation be made of returns that a division and the overall company are earning on invested capital. Most companies have elaborate systems for authorizing capital expenditures. Measurement of investment center performance can be viewed as the evaluation of an aggregation of past and present capital projects as opposed to the evaluation of each project individually. Such a measurement also provides an incentive for division managers to monitor capital investments carefully while managing their operations. The managers will also be motivated to watch the levels of inventory and receivables since these accounts will almost always be included in that investment base.

Despite the intuitive appeal investment centers, many conceptual and measurement problems may arise in the construction of a particular measure. Some of the problems and other issues are discussed under the following aspects:

- Choice of an appropriate measure: Return on Investment, Residual Income, Cash Recovery Rate
- Choice depreciation method
- Measurement of assets: Current Cost or Historical Cost

Return on Investment [ROI]: The most common measure of evaluation for an investment center is the return on investment. It is a better test of profitability and is defined in general as the division's net income before taxes divided by some measure of assets employed in the division. Consider a division with assets of Rs.2 00 000 and net income before taxes of Rs.50 000. Its ROI is 25 per cent.

$$\text{ROI} = \frac{\text{Net Income} \times 100}{\text{Invested Capital}} = \frac{\text{Rs. } 50{,}000 \times 100}{\text{Rs. } 2{,}00{,}000} = 25\%$$

The two major ingredients of ROI are net income and invested capital. The net income when related to sales revenue gives the Net Profit ratio and when sales revenue is related to invested capital, it will give the capital turnover ratio. Then the ROI can be derived from these two ratios as follows:

$$\text{ROI} = \frac{\text{Net Income}}{\text{Sales Revenue}} \times \frac{\text{Sales Revenue}}{\text{Invested Capital}}$$

ROI = Net Profit Ratio x Capital Turnover ratio

Hence, the ROI is the product of these two ratios. An improvement in either without changing the other will improve the ROI. For example, the net profit ratio is 16% and capital turnover ratio is 1.25. Then the ROI is equal to 20% [16% x 1.25]. An increase in net profit ratio by 2% will result in increase in ROI to 22.5% [18% x 1.25]. Similarly an increase in capital turnover ratio to 1.5 will increase the ROI to 24% [16% x 1.25].

There are many positive aspects of ROI computation. It is generally an objective measure based on historical accounting data. It facilitates a comparison among divisions of different sizes and in different lines of business. It is a common measure, since it is similar to a cost of capital for which external referents exist in capital market s. while evaluating the overall corporate profitability; the use of this measure for evaluating divisional performance encourages goal congruence between the division and the firm.

Actions taken by a division to increase its ROI may often increase the overall profitability. Most important, perhaps, the measure focuses the division manger's attention on the assets employed in the division and motivates the manager to invest in assets only to the extent that an adequate return can be earned on them. If a manager were evaluated only on the level of profits, without regard to assets employed, then the tendency would be to expand assets and thereby increase profits. Such actions would lower the ROI and, therefore, will not take place when ROI is used as a performance measure.

Defects of ROI Measure: Actions that increase the divisional ROI may make the division worse off and conversely, actions that decrease divisional ROI may increase the economic wealth of the division. For example, assume the cost of capital to the division mentioned above [with ROI of 25%] is say 15%. Suppose the division finds an opportunity of a new investment of Rs.50 000 that will earn Rs.10 000 per annum. The return on this investment is 20% well above the cost of capital. But the new ROI for the division will be 24% as shown below:

$$\text{ROI} = \frac{\text{Rs. } 50{,}000 + 10{,}000}{\text{Rs. } 2{,}00{,}000 + 50{,}000} \times 100 = 24\%$$

That is a decrease from the previous level of 25%. Therefore, the divisional manager may refuse this investment. Conversely, if the division has an asset costing Rs.50 000 that is earning Rs.10 000 per year [i.e., 20% return], the division can increase its ROI by disposing of this asset even if its return is above cost of capital:

$$\text{ROI} = \frac{\text{Rs. } 50{,}000 - 10{,}000}{\text{Rs. } 2{,}00{,}000 - 50{,}000} \times 100 = 26.67\%$$

A similar problem may arise when two divisions with different investment bases are compared. The ROI of two divisions say, A and B are 25% and 30% with capital investments of Rs. 2,00,000 and Rs. 1,00,000 respectively. It might appear that division B is profitable. But on closer examination we find that division A has Rs.1 00 000 more in assets with an incremental earnings of Rs.20 000. Its incremental ROI is 20%, well above the cost of capital of 15%. Hence, division A is more profitable, after deducting capital costs than division B. unfortunately these things may tempt the divisional manager to manipulate the investment bases in order to maximize ROI. This problem is caused by evaluating divisional performance attempting to maximize the ratio [ROI].

Residual Income [RI]: To eliminate the problems associated with using a ratio as a performance measure, many companies use the RI approach. RI is the difference between actual income earned by the division on an investment and the desired income on the investment as specified by minimum desired rate of return. It is calculated as follows:

RI = Actual Income – Desired income [maximum desired rate of return x invested capital]

In effect RI is the excess of earnings above the minimum desired earnings. If the firm sets its minimum rate of return at its cost of capital, it must earn an ROI that is at least equal to the cost of funds used in making the investment. Any amount of income earned above the cost of capital is the profit to the firm. The more the income earned above the capital charge, the better off the firm will be. In short, a firm has to maximize its RI.

Computation of RI: The invested capital for two divisions A and B are Rs.2 00 000 and Rs.1 00 000 and net income for A Rs.50 000 and for B Rs.30 000. If the firm's cost of capital [desired return] is 15%, then the residual income will be as shown below:

Statement of Residual Income

	Division A	Division B
	Rs.	Rs.
Invested capital	2,00,000	1,00,000
ROI	25 %	30 %
Net income	50,000	30,000
Less: Capital charge [15% on Invested capital]	30,000	15,000
Residual income	20,000	15,000

The computation shows that division A is more profitable than division B, since its RI is higher. The excess residual income of Rs.5 000 is from the incremental investment of Rs.1 00 000. As long as the incremental ROI of any division is above the cost of capital, its residual income will be more significant RI measure.

The RI measure will always increase when investments earning above the cost of capital or eliminate investment earning below the cost of capital. Therefore, there is goal congruence between the evaluation of the division and actions that maximize the economic wealth of the division and the firm. The firm will always prefer the division to have a higher residual income. In this regard, RI offers significant advantage over the ROI measure. The RI measure is also more flexible, since a different percentage can be applied to investments of different risk. The cost of capital will reflect a risk premium for the different kinds of risky assets. Hence, in principle, an RI evaluation permits the recognition of different risk-adjusted capital costs, whereas the simple ROI evaluation does not.

Weaknesses of RI measure: RI is a less convenient measure than ROI because it is an absolute number, not deflated by the size of the division. It is easier for a much larger division to earn a given amount of residual income than a small division. For example, consider two divisions, one with Rs.5 lakhs in assets and the second with Rs.10 lakhs in assets; both have a cost of capital of 15%. In order to earn a residual income of Rs.50 000, the first division would need to earn a net income of Rs.1 25 000 [an ROI of 25%] whereas the second division would have to earn Rs.2 00 000 [an ROI of 20%]. For this reason, most companies using RI evaluation will not simply direct managers to maximize residual income. Rather they will set budgeted levels of residual income, appropriate for the asset structure of each division, evaluate divisional managers by comparing actual to budgeted residual income. However, this measure also suffers from the same limitation of ROI with regard to the maximization of economic wealth of the firm.

ROI vs. RI

RI is favoured for reasons of goal congruence and managerial effort. Under ROI the basic objective is to maximize the rate of return percentage. Thus, managers of highly profitable divisions may be reluctant to invest in the projects with lower ROI than the current rate because their average ROI would be reduced. On the other hand, under RI the manager would be inclined to invest in the projects earning more than the desired rate of return, i.e., the risk-adjusted cost of capital. Despite its known disadvantages, most managers agree that the rate of return on invest is the ultimate test of profitability. Intelligently used ROI can help decision-making. However, with both measures, there remain significant problems of interpretation and measurement. It all depends on how investment and income in a decision are measured and interpreting the accounting rate of return as if it be analogous to the cost of capital. Some of the problems are discussed below:

Accounting Vs, True Rate of Return: The accounting rate of return i.e., net income divided by investment is a popular measure because it has been interpreted as representing the true underlying economic rate of return for investment in the division. Unfortunately, except in very special circumstances, the accounting ROI will not equal the underlying yield of the assets in the division. Mainly this is because of using straight-line method of depreciation for the accounting measure. In order for the accounting ROI equal the actual yield [internal rate of return], one must use a depreciation derived from the decline in the present value of the asset.

Present-value Depreciation Method: The present value depreciation method is derived directly from the cash flow schedule used for the appraisal of capital investments, i.e., from the discounted cash flow approach. In this way, a periodic ROI performance measure can be determined such that when actual cash flows equal forecasted cash flows, then each year's ROI figure will equal the yield [internal rate of return] of the asset. When an asset yields equal cash flows over its economic life, the present value depreciation method will be identified to the annuity depreciation method. The present value method while incorporating the RI computation produces more satisfying results. It also offers significant advantages over the straight-line method for evaluating the performance of investment centers.

Price Level Changes: The price level changes have become a common phenomenon and will introduce entirely new distortions into ROI and RI measures. The principal distortion s occurs because revenues and cash costs are measured at current prices, while the investment cost and depreciation charge are measured at historical prices used to acquire the assets. Depreciation based on historical cost will be different from the depreciation based on current cost. This results in overstating the firm's income. At the same time the firm's investment is understated because most of the firm's assets were acquired at lower prices than those prevailing currently. The combination of overstated income and understated investments would distort the ROI and RI measures very much. The higher values of these measures may not a true indicator of higher profitability; it is mainly due to a failure to adjust for inflationary effects. When the returns are related to new investments at current price levels it may show lower returns. And divisions with new assets will tend to show lower ROI and RI measures than divisions whose assets were purchased at lower price levels. Hence, it requires some adjustment to eliminate such inflationary effects in order managers to make new investments in their divisions.

There are two methods to adjust for inflation – general price level adjustment and current replacement cost or market value measures. Under the first method general prices are used to convert the historical cost in to current cost. For the purpose the ratio of current year's price index to the value of the index in the year the asset was purchased. This will enable all assets to be measured and depreciated at the same units that represent the current year's purchasing power. This simple adjustment will remove much of the inflationary effects from ROI and RI measures. However some people consider this method as unrealistic and recommend for the application of the current replacement cost method.

Advocates of the second method claim that replacement cost or market value provides a better estimate of the current investment base of the decision. The simplest way to perform the adjustment to current cost is to use an index specific to each asset class. Government and trade associations publish a number of indices for specific class of assets. But these specific indices fail to reflect the change in technological developments. Hence, measurement of current value can be decided by independent appraisal or by making comparisons to the selling prices of recently traded comparable assets. In making these adjustments it is important to use an objective method such as indexing. The objective for making inflationary adjustments must be to prevent distortions in the evaluation of investment center performance.

Inflation adjustments are needed for depreciation and cost of goods sold while computing net income and for the inventory and fixed capital included in the investment base. Index methods – general or specific – will provide a good basis for making adjustments for inflation. Index methods are least expensive and provide objectivity and freedom from manipulation necessary for a system of measuring the divisional performance rationally. One more item to be adjusted is the cost of capital. Necessary adjustments to the divisional cost of capital must be done as part of either the capital budgeting process or performance evaluation measure.

Capital Expenditure Vs. Revenue Expenditure: For certain expenditures, particularly on intangibles, there is discretion to treat such expenditures as revenue or capital expenditures. There are no hard and fast rules in this regard. When expenditures with expected future benefits are capitalized the earnings in the short run will be affected and ROI and RI be overstated since the expenditure on tangibles will not be included in the measured investment base. Hence, divisions with a high proportion of expenditures on intangibles [say, marketing] will tend to show a higher ROI than other divisions with high proportion of tangible assets [say, manufacturing division]. Such factors should be taken into consideration while evaluating divisional performance.

Investment Base: The investment base used for the computation of ROI and RI measures influence them very much. While determining the investment base, the primary purpose of performance evaluation should be decided first. If the purpose is to evaluate the divisional manager, then only those assets that are under his control should be included in the investment base. Other assets controlled by the central management should be excluded. With this approach, he would be held responsible for divisional property, plant and equipment and inventories. If he has control over credit policy and sales terms the divisional receivables should also be included. Similarly, if he has control over payment terms to suppliers then accounts payables should be deducted from the investment base. This narrowly defined investment may be referred to as controllable divisional investment. Assets, which are not under his direct control of the divisional manager, are called non-controllable investment. If the purpose is to evaluate the division's performance and it is based on solely on controllable investments, then the division's actual profitability will be overstated. Further no division could operate without receiving services from the corporate assets. Hence, many decentralized firms allocate investments in cash, marketable securities, and other corporate assets to division when computing the investment base. Such allocation of non-controllable investments will be mostly arbitrary, based on measures such as sales, space occupied, and personnel employed, etc.

Some firms exclude idle assets from the division's investment base, if such assets are not controllable at the divisional level. However, the central management can transfer them to other divisions where they may be needed. Another minor issue is whether to use beginning, average or closing values of assets. Since income is earned continuously over the period, it is always better to use the average level of assets during the period. One way clever way is that the investment center manager may lease the assets, instead of purchasing them. This will increase the ROI and RI values and distort the performance evaluation procedure. The exclusion of leased assets provides an incentive for a division even there is no apparent economic advantage. However, the leased assets should be included in the investment base at their fair market value. If an independent estimate of the cost of the asset is not available, then the leased asset may be valued at the discounted present value of the lease payments.

Cash Flow Accounting: Most of the problems of performance evaluation arise from the earnings based performance measures such as ROI and RI. Investment evaluation measures including net present value, internal rate of return, and payback period are computed using cash flows. But the results of these decisions [i.e., performance evaluation] are evaluated using accounting return or earnings. Hence, there is inconsistency between the two types of measurement. However, in order to make the evaluation more congruent, the performance evaluation should be based on cash flows. For 'he purpose a cash recovery rate [CRR] may be used. The CRR is simply defined as follows:

$$\text{CRR} = \frac{\text{Cash flow operations}}{\text{Gross Assets}}$$

Where cash flow from operations includes the proceeds from disposal of long-term assets and changes in net working capital and gross assets is the average value of the historical [undepreciated] cost of all assets in operation.

The CRR is the reciprocal of the payback period if projects have uniform cash flows. For long-lived assets [n > 15 years] the CRR provides a reasonable approximation to IRR. However, the problem with CRR is that it is a ratio and therefore, has many problems similar to using ROI to measure the divisional performance. Managers being evaluated by CRR might turn down investments returning above the cost of capital but whose adoption would lower the average CRR for the division. Therefore, a residual cash flow measure similar to RI measure might provide a better basis for evaluating the performance of divisional managers. Residual cash flow is the remainder after the cost of capital is multiplied by gross investment and deducted from cash flows.

Practical problems

Illustration 1. A division has assets of Rs.5 00 000 and operating income of Rs.1 50 000.

[a] What is the division's ROI?

[b] If interest is imputed at 16% what is the RI?

[c] What effects on management behaviour can be expected if ROI is used to evaluate performance?

[d] What effects on management behaviour can be expected if RI is used to evaluate performance?

Solution

$$[a]\ \text{ROI} = \frac{\text{Operating income}}{\text{Investment}} \times 100 \frac{\text{Rs.}1{,}50{,}000 \times 100}{\text{Rs. }5{,}00{,}000} = 30\%$$

$$\begin{aligned}[b]\ \text{RI} &= \text{Operating income} - \text{Imputed interest}\\ &= \text{Rs. }1{,}50{,}000 - [0.16 \times \text{Rs.}5{,}00{,}000]\\ &= \text{Rs. }1{,}50{,}000 - \text{Rs. }80{,}000 = \text{Rs. }70{,}000\end{aligned}$$

[c] If ROI is used; the manager would like to reject projects, which do not earn an ROI of at least 30%. From the company's point of view as a whole, they may not be desirable because its best investment opportunities may lie in a decision at a rate of, say, 25%. If a division enjoys a high ROI, it may less likely expand when judged through ROI.

[d] If RI is used, the manager may like to accept all projects whose ROI exceeds the minimum desired rate. The division may expand more rapidly because the manager's goal is to maximize the quantum of profit rather than a rate.

Illustration 2: [Variable cost as a transfer price]

A product's variable cost is Rs.20 and its market value at a transfer point from division A to division B is Rs.30. Division B's variable cost of processing the product further is Rs. 22.5 and the selling price of the final product is Rs.47.5. Prepare a tabulation of contribution margin per unit of division A, performance and overall performance under the two alternatives of [a] processing further, and [b] selling to outsiders at the transfer point.

Also explain as Division A manager, which alternative you would choose.

Solution

Performance Evaluation Report

Sale at transfer point		Further processing	
Division A	Rs.	Division B	Rs.
Market value at transfer point	30.00	Sale value	47.50
Variable cost	20.00	variable cost:	
Contribution margin per unit	10.00	Division A	Rs.20.00
		Division B	22.50
		Contribution margin per unit	42.50
			5.00

If the product is further processed, the overall contribution margin decreases by Rs.5.00. Hence, it is better to sell the product at the transfer point in order to maximize the overall margin.

Illustration 3 [Cost plus a return on investment]

A company has the practice of fixing the inter-divisional transfer price for its products on the basis of cost plus a return on investment in the division. The budget for Division A for 2005 – 2006 is as follows:

Total investment in the division	Rs. 15,00,000
Annual fixed costs for the division	10,00,000
Variable cost per unit of the product	10.00
Annual budgeted volume 5,00,000 units	
Desired ROI 25%	

Determine the transfer price for Division A.

Solution

Computation of Transfer Price for Division A

Total investment	Rs. 15,00,000
Desired ROI	25%
Desired Profit margin	Rs. 3,75,000
Variable cost per unit	Rs. 10.00
Fixed cost per unit [Rs.10 00 000/5 00 000]	2.00
Profit margin per unit [Rs.3 75 000/ 5 00 000]	0.75
Transfer price per unit	12.75

Illustration 4

A company has two divisions A and B, which are operated as profit centers. Division A has been selling a part of its production to Division B at Rs.200 per unit. Annual output of Division A is 10 000 units. Sales are as follows:

To Division B	4,000 units
To outside customers	6,000 units

Per unit cost in Division A are as follows:

Fixed cost	Rs.75
Variable cost	100
Total cost	175

Division has found that it can negotiate a contract to buy from an outside supplier at Rs.150 per unit. Should Division B be allowed to buy from outside? In the light of its implications, can you suggest an alternative ?

Solution

No. Division B should continue to buy its requirements from Division A as the variable cost of making the product is Rs.100 per unit, as compared to the buying cost of Rs.150. buying from outside will lower profits by Rs.2 00 000 [4000 x Rs.50 being the excess price per unit].

An alternative arrangement could be the institution of dual prices on the basis of transfer price in terms of which the Division A would be credited with Rs.200 and Division B would be charged with Rs.150 only.

Illustration 5 [Responsibility Accounting Report]

The following control report has been prepared for Department A in a factory:

Overheads directly assigned to Department A	Rs.	Rs.
Indirect materials [as per actual requisitions]	6,000	
Indirect labour [job cards]	5,600	
Overtime charges	400	
Depreciation on equipment	3,000	15,000
Allocated factory overheads [40% of factory space]		8 000
Repairs [allocated 60%of repairs done for Dept. A]		6 800
Administrative overheads [allocated on agreed basis]		15 500
Total department expenses		45 300

Prepare a revised control report assuming Department as responsibility center.

Solution

Revised Control Report – Department A

Fully controllable costs:	Rs.	Rs.
Indirect materials	6,000	
Indirect labour	5,600	
Overtime charges	400	12,000
Partially controllable costs:		
Allocated repair charges		6,800
Total department expenses		18,800

Note: Department A has no control on other allocated items – depreciation, factory overheads, administrative overheads, since they depend on overall management policy and therefore are not controllable.

Illustration 6: [Transfer Pricing – contribution approach]

Division A of BM ltd. has been given a budgeted target of selling 2 00 000 components, it manufactures at a price, which gives a return of 25% on the average assets employed by it. The following information is relevant:

Fixed overheads	Rs. 4,00,000
Variable cost	Re. 1 per unit
Average assets employed:	
Sundry debtors	Rs. 2,00,000
Stocks	6,00,000
Plant and other assets	4,00,000

However, the marketing department finds out by a survey that the maximum number of components, the market can take is only 1 40 000 units. Fortunately, Division B is willing to purchase the balance 60 000 units. Division A is willing to sell to B at a concessional price of Rs.4 per unit. But Division B is ready to pay only Rs.2.25 per unit. But Division A feels that the price is low and plans to manufacture and sell only 1,40,000 units. By this the department could reduce Rs. 80,000 in stocks, Rs. 1,20,000 of plant and other assets, and Rs. 40,000 in selling and administration expenses.

As a Cost Accountant work out the various computations and show that selling 60,000 units to Division B at Rs. 2.25 per unit would be in the best interest of the company.

Solution

Division A of BM ltd. expects a return of 25% on average assets of Rs.12 00 000

Expected profit Rs.12 00 000 x 25% = Rs.3 00 000

Variable cost 2 00 000 x Re.1 per unit = Rs.2 00 000

Fixed cost = Rs.4 00 000

Total sales value Rs.9 00 000

Selling price per unit [9 00 000/2 00 000] = Rs.4.50

Comparative Statement of Profitability

	Transfer to Division B Plus sales to outsiders	Sales to outside parties only
Sales [units]	2,00,000 units	1,40,000 units
Sales value [1,40,000 × 4.50]	Rs. 6,30,000	Rs. 6,30,000
[60 000 × 2.25]	1,35,000	
Total sales value	7,65,000	6,30,000
Less: Variable cost [Re.1 per unit]	2,00,000	1,40,000
Contribution margin	5,65,000	4,90,000
Less: Fixed costs	4,00,000	3,60,000*
Net profit	1,65,000	1,30,000
Average assets employed	12,00,000	10,00,000*
Return on Investment	13.75%	13.00%
[Net Profit/Average Assets]		

Recommendation. Producing and selling/transferring to B 2 00 000 units is more profitable since the contribution, net profit and return on investment are more than the alternative proposal of Division A. Hence. Selling the component to Division B at Rs.2.25 per unit is in the overall interest of the company.

* Reduction of selling and administration expenses [fixed cost] by Rs.40 000 and reduction of assets by Rs.2 00 000.

Illustration 7 [Transfer pricing – opportunity cost approach]

Division A is a profit center. It produces three products X, Y, and Z. Each product has an external market.

	X	Y	Z
External market price per unit	Rs. 48	Rs. 46	Rs. 40
Variable cost per unit in Division A	Rs. 33	Rs. 24	Rs. 28
Labour hours required per unit in A	3	4	2

Product Y can be transferred to Division B, but the maximum quantity required for transfer is 300 units of Y. The maximum external sales are:

Product X 800 units; Product Y 500 units; Product Z 300 units

Instead of receiving transfers of Product Y from Division A, B could buy similar product in the open market at a slightly cheaper price of Rs.45 per unit.

What should the transfer price per unit be for 300 units of Product Y, if the total labour hours available in Division A are: [a] 3 800 hours, [b] 5 600 hours.

Solution

Statement showing Contribution per unit of Key factor [Labour hour]

	Product X	Product Y	Product Z
Selling price per unit	Rs. 48	Rs. 46	Rs. 40
Variable cost per unit	33	24	28
Contribution per unit	15	22	12
Labour hours required per unit	3	4	2
Contribution per hour	Rs. 5	5.5	6
Ranking	III	II	I

[a] When labour is the key factor the available hours should be used to produce products based on contribution per unit.

If only 3800 hours are available in Division A, they should be used as follows:

300 units of Z [Maximum], which will take 300 × 2 = 600 hours

500 units of Y [Maximum], which will take 500 × 4 = 2 000 hours

400 units of X to use remaining hours [3,800 – 2,600] = 1,200 hours.

Total contribution will be [300 × 12] + [500 × 22] + [400 × 15] = Rs. 20,600

If 300 units of Y are to be transferred to Division B, then 1,200 hours will have to be used for production of Y instead of X. It means that Division A gives up 400 units of X, which yields at Rs.5 per hour. Given above is the optimum production mix for Division A for 3 800 hours. If 300 units of Y are to be transferred to Division B with time constraint of 3 800 hours, then additional 300 units of Y will have to be produced foregoing the production of 400 units of X, which is yielding contribution. Hence, the transfer price should cover both the variable cost and contribution sacrificed, which should be calculated as follows:

Transfer price if 3 800 hours are available:

Variable cost per unit of Y	Rs. 24.00
[Opportunity cost]	
Contribution from X foregone [4Hrs × Rs. 5]	20.00
Transfer Price should be	= 44.00

Y takes 4 hours and in each hour of production of X, it would have generated contribution at the rate of Rs. 5.

[b] If 5 600 hours are available, the hours required to meet maximum external demand would be as follows:

Product X	800 units × 3 hours per unit	= 2,400 hours
Product Y	500 × 4 hours per unit	= 2,000 hours
Product Z	300 × 2 hours per unit	= 600 hours
	Total	= 5,000 hours

It means that 600 hours extra can be used for producing 150 units of Y [150 x 4 = 600 hours] and the transfer price will be only the variable cost.

That is, the cost for producing 150 units at Rs. 24 per unit = Rs. 3,600

For producing additional 150 units the cost will be:

Variable cost 150 × 24	= Rs. 3,600
Contribution foregone 600 hrs × Rs. 5 per hour = Rs. 3,000	
	6,600
Total price for 300 units	Rs. 10,200

Therefore, the average transfer price should be [Rs.10 200/300] Rs. 34 per unit.

REVIEW QUESTIONS

1. Define Responsibility Accounting.
2. Explain the meaning and types of responsibility centers.
3. Distinguish between investment center and profit center.
4. How does Responsibility center differ from Cost center?
5. Write a note on 'Measurement of segment performance'.
6. How can the performance of a profit center be measured?
7. What is variable contribution margin?
8. Describe the meaning and various methods of transfer pricing.
9. Discuss the problems involved in determining transfer price.
10. What are the bases normally used for arriving at transfer prices?
11. What is negotiated transfer pricing? What are its advantages and limitations?
12. Write a critical note on 'ROI' as a measure of segment performance.
13. Explain how RI is a better measure of performance over ROI.
14. Explain the effect of price level changes on ROI and RI measures.
15. What is cash flow accounting? What is its role?
16. Explain the meaning and various methods of cost-based transfer pricing.
17. A company has two decentralized divisions D1 and D2. Division D1 has always purchased certain units from Division D2 at. 300 per unit. As division D2 plans to raise the price to Rs.400 per unit, division D1 desires to purchase these units from outside suppliers for Rs.300 per unit. The costs of D2 are as follows:

Variable cost per unit	Rs. 250
Annual fixed costs	Rs. 50,000
Annual production for division D1	1,000 units

If division D1 buys from an outside supplier, the facilities, division D2 uses to manufacture these units would remain idle. From the point of the company as a whole, should division D1 purchase from division D2 at Rs.400 per unit or from outside at Rs.300 per unit?

[Answer: D1 should buy from D2 and not from outside; advantage Rs. 50,000]

18. A company has two divisions, A and B, which are operated as profit centers. Division A has been selling a part X of its production to Division B at Rs.200 per unit. Annual output of Division A is 10 000 units. Sales are as follows:

Division B	4,000 units
Outside companies	6,000 units

Unit cost in Division A are as follows:

Fixed cost	Rs. 75
Variable cost	Rs. 100

Division B has found that it can negotiate a contract to buy from an outside supplier at Rs.150 per unit. Should Division B be allowed to purchase from outside? In the light of its implications, can you suggest an alternative?

[Answer: B should buy from A as it variable cost is less than the purchase price. Alternative two way prices credit to A Rs.200 and debit to B Rs.150]

19. A company operates a number of divisions located in different regions. Division A has incurred losses in the first half of current year. Relevant data relating to Division A are as follows:

Sales revenue	Rs. 1,30,000
Controllable variable costs	70,000
Controllable fixed costs	40,000
Attributable segment costs	10,000
Common costs allocated to division A	12,000
Loss	2,000

Prepare a Performance Evaluation Report of Division A and advise the management whether its operations should be continued or shut down?

[Answer: Controllable contribution margin Rs. 60,000; controllable segment margin Rs. 20,000; segment profit contribution Rs. 10,000; Loss Rs. 2,000. Continued segment profit is positive]

21

ACTIVITY BASED COSTING

1 Concept

ABC has been defined by CAM-1 organization of Arlinton Taxes as "the collection of financial and operation performance information tracing the significant activities of the firm of product costs".

ABC is a recent development in Cost Accounting which attempts of absorbs overheads in to product costs on a more realistic basis. Supporters of the technique argue that many costs ate unnecessarily treated as common costs and are arbitrarily absorbed using a basis such as direct labour hours, machine hours, etc. many organizations have now adopted Advanced Manufacturing Technology (AMT) with the result that overheads are increasing and labour costs are becoming a smaller portion of total costs portion of total costs. Costing system which absorb overheads on a direct labour basis are therefore, not relevant in a AMT environment. The basic idea of ABC is that costs are grouped according to what drives them or causes them to be incurred. The cost drivers are then used as an absorption base.

The CIMA official terminology defines ABC as "Cost attribution to cost units on the basis of benefit received from indirect activities e.g., ordering, setting up, assuring quality".

2. Kaplan and Cooper's approach to ABC

Kaplan and Cooper of Harvard Business School, who have developed this new approach in costing to calculate product costs, claim that the costs should be classified as long-term variable costs and short-term variable costs. Traditionally short-term variable costs are known as variable costs and long-term variable costs are known as fixed costs. Short-term variable costs are volume related and change proportionately with the volume of production. Long-term variable costs vary in long-term but not instantaneously. For example, production scheduling cost can be changed in the long-term by changing number of runs rather than changing number of units produced.

They further claim that this approach related overhead costs to the forces behind them. The forces behind overhead costs are named 'Cost drivers'. Cost drivers can be defined as those activities or transactions that are significant determinants of costs. Under ABC system, product cost is determined by obtaining a greater understanding of cost behaviour and using new measures of quantity of resources consumed by each product. A cost driver is 'an activity which generates cost'. ABC system is based on the belief that activities cause costs and that a link should therefore be made between activities and products by assigning costs of activities to products based on an individual products's demand for each activity.

3. Characteristics of ABC

The important characteristics of ABC are noted below:

Simple traditional distinction made between fixed and variable cost is not enough guide to provide quality of information to design a cost system.

- The more appropriate distinction between cost behaviour patterns are volume (scale) related, diversity (scope) related, events (decisions) related and time related.
- Cost drives need to be identified. A cost driver is a structural determinant, of cost related activity. The logic behind is that the cost behaviour pattern must be understood so that, behaviour pattern is dictated by cost drivers. In tracing overhead cost product, a cost behaviour pattern must be understood so that appropriate cost driver could be identified.

4. How do develop an ABC system?

The following are the three key areas of ABC:

- Product cost differentiation.
- Activities and their cost drivers.
- Identification of non-value added cost.

In ABC system a cost centre is established for each cost driver and identification, measurement and control of cost drivers is essential in ABC.

ABC is the planed and systematic study and determination of cost of each of the branches of business activities that add to the value of product and services. The matrix of activities showing the short-term and long-term cost strategy is presented as follows:

Short Term	Long-term
Product value	Value addition
Pricing	Corporate growth

Steps to develop ABC system:

The steps required to develop an ABC system are as follows:

Identify the main activities performed in the organization, such as manufacturing, assembly etc., as well as support activities, including purchasing, packing and dispatching.

- Identify the factors which influence the cost of each activity-the cost drivers.
- Collect accurate data on direct labour, material and overhead costs.
- Establish the demands made by particular products on activities, using the cost drivers as a measure of demand.
- Trace the cost of activities to product according to a product's demand for each activity.

The rules developed by Kaplan and Cooper for this process is:

- Focus on expensive resources, thus directing attention to resource categories where the new costing process has the potential to make big differences on product costs,
- Emphasis resources whose consumption varies significantly by product and product type-look for diversity, and
- Focus whose demand patterns are un-correlated with traditional allocation measures.

6. How to implement ABC System?

In ABC the hidden weaknesses and high cost segments are identified for maximum effectiveness of cost accounting system. The process of designing and implementing an ABC system for support departments usually by way interviewing the concerned departmental heads to have an insight into the departmental operations and in to the departmental operations and into the factors that trigger departmental activies. Subsequent analyses trace these activities to specific products. Suppose the inventory control department is responsible for raw material and purchased components. The relevant questions that could be asked are

- How many people work in the department?
- What do they do?
- What determines the time required to process an incoming shipment? Does it matter if the shipment is large or small?

- What other factors affect your department's work load?
- Do you usually disburse the total amount of material required for a production run all at once or does it go out in smaller quantities?

7. How ABC System Supports Corporate Strategy?

ABC supports corporate strategy in many ways such as:

- ABC system can effectively support the management by furnishing data, at the operational level and strategic level. Accurate product costing will help the management to compare the profits that various customers, product lines, brands or regions generate and to decide on pricing strategy, dropping unprofitable products, lines etc.,
- Information generated by ABC system can also encourage management to re-design the products,
- ABC system can change the method of evaluation of new process technologies, to reduce setup times, rationalization of plant layout in order to reduce or lower material handling cost, improve quality etc.
- ABC system will report on the resource spending vis-à-vis resource consumption, and reduced demand in organizational resources lead to increase in profits.
- ABC analysis helps managers focus their attention and energy on improving activities and the actions allow the insights from ABC to be translated into increased profits.
- The cost driver's rates established by the system can be used to measure activity performance and efficiency and provide a more suitable basis for budgeting.
- The accurate feedback can be provided to cost centre managers on their performance based on their consumption of resources during a period rather than the allocations of cost over which they have no control, and
- The provision of accurate information of product costs enables better decisions to be made on pricing, marketing design and product mix.

Illustration 1:

A Company manufactures two products A and B using the same equipment and similar processes. An extract of the production data for these products in one period is shown below:

Particulars	A	B
Quantity produced (Units)	5,000	7,000
Direct labour hours per unit	1	1
Machine hours per unit	3	1
Setups in the period	10	40
Orders handled in the period	15	60

Overhead costs

Relating to machine activity	2,20,000
Relating to production run set-up	20,000
Relating handling of orders	45,000
	2,85,000

Required

Calculate the production overheads to be absorbed by one unit of each of the products using the following costing methods:

(a) A traditional costing approach using a direct labour hour rate to absorb overheads.

(b) An activity based costing approach, using suitable cost drivers to trace overheads to products.

(a) Direct labour hours

Product A	(5,000 units × 3 hours)	5,000
Product B	(7,000 units × 1 hour)	14,000
Total		19,000

$$\therefore \quad \text{Overhead absorbed rate} = \frac{\text{Rs. } 2{,}85{,}000}{19{,}000 \text{ DLH}} = \text{Rs. } 15 \text{ per hour}$$

Product A	(1 hour × Rs. 15)	Rs. 15 per unit
Product B	(2 hour × Rs. 15)	Rs. 30 per unit

(b) Machine hours

Product A	(5,000 units × 3 hours)	15,000
Product B	(7,000 units × 1 hour)	7,000
Total		22,000

Using ABC the overhead costs are absorbed according to the cost drivers.

Machine – hour driven costs	(Rs. 2, 20,000/22,000 M.H)	= Rs. 10 per M.H.
Setup driven costs	(Rs. 20,000/50 set ups)	= Rs. 400 per setup
Order – driven costs	(Rs. 45,000/75 orders)	= Rs. 600 per order

Overhead costs:

Particulars	Product A	Rs.	Product B	Rs.
Machine driven cost	(15000 hrs. × Rs. 10)	1,50,000	(7,000 hrs. × Rs. 10)	70,000
Setup costs	(10 × Rs. 400)	4,000	(40 × Rs. 400)	16,000
Order handling costs	(15 × Rs. 600)	9,000	(60 × Rs. 600)	36,000
		1,63,000		1,22,000

Units produced	5,000	7,000
Overhead cost per unit	Rs. 32.60	Rs. 17.43

These figures suggest that product B absorbs an unrealistic amount of overhead using a direct labour hour basis. Overhead absorption should be based on the activities which drive the costs, in this case machine hours, the number of production run setups and the number of orders handled for each product.

REVIEW QUESTIONS

1. Explain the concept of ABC.
2. Explain the Kaplan and Cooper's approach to ABC.
3. What are the characteristics of ABC?
4. How to develop an ABC system?
5. Explain the steps to develop an ABC system.
6. How to implement ABC system?
7. What are the benefits from adoption of ABC system?
8. When to use ABC?

22

TARGET COSTING

1. Definition of Target Costing

Target costing is "as a cost management tool for reducing the overall cost of a product over its entire life cycle with the help of the production, engineering, R&D."

The target cost is the estimated cost of a product that enables a company to remain and complete in the market in the long run. Sakurai discusses the most common procedure of target costing as follows:

– To plan and design high quality products that meet customer's needs.

– To set a target cost for the products through the use of value engineering.

– To attain the target cost at the production stage by use of standard costs.

2. Meaning of Target Costing

The idea of target costing, originally promoted in Japan, is about going upstream to achieve cost reduction. Target costing is not really a method of costing. But it is a technique used in cost management. The intent of target costing is to reduction is aimed at the entire life cycle of any product. Target costing can also help in achieving certain broader objectives, such as, identifying and delivering various customer requirements in a product in a product through effective management of different processes.

The target cost is maximum allowable cost at a particular point of time and is specified by reference to the successive stages in a product's life cycle. The important feature of the target costing is that it is used only after the product has reached its established production phase. However, it follows the conventional material, labour and overhead classification.

3. Features

The important feature of target costing is its market orientation i.e. it involves ascertaining of the product cost before hand by working back from an expected future market price. Thus, it includes the following two fundamental steps:

- Keeping track of the external market information which would affect the organization decision making.
- Internal cost planning process that is based on the external market information.

This technique is a powerful tool for reducing cost not only the production stage but also at the planning and design stages of the product life-cycle. Target costing is an approach that is widely used by Japanese companies, and has recently received a considerable amount of attention in the USA and European accounting literature. Target costing is driven by external market factors.

4. Nature of Target Costing

The target costing makes the system to support the cost reduction process not only in the manufacturing phase of the existing product but also the developing and designing phase of an entirely new product. It acts as a motivator of much of the creative and innovative activity in an organization. The following may be construed as the components in the product target costing:

– Type of product
– Technical specification
– Technical requirements
– Customer
– Resource consumption (Acquisition price)
– Resource consumption (Cost)

Another important aspect of the target costing is the concept of design to cost. This concept which originated in 1975. Find its use in the target costing by setting the largest cost at level which can be achieved with the greatest possible efforts from planners and it aims at improving the internal capabilities of an organisation. The approach of design to cost coupled with the market-based target cost provides an excellent basis for cost management.

5. Target Costing Methodology

Target costing forces and organization to '*manage upstream*', during product planning and design stage and provides a frame work of strategic targets to guide to '*managing downstream*', during production and later phases. By employing concurrent engineering analyses of market forces, customer needs, relevant technology, competitors' models, product configuration and performance features, design alternatives, process capabilities, maintenance and services requirements etc. and life cycle costs. Such analyses reveal innovative possibilities in several areas, especially for:

– Reducing cycle times for design, development, manufacturing and service.
– Reducing costs for design, development, manufacturing and service.
– Reducing the number of total parts.
– Reducing the number of unique parts per model.
– Reducing the rate of design, rework and repair.

The end result is a product design that builds in competitive barriers and guarantees a target profit and a target cost against a planned selling price. A new product or a derivative will be approved for productions only after all concerned managers are satisfied that the targets are aggressive enough and can be achieved.

A firm's business plan and product market strategies provide the framework and basic guidelines for applying the target costing methodology. Specific steps involved in target costing may be summarized as follows:

– Determine customer wants precisely.
– Translate them into the desired product performance feature.
– Estimate the proportion of value added by each feature and component.
– Choose a product design assures a targeted profit, and cost targets for each component in total.
– Choose manufacturing designs that assure targeted costs.
– Choose suppliers that assure buying at targeted costs.
– After each cost review, conduct value engineering to reduce target costs.
– Monitor initial production sure that all product performance, cost, profit, targets are met.

Target costing is a method used in product design that involves estimating a target cost for a new product, then designing the product to meet the cost.

Customer requirements:

The first element of target costing understands customer requirements, including the performance and cost characteristics of competitors' products. Target costing can then be applied during the product design phase to create a product that meets the customer's requirements and beats the competition.

Gathering market information

Gathering market information is an important step in the target costing and product development process. The characteristics of selected product available in the market should reflect customer values and expectations about:

– Price
– Quality
– Delivery
– Service
– Technology
– Product Performance

Documenting customer requirements

A structures method for documenting customer requirements and competitor comparisons helps ensure that all relevant market factors and product characteristics are considered during product development. The frame work of documentation should take into consideration the following:

– Product characteristics
– Competitor performance comparisons
– Target performance values
– Customer rating comparisons

The above data is obtained from:

– Customer surveys
– Experience with previous products.
– Market research studies.
– Calculations and Modelling
– Experimentation

Comparing competitors' Products: When developing a competitive comparison, a manufacturer should select two sets of comparisons:

– Competitors that represent a cross section of global market.

– Upcoming competitors not having significant market share.

– The representative products of each competitor chosen should have price and performance parameters similar to those planned for the new product. The data used to make the decision are based on:

– Published performance data and specifications.

– Customer input.

– Comparative test data.

– Information from annual reports trade shows and other external sources of information that may provide insight into plans for new products.

Once selection process is completed, the manufacturer should obtain several samples of each chosen product for performance testing and reverse engineering.

Applying Reverse Engineering: Reverse engineering determines design characteristics and provides information about competitor's materials and processes. The purpose of this information is to help the manufacturer in ascertainment of target cost. Reverse engineering should involve a cross functional team of people from product and process engineering, manufacturing, industrial engineering, procurement and estimating.

- **Cost Structure Analysis:** The target costing makes the target cost development an aspect of ongoing design process. The manufacture should develop estimated of competitor's cost structures by analyzing the internal costs of existing products, categorizing them by cost driver and developing comparative ratios by cost driver to translate internal costs into estimated competitor costs.
- **Best Practices Model:** The model of best practices consider the best design characteristics, best manufacturing process and best economics as factors. The product costs determined through the modeling of best levels of performances are an indication of improvement over the competitors.
- **Competitor Information:** Depending on the level of accuracy required for the target cost, competitor information is available from a variety of sources. The external data sources include;
  - Annual reports
  - Marketing broachers
  - Commercially available information databases
  - Government reports
  - News papers and other industry and commercial publications
- **Product Design:** The target costing is considering the impact of various cost drivers during product design can help a company create a different perspective. This information allows the engineers to factors in many costs saving design process.
- **Value Engineering:** Once a conceptual design is complete, internal cost models can help estimate the cost of the new product. The internal cost models give value engineering team's detailed information about current production costs.
- **JIT Environment:** Target costing provides a frame work for justifying changes in the production environment. It provides a means for identifying benefits that could result from the comprehensive application of JIT.
- **Coordination:** The primary element in the concept of target costing is that of coordination. A target costing project works by bringing together all concerned (functions, units and supply-chain partners to develop a product, with its related cost that can be achieved. The cost must be capable of being kept at the target, and this may mean that the group will continue to work together in an operational sense.

7. Methods of Establishment of Targets Costs

Three basic methods are used for setting target costs:

- First, there is the subtraction method which is based on the price of competitor's product, where the target cost is worked backwards from the market price. The result may represent a very rigorous target, and it may be impossible to achieve.
- The second method of settings up the target costs is the addition method which is based on the existing technology and past cost data of the company. Normally it results achievable targets because it is basically an extension of what has already been happening with in the company. The greatest disadvantage of this method is that it is very inward looking and grossly ignores the market situation.
- The third method is the integrated method, a mixture of the subtraction and addition methods. However, in practice this integrated method involves many difficult problems.

Illustration:

In a period a company has the following transactions:

Purchase of raw materials	(Rs.)	85,000
Conversion	(Rs.)	68,600
Production	(units)	4,900
Sales	(units)	4,850

There were no opening stocks of raw materials, WIP of finished goods. The standard cost per unit is Rs. 31 (Rs. 17 Materials + Rs. 14 Conversion cost). There was no closing WIP at the end of the period.

Show the journal entries for a back-flush accounting system using a Raw material and In Process Account.

Journal entries under back-flush accounting system

Particulars		*Debit*	*Credit*
RIP A/c	Dr.	85,000	
To Creditors			85,000
(Being purchase of raw materials on credit)			
Finished goods Stock A/c	Dr.	1,51,900	
To RIP A/c			83,300
To Conversion Cost Control A/c			68,600
(Being cost of goods produced for 4,900 units)			
Cost of Sales A/c	Dr.	1,50,350	
To Finished Goods Stock A/c			1,50,350
(Being cost of goods sold for 4,850 units)			

At the end of the period there will be two separate stock balances:

RIP Account (85,000 – 83,300) = Rs. 1,700

Finsihed goods (50 @ Rs. 31) = Rs. 1,550

Notes: (a) All the entries shown above are at standard cost.

(b) For simplicity the figures have been chosen so that no variance arise.

REVIEW QUESTIONS

1. Define Target Costing.
2. Discuss the features of Target Costing.
3. Explain the importance of Target Costing.

23

FINAL ACCOUNTS OF COMPANIES

Learning Objectives

After going through this chapter, you should be able to:

— Know the position of each item in the financial accounts and balance sheet

— Prepare the layout of the final accounts and balance sheet

— Learn the process of adjustments

— Know about segment reporting

Introduction

Financial statements of a company are written records that convey the financial performance of the company and its business activities. The three major financial statements are balance sheet, income statement and cash flow statement.

Financial statements for a company are required to comply with the Companies (Accounting Standards) Rules, 2006 (substituted as Division I in the Companies Act, 2013, Schedule III for the heading "General Instructions for Preparation of Balance Sheet and Statements of Profit and Loss of Company").

Financial statements for a company are drawn up in compliance of the Companies (Indian Accounting Standards) Rules, 2015 (inserted as Division II in the Companies Act, 2013, Schedule III, at the end).

Every company to which Indian Accounting Standards apply shall prepare its financial statements in accordance with this Schedule or with such modification as maybe required under certain circumstances.

Where compliance with the requirements of the Act including Indian Accounting Standards except the option of presenting assets and liabilities as provided by the relevant Indian Act as applicable to the companies require any change in treatment or disclosure including addition amendment, substitution or deletion in the head or sub-head or any changes in the financial statements forming part of the same shall be made and the requirements under this Schedule shall stand modified accordingly.

Schedule III of the Companies Act, 2013 sets out the minimum requirements for disclosure on the face of the Financial Statements, i.e. Balance Sheet, Statement of Changes in Equity for the Period, the Statement of Profit and Loss for the Period (The term 'Statement of

Profit and Loss' has the same meaning as 'Profit and Loss Account) and Notes. Cash flow statement shall be prepared, where applicable, in accordance with the requirements of the relevant Indian Accounting Standard.

Line items, sub-line items and sub-totals shall be presented as an addition or substitution on the face of the Financial Statements when such presentation is relevant to an understanding of the company financial position or performance or to cater to industry or sector-specific disclosure requirements or when required for compliance with the amendments to the Companies Act, 2013 or under the Indian Accounting Standards.

Books of Accounts to be Maintained by a Company

Section 128 of the Companies Act, 2013 requires that every company shall prepare and keep at its registered office books of accounts and other relevant books and papers and financial statements for every financial year which give a true and fair view of the state of affairs of the company, including that of its branch office or offices, if any, and explain the transactions effected both at the registered office and its branches and such books will be kept on accrual basis and according to the double entry system of accounting.

All or any of the books of account aforesaid and other relevant papers may be kept at such other place in India as the Board of Directors may decide and where such a decision is taken, the company shall, within seven days thereof, file with the Registrar a notice in writing giving full address of that other place.

The company may keep such books of account or relevant papers in electronic mode in such manner as may be prescribed.

The books of account and other books and papers maintained by the company within India shall be open for inspection at the registered office of the company or at such other place in India by any director during business hours and in the case of financial information, if any, maintained outside the country, copies of such financial information shall be maintained and produced for inspection by any director subject to such conditions as may be prescribed. The officers and other employees of the company shall give to the person making such inspection all assistance in connection with the inspection which the company may reasonably be expected to give.

The books of account of every company relating to a period of not less than eight financial years immediately preceding a financial year, or where the company had been in existence for a period less than eight years, in respect of all the preceding years together with the vouchers relevant to any entry in such books of account shall be kept in good order.

Section 129 of the Companies Act, 2013 requires that the financial statements shall give a true and fair view of the state of affairs of the company or companies, comply with the accounting standards under Section 133 and shall be in the form or forms as may be provided for different class or classes of companies in Schedule III.

At every annual general meeting of a company, the Board of Directors of the company shall lay before such meeting financial statements for the financial year.

Where a company has one or more subsidiaries, it shall in addition to its financial statements, prepare a consolidated financial statements of the company and of all the subsidiaries in the same form manner as that of its own which shall also be laid before the annual general meeting of the company along with the laying of its financial statements.

If a company contravenes the provision of Section 129 of the Companies Act, 2013, the managing director, the whole-time director in charge of finance, the chief Financial Officer or any other person charged by the Board with the duty of complying with the requirements of this Section and in the absence of any of the officers mentioned above, all the directors shall be punishable with imprisonment for a tern, which may extend to one year or with fine which shall not be less than fifty thousand rupees but which may extend to five lakh rupees, or with both.

It is further stated that the books of accounts should be maintained on accrual basis and according to the double entry system of accounting to ensure that these represent true and fair view of the affairs of the company or branch office, as the case may be.

"The Act requires that proper stock records should form a necessary part of proper books of accounts and also that the books of accounts and the relevant vouchers must be preserved for a minimum period of eight years in good order."

Compliance with the Accounting Standards

According to Section 129 of the Companies Act, 2013, the financial statements shall give a true and fair view of the state of affairs of the company or companies, comply with the accounting standards and shall be in the form or forms as may be provided for different class or classes of companies in Schedule III. It is further provided that items contained in such financial statements shall be in accordance with the Indian Accounting Standards. As per Section 133 of the Companies Act, 2013, the Indian Accounting Standards recommended by the Institute of Chartered Accountants of India and prescribed by the Central Government in consultation with National Financial Reporting Authority are mandatory and applicable to all companies.

PART I – BALANCE SHEET

Name of the Company ....

Balance Sheet as at ....

(Rupees in ......)

	Particulars	Note No.	Figures as at the end of current reporting period	Figures as at the end of previous reporting period
	1	2	3	4
	ASSETS			
(1)	**Non-Current Assets**			
	(a) Property, plant and equipment			
	(b) Capital work-in-progress			
	(c) Investment property			
	(d) Goodwill			
	(e) Other intangible assets			
	(f) Intangible assets under development			
	(g) Biological assets other than bearer plants			
	(h) Financial assets:			
	(i) Investments			
	(ii) Trade receivables			
	(iii) Loans			
	(iv) Others (to be specified)			
	(i) Deferred tax assets (net)			
	(j) Other non-current assets			

(2)	**Current Assets:**			
	(a) Inventories			
	(b) Financial assets			
	(i) Investments			
	(ii) Trade receivables			
	(iii) Cash and cash equivalents			
	(iv) Bank balances other than (iii) above			
	(v) Loans			
	(vi) Others (to be specified)			
	(c) Current tax assets (Net)			
	(d) Other current assets			
	Total Assets			
	EQUITY AND LIABILITIES			
	Equity			
	(a) Equity share capital			
	(b) Other equity			
	Liabilities			
(1)	**Non-Current Liabilities**			
	(a) Financial liabilities:			
	(i) Borrowings			
	(ii) Trade payables			
	(iii) Other financial liabilities (other than those specified in item (b), to be specified)			
	(b) Provisions			
	(c) Deferred tax liabilities (Net)			
	(d) Other non-current liabilities			
(2)	**Current Liabilities**			
	(a) Financial Liabilities:			
	(i) Borrowings			
	(ii) Trade payables			
	(iii) Other financial liabilities (other than those specified in item (c)			
	(b) Other current liabilities			
	(c) Provisions			
	(d) Current tax liabilities (Net)			
	Total Equity and Liabilities			

See accompanying notes to the Financial Statements

STATEMENT OF CHANGES IN EQUITY

Name of the Company ………..
Statement of the Changes in Equity for the period ended ……..

(Rupees in ……)

A. Equity Share Capital

Balance at the beginning of the reporting period	Changes in equity share capital during the year	Balance at the end of the reporting period

B. Other Equity

	Share application money pending allotment	Equity component of Compound financial instruments	Reserves and Surplus				Debt instruments through other Comprehensive Income	Equity instruments through other Comprehensive Income	Effective portion of Cash Flow Hedges	Revaluation Surplus	Exchange differences on translating the financial statements of foreign operation	Other items Comprehensive income (specify nature)	Money received against share warrants	Total
			Capital Reserve	Securities Premium Reserve	Other Reserves (specify nature)	Retained Earnings								
Balance at the beginning of the reporting period														
Changes in according policy or prior period errors														
Restated balance at the beginning of the reporting period														
Total comprehensive income of the year														
Dividends														
Transfer to retained earnings														
Any other change (to be specified)														
Balance at the end of the reporting period														

Note: Remeasurement of defined benefit plans and fair value changes relating to own risk of liabilities designated at fair value through profit or loss shall be recognized as a part of retained earnings with separate disclosure of such items along with the relevant amounts in the notes.

Notes:

GENERAL INSTRUCTIONS FOR PREPARATION OF BALANCE SHEET

1. An entity shall classify an asset as current when:
   (a) it expects to realise the asset, or intends to sell or consume it, in its normal Operating cycle;
   (b) it holds the asset primarily for the purpose of trading;
   (c) it expects to realise the asset within twelve months after the reporting period; or
   (d) the asset is cash or a cash equivalent unless the asset is restricted from being exchanged or used to settle a liability for at least twelve months after the reporting period.

   An entity shall classify all other assets as non-current.
2. The operating cycle of an entity is the time between the acquisition of assets for processing and their realisation in cash or cash equivalents, when the entity's normal operating cycle is not clearly identifiable, it is assumed to be twelve months.
3. An entity shall classify a liability as current when:
   (a) It expects to settle the liability in its normal operating cycle;
   (b) It holds the liability primarily for the purpose of trading;
   (c) The liability is due to be settled within twelve months after the reporting period; or
   (d) It does not have an unconditional right to defer settlement of the liability for at least twelve months after the reporting period. Terms of a liability that could, at the option of the counterparty, result in its settlement by the issue of equity instruments do not affect its classification.

   An entity shall classify all other liabilities as non-current.
4. A receivable shall be classified as a 'trade receivable' if it is in respect of the amount due on account of goods sold or services rendered in the normal course of business.
5. A payable shall be classified as a 'trade payable' if it is in respect of the amount due on account of goods purchased or services received in the normal course of business.
6. A company shall disclose the following in the Notes:

A. Non-Current Assets

I. Property, Plant and Equipment:
   (i) Classification shall be given as:
      (a) Land
      (b) Buildings
      (c) Plant and equipment
      (d) Furniture and fixtures
      (e) Vehicles
      (f) Office equipment
      (g) Bearer plants
      (h) Others (specify nature)
   (ii) Assets under lease shall be separately specified under each class of assets.
   (iii) A reconciliation of the gross and net carrying amounts of each class of assets at the beginning and end of the reporting period showing additions, disposals, acquisitions through business

combinations and other adjustments and the related depreciation and impairment losses or reversals shall be disclosed separately.

II. Investment Property:

A reconciliation of the gross and net carrying amounts of each class of property at the beginning and end of the reporting period showing additions, disposals, acquisitions through business combinations and other adjustments and the related depreciation and impairment losses or reversals shall be disclosed separately.

III. Goodwill:

A reconciliation of the gross and net carrying amount of goodwill at the beginning and end of the reporting period showing additions, impairments, disposals and other adjustments,

IV. Other Intangible Assets:

(i) Classification shall be given as:

(a) Brands or trademarks

(b) Computer software

(c) Mastheads and publishing titles

(d) Mining rights

(e) Copyrights, patents, other intellectual property rights, services and operating rights

(f) Recipes, formulae, models, designs and prototypes

(g) Licenses and franchises

(h) Others (specify nature)

(ii) A reconciliation of the gross and net carrying amounts of each class of assets at the beginning and end of the reporting period showing additions, disposals, acquisitions through business combinations and other adjustments and the related amortization and impairment losses or reversals shall be disclosed separately.

V. Biological Assets Other than Bearer Plants:

A reconciliation of the carrying amounts of each class of assets at the beginning and end of the reporting period showing additions, disposals, acquisitions through business combinations and other adjustments shall be disclosed separately.

VI. Investments:

(i) Investments shall be classified as:

(a) Investments in equity instruments;

(b) Investments in preference shares;

(c) Investments in government or trust securities;

(d) Investments in debentures or bonds;

(e) Investments in mutual funds;

(f) Investments in partnership firms; or

(g) Other investments (specify nature).

Under each classification, details shall be given of names of the bodies corporate that are:

(i) Subsidiaries;

(ii) Associates;

(iii) Joint ventures; or

(iv) Structured entities,

in whom investments have been made and the nature and extent of the investment so made in each such body corporate (showing separately investments which are partly-paid). Investments in partnership firms along with names of the firms, their partners, total capital and the shares of each partner shall be disclosed separately.

(ii) The following shall also be disclosed:

(a) Aggregate amount of quoted investments and market value thereof;

(b) Aggregate amount of unquoted investments; and

(c) Aggregate amount of impairment in value of investments;

VII. Trade Receivables:

(i) Trade receivables shall be sub-classified as:

(a) Secured, considered good;

(b) Unsecured considered good; and

(c) Doubtful;

(ii) Allowance for bad and doubtful debts shall be disclosed under the relevant heads separately.

(iii) Debts due by directors or other officers of the company or any of them either severally or jointly with any other person or debts due by firms or private companies respectively in which any director is a partner or a director or a member should be separately stated.

VIII. Loans:

(i) Loans shall be classified as:

(a) Security deposits;

(b) Loans to related parties (giving details thereof); and

(c) Other loans (specify nature).

(ii) The above shall also be separately sub-classified as:

(a) Secured, considered good;

(b) Unsecured, considered good; and

(c) Doubtful.

(iii) Allowance for bad and doubtful loans shall be disclosed under the relevant heads separately.

(iv) Loans due by directors or other officers of the company or any of them either severally or jointly with any other persons or amounts due by firms or private companies respectively in which any director is a partner or a director or a member should be separately stated.

IX. Bank deposits with more than 12 months maturity shall be disclosed under 'other financial assets';

X. Other non-current assets: Other non-current assets shall be classified as:

(i) Capital Advances; and

(ii) Advances other than capital advances;

(1) Advances other than capital advances shall be classified as:

(a) Security Deposits;

(b) Advances to related parties (giving details thereof; and

(c) Other advances (specify nature).

(2) Advances to directors or other officers of the company or any of them either severally or jointly with any other persons or advances to firms or private companies respectively in which any director is a partner or a director or a member should be separately stated. In case advances are of the nature of a financial asset as per relevant Ind AS, these are to be disclosed under 'other financial assets' separately.

(iii) Others (specify nature).

B. Current Assets

I. Inventories:

(i) Inventories shall be classified as:

(a) Raw materials;

(b) Work- in-progress;

(c) Finished goods;

(d) Stock-in-trade (in respect of goods acquired for trading);

(e) stores and spares ;

(f) Loose tools; and

(g) Others (specify nature).

(ii) Goods-in-transit shall be disclosed under the relevant sub-head of inventories.

(iii) Mode of valuation shall be stated.

II. Investments:

1. Investments shall be classified as:

(a) Investments in equity instruments;

(b) Investment in preference shares;

(c) Investments in government or trust securities;

(d) Investments in debentures or bonds;

(e) Investments in mutual funds;

(f) Investments in partnership firms; and

(g) Other investments (specify nature).

Under each classification, details shall be given of names of the bodies corporate that are:

(i) Subsidiaries;

(ii) Associates;

(iii) Joint ventures; or

(iv) Structured entities,

in whom investments have been made and the nature and extent of the investment so made in each such body corporate (showing separately investments which are partly-paid).

2. The following shall also be disclosed:

(a) Aggregate amount of quoted investments and market value thereof;

(b) Aggregate amount of unquoted investments;

(c) Aggregate amount of impairment in value of investments.

III. Trade Receivables:

(i) Trade receivables shall be sub-classified as:

(a) Secured, considered good;

(b) Unsecured, considered good; and

(c) Doubtful.

(ii) Allowance for bad and doubtful debts shall be disclosed under the relevant heads separately,

(iii) Debts due by directors or other officers of the company or any of them either severally or jointly with any other person or debts due by firms or Private companies respectively in which any director is a partner or a director or a member should be separately stated.

IV. Cash and cash equivalents: Cash and cash equivalents shall be classified as:
- (a) Balances with Banks (of the nature of cash and cash equivalents);
- (b) Cheques, drafts on hand;
- (c) Cash on hand; and
- (d) Others (specify nature).

V. Loans:
- (i) Loans shall be classified as:
  - (a) Security deposits;
  - (b) Loans to related parties (giving details thereof); and
  - (c) Others (specify nature).
- (ii) The above shall also be sub-classified as:
  - (a) Secured, considered good;
  - (b) Unsecured, considered good; and
  - (c) Doubtful.
- (iii) Allowance for bad and doubtful loans shall be disclosed under the relevant heads separately.
- (iv) Loans due by directors or other officers of the company or any of them either severally or jointly with any other person or amounts due by firms or private companies respectively in which any director is a partner or a director or a member shall be separately stated.

VI. Other current assets (specify nature). This is an all-inclusive heading, which incorporates current assets that do not fit into any other asset categories. Other current assets shall be classified as-
- (i) Advances other than capital advances
  - (1) Advances other than capital advances shall be classified as:
    - (a) Security Deposits;
    - (b) Advances to related parties (giving details thereof);
    - (c) Other advances (specify nature).
  - 2. Advances to directors or other officers of the company or any of them either severally or jointly with any other persons or advances to firms or private companies respectively in which any director is a partner or a director or a member should be separately stated.
- (ii) Others (specify nature)

C. Cash and Bank Balances

The following disclosures with regard to cash and bank balances shall be made:
- (a) Earmarked balances with banks (for example for unpaid dividend) shall be separately stated.
- (b) Balances with banks to the extent held as margin money or security against the borrowings, guarantees, other commitments shall be disclosed separately.
- (c) Repatriation restrictions, if any, in respect of cash and bank balances shall be separately stated.

D. Equity

I. Equity Share Capital: For each class of equity share capital:
- (a) the number and amount of shares authorised;
- (b) the number of shares issued, subscribed and fully paid, and subscribed but not fully paid;
- (c) par value per share;

(d) a reconciliation of the number of shares outstanding at the beginning and at the end of the period;

(e) the rights, preferences and restrictions attaching to each class of shares including restrictions on the distribution of dividends and the repayment of capital;

(f) shares in respect of each class in the company held by its holding company or its ultimate holding company including shares held by subsidiaries or associates of the holding company or the ultimate holding company in aggregate;

(g) shares of the company held by each shareholder holding more than five per cent. Shares specifying the number of shares held;

(h) shares reserved for issue under options and contracts or commitments for the sale of shares or disinvestment, including the terms and amounts;

(i) for the period of five years immediately preceding the date at which the Balance Sheet is prepared.

- aggregate number and class of shares allotted as fully paid up pursuant to contract without payment being received in cash;
- aggregate number and class of shares allotted as fully paid up by way of bonus shares; and
- aggregate number and class of shares bought back;

(j) terms of any securities convertible into equity shares issued along with the earliest date of conversion in descending order starting from the farthest such date;

(k) calls unpaid (showing aggregate value of calls unpaid by directors and officers);

(l) forfeited shares (amount originally paid up).

II. Other Equity:

(i) 'Other Reserves' shall be classified in the notes as:

(a) Capital Redemption Reserve;

(b) Debenture Redemption Reserve;

(c) Share Options Outstanding Account; and

(d) Others–(specify in the nature and purpose of each reserve and the amount in respect thereof);

(Additions and deductions since last balance sheet to be shown under each of the specified heads);

(ii) Retained Earnings represents surplus i.e balance of the relevant column in the Statement of Changes in Equity;

(iii) A reserve specifically represented by earmarked investments shall disclose the fact that it is so represented;

(iv) Debit balance of Statement of Profit and Loss shall be shown as a negative figure under the head 'retained earnings'. Similarly, the balance of 'Other Equity', after adjusting negative balance of retained earnings, if any, shall be shown under the head 'Other Equity' even if the resulting figure is in the negative; and

(v) Under the sub-head' Other Equity', disclosure shall be made for the nature and amount of each item.

E. Non-Current Liabilities

I. Borrowings:

(i) Borrowings shall be classified as:

(a) Bonds or debentures

(b) Term loans

(I) from banks

(II) from other Parties

(c) Deferred payment liabilities

(d) Deposits

(e) Loans from related Parties

(f) Long term maturities of finance lease obligations

(g) Liability component of compound financial instruments

(h) Other loans (specify/nature);

(ii) borrowings shall further be sub-classified as secured and unsecured. Nature of security shall be specified separately in each case.

(iii) where loans have been guaranteed by directors or others, the aggregate amount of such loans under each head shall be disclosed;

(iv) bonds or debentures (along with the rate of interest, and particulars of redemption or conversion, as the case may be) shall be stated in descending order of maturity or conversion, stating from farthest redemption or conversion date, as the case may be, where bonds/debentures are redeemable by installments, the date of maturity for this purpose must be reckoned as the date on which the first installment becomes due;

(v) particulars of any redeemed bonds or debentures which the company has power to reissue shall be disclosed;

(vi) terms of repayment of term loans and other loans shall be stated; and

(vii) period and amount of default as on the balance sheet date in repayment of borrowings and interest shall be specified separately in each case

II. Provisions: The amounts shall be classified as:

(a) Provision for employee benefits; and

(b) Others (specify nature).

III. Other non-current liabilities:

(a) Advances; and

(b) Others (specify nature).

F. Current Liabilities

I. Borrowings:

(i) Borrowings shall be classified as:

(a) Loans repayable on demand

(I) from banks

(II) from other parties

(b) Loans from related parties

(c) Deposits

(d) Other loans (specify nature);

(ii) borrowings shall further be sub-classified as secured and unsecured. Nature of security shall be specified separately in each case

(iii) where loans have been guaranteed by directors or others, the aggregate amount of such loans under each head shall be disclosed

(iv) Period and amount of default as on the balance sheet date in repayment of borrowings and interest, shall be specified separately in each case.

II. Other Financial Liabilities: Other Financial liabilities shall be classified as:

(a) Current maturities of long-term debt;

(b) Current maturities of finance lease obligations;

(c) Interest accrued;

(d) Unpaid dividends;

(e) Application money received for allotment of securities to the extent refundable and interest accrued thereon;

(f) Unpaid matured deposits and interest accrued thereon;

(g) Unpaid matured debentures and interest accrued thereon; and

(h) Others (specify nature).

'Long term debt' is a borrowing having a period of more than twelve months at the time of origination.

III. Other current liabilities:

The amounts shall be classified as:

(a) Revenue received in advance;

(b) other advances (specify nature); and

(c) others (specify nature);

IV. Provisions: The amounts shall be classified as:

(a) Provision for employee benefits; and

(b) Others (specify nature).

G. The presentation of liabilities associated with group of assets classified as held for sale and non-current assets classified as held for sale shall be in accordance with the relevant Indian Accounting Standards (Ind AS).

H. Contingent Liabilities and Commitments:

(to the extent not provided for)

(i) Contingent Liabilities shall be classified as:

(a) claims against the company not acknowledged as debt;

(b) guarantees\excluding financial guarantees; and

(c) Other money for which the company is contingently liable.

(ii) Commitments shall be classified as:

(a) estimated amount of contracts remaining to be executed on capital account and not provided for;

(b) uncalled liability on shares and other investments partly paid; and

(c) Other commitments (specify nature).

I. The amount of dividends proposed to be distributed to equity and preference shareholders for the period and the related amount per share shall be disclosed separately. Arrears of fixed cumulative dividends on irredeemable preference shares shall also be disclosed separately.

J. Where in respect of an issue of securities made for a specific purpose the whole or part of amount has not been used for the specific purpose at the Balance sheet date, there shall be indicated by way of note how such unutilized amounts have been used or invested.

7. When a company applies an accounting policy retrospectively or makes a restatement of items in the financial statements or when it reclassifies items in its financial statements, the company shall attach to the Balance Sheet, a "Balance Sheet" as at the beginning of the earliest comparative period presented.
8. Share application money pending allotment shall be classified into equity or liability in accordance with relevant Indian Accounting Standards. Share application money to the extent not refundable shall be shown under the head Equity and share application money to the extent refundable shall be separately shown under 'Other financial liabilities'.
9. Preference shares including premium received on issue, shall be classified and presented as 'Equity' or 'Liability' in accordance with the requirements of the relevant Indian Accounting Standards. Accordingly, the disclosure and presentation requirements in this regard applicable to the relevant class of equity or liability shall be applicable mutatis mutandis to the preference shares. For instance, redeemable preference shares shall be classified and presented under 'non-current liabilities' as 'borrowings' and the disclosure requirements in this regard applicable to such borrowings shall be applicable mutatis mutandis to redeemable preference shares.
10. Compound financial instruments such as convertible debentures, where split into equity and liability components, as per the requirements of the relevant Indian Accounting Standards, shall be classified and presented under the relevant heads in 'Equity' and 'Liabilities'
11. Regulatory Deferral Account Balances shall be presented in the Balance Sheet in accordance with the relevant Indian Accounting Standards.

PART II – STATEMENT OF PROFIT AND LOSS

Name of the Company ....

Statement of Profit and Loss for the period ended ...... (Rupees in .....)

	Particulars	Note No.	Figures for the current reporting period	Figures for the previous reporting period
I	Revenue from operations			
II	Other income			
III	Total income (I + II)			
IV	**EXPENSES**			
	Cost of materials consumed			
	Purchases of stock-in-trade			
	Changes in inventories of finished goods, stock-in-trade and work-in-progress			
	Employee benefits expense			
	Finance costs			
	Depreciation and amortization expense			

	Other expenses Total expenses (IV)					
V	Profit (loss) before exceptional items and tax (I – IV)					
VI	Exceptional Items					
VII	Profit/Loss before tax (V – VI)					
VIII	Tax expense: (1) Current tax (2) Deferred tax					
IX	Profit (loss) for the period from continuing operations (VII – VIII)					
X	Profit (loss) from discontinued operations					
XI	Tax expense of discontinued operations					
XII	Profit/(loss) from discontinued operations (after tax) (X – XI)					
XIII	Profit/(loss) for the period (IX + XII)					
XIV	Other comprehensive expense: **A:** (i) Items that will not be reclassified to profit or loss (ii) Income tax relating to items that will not be reclassified to profit or loss **B:** (i) Items that will be reclassified to profit or loss (ii) Income tax relating to items that will be reclassified to profit or loss					
XV	Total comprehensive income for the period (XIII + XIV) (comprising profit (loss) and other Comprehensive for the period)					
XVI	Earnings per equity share (for continuing operation): (1) Basic (2) Diluted					
XVII	Earnings per equity share (for discontinued operation): (1) Basic (2) Diluted					
XVIII	Earnings for Equity Share (for discontinued and continuing operations) (1) Basic (2) Diluted					

see accompanying notes to the Financial Statements

Notes:

GENERAL INSTRUCTIONS FOR THE PREPARATION OF STATEMENT OF PROFIT AND LOSS

1. The provisions of this Part shall apply to the income and expenditure account, in like manner as they apply to a Statement of Profit and Loss,
2. The Statement of Profit and Loss shall include:
   (i) Profit of loss for the period;
   (ii) Other comprehensive income for the period.
   The sum of (1) and (2) above is 'Total Comprehensive Income'.
3. Revenue from operations shall disclose separately in the notes
   (a) sale of products (including excise duty).
   (b) sale of services. and
   (c) other operating revenues.
4. Finance Costs: Finance costs shall be classified as:
   (a) Interest;
   (b) Dividend on redeemable preference shares;
   (c) Exchange differences regarded as an adjustment to borrowing costs; and
   (d) other borrowing costs (specify nature).
5. Other income: other income shall be classified as:
   (a) Interest income;
   (b) Dividend income; and
   (c) Other non-operating income (net of expenses directly attributable to such income).
6. Other Comprehensive Income shall be classified into:
   (A) Items that will not be reclassified to profit or loss
      (i) Changes in revaluation surplus;
      (ii) Remuneration of the defined benefit plans;
      (iii) Equity Instruments through Other Comprehensive Income;
      (iv) Fair value changes relating to own credit risk of financial liabilities designated at fair value through profit or loss
      (v) Share of Other Comprehensive Income in Associates and joint Ventures, to the extent not to be classified into profit or loss and
      (vi) Others (specify nature).
   (B) Items that will be reclassified to profit or loss
      (i) Exchange differences in translating the financial statements of a foreign operation;
      (ii) Debt instruments through Other Comprehensive Income;
      (iii) The effective portion of gains and loss on hedging instruments in a cash flow hedge;
      (iv) share of other comprehensive income in Associates and joint ventures, to the extent to be classified into profit or loss; and
      (v) Others (specify nature).

7. Additional Information: A Company shall disclose by way of notes, additional information regarding aggregate expenditure and income on the following items:
   (a) Employee benefits expense showing separately (i) salaries and wages, (ii) contribution to provident and other funds, (iii) share based payments to employees, (iv) staff welfare expenses.
   (b) Depreciation and amortization expense;
   (c) Any item of income or expenditure which exceeds one per cent of the revenue from operations or Rs.10,00,000, whichever is higher, in addition to the consideration of 'materiality' as specified in clause 7 of the General Instructions for Preparation of Financial Statements of a Company;
   (d) Interest Income;
   (e) Interest Expense;
   (f) Dividend income;
   (g) Net gain or loss on sale of investments;
   (h) Net gain or loss on foreign currency transaction and translation (other than considered as finance cost);
   (i) payments to the auditor as (a) auditor, (b) for taxation matters, (c) for company law matters, (d) for other services, (e) for reimbursement of expenses;
   (j) in case of companies covered under section 135, amount of expenditure incurred on corporate social responsibility activities; and
   (k) details of items of exceptional nature;
8. Changes in Regulatory Deferral Account Balances shall be presented in the Statement of Profit and Loss in accordance with the relevant Indian Accounting Standards

PART III – GENERAL INSTRUCTIONS FOR THE PREPARATION OF CONSOLIDATED FINANCIAL STATEMENTS

1. Where a company is required to prepare Consolidated Financial Statements, i.e., consolidated balance sheet, consolidated statement of changes in equity and consolidated statement of profit and loss, the company shall mutatis mutandis follow the requirements of this Schedule as applicable to a company in the preparation of balance sheet, statement of changes in equity and statement of profit and loss in addition, the consolidated financial statements shall disclose the information as per the requirements specified in the applicable Indian Accounting Standards notified under the Companies (Indian Accounting Standards) Rules 2015, including the following, namely:
   (i) Profit or loss attributable to 'non-controlling interest' and to 'owners of the parent' in the statement of profit and loss shall be presented as allocation for the period. Further, 'total comprehensive income' for the period attributable to 'non-controlling interest' and to 'owners of the parent' shall be presented in the statement of profit and loss as allocation for the period. The aforesaid disclosures for 'total comprehensive income' shall also be made in the statement of changes in equity. In addition to the disclosure requirements in the Indian Accounting Standards, the aforesaid disclosures shall also be made in respect of 'other comprehensive Income'.
   (ii) 'Non-controlling interests' in the Balance Sheet and in the Statement of Changes in Equity, within equity, shall be presented separately from the equity of the 'owners of the parent'.
   (iii) Investments accounted for using the equity method.

2. In consolidated financial statements, the following shall be disclosed by way of additional information:

Name of the entity in the Group	Net Assets, i.e., total Assets minus total Liabilities		Share in Profit or Loss		Share in other comprehensive income		Share in total comprehensive income	
	As % of consolidated net assets	Amount	As % of consolidated profit or loss	Amount	As % of consolidated other comprehensive income	Amount	As % of total comprehensive income	Amount
Parent								
Subsidiaries								
Indian								
1.								
2.								
3.								
Subsidiaries								
Foreign								
1.								
2.								
3.								
Non-controlling interest in all Subsidiaries								
Associates (investment as per the equity method)								
Indian								
1.								
2.								
3.								
Foreign								
1.								
2.								
3.								
Joint Ventures (investment as per equity method)								
Indian								
1.								
2.								
3.								
Foreign								
1.								
2.								
3.								
Total								

3. All Subsidiaries, associates and joint ventures (whether Indian or foreign) will be covered under consolidated financial statements.
4. An entity shall disclose the list of Subsidiaries or associates or joint ventures which have not been consolidated in the consolidated financial statements along with the reasons of not consolidating.

Dividends

Shareholders expect some return for the money invested by them in the company. They get the return on their investment in the form of dividends given to them from time to time. Thus, dividends are the profits of the company distributed amongst the shareholders. The company may declare dividends in general meeting, but no dividend shall exceed the amount recommended by the Board of Directors. Thus, shareholders in annual general meeting can only reduce the amount of dividends but cannot increase the amount of dividends recommended by the Board of Directors. It is so because directors are familiar with the financial affairs of the company and as şuch are considered as the experts to decide the amount to be distributed as dividend among shareholders. The directors may not recommended dividend even if there are profits if they link that distribution of dividend will impair the financial position of the company.

Sources of Declaring Dividend

As per Section 205 of the Companies Act, 1956 dividend may be declared out of the following three sources:

(i) **Out of Current Profits.** Dividend may be declared out of the profits of the company for the current year after providing depreciation. The company must transfer the prescribed percentage of its profits to general reserve before declaring dividends. This percentage depends on the percentage of dividend declared.

(ii) **Out of past reserves.** Dividend may be declared out of the profits of the company for any previous financial year or years arrived at after providing for depreciation in accordance with the provisions of section 205 of the Company Act, 1956 and remaining undistributed. Section 205A (3) of the Act, requires that dividend can be declared out of the reserves only in accordance with the rules framed by the Central Government in this behalf.

(iii) **Out of money provided by the Government.** A company can also declare dividend out of the moneys provided by the Central Government for payment of such dividend in pursuance of guarantee given by the Government.

Types of Dividend

Dividends may be of the following two types:

1. Interim Dividend. 2. Final Dividend.

1. **Interim Dividend.** This dividend is declared between two annual general meetings. As per regulation 86 of Table A, the Board may from time to time pay to the shareholders such interim dividends as appear to it to be justified keeping in view the profits of the company. The articles of association may allow for the payment of such a dividend if Table A has not been adopted by a company.
2. **Final Dividend.** It is a dividend which is declared at the annual general meeting of the shareholders and is declared by the shareholders only on the recommendation of the directors. The dividend proposed by the directors is provided for in the final accounts of the company and is paid only after it has been passed at the annual general meetings of the shareholders.

Corporate Dividend Tax: As per the Finance Act, 1997 dividends paid or declared are subject to corporate dividend tax @ 10% with effect from 1st June, 1997. Such corporate dividend tax is deducted from Surplus sub-head in the Balance Sheet and it is also shown under the heading

'Short-term Provisions' as a current liability till it is paid. But as per recent Finance Act, the rate of this tax is 15% plus 10% surcharge and cess of 2% thereon. Total corporate dividend tax including surcharge and cess may be taken as 17% approximately.

Accounting Entries Relating to Dividend

(1) When the dividend is proposed by the directors:

Surplus Account Dr.

To Proposed Dividend Account

(Being dividend proposed by the directors)

(2) When the dividend recommended by the directors is passed by the shareholders at the annual general meeting:

Proposed Dividend Account Dr.

To Dividend Account

To Income Tax Account

(Being dividend proposed by the directors passed at the annual general meetings of shareholders apportioned between net amount payable to shareholders as dividend and income-tax on dividend deductible at source)

(3) On opening a separate Bank Account for the payment of dividend:

Dividend Banking Account Dr.

To Bank Account

(Being amount payable to the shareholders as dividend transferred from the General Bank Account to Dividend Banking Account)

(4) On payment of Dividends—

Dividend Account Dr.

To Dividend Banking Account

(5) When the amount of unpaid dividend is transferred to Unpaid Dividend Account declaration of the dividend:

Unpaid Dividend Account (with Bank) Dr.

To Dividend Banking Account

(Being unpaid dividend transferred from Dividend Banking Account to Unpaid Dividend Account opened with a schedule bank as per provisions of the law)

(6) If the unpaid dividend is not claimed by the shareholders within 3years

Dividend Account Dr.

To Unpaid Dividend Account

(Being amount of unpaid dividend not claimed for a period of three years withdrawn from Unpaid Dividend Account and deposited in General Revenue Account of the Central Government liability of unpaid dividend discharged by depositing the amount in General Revenue Account. After a period of 3 years, shareholders can claim dividend from the Central Government so dividend unpaid is no more a liability of the company).

Capital Profits: Capital profits are not earned during the normal course of the business and arise in the following special circumstances:

(a) Excess of sale proceeds over the cost of the fixed assets.

(b) Profit on sale of the under taking or part of it.

(c) Profits on purchase of business, such profit arises when the value of assets taken over minus the liabilities taken over is more than the amount paid for the purchase of the business.

(d) Profit on revaluation of fixed assets and liabilities.

(e) Profit prior to incorporation.
(f) Premium received on issue of shares or debentures.
(g) Balance left in Forfeited Shares Account after the reissue of forfeited shares.
(h) Profit made on redemption of debentures.
(i) Profit set aside for redemption of preference shares.

Provision for Taxation

A company is liable to pay income-tax or tax on profits under the Income-tax Act, 1961 and such tax is treated as a charge against the profits of the accounting year, although the profits are assessed and actual liability for tax is determined in the following year. Moreover, the assessable profits (taxable profits) are seldom the same as accounting profits. As such it is not possible to determine the actual amount of tax payable at the time the final accounts are prepared. Therefore, liability for tax is estimated and provided for while preparing the final accounts. Such provision is a charge against profit and loss statement and credited to provision for taxation account.

While making the estimate of provision for taxation, due consideration should be given to the following points:

(i) Whether the net profit has been determined after deducting depreciation according to Income–Tax Act and managerial remuneration.
(ii) Whether income-tax has been computed at the rates prescribed.
(iii) Whether profit sur-tax is payable or not.
(iv) Whether capital gains tax is payable or not.
(v) Whether penalty is payable under any tax laws.
(vi) Whether rebate are available for double taxation.
(vii) Whether investment allowance, extra shift allowance, etc., if any, have been duly deducted or not in estimating the tax liability.
(viii) Whether adjustment has made for the last year's actual tax liability or not.

MANAGERIAL REMUNERATION

The Companies Act lays down restrictions on the remuneration to be paid to directors, manager, and managing director. Under Section 197 of the Companies Act, the total remuneration payable by a public company to directors, manager and managing director in any financial year should not exceed 11% of the net profits of the company for that financial year computed in the manner laid down in Sections 198 of the Companies Act, 2013. For the purpose of Section 198 and other related Sections, however, remuneration shall include:

(a) any expenditure incurred buy the company in providing any rent-free accommodation, or any other benefits or amenity in respect of accommodation free of charge, to any of the managerial personnel;
(b) any expenditure incurred buy the company in providing any other benefit or amenity free of charge or at concessional rate to them:
(c) any expenditure incurred buy the company in respect of any obligation or service which but for such expenditure by the company would have been incurred by any of the managerial personnel; and
(d) any expenditure incurred buy the company to effect any insurance on the life of, or to provide any pension, annuity, or gratuity for any of the managerial personnel, or his spouse or child.

It shall, however, exclude any fee payable to the directors for attending the meeting of the Board or a committee thereof.

Remuneration in Case of Nil or Inadequate Profits

Notwithstanding anything contained in this Part, where any financial year during the currency of tenure of the managerial person, a company has no profits or its profits are inadequate, it may pay remuneration to a managerial person by way of salary, dearness allowance, perquisites and any other allowance as per Part II of Schedule III as given below:

Where the effective capital of Company is	Yearly remuneration payable shall not exceed (Rupees)
(i) Negative or less than rupees 5 crores	30 lakhs
(ii) 5 crores and above but less than rupees 100 crores	42 lakhs
(iii) 100 crores and above but less than rupees 250 crores	60 lakhs
(iv) rupees 250 crores and above	60 lakhs plus 0.01% of the effective capital in excess of Rs. 250 crores

Provide that the above limits shall be doubled if the resolution passed by the shareholders is a special resolution.

For a period less than one year the limit shall be prorated.

Provided that the ceiling limits specified under this sub-paragraph shall apply, if:

I. payment of remuneration is approved by a resolution passed by the Remuneration Committee;
II. the company has not made any default in repayment of any of its debts (including public deposits) or debentures or interest payable thereon for a continuous period of thirty days in the preceding financial year before the date of appointment of such managerial personnel;
III. a special resolution has been passed at the general meeting of the company for payment of remuneration for a period not exceeding three years;
IV. a statement along with a notice calling the general meeting referred to in clause (iii) is given to the shareholders.

SIMPLE PROBLEMS ON COMPANY BALANCE SHEET AS PER REVISED SCHEDULE III

***Illustration* 1**

From the following is the trial balance of ABC Ltd., prepare the Balance Sheet of the company as on 31st March 2016 as per Schedule III of the Companies Act.

Trial Balance as on 31st March 2016

Particulars	Dr. (Rs.)	Particulars	Cr. (Rs.)
Advances to employees	3,00,000	Equity share capital	52,00,000
Cash at bank	3,14,320	Capital reserve	60,000
Furniture and fixture	7,50,000	Loan from SBI	8,00,000
Premises	41,09,940	Provision for Employees Welfare Fund	6,00,000
Patents	10,00,000	Proposed dividend	1,64,000
Discount on issue of shares (unwritten off)	25,000	Short term loan from bank	4,90,200
		Unpaid dividend	64,800
Trade receivables	3,66,240	Profit and Loss A/c	42,980

Advance tax	50,000	Bills payable	85,100
8% Govt. bonds	3,36,000	Sundry creditors	1,00,020
Stock in trade	3,55,600		
	76,07,100		76,07,100

Balance Sheet of ABC Ltd as on 31st March 2016

Particulars	Note No.	Amount (Rs.)
ASSETS		
1. Non-Current Assets:		
(a) Property plant and equipment	1	48,59,940
(b) Other intangible assets		10,00,000
(c) Other non-current assets		25,000
2. Current Assets:		
(a) Inventories		3,55,600
(b) Financial assets:		
(i) Current investments		3,36,000
(ii) Trade receivables		3,66,240
(iii) Cash and cash equivalents		3,14,320
(iv) Short-term loans and advances		3,00,000
(c) Other current assets		50,000
Total Assets		**76,07,100**
EQUITY AND LIABILITIES		
Equity		
(a) Equity share capital		52,000
(b) Other equity	2	6,00,000
Liabilities		
1. Non-Current Liabilities		
(a) Financial liabilities:		
(i) Long term borrowings		8,00,000
(ii) Other financial liabilities		6,00,000
2. Current Liabilities		
(a) Financial liabilities:		
(i) Short term borrowings		4,90,000
(ii) Trade payables	3	1,85,000
(iii) Other financial liabilities		64,800
(b) Short term provisions		1,64,000
Total Equity and Liabilities		**76,07,100**

Solution:

Notes to the Financial Statement:

1. Property Plant and Equipment

Premises	41,09,940
Furniture and fixture	7,50,000
Total	**48,59,940**

2. Other Equity

Capital reserve	60,000
Profit and Loss A/c (Cr. Bal.)	42,980
Total	**1,02,980**

3. Trade Payables

Sundry creditors	1,00,020
Bills payable	85,100
Total	**1,85,120**

***Illustration* 2**

From the following Ledger balances of Ramky Ltd., prepare the Balance Sheet of the company as on 31st March 2016 as per Schedule III of the Companies Act.

Particulars	Rs.	Particulars	Rs.
Plant and machinery	6,00,000	Immovable property	10,00,000
8% Debenture	8,00,000	Public deposit	5,00,000
Employee's provident fund	1,30,000	Provision for taxation	1,80,000
Securities premium	80,000	Drafts on hand	5,00,000
Cash at bank	34,000	Bills receivable	2,40,000
24000 fully paid Equity shares of Rs.100 each Rs. 50 called up	12,00,000	Brokerage on issue of shares	1,10,000
		Bank overdraft	1,50,000
Sundry creditors	1,16,000	Security deposit	1,24,000
Loan to manager	70,000	Trade marks	1,80,000
Deposits with ICICI Bank (5 years)	1,98,000		
Prepaid insurance	1,00,000		

Solution:

Balance Sheet of RAMKY Ltd. as on 31st March 2016

Particulars	Note No.	Amount (Rs.)
ASSETS		
1. Non-Current Assets:		
(a) Property plant and equipment	1	16,00,000
(b) Intangible assets		1,80,000
(c) Financial Assets		
(i) Investments		1,98,000
(ii) Long term loans and advances		1,24,000
(d) Other non-current assets		1,10,000

2. Current Assets:		
(a) Financial Assets:		
(i) Trade receivables		2,40,000
(ii) Cash and cash equivalents	2	5,34,000
(iii) Short-term loans and advances		70,000
(b) Other current assets		1,00,000
Total Assets		**31,56,000**
EQUITY AND LIABILITIES		
Equity		
(a) Equity share capital	3	12,00,000
(b) Other equity		80,000
Liabilities		
1. Non-Current Liabilities		
(a) Financial liabilities:		
(i) Long term borrowings	4	13,00,000
(b) Long term provisions		1,30,000
2. Current Liabilities		
(a) Financial liabilities:		
(i) Short term borrowings		1,50,000
(ii) Trade payables		1,16,000
(b) Short term provisions		1,18,000
Total Equity and Liabilities		**31,56,000**

Notes to the Financial Statement

1. Property Plant and Equipment

Plant and machinery	6,00,000
Immovable property	10,00,000
Total	**16,00,000**

2. Cash and Cash Equivalent

Cash in hand	34,000
Drafts on hand	5,00,000
Total	**5,34,000**

3. Equity

Authorised Capital (24,000 Equity shares of Rs. 100 each)	24,00,000
Issued and Subscribed Capital (24,000 Equity shares of Rs. 100 each)	24,00,000
Called up and Paid up capital (24,000 Equity shares of Rs. 80 each)	12,00,000
Total	**12,00,000**

4. Long Term Borrowings

8% Debentures	8,00,000
Public deposits	5,00,000
Total	**13,00,000**

***Illustration* 3**

From the following ledger balances of XY Ltd as on 31st March 2017, you are required to prepare the Balance Sheet as on 31st March 2017 as per Revised schedule III of the Indian Companies Act.

Particulars	Rs.	Particulars	Rs.
Office equipment	4,80,600	General reserve	4,15,000
9% Debentures in APCO Ltd,	2,45,000	Creditors for goods	1,68,500
Loose tools	1,63,000	Creditors for expenses	36,000
Plant and machinery	18,00,000	Cash credit	75,000
Computer software	83,250	Mortgage loan	3,10,000
Debtors for goods	1,90,000	8% Preference share capital	5,50,000
Advertisement	30,000	Equity sharecapital (unwritten off)	15,00,000
Stores and spares	1,00,200	Staff welfare fund	85,000
Interest accrued on investment	51,000	Provision for taxation	26,550
Cash at bank	23,000		

Solution:

Balance Sheet of XY Limited as on 31st March 2017

Particulars	Note No.	Amount (Rs.)
ASSETS		
1. Non-Current Assets:		
(a) Property, plant and equipment	1	22,80,000
(b) Intangible assets		83,250
(c) Other non-current assets		30,000
2. Current Assets:		
(a) Financial Assets:		
(i) Current investments		2,45,000
(ii) Trade receivables		1,90,000
(iii) Cash and cash equivalents		23,000
(b) Inventories	2	2,63,200
(c) Other current assets		51,000
Total Assets		**31,66,050**
EQUITY AND LIABILITIES		
Equity		
(a) Equity share capital		15,00,000
(b) Other equity		9,65,000
Liabilities		
1. Non-Current Liabilities		
(a) Financial Liabilities:		
(i) Long term borrowings		3,10,000
(b) Long term provisions		85,000
2. Current Liabilities		
(a) Financial Liabilities:		
(i) Short term borrowings		75,000
(ii) Trade payables	3	20,45,000
(b) Short term provisions		26,550
Total Equity and Liabilities		**31,66,050**

Notes to the Financial Statement:

1. Property, plant and equipment

Office equipment	4,80,600
Plant and machinery	18,00,000
Total	**22,80,600**

2. Inventories

Loose tools	1,63,000
Stores and spares	1,00,200
Total	**2,63,200**

3. Trade payables

Creditors for goods	1,68,500
Creditors for expenses	36,000
Total	**2,04,500**

***Illustration* 4**

Prepare Balance sheet of Boat Ltd., in the prescribed pro forma as on 31st March 2016 from the following Trial balance

Trial Balance as on 31st March 2016

Particulars	Rs.	Particulars	Rs.
Leasehold property	16,00,000	Share capital	20,65,000
Bank balance	1,05,000	Staff provident fund	8,00,000
Plant and machinery	9,00,000	Capita redemption reserve	2,20,000
Goodwill	3,00,000	General reserve	1,90,000
Investment in a subsidiary Co.	11,50,000	Deposits from public	9,00,000
P & L A/c	70,000	Accounts payable	2,10,000
Stock of finished goods	1,20,000	Short term loan from SBI	1,78,000
Accounts receivable	2,40,000	Unclaimed dividend	6,000
Preliminary expenses	39,000		
Underwriting commission	45,000		
	45,69,000		**45,69,000**

Solution:

Balance Sheet of Boat Ltd as on 31st March 2016

Particulars	Note No.	Amount (Rs.)
ASSETS		
1. Non-Current Assets:		
(a) Property, plant and equipment	1	25,00,000
(b) Intangible assets		3,00,000

(c) Financial Assets:		
(i) Non-current investments		11,50,000
(d) Other non-current assets	2	84,000
2. Current Assets:		
(a) Inventories		1,20,000
(b) Financial Assets:		
(i) Trade receivables		2,40,000
(ii) Cash and cash equivalents		1,05,000
Total Assets		**44,99,000**
EQUITY AND LIABILITIES		
Equity		
(a) Equity share capital		20,65,000
(b) Other equity	3	3,40,000
Liabilities		
1. Non-Current Liabilities		
(a) Financial Liabilities:		
(i) Long term borrowings		9,00,000
(b) Long term provisions		8,00,000
2. Current Liabilities		
(a) Financial Liabilities:		
(i) Short term borrowings		1,78,000
(ii) Trade payables		2,10,000
(b) Other current liabilities		6,000
Total Equity and Liabilities		**44,99,000**

Notes to the Financial Statement

1. Property, plant and equipment

Leasehold property	16,00,000
Plant and machinery	9,00,000
Total	**25,00,000**

2. Other non-current assets

Underwriting commission	45,000
Preliminary expenses	39,000
Total	**84,000**

3. Other Equity

Capital redemption reserve	2,20,000
General reserves	1,90,000
Debit balance of P & L	70,000
Total	**3,40,000**

***Illustration* 5**

From the following ledger balances of Sundar Ltd., prepare the Balance Sheet of the company as on 31st March 2016 as per Schedule III of the Companies Act.

Particulars	Rs.	Particulars	Rs.
Equity share capital	26,00,000	Discount on issue of debentures	
General reserves	30,000	(unwritten off)	12,500
12% Debenture	4,00,000	Tools and equipment	3,75,000
Land and buildings	15,54,970	Gratuity fund	3,00,000
Goodwill	10,00,000	Debtors	1,38,520
Bank overdraft	2,45,100	Cash at bank	1,57,160
Proposed dividend	82,000	Stores and spares	1,77,800
Prepaid insurance	25,000	Profit and loss A/c (credit)	21,490
Mutual fund	1,68,000	Bills receivable	44,600
Interest payable	32,400	Sundry creditors	92,560
Advances to employees	1,50,000		

Solution:

Balance Sheet of Sundar Company Limited as on 31st March 2016

Particulars	Note No.	Amount (Rs.)
ASSETS		
1. Non-Current Assets:		
(a) Property, plant and equipment	1	19,29,970
(b) Intangible assets		10,00,000
(c) Other non-current assets		12,500
2. Current Assets:		
(a) Inventories		1,77,800
(b) Financial Assets:		
(i) Current investments		1,68,000
(ii) Trade receivables	2	1,83,120
(iii) Cash and cash equivalents		1,57,160
(iv) Short term loans and advances		1,50,000
(c) Other current assets		25,000
Total Assets		**38,03,550**
EQUITY AND LIABILITIES		
Equity		
(a) Equity share capital		26,00,000
(b) Other equity	3	51,490
Liabilities		
1. Non-Current Liabilities		
(a) Financial liabilities:		
(i) Long term borrowings		4,00,000
(b) Long term provisions		3,00,000

2. Current Liabilities	
(a) Financial Liabilities:	
(i) Short term borrowings	2,45,100
(ii) Trade payables	92,560
(b) Other current liabilities	32,400
(c) Short term provisions	82,000
Total Equity and Liabilities	**38,03,550**

Notes to the Financial Statement:

1. Property, plant and equipment

Land and buildings	15,54,970
Tools and equipment	3,75,000
Total	**19,29,970**

2. Trade Receivables

Sundry debtors	1,38,520
Bills receivable	44,600
Total	**1,83,120**

3. Other Equity

General reserve	30,000
Profit and loss A/c (Cr. Bal.)	21,490
Total	**51,490**

SIMPLE PROBLEMS ON COMPANY FINANCIAL ACCOUNTS AS PER REVISED SCHEDULE III

Problem 1

You are given the following information from the books of Suraj Co. Ltd., as on 31st March 2016.

Suraj Co. Ltd.
Trial Balance as on 31st March, 2016

Particulars	Amount	Particulars	Amount
Depreciation on premises	8,000	Sales	12,40,000
Materials consumed	8,00,000	Equity share capital	8,00,000
Opening stock	40,000	Outstanding wages	6,000
Salaries	1,14,000		
Bad debts	3,800		
Bonus to employees	20,000		
Interest on loan	16,000		
Depreciation on machinery	18,000		

Conveyance	4,000		
Loss on sale of machinery	20,000		
Insurance	16,200		
Sales returns	40,000		
Provision for tax	60,000		
Machinery	6,00,000		
P. F. Contribution	86,000		
Premises	1,60,000		
Computer	40,000		
	20,46,000		**20,46,000**

Additional information:

Closing stock was valued at Rs.1,20,000.

Solution:

Suraj Co. Ltd.

Statement of Profit and Loss as on 31st March, 2016

Particulars	Note No.	Amount
(I) Revenue from operations	1	12,00,000
(II) Other income		–
(III) Total income [(I) + (II)]		**12,00,000**
(IV) EXPENSES:		
(a) Material consumed		8,00,000
(b) Purchases		–
(c) Changes in inventories	2	(80,000)
(d) Employees benefit expenses	3	2,20,000
(e) Finance cost		16,000
(f) Depreciation and amortization expenses	4	26,000
(g) Other expenses	5	44,000
Total expenses (IV)		**10,26,000**
(V) Profit/(Loss) before tax [(III – IV)]		**1,74,000**
(VI) Provision for tax		(60,000)
(VII) Profit/(Loss) after tax [(V – VI)]		**1,14,000**

Notes:

1. Revenue from operations

Sales	12,40,000
Less: Sales returns	40,000
	12,00,000

2. Changes in inventories

Opening stock	40,000
Less: Closing stock	(1,20,000)
	(80,000)

3. Employees benefit expenses

Salaries	1,14,000
PF contribution	86,000
Bonus to employees	20,000
	2,20,000

4. Depreciation and amortisation

Depreciation on premises	8,000
Depreciation on machinery	18,000
	26,000

5. Other expenses

Bad debts	3,800
Conveyance	4,000
Loss on sale of machinery	20,000
Insurance	16,200
	44,000

Problem 2

From the following Trial balance of Glady Ltd., as on 31st March 2016. Prepare a statement of P & L A/c as per schedule III of the companies Act. Glady Ltd.

Trial Balance as on 31st March, 2016

Particulars	Amount	Particulars	Amount
Interest on debentures	32,400	Share transfer fees	15,000
Travelling expenses	10,200	12% Debentures	2,70,000
Delivery van expenses	5,100	Commission received	7,400
Bad debts	6,500	Sales	6,45,500
Discount	7,000	Share capital	5,00,000
Purchases	3,15,800		
Opening stock	72000		
Freight outward	8,400		
Free samples	5,000		
Depreciation	38,900		
Showroom expenses	11,400		
Bank balance	1,58,600		
Wages	93,000		
Land and building	4,00,000		
Office equipment	1,45,000		
Insurance	6,000		
Furniture	1,22,600		
Total	**14,37,900**	**Total**	**14,37,900**

Additional information:

Closing stock was valued at Rs. 85,500

Solution:

Glady Ltd.

Statement of Profit and Loss as on 31st March, 2016

Particulars	Note No.	Amount
(I) Revenue from operations		6,45,500
(II) Other income	1	22,400
(III) Total income [(I) + (II)]		**6,67,900**
(IV) Expenses:		
(a) Material consumed		0
(b) Purchases		3,15,800
(c) Changes in inventories	2	(13,300)
(d) Employees benefit expenses		93,000
(e) Finance cost		32,400
(f) Depreciation and amortization exp		38,900
(g) Other expenses	3	59,600
Total expenses (IV)		**5,26,400**
(V) Profit/(loss) before tax [(III – IV)]		**1,41,500**
(VI) Provision for tax		0
(VII) Profit/(loss) after tax [(V – VI)]		**1,41,500**

Notes:

1. Other income

Share transfer fees	15,000
Commission received	7,400
	22,400

2. Changes in inventories

Opening stock	72,000
Less: Closing stock	(85,500)
	(13,500)

3. Other expenses

Travelling expenses	10,200
Delivery van expenses	5,100
Bad debts	6,500
Discount	7,000
Freight outward	8,400
Free samples	5,000
Showroom expenses	11,400
Insurance	6,000
	59,600

Problem 3

You are given the following extracts of ledger balances taken from Vikas Ltd., for the year ending 31st March 2017. Prepare a statement of P & L A/c as per revised schedule III.

Particulars	Amount	Particulars	Amount
Excise duty	8,000	Returns inward	5,000
Provision for tax	10,000	Purchases	2,35,000
Depreciation on machinery	3,300	Closing stock	75,000
Sundry expenses	7,000	Opening stock	82,000
Rent	4,000	Wages	30,000
Salaries	7,500	Bank loan	40,000
Materials consumed	90,000	Interest on bank loan	4,000
Machinery	25,000	Interest on investment	5,000
Directors remuneration	20,000	Rent received	3,000
Factory expenses	2,500	Motive power	12,000
Sales	4,55,000	Transport charges	1,000

Solution:

Vikas Ltd.

Statement of Profit and Loss as on 31st March, 2017

Particulars	Note No.	Amount
(I) Revenue from operations	1	4,42,000
(II) Other income	2	8,000
(III) Total income [(I) + (II)]		**4,50,000**
(IV) Expenses:		
(a) Material consumed		90,000
(b) Purchases		2,35,000
(c) Changes in inventories	3	7,000
(d) Employees benefit expenses	4	37,500
(e) Finance cost		4,000
(f) Depreciation and amortization exp.		3,300
(g) Other expenses	5	46,500
Total expenses (IV)		**4,23,300**
(V) Profit/(loss) before tax [(III – IV)]		**26,700**
(VI) Provision for tax		10,000
(VII) Profit/(loss) after tax [(V – VI)]		**16,700**

Notes:

1. Revenue from operations

Sales	4, 55,000
Less: Sales returns	5,000
Less: Excise duty	8,000
	4, 42,000

2. Other income

Interest on investment	5,000
Rent received	3,000
	8,000

3. Changes in inventories

Opening stock	82,000
Less: Closing stock	75,000
	7,000

4. Employees benefit expenses

Salaries	7,500
Wages	30,000
	37,500

5. Other expenses

Sundry expenses	7,000
Rent	4,000
Directors remuneration	20,000
Factory expenses	2,500
Motive power	12,000
Transport charges	1,000
	46,500

Problem 4

You are given the following extracts of ledger balances taken from Chandar Ltd., for the year ending 31st March 2016. Prepare a statement of P & L A/C as per revised schedule III.

Particulars	Rs.	Particulars	Rs.
Opening stock of finished goods	1,90,500	Provision for taxation	30,000
Cost of material consumed	2,92,000	Goodwill written off	18,000
Salaries to office staff	68,000	Sales returns	17,000
Closing stock of finished goods	2,03,000	Provision for bad debts	8,200
Interest on debentures paid	16,250	Delivery expenses	7,200
General expenses	8,250	Printing and stationery	22,600
Discount earned	4,900	Factory expenses	82,000
Cash sales	2,66,000	Bonus to employees	32,000
Credit sales	3,87,500	Depreciation on plant and	
Income tax refund	11,500	machinery	50,000

Solution:

Chandar Ltd.,
Statement of Profit and Loss as on 31st March, 2016

Particulars	Note No.	(Rs.)
(I) Revenue from operations	1	6,36,500
(II) Other income	2	16,400
(III) Total income [(I) + (II)]		**6,52,900**
(IV) Expenses:		
(a) Material consumed		2,92,000
(b) Purchases		0
(c) Changes in inventories	3	(12,500)
(d) Employees benefit expenses	4	1,00,000
(e) Finance cost		16,250
(f) Depreciation and amortization expenses	5	68,000
(g) Other expenses	6	1,28,250
Total expenses (IV)		**5,92,000**
(V) Profit/(loss) before tax [(III) – (IV)]		**60,900**
(VI) Provision for tax		(30,000)
(VII) Profit/(loss) after tax [(V) – (VI)]		**30,900**

Notes:

1. ***Revenue from Operations:***

	(Rs.)
Cash sales	2,66,000
Credit sales	3,87,500
Less: Sales returns	(17,000)
	6,36,000

2. ***Other Income:***

Discount earned	4,900
Income tax refund	11,500
	16,400

3. ***Changes in Inventories:***

Opening stock	1,90,500
Less: closing stock	(2,03,000)
	(12,500)

4. ***Employees Benefit Expenses:***

Salaries to office staff	68,000
Bonus to employees	32,000
	1,00,000

5. ***Depreciation and Amortisation:***

Goodwill written off	18,000
Depreciation on plant and machinery	50,000
	68,000

6. ***Other Expenses:***

General expenses	8,250
Provision for bad debts	8,200
Freight on purchases	7,200
Printing and stationery	22,600
Factory expenses	82,000
	1,28,250

Problem 5

The authorized capital of Y Ltd. is Rs. 5,00,000 consisting of 2,000 6% preference shares of Rs. 100 each and 30,000 equity shares of Rs.10 each. Following was the Trial Balance of Y Limited as on 31-3-2016:

TRIAL BALANCE
as on 31-3-2016

Particulars	Dr (Rs.)	Cr (Rs.)
Investment in shares at cost	50,000	
Purchases	4,90,500	
Selling expenses	79,100	
Stock on 1-4-2015	1,45,200	
Salaries and wages	68,500	
Cash on hand	12,000	
Interim preference dividend for the half-year to 30-9-2015	6,000	
Bills receivable	41,500	
Interest on bank overdraft	7,800	
Interest on debentures upto 30-9-2015	3,750	
Sundry debtors and creditors	50,100	87,850
Freehold property at cost	4,86,500	
Furniture at cost less depreciation of Rs.15,000	35,000	
6% Preference share capital		2,00,000
Equity share capital fully paid up		2,00,000
5% Mortgage debentures secured on freehold properties		1,50,000
Income tax paid in advance for 2015-16	10,000	
Dividends		4,250
Surplus A/c (1-4-2015)		28,500
Sales (net)		6,70,350
Bank overdraft secured by hypothecation of stocks and receivables		1,50,000
Audit fees	5,000	
	14,90,950	14,90,950

You are required to prepare the Statement of Profit and Loss for the year ended 31-3-2016 and the Balance Sheet as on that date after taking into account the following:

1. Closing stock was valued at Rs. 1,42,500
2. Purchase includes Rs.5,000 worth of goods and articles distributed among valued customers.
3. Salaries and wages include Rs.2,000 being wages incurred for installation of electrical fitting, which were recorded under "Furniture".
4. Bills receivable include Rs.1,500 being dishonoured bills, 50% of which had been considered irrecoverable.
5. Bills receivable of Rs.2,000 maturing after 31-3-2016 were discounted.
6. Depreciation on furniture is to be charged at 10% on written down value.
7. Interest on debentures for the half-year ending on 31-3-2016 was due on that date.
8. Provide provision for taxation Rs.4,000.
9. Salaries and wages include Rs.10,000 being the Director's remuneration.
10. Sundry debtors include Rs.6,000 debts due for more than six months.
11. Corporate dividend tax is to be ignored.

Solution:

Y Ltd
Statement of Profit and Loss
for the Year Ending 31st March, 2016

(Rs. in '000)

Particulars	Note No.	Year Ending 31-3-2016	Year Ending 31-3-2015
(I) Revenue from operations	1	670.350	
(II) Other income: Dividends		4.250	
(III) Total income [(I) + (II)]		**674.600**	
(IV) Expenses:			
Cost of goods sold	2	488.200	
Employee benefits expense	3	56.500	
Finance Costs	4	15.300	
Depreciation	5	3.700	
Other expenses	6	99.850	
Total expenses (IV)		**663.550**	
(V) Profit before tax [(III) – (IV)]		**11.050**	
(VI) Tax expenses: Provision for taxation		4.000	
(VII) Profit for the Period [(V) – (VI)]		**7.050**	

Notes: Forming Part of Statement of Profit and Loss

1. Revenue from Operations (Rs. in '000)

	Year Ending 31-3-2016	Year Ending 31-3-2015
Sales (Net)	670.350	

2. Cost of Goods Sold (Rs. in '000)

		Year Ending 31-3-2016	Year Ending 31-3-2015
Opening stock		145.200	
Add: Purchases	490.500		
Cost of goods distributed among valued customers treated as advertisement	–5.000	485.500	
		630.700	
Less: Closing stock		142.500	
		488.200	

3. Employee Benefit Expense (Rs. in '000)

	Year Ending 31-3-2016	Year Ending 31-3-2015
Salaries and wages	68.500	
Less: Wages for installation of electrical fittings capitalized	2.000	
	66.500	
Less: Director's remuneration.	10.000	
	56.500	

4. Finance Cost (Rs. in '000)

	Year Ending 31-3-2016	Year Ending 31-3-2015
Interest on bank overdraft	7.800	
Interest on Debentures (3,750 + 3,750 Outstanding)	7.500	
	15.300	

5. Depreciation and Amortisation Expense (Rs. in '000)

	Year Ending 31-3-2016	Year Ending 31-3-2015
Depreciation on furniture–10% on Rs. 37.00	3.700	

6. Other Expense (Rs. in '000)

	Year Ending 31-3-2016	Year Ending 31-3-2015
Selling expenses	79.100	
Advertisement expenses (goods distributed among valued customers)	5.000	
Directors' remuneration	10.000	
Audit fees	5.000	
Bad debts	0.750	
	99.850	

Y Ltd.
Balance Sheet as at 31-3-2016

Particulars	Note No.	Amount (Rs.)
ASSETS		
1. Non-Current Assets:		
(a) Property, plant and equipment	1	519.80
(b) Financial Assets:		
(i) Non-current investments	2	50.00
2. Current Assets:		
(a) Inventories	3	142.50
(b) Financial Assets:		
(i) Trade receivables	4	90.85
(ii) Cash and cash equivalents	5	12.00
(c) Other current assets	6	10.00
Total Assets		**825.15**
EQUITY AND LIABILITIES		
Equity		
(a) Equity share capital	7	400.00
(b) Other equity	8	29.55
Liabilities		
1. Non-Current Liabilities		
(a) Financial Liabilities:		
(i) Long term borrowings	9	150.00
2. Current Liabilities		
(a) Financial Liabilities:		
(i) Trade payables		87.85
(b) Other current liabilities	10	153.75
(c) Short term provisions	11	4.00
Total Equity and Liabilities		**825.15**

Notes: Forming Part of Balance Sheet.

1. Property, Plant and Equipment (Rs. in '000)

		31-3-2016	31-3-2015
Freehold property (at cost)		486.500	
Furniture at cost (35 + 15 depreciation + 2 addition)	52.00		
Less: Depreciation to date (15 + 3.7)	18.70		
		33.300	
		519.800	

2. Non-Current Investments

(Rs. in '000)

	31-3-2016	31-3-2015
Investment in shares (at cost)	50.00	

3. Inventories

(Rs. in '000)

	31-3-2016	31-3-2015
Closing stock (finished goods assumed)	142.50	

4. Trade Receivables

(Rs. in '000)

				31-3-2016	31-3-2015
Sundry Debtors:					
(a) Debtors outstanding for a period exceeding 6 months			6.00		
(b) Other debtors		44.100			
Dishonoured bill	1.50				
Less: Bad debt (50%)	0.75	0.750			
			44.85	50.85	
Bills receivable			41.50		
Less: Bills dishonored			1.50	40.00	
				90.85	

5. Cash and Cash Equivalents

(Rs. in '000)

	31-3-2016	31-3-2015
Cash-in-hand	12.00	

6. Other Current Assets

(Rs. in '000)

	31-3-2016	31-3-2015
Advance income tax for 2015-16	10.00	

7. Equity Share Capital

(Rs. in '000)

	31-3-2016	31-3-2015
Authorised		
2,000 6% Preference shares of Rs.100 each	200.00	
30,000 Equity shares of Rs.10 each	300.00	
	500.00	
Issued, subscribed and paid-up capital		
2,000 6% Pref. shares of Rs.100 each fully paid up	200.00	
20,000 Equity shares of Rs.10 each fully paid up	200.00	
	400.00	

8. Other Equity (Rs. in '000)

		31-3-2016	31-3-2015
Surplus			
Balance as on 1-4-2015		28.500	
Net Profit for the year ending 31-3-2016	7.05		
Less: Interim preference dividend	6.00	1.050	
		29.550	

9. Long-Term Borrowings (Rs. in '000)

	31-3-2016	31-3-2015
5% Mortgage debentures (secured on freehold property)	150.00	

10. Other Current Liabilities (Rs. in '000)

	31-3-2016	31-3-2015
Interest on debentures Outstanding	3.750	
Bank overdraft (Secured by hypothecation of stocks and receivables)	150.000	
	153.750	

11. Short-Term Provisions (Rs. in '000)

	31-3-2016	31-3-2015
Provision for taxation	4.00	

Contingent Liabilities and Commitments

1. A contingent liability for bills discounted Rs.2,000, which will mature after 31-3-2016
2. Fixed preference dividend for half year @ 6% p.a. on Rs.2,00,000 preference capital is not provided for in the accounts.

Working Notes:

1. *Calculation of Depreciation and Gross Value of Furniture:*

		(Rs.)
Furniture at cost less depreciation as on 1-4-2015		35,000
Add: Installation of electrical fittings		2,000
		37,000
Less: Depreciation 10% for 2015-16		3,700
Book value as at 31-3-2016		33,300
Add: Accumulated depreciation up to 31-3-2015	15,000	
Depreciation for 2015-16	3,700	
		18,700
Furniture at cost		52,000

Problem 6

The authorized capital of X Ltd. is Rs 7,50,000 consisting of 3,000 6% cumulative preference shares of Rs 100 each and 45,000 equity shares of Rs.100 each. Following was the trial balance drawn up on 31-3-2016:

Particulars	(Rs.)	Particulars	(Rs.)
Paid-up capital:		General expenses	1,000
3,000 6% cumulative preference		Furniture at cost	75,000
shares	3,00,000	Sales	9,18,000
3,000 equity shares (Rs 75 per		Purchases	4,76,500
share called up)	2,25,000	Bills receivable	6,000
Goodwill	1,00,000	Freight and carriage inward	3,750
5% first mortgage debentures		Investments:	
(secured on freehold properties)	2,10,000	600 shares of Rs.100 each in	
Trade debtors	1,67,500	Sunrises Limited	60,000
Trade creditors	1,25,520	Debenture interest (half-year to	
Freehold properties at cost	3,90,000	September, 2015)	5,250
Stock on 1st April, 2015	2,41,500	Final dividend for 2014-15	20,250
General Reserve	82,725	Preference dividend (half-year to	
Salaries	1,03,500	30th September, 2015)	9,000
Surplus Account (Cr.)	58,500	Balance at bank in current account	97,500
Reserve for taxation	8,800	Cash in hand	14,145
Delivery expenses	1,02,000	Shares forfeited account	2,000
Rent and rates	38,250		

(a) The value of stock on March 31, 2016 was Rs. 2,15,000

(b) Depreciation on freehold properties is to be provided at 2.5% and on furniture at 6%

(c) The directors propose to pay the second half-year's dividend on preference shares and a 10% dividend on equity shares

(d) Shares were forfeited on non-payment of Rs. 35 per share.

(e) Corporate dividend tax need not be provided.

You are required to prepare final accounts of the company.

Solution:

X Ltd.
Statement of Profit and Loss
for the Year Ending 31st March, 2016

(Rs. in '000)

Particulars	Note No.	Year Ending 31-3-2016	Year Ending 31-3-2015
(I) Revenue from operations	1	918.600	
(II) Other income		NIL	
(III) Total income [(I) + (II)]		**918.600**	

(IV) Expenses:			
Cost of goods sold	2	506.750	
Employee benefits expense	3	103.500	
Finance costs	4	10.500	
Depreciation amortisation expense	5	14.250	
Other expenses	6	161.250	
Total expenses (IV)		**796.250**	
(V) Profit before tax [(III) – (IV)]		**122.350**	

Notes: Forming Part of Statement of Profit and Loss.

1. Revenue from Operations

(Rs. in '000)

	Year Ending 31-3-2016	Year Ending 31-3-2015
Sales	918.600	

2. Cost of Goods Sold

(Rs. in '000)

		Year Ending 31-3-2016	Year Ending 31-3-2015
Opening stock		241.500	
Purchases	476.500		
Add: Freight and carriage	3.750	480.250	
		721.750	
Less: Closing stock		215.000	
		506.750	

3. Employee Benefits Expense

(Rs. in '000)

	Year Ending 31-3-2016	Year Ending 31-3-2015
Salaries	103.500	

4. Finance Cost

(Rs. in '000)

		Year Ending 31-3-2016	Year Ending 31-3-2015
Debenture interest	5.250		
Add: Interest outstanding for 1/2 year	5.250	10.500	

5. Depreciation and Amortisation Expense

(Rs. in '000)

	Year Ending 31-3-2016	Year Ending 31-3-2015
Depreciation @ 2 ½ % on freehold property	9.750	
Depreciation @ 6% on furniture	4.500	
	14.250	

6. Other Expense

(Rs. in '000)

	Year Ending 31-3-2016	Year Ending 31-3-2015
Rent and rate	38.250	
Delivery expenses	102.000	
General expenses	21.000	
	161.250	

X Ltd.

Balance Sheet as at 31-3-2016

Particulars	Note No.	Amount (Rs.)
ASSETS		
1. Non-Current Assets:		
(a) Property, plant and equipment	1	450.750
(b) Intangible assets	2	100.000
(c) Financial Assets:		
(i) Non-current investments	3	60.000
2. Current Assets:		
(a) Inventories	4	215.000
(b) Financial Assets:		
(i) Trade receivables	5	173.500
(ii) Cash and cash equivalents	6	111.645
(c) Other current assets		Nil
Total Assets		**1110.895**
EQUITY AND LIABILITIES		
Equity		
(a) Equity share capital	7	527.000
(b) Other equity	8	211.625
		738.625

Liabilities		
1. Non-Current Liabilities		
(a) Financial Liabilities:		
(i) Long-term borrowings	9	210
2. Current Liabilities		
(a) Financial Liabilities:		
(i) Trade payables		125.520
(b) Other current liabilities	10	5.250
(c) Short term provisions	11	31.500
Total Equity and Liabilities		**1110.895**

Notes to the Balance Sheet:

1. Property, Plant and Equipment

(Rs. in '000)

		31-3-2016	31-3-2015
Freehold properties at cost	390.000		
Less: Depreciation at @ 2.5%	9.750	380.250	
Furniture at cost	75.000		
Less: Depreciation @ 6%	4.5000	70.500	
		450.750	

2. Intangible Assets

(Rs. in '000)

	31-3-2016	31-3-2015
Goodwill	100.000	

3. Non-Current Investments

(Rs. in '000)

	31-3-2016	31-3-2015
600 shares of Rs.100 each in Sunrise Ltd	60.000	

4. Inventories

(Rs. in '000)

	31-3-2016	31-3-2015
Stock	215.000	

5. Trade Receivables

(Rs. in '000)

	31-3-2016	31-3-2015
Trade Debtors (assumed to be less than 6 months)	167.500	
Bills Receivable	6.000	
	173.500	

6. Cash and Cash Equivalents

(Rs. in '000)

	31-3-2016	31-3-2015
Cash in hand	14.145	
Balance at bank in Current A/c	97.500	
	111.645	

7. Equity Share Capital

(Rs. in '000)

	31-3-2016	31-3-2015
Authorised		
3,000 6% cumulative preference shares of Rs.100 each	300.00	
4,500 Equity shares of Rs.100 each	450.00	
	750.00	
Issued, Subscribed and Paid-up Capital		
3,000 6% Preference shares of Rs.100 each, fully called up and paid up	300.00	
3,000 Equity shares of Rs.100 each, Rs.75 per share called up and paid up	225.000	
Shares Forfeited Account	2.000	
	527.00	

8. Other Equity

(Rs. in '000)

		31-3-2016	31-3-2015
General reserve		82.725	
Reserves for taxation		8.800	
Surplus: Balance as on 1-4-2015	58.500		
Add: Profit for the year	122.350		
	180.850		
Less: Final dividend for 2014-15	20.250		
Preference dividend for ½ year to 30-9-2015	9.000		
Proposed Dividend:			
On preference shares for the second ½ year to 31-3-2015	9.000		
On equity shares @ 10% on Rs. 2,25,000	22.500		
	60.750	120.100	
		211.625	

9. Long-Term Borrowings

(Rs. in '000)

	31-3-2016	31-3-2015
5% First mortgage debentures (secured on freehold properties)	210.00	

10. Other Current Liabilities (Rs. in '000)

	31-3-2016	31-3-2015
Interest on debentures outstanding	5.250	

11. Short-Term Provisions (Rs. in '000)

	31-3-2016	31-3-2015
Proposed dividend on preference shares @ 6% p.a. for ½ year on Rs. 3,00,000	9.000	
Proposed dividend on equity shares @ 10 % on Rs. 2,25,000	22.500	
	31.500	

Problem 7

Prepare a Balance Sheet in vertical form as at 31st March, 2016 from the following information of X Ltd. as required under Part I of Schedule III of the Companies Act, 2015:

	(Rs.)		(Rs.)
Term loan	10,00,000	Loss for the year	3,58,000
Sundry creditors	11,45,000	Sundry debtors	12,25,000
Advances	3,72,000	Loans from debtors	2,00,000
Cash and bank balances	2,75,000	Provision for doubtful debts	20,200
Staff advances	55,000	Stores	4,00,000
Taxes payable	1,70,000	Fixed assets (WDV)	51,50,000
Securities premium reserve	4,75,000	Finished goods	7,50,000
Loose tools	50,000	General reserve	20,50,000
Investments	2, 25,200	Capital work-in-progress	2,00,000

Additional Information:

1. Share capital consists of–
   (a) 3,000 equity shares of Rs.100 each fully paid up.
   (b) 10,000—10% redeemable preference shares of Rs.100 each fully paid up.
2. Term loans are secured.
3. Depreciation on assets Rs.5, 00,000.
4. Schedules need not be given. However, groupings should form part of the answer.

Solution:

X Ltd.
Balance Sheet
as at 31-3-2016

Particulars	Note No.	As on 31-3-2016	As on 31-3-2015
ASSETS			
1. Non-Current Assets:			
(a) Property, plant and equipment	1	53,50,000	

Particulars	Note	Rs.
(b) Financial Assets:		
(i) Non-current investments (assumed to be non-current)		2,25,200
2. Current Assets:		
(a) Inventories	2	12,00,000
(b) Financial Assets:		
(i) Sundry debtors	3	12,04,800
(ii) Cash and cash equivalents	4	2,75,000
(iii) Short term loan and advances	5	4,27,000
Total Assets		**86,82,000**
EQUITY AND LIABILITIES		
Equity		
(a) Equity share capital	6	13,00,000
(b) Other Equity	7	21,67,000
Liabilities		
1. Non-Current Liabilities		
(a) Financial Liabilities:		
(i) Long term borrowings		10,00,000
2. Current Liabilities		
(a) Financial Liabilities		
(i) Trade payables		11,45,000
(b) Other current liabilities	8	3,70,000
Suspense account (balancing figure)		27,00,000
Total Equity and Liabilities		**86,82,000**

Accompanying notes to the Balance Sheet: (Rs.)

1. Property, plant and equipment	
Fixed asset at cost	56,50,000
Less: Depreciation	(5,00,000)
Capital work-in-progress	2,00,000
	53,50,000
2. Inventories	
Finished goods	7,50,000
Stores	4,00,000
Loose tools	50,000
	12,00,000

3. Sundry Debtors	12,25,000
Less: Provision for doubtful debts	20,200
	12,04,800
4. Cash and Cash Equivalents:	
Cash and bank balances	2,75,000
5. Loans and Advances:	
Advances	3,72,000
Staff advances	55,000
	4,27,000
6. Equity:	
3,000 Equity shares of Rs. 100 each	3,00,000
10,000—10% Redeemable preference shares of Rs. 100 each	10,00,000
	13,00,000
7. Other Equity:	
Securities premium reserve	4,75,000
General reserve	20,50,000
	25,25,000
	3,58,000
	21,67,000
8. Other Current Liabilities:	
Loan from debtors	2,00,000
Taxes Payable	1,70,000
	3,70,000

Problem 8

Following balances have been extracted from the books of X Ltd. as on 31-3-2016.

Particulars	(Rs.)	Particulars	(Rs.)
Freehold land	2, 00,000	Income from investment (net)	4,000
Building	1, 75,000	Provision for bad and doubtful debts	2,000
Furniture	25,000	Creditors	30,000
Debtors (unsecured)	1, 50,000	Provision for depreciation	
Stock	60,000	on 1-4-2015	
Cash at bank	5,000	Building	15,000

Cash in hand (secured on freehold		Furniture	6,000
properties)	1,000	Suspense	6,000
Cost of goods sold	3, 10,000	Equity share capital	3, 66,500
Salaries and wages	20,000	9% Cumulative preference shares	
Miscellaneous expenses	8,000	of Rs.100 each	1, 00,000
Investments in shares	1, 80,000	Securities premium reserve	10,000
Interest	3,000	Bank overdraft	1, 52,500
Bad debts	1,000	Sales	4, 50,000
Repairs and maintenance	1,500	Surplus account 1-4-2015	3,500
Advance payment if income-tax	6,000		
	11, 45,500		11, 45,500

Following particulars may be taken into account:

1. The land was revalued by an expert value on 1st January, 2015 at Rs. 3,00,000, but this was not given effect to, although the directors had decided to give effect of this.
2. Provision for doubtful debts is to be adjusted to 5% of the amount of debtors.
3. Equity share capital comprised of Rs. 10 shares, 36,400 fully paid and 500 shares on which final call of Rs. 5 remains unpaid.
4. Suspense includes (i) Rs.1,000 representing surplus found on physical verification of closing stock, pending investigation and (ii) money received from a new allottee for the reissue of 500 shares forfeited during the year non-payment of final call, but no entry for adjustment thereof has been made.
5. Provision for taxation is to be made at 50%.
6. Market value of investment was Rs.1,90,000 on 31st March, 2016.
7. The company is managed by a Managing Director, who is entitled to 5% remuneration on the annual net profits.
8. Depreciation is to be charged on written down value on building @ 2% and on furniture at 10% p.a.
9. The company has arrangements with a bank for overdraft upto a limit of Rs 2,50,000 secured on land and building of the company.
10. Dividend on preference Shares was in arrears for 5 years upto 31st March, 2016. The directors decided to pay the dividend for four years.
11. Income tax deducted from the income from investments amounted to Rs. 500.

Prepare Statement of Profit Loss for the year ended 31st March, 2016 and Balance Sheet as on that date, after making such assumptions as may be considered necessary. Ignore previous year's figures.

Solution:

X Ltd.
Statement of Profit and Loss
for the Year Ending March 31, 2016

(Rs. in '000)

	Note No.	Year Ending 31-3-2016	Year Ending 31-3-2015
(I) Revenue from operations	1	450.000	
(II) Other income	2	4.500	
(III) Total income [(I) + (II)]		**454.500**	
(IV) Expenses:			
Cost of goods sold	3	310.000	
Employee benefits expense	4	20.000	
Finance costs	5	3.000	
Depreciation and amortisation expense	6	5.100	
Other expenses	7	21.020	
Total expenses (IV)		**359.120**	
(V) Profit before tax [(III) – (IV)]		**95.380**	
(VI) Tax expenses (b)		**47.690**	
(VII) Profit for the period [(V) – (VI)]		**47.690**	

Accompanying Notes to the Balance Sheet

1. Revenue from Operations (Rs. in '000)

	Year Ending 31-3-2016	Year Ending 31-3-2015
Sales	450.000	

2. Other Income (Rs. in '000)

		Year Ending 31-3-2016	Year Ending 31-3-2015
Income from investment:			
Net	4.000		
Add: Income tax deducted	0.500	4.500	

3. Cost of Goods Sold (Rs. in '000)

	Year Ending 31-3-2016	Year Ending 31-3-2015
Cost of goods sold (details not given)	310.00	

4. Employee Benefits Expense (Rs. in '000)

	Year Ending 31-3-2016	Year Ending 31-3-2015
Salaries and wages	20.000	

5. Finance Costs (Rs. in '000)

	Year Ending 31-3-2016	Year Ending 31-3-2015
Interest	3.000	

6. Depreciation and Amortisation Expense (Rs. in '000)

	Year Ending 31-3-2016	Year Ending 31-3-2015
2% Depreciation on W.D.V. Rs. 1,60,000 of building	3.200	
10% Depreciation on W.D.V. Rs. 19,000 of furniture	1.900	
	5.100	

7. Other Expenses (Rs. in '000)

		Year Ending 31-3-2016	Year Ending 31-3-2015
Repairs and maintenance		1.50	
Bad debts	1.000		
Add: Provision for doubtful debts required 5% on Rs.1,50,000	7.500		
	8.500		
Less: Existing provision for doubtful debts	2.000	6.500	
		5.020	
Managing Director's remuneration (a)		8.000	
Miscellaneous expenses		21.020	

Working Notes:

(a) Calculation of Managing Director's Remuneration:

	(Rs. in '000)	(Rs. in '000)
Total revenue		454.500
Less: Cost of goods sold	310.000	
Salaries and wages	20.000	
Interest	3.000	
Depreciation	5.100	
Repairs and maintenance	1.500	
Bad debts	6.500	
Miscellaneous expenses	8.000	354.100
Profit for commission purpose		100.400

Managing Director's remuneration @ 5% on Rs. 100.400 thousands 5.020

(b) Calculation for provision for taxation:

	(Rs. in '000)
Profit for Commission purpose	100.400
Less: Managing Director's remuneration	5.020
Profit for taxation purpose	95.380
Income tax provision @ 50%	47.690

X Ltd
Balance Sheet
as at 31-3-2016

(Rs. in '000)

Particulars	Note No.	As on 31-3-2016	As on 31-3-2015
ASSETS			
1. Non-Current Assets:			
(a) Property, plant and equipment	1	473.900	
2. Current Assets:			
(a) Financial Assets:			
(i) Current investments (assumed to be current)	3	180.000	
(ii) Trade receivables	4	142.500	
(iii) Cash and cash equivalents	5	6.000	
(iv) Short-term loan and advances	6	6.500	
(b) Inventories	2	60.000	
Total Assets		**868.900**	
EQUITY AND LIABILITIES			
Equity			
(a) Equity share capital	7	469.000	
(b) Other equity	8	121.570	
Liabilities			
1. Non-Current Liabilities			
(a) Financial Liabilities:			
(i) Long-term borrowings		Nil	
2. Current Liabilities			
(a) Financial Liabilities:			
(i) Trade payables		30.000	
(b) Other current liabilities	9	158.520	
(c) Short-term provisions	10	89.810	
(d) Contingent liabilities	11	18.000	
Total Equity and Liabilities		**868.900**	

Accompanying notes to the Balance Sheet

1. Property, Plant and Equipment

(Rs. in '000)

		31-3-2014	31-3-2013
Land at cost	200.000		
Add: Appreciation	100.000	300.000	
Buildings at cost	175.000		
Less: Accumulated depreciation	18.200	156.800	
Furniture at cost	25.000		
Less: Accumulated depreciation to date	7.900	17.100	
		473.900	

2. Inventories

(Rs. in '000)

	31-3-2016	31-3-2015
Stock at cost	60.000	

3. Current Investments

(Rs. in '000)

	31-3-2014	31-3-2013
Investment in shares at cost (market value of Rs. 1,90,000 assumed to be same as it was on 31-3-2013)	180.000	

4. Trade Receivables

(Rs. in '000)

	31-3-2016	31-3-2015
Debtors (Unsecured assumed to be less than 6 months)	150.000	
Less: Provision for doubtful debts	7.500	
	142.500	

5. Cash and Cash Equivalents

(Rs. in '000)

	31-3-2016	31-3-2015
Cash in hand	1.000	
Cash at bank	5.000	
	6.000	

6. Short- Term Loans and Advances

(Rs. in '000)

	30-9-2016	30-9-2015
Income tax paid in advance	6.000	
Income tax deducted at source	0.500	
	6.500	

7. Equity Share Capital

(Rs. in '000)

	31-3-2014	31-3-2013
Authorised:		
Equity shares of Rs.10 each	–	
9% Cumulative preference shares of Rs.10 each	–	
Issued, subscribed and paid-up capital:		
36,900 Equity shares of Rs.10 each fully paid	3,69,000	
1,000 9% Cumulative preference shares of Rs.100 each fully paid up	1,00,000	
	4,69,000	

8. Other Equity

(Rs. in '000)

		31-3-2014	31-3-2013
Capital Reserves			
Profit on reissue of Forfeited Shares (i)	2.500		
Appreciation in value of Land	100.00	102.500	
Securities premium reserve		10.000	
Surplus A/c	3.500		
Balance as on 1-4-2013	47.690		
Profit for the year			
Less: Preference share			
dividend for 4 years.			
@ 9% on Rs. 100.00	36.000		
Provision for corporate dividend tax @ 17%	6.120		
	5.570	9.070	
		121.570	

9. Other Current Liabilities

(Rs. in '000)

	31-3-2014	31-3-2013
Bank overdraft	152.500	
Managing Director's remuneration due	5.020	
Stock surplus pending investigation	1.000	
	158.520	

10. Short-Term Provisions

(Rs. in '000)

	31-3-2014	31-3-2013
Provision for taxation	47.690	
Proposed dividend on preference shares	36.000	
Provision for corporate dividend tax	6.120	
	89.810	

11. Contingent Liabilities and Commitments (Rs. in '000)

	31-3-2016	31-3-2015
Advance of dividend @ 9% on cumulative preference shares for 2 years	18.000	

Working Note:

(i) ***Calculation of Profit on Reissue of Forfeited Shares*** (Rs.)

	(Rs.)
Amount received on reissue of 500 shares @ Rs.10 per share	5,000
Less: Calls in arrears on 500 shares @ Rs. 5	2,500
Capital reserve	2,500

COMPREHENSIVE PRACTICAL PROBLEM

From the following Trial Balance of XYZ Ltd. for the two comparative years 2016-17 and 2015-16, prepare Profit and Loss A/c and Balance Sheet as on date by following the recent Companies Act, 2013 revision as per Schedule III.

XYZ Ltd.
Trial Balance as on 31st March 2017

Particulars	2016-17		2015-16	
	Dr.	Cr.	Dr.	Cr.
Share capital		95,00,000		95,00,000
TDS payable-interest		0		139
TDS professional fee		38,712		21,500
TDS-salary		1,16,240		57,584
TDS-rent-company		3,500		0
Professional tax deduction		200		0
Deferred tax liability	40,101		33,058	
Annual benefits payable		2,32,272		1,82,901
EPF payable		64,842		52,785
ESI payable		7,375		1,001
Expenses payable		9,205		12,479
Provision for income tax		9,60,000		6,20,000
Service tax input/payable	3,233	38,160	82,501	
Sundry creditors		1,04,404	1,250	2,17,761
Air conditioner	68,600		68,600	
Computers	2,89,490		2,46,490	
Furniture and fixtures	2,20,928		2,20,928	
Office equipment	7,000		0	
Software	2,82,000		2,82,000	
Depreciation reserve		5,54,333		3,83,272
Fixed deposit- CUB bank Ltd-lien	12,42,469		11,46,728	
Staff loan	1,35,408		1,66,055	
Deposit-Rent CJB	1,00,000		1,00,000	
Deposit-Rent Bangalore	1,00,000			
Deposit-Rent Chennai	2,50,000			

Prepaid expenses	1,00,153		96,584	
Tax deducted at source (TDS receivable)	52,19,021		45,02,528	
Sundry debtors	19,67,344		7,87,409	1,932
Cash in hand	8,905		2,110	
Bank 1	9,95,591			98,385
Bank 2	20,155		13,254	
Bank 3	22,751		53,268	
Bank 4	24,894		24,894	
Bank 5	24,64,500		119,358	
Fixed deposit	11,24,957		4,965,023	
Commission received - export		506,580		
Commission received - non-life		13,880,527		1,24,72,053
Commission received - life		10,226		3,000
Interest received		626,285		5,38,381
Other income-profit on exchange fluctuation	7,074			
Other income- service charges				2,15,776
Directors remuneration	27,60,000		21,60,000	
Salaries and wages-basic	22,67,701		20,58,220	
Salaries and wages-HRA	8,18,771		7,46,428	
Salaries and wages-conveyance	3,66,950		3,37,140	
Salaries and wages-other allowance	11,18,962		9,41,378	
Salaries and wages-medical	2,60,799		2,40,000	
Food coupons	2,69,392		2,54,520	
Salaries and wages-education allowance	1,24,528		1,21,200	
Staff annual benefits	3,78,276		3,40,720	
Gratuity	2,910		3,50,260	
ESI contribution	15,944		11,389	
PF contribution	3,30,144		2,93,348	
PF administration charges	34,751		30,853	
Consultancy charges	1,19,000		24,005	
Retainer fees	10,50,000		11,05,000	
Professional fee	66,500		47,500	
Audit fees	50,000		50,000	
Internal audit fee	50,000		50,000	
Repairs and maintenance	61,554		43,592	
Office maintenance	7,790		6,707	
Repairs and maintenance-AMC	15600		11,805	
Computer maintenance	44,104		43,907	
Membership and subscription	38,084		1,125	
Insurance-assets	4,157		4,989	
Insurance-group mediclaim	1,41,203		99,418	
Insurance-personal accident	3,532		3,143	

Insurance - prof indemnity policy	77,474		72,060	
Postage and Telegram, courier charges	21,134		17,985	
Telephone, telex and mobile charges	1,16,131		1,26,678	
Telephone, telex and internet	1,11,536		1,04,908	
Conveyance	4,16,988		394,106	
Travelling expenses	4,03,481		10,32,206	
Printing and stationery	45,990		33,905	
Professional tax contribution	11,464		11,069	
Rates and taxes	38,285		2,576	
Staff welfare expenses	96,620		121,752	
Staff welfare expenses-coffee/tea expenses	35,297		34,207	
Training expenses	9,600		10,500	
Depreciation	2,57,456		245,808	
Advertisement			100,000	
Business development expenses	11,961		51,251	
Sundry expenses		4,742	14,969	
Bank charges	5,834		7,121	
Interest paid	382		35,295	
Electricity charges	3,913		3,786	
Deferred tax expenses a/c		7,043		20,101
Income tax	7,00,000		2,60,000	
Profit and loss account		17,62,300		12,68,509
Rent	3,38,100		1,92,000	
Fees	72,972		56,494	
Web design charges			3,730	
Co-broking commission/brokerage	142,121		2,27,394	
Bad-debts	30,497		39,074	
IT relating to earlier year		5,516		
Management fee	3,90,000		1,80,000	
Total	**2,84,32,462**	**2,84,32,462**	**2,56,67,559**	**2,56,67,559**

Solution:

Part I - Balance Sheet

XYZ Ltd.

Balance Sheet as at 31st March, 2017

Particulars	Note No.	Figures as at the end of the current reporting period	Figures as at the end of the previous reporting period
ASSETS			
1. Non-Current Assets			
(a) Property, plant and equipment	1	2,35,378	2,22,184
(b) Goodwill		–	
(c) Other intangible assets	1a	78,308	2,12,562

(d) Financial assets:			
(i) Trade receivables		–	–
(ii) Others		–	–
(e) Deferred tax assets(net)		40,101	33,058
(f) Other non-current assets	2	4,50,000	1,00,000
2. Current Assets			
(a) Financial Assets:			
(i) Trade receivables	3	19,67,344	7,87,409
(ii) Cash and cash equivalents	4	35,36,796	1,14,499
(iii) Bank balances other than (ii) above		23,67,426	61,11,751
(iv) Others		–	–
(b) Current tax assets (net)	5	42,59,021	38,82,528
(c) Other current assets	6	2,38,794	3,46,390
Total Assets		**1,31,73,168**	**1,18,10,381**
EQUITY AND LIABILITIES			
Equity			
(a) Equity share capital	7	95,00,000	95,00,000
(b) Other equity	7a	30,58,257	17,62,299
Liabilities			
1. Non-Current Liabilities			
(a) Deferred tax liabilities (net)			
2. Current Liabilities			
(a) Other current liabilities	8	4,28,885	2,64,056
(b) Provisions	9	1,86,026	284,026
Total Equity and Liabilities		**1,31,73,168**	**1,18,10,381**

PART II - Statement of Profit and Loss

XYZ Ltd.

Statement of Profit and Loss for the Year Ended 31st March 2017

S. No	Particulars	Sch. No.	Figures for the current reporting period	Figures for the previous reporting period
(I)	Revenue from operations			
	(a) Brokerage income	10	1,43,97,333	1,26,90,829
	(b) Other operating revenues		–	–
(II)	Other Income	11	6,26,285	5,38,381
(III)	**Total income (I) + (II)**		**1,50,23,618**	**1,32,29,210**
(IV)	(a) Employee benefit expense	12	90,00,629	8,123,623
	(b) Financial costs	13	382	35,295
	(c) Depreciation and amortization expense		2,57,456	2,45,808
	(d) Other administrative expenses	14	37,81,753	40,90,795
	Total Expenses (IV)		**1,30,40,220**	**1,24,95,521**

(V)	Profit before exceptional and extra-ordinary items and tax (III – IV)			19,83,398		7,33,689
(VI)	Exceptional Items			–		
(VII)	Profit before extraordinary items and tax [(V) – (VI)]			19,83,398		7,33,689
(VIII)	Extraordinary Items			–		–
(IX)	Profit before tax [(VII) – (VIII)]			**19,83,398**		**7,33,689**
(X)	**Tax expense:**					
	(1) Current tax		7,00,000		2,60,000	
	(2) Deferred tax		(7,043)	6,92,957	(20,101)	2,39,899
(XI)	Profit after tax (IX – X)			**12,90,441**		**4,93,790**
(XII)	Earning per equity share:					
	(1) Basic			1.36		0.52
	(2) Diluted			1.36		0.52

XYZ Ltd.

Cash Flow Statement for the Year Ended 31st March 2017

(As per Accounting Standard AS(3) Issued by

The Institute of Chartered Accountants of India)

Particulars	Figures as at the end of the current reporting period	Figures as at the end of the Previous reporting period
A. Cash Flow from Operating Activities		
Net profit after taxation and extraordinary items:	12,90,441	4,93,790
Additions:		
Depreciation	2,57,456	2,45,808
Deferred tax	(7,043)	(20,101)
Interest income, dividend and commission received	(6,26,285)	(5,38,381)
Interest expenses	382	35,295
Cash Generated Before Working Capital Changes	9,14,951	2,16,411
Adjustments For:		
(Increase)/Decrease in sundry debtors	(11,79,935)	8,17,601
(Increase)/Decrease in loans and advances	(2,42,404)	(1,47,110)
(Decrease)/Increase in sundry creditors	66,829	(32,972)
Cash Generated from Operations	**(13,55,510)**	**6,37,519**
Direct taxes paid	(3,76,493)	(6,13,347)
Net cash flow from operation before extraordinary items	(8,17,052)	2,40,583
B. Cash Flow from Investing Activities		
Purchase of fixed assets including working in progress	(1,36,395)	(3,80,000)
Interest received	6,26,285	5,38,381
Net cash from/(used in) Investing activities	4,89,890	1,58,381

C. Cash Flow from Financing Activities		
IT relating to earlier year	5,516	
Interest expenses	(382)	(35,295)
Net cash from Financing Activities	5,134	(35,295)
Net Increase in Cash and Cash Equivalents	**(3,22,028)**	**3,63,669**
Cash and cash equivalents at the beginning of the year	62,26,250	58,62,581
Cash and cash equivalents at the end of the year	59,04,222	62,26,250
Change in Cash and Cash Equivalents	**(3,22,028)**	**3,63,669**

XYZ Ltd.

Notes on Accounts for the Year Ended 31st March 2017

1 Property Plant and Equipment (Non Current Assets)

Particulars	Figures as at the end of current reporting period	Figures as at the end of previous reporting period
Property Plant & Equipment	2,53,378	2,22,184
Total	**2,53,378**	**2,22,184**

1a Other Intangible Assets (Non Current Assets)

Particulars	Figures as at the end of current reporting period	Figures as at the end of previous reporting period
Other Intangible Assets	73,808	2,12,562
Total	**73,808**	**2,12,562**

2 Other Non-Current Assets

Particulars	Figures as at the end of current reporting period	Figures as at the end of previous reporting period
(A) Capital Advances		
Unsecured considered good	–	–
(B) Security Deposits		
Unsecured considered good	4,50,000	1,00,000
Total	**4,50,000**	**1,00,000**

3 Trade Receivables (Current Assets: Financial Assets)

Particulars	Figures as at the end of current reporting period	Figures as at the end of previous reporting period
(A) Trade receivables outstanding for a period less than twelve months from the date they are due for payment		
From the date they are due:		
(i) Secured, Considered good		
(ii) Unsecured, Considered good	19,67,344	7,87,409
(B) Others		
Total	**19,67,344**	**7,87,409**

4 Cash and Cash Equivalents (Current Assets: Financial Assets)

Particulars	Figures as at the end of current reporting period	Figures as at the end of previous reporting period
(A) Balances with banks (i) Bank balances held as margin money or as security against: (a) Letter of credit (b) Other commitments (Fixed deposit against lien with IRDA)	12,42,469	11,46,728
(ii) Other bank balances		
(a) Others including balances in current account	35,27,891	1,12,389
(b) Bank balances other than (a) above	11,24,957	49,65,023
(B) Cash in hand	8,905	2,110
Total	**59,04,222**	**62,26,250**

5 Other Current Assets [Current Tax Assets (Net)]

Particulars	Figures as at the end of current reporting period	Figures as at the end of previous reporting period
Unsecured, considered good		
Secured, considered good	–	–
Current tax assets (Net)	42,59,021	38,82,528
Total	**42,59,021**	**38,82,528**

6 Other Current Assets

Particulars	Figures as at the end of current reporting period	Figures as at the end of previous reporting period
Unsecured, considered good		
Secured, considered good	–	–
Advances to Employees	1,35,408	1,66,055
Others (advance for prepaid expenses and other trade advances)	1,03,386	1,80,335
Total	**12,38,794**	**3,46,390**

7 Equity Share Capital

Particulars	Figures as at the end of current reporting period	Figures as at the end of previous reporting period
Equity Share Capital	95,00,000	95,00,000
Total	**95,00,000**	**95,00,000**

7a Other Equity

Particulars	Figures as at the end of current reporting period	Figures as at the end of previous reporting period
Other Equity	30,58,257	17,62,299
Total	**30,58,257**	**17,62,299**

8 Other Current Liabilities

Particulars	Figures as at the end of current reporting period	Figures as at the end of previous reporting period
Accrued Salaries and Incentives		
Salaries and benefits		–
Bonus and Incentives	2,32,273	1,82,901
Taxes payable	1,96,612	79,223
Trade advances (Cr. balance in sundry debtors)	–	1,932
Total	**4,28,885**	**2,64,056**

9 Provisions

Particulars	Figures as at the end of current reporting period	Figures as at the end of previous reporting period
(a) Provision for income tax	–	–
(b) Provision for expenses	1,86,026	2,84,026
Total	**1,86,026**	**2,84,026**

Notes on Accounts for the Year Ended 31st March 2017

Particulars	Figures as at the end of current reporting period		Figures as at the end of Previous reporting period	
10 Brokerage Income				
Gross receipts	1,64,61,637		1,44,27,295	
Less: Service tax	20,64,304	1,43,97,333	17,36,466	1,26,90,829
11 Other Income				
(a) Interest income	6,26,285		5,38,381	
(b) Other non-operating income	–	6,26,285	–	5,38,381
12 Expenses				
Employee benefits expense				
(i) Salaries and wages	56,05,379		5,759,606	
(ii) Directors remuneration	27,60,000		1,440,000	
(ii) Contribution to provident and other funds	3,48,998		6,54,997	
(iii) Staff welfare expenses	2,86,252	90,00,629	2,69,020	81,23,623
13 Finance Costs				
Interest expenses		382		35,295
14 Other Expenses				
(a) Power and fuel	3,913		3,786	
(b) Rent	3,38,100		1,92,000	
(c) Repairs to machinery	59,704		55,712	
(d) Insurance	81,631		77,049	
(e) Rates and taxes	84,500		44,498	
(f) Miscellaneous expenses	33,342		19,824	
(g) Repairs and maintenance to others	69,344		50,299	
(h) Travelling and conveyance	8,20,469		14,26,312	

(i) Bank charges	5,834		7,121	
(j) Professional fees	1,80,500		86,505	
(k) Retainer fees	10,50,000		11,05,000	
(l) Postage and communication expenses	2,48,801		2,49,571	
(m) Printing and stationery	45,990		33,905	
(n) Fees/ Payments to IRDA	72,972		56,494	
(o) Co broking commission	1,42,121		2,27,394	
(p) Bad debts	30,497		39,074	
(q) Management fee	3,90,000		1,80,000	
(r) Advertisement and selling expenses	11,961	36,69,679	1,51,251	40,05,795
(s) Net gain or loss on foreign currency transaction (other than considered as finance cost)		7,074		0
(t) Payments to the auditor as:				
(i) Auditor	50,000		50,000	
(ii) For taxation matters	20,000		20,000	
(iii) For Other services	35,000		15,000	
(iv) For reimbursement of expenses	–	1,05,000	–	85,000
Total		**37,81,753**		**40,90,795**
15 Extraordinary Items-Prior period Expenses		–		–

REVIEW QUESTIONS

1. What is meant by revenue from operations?
2. Name any two items that appear under other income.
3. Give the meaning of costs of materials consumed.
4. Name any two items that appear under employees benefit expenses.
5. Name any two items that appear under finance costs.
6. How will you deal with preliminary expenses in final account of companies?
7. Write a short note on shareholder's funds.
8. State the meaning of non-current liabilities.
9. What do you understand by current liabilities?
10. What are tangible assets?
11. Give some examples for intangible assets.
12. Define current assets.
13. How will you deal with provision for tax in final accounts of companies?
14. Explain briefly the major changes related to statement of profit and loss introduced by Revised Schedule III to the Companies Act, 2013.
15. Discuss briefly the major changes related to balance sheet introduced by Revised Schedule III to the Companies Act, 2013.
16. Give the format of statement of profit and loss as per Revised Schedule III.
17. Give the format of balance sheet as per Revised Schedule III.

REVIEW PROBLEMS

1. The following Trial Balance has been extracted from the books of ABC Ltd. on 31.03.2015:

Trial Balance as on 31st March 2015

Particulars	Cr. (Rs.)	Particulars	Dr. (Rs.)
Plant and machinery	9,00,000	Sinking fund	1,00,000
Stock of raw material	1,75,000	Sundry creditors	1,00,000
Live stock	4,30,000	Equity share capital	15,00,000
Loan to director	1,35,000	15% Debentures	25,000
IFCI bonds	2,00,000	Outstanding salary	10,000
Profit and Loss A/c	10,000	Proposed dividend	2,00,000
Patents	3,74,000	Revaluation reserve	1,65,000
Discount on issue of shares	25,000	Mortgage loan	2,54,000
Interest accrued	1,05,000		
	23,54,000		23,54,000

Prepare the Balance Sheet of the company as per Revised Schedule III of the Companies Act, 2013.

2. Prepare Balance sheet of Samarth Ltd. in a prescribed pro forma as on 31-03-2015 from the following Trial Balance:

Trial Balance as on 31st March 2015

Particulars	Dr. (Rs.)	Particulars	Cr. (Rs.)
Lease hold premises	13,00,000	Debenture redemption reserve	3,75,000
Plant and equipment	9,45,000	Provision for warranties	1,35,000
Book debts	3,44,000	Short term loan from Ambica Ltd.	2,65,000
Bank balance	1,45,000	Profit and loss A/c	2,69,000
Advance income tax	85,000	12% Debentures	4,55,000
Licenses and franchise	2,25,000	Commission payable	44,000
Redeemable preference shares in Sonata Ltd.	6,30,000	32,000 equity shares of Rs. 100 each, Rs.50 called up	16,00,000
Cheques on hand	95,000	Provision for tax	46,000
Rent paid in advance	36,000	Interest accrued	54,000
		Mortgage loan from IDBI	5,62,000
	38,05,000		38,05,000

3. From the following Ledger balances of Mahan LTD., prepare a Balance Sheet of the company as on 31st March 2014 as per Revised Schedule III of the Companies Act, 2013.

Particulars	(Rs.)	Particulars	(Rs.)
Furniture and fixtures	5,00,000	Free hold property	32,00,000
Public issue of 7% bonds	15,00,000	8% Government bonds	8,00,000
Provident fund	4,60,000	Provision for taxation	1,40,000
General reserve	5,40,000	Cash in hand	5,00,000
10% Preference share capital	15,00,000	Acceptances received	7,20,000
Equity share capital	26,00,000	Discount on issue of shares	1,30,000
Outstanding printing and stationery	86,000	Bank overdraft	4,50,000
Payment due to suppliers	9,00,000	Loan to Managing Director	3,72,000
Trade investment	3,24,000	Goodwill	5,40,000
Interest accrued on investment	48,000	Cash at bank	10,42,000

4. From the following Ledger Balances of Premier Co. Ltd., prepare a Balance Sheet of the company as on 31st March 2015 as per Revised Schedule III of the Companies Act, 2013.

Particulars	(Rs.)	Particulars	(Rs.)
Plant and machinery	3,00,000	Premises	5,00,000
6% Debenture	4,00,000	Fixed deposits with banks	2,50,000
Provision for workmen compensation	65,000	Provision for taxation	90,000
General reserves	40,000	Loan from Bank of India	2,50,000
Cash in hand	17,000	Discount on issue of debentures	55,000
Equity share capital	6,00,000	(unwritten off)	
Sundry creditors	58,000	Bills receivable	1,20,000
Advance salary to staff	35,000	Bank overdraft	75,000
Shares of Reliance Co. Ltd.	99,000	Security deposits	62,000
Commission receivable	50,000	Goodwill	90,000

5. From the following Ledger Balances of Akshar Co. Ltd., prepare a Balance Sheet of the company as on 31st March 2015 as per Revised Schedule III of the Companies Act, 2013:

Particulars	(Rs.)	Particulars	(Rs.)
Equity share capital	26,00,000	Advances to employees	1,50,000
General reserves	30,000	Discount on issue of debentures(unwritten off)	12,500
12% Debenture	4,00,000	Tools and equipment	3,75,000
Land and buildings	15,54,970	Gratuity fund	3,00,000
Goodwill	10,00,000	Debtors	1,38,520
Bank overdraft	2,45,100	Cash at Bank	1,57,160
Proposed dividend	82,000	Stores and spares	1,77,800
Prepaid insurance	25,000	Profit and loss A/c [Cr.]	21,490
Mutual fund	1,68,000	Bills receivable	44,600
Interest payable	32,400	Sundry creditors	92,560

6. Following balance have been extracted from the books of Jenins Company Ltd. as on 31st March 2014:

Particulars	Dr. (Rs.)	Cr. (Rs.)
Machinery	1,60,000	
Land and building	6,74,000	
Depreciation on machinery	16,000	
Purchase (adjusted)	4,00,000	
Closing stock	1,50,000	
Wages	1,20,000	
Sales		10,00,000
Salaries	80,000	
Bank overdraft		2,00,000
10% Debentures (issued on 1st April 2013)		1,00,000
Equity share capital—shares of Rs.100 each (fully paid)		2,00,000
Preference share capital—1,000 6% Shares of Rs.100 each (fully paid)		1,00,000

The Board of Directors of Jenins Company Ltd. Had decided to make the following appropriations:

I. To declare an equity dividend @10% on paid up capital
II. To pay dividend on the preference share capital in full
III. To transfer Rs. 2,00,000 to general reserve.

Prepare statement of profit and loss for the year ended 31st March 2014 and Balance sheet as at that date. Ignore the income tax.

(Ans. Revenue from operations Rs. 10,00,000:cost of goods sold Rs. 4,00,000; Employee benefits expenses Rs. 2,00,000; Finance cot Rs.10,000: Dep. and amortised exp. Rs. 16,000; profit Rs. 3,74,000; shareholder's funds. Rs, 6,43,580; Non-current liabilities: Rs. 1,00,000; Current liabilities Rs. 2,40,420; Non-current assets: Rs. 8,34,000; Current assets Rs. 1,50,000; B/S total Rs.9,84,000)

7. A limited company was registered with an authorised capital of Rs. 30,00,000 in equity shares of Rs.10 each. The following is the list of balance extracted from its books on 31.12.2014:

	(Rs.)
Purchase	9,25,000
Wages	4,24,325
Manufacturing expenses	65,575
Salaries	70,000
Bad debts	10,550
Directors fees	31,125
Debenture interest paid	45,000
Preliminary expenses	25,000
Calls-in arrears	37,500
Plant and Machinery	15,00,000
Premises	16,50,000
Interim dividend paid	1,87,500
Furniture and fittings	35,000
Sundry debtors	4,36,000
General expenses	84,175
Stock on 1.1.94	3,75,000
Cash in hand	1,00,000
Goodwill	28,750
Cash at bank	1,99,500
Subscribed and fully called up capital	20,00,000
Profit and Loss A/c (Cr)	72,500
6% Debentures	15,00,000
Sundry creditors	2,90,000
Bills payable	1,67,500
Sales	20,75,000
General reserve	1,25,000

You are required to prepare statement of profit and loss for the year ended 31.12.2014 and the Balance sheet as on that date, after making the following adjustment.

Depreciates Plant and Machinery by 10%. Provide half year's interest on debentures. Also write off preliminary expenses and make provision for bad and doubtful debts of Rs. 4,250 on sundry debtors. Stock on 31st December 2014 was Rs. 4,55,000. Provided for corporate dividend tax@17%

(Ans. Revenue from operations Rs. 20,75,000; cost of goods sold Rs. 8,45,000; Employee benefits benefits expenses Rs. 4,94,325; Finance cost Rs. 90,000; Dep and amortised exp. Rs.1,75,000; other expenses Rs. 1,95,675: profit Rs. 2,75,000; Shareholders funds: Rs. 22,15,625: Non-current assets: Rs.30,63,750; Current assets Rs.11,86,250; B/S total Rs.42,50,000)

8. From the following is the Trial Balance of ABC Company Ltd. as on 31.12.2014, prepare Statement of Profit and Loss Account Balance Sheet:

	Dr. (Rs.)	Cr. (Rs.)
Authorised capital: 50,000 shares of Rs.10 each	–	5,00,000
Subscribed capital:10,000 share of Rs.10 each		1,00,000
Calls-in- arrears	6,400	
Land	10,000	
Building	25000	
Machinery	15,000	
Furniture	3,200	
Carriage inwards	2,300	
Wages	21,400	
Salary	4,600	
Bad debts reserve(1.1.2014)		1,400
Sales		80,000
Sales returns	1,700	
Bank charges	100	
Coal	700	
Rates and taxes	800	
Purchase	50,000	
Purchase return		3,400
Bills receivable	1,200	
General expenses	1,900	
Sundry debtors	42,800	
Sundry creditors		13,200
Stock on 1.1.2014	25,000	
Fire insurance	400	
Cash at bank	13,000	
Cash in hand	2,500	
Securities premium	–	6,000
General reserve	–	24,000
	2,28,00	2,28,000

Charge depreciations on building at 2 ½% on Machinery at 10% and on Furniture at 10%.
Make a reserve of 5% on debtors for bad debts.
Carry forward the following unexpired amount
Fire insurance Rs. 120
Provide for liabilities
Wages Rs. 3,200. Salaries Rs.500 and Rates. Rs. 200.
The value of stock on 31.12.2014 was Rs.30,000.

(Ans. Revenue from operations Rs. 78,300;Cost of goods sold Rs.43,900; Employee benefits expenses Rs. 29,700; Dep. and amortised exp. Rs. 2,445; other expenses Rs. 4,720; Loss Rs. 2,465; Shareholder's funds; Rs. 1,21,135; Current liabilities Rs, 17,100; Non- current assets: Rs. 50,755; Current assets Rs.87,480; B/S total Rs.1,38,235.

9. The following Trial Balance of Nallis Ltd. as at 30th Dec. 2008 is given to you:

Particulars	Dr. (Rs.)	Particulars	Cr. (Rs.)
Stock (1.1.2008)	80,000	8,000 equity shares of Rs. 100	
Bank	17,600	each, Rs.75 paid	6,00,000
Patents	60,000	6% debentures	2,00,000
Calls-in arrears	20,000	Sundry creditors	1,00,000
Returns inwards	30,000	General reserve	80,000

Purchase	7,72,000	Sales	10,00,000
Wages	1,08,000	Returns outward	20,000
Insurance prepaid	400	P and L A/c	12,000
Bills receivable	30,000		
Sundry debtors	80,000		
Discount on issues of debentures			
Plant and machinery	10,000		
Land and Building	4,00,000		
Insurance	3,00,000		
General expenses	4,000		
Establishment expenses	40,000		
	60,000		
	20,12,000		20,12,000

Additional Information:

(i) The value of stock on 31st Dec. 2008 was Rs.74,000.

(ii) Outstanding wages totaled Rs. 10,000.

(iii) A provision 5% is to be created on sundry debtors for doubtful debts.

(iv) Depreciate patents @10% and Plant and Machinery @ 7/ ½% and on the Land and Building @4%.

You are required to prepare Statement of profit and Loss for the ended 31.12.2008 and Balance sheet as on that date.

(Ans. Revenue from operations Rs. 9,70,000; cost of goods sold Rs. 7,58,000; Employee benefit expenses Rs. 1,18,000; Dep. and amortised exp. Rs. 48,000; other expenses Rs. 1,08,000; Loss Rs. 62,000; Shareholders funds: Rs. 6,10,000; Non-current assets:Rs.2,00,000; Current liabilities Rs.1,10,000; Non-current assets; Rs.7,12,000: Current assets Rs.2,08,000; B/S total Rs. 9,20,000)

10. From the following balances as on 31st Dec.2008 of a Limited company, prepare the Statement of Profit and Loss for the year ended and Balance Sheet as on that date:

Particulars	Dr. (Rs.)	Particulars	Cr. (Rs.)
Stock 1.1.2010	33,380	Subscribed and paid up capital	50,000
Discounts	6,788	Sales	1,46,268
Land	22,000	Sundry receipts	200
Plant and machinery	10,700	Creditors	39,532
Purchase	91,888	Provision for bad debts	5,300
Furniture	2,750	Discounts (Cr.)	5,904
Debtors	63,600	Bank overdraft	13,823
P and L A/c (Dr.)	4,960	Customer's deposit	400
Carriage	3,780		
Wages	9,016		
Bad debts	1,820		
Office expenses	10,275		
Cash in hand	470		

The following adjustments have to be made:

(a) Stock on 31.12.2010 Rs.35,460

(b) Depreciation on Plant and Machinery at 10% and furniture at 6%.

(c) Provide 10% for bad and doubtful debts.

(d) Customers deposit has been forfeited.

(e) Proposed dividend at 10%

(f) Provision for taxation Rs. 7,500

(g) The Managing director is entitled to 10% commission on net profit before charging such commission.

(Ans. Revenue from operations Rs. 1,46,268; other income Rs. 6,504; cost of goods sold Rs. 93,588; Employee benefit expenses Rs. 9,016; Dep. and amortised exp. Rs. 1,235; other expenses Rs. 23,478; profit after tax Rs. 17,955; Shareholder's funds: Rs.57,145; Current liabilities Rs. 70,240; Non-current assets: Rs. 34,215; Current assets Rs.93,170; B/S total Rs.1,27,385)

Hint: Profit for M.D's commission is arrived at after adding back provision for tax and PBDD.

11. Following is the Trial balance extracted from the books of Foster Company Ltd.

Particulars	Dr. (Rs.)	Particulars	Dr. (Rs.)
Stock on 1.1.2006	7,000	Authorised capital:	
Purchase	30,000	2,000 equity shares of Rs.100 each	2,00,000
Wages	8,000	Issued share capital	1,00,000
Carriage	2,000	Rent received	3,500
Building	50,000	Sales	1,05,000
Motor vehicle	37,000	Sundry creditors	16,800
Sundry debtors	9,600	Bank overdraft	12,200
Salaries	15,000	Profit and Loss A/c	22,500
Bank interest and charges	400		
Travelling expenses	4,000		
Machinery	80,000		
Discount allowed	1,500		
Cash in hand and at Bank	1,000		
Printing and Stationary	2,000		
Repairs and renewals	1,500		
Director's remuneration.	2,500		
Audit fees	500		
Calls-in arrears	3,000		
Interim dividend	5,000		
	2,60,000		2,60,000

Adjustments:

(i) Closing stock on 31.12.2006 was Rs. 6,000

(ii) Outstanding wages were Rs. 1,000

(iii) Depreciate machinery by Rs.2,000, Building by Rs. 7,000 and Motor vehicle by Rs. 60.

(iv) Directors declared a final dividend at 20% on paid up capital.

(v) Create a provision for bad debts at 5 on debtors.

(vi) There is a contingent liability of Rs. 2,000 for the compensation claim against the company pending in the court.

(vii) Provide for corporate dividend tax@ 17% on interim dividend and proposed dividend.

You are required to prepare Profit and Loss Account for the year ended 31.12.2006 and Balance sheets as on that date.

(Ans. Revenue from operations Rs. 1,05,000; other income Rs. 3,500; cost of goods sold Rs. 33,000; Employee benefit expenses Rs. 24,000; Dep. and amortised exp. Rs. 9,620; other expenses Rs. 12,880; profit Rs. 29,000; Shareholder's funds: Rs. 1,19,952; Current liabilities 53,548; Non-current assets: Rs.1,57,380; Current assets Rs.16,120; B/S total Rs. 1,73,500)

24

ACCOUNTING IN COMPUTERIZED ENVIRONMENT

Learning Objectives

After going through this chapter, you should be able to:

- Discuss the meaning and role of Computer in Accounting System.
- State the merits and demerits of Computerized Accounting System.
- Know about the usage of the Accounting Software.
- Differentiate Computer Accounting from Manual Accounting system.
- Describe various Computer Accounting Problems.
- Understand simple accounting and financial problems.

Computer Applications in Business

Computers are, in recent times, are being used in diversified fields such as business and industry, services, engineering, health care, education, etc. A computer can be applied in almost all types of accounting, technical and managerial matters of business and industry. Some of the areas where computers are used in business and industry are as follows: [a] Inventory Control, [b] Production Planning, [c] budgeting and Variance Analysis, [d] Plant Capacity Utilization, [e] Quality Control, [f] Market Research, [g] Purchase Accounting, [h] Sales Accounting, [i] Payroll Accounting, [j] Information Management, and so.

Role of Computer

With the expansion of business activities, the volume of business transactions has increased. The manual method of maintaining books of accounts is found to be unmanageable and gradually computers have replaced the manual method of accounting. And finally the database technology has revolutionized the accounting departments of business organizations. Computer is an electronic device that can perform a variety of operations in accordance with a set of instructions called program. It is fast electronic data processing machine, which can provide solutions to all complicated situations. It accepts data from the user, converts the data into information, and provides the desired results. Hence, computer accepts the data, stores data, processes data as desired, retrieves the stored data as when required and print the results in desired format.

Characteristics of Computer

- **Speed.** Computer can access and process data at a very high speed and can store data and information in its memory, process them and produce the desired results. It is used essentially as a data processor.
- **Storage.** Computer has the capability of storing vast amount of data and information. It is also capable of storing pictures and sound in digital form.
- **Accuracy.** The accuracy of computer is very high in processing the data and providing desired results. If there are any errors, which would be because of the human errors such as wrong program or inaccurate data, etc.
- **Versatility.** Computer can perform wide range of jobs with speed, accuracy, and diligence.
- **Communication.** Computer can be used as a power communication tool within the office and outside through network of computer.

Components of Computer

The major components of a computer are Input Unit, Central Processing Unit, and Output Unit. These components may be presented diagrammatically as follows:

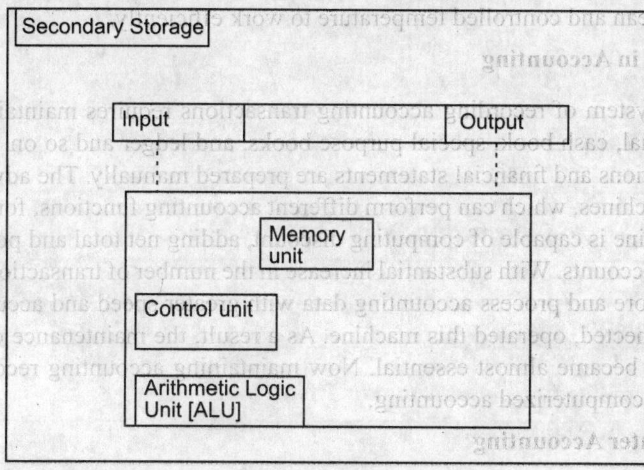

Major Components of Computer

Input Unit: Input unit is controlling the various devices that are used for entering data into the computer. Keyboard, mouse and scanner are the mostly used input devices. Other such devices are magnetic tape, magnetic disk, light pen, bar code reader, smart card reader, etc. In addition there are other devices that respond to voice and physical touch. The input unit is responsible for taking input and converting it into binary system. For example, the physical touch system is installed at airport for obtaining the online information about departure and arrival of flight.

Central Processing Unit [CPU]: The CPU is the control center for a computer. It guides, directs, and governs its performance. It is the brain of the computer. It is the main unit inside the computer. It is used to store program, photos, graphics, and data and obey the instructions in program. It is divided into three units – Control unit, Memory unit and Arithmetic Logic Unit [ALU]. Control unit accepts input data and converts it into computer binary system. It controls and coordinates the activities of all the components of the computer. Memory unit stores data before being actually processed. The data so stored and the instructions for accessing and processing are also stored in the memory section of the computer. Arithmetic and Logic unit is responsible for performing all the arithmetical calculations and computations such as addition, subtraction, multiplication, and division. It also performs logical functions involving comparisons among variable and data items.

Output Unit converts the processed data into human readable form, which is understandable by the user. The commonly used output devices include like monitor, also called visual display unit, printer, etc.

Limitations of Computer: The limitations of computer are depending upon the operating environment. Some of these limitations are as follows:

Cost of Installation: The cost of installation and maintenance is very heavy. Computer hardware and software should be updated from time to time with the availability of new versions.

Cost of Training: New versions of hardware and software are introduced in order to ensure efficient use of computer. This requires training and cost is incurred to train the employees.

Self Decision –Making: The computer cannot make a decision like human beings. It is to be guided by the user.

Health Problems: Extensive use of computer may lead to many health problems such as muscular pain, eyestrain, and backache, etc. This affects adversely the working efficiency and increases medical expenditure.

Maintenance of Computer: Computer needs proper maintenance in order to function efficiently. It requires a neat, clean and controlled temperature to work efficiently.

Role of Computers in Accounting

The manual system of recording accounting transactions requires maintaining books of accounts such as journal, cash book, special purpose books, and ledger and so on. From these books summary of transactions and financial statements are prepared manually. The advanced technology involves various machines, which can perform different accounting functions, for example a billing machine. This machine is capable of computing discount, adding net total and posting the requisite data to the relevant accounts. With substantial increase in the number of transactions, a new machine was developed to store and process accounting data with greater speed and accuracy. A computer, to which it was connected, operated this machine. As a result, the maintenance of accounting data on a real-time basis became almost essential. Now maintaining accounting records become more convenient with the computerized accounting.

Meaning of Computer Accounting

Accounting is the language of the business. Different parties such as shareholders, stakeholders, tax authorities, stock exchanges, etc. are interested in the accounting information for their varied needs. A full disclosure is insisted by Securities Exchange Board of India [SEBI] and therefore, full information and its neat, simple, and quick presentation has become very essential. Manually maintained accounting system may not be able to provide all these facilities. In recent times, computers are being used to maintain the accounting records and for the preparation, analysis, and interpretation of accounting statements. Hence, the system operated through computers is called as computerized accounting or simply, accounting in computerized environment.

Special Features of Computerized Accounting System

- It leads to quick preparation of accounts and makes available the accounting statements and records on time.
- It ensures control over accounting work and records.
- Errors and mistakes would be at minimum in computerized accounting.
- Maintenance of uniform accounting statements and records is possible.
- Easy access and reference of accounting information is possible.

- Flexibility in maintaining accounts is possible.
- It involves less clerical work and is very neat and more accurate.
- It adapts to the current and future needs of the business.
- It generates real-time comprehensive MIS reports and ensures access to complete and critical information instantly.

Usage of Accounting Software

The computerized accounting uses the concept of databases. For this purpose an accounting software is used to implement a computerized accounting system. It does away the necessity to create and maintain journals, ledgers, etc. Some of the commonly used accounting software is Tally, Cash Manager, Best Books, etc. Accounting software is basic software, which allows access to the data contained in the data base. It is a system to manage collection of data insuring at the same time that it remains reliable and confidential. Typical computerized accounting software will offer a number of different facilities, such as follows:

- On-screen input and print out of sales invoices
- Automatic updating of customer accounts in the sales ledger
- Recording of suppliers' invoice
- Automatic updating of suppliers' accounts in the purchase ledger
- Recording of bank receipts
- Making payments to suppliers and for expenses
- Automatic updating of general ledger
- Automatic adjustment of stock records
- Integration of database with the accounting program
- Automatic calculation of pay rolls and associated entries
- Computerized accounting programs can provide instant reports for management, for example: Aged debtors summary – a summary of customer accounts showing overdue amounts, Trial Balance, Trading and Profit and Loss Account and Balance Sheet, Stock Valuation, Sales Analysis, Budget Analysis, Variance Analysis, GST/VAT Returns, and Pay Roll Analysis.

When using computerized accounting system on the computer, the input screens have been designed for ease of use. The main advantage is that each transaction needs to be inputted only once, unlike a manual double entry system where two or three entries are required.

While selecting accounting software the following points need to be taken into consideration:

- The requirements of the particular business should match with the available solutions. The software that fulfils the maximum requirement should be selected.
- Costs of the various packages should be considered before final selection.
- It should very simple and easy to use.
- Vendor's credentials should also be verified. A vendor who is prepared to supply updates has to be preferred.

Customized Accounting Software

Customized software is one, which is developed on the basis of the requirement specifications provided by the business unit. A feasibility study is done in order to ascertain the requirements of the unit. Based on these requirements, a requirement specification report is prepared for submission to the top management for approval. After approval, the designing process starts. After testing, it is implemented.

Advantages: [a] It covers all functional areas as per requirement. [b] For ease of data entry, the input screens would be tailor-made to match input documents. [c] The reports would be as per the specifications of the business unit. [d] Bar-code scanners can be used as input devices suitable for its specific needs.

Disadvantages: [a] If requirement specification or documentation is incomplete or control measures are inadequate, the system may work defectively. [b] Inadequate testing may result in bugs in the software. [c] Vendor may not give full support for the operation of the software.

Objects of Introduction of Computers in Accounting

- **Labor Saving:** Labor saving is the main aim of introduction of computers in accounting. It refers to annual savings in labor cost or increase in the volume of work handled by the existing staff.
- **Time Saving:** Savings in time is another object of computerization. Computers should be used whenever it is important to save time. It is important that jobs should be completed in a specified time such as the preparation of pay rolls and statement of accounts. Time so saved by using computers may be used for other jobs.
- **Accuracy:** Accuracy in accounting statements and books of accounts is the most important in business. This can be done without any errors or mistakes with the help of computers. It also helps to locate the errors and frauds very easily.
- **Minimization of Frauds:** Computer is mainly installed to minimize the chances of frauds committed by the employees, especially in maintaining the books of accounts and handling cash.
- **Effect on Personnel:** Computer relieves the manual drudgery, reduces the hardness of work and fatigue, and to that extent improves the morale of the employees.

Components of Computerized Accounting Software

- **Preparation of Accounting Documents:** Computer helps in preparing accounting documents like Cash Memo, Bills, and Invoices, etc., and preparing accounting vouchers.
- **Recording of Transactions:** Every day business transactions are recorded with the help of computer software. Logical scheme is implied for codification of account and transaction. Every account and transaction is assigned a unique code. The grouping of accounts is done from the first page. This process simplifies the work of recording the transactions.
- **Preparation of Trial Balance and Financial Statements:** After recording the transaction, the data is automatically transferred into ledger account by the computer. The Computer prepares the Trial Balance to check the accuracy of the records. With the help of trial balance, the computer can be programmed to prepare the Trading account, Profit and Loss account, and Balance Sheet.

Recording of Transaction

In respective voucher

Sales **Purchases**

Ledger

Trial Balance

Trading and P & L A/c **Balance Sheet**

Transaction Processing System [TPS]: It is the first stage of computerized accounting system. Its purpose is to record, process, validate and store transactions that occur in various functional areas of a business for subsequent retrieval and usage. The following steps are involved in processing a transaction: Data Entry, Data Validation, Processing, and Revalidation, Storage, Information and Reporting. TPS is one of transaction processing systems, which is concerned with financial transactions only. When a system contains only human resources, it is called manual system. When it uses computer resources, it is called computerized system. When both computer and human resources are used, it is called computer-based system. These steps may be explained with an example making use of Automatic Teller Machine [ATM] facility by a Bank – Customer.

- **Data Entry.** Processing presumes data entry. A bank customer operates an ATM facility to make a withdrawal. The actions taken by the customer constitute the data, which is processed after validation by the computerized personal banking system.
- **Data Validation.** It ensures the accuracy and reliability of input data by comparing the same with some predefined standards or known data. 'Error Detection' or Error Correction' procedures do this validation. Error detection control mechanism ensures to detect errors by comparing the actual data with the predetermined norm. And the Error correction mechanism makes suggestions for entering correct data input. The Personal Identification Number [PIN] of the customer is validated with known data. If the PIN is wrong, a suggestion is made to indicate the PIN is invalid. Once the PIN is validated, the amount of withdrawal being made is also checked to ensure that it does not exceed a pre-specified limit of withdrawal.
- **Processing and Revalidation.** The processing of data occurs almost instantaneously in case of Online Transaction Processing [OLTP] provided a valid data has been fed to the system. This is called check input validity. Revalidation occurs to ensure that the transaction in terms of delivery of money by ATM has been duly completed. This is called check output validity.
- **Storage.** Processed actions, as described above, result into financial transaction data. That is, withdrawal money by a particular customer is stored in transaction database of computerized personal banking system. This ensures that only valid transactions are stored in the database. The stored data is processed making use of the Query facility to produce the desired information.
- **Reporting.** Reports can be prepared on the basis of the required information content according to the decision usefulness of the report.

Need for Computerized Accounting

The need for computerized accounting arises from advantages of speed, accuracy and lower cost of handling the business transactions.

- **Numerous Transactions.** The computerized accounting system is capable of large number of transactions with speed and accuracy.

- **Instant Reporting.** It is capable of offering quick and quality reporting because of its speed and accuracy.
- **Reduction in Paper work.** Manual accounting system requires large storage space to keep accounting records/books, and vouchers/documents. The requirement of books and stationery and books of accounts along with vouchers and documents is directly dependent on the volume of transactions beyond certain point. There is a dire need to reduce the paper work and dispense with large volume of books of accounts. This can be achieved with the help of computerized accounting system.
- **Flexible Reporting.** The reporting is flexible in computerized accounting system. It is capable of generating reports of any balance as when required and for any duration which is within the accounting period.
- **Accounting Queries.** There are accounting queries, which are based on some external parameters. For example, a query relating to overdue customers' accounts can be easily answered by using the structured query language [SQL] support of database technology in the computerized accounting system. Such an exercise would be quite difficult and expensive in manual accounting system.
- **Online Facility.** Computerized accounting system offers online facility to store and process transaction data so as to retrieve information to generate and view financial reports.

  Accuracy. The information and reports generated are accurate and quite reliable for decision-making. In manual accounting system, as many people do the job and the volume of transactions is quite large, such information and reports are likely to be distorted and unreliable and inaccurate.
- **Security.** This system is highly secured and the data and information can be kept confidential, when compared to manual accounting system.
- **Scalability.** The system can cope easily with the increase in the volume of business. It requires only additional data operators for storing additional vouchers.

Basic requirements of the Computerized Accounting System

Accounting Framework: A good accounting framework in terms of accounting principles, coding and grouping structure is a pre-condition. It is the application environment of the computerized accounting system.

Operating Procedure: A well-conceived and designed operating procedure blended with suitable operating environment is necessary to work with the computerized accounting system. The computer accounting is one of the database-oriented applications, wherein the transaction data is stored in well organized database. The user operates on such database using the required interface. And he takes the required reports by suitable transformations of stored data into information. Hence, it includes all the basic requirements of any database-oriented application in computers.

Advantages of Computerized Accounting

- **Better Quality Work:** The accounts prepared with the use of computers are usually uniform, neat, accurate, and more legible than manual job.
- **Lower Operating Costs:** Computer is a labor and time saving devise. Hence, the volume of job handled with the help of computers results in economy and lower operating costs.
- **Improved Efficiency:** Computer brings speed and accuracy in preparing the records and accounts and thus, increases the efficiency of employees.
- **Facilitates Better Control:** From the management point of view, greater control is possible and more information may be available with the use of computer in accounting. It ensures efficient performance in accounting work.

- **Greater Accuracy:** Computerized accounting ensures accuracy in accounting records and statements. It prevents clerical errors and omissions.
- **Relieve Monotony:** Computerized accounting reduces the monotony of doing repetitive accounting jobs, which are tiresome and time consuming.
- **Facilitates Standardization:** Computerized accounting facilitates standardization of accounting routines and procedures. Therefore, standardization in accounting is ensured.
- **Minimizing Mathematical Errors:** While doing mathematics with computers, errors are virtually eliminated unless the data is entered improperly in the first instance.

Disadvantages of Computerized Accounting

- **Reduction of Manpower:** The introduction of computers in accounting work reduces the number of employees in an organization. Thus, it leads to greater amount of unemployment.
- **High Cost:** A small firm cannot install a computer accounting system because of its high installation and maintenance cost. To be more economical there should be large volume of work. If the system is not used to its full capacity, then it would be highly uneconomical.
- **Require Special Skills:** Computer system calls for highly specialized operators. The availability of such skilled personnel is very scarce and very costly.
- **Other Problems:** Frequent repair and power failure may affect the accounting work very much. Computers are prone to viruses. Often time's people will assume the computer is doing things correctly and problems will go unchecked for long period of time.

Distinctions between Manual Accounting and Computerized Accounting

Functions	Manual Accounting	Computerized Accounting
Recording	Recording of financial transactions is through books of original entry.	Data content of these transactions is stored in well-designed database.
Classification	Transactions recorded in the books of original entry are further classified by posting them into ledger accounts. This results in transaction data duplicity.	No such data duplication is done. In order to produce ledger accounts, the stored transaction data is processed to appear as classified so that the same is presented in the form of report.
Summarizing	Transactions are summarized to produce trial balance by ascertaining the balances of various ledger accounts.	No ledger accounts are necessary to prepare a trial balance.
Adjusting entries	Adjusting entries are made in order to follow the matching principle.	No adjusting entries for errors and rectifications are made.
Financial Statements	The preparation of financial statements depends on the availability of trial balance.	The preparation of financial statements is independent of the preparation of trial balance.

Internal Control in Accounting Systems

Controls in Manual Accounting System

- Independent reconciliation of external data like using bank statement to reconcile to the company's bank account or using external supplier statement of account to reconcile with individual creditor account;

- Using Control or Total Account;
- Review of the Trial balance to ensure debit is equal to credit.

Controls in Computerized Accounting System

- **Proper transaction authorization.** Input controls needs to be instituted like input data needs to be verified for accuracy and completeness by a person different from the one who is keying in the data.
- **Besides the above input control,** there should be processing and output controls to ensure integrity of the transaction data intact.
- **No authorized access to computer files, data, etc.** All should be kept under lock and key and proper log is maintained.
- **Uses of pass word control to access data.**

Storage of Data in Files

In a computer system any information, which is required to be stored in a secondary storage medium must be in the form of a file. A file consists of a collection of records of the same context. A record comprises information about an entity and/or event pertaining to the organization as, for example, a purchase, a sale, an employee, etc. All data processing systems use certain data items, which are to a greater extent, permanent in nature. Even if changes occur, they occur very largely. Name, address, date of birth etc., are some examples of such data items. Most data processing systems, therefore, store these data in a separate file, which is called a Master file.

The Transaction files are those files where data are frequently fed into, to update the data availability. The items that are stored in a master file are not keyed in again and again in transactions. For example, once the name or date of birth of employees is stored in a master file, they are retrieved from there as when required for any program. Since such data items are entered and stored to be used respectively repetitively in different programs at various points of items. Once wrong data is stored in a master file, all the outputs in which they appear will contain wrong information. Hence, it is important to ensure the accuracy of data in master files

Data Processing

The work done by a computer is termed as data processing. The computer processes the data into meaningful information. This information forms the basis for further action to be initiated by the user or computer itself. The documents from which the data are taken out for processing is called **source documents,** say for example, ledgers. The various types of data used in a computer are numeric data, character data, or alphabetic data, alphanumeric data and logical data. Data processing involves the following functions:

- Input/output invoicing, Recording, coding, storing, selecting, etc.
- Data transformation involving calculation, summarization, sorting, merging, etc.
- Information output like display, reproduction, telecommunication, etc.

Data Processing Methods

There are three methods of data processing. They are Batch processing, On-line processing, and Real time processing.

Batch Processing: The term batch processing applies to those situations where similar types of transactions are collected to a cutoff point and then grouped to form a batch for processing. It involves the following two essential steps:

- Sorting of the transaction data in the same sequence as existing in the master file, and
- Updating of records in the master file.

The sorting and updating process are carried out using record keys. The records so sequenced are processed serially one after another. Hence, batch processing is also termed as sequential file processing. Typically, it is carried out in several stages, each stage requiring a separate computer run. The final output is available to the user only after the last run.

On-line Processing: Under this method telecommunication equipment replaces the manual collection of records, as in batch processing and data entry takes place on-line. It is also known as direct access or non-sequential method of file processing. This method has two basic requirements as follows:

- Terminal at various locations connected and controlled by a central computer.
- Storage of records on direct access media like disks, to that the computer can randomly access the required records.

Real-time Processing: Under this method the data relating to each individual transaction, received through the telecommunication line, is treated as batch, and the processed results are communicated back instantaneously. It enables to make decisions on the basis of latest information. This method is suitable where the processed information is required immediately and the on-line processing method is considered very slow. This method is also called as transaction processing. The time taken by the system to respond to an input of data and the display of the required updated information is termed response time. The basic requirements of this method are as follows:

- Large memory to accommodate software and operating system requirements
- Large disk memory
- Stand by facilities to take care of such events as system
- Complex communication system
- Maintenance of audit trails, as well as security of program and data.

Data coding

Coding is a convenient representation of each value of an item of data. It is done in order to make the communication possible between a computer and the user. The data is coded in such a way that is understandable to the computer and the information supplied by the computer through data processing is decoded in the form understandable to the user. The coding is done in order to convert numeric and alphanumeric information in terms of binary digits 0 and 1 and to transmit correct data to the computer. Though the binary codes are less intelligible to a person, it is more useful for the computer. The codes and data can be cross-referenced. The basic requirements of data coding are as follows:

- The code should be designed to identify the characteristic of the item of the data it represents.
- Each code should represent one and only one value of the data.
- The code should be as compact as possible to minimize storage requirements.
- The code should be so designed as to be secure in the case of sensitive data and not amenable to conversion back to the original data.
- The code should be so designed to minimize errors in hounding.
- The code must contain sufficient ciphers to represent all possible values of the data.

Advantages of Data Coding

- Codes occupy less computer storage space.
- Coding enables to save time in entering the data.
- It helps to save time and cost in data transmission.
- It reduces the chances of error in entering the data.
- It facilitates classification, grouping and selection of data.
- Coding provides consistency and unique identification for data entries.

General Problems faced in Computerized Accounting System

User Training: The user, for using computer accounting software, needs to understand the concepts of the software. Hence, he should undergo proper training. A computer operator must learn the basics of computer, concepts of software, working with the operating system software [such as Windows/DOS] and the accounting software.

System Dependency: Using a computer solution makes the user to depend fully on the computer system and necessitates the availability of computer at all times. If the system is not available [due to hardware failure or power cut], it would be difficult to verify the accounts.

Hardware Requirements: A full-fledged computer system with a printer is required to operate the computerized accounting system. Most small organizations may not afford to have such facility with necessary software.

System Failure: When there is a system crash [hard disk crash], there is high risk of losing the data available on the hard disk drive at any point of time. It would be highly painful, if the problem occurs at end of the financial year, when the financial statements should be ready.

Backups and Prints: Backups of the data should be done regularly so that, when the data is lost, it can be restored from floppies [backups]. Regular print outs of the system information would be useful as manual records.

Voucher Management: Accounting software allows easy alteration of data. If a voucher is wrongly placed in a wrong head, it would be very difficult to sort out and bring back the voucher. A good voucher management is very essential.

Security: Additional security has to be provided because improper handling of the system [hardware/software] could be dangerous. Passwords, locks, etc., have to be set so that no unauthorized person can handle the system.

Security Problems

Security is an important aspect in any organization using computers. It is the method of enforcing restrictions on personnel who handle the computer system or its parts. It is a means keeping computer crime on hold. Some of the security problems are as follows:

Theft of Computer Time: Information created by one person may be easily copied by another person who can claim that the data is his own and he is the actual creator. In computers there is nothing like original copy and duplicate copy.

Manipulation of Programs: An intruder, rival or competitor can manipulate, modify or delete one or more programs of a company making the complete software unusable.

Theft of Data: Data stored in a computer can be copied into floppies and could be delivered to competitors. With modern communication networks available, insiders of the company may send confidential information of a company to another. Hackers can connect to network and steal data.

Stealing Software: This is the most commonly committed crime in computers. An employee of the company may copy the software purchased by a company and copy it in his home computer. Precautions and controls can be employed for protecting hardware and software from illegitimate use.

Controlling Access: Controlling of hardware and software should be the first system security. The system should be under lock and key to prevent hardware theft. Physical and electronic access control techniques including keyboard locks, automatic logs, restricted access to systems and limited after-hour use.

Passwords: Passwords should be provided at all levels of system. They should be changed frequently or as and when needed so that unauthorized users cannot enter into the system.

Backup Copies: It is necessary to take frequent backups of all software and keep them separate from the usual media. Backups are often taken on tapes and are used to restore data when the primary data from the system fails. Software programs should also be taken if necessary.

Security for Backup: Backups should be kept in secure place. Loss of backups means disaster for the company. Protection of backups includes fireproof containers and away from the computer installation site to avoid any natural disaster.

Network Control: Most companies may have computers that exchange data with each other using a networking architecture. In such cases, PC users can connect with another person/users and access files or services from the machine. Since outsiders [competitors] can also get connected to our network, special interest should be shown on security of systems and data located on the internet.

Data Encryption: It refers to the means of converting data into an unrecognizable form, transmitting it over a network and decrypting it back so that the original contents can be revealed. If an unauthorized person taps into the file, could not go through its contents.

Computer VIRUS Problems

VIRUS stands for Virtual Information Resource under Seize. A virus is a computer program that spreads itself [infects or replicates] and interferes with the normal functioning of a computer system. A virus may be 'corrupting' user data or formatting hard disk, rebooting system all of a sudden or does something else with which a computer user is affected. A virus spreads itself infecting every user program thereby destroying one or more user programs on the system. A virus attaches its signature to a program file. The virus gets into the memory of the system when the user executes by running the program. Normally, deletion of the infected program file cannot solve this problem.

Viruses that infect files usually add its signature to the last or the starting of the program. This results in the increase or decrease of the file size. They then store the increased bytes within themselves, which makes us feel that there is no increase in the file size. Viruses are programs inserted into another program. They get activated by its host program. They replicate themselves and spread to others through floppy transfer. A virus infects data or program every time the user runs the infected program and the virus takes the advantage and replicates itself.

Types of Viruses

Parasitic Virus: This virus attaches itself to other programs and is activated when the host program is executed. It tries to get attached to more programs so that the chances of getting the virus activated are more. It spreads to other computers when the affected programs are copied. Jerusalem and Data-crime are the best examples for parasitic virus.

Boot Virus: This virus attaches to the boot sector of a storage device such as a floppy or hard disk drive. Thus whenever the floppy or the hard disk drive is booted, the virus gets into the memory. It is designed to enter the boot sector of a floppy disc. It works by replacing the first sector on the disc with part of itself. It hides the rest of the virus code elsewhere on the disc. The virus is loaded by the built in program when the machine is switched on. The boot virus attaches on the DOS boot sector or master boot sector on a hard disk.

Polymorphic Virus: It is a virus, which changes its source code as and when it infects a file. The virus program encrypts the destruction part of the program and infects the system thus escaping from antivirus software. It often comes with a special Mutation Engine, which contains the destruction code.

Macro Viruses: These viruses affect files that were created in MS Office software. They destroy the data in a Microsoft word file or change values in an Excel spreadsheet. These viruses do not affect and its software however; data in MS Office documents will be affected.

Examples of viruses: There are many viruses that affect computer systems. These include C Brain, Microangelo, Love Bug, Mellisa, etc.

Avoiding Viruses

It is always better to avoid a viral attack. To do so,

- Floppies from outside should be used only after proper virus scan.
- Always backup copies of all data should be kept in a separate place [usually on a floppy]
- Protect floppies should be written.
- Games brought from a different system should be avoided. Games are the most common medium through which viruses spread.
- The system should be loaded with Anti Virus Software.

Anti Virus software is a program, which loads itself into the memory every time the machine is on. It searches for virus or virus-like activity. Antivirus software also cleans the virus if detected. It tries to remove virus code of a system. Examples of popular antivirus software include Norton Antivirus, Trend Pc-Cillin, MacAfee Virus Scan, etc.

Worm is a self propagating program, which often does not cause any destruction to the user data. Instead, the worm tries to unearth the security problems and tries to cause unwanted delay in processing of the CPU.

Trojan Horse is a innocuous program, which looks like a safe program to the user but opens a 'trap door', which is used to transfer user data to another system or cause destruction to user data without the knowledge of the user.

Program for Simple Book keeping System

The necessary accounting reports include:

- A trial balance
- An income statement
- A balance sheet and
- A post closing trial balance

A typical general purpose journal should provide the following information:

[1] Date [2] journal entry number, [3] account to be debited, [4] debit amount, [5] account to be credited, [6] credit amount

The operation of this computer book-keeping system is similar to the operation of a manual system, with the exception of the assistance the computer offers in each of the steps. The sequence of actions listed below illustrates the operation of the system. BCREATE, BPOST, BTRIAL, BINCOME, BSHEET, BJOURNAL, BPRINT, AND BCLOSE are the program names used here.

Time	Action	Program of Manual
Initialization at start of the year	• Determine required accounts • Initialize files	Manual B CREATE
Throughout accounting period	• Gather transactions and post journal • Post entries to files	Manual B POST
End of accounting period	• Prepare trial balance • Prepare Income statement • Post net income/loss to capital accounts • Prepare Balance Sheet • Enter closing journal entries • Close accounts	B TRIAL B INCOME B POST B SHEET B POST and Manual B CLOSE
As required	• List account file contents • Recreate Journal entries • Correct account information • Display accounts	B FLIST B JOURNAL B PRINT B PRINT

General Financial Programs

- **Break even Analysis**

The program must accept cost and price information from the operation and produce a table describing the product's breakeven point and the cost break down for that level of production.

```
10 INPUT "Enter FIXED COSTS" = F
20 INPUT "Enter VARIABLE COST PER UNIT" = V
30 INPUT "Enter UNIT PRICE" = P
40 Q = F/ [P – V]
50 V = V x Q
60 R = P x Q
70 C = P + [V x Q]
80 U = C / Q
85 PRINT "BREAKEVEN POINT"
90 PRINT "BREAKEVEN QUANTITY"; TAB [25] =Q
100 PRINT "BREAKEVEN REVENUES"; TAB [24]; R
110 PRINT "FIXED COSTS"; TAB [15]; F
120 PRINT "VARIABLE COSTS"; TAB [24]; V
130 PRINT "TOTAL COSTS"; TAB [15]; C
140 PRINT "UNIT COST" = TAB [15]; U
```

When we execute this program we will get the following display

Enter FIXED COST > 10000 [operator entry]

Enter VARIABLE COSTS per unit > 4 [operator entry]

Enter UNIT PRICE > 6 [operator entry]

The result will be as follows.

BREAKEVEN QUANTITY		50 000
BREAKEVEN REVENUES		30 000
FIXED COSTS	10 000	
VARIABLE COSTS	20 000	
TOTAL COSTS	30 000	
UNIT COST	6	

- **Ratio Analysis:** This Process calculates and prints a number of ratios that have been found to be useful in business. Some of the useful ratios are: Current Ratio, Acid Test Ratio, Net Profits on Sales Ratio, Investment Turnover Ratio, Return on Investment Ratio, and Inventory Turnover Ratio.
- Cash Flow and Budget Analysis
- Equipment Comparison
- Depreciation
- Amortization Table
- Return on Investment [ROI]
- Mortgage Comparison, etc

Outsourcing of Accounting Function

The accounting function may be outsourced to outside party for a fee. It is done to save cost and utilize the expertise of outside party. The accounting software is used by outside party. He processes the data and hands over different reports to the client from time to time.

Advantages: [a] It saves time and enables the business unit to concentrate on core area of business activity. [b] It is more economical. [c] It enables to obtain the expertise of the outside party. [d] The organization need not bother about the efficiency of the accounting department.

Disadvantages: [a] As the data of the organization lies with the outside party, it may endanger the security and confidentiality of the business data. [b] Sometimes, because of the inefficiency of the outside party, the system may prove to be costly. [c] If the outside party is very busy, he may make delays and organization's reporting work may suffer.

REVIEW QUESTIONS

- Briefly explain the computer applications in business.
- State the meaning and characteristics of computer.
- Explain the components of computer.
- What are the limitations of a computer?
- Explain the role of computers in Accounting.
- Differentiate computerized accounting from manual accounting.
- State the meaning and special features of computerized accounting system.

- State the objects of introducing computer in accounting.
- Enumerate the advantages and disadvantages of computer accounting.
- What are Master Files and Transaction Files?
- What is Data Processing?
- Describe the Data Processing Methods.
- State the meaning and advantages of Data Coding.
- Describe a program for simple Book keeping system.
- Mention a few general financial programs for computer applications.
- Write a note on: [a] Computer Security Problems [b] VIRUS Problems
- Write a note on Outsourcing of Accounting Function.

25

MISCELLANEOUS TOPICS

Learning Objectives

After Reading this chapter, you should be able to:

— Segment Reporting

— Interim Financial Reporting

— Accounting for Investments

— The Effect of Changes in Foreign Exchange Rates

AS 17- Segment Reporting

If there is neither more than one business segment nor more than one geographical segment, segment information as per AS 17 is not required to be disclosed. (Accounting Standards Interpretation 20)

What is the objective of AS 17

Now a days, there are a large number of enterprises that deal in multiple products and services and also operate in different geographical areas. The profitability, risks, future prospects, etc. in these differ considerably. Aggregate information fails to throw much light on the performance of a single segment. This calls for reporting of segment information. Such an information when presented helps users of financial statements:

(*a*) Better understand the performance of the enterprise;

(*b*) Better assess the risks and returns of the enterprise; and

(*c*) make more informed judgements about the enterprise as a whole.

The objectives of AS 17 is to establish principles for reporting segment-wise financial information.

Which accounting policies are to be followed for segment reporting

Segment information should be prepared in conformity with accounting policies adopted for preparing and presenting the financial statements of the enterprise as a whole. However, if an enterprise wants to disclose additional segment information prepared on a basis other than the accounting policies adopted for the enterprise financial statements then it can do so on satisfaction of the following conditions:

(*a*) The information is reported internally to the board of directors and the CEO for purposes of making decisions about allocating resources tc the segment and assessing its performance, and

As 17 at a glance

OBJECTIVE

To establish principles for reporting segment wise financial information to enable users of FS to assess risk & returns of a diversified and/or multi-locational enterprise

↓

SEGMENT

Distinguishable component of an enterprise – could be business segment or geographical (based on location of assets or location of customers) segment

↓

REPORTABLE SEGMENT

To be reported if any one or more conditions applicable

- Revenue Atleast 10%
- Profit Or Loss Atleast 10%
- Segment Assets Atleast 10%
- If Reported In Preceding
- Total Revenue Attributed Less Than 75%
- Management Discretion

TO BE REPORTED IN

Primary & Secondary Reporting Format

Business Segment Primary & Geographic Secondary when there are

- Differences in products & services that the enterprise produces, or
- There are difference in products & services as well as geographic location

Geographic Segment Primary & business & business segment secondary when there are

- Differences in geographic location (of assets or customers)

ACCOUNTING POLICIES

Segment information to be prepared in conformity with accounting policies adopted for FS of enterprise as a whole

PRIMARY DISCLOSURES SECONDARY DISCLOSURES OTHER DISCLOSURES

DISCLOSURES

To be disclosed in both primary & secondary format

When Primary is	Secondary is
1. Business Segment	• Geographic -Location of Assets (LOA) -Location of Customers (LOC)
2. Geographic (LOA)	• Business Segment • Geographic (LOC)
3. Geographic (LOC)	• Business Segment • Geographic (LOA)

(a) Revenue from external
(b) Inter – segment revenue
(c) Segment results
(d) Total carrying amount of segment assets
(e) Total segment liabilities
(f) Cost of acquiring tangible & in tangible FA during the period
(g) Depreciation and amortization expenses
(h) Other significant non – cash expenses
(i) Reconciliation of revenue, segment results, assets & liabilities

- Basics of pricing inter-segment transfer & any charges therein
- Changes in segment accounting policies
- Types of products & services in each business segment
- Composition of each geographical segment

(*b*) The basis of measurement for this additional information is clearly stated.

Further, assets and liabilities that relate jointly to two or more segments should be allocated to segments only if their related revenues and expenses are also allocated to such segments e.g. a fixed asset should be included in segment assets only if the related depreciation is included in the segment expense.

Examples

1. Satyam Computer Services Ltd., year ending March 31,2008

Segment Reporting

The company has identified geographic segments as its primary segment and industry segments as its secondary segment.

Geographic segments of the Company are Americas, Europe, India and Others.

Secondary segments of the Company are Banking, Financial Services and Insurance (BFSI), which are considered as single segment, Manufacturing, Retail and Distribution, Telecom and Others. Others comprise Transportation, Life Sciences and Healthcare, Energy and utilities, s-Governance, Media and Entertainment, Travel and Hospitality services and sale of products, etc.

Revenue and expense directly attributable to segments are reported under each reportable segment. Expenses incurred in India on behalf of other segments and not directly identifiable to each reportable segment have been allocated to each segment on the basis of associated revenues of each segment. All other expenses which are not attributable or allocable to segments have been disclosed as unallocable expenses.

Assets and liabilities that are directly attributable to segment are disclosed under each reportable segment. All other assets and liabilities are disclosed as unallocable. Fixed assets have not been allocated between segments as these are used interchangeably between segments.

Year ended March 31,2008

Particulars	Geographic Segment				(Rs. in cores)
	Americas	Europe	India	Others	Total
Reveue	**10460.75** 8899.62	**5355.86** 4105.58	**1590.47** 1189.63	**1123.64** 745.14	**18533.72** 14939.97
Identified operating expenses	**5831.68** 5124.69	**2713.95** 2180.66	**1169.46** 769.50	**698.40** 473.71	**10413.49** 8548.56
Allocated expenses	**1388.14** 958.11	**757.76** 469.91	**187.87** 140.46	**113.60** 93.35	**2447.37** 1661.83
Segment result	**3240.93** 2816.82	**1884.15** 1455.01	**233.14** 279.67	**314.64** 178.08	**5672.86** 4729.58
Unallocable expense (net)					**1114.95**

Particulars	**Geographic Segment**				**(Rs. in cores)**
	Americas	**Europe**	**India**	**Others**	**Total**
					775.45
Operating income					4557.91 3954.13
Other income					445.95 216.55
Profit before taxes					5003.86 4170.68
Tax expense					495.10 413.39
Net profit					4508.76 3757.29

As at March 31, 2008

	Americas	**Europe**	**India**	**Others**	**Total**
Segment assets	1621.00 1100.24	1994.43 1574.20	1380.21 887.34	740.98 473.91	5736.62 4035.69
Unallocable assets					8999.44 6679.20
Total assets					14736.06 10714.89

Segment liabilities	**1320.99** **821.70**	**754.75** **702.69**	**407.59** **218.50**	**228.60** **180.21**	**2711.93** **1923.10**
Unallocable liabilities					1019.32 732.80
Total liabilities					3731.25 2655.90

Business Segment

The following business segments individually contribute 10 per cent or more of the Company's revenues and segment assets:

Industry Segment

	Revenues for the year ended March 31,2008	**Segment Assets as at March 31,2008**
	(Rs. In crores)	(Rs. In crores)
Banking, financial Services and Insurance	**7554.28** 6088.22	**1545.95** 1165.91
Manufacturing	**1838.41** 1991.11	**402.57** 320.96
Retail and Distribution	**1326.25** 970.97	**282.85** 169.13
Telecom	**3561.13** 2732.22	**1245.00** 797.06

AS 25 at a glance

OBJECTIVE

To lay down what information should be provided in interim financial reports & to prescribe the recognition and measurement principles

↓

SCOPE

To be followed only when an enterprise is otherwise required to prepare & present interim financial statements (IFS)

↓

FORM & CONTENTS

- Minimum components
  - Condenses balance sheet, P&L A/c, cash flow statements [(CFS) containing at a minimum each of the heading & sub-heading of latest annuals FS]
  - Selected explanatory notes (to be disclosed on a year to date basis)
- Basic Diluted EPS to be presented if it also presented in annual FS
- Should include CFS if annual financial report also contain CFS

↓

PERIOD FOR WHICH COMPONENT TO BE PRESENTED

- Balance sheet
  - As on end of current interim period
  - Comparative as at the end of immediately preceding financial year (FY)
- Profit & Loss Account
  - For the current interim period & year to date
  - Comparative for current interim period & year to date of immediately preceding FY
- Cash flow statements
  - Year to date current FY
  - Comparative year to date for immediately preceding FY
- For seasonal business
  - Additional reporting for 12 months ending on interim reporting date and comparative for prior 12 months period

↓

RECOGNITION AND MEASUREMENT PRINCIPLES

- Same as in annual FS
- Revenues received seasonally or occasionally & cost incurred unevenly to be anticipated or deferred at an interim date only if it would have been appropriate at year end

↓

OTHER KEY ISSUES

- Nature & amount of charges in accounting estimates relating to final interim period to be disclosed as a note in the annual FS if, separate IFS are not prepared for final interim period
- A change in accounting policy for which transition not specified by any AS, to be applied retrospectively to prior interim periods of current FY
- Accounting policy changes made in the current period (and, hence, could not be presented in the latest annual FS) to be incorporated in the IFS of current period

↓

TRANSITIONAL PROVISIONS

- No need to present following statements for all the interim periods of a FY for which IFS are presented for the first time
  - Comparative current & year to date statement of profit and loss for the immediately preceding FY
  - Comparative CFS for the comparable year to date period of the immediately preceding FY

AS 25 – Interim Financial Reporting

The presentation and disclosure requirements contained in AS 25 should be applied only if an enterprise prepares and presents an 'interim financial report' as defined in AS 25. Accordingly, presentations and disclosure requirements contained in AS 25 are not required to be applied in respect of interim financial results (which do not meet the definition of 'interim financial report' as per AS 25) presented by an enterprise. For example, quarterly financial results presented under Clause 41 of the Listing Agreement entered into between Stock Exchanges and the listed enterprises do not meet the definition of 'interim financial report' as per AS 25. However, the recognition and measurement principles laid down in AS 25 should be applied for recognition and measurement of items contained in such interim financial results. (Accounting Standards Interpretation 27)

What is the objective of AS 25

Timely and reliable financial information helps the investors, creditors and other stakeholders in an organisation to understand an enterprise's capacity to generate earnings and cash flows, its financial condition and liquidity, etc. However, financial statements prepared on an annual basis fail to meet this objective fully. Hence, the need for interim financial reporting araises. But at the same time due to time and cost constraints only condensed information can be provided in the interim financial statements. Now this information should be such that it provides an update on the latest annual financial statements and not the one which is merely a duplication of the information previously reported. AS 25 has been issued to meet this very objective laying down what information to be provided in the interim financial reports.

What are the minimum components of an interim financial report

An interim financial report should have atleast the following components:

(*a*) Condensed balance sheet;
(*b*) Condensed statement of profit and loss;
(*c*) Condensed cash flow statements; and
(*d*) Selected explanatory notes.

What should be the form and content of interim financial statements if an enterprise prepares and presents:

(*a*) A complete set of financial statements in its interim financial report;

(*b*) A set of condensed financial statements.

(a) If an enterprise prepares and presents a complete set of financial statements in its interim financial report then, the form and content of those statements should confirm to the requirements that are applicable to annual complete set of financial statements.

(b) If an enterprise prepares and presents only a set of condensed financial statements then those condensed statements should include, at a minimum, each of the headings and sun-headings that were included in its most recent annual financial statements and the selected explanatory notes as required by this standard, Additional line items or notes should be included if their omission would make the condensed interim financial statements misleading.

AS 13 – Accounting for Investments

Status: Mandatory

The Standards does not deal with:-

(*i*) *The bases for recognition of interest, dividends and rentals on investments as these are covered by Accounting Standard 9 on Revenue Recognition*;

(*ii*) *Operating or financial leases*;

(*iii*) *Investments of retirement benefit plans and life insurance enterprises; and*

(*iv*) *Mutual funds and/or the related assets management companies, banks and public financial institutions formed under a Central or state Government Act or so aeclared under the Companies Act, 1956.*

Further, pursuant to a limited revision to AS 13, the Standard is also not applicable to venture capital funds in respect of accounting periods commencing on or after 1-4-2002.

What is the objective of AS 13

The objective of AS 13 is to prescribe the accounting treatment for investments in the financial statements of an enterprise and the related disclosure requirements.

What are the key terms that have been defined in AS 13

AS 13 has defined the following terms which are to be used, for the purpose of AS 13, with the meanings specified below:

Investments: Investments are assets held by an enterprise for earning income by way of dividends, interest and rentals, for capital appreciation, or for other benefits to the investing enterprise, e.g., investment in shares, debentures, etc. Assets held to stock-in-trade are not 'investments'.

Current investment: A current investment is an investment that is by its nature readily realisable and is intended to be held for not more than one year from the date on which such investment is made.

Long-term investment: A long-term investment is an investment other than a current investment, e.g., surplus funds invested in shares to be held for 2-3 years.

Investment property: An investment property is an investment in land or buildings that not intended to be occupied substantially for use by, or in the operations of, the investing enterprise.

Thus, investment property is essentially a long-term investment.

Fair value: Fair value is the amount for which an asset could be exchanged between a knowledgeable, willing buyer and a knowledgeable, willing seller in an arm's length transaction. Under appropriate circumstances, market value or net realizable value provides an evidence of fair value.

Market value: Market value is the amount obtainable from the sale of an investment in an open market, net of expenses necessarily to be incurred on or before disposal.

What are the various criteria on the basis of which investments can be classified

The following chart summarises the various criteria on the basis of which investments can be classified:

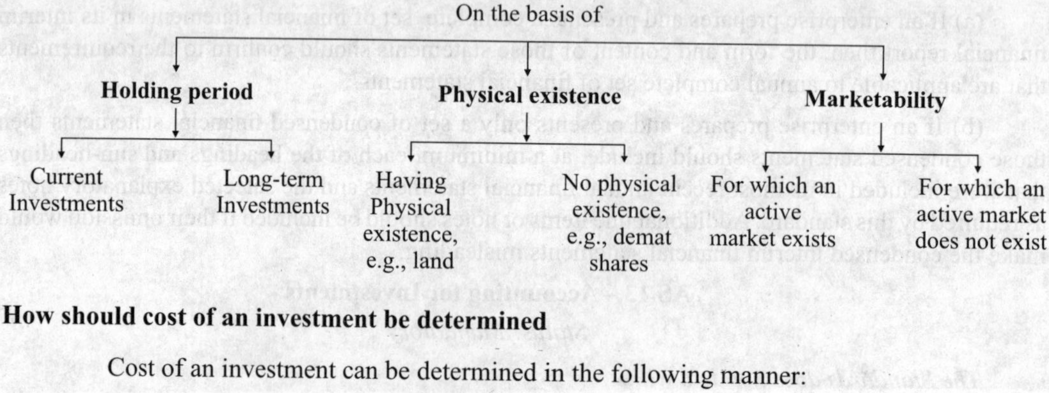

How should cost of an investment be determined

Cost of an investment can be determined in the following manner:

How to compute purchase price: Calculation of purchase price does not involve complexities when actual cash has been paid for acquiring the investments. However, when this is not the case, certain basis need to be adopted for computing purchase price. Under such circumstances, AS 13 prescribes the following guidelines for computing purchase price:

When the investment is acquired (fully or partly)

- **Bu issue of shares or other securities**
  - Acquisition cost is the fair value of the securities issued
- **In exchange (or part exchange) for another asset**
  - Acquisition cost is determined by reference to the fair value of the asset given up or fair value of the investment acquired, whichever is more clearly evident

AS 13 at a glance

OBJECTIVE

To prescribe accounting treatment for investments in the financial statements of an enterprise & related disclosure requirements

TYPES OF INVESTMENTS

- Current
  - Ready realizable
  - To be held for one year or less
- Long Term
  - Intended to held for long period

COMPUTATION OF COST

Purchase price
+ Incidental expenses
- Pre-acquisition income

- ♦ Purchase price when actual cash has been paid
  - Take actual cash price
- ♦ Acquired for consideration other than cash (fully or partly)
  - Issue of securities
    - Fair value of securities issued
  - In exchange for another asset
    - Fair value of asset given up or fair value of investment, whichever is more clearly evident

CARRYING AMOUNT

- Not to be valued on global basis

Current Investment

- Lower of cost & Fair value
- Reductions to fair value & any reversals thereof taken to P&L A/c

Long-term Investment

- Cost
- Permanent reduction to be charged to P&L A/c
- Permanent reduction can be reversed when value of investment rises

DISPOSAL OF INVESTMENT

Investment fully sold

Ascertain carrying amount (a)
Ascertain Net disposal proceeds (b)
If a>b, charge difference to P&L A/c

Investment partly sold

- Ascertain proportionate carrying amount (through FIFO, Average Cost, etc) (a)
- Ascertain Net disposal proceeds (b)

If a>b, charge difference to P&L A/c
a=b, No further action required
a<b, Credit difference to P&L A/c

DISPOSAL OF INVESTMENT

Current to Long-term

Transfer at Lower of Cost & Fair Value at the date of

Long-term to Current

Transfer at Lower of Cost & Carrying Amount at the date

DISCLOSURE

- Accounting policies adopted for determination of carrying amounts
- Gross Income from interest, dividends, rentals separately from long-term & current investments
- TDS on gross income under 'Advances Taxes Paid'.
- Profits and losses on disposal of current investments & long-term investments, alongwith their carrying amounts
- Significant restrictions on right of ownership, realisability of investments or the remittance of income & proceeds of disposal
- Aggregate amount of quoted & unquoted investments
- Aggregate market value of quoted investments

AS 11 (Revised 2003) at a glance

OBJECTIVE

To lay down principles for deciding which exchange rates to be used and how to recognize the financial effect of changes in exchange rates

REPORTING & RECOGNITION PRINCIPLES

Initial Recognition

- Rate on the date of transactions, or
- If no significant fluctuations, average rate if it approx. actual rate

Effects of changes in exchange rate subsequent to initial recignition

- Monetary Items
  - Closing Rate or other realistic rate
- Non-monetary items, carried in terms of
  - Historical Cost
  - Fair value

Exchange differences on monetary items

- ♦ Relating to an enterprise's net investment in a non-integral foreign
  - To be accumulated in a foreign currency translation reserve until the disposal of net investment
- ♦ Others
  - Income or expense of the period

Forward Exchange Contracts

- ♦ Others
  - Ignore premium of discount
  - Mark the value of contract to its current market value on each balance sheet date and recognize the gain or loss
- ♦ For trading or speculative purposes
  - Amortise premium/discount arising at the inception of the contract over the life of contract
  - Recognise the exchange difference in the profit and loss account in the reporting period in which exchange rates change
  - Recognise profit or loss arriving on cancellation or renewal, as income/expense for the period

TRANSLATION OF FINANCIAL STATEMENTS OF FOREIGN OPERATIONS

Non-Integral Foreign Operations

- Assets & liabilities (monetary & non-monetary)
- Income & expense
- Contingent liabilities
- G/W or capital Reserve on acquisition

Integral Foreign Operations

- Individual item in FS of foreign operation
- Cost & depreciation of tangible FA
  (a) When FA carried at cost –Rate at the date of purchase
  (b) When FA carried at fair value - Rate that existed on the date of valuation
- Inventories
  (a) Cost-Rule when cost was incurred
  (b) NRV – When NRV is determined, usually the closing rate

OTHER ISSUES

- Disposal of non-integral foreign operation
  → Recognise the cumulative amount of the exchange differences that have been deferred and which relate to that operation, as income/expense in the period in which gain/loss on disposal is recognised
- Tax effects of exchange differences
  → Apply AS 22
- Change in classification of a foreign operation
  → Apply the translation procedures to the revised classification from the date of change in the classification
  - Integral to non – integral
    - Accumulate the exchange differences arising on translation of non-monetary assets at the date of re-classification, in foreign currency translation reserve
  - Non-integral to integral
    - Translated amount of non-monetary items at the date of change treated as historical cost
    - Exchange differences lying in foreign currency translation reserve not to be recognized as income/expense till the disposal of operation

DISCLOSURES

- Exchange differences included in net profit or loss for the period
- Net exchange differences accumulated in foreign currency translation reserve as a separate component of shareholders' funds, and a reconciliation of the amount of such exchange differences at the beginning and end of the period.
- Reason for using a different currency, when the reporting currency is different from the currency of the country in which the enterprise is domiciled
- When there is a change in classification
  - Nature and reason for change
  - Impact of change on shareholders' funds
  - The impact on net profit or loss for each prior period presented had the change occurred at the beginning of the earliest period presented.

AS 11 (Revised 2003) – The Effect of Changes in Foreign Exchange Rates

The revised standards supersedes Accounting Standard (AS) 11, Accounting for the effects of changes in Foreign Exchange Rates (1994(, except that in respect of accounting for transactions in foreign currencies entered into by the reporting enterprise itself or through its branches before the date this Standard comes into effect, AS 11 (1994) will continue to be applicable.

What is the objective of AS 11 (Revised 2003)

The objective of the Standard is to lay down the principles in deciding which exchange rate to use and how to recognize in the financial statements the financial effect of changes in exchange rates.

What is the scope of the Standards

AS 11 (Revised 2003) is to be applied by an enterprise:

(*i*) In accounting for transactions in foreign currencies; and

(*ii*) In translating the financial statements of foreign operations;

(*iii*) In accounting for foreign currency transactions in the nature of forward exchange contracts (except the ones that are entered into to hedge the foreign currency risk of a 'firm commitment' or 'highly portable forecast transaction').

However, the Standards is not applicable to:

(*i*) The restatement of an enterprise's financial statements from its reporting currency into another currency for the convenience of users accustomed to that currency or for similar purposes.

(*ii*) The presentation in a cash flow statements of cash flows arising from transactions in a foreign currency and the translation of cash flow of a foreign operation.

(*iii*) Exchange differences arising from foreign currency borrowings to the extent that they are regarded as an adjustment to interest costs.

How to account for exchange differences

(*i*) Exchange differences relating to net investment in a non-integral foreign operation: Exchange differences arising on a monetary item that, in substance, forms part of an enterprise's net investment in a non-integral foreign operation should be accumulated in a foreign currency translation reserve in the enterprise's financial statements until the disposal of the net investment.

On the disposal of a non-integral foreign operations, the cumulative amount of the exchange differences which have been deferred and which relate to that operation should be recognized as income or as expenses in the same period in which the gain or loss on disposal is recognized.

(*ii*) Other exchange differences: Other exchange differences arising on the settlement of monetary items or on reporting an enterprise's monetary items at rates different from those at which they were initially recorded during the period, or reported in previous financial statements should be recognized as income or expense in the period in which they arise.

REVIEW QUESTIONS

1. Explain segment reporting?
2. Discuss interim financial reporting?
3. Enumerate accounting for investments?
4. Explain the effect of changes in foreign exchange rates?

APPENDIX

UNIVERSITY QUESTION PAPERS

University of Madras - M.B.A. Degree Examinations

MANAGEMENT ACCOUNTING, APRIL 2001

Time: 3 Hours **Part A** Maximum: 80 or 75 Marks

Answer any 8 questions for New Regulation and 7 questions for Old Regulations.

($8 \times 5 = 40$) or ($7 \times 5 = 35$)

All questions carry equal marks.

1. What are the limitations of Financial Accounting?
2. What are the principal methods employed for ascertaining the profitability of capital expenditure projects?
3. Explain the meaning and objectives of financial statement analysis.
4. What are the uses of the Funds flow Statement?
5. What are the objectives of budgetary control?
6. What are the main features of Job-order costing?
7. Explain the general principles of Process Costing. Name three industries where process costing can be applied.
8. What is the significance of 'Contribution' in marginal costing?
9. Explain the various sales margin variances.
10. What are the points to be borne in mind while presenting cost report to management?
11. How do standard costs differ from estimated costs?
12. Explain the various elements of cost.

Part B (40 Marks)

Answer Questions No. 13 and Two other questions.

Question No. 13 carries 20 marks and others 10 each.

13. A job, which is presently done entirely by manual labour has a labour cost of Rs. 46.00 a year. it is proposed to install a machine to do the job, which involves an investment of Rs. 80,000 and an additional operating cost of Rs. 10,000. Assume the machine can be written off in 5 years on straight-line depreciation basis for tax purposes. Salvage value at the end of its economic life is zero. The tax rate is 55%. Analyze the economic implications of the proposal by return on Investment and Internal rate of Return method.

(Answer: 11.25% or 22.5%; IR 17%)

14. From the following information, prepare a Balance Sheet:

	Rs.		Rs.
Working Capital	75,000	Reserves and Surplus	1,00,000
Bank Overdraft	60,000	Current Ratio	1.75:1
Liquid Ratio	1.15:1	Fixed Assets to Proprietor's funds	0.75
Long-term liabilities	Nil		

(Answer: FA Rs. 2,25,000; Stock Rs. 129000; Liquid Assets Rs. 46,000; Share Capital Rs. 2,00,000; Creditors Rs. 40,000; B/S total Rs. 4,00,000)

15. From the following determine the 'funds from operations':

	Rs.		Rs.
Net loss	12,000	Depreciation on machinery	14,000
Amortization of Goodwill	12,000	Loss on sale of Plane	4,000
Profit on sale of Land	8,500	Provision for likely bad debts	2,000

(Answer: Rs. 9,500)

16. Given

	Sales (Rs.)	Profit (Rs.)
1976	16,000	800
1977	20,000	2,000

Calculate: (i) P/V Ratio, (ii) Profit when sales are Rs. 18,000 and (iii) Sales required to earn a profit of Rs. 2,400.

(Answer: (i) 30%, (ii) Rs. 1,400, (iii) Rs. 21,333.)

M.B.A. Degree Examinations, November 2001

MANAGEMENT ACCOUNTING

Time: 3 Hours **Part A** Maximum: 80 or 75 Marks

Answer any 8 questions for New Regulation and 7 questions for Old Regulations.

(8 × 5 = 40) or (7 × 5 = 35)

Each answer should not exceed a page

1. Distinguish between cost accounting and financial accounting.
2. What are the various classification of ratios?
3. What are the advantages and disadvantages of pay back period?
4. Explain the steps in the installation of a system of budgetary control.
5. What do you mean by elements of cost?
6. What are the advantages of standard costing?
7. Explain the overhead variances.
8. What is break-even analysis? Explain its significance.
9. Explain the important qualities, which a project report should have.
10. Explain normal wastage and abnormal wastage and state how they should be dealt with in process accounts.
11. Explain the advantages and limitations of Job-order cost accounting.
12. Explain the procedure for preparing fund flow statement.

Part B (40 Marks)

Answer Questions No. 13 and Two other questions.

Question No. 13 carries 20 marks and others 10 each.

13. The following are the Balance Sheets of a Limited Company on 31st December 1998 and 1999.

	1998	1999
Liabilities:	(Rs.)	(Rs.)
Share Capital	1,00,000	1,50,000
Premium on issue of shares	—	5,000
General Reserves	50,000	60,000
Profit and Loss account	10,000	17,000
15% Debentures	70,000	50,000
Accumulated depreciation	50,000	56,000
Sundry Creditors	86,000	95,000
	3,66,000	4,33,000
Assets:		
Freehold land	1,00,000	1,00,000
Plant at cost	1,04,000	1,04,000
Furniture at cost	7,000	9,000
Investments at cost	60,000	80,000

Debtors	30,000	70,000
Stock	35,000	29,000
Cash	30,000	41,000
	3,66,000	4,33,000

During 1999, a machine that had been purchased for Rs. 4,000 and on which Rs. 2,000 had been provided as depreciation was sold for Rs. 1,000. You are required to prepare fund flow statement

Ans: Net increase in working capital Rs. 36,000; Total sources Rs. 82.000; Total Applications Rs. 46,000

14. Current liabilities of a company are Rs. 3,00,000. Current Ratio is 3 : 1 and Quick Ratio is 1:1. Calculate the value of the stock in trade.

    Ans: Stock Rs. 6,00,000; C.A. Rs. 9,00,000: Liquid assets Rs. 3,00,000

15. The position of Ram Ltd. in the year 1999 was as follows:

	Rs.
Sales	4,00,000
Less: Variable costs	3,00,000
Gross profit	1,00,000
Less: Fixed cost	30,000
Net profit	70,000

Find out the following: (a) P/V Ratio (b) B.E.P. (c) Net profit for the sales of Rs. 6,00,000 (d) Sales required earning a net profit of Rs. 1,40,000.

Ans: (a) 25% (b) Rs. 1,20,000; (c) Rs. 1,20,000; (d) Rs. 6,80,000.

16. A product passes through three processes, A, B and C. The normal wastage of each process is as follows: Process A – 3%. Process B –5% and Process C–8%. Wastage of process A was sold at 25 Ps. per unit and that of process B at 50 Ps. per unit and that of process C at Re. 1 per unit. 10,000 units were issued to process A in the beginning of October 1998 at a cost of Re. 1 per unit. The other expenses were as follows:

	Process A (Rs.)	Process B (Rs.)	Process C (Rs.)
Sundry Materials	1,000	1,500	500
Labour	5,000	8,000	6,500
Direct expenses	1,050	1,188	2,009
Actual output [in units]	9,500	9,100	8,100

Ans: Process A – Rs. 1.75 per unit, Abnormal loss 200 units – Rs. 350; Process B – Rs. 3 per unit, Abnormal gain 75 units – Rs. 225; Process C – Rs. 4.25 per unit, Abnormal loss 272 units – Rs. 1,156.

M.B.A. Degree Examinations, April 2002

MANAGEMENT ACCOUNTING

Time: 3 Hours **Part A** Maximum: 80 or 75 Marks

Answer any 8 questions for New Regulation and 7 questions for Old Regulations.

(8 × 5 = 40) or (7 × 5 = 35)

Each answer should not exceed one page.

1. Discuss the utility and significance of financial statements to various parties interested in business concern.
2. What are the different techniques used for the analysis and interpretation of financial statements?
3. What is a fund flow statement? Explain its uses and significance for management.
4. Explain the concept of budgetary control. How does it operate as a tool of management control?
5. How do you calculate the accounting rate of return? What are its limitations?
6. Describe in brief the three major elements of cost.
7. In the concept of marginal costing, what is meant by limiting factor? Discuss its utility.
8. The basic variances are price and usage variances. Discuss this statement in relation to material, labour and overheads.
9. Explain normal and abnormal wastage and state how they would be dealt with in process accounts.
10. What are the essential characteristics of a good report to management?
11. Discuss the use of management accounting as a tool in decision-making.
12. Distinguish between cost center and profit center.

Part B (40 Marks)

Answer question No. 13 and *any* two other questions.

Question No. 13 carries 20 marks and others ***ten*** each.

13. From the following details prepare statement of proprietor's funds:

	Rs.		Rs.
Current Ratio	2.5	Liquid Ratio	1.5
Proprietary Ratio (Fixed Assets/Proprietor's Funds)			0.75
Working Capital	60,000	Reserves and Surplus	40,000
Bank Overdraft	10,000		

There are no long-term loans.

(Answer: Refer Illustration No. 12 in Chapter 8)

14. The initial cash outlay of a project is Rs. 50,000 and it generates cash inflows of Rs. 20,000, Rs. 15,000, Rs. 25,000 and Rs. 10,000 in four years. Using Net Present Value method appraise

(Answer: NPV = Rs. 6,175)

15. From the following figures calculate (a) Break even point (b) Sales to earn a profit of Rs. 1,20,000.

	Rs.
Sales	6,00,000
Variable costs	3,75,000
Fixed costs	1,80,000

(Answer: P/V Ratio – 37.5%; (a) Rs. 4,80,000; (b) Rs. 8,00,000)

16. From the following balance sheets prepare schedule of changes in working capital:

Liabilities	Dec. 1980 (Rs.)	Dec. 1981 (Rs.)	Assets	Dec. 1980 (Rs.)	Dec. 1981 (Rs.)
Share Capital	2,00,000	2,50,000	Cash	30,000	47,000
Creditors	70,000	45,000	Debtors	1,20,000	1,15,000
Retained Earnings	10,000	23,000	Stock	80,000	90,000
			Land	50,000	66,000
	2,80,000	3,18,000		2,80,000	3,18,000

(Answer: Increase in Working Capital Rs. 47,000

17. What are the limitations of financial statements?
18. State and explain the components of total cost.

M.B.A. Degree examinations, October 2002

MANAGEMENT ACCOUNTING

Time: 3 Hours **Part A** Maximum: 80 or 75 Marks

Answer any 8 questions for New Regulations and 7 questions for Old Regulations.

(8 × 5 = 40) or (7 × 5 = 35)

All questions carry equal marks.

Each answer should not exceed a page

1. Describe the characteristics of a good or ideal financial statement.
2. What are the various financial statements?
3. What are the limitations of funds flow statement?
4. What do you understand by budgetary control? Explain is objectives.
5. What is the purpose of capital expenditure budget?
6. Define direct and indirect costs. Give examples.
7. Explain clearly what do you understand by "contribution" in a cost accounting sense.
8. What are the advantages of standard costing?
9. What are basic differences between job and process costing?
10. Describe the general principles of a reporting system.
11. "Management Accounting has been evolved to meet the needs of management"– Explain.
12. Distinguish between historical cost and predetermined cost.

Part B (40 Marks)

Answer Question No. 13 and Two other questions.

Question No. 13 carries 20 marks and others 10 marks each.

13. From the following details prepare a balance sheet.

Stock velocity	–	6 times
Debtors's velocity	–	2 months
Capital turnover	–	2 times
Creditors's velocity	–	73 days
Fixed assets turnover	–	4 times
Gross profit Ratio	–	20%

Gross profit was Rs. 60,000. Reserves and Surplus Rs. 20,000, Closing stock was Rs. 5,000 in excess of opening stock.

(Answer: Refer illustration No. 14 in Chapter 8)

14. An investment proposal would initially cost Rs. 25,000 and would generate year-end cash inflows of Rs. 9,000, Rs. 8,000, Rs. 7,000, Rs. 6,000 and Rs. 5,000 in five years. The required rate of return is 10%. Calculate net present value.

(Answer: NPV – Rs. 2249)

15. Calculate P/V Ratio and Break even point from the following particulars:

	Rs.
Sales	5,00,000
Fixed expenses	1,00,000
Profit	1,50,000

(Answer: 50% and Rs. 2,00,000)

16. From the following balance sheets prepare schedule of changes in working capital:

Liabilities	Dec. 1981	Dec. 1982	Assets	Dec. 1981	Dec. 1982
Share Capital	3,00,000	4,00,000	Cash	1,10,000	1,70,000
Creditors	1,00,000	70,000	Debtors	1,60,000	1,50,000
Retained earnings	15,000	30,000	Stock	85,000	1,05,000
			Furniture	10,000	15,000
			Plant and Machinery	50,000	60,000
	4,15,000	5,00,000		4,15,000	5,00,000

(Answer: Increase in working capital Rs. 1,00,000)

17. State and explain various elements of cost.
18. State the uses of fund flow statement.

M.B.A. Degree Examinations, October 2002 (ICE)

MANAGEMENT ACCOUNTING

Time: 3 Hours **Part A** Maximum: 80

(5 × 5 = 25 marks)

Answer any Five questions.
Each question carries 5 marks.
Each answer should not exceed 2 pages.

1. Define management accounting. Identify the factors, which made management accounting a necessity.
2. XYZ company produces two products X and Y. the operating results of the two products are given below. Compute gross profit ratio for each product and the company and comment.

	Product X	Product Y	Company
			(Rs. In lakhs)
Sales revenue	12	6	18
Production costs	8	5	13
Sales volume (units)	5,000	4,000	9,000

(Answer: 33 1/3%; 16 2/3%; 27 7/9%)

3. Explain the advantages and limitations of budgetary control.
4. Compute the Overhead variances from the data:

	Standard	Actual
Labour hours	1,000	1,200
Output (units)	500	400
Fixed overheads (Rs.)	300	300
Variable overheads (Rs.)	200	300

(Answer: VOHV = 140(A) = 60(A) + 80(A);
FOHV = 60(A) = 0 + 60(F) + 120(A))

5. State the fundamental principles of managerial reports.
6. A company's turnover is Rs. 50 lakhs. Its profit is Rs. 5 lakhs. P/V Ratio is 40%. Find break-even point. (Answer: BEP Rs. 37 50,000; FC Rs. 15 lakhs)
7. A project costs Rs. 36,000 and is expected to generate even cash flows annually of RS. 11 200 for 5 years. The decision rule is to accept the project if rate of return is 16% or above. Do you accept the project? (PV of annuity of one rupee for 16% is 3.274, for 17% – 3.199 and for 15% is .352)

   (Answer: NPV at 16% – 668.80; at 17% – (171.20); at 15% – 1 542.40; Yes, IRR is above 16%)

Part B (4 × 10 = 40 Marks)

Answer any four questions.

Each question carries 10 marks, Each answer should not exceed 4 pages.

8. Develop proforma income statement for the months of July, August and September for a company from the following information:

(a) Sales are projected at Rs. 2,25,000, Rs. 2,40,000, and Rs. 2,15,000 for July, August, and September respectively.

(b) Cost of goods sold is Rs. 50,000 plus 30% of selling price per month.

(c) Selling expenses are 3% of sales.

(d) Rent Rs. 7,500 per month. Administration expenses for July are expected to be Rs. 60,000 but expected to rise 1% per month over previous month's expenses.

(e) The company has Rs. 3,00,000 of 8% loan, interest payable monthly.

(f) Corporate tax rate is 70%.

(Answer: G.P Rs. 1,07,500, 1,28,000, 1,00,500; N.P. Rs. 30,500, 50,300, 22,944; PAT Rs. 9,255, 15,090, 6,883)

9. The following extract of financial information relate to Curious Ltd.

Comparative Balance Sheet as on 31st December: (Rs. in laksh)

	2002	2001
Share capital	10	10
Reserves and surplus	30	10
Loan funds	60	70
Current liabilities	30	20
Fixed Assets	30	30
Stock	30	20
Debtors	30	30
Cash and Bank balances	10	20
Other current assets	30	10
Sales	270	300

(a) Calculate for the two years Debt-equity Ratio, quick ratio, and working capital turnover ratio.

(b) Find the sales volume that should have been generated in 2002, if the company were to have maintained its working capital turnover ratio.

(Answer: (a) 3:2, 7:2, 3:1, 3 1/7, 5. (b) Rs. 350 lakhs)

10. From the following information, prepare a fund flow statement for Excellence Ltd. for the year ended 31.3.2002.

Comparative Balance Sheets of Excellence limited

	As on 31st March	
	2002 (Rs.)	2001 (Rs.)
Liabilities and Capital		
Share Capital	50,00,000	40,00,000
Reserves and surplus	15,00,000	5,00,000

Sundry creditors	35,00,000	40,00,000
Current liabilities	50,00,000	60,00,000
	150,00,000	1,45,00,000
Assets:		
Fixed assets	31,00,000	30,00,000
Investments	1,50,000	–
Cash and Bank	2,50,000	1,25,000
Work in progress	75,00,000	78,75,000
Sundry debtors	40,00,000	35,00,000
	150,00,000	1,45,00,000

(a) The net profit for the year after adjustment in respect of provision for dividends, taxation was Rs. 10,000.

(b) Additions to fixed assets during the year Rs. 4,00,000 and depreciation Rs. 3,00,000

(Answer: Increase in working capital Rs. 17.5 lakhs. FFS – sources Rs. 23 lakhs, applications Rs. 5.5 lakhs.)

11. A plastic manufacturing company is considering replacing an lder machine, which was fully depreciated for tax purposes with a new machine costing Rs. 40,000. The new machine will be depreciated over its eight-yea life. It is estimated that the new machine will reduce the labour costs by Rs. 8,000 per year. The management believes that there will be no change in other expenses and revenues of the firm due to the machine. The company requires an after tax return of investment of 10%. The tax rate is 35%. The company's income statement for the current year is given below.

		(Rs.)
Sales		5,00,000
Less: Costs		
Materials	1,50,000	
Labour	2,00,000	
Factory and Admn.	40,000	
Depreciation	40,000	4,30,000
Net income before taxes		70,000
Taxes (at 35%)		24,500
Earnings after taxes		45,500

Should the company buy the new machine? You may assume the company follows straight-line method of depreciation. (PV factor at 10% and 8 years is 5.335)

(Answer: Increase in cash inflows = Rs. 8,000 less depreciation Rs. 5,000 = 3,000 less tax 35% = 1950 plus depreciation Rs. 5,000 = 6,950. NPV 6,950 × 5.335 = 37,078.25 – 40,000 = (2921.75). Since NPV is negative the decision is not to buy).

12. A company estimates variable costs to be Rs. 5 per unit and fixed cost to be Rs. 2,50,000 per year. Plant capacity is set at 2,25,000 units per year. It is estimated that 1,00,000 units can be sold at a price of Rs. 10 and 1,25,000 units at Rs. 9 and 2,00,000 units at Rs. 8. Recommend a suitable price. At what price the company can sell 2,25,000 units with the same profit it gets at Rs. 8 price?

(Answer: Profit at Rs. 8 = Rs. 3,50,000; Selling Price at 2,25,000 units level = Rs. 7.67)

13. Prepare a production budget for each month and a summarized production cost budget for the six months period ending 31st December, 2002 from the following data of product X.

(a) The units to be sold for different months are as follows:

2002	July	1100
	August	1100
	September	1700
	October	1900
	November	2500
	December	2300
2003	January	2000

(b) There will be no work in progress at the end of any month.

(c) Finished units equal to half of the sales for the next month will be in stock at the end of each month (including June 2002).

(d) Budgeted production and production cost for the year ending 31st December 2002 are as follows:

Production (units)	2,200
Direct material per unit	Rs. 10
Direct wages per unit	Rs. 4
Total factory overheads (Apportioned to product)	Rs. 88

(Answer: Production: 1100, 1400, 1800, 2200, 2400, 2150 = 11050; Rs. 1,55,142)

Part C (1 × 15 = 15 Marks)

14. The installed capacity of a company is one-lakh units per annum. It is licensed only to produce 75% of capacity. But it is given option by government to produce up to full capacity if the company could export and earn foreign exchange on the extra production. The operating costs at the installed capacity are:

Direct materials	Rs. 3 per unit
Direct labour	Rs. 2 per unit
Variable overheads	Rs. 3 per unit
Fixed overheads	Rs. 2,50,000

No increase in the material and labour, etc. costs is anticipated during the current year. The company has received an overseas offer for 20,000 units, which if accepted, would involve an extra expenditure of Rs. 11,000 towards special packing, commission, etc. If the offer materializes, the company obtains raw materials required for the export order at concessional rate of 40% below the present cost.

Submit a report to your managing director suggesting the selling prices you recommend if the company is to earn the same profit margin as on local sales at Rs. 12 per unit of installed capacity.

(a) Before getting the export order (b) After getting the export order.

(Answer: (a) Profit Rs. 1,00,000; (b) Percentage of profit 16 2/3%, Selling price Rs. 8.82)

ANNA UNIVERSITY

M.B.A. DEGREE EXAMINATIONS,

NOVEMBER/ DECEMBER 2002

ACCOUNTING FOR MANAGEMENT

Time: 3 Hours Maximum: 100 marks

PART A

(10 × 2 = 20 marks)

Answer ALL questions.

1. Explain accounting cycle.
2. Give any four managerial applications of accounting information.
3. Explain sectional balancing system.
4. Give any two limitations of cash flow analysis.
5. Define imputed costs.
6. Give any four common bases of apportioning factory overheads.
7. Explain Zero-base budget.
8. Define cost center.
9. Explain direct material cost variances.
10. Explain profit/volume ratio.

PART B (5 × 16 = 80 Marks)

11. Discuss the significance of accounting information from the viewpoint of business stakeholders.

12. (a) (i) Explain the objectives of providing depreciation. (8)

(ii) X Ltd. purchased a machine for Rs. 60,000 on 1.1.1998. Depreciation is provided @ 10% p.a. on diminishing balance method. Prepare machinery account for the year 2000 in each of the following alternative cases:

(1) If the machine is sold on 1.7.2000 for Rs. 28,600

(2) If a new machine costing Rs. 60,000 is purchased on 1.7.2000 after surrendering the old machine and paying cash Rs. 35,000. (8)

(Answer: (1) Loss on sale Ras. 17,570; (2) Loss Rs. 21,170)

OR

(b) (i) Explain factors affecting valuation of shares. (8)

(ii) ABC Ltd. has 15,000 equity shares of Rs. 100 each, Rs. 80 paid. Also 3,000 – 8% preference shares of Rs. 100 each fully paid. The company transfers 15% of its profits to General reserve every year. The company expects profits of Rs. 8,00,000 (before tax). The rate of tax is 40%. You are required to calculate the value of equity shares. The normal rate of dividend is 25%.

(Answer: DPS Rs. 30.4 or ROE – 38%; Value Rs. 121.60)

13. (a) (i) Explain the difference between cash flow analysis and funds flow analysis.

(ii) Statement of financial position of Mr. A is given below:

	1.1.2000 (Rs.)	31.12.2000 (Rs.)
Account payable	29,000	25,000
Capital	7,39,000	6,15,000
	7,68,000	6,40,000
Cash	40,000	30,000
Debtors	20,000	17,000
Stock	8,000	13,000
Building	1,00,000	80,000
Other Fixed assets	6,00,000	5,00,000
	7,68,000	6,40,000

Additional information:

There were no drawings.

There were no purchase or sale of either building or fixed assets.

Prepare Statement of Cash Flow. (8)

OR

(b) (i) Explain the assumptions of cost-volume-profit analysis. (8)

(ii) S & Co., Ltd., has three divisions, each of which makes a different product. The budgeted data for the next year is as follows:

Divisions	A (Rs.)	B (Rs.)	C (Rs.)
Sales	1,12,000	56,000	84,000
Costs:			
Direct material	14,000	7,000	14,000
Direct labour	5,600	7,000	22,400
Variable overheads	14,000	7,000	28,000
Fixed costs	28,000	14,000	28,000
Total costs	61,600	35,000	92,400

The management is considering closing down Division C. There is no possibility of reducing fixed costs. Advise whether or not division C should be closed down.

(Answer: C should not be closed down. Profits will decrease from Rs. 63,000 to 43,000)

14. (a) (i) Outline the usefulness of Process Costing. (8)

(ii) Fifty units are introduced into a process at a cost of Rs. 50. The total additional expenditure incurred by the process is Rs. 30. Of the units introduced 10% are normally spoilt in the course of manufacture; these possess a scrap value of Re. 0.25 each. Owing to an accident only 40% units are produced. You are required to prepare a process account. (8)

(Answer: Normal loss 5 units Rs. 1.25; Abnormal loss 25 units Rs. 43.75; Transfer to next process 20 units Rs. 35.00; Cost per finished unit Rs. 1.75)

OR

(b) (i) Explain the application of marginal cost analysis for managerial decision-making. (8)

(ii) A product X takes 5 hours to be produced on a machine, which is used to full capacity. Its selling price is Rs. 60 and marginal cost Rs. 30. A component Z, used in the production of X, can be made on the same machine in 2 hours. The marginal cost of producing Z is Rs. 10 It can be bought at the net rice of Rs. 12 from the market. Should the firm make or buy the component? (8)

(Answer: Profitability of X – Rs. 6 per hour; Component Z – Re. 1 per hour. Better to buy)

15. (a) (i) Explain the features of a flexible budget.

(ii) XY Industries Ltd. is preparing its comprehensive budget for the next year. The sales manager has said that he does not wish to have a single estimate of sales, but would prefer to give four forecasts along with his estimates of the probabilities he attaches to them.

Sales forecasts (Rs)	Probabilities
16,00,000	0.4
20,00,000	0.3
24,00,000	0.2
30,00,000	0.1

Variable costs are 40% of the sales and total fixed costs are Rs. 8,00,000 per year. Prepare budgeted income statement based on each of the four forecasts. (8)

(Answer: Budgeted Income)

= Rs. 64,000 + 1,20,000 + 1,28,000 + 1,00,000 = Rs. 4,12,000

OR

(b) (i) Explain standard costing as a control technique. (8)

(ii) You have been appointed as financial executive attached to the central office of AB Ltd. with special responsibility for monitoring the performance of the divisions within the company. Each division is treated as an investment center. Summaries of the Divisions X and Y for the year ending 31st December 2000 are given below:

Particulars	X (Rs.)	Y (Rs.)
Sales	7,00,000	9,50,000
Variable costs	3,20,000	4,10,000
Fixed overheads	2,00,000	2,90,000
Divisional assets	2,50,000	3,75,000

You are required to assess the performance of the divisions with the help of ROI.

(Answer: X – 72%; Y – 66 2/3%)

Question Paper

M.B.A. DEGREE EXAMINATION, APRIL/MAY 2004

First semester

BA 105 – ACCOUNTING FOR MANAGEMENT

Time: Three hours | Maximum: 100 marks

Answer ALL questions.

PART – (10 × 2 = 20 marks)

1. What is Shareholders Equity ?
2. Give any two defects of historical costing.
3. What does a low inventory turnover ratio indicate ?
4. Calculate Break Even point in sales value

Output = 3000 units
Selling price per unit = Rs. 30
Variable cost per unit = Rs. 20
Total fixed cost = Rs. 20,000.

Ans:-
Selling price = Rs.30
Less Variable cost = Rs.20
Contribution Rs.10

P/V Ratio $= \frac{\text{Contribution}}{\text{Sales}} \times 100 = \frac{10}{30} \times 100 = 33\ 1/3\ \%$

BE Point $= \frac{\text{Fixed Cost}}{\text{P/V Ratio}} = \frac{20,000}{33\ 1/3\%} = \text{Rs. } 60,000$

5. What is Receivables Management?
6. Define differential cost?
7. Mention any two objectives of providing depreciation.
8. Give the formula for calculating material cost variance.
9. What is Zero base budgeting?
10. What do you mean by cost allocation?

XC

11. Design a Basic Accounting Model as applicable for a medium scale organization manufacturing and marketing consumer durable item.

12. (a) The following details are available from a company:

	31.12.95	31.12.96		31.12.95	31.12.96
	Rs.	Rs.		Rs.	Rs.
Share capital	70,000	74,000	Cash	9,000	7,800
Debentures	12,000	6,000	Debtors	14,900	17,700
Reserve for doubtful			Stock	49,200	42,700
Dedts	700	800	Land	20,000	30,000
Trade creditors	10,360	11,840	Goodwill	10,000	5,000
P/L A/c	10,040	10,560			
	1,03,100	1,03,200		1,03,100	1,03,200

The following additional information are given:

(i) Dividend paid in total Rs. 3,500

(ii) Land was purchased for Rs. 10,000

(iii) Amount provided for amortization of goodwill Rs.5,000

(iv) Debentures paid off Rs. 6,000.

Prepare cash flow statement.

ANS:

Calculation of funds from operation and cash from operation.

	Net Profit (10,560 – 10,040)		520
Add	Amortization of Goodwill	5,000	
	Dividend Paid	3,500	
			8,500
	Funds from operation		9,020
Add	Decrease in stock	6,500	
	Increase in for bad debts	100	
	Increase in Trade Creditors	1,480	8,080
			17,100
Less	Increase in Sundry Debtors		2,800
	Cash from operation		14,300

<u>Cash flow Statement:-</u>

	Opening Balance of Cash A/c		9,000
Add	inflows		
	Cash from operation	14,300	
	Issue of share capital	4,000	
			18,300
			27,300
Less	outflows		
	Purchase of Land	10,000	
	Repayment to Debenture Holders	6,000	
	Payment of dividend	3,500	
			19,500
	Closing balance of cash A/c		7,800

(b) (i) Explain the different methods used for the analysis and interpretation of Financial statement. (10)

(ii) Briefly explain the factors influencing the size of receivables in an Organization. (6)

13. (a) The comparative statements of income and financial position are given below ;

	1990	1991
	Rs.	Rs.
Net sales	1,00,000	1,50,000
Less: Cost of sales	70,000	1,10,000
Gross profit	30,000	40,000
Less : Operating expenses	20,000	25,000
Net Profit	10,000	15,000
Cash in hand	5,000	8,000
Cash at Bank	4,000	2,000
Debtors	40,000	25,000
Stock at cost	15,000	10,000
Fixed Asset (Net)	56,000	65,000
	1,20,000	1,10,000
Creditors	36,000	12,000
Bills payable	2,000	1,000
Mortgage loan	10,000	20,000
Equity share capital	60,000	70,000
Reserves and surplus	12,000	7,000
	1,20,000	1,10,000

Calculate the following ratios for both the years :

(i) Current Ratio (4)

(ii) Acid Test Ratio (4)

(iii) Debtors Turnover Ratio (4)

(iv) Stock Turnover Ratio (4)

ANS:

(i) Current Ratio $= \dfrac{\text{Current Assets}}{\text{Current Liabilities}}$

For the year 1990 $= 5{,}000 + 4{,}000 + 40{,}000 + 15{,}000$

$= 64{,}000$

Current Liabilities $= 36{,}000 + 2{,}000 = 38{,}000$

$\therefore$ Current Ratio $= \dfrac{64{,}000}{38{,}000} = 1.68$ times

For the year 1991

Current Assets $= 8{,}000 + 2{,}000 + 25{,}000 + 10{,}000$

$= 45{,}000$

Current Liabilities $= 12{,}000 + 1{,}000 = 13{,}000$

$\therefore$ Current Ratio $= \dfrac{45{,}000}{13{,}000} = 3.46$ times.

(ii) Acid text Ratio $= \dfrac{\text{Current Assets} - \text{Inventory}}{\text{Current Liability}}$

<u>For the year 1990:</u>

Current Assets – Inventory $= 64{,}000 - 15{,}000 = 49{,}000.$

$\therefore$ Acid test Ratio

$$= \frac{49{,}000}{38{,}000} = 1.29 \text{ times.}$$

<u>For the year 1991</u>

Current Assets Inventory $= 45{,}000 - 10{,}000 = 35{,}000$

$$\therefore \text{Acid test Ratio} = \frac{35{,}000}{13{,}000} = 2.69 \text{ times.}$$

$$\text{(iii) Debtors Turnover Ratio} = \frac{\text{Net (credit) Sales}}{\text{Debtors}}$$

<u>For the year 1990:-</u>

$$\text{Debtors Turnover Ratio} = \frac{1{,}00{,}000}{40{,}000} = 2.5 \text{ times}$$

<u>For the year 1991</u>

$$\text{Debtors Turnover Ratio} = \frac{1{,}50{,}000}{25{,}000} = 6 \text{ times.}$$

$$\text{(iv) Stock Turnover Ratio} = \frac{\text{Cost of Goods sold}}{\text{Inventory}}$$

<u>For the year 1990:-</u>

$$\text{Stock Turnover Ratio} = \frac{70{,}000}{15{,}000} = 4.667 \text{ times}$$

<u>For the year 1991:-</u>

$$\text{Stock Turnover Ratio} = \frac{1{,}10{,}000}{25{,}000} = 4.4 \text{ times}$$

OR

13. (b) (i) From the following information calculate :

(1) P/V Ratio

(2) Break-even point

(3) Margin of safety

Total Sales	Rs. 3,60,000
Selling price per unit	Rs. 100
Variable Cost per unit	Rs. 50
Fixed cost	Rs. 1,00,000

(4) If the selling price is reduced to Rs.90 by how much is the margin of Safety reduced? (10)

(ii) Explain the managerial application of differential cost analysis. (6)

Ans:-

$$\text{(1) P/V Ratio} = \frac{\text{Contribution}}{\text{Sales}} \times 100$$

Contribution $= 100 - 50 = \text{Rs.}50$

P/V Ratio $= \frac{50}{100} \times 100 = 50\%$

(2) Break even Point $= \frac{\text{Fixed cost}}{\text{P/V Ratio}}$

$= \frac{1,00,000}{50\%} = \text{Rs. } 2,00,000$

(3) Margin of Safety = Actual Sales – BEP sales
= 3,60,000 – 2,00,000
= Rs. 1,60,000

(4) When the selling price is reduced to Rs. 90 how much margin of safety reduced:

New total Sales will be $= \left\{\frac{360000}{100} \times 90\right\} 3,24,000$

New P.V. Ratio $= \frac{(90 - 50)}{90} \times 100 = 44.44\%$

New Break even point $= \frac{1,00,000}{44.44\%}$
= 2,25,000

New Margin of safety = 3,24,000 – 2,25,000
= 99,000

When the selling price reduced to Rs.90.
Margin of safety is reduced by Rs. 61,000

14. (a) Following are the particulars for the production of 2000 Sewing Machines of Nath Engineering Co. Ltd., for the year 2002:

	Rs.
Cost of materials	1,60,000
Wages	2,40,000
Manufacturing expenses	1,00,000
Salaries	1,20,000
Rent, Rates and Insurance	20,000
Selling expenses	60,000
General expenses	40,000
Sales	8,00,000

The company plans to manufacture 3,000 Sewing Machines during 2003. Prepare a statement showing the price at which machines would be sold so as to show a profit of 10% on selling price. The following additional information is given:

(i) Price of materials is expected to rise by 20%.
(ii) Wages rates are expected to show an increase of 5%
(iii) Manufacturing expenses will raise in proportion to the combined cost of materials and wages.
(iv) Selling expenses per unit will remain the same.
(v) Other expenses will remain unaffected by rise in output.

Ans:-

Statement showing cost and profit for 3000 Sewing Machines of Nath Engineering Co.

Cost of materials (W.N.1)	2,88,000
Wages (W.N.2)	3,78,000
Manufacturing EX (W.N.3)	1,66,500
Salaries *	1,20,000
Rent Rates and Insurance *	20,000
Selling Expenses (W.N.4)	90,000
General Expenses *	40,000
Total Cost	11,02,500
ADD	
Profit 10% on sales ie. on cost (11,02,500 X 10 / 90)	1,22,500
Sales price of 3000 Sewing machines	12,25,000

Working No: 1

Cost of material per unit $= \dfrac{160000}{2000} = 80$

New material cost = 80 + 20 % of 80 = 96

Cost of material for 3000 Sewing Machines = 3000 × 96 = 2,88,000

Working No: 2

Wages Per unit $= \dfrac{240000}{2000} = 120$

New Wages per unit = 120 +5% of 120 = 126.

Wages for 3000 Sewing Machines = 3000 × 126 = 3,78,000

Working No: 3

% of manufacturing expenses on cost of material and wages $= \dfrac{100000}{400000} \times 100$

$= 25\%$

Manufacturing Expenses for 3000 Sewing Machines = (2,88,000 + 3,78,000) X 25%

= 1,66,500

Working No: 4

Selling Expenses per unit $= \dfrac{60,000}{2000} \times 30$

Selling Expenses per 3000 unit = 30 × 3000 = 90,000

* = These expenses are constant, in spite of increase in volume of production.

OR

14. (b) Bengal Chemical Co. Ltd. Produced three chemicals during the month of July, 1998 by three consecutive processes. In each process 2% of the total weight put in is lost and 10% is scrap which from each processes (1) and (2) realizes Rs. 100 a ton and from process (3) Rs. 20 a ton.

The products of three processes are dealt with as follows:

Particulars	Process 1	Process 2	Process 3
Passed on to the next process	75%	50%	–
Sent to warehouse for sale	25%	50%	100%

Expenses incurred:

	Process 1		Process 2		Process 3	
	Rs.	Tons	Rs.	Tons	Rs.	Tons
Raw materials	1,20,000	1,000	28,000	140	1,07,840	1,348
Manufacturing						
Wages	20,500	–	18,520	–	15,000	–
General Expenses	10,300	–	7,240	–	3,100	–

Prepare Process Cost Accounts showing the Cost per ton of each product.

Ans:-

Process 1 Account

Dr Cr

Particulars	Tons	Amount	Particulars	Tons	Amount
To Raw material	1000	1,20,000	By loss in weight (2% of 1000)	20	–
To Manufacturing Wages		20,500	By sale of scrap (10% of 1000)	100	10,000
To General Expen		10,300	By Transferred to warehouse A/c	220	35,200
			By Process 2 A/c	660	1,05,600
	1000	1,50,800		1000	1,05,800

Process 2 Account

Dr Cr

Particulars	Tons	Amount	Particulars	Tons	Amount
To Process 1 A/C (Transfer)	660	1,05,600	By Loss in weight (800X2%)	16	
To Raw materials	140	28,000	By Sale of scrap (10% of 800)	80	8,000
To Manufacturing wages	–	18,520	By Transferred to Ware house A/C	352	75,680
To General Ex		7,240	By Process 3 A/C	352	75,680
	800	1,59,360		800	1,59,360

Process 3 Accounts

Dr Cr

Particulars	Tons	Amount	Particulars	Tons	Amount
To Process 2 A\c	352	75,680	By Loss in weight (2% of 1700)	34	–
			By Sales of scrap (1700X10%)	170	3,400
To Raw materials	1,348	1,07,840	By Transferred to Ware House A/C	1,496	1,98,220
To Manufacturing wages	–	15,000			
		3,100			
To General Ex	1700	2,01,620		1,700	2,01,620

15. (a) Using the following information calculate:

(i) Labour Cost Variance (4)

(ii) Labour rate of Pay Variance (4)

(iii) Labour Efficiency Variance (4)

(iv) Idle Time Variance. (4)

Gross direct wages = Rs.3,000

Standard hours produced = 1600

Standard rate per hour = Rs.1.50

Actual hours paid 1500 hours, out of which hours not worked (abnormal idle time) are 50.

Ans:

(i) Labour Cost Variance = Standard wages – Actual Wages.
(LCV)

= (1600 X 15) – 3000

= 600 (A)

(ii) Labour Rate Pay Variance = Actual Hours (std. Rate - Actual Rate)
(LRV)

$$\text{Actual Rate} = \frac{3000}{1500} = \text{Rs. } 2$$

Labour Rate Pay Variance = 1500 (1.5 – 2)

= 750 (A)

(iii) Labour Efficiency Variance = Std. Rate (Std. Hours – Actual time
(LEV) Timed Worked)

Actual Time Worker = 1500 – 50 = 1450 Hours.

Labour Efficiency Variance = 1.5 (1600 – 1450)

= 225 (F)

(iv) Idle Time Variance = Std.Rate X Idle Time
(ITV)

= 1.5 x 50

= 75 (A)

Verification :-

LCV = LRV + LEV + ITV

600 (A) = 750 (A) + 225 (F) + 75 (A)

600 (A) = 600 (A)

(b) From the following forecast of income and expenditure prepare a budget for the months January to April 1996:

Months	sales (Credit)	Purchase (Credit)	Wages	Manufac turing expenses	Admini strative expenses	Selling expenses
	Rs.	Rs.	Rs.	Rs.	Rs.	Rs.
95 Nov.	30,000	15,000	3,000	1,150	1,060	500
Dec.	35,000	20,000	3,200	1,225	1,040	550
96 Jan.	25,000	15,000	2,500	990	1,100	600
Feb.	30,000	20,000	3,000	1,050	1,150	620
March	35,000	22,500	2,400	1,100	1,220	570
April	40,000	25,000	2,600	1,200	1,180	710

Additional information is as follows:

(i) The customers are allowed a credit period of 2 months

(ii) A dividend of Rs.10,000 is payable in April

(iii) Capital expenditure to be incurred : Plant purchased on 15th of January for Rs.5,000; a building purchased on 1st March and the payments are to be made in monthly installments of Rs. 2,000 each.

(iv) The creditors are allowing a credit of 2 months.

(v) Wages are paid on the 1st of next month.

(vi) Lag in payment of other expenses is one month

(vii) Balance of cash in hand on 1st January 1996 is Rs.15,000.

Ans:-

Cash Budget for the month of January ,February , March and April of 1996.

Particulars	January Z	February	March	April
Opening Balance	15,000	23,985	31,795	33,975
ADD Receipts				
Collection from debtors	30,000	35,000	25,000	30,000
Total (A)	45,000	58,985	56,795	63,975
Payments				
Payments to creditors	15,000	20,000	15,000	20,000
Wages	3,200	2,500	3,000	2,400
Manufacturing Ex	1,225	990	1,050	1,100
Administrative Ex	1,040	1,100	1,150	1,220
Selling Ex	550	600	620	570
Payment of Dividend	–	–	–	10,000
Payment of installment for Plant	–	2,000	2,000	1,000
Payment of installment for Building	–	–	–	2,000
Total of Payments (B)	21,015	27,190	22,820	38,290
Closing balance (A-B)	23,985	31,795	33,975	25,685

Y 7044

M.B.A. DEGREE EXAMINATION, MAY/JUNE 2005.

ANNA UNIVERSITY

First Semester

BA. 105 – ACCOUNTING FOR MANAGEMENT

Time : Three hours Maximum: 100 Marks

Answer All Questions.

Part – (10 × 2 = 20 marks)

1. Define accounting cycle.

2. How would you differentiate between current assets and current liabilities ?

3. Define budget and budgetary control.

4. What do you mean by the term Batch costing ?

5. Define marginal costing.

6. Bring out any two differences between job costing and process costing.

7. What is meant by overhead charges?

8. What is a direct or chargeable expenses?

9. What is a cash budget ?

10. How does Zero-base budgeting differ from traditional budgeting ?

PART – (5X16 = 80 marks)

11. Explain the different techniques of analysis and interpretation of financial statements.

12. (a) Kailash Ltd. is presently selling a product @ Rs. 10 per unit. The present sales are 30,000 units, and the variable cost per unit is Rs. 6 and the fixed costs amounted to Rs.60,000. The average Collection period is of 30 days.

The company proposes to relax its credit standard resulting in a 15 percent increase in unit sales. The average collection period is expected to increase to 45 days. However, there is to be no Change in losses on account of bad debts and collection Expenses. The company expects a return on investment at 15%. You are required to advise whether the company should Relax its credit standard.

Ans:

	@ Present situation	@ Proposed situation
Average collection period	30 days	45 days
Sales	30,000 × 10 = Rs. 3,00,000	(30,000 × 115%) × 10 = 34,500 × 10 = 3,45,000
Average investment in Debtors	$\frac{3,00,000 \times 30}{360}$ = Rs.25,000	$= \frac{3,45,000 \times 45}{= 360}$ = Rs. 43,125
Profit = Sales–VC– FC	3,00,000–1,80,000-60,000 = Rs. 60,000	3,45,000-2,07,000-60,000 = Rs. 78,000

Incremental Investment in Debtors = Rs.18,125
(43,125 – 25,000)

Incremental Profit (Actual Return) =Rs.18,000.
(78,000 – 60,000)

Expected Return on Investment =Rs.2718.75
(18,125 × 15%)

Conclusion :- Actual return is more than the expected return. The company can relax its credit standard.

OR

(b) The major objectives of inventory management is 'to minimize cash outlays for inventories" Explain how this is sought to be achieved.

13. (a) From the following Balance Sheet as on 31st December, you are required to prepare a cash flow statement:

Liabilities	2002 Rs.	2003 Rs.	Assets	2002 Rs.	2003 Rs.
Share capital	1,00,000	1,50,000	Fixed Assets	1,00,000	1,50,000
Profit and loss A/c	50,000	80.000	Goodwill	50,000	40,000
General reserve	30,000	40,000	Inventories	50,000	80,000
16% Bonds	50,000	60,000	Debtors	50,000	80,000
Sundry Creditors	30,000	40,000	Bills receivables	10,000	20,000
Expenses O/S	10,000	15,000	Bank	10,000	15,000
	2,70,000	3,85,000		2,70,000	3,85,000

Ans:

<u>Calculation of funds from operation and cash from operation</u>

		Amount	Amount
Net Profit (80,000 – 50,000)			30,000
Add Goodwill written off		10,000	
	Transferred to General reserve	10,000	20,000
	Fund from operation		50,000
Add Increase in sundry creditors		10,000	
	Increase in out standing Ex	5,000	15,000
			65,000
Less	Increase in Inventories	30,000	
	Increase in Debtors	30,000	
	Increase in Bills Receivable	10,000	70,000
	Cash Outflow from operations		5,000

<u>Cash flow statements:</u>

	Opening Balance of Bank A/C		10,000
Add Inflows: Issue of share capital		50,000	
	Issue 16% Bonds	10,000	60,000
			70,000
Less Out flow: - Purchase of fixed assets		50,000	
	Cash outflow from Operations	5,000	55,000
	Closing Balance of Bank A/C		15,000

OR

(b) What do you understand by classification, allocation and apportionment in relation to overhead expenses ?

14. (a) from the following figures prepare raw materials purchase budget for January :

Materials (Units)

	A	B	C	D	E	F
Estimated stock on 1st January	16,000	6,000	24,000	2,000	14,000	28,000
Estimated stock on 31st January	20,000	8,000	28,000	4,000	16,000	32,000
Estimated consumption	1,20,000	44,000	1,32,000	36,000	88,000	1,72,000
Standard price per unit	25 paise	5 paise	15 paise	10paise	20paise	30Paise

Ans:-

Purchase= Raw material consumption + closing stock
– opening stock

Material purchase Budget for January

Particulars	A	B	C	D	E	F
Raw Material consumption (units)	1,20,000	44,000	1,32,000	36,000	88,000	1,72,000
ADD						
Stock on 31 Jan (Unit)	20,000	8,000	28,000	4,000	16,000	32,000
	1,40,000	52,000	1,60,000	40,000	1,04,000	2,04,000
LESS						
Stock on 1st Jan (unit)	16,000	6,000	24,000	2,000	14,000	28,000
Purchase (units) Standard	1,24,000	46,000	1,36,000	38,000	90,000	1,76,000
Price						
Per unit	25Paise	5Paise	15Paise	10paise	20paise	30paise
Purchase to be Made (in value)	Rs. 31,000	Rs. 2,300	Rs. 20,400	Rs. 3,800	Rs. 18,000	Rs. 52,800

(b) A company working at 50% capacity manufactures 10,000 units of a product. At 50% capacity the product cost is Rs.180 and sale price is Rs.200. The break up of the cost is as below:

	Cost per unit
Material	Rs.100
Wages	30
Factory	30 (40% fixed)
Administration	20 (50% fixed)

At 60% working raw material cost goes up by 2% and sales price falls by 2%. At 80% working the raw material cost increases by 5% and Sale price decreases by same percentage i.e. 5% Prepare a statement to show profitability at 60% and 80% capacity.

14. (b) Statement showing profit @ 50% ; 60% and 80% level.

@ 50% capacity, @60% capacity, @80% capacity

Particulars	Unit Cost	Amount (10000 units)	Unit Cost	Amount (12000 units)	Unit cost	Amount (16000 units)
Variable cost						
Material	100	10,00,000	102	12,24,000	105	16,80,000
Wages	30	3,00,000	30	3,60,000	30	4,80,000
Factory OHS	18	1,80,000	18	2,16,000	18	2,88,000
	10	1,00,000	10	1,20,000	10	1,60,000
Administration OHs						
Fixed Cost	12	1,20,000	10	1,20,000	7.5	1,20,000
Factory OHS	10	1,00,000	8.33	1,00,000	6.25	1,00,000
Administration OHs						
Total Cost	180	18,00,000	178.33	21,40,000	176.75	28,28,000
Profit (sales –TC)	20	2,00,000	17.67	2,12,000	13.25	2,12,000
Sales	200	20,00,000	196	23,52,000	190	30,40,000

15. (a) The budgeted sales for one month and the actual results achieved under

Product	Qty. Nos	Budget Rate Rs	Amount Rs.	Qty. Nos	Actual Rate Rs.	Amount
A	1,000	100	1,00,000	1,200	125	1,50,000
B	700	200	1,40,000	800	150	1,20,000
C	500	500	2,50,000	600	300	1,80,000
D	300	500	1,50,000	400	600	2,40,000
	2,500		6,40,000	3,000		6,90,000

Calculate in respect of each product, the sales variances.

Ans:

(1) Total sales value variance = actual sales value – standard sales value (TSN)

Actual sales value = 6,90,000

Standard sales value = 5,40,000

Total sales value variance = 6,90,000 – 6,40,000 = 50,000 (F)

(2) Sales value price variance = AQ(AP-SP) (SVPB)

Product - A = 1200 (125 – 100) = 30,000 (F)

Product - B = 800 (150 – 200) = 40,000 (A)

Product - C = 600 (300 – 500) = 1,20,000 (A)

Product - D = 400 (600 – 500) = 40,000 (F)

Sales value price Variance (SVPV) 90,000 (A)

(3) Sales Value Volume Variance = SP (AQ – SQ)

Product A = 100 (1200 – 1000) = 20,000 (F)

Product B = 200 (800 – 700) = 20,000 (F)

Product C = 500 (600 – 500) = 50,000 (F)

Product D = 500 (400 – 300) = 50,000 (F)

1,40,000 (F)

(4) Sales Value Mix Variance = SP (AQ – RSQ) (SVMV)

<u>Calculation of Revised Standard Quantity</u> :- (RSQ)

$A = \frac{2500}{3000} \times 1200 \quad = \quad 1000 \text{ units}$

$B = \frac{2500 \times 800}{30000} \quad = \quad 66 \text{ units}$

$C = \frac{2500 \times 600}{3000} \quad = \quad 500 \text{ units}$

$D = \frac{2500 \times 400}{3000} \quad = \quad 333 \text{ units}$

SVMV = SP (AQ – RSQ)

A	=	100 (1200 – 1000)	= 20,000 (F)
B	=	200 (800 – 667)	= 26,600 (F)
C	=	500 (600 – 500)	= 50,000 (F)
D	=	500 (400 – 333)	= 33,500 (F)
			1,30,100 (F)

(5) Sales Value Quantity Variance = SP (RSQ – SQ

A	= 100 (1000 – 1000)	= 0
B	= 200 (667 – 700)	= 6,600 (A)
C	= 500 (500 – 500)	= 0
D	= 500 (333 – 300)	= 16,500 (F)
		23,100 (F)

Verification:

TSVV = SVPV + SVV

50,000(F) = 90,000 (A) + 1, 40,000 (F)

50,000 (F) = 50,000 (F)

SVVV = SVMV + SVQV

1,40,000(F) = 1,30,100(F) + 9,900(F)

1,40,000 (F) = 1,40,000 (F)

(b) Define and explain the following terms:

(i) Material Price variance

(ii) Material usage variance

(iii) Material mix variance

(iv) Material yield variance

ACCOUNTING FOR MANAGEMENT
MADRAS UNIVERSITY – 05

Time : Three hours Maximum : 100 Marks

PART – A (8 × 4 = 32 marks)
Answer any eight questions
All questions carry equal marks

1. State the objectives of Management Accounting .
2. What are the Nature of Financial Statements ?
3. Mention the limitations of ratio analysis.
4. Explain 'Funds Flow Statement'.
5. Explain the uses of cash flow statement.
6. Describe the concept of marginal costing.
7. What are the assumption of Break Even Analysis?
8. Write a note on 'Budgetary Control'.
9. Explain 'Flexible Budget'.
10. Define ' Report'.
11. What do you mean by 'Adhoc Report '?
12. Explain 'short term solvency ratios'.

PART B – (3 × 12 = 36 marks)
Answer any THREE questions.
All questions carry equal marks.

13. From the following details, you are to calculate
(a) Purchases for the year (b) rate of stock turnover (c) Percentage of gross profit to turnover:

	Rs.
Sales	3, 39,845
Sales returns	380
Stock at the beginning	1,378
Stock at the end	1,814
Gross profit for the year	8,068

Ans:
CALCULATION OF PURCHASE:-

TRADING ACCOUNT

To opening stock	1,378	By Sales	33,984
To Purchase (bal. in fig.)	25,972	less:-sales return	380
			33,604
To gross profit	8,068	By closing stock	1,814
	35,418		35,418

$$\text{Rate of stock turnover} = \frac{\text{Cost of goods sold}}{\text{Av. Stock}}$$

Cost of goods sold = Net sales – gross profit
= 33,604 – 8068
= 25,536.

$$\text{Av. Stock} = \frac{\text{Opening stock + closing stock}}{2}$$

$$= \frac{1378 + 1814}{2}$$

= 1596.

(2) Rate of stock Turnover $= \frac{25,536}{1596}$

= 16 times.

(c) Percentage of gross profit to turnover $= \frac{\text{Gross profit}}{\text{Net sales}} \times 100$

$$= \frac{8068}{33,604} \times 100 = 24\%$$

14. from the following balances calculate the cash form operations:

	December 2001 Rs.	December 2002 Rs.
Debtors	10,000	9,400
Bills receivable	2,000	2,500
Creditors	4,000	5,000
Bills payable	1,600	1,200
Out standing expenses	200	240
Prepaid expenses	160	140
Income received in advance	60	50

Current year profit Rs. 26,000

Ans:

<u>Calculation of cash from operation:-</u>

Current year profit		26,000
Add:-		
Decrease in debtors	600	
Increase in creditors	1000	
Increase in outstanding	40	
Decrease in prepaid Exp	20	
		1,660
		27,660
Less:-		
Increase in bills receivable	500	
Decrease in bills payable	400	
Decrease in income received In advance	10	910
Cash from operation		26,750

15. From the following particulars, calculate BEP:-

Sales Rs. 1, 00,000

Variable cost Rs. 60,000

Fixed overheads Rs.15,000

Also calculate, New BEP

(A) when selling price is reduced by 10%

(B) When variable cost is increased by 10%.

ANS:

Calculation of BEP:-

Sales	1, 00,000
Less:- variable cost	60,000
Contribution	40,000

$$\text{P/V. Ratio} = \frac{40,000}{1,00,000} \times 100 = 40\%$$

$$\text{BEP} \quad = \frac{\text{Fixed cost}}{\text{P/V. ratio}}$$

$$= \frac{15000}{40} \times 100 = 37,500.$$

(a) When the selling price is reduced by 10%

Sales (1,00,000 – 10,000)	90,000
Less: variable cost	60,000
Contribution	30,000

$$\text{P/V ratio} = \frac{30000}{90000} \times 100$$

$$= 33.333\%$$

$$\text{BEP} \quad = \frac{15000}{33.333} \times 100 = 45,000$$

(b) When variable cost in increased by 10%

Sales	1,00,000
Less:- variable cost(60000 + 6000)	66,000
Contribution	34,000

$$\text{P/V Ratio} = \frac{34,000}{1,00,000} \times 100 = 34\%$$

$$\text{BEP} \quad = \frac{15,000}{34} \times 100$$

$$= 44,118$$

16. Jai ltd. Plans to sell 1,10,000 units of a certain product line in the first fiscal quarter; 1,20,000 units in the second quarter; 1,30,000 units in the third quarter and 1,50,000 units in the fourth quarter and 1,40,000 units in the first quarter of the following year. At the beginning of the first quarter of the current year, there are 14,000 units of products in stock. At the end of each quarter, the company plans to have an inventory equal; to 1/5th of the sales for the next fiscal quarter. How many units must be manufactured in each quarter of the current year?

Manufacting Budget

Particulars	1st Quarter	2nd Quarter	3rd Quarter	4th Quarter
Sales	1,10,000	1,20,000	1,30,000	1,50,000
ADD: Closing stock *	24,000	26,000	30,000	28,000
	1,34,000	1,46,000	1,60,000	1,78,000
LESS: opening stock	14,000	24,000	26,000	30,000
No of unit to be manufactures	1,20,000	1,22,000	1,34,000	1,48,000

Note: 1/5 of 2nd quarter sales will be closing stock for 1st Quarter, 1/5 of 3rd Quarter sales will be closing stock for 2nd Quarter and so on.

1st Quarter closing stock will be opening stock for 2nd quarter and so on.

17. Distinguish between funds flow statement and cash flow statement.

PART – C

Answer any two questions.

All questions carry equal marks

18. Discuss the advantages and disadvantages of management accounting

19. From the following information prepare Balance Sheet of Anbu Ltd.:

(a) Stock turnover ration 6
(b) Capital turnover ratio 2
(c) Fixed assets turnover ratio 4
(d) Gross profit turnover ratio 20%
(e) Debtors velocity 2 months
(f) Creditor's velocity 73 days.

The gross profit was Rs. 60,000. Reserves and surplus Rs. 20,000. Closing stock was Rs. 5,000 in excess of opening stock.

Ans :

Gross profit Rs. 60,000.

Gross Profit Turnover Ratio = 20%

$$\therefore \text{ Sales} = \frac{60000}{20} \times 100 = \text{Rs.3, 00,000.}$$

Cost of Goods sold = Sales – Gross profit
= 3,00,000 – 60,000
= 2,40,000.

Stock Turnover Ratio = 6

$$= \frac{\text{Cost of Goods sold}}{\text{Av. Stock}} = 6$$

$$= \frac{2,40,000}{\text{Av. Stock}} = 6$$

$\therefore$ Av. Stock $= \dfrac{2,40,000}{6} = 40,000$

Av. Stock $= \dfrac{\text{op. Stock + Cl. Stock}}{2}$

Let opening stock be x

$\therefore$ Closing stock x + 5000 i.e. 5000 in exceed of opening stock

$40,000 = \dfrac{x+(x+5000)}{2}$

$80,000 = x + x + 5,000.$

$80,000 = 2x + 5,000.$

$75,000 = 2x$

$\therefore$ $x = 75,000\backslash 2 = 37,500$

Opening stock = 37,500

Closing Stock = 37,500 + 5000 = 42,500

Capital turnover Ratio = 2

$= \dfrac{\text{Cost of goods sold}}{\text{Net worth}} = 2$

$= \dfrac{2,40,000}{\text{Net worth}} = 2$

$\therefore$ Net worth $= \dfrac{2,40,000}{2} = 1,20,000$

Share capital = Net worth – Reserve and surplus

= 1,20,000 – 20,000

= 1,00,000.

Fixed assets Turnover Ratio = 4

$\dfrac{\text{Cost of Goods sold}}{\text{Fixed Assets}} = 4$

$\dfrac{2,40,000}{\text{Fixed Assets}} = 4$

$\therefore$ Fixed assets $= \dfrac{2,40,000}{4} = 60,000$

Debtors Velocity = 2 months

$\therefore$ Debtors turnover ratio $= \dfrac{12}{2} = 6$ times

$\dfrac{300000}{\text{Debtors}} = 6$

$\therefore$ Debtors $= \dfrac{300000}{6} = 50,000$

Creditors Velocity = 73 days.

$\therefore$ Creditors Turnover Ratio = $\frac{365}{73}$ = 5 times

Creditors Turnover Ratio = $\frac{\text{Net Credit purchase}}{\text{Creditors}}$.

Net Credit purchase = cost of goods sold + closing stock – opening stock

= 24000 + 42,500 – 37, 5000

= 24, 5000

$5 = \frac{24,5000}{\text{Creditors}}$

$\therefore$ Credit = $\frac{245000}{5}$ = 49,000

Balance sheet

Share Capital	1,00,000	Fixed assets	60,000
Reserves & Surplus	20,000	Debtors	50,000
Creditors	49,000	Closing stock	42,500
		Other current Assets	16,500
	1,69,000		1,69,000

20. Assuming that the cost structure and selling price remains the same in periods I and II, find out :

(a) Profit volume ratio

(b) B.E.P. sales

(c) Profit when sales are of Rs. 1,00,000

(d) Sales required to earn a profit of Rs. 20,000

Period	Sales Rs.	Profit Rs.
I	1,20,000	9,000
II	1,40,000	13,000

Ans:

(a) P/V Ratio = $\frac{\text{Change in profit}}{\text{Change in sales}} \times 100$

$= \frac{4000}{20,000} \times 100$

= 20%

(c) BEP Sales = $\frac{\text{Fixed cost}}{\text{P/V Ratio}}$

Fixed cost = Contribution – Profit

= (120000 x 20%) – 9000

= 24000 – 9000

= 15000.

$$\text{BEP Sales} = \frac{15000}{20\%}$$

$$= \frac{15000}{20} \times 100$$

= Rs. 75,000

(c) Profit when sales are Rs. 1, 00,000

Profit = contribution – fixed x cost

= (100000 X 20%) – 15,0000

= 20,000 – 15,000

= 5000.

(d) Sales required to earn a profit of Rs. 20,000

$$\text{Sales} = \frac{\text{Fixed cost + Desired profit}}{\text{P/V Ratio}}$$

$$= \frac{15000 + 20000}{20} \times 100$$

= 1,75,000.

21. Usha Ltd. Wishes to arrange over draft facilities wit its bankers during April to June 2003. Prepare a cash budget for the above periods from the following data:

2003	Sales	Purchase Rs.	Wages Rs.
Feb.	90,000	62,400	6,000
Mar.	96,000	72,000	7000
Apr.	54,000	1,21,500	5,500
May	87,000	1,23,000	5000
June	63,000	1,34,000	7,500

50% credit sales are realized in the month following the sales and the remaining 50% in the second month following. Creditors are paid in the month following the month of purchase. Cash at Bank on 1.4.2003 Rs. 12.500.

Cash budget for the month of April, May and June.

Particulars	April	May	June
Opening balance	12,500	28,000	23,500(OD)
Add;- Receipts			
Cash from Debtors	93,000	75,000	70,500
Total (A)	1,05,500	1,03,000	47,000
Payments:-			
Payment to crds	72,000	1,21,500	1,23,000
Wages	5,500	5,000	7,500
Total (B)	77,500	1,26,500	1,30,500
Closing balance (A-B)	28,000	23,500(OD)	83,500(OD)